LANDMARKS IN RHETORIC AND PUBLIC ADDRESS

LANDMARKS IN RHETORIC AND PUBLIC ADDRESS

David Potter, *General Editor*

CHIRONOMIA

OR

A Treatise on Rhetorical Delivery

BY

GILBERT AUSTIN

Edited by Mary Margaret Robb
and Lester Thonssen

Foreword by David Potter

Southern Illinois University Press

Carbondale and Edwardsville

FOREWORD

By David Potter

For almost a century after its publication in 1806, Gilbert Austin's *Chironomia* exerted a profound influence upon the history and teaching of rhetoric and oral interpretation in Europe and, especially, in America. Within the past fifty years, however, copies have become exceedingly rare. Consequently, scholars have been forced to resort to the inconvenient and relatively inaccessible microprint copies or to rely upon the interpretations of critics. The result has been a recent tendency to brand the volume as purely mechanical and to dismiss it as a curiosity.

In order to correct this misinterpretation and make available to the student of speech a truly handsome example of the bookmaker's art as well as a scholarly and entertaining attempt to place *actio* in its proper perspective, this offset version of the first edition has been conceived. In a brief but succinct introductory essay, editors Mary Margaret Robb and Lester Thonssen have examined the purposes of the Irish clergyman-teacher-author, gathered what pertinent bits of information are available about Austin and his background, and assisted the scholar by providing a list of books to which Austin has referred in the *Chironomia*.

Robb and Thonssen have been carefully selected for this editorial responsibility. For many years Professor of Speech at the City College of New York, Lester Thonssen is teaching at Metropolitan State College of Colorado. Author of many articles and books, Thonssen is most widely recognized for his annual series of *Representative American Speeches*, the *Bibliography of Speech Education*, and, with A. Craig Baird, the monumental *Speech Criticism*. Professor of Speech at the University of Colorado, Margaret Robb has been published extensively in the professional journals. In 1950 she collaborated with Lester and Dorothea Thonssen on a supplement to the *Bibliography of Speech Education.* Her most influential publication to date has been the *Oral Interpretation of Literature in American Colleges and Universities,* 1941.

CONTENTS

EDITORS' INTRODUCTION

By Mary Margaret Robb
and Lester Thonssen

ONE OF THE BEST REASONS for writing a textbook is to protest prevailing practices and neglects and to present a new or different theory and plan of instruction. This motive has the genuine flavor of hope about it, hope that some change although, perhaps, small will be beneficial to the student in his pursuit of knowledge and skill. When the concern is for the student rather than for the prestige of the author, the writing is of interest, especially to scholars who look backward as well as forward as they study contributions to the fields of knowledge. The Reverend Gilbert Austin wrote *Chironomia* because he wished to dispel a "strange prejudice" against rhetorical delivery, especially against gesture and bodily action.[1] Published in England in 1806, the book affected the teaching of delivery, particularly in America, throughout the nineteenth and well into the present century.

Moreover, Austin's interest in gesture had a certain focus in history. Through an elaborate notational scheme he hoped not only to facilitate the training of speakers and actors, but also to make possible the preservation of patterns of delivery. In effect, he anticipated the electronic wizardry of tape and disc that today preserves the images and the voices of poets, actors, orators, and public officials who record memories for the archives of oral history projects.

The reader will probably look first at the steel engravings which illustrate the book. They explain that Austin's system of gesture and movement is based upon the speaker's position in an imaginary sphere, and that notations are made to indicate changes of position, especially of the arms as they move in the sphere. The notations for arms, hand, and head are placed above the line of literature to be read, and the movement about the stage indicated below; for example, *AR2* means that the speaker advances two steps to the right. The reaction of the reader is probably one of disbelief that any such method could be followed except with disastrous results. But it is only fair to begin at the beginning and to discover Austin's theory of delivery and his concept of the whole field of rhetoric. *Chironomia* then becomes not only an example of fine bookmaking but of eighteenth-century scholarship.[2]

A gifted student of languages, Austin combined his scholarship and respect for the past with an impelling interest in experimentation. He may well set an example for the present-day writer and teacher who becomes enamored with the new machines and methods of testing and recording without relating them to traditional principles of education. In *Chironomia*, Austin proceeds in a logical fashion. He presents his purpose, defines his terms, and explains how he devised the method of notation which he hopes will correct the obvious deficiencies: lack of expressiveness in speaking and the lack of a method for recording a speech as delivered. His explanation of "the origin, the progress, and the objects of the work" is clear and complete; [3] it might be a model for the introduction to a doctoral dissertation.

According to Austin, the first deficiency in rhetorical training was the neglect of the fifth part of classical rhetoric—*pronuntiatio* or *actio*. Although he felt that attention was being paid to the other parts, a well-reasoned and organized speech was dull if the speaker did not deliver it well.[4] He found support in the writings of the older rhetoricians, especially Cicero and Quintilian, and quoted them at length. He also quoted contemporary writers—Walker, Sheridan, Burgh, Engel, and Abbé Maury—but he observed that these writers often neglected the ancients and for that reason he purposely "placed these authorities [the ancients] before the eyes of the reader." [5]

The second deficiency which Austin observed, as had many others before him, arose from the ephemeral quality of the spoken word. Writing was preserved for later generations but the eloquence of the speaker or actor died with him. Joshua Steele in *Prosodia Rationalis,*

1775, attempted to devise notations to record the variations in the voice as it was used in speaking, much as the notes for a musical score indicated vocal production for song.[6]   The schemes devised by Steele and Austin may not impress the student today.   Keep in mind, however, that these men worked in a "scientific manner" with the tools at their disposal.   "The laborious duty of teaching declamation" was Austin's first incentive.   He experimented with notations.   His original intention was to relieve his own labor, but as he extended his inquiries he envisioned rules that would be helpful in solving the problems which he observed to be of general concern.   His field of interest became not only the elementary principles of rhetorical action but also "whatsoever appeared to me most intimately connected with the improvement and perfecting of public speaking in general." [7]

Before offering his ideas to the public, Austin felt obliged to examine, as far as possible, all the work that had been done in the field.   His research was extensive and included French writers as well as English. In quoting from Ludovicus Cresollius, a Jesuit of Brittany who wrote a treatise on perfect action and pronunciation in 1620, Austin remarks that there is some consolation that other nations have "cause to complain of deficiency and neglect in this important branch of oratory." [8] He does not mention John Bulwer's *Chirologia* and *Chironomia* published in England in 1644, however, and may never have seen it.[9]

After his research and because of his experience both as a teacher and as a member of many audiences, especially in the theatre, he was encouraged "to produce a language of symbols so simple and so perfect as to render possible with facility to represent every action of an orator throughout his speech, or of an actor throughout the whole drama, and to record them for posterity, and for repetition and practice." [10]   He hoped to be of help to four different professions: the clergy, the members of parliament, lawyers, and actors.   Although he felt that the actor was in a better position to learn than the orator because he had models of "almost absolute perfection" to imitate, his performances would be lost if not recorded.   He mentions Garrick and

Kemble, in particular, whose acting must be recorded for those who could never see them and had only paintings to suggest their unusual impressiveness and grace.[11]   He also makes clear that the different professions make different demands upon the speaker and that their techniques are not interchangeable; the clergyman must not sound like the actor.   He proposed to "distinguish the character of the delivery belonging to each profession, to discriminate their peculiar manner, force, and expression, and if possible to mark the limits of each distinctly." [12]   It is doubtful that Austin felt satisfied with the distinctions which he made but he was sure of a general canon: action should assist and not decorate speech.

There were many elocutionists who suggested that the natural manner was the best manner, but Austin did not believe that nature could be relied upon for the right gesture at the right time.   The exception was the genius who knew instinctively what to do and devised his own rules.   In addition, Austin believed that the speaker must work as a complete human being—mind and body together. He suggested that the perfection of bodily control may instead of increasing gestures decrease them and serve the same purpose which the father desired when he sent his son to dancing school to learn to stand still.[13]

Although usually grouped with the English elocutionists, the Reverend Gilbert Austin was an Irish clergyman who conducted a private school for the sons of Irish nobility.   He was a man of many interests and abilities.   His education in Trinity College (Dublin University) was thorough.   According to Constantia Maxwell, in the *History of Trinity College, Dublin*, Lord Chesterfield considered the Irish schools and universities superior to the English during the eighteenth century.[14]   There were only three provosts in Trinity College from 1717 to 1795, all able leaders who built the college physically and educationally. During this century, under the influence of John Locke, whose *Essay Concerning Human Understanding*, 1690, and *Some Thoughts Concerning Education*, 1693, questioned the authority of the past, scholasticism began to give way to modern philosophy.[15]   Maxwell lists the subjects taught in 1759 as: "Classical Learning; Oriental, Ancient and Modern Languages; Criticism; Sacred and Profane History; Oratory; Logick; Ethics and Metaphysicks; Natural and Experimental Philosophy; Anatomy, Botany, and Chymistry; the Mathematicks, in theory and practice; Civil and Canon Laws; Theology Controversy, and Ecclesiastical History." The same essay states that the Newtonian Philosophy, Boyle's experimental Philosophy, and Locke's Metaphysics "prevail much in the College of Dublin: which for extent, convenience, magnificence, and a most sumptuous library, exceeds any one college in Europe." [16] Nevertheless, lectures in subjects such as logic and astronomy continued to be given in the ancient languages, either Latin or Greek, as were the declamations and disputations. As late as 1845, students taking B.A. and M.A. degrees were required to give two declamations, one in Latin and one in Greek, and to take part in the final disputations as part of their graduating exercises.[17] Such emphasis upon the traditional program was found in our own early education which was patterned upon that of the British Isles.

Many changes were made in the offerings at Trinity College during the eighteenth century. For example, oratory was separated from history; the two had been taught by one professor, but in 1762, two distinct positions were created. In 1777, two professorships in modern language were added: French and German; Spanish and Italian. Although there had been lectureships or professorships in Divinity and also in Laws since the early days, in 1761 a Regius Professorship of Divinity was established and a Professorship of Feudal and English Law. A Professorship of Music was established in 1764. In 1785 similar chairs of Chemistry and Botany were instituted. Provost Francis Andrews, who died in 1774, endowed a professorship of Astronomy and left the College three thousand pounds to erect and equip an astronomical observatory, and additional funds for an assistant to operate the equipment. A professorship of Anatomy was established in 1785; a laboratory and anatomical theatre had been built in 1710.[18]

This century was an exciting period because of the emphasis upon the intellectual powers and potentials of man; it was, in truth, a period of enlightenment which stimulated theorizing in education and politics and empiricism in science.

It was a relatively quiet period politically until the last decade. The French Revolution stirred the pot and much discontent arose in Ireland which chafed under the English rule. The revolution which had been fermenting for a long time broke out in 1798. The government quickly suppressed it and passed The Act of Union to prevent further trouble. Many changes took place in Trinity College at this time: one of its two parliamentary representatives was removed and since the parliament was absorbed by the English Parliament, the strong relationship with Trinity College was broken. Agitation for Irish independence did not slacken, however, especially among the younger men.[19]

It is not surprising that the Debating Club, probably the first of its kind, originated in Trinity College in 1747. The founder was Edmund Burke, and the purpose as stated "for improvement of its members in the more refined, elegant and usefull parts of Literature, these seeming the most likely means for attaining the great end in view—the formation of our minds and manners for the functions of Civil Society." The Debating Club later became the College Historical Society and by 1780 had some 700 members. Many of the Irish leaders were given their first training in this club, which met twice a week and debated the questions of the day.[20] Austin mentions the society as a training place but does not say whether he belonged.[21] Many of the outstanding political leaders were members, men such as: Isaac Cory, Henry Grattan, Robert Emmet, Wolfe Tone, and William Conyngham Plunket. The purpose of the Historical Society as stated in its constitution was to cultivate historical knowledge and to give practice in oratory and composition (in English, not in the learned languages). The Club was, perhaps, too political to suit the professors who were responsible to the Parliament, and stringent rules were imposed that caused the group to disband in 1815. Later, in 1843, the Historical Society was reactivated and continued to be a training ground for public speakers.[22]

According to Thomas U. Sadlier's *Alumni Dublinenses,*[23] Gilbert Austin entered Trinity College in February 1770, at the age of seventeen, as a pensioner (the largest and middle group). The highest group were the sons of nobility and the fellow commoners who paid higher fees, wore more elaborate gowns and were given special favors, the most important being the B.A. degree in three instead of four years. The lowest rank of students was the sizars who paid no fees and performed menial tasks for the fellows. Austin was awarded the B.A. in the spring, 1774, and the M.A. in the summer, 1780. Although he became a clergyman, his degrees do not indicate that he was a divinity student. He was fortunate to have been a student during the time that Provost Andrews was in office because during this period, 1758–74, Trinity College flourished. New professorships were added and an extensive building program begun. Dr. Andrews represented the gentleman and scholar so admired in this period. He was trained as a lawyer, became a member of Parliament where he distinguished himself as a fine speaker, and was well known for his wit and social graces.[24]

In W. B. S. Taylor's *History of the University of Dublin,* 1845, a list of some three hundred famous graduates is given with some facts about their lives. Gilbert Austin is there in company with William Congreve, Edmund Burke, Dean Swift, Thomas Sheridan, Richard Brinsley Sheridan, George Berkeley, Rev. John Lawson (a professor of Oratory and History), Henry Grattan, and Thomas Moore. Since this is the only biographical source on Austin suggested by the present Director of the Dublin University Library, perhaps it should be quoted in full.

> This accomplished scholar and estimable man was a native of Dublin, who graduated in its University. He afterwards established a school for the education of a limited number of the sons of the higher classes in Ireland, in which profession he was eminently successful. His high endowments in ancient learning were directed by an elegance and purity of

taste which could scarcely be surpassed, and which was equally conspicuous in the classical character of his English productions. In morals and manners this gentleman stood equally high in the opinions of his friends, and of course his acquaintance was eagerly sought by the best people in society. With the late Duke of Leinster, he was an especial favourite; his Grace placed his only son, the present duke, under the care of Dr. Austin; and the best proof we can give of the esteem the young nobleman felt for his learned preceptor was, that soon after he had succeeded to the dukedom, he presented him to a very valuable living which had then become vacant.

Dr. Austin was also a very much admired preacher. The works he published are:

A Sermon, preached at the Magadalen Asylum, Dublin; a very elegant and powerful composition. 1791.—Chironomia; or, a Treatise on Rhetorical Delivery, comprehending many precepts both ancient and modern, for the proper regulation of the Voice, the Countenance, and Gesture, and a new method of the Notation thereof, illustrated with figures. Lond. 1806.—Description of a portable Barometer.—Description of an Apparatus for impregnating Water and other substances strongly with Carbonic Acid Gas.—Description of an Apparatus for transferring Water over Gases or Mercury. These are in the Transactions of the Royal Irish Academy, 4th, 8th, and 10th vols.—Also on a New Construction of a Condenser and Air Pump. Phil. Trans., 1813.[25]

According to J. B. Leslie's *Ossory Clergy and Parishes,* Enniskillen, 1933, Austin was a minor canon of St. Patrick's Cathedral, Dublin, 1798, Vicar of Laraghbryan 1816–37, and held the prebendary of Blackrathe 1821 until 1835. He died in 1837.[26] His *Sermons on Practical Subjects* was published in 1795. He speaks of his greater familiarity with the profession of the clergyman than with any other when he discusses the different kinds of professions which demand effective speaking. His other activities, including teaching, evidently were in addition to his professional duties as a clergyman in the Church of Ireland, an extension of the Church of England.

Austin's most unusual interest was in scientific research.   The

Royal Irish Academy, in which he was a contributing member, was founded in 1785. The weekly meetings were devoted to essays or reports given by members, and later published as the *Transactions of the Society*. The first paper read was "An Account of the Observatory belonging to Trinity College" by Rev. H. Ussher, D.D., the professor of Astronomy. Although the "new science" consisted mainly in observations and ordering of information, giving nomenclature and determining categories, it was the spark for intellectual activity. There was a brief hiatus in this activity during the rebellion of 1798; for a time Dublin was under martial law and no one could leave his house after eight o'clock in the evening.[27] It must have been brief as far as the Royal Irish Academy was concerned, though, because the eighth volume of *Transactions* was published in 1799, and in it we find Austin's account of his experiment in impregnating water with carbonic acid gas.[28] This highly inventive mind, when confronted with the problem of "total want of any regular system of . . . rules for rhetorical delivery" and "the reproach of frigid indifference" among speakers, would, of course, develop a system such as *Chironomia* presents.

The influence of *Chironomia* upon the teaching of speech in England and America is hard to assess. Until the appearance of Delsarte, however, Austin was the authority on teaching gesture. He was widely quoted, often with no acknowledgment of the source, and perhaps with no knowledge of it.

Dr. Jonathan Barber's *Practical Treatise on Gesture,* 1831, gave full credit to Austin, stating at the beginning that it was chiefly abstracted from *Chironomia* and designed for the students at Harvard College. Dr. Barber, English physician turned elocutionist, served as Dr. Edward T. Channing's assistant from 1829 to 1835. Channing, a very successful teacher of rhetoric, asked for an assistant who would work with individual students to polish their delivery for declamations, and to give some lectures. Evidently Barber was not wholly successful. One morning he found his bamboo sphere on the top of a barber's pole

(the sphere was undoubtedly used in teaching Austin's system).[29]
Soon Barber resigned.   The students found his teaching too mechanical and demanding.

Increase Cooke's *The American Orator,* 1819, was one of the earliest American books to show Austin's influence.[30]   In 1818, Christian F. Michaelis published a book in German based on *Chironomia* titled *Die Kunst der rednerischen und theatralischen Declamation.*[31]   A. M. Hartley's *Oratorical Class-book,* published in Glasgow in 1824, called *Chironomia* "the ablest treatise on delivery in our language." [32]   Dr. C. P. Bronson's book on elocution, 1845,[33] and Rufus Claggett's *Elocution Made Easy,*[34] used the illustrations but gave no credit to Austin, but Merritt Caldwell's *A Practical Manual of Elocution* published the same year quotes him as an authority.[35]   William Russell, although more interested in following Dr. Rush's system for training the voice, treats gesture briefly and mentions the importance of *Chironomia.*[36]   In his lectures published in 1881, Charles J. Plumtre, an instructor of elocution at King's College, London, refers to Austin as a respected authority on teaching rhetorical action.[37]   R. I. Fulton and T. C. Trueblood [38] mention Austin in the preface to their book, as does Joseph A. Mosher in the preface to *The Essentials of Effective Gestures,* 1916.[39]   Albert M. Bacon's *Manual of Gesture,* 1872,[40] relied upon the Austin techniques for teaching delivery because "gesture is thus reduced to a science; and the student is relieved of inventing for himself a system of action"; the writer was relieved in the same manner. Perhaps the most recent reference to Austin is to be found in *Public Speaking as a Liberal Art* by John F. Wilson and Carroll C. Arnold, published in 1964.[41]   Some of the steel engravings are used for decoration and perhaps to suggest the long tradition of rhetoric as a liberal art.   Or perhaps they were used to evoke a smile from teacher and student because Austin's system of gesture, happily, is not applicable to the teaching of speech today.

It is true that *Chironomia* enjoyed its great popularity because of Austin's system for teaching rhetorical delivery, but it would be a mistake to think that this is its only contribution. It is so much more: not just an interesting example of early elocutionary theory but a rather complete resumé of the theories of ancient and modern writers and teachers concerning the use of the voice, the countenance, action, and pantomime; in addition, discussions of reading, of giving orations and declamations, of acting, and of public speaking in general. Because he used Cicero and Quintilian as irrefutable sources, he must be called a classicist in his approach to the subject of rhetoric, but his wide reading in the later related literature not only of the rhetoricians and elocutionists but also of the historians, the philosophers, and the artists indicates that he is also a modern scholar. His copious footnotes make a kind of anthology of material that has seldom been brought together in such an easy and readable treatise. This is eclecticism at its best and the reader finds many ideas that he holds dear and few that he can consider outdated. The Reverend Gilbert Austin reveals not only an original mind but a discriminating and practical one.

In the discussion of the use of the voice as an important part of delivery, Austin emphasizes the importance of training. The voice is the "organ of eloquence, and has the entire dominion over one sense [auditory]." [42] If the student has an imperfect voice that cannot be improved, he, of course, should be urged to turn his talents to writing instead of speaking, but for the student with a moderately good voice when "the ear is not wholly depraved," he must be directed to cultivate the different parts of speech: articulation, pronunciation and accent, emphasis, pauses, pitch, quantity, modulation and variety, and tones. He considered the quality and management of the voice to be of the highest importance to the public speaker, attributing the former to nature and the latter to art.[43] Gesture would, according to Austin, come second in order of training. It was not because he thought action the most important part of delivery but because he felt that it was the most neglected that he presented his "system in the sphere."

We know of no writer before Dr. James Rush who describes in more detail or in clearer fashion, the use of the voice. It is sometimes said that Rush in *Philosophy of the Human Voice* was the first to analyze the quality of the voice, but Austin lists the following descriptive terms in contrasting pairs: clearness, indistinctness; sweetness, harshness; evenness, broken or cracked; and adds that the good voice must have variety and flexibility instead of monotony and rigidity.[44] These are terms that may be heard in any classroom today. He speaks of the quantity of the voice as referring to its "body or volume, the compass, the soundness and durability."

He explains the rhetorical pause, and says that phrases may be read without observing all the punctuation marks. He regards good articulation as an essential of intelligibility. He has observed speech defects such as stammering and hissing of the letter *S,* also the denasalization of *M* and *N.*[45] He has also observed that it is much easier to raise the pitch than to lower it and warns the speaker not to raise the pitch when he increases the volume.[46]

The discussion of reading, which he considers the easiest form of speech, is delightfully modern even to a description of group readings which today would probably be called Readers' Theatre. Reading may be of several different kinds depending upon the occasion and the material read; first it is *intelligible,* then it may advance to *correct;* if it requires more feeling and involvement, it will be *impressive;* if in tune with the oratorical it will be *rhetorical,* if a play is being read, *dramatic,* or perhaps *epic.*[47] Much attention is given to the minister and his problems in reading; part of his difficulty Austin believes to be caused by the pulpit which is so high and the speaker so boxed up that it appears that "some juggling were to be performed within." [48] The styles of reading as in speaking must be governed by good judgment and taste. Austin believed that delivery must change according to different circumstances, different audiences, and different sentiments, and that the actor, the minister, the lawyer, and the political orator must be their own judges as to the manner chosen. Training of the voice and the body depended upon much laborious practice and the techniques learned must be adapted to each occasion.[49]

Modern students and teachers will view *Chironomia* in a variety of ways. To those who look carefully there will be helpfully guided instruction in delivery. Others will look upon the seemingly strange diagrams, nomenclature, and detailed advice as an intriguing but mildly archaic reminder of a day that is happily past. All will doubtless agreee, however, that Gilbert Austin's handsome volume is a noteworthy example, historically and pedagogically, of sound scholarship, creative imagination, and uncommon knowledge.

Virtually inaccessible to scholars for many years, except in larger libraries, *Chironomia* is, through this reprinting, once more made available to a wide reading public. The treatise will tell us again how one man, distressed by the "irremediable privation" arising from the removal of great speakers and actors from the scene, sought to preserve their patterns of voice and action, as well as provide instruction for others, through an elaborate and ingenious system of notational symbols.

NOTES TO THE INTRODUCTION

[1] Gilbert Austin, *Chironomia: or a Treatise on Rhetorical Delivery* (London, 1806), p. 5.

[2] Frederick W. Haberman, "English Sources of American Elocution," *History of Speech Education*, ed. Karl R. Wallace (New York, 1954), pp. 117–118. There was one British edition and no American. It cost £2, s2, and it seems possible that students used a library copy instead of owning it as a textbook. The copy in the University of Colorado library still retains its leather binding.

[3] *Chironomia*, p. iv.

[4] *Ibid.*, pp. 13–18.

[5] *Ibid.*, pp. v–vi. Haberman, *op. cit.*, calls the footnotes an anthology of the rhetorician's theories and methods. They may pose a problem for the reader who does not read Latin, Greek, and French but show Austin to be a thorough scholar. His wish was to present accurate references for the reader's "greater convenience."

[6] Joshua Steele, *Prosodia Rationalis* (London, 1775). Austin states that Mr. Steele has most ingeniously and perfectly recorded the delivery of the actor Garrick "as to the modulation of the voice." *Chironomia*, p. 290.

[7] *Chironomia*, p. v.

[8] *Ibid.*, pp. 9–11. Ludovicus Cresollius, *Vactiones Autumnales sive de perfecta Oratoris* (Paris, 1620).

[9] John Bulwer, *Chirologia . . . Chironomia* (London, 1644), 2 vols. in 1. Both writers were motivated by the need to improve rhetorical delivery and both preferred to use Greek words rather than the current term, *elocution*. Austin thought it improper to use *elocutio* for *actio* and shows himself to be a conservative rhetorician in this respect and in many others. See Wilbur Samuel Howell's discussion of the change in terms in "Sources of the Elocutionary Movement in England 1700–1743," *QJS*, 45 (February, 1959), 1–18.

[10] *Chironomia*, pp. 274–75.

[11] *Ibid.*, pp. 15, 279.

[12] *Ibid.*, pp. 134–35.

[13] *Ibid.*, p. 137 ff.

[14] Constantia Maxwell, *A History of Trinity College, Dublin 1591–1892* (Dublin, 1946), p. 156.

[15] *Ibid.*, p. 80.

[16] *Ibid.*, pp. 148–49.

[17] *Ibid.*, p. 149. See *Laws of Harvard College, 1814*, pp. 18–20.

[18] *Ibid.*, pp. 120, 124, 148, 158.

[19] W. B. S. Taylor, *History of the University of Dublin* (London, 1845), pp. 115–16.

[20] W. MacNeil Dixon, *Trinity College, Dublin* (London, 1902), pp. 131–36. See Maxwell, pp. 141–43, and Taylor, pp. 198–204.

[21] *Chironomia*, pp. 212–13.

[22] Maxwell, p. 240.

[23] Thomas U. Sadlier and George D. Burtchaell, comp., *Alumni Dublinneses, A register of students, graduates, professors, and provosts of Trinity College 1593–1860* (Dublin, 1869), New ed., 1935.

[24] Maxwell, p. 132.

[25] Taylor, pp. 438–39.

[26] J. B. Leslie, *Ossory Clergy and Parishes* (Enniskillen, 1933), p. 118.

[27] Maxwell, pp. 179–180.

[28] Is it possible that Austin's experiment was the beginning of the soft drink industry?

[29] Andrew Peabody, *Harvard Reminiscences* (Boston, 1888), pp. 90–91.

[30] Increase Cooke, *The American Orator* (New Haven, 1819). Although credit is given to Chapman's *Orator,* many sentences come directly from Austin. *cf.* pp. 54–56 with Austin, pp. 294–95.

[31] Christian F. Michaelis, *Die Kunst der rednerischen und theatralischen Declamation durch 152 Figuren erlāutert für Offentliche Redner, Schauspieler, und Kunstler* [Founded on G. Austin's *Chironomia*] (Leipzig, 1818).

[32] A. M. Hartley, *The Oratorical Class-Book* (Glasgow, 1824), p. 7.

[33] C. P. Bronson, *Elocution; or Mental and Vocal Philosophy* (Louisville, Ky., 1845), 5th ed.

[34] Rufus Claggett, *Elocution Made Easy* (New York, 1845).

[35] Merritt Caldwell, *A Practical Manual of Elocution* (Philadelphia, 1845).

[36] William Russell, *American Elocutionist* (Boston, 1844), p. 200.

[37] Charles J. Plumtre, *Kings College Lectures on Elocution* (London, 1881), pp. 106–7, 293.

[38] R. I. Fulton and T. C. Trueblood, *Practical Elements of Elocution* (Boston, 1893).

[39] Joseph A. Mosher, *Essentials of Effective Gestures* (New York, 1916).

[40] Albert M. Bacon, *A Manual of Gesture* (New York, 1872).

[41] John F. Wilson and Carroll C. Arnold, *Public Speaking as a Liberal Art* (New York, 1964).

[42] *Chironomia*, p. 29.

[43] *Ibid.*, pp. 30–36.

[44] *Ibid.*, p. 33.

[45] *Ibid.*, pp. 40–44, 52.

[46] *Ibid.*, p. 59.

[47] *Ibid.*, pp. 204–5.

[48] *Ibid.*, pp. 233 ff.

[49] *Ibid.*, p. 462.

BIBLIOGRAPHY

Austin used many reference books and for only a few did he use a translation. An effort has been made to list early editions and also English translations for the convenience of present-day readers who are not as well trained in Latin and Greek as the eighteenth-century scholar. The location of the books is indicated in the following manner: *Library of Congress,* L; *British Museum,* B; and *Bibliotheque Nationale,* N. There are many editions of almost all of the books listed below; many of them are to be found in college and university libraries.

Addison, Joseph. "The Spectator," Nos. 147, 490, August 18, 1711. In *Works of Joseph Addison.* Birmingham: J. and R. Tonson, 1761 [L,B].

Alcuin (Flaccus Albinus). "Albinin Alcuini de Arte Dialogus," in *Antiqui Rhetores Latini,* ed. Rutilius Lupus. Parisiis, 1559 [B,N].

———. *The Rhetoric of Alcuin and Charlemagne.* English trans. Wilbur Samuel Howell. Princeton: Princeton University Press, 1941 [L,B].

Algarotti, Francesco (Comte). *Saggio Sopra L'Opera in Musica.* Livorno, 1763 [B].

Apuleius, Lucius. *Apuleii Metamorphoses.* Venetiis: Aldi and Andreae Soceri, 1521 [B,N].

———. *Lucii Apulei Metamorphoseon.* Lipsiae: B. G. Teubneri, 1897 [L].

Aristotle. *Aristotelis de Arte Rhetorica.* Basileae, 1546 [B,N].

———. *De Arte Poetica.* Parisiis: G. Morelium, 1555 [B,N]. English trans. Thomas Twing. London, 1789 [L,B].

Athenaeus, Naucratitia. *Deipnosophistae.* Venetiis: Aldi and Andreae Soceri, 1514 [B]. English trans. C. D. Yonge. London, 1854 [L,B].

Augustine, Saint (Bishop of Hippo). *D. Aurelii Augustini Confessionum,* libri tredecim. Strasburg: Johann Mentelin, 1470 [B]. Louanii: H. Wellaeum, 1573 [N]. English trans. William Watts. London, 1631 [L,B].

Barrow, William (Rev.). *An Essay on Education.* London: F. C. Rivington, 1802 [L,B].

Barthélemy, Jean-Jaques (Abbé). *Voyage du jeune Anacharsis en Grece dans le millieu du quatrieme siecle avant l'ere vulgaire.* Paris, 1789 [L,B,N]. English trans. J. Robinson. London, 1790–91 [B].

Buffon, Georges-Louis Leclerc (Comte). *Histoire Naturelle.* 44 Vols. Paris, 1749 [B,N]. English trans. William Smellie. London, 1785 [B].

Burke, Edmund. *A Philosophical Enquiry into the Origin of our Ideas of the Sublime and Beautiful.* London, 1757 [B]. London, 1770 [L,B].

Cassiodorus Senator (Flavius Magnus Aurelius). "Rhetoricae Compendium" from *Institutiones*. Paris: Wechelum, 1541 [B,N]. English Trans. Oxford, 1937 [L].

Caussin, Le P. Nicolas. *De Eloquentia Sacrae et Humanae*. 16 vols. Parisiis, 1619 [N], 1630 [B].

Cibber, Colley. *An Apology for the Life of Mr. Colley Cibber*. London, 1740 [B].

Cicero, Marcus Tullius. *De Oratore*. Rome: U. Han, 1468 [B,N]. Trans. William Guthrie. London, 1742 [B]. Trans. J. S. Watson. New York: Harper and Bros., 1881 [L].

————. *Brutus seu de Claris Oratoribus*. Parisiis, 1535 [N]. Romae: P. Marottum, 1629 [B]. Trans. H. M. Hubbell. Cambridge, 1939 [L].

————. *Rhetorica ad C. Herennium*. Veniis: N. Jenson, 1470 [B]. Often attributed, perhaps erroneously, to Cicero.

Condillac, Étienne Bonnot de. *Traité des Sensations*. 2 vols. London, Paris, 1754 [B,N].

Cresollius, Ludovicus. *Vacationes Autumnales sive De perfecta Oratoris Actione et Pronunciatione*. 3 vols. Paris, 1620 [B,N].

Darwin, Erasmus. *Zoonomia: or the Laws of Organic Life*. London: J. Johnson, 1794 [L,B].

Dionysius Halicarnassus. *The Roman Antiquities*. Latin, French, English [L,B,N].

Dubos, Jean Baptiste. *Reflexiones sur la Poesie et sur la Peinture*. 3 vols. Paris: J. Mariette, 1719 [B,N]. English trans. J. Nourse. London, 1748 [L].

Dubroca, Louis. *Principes sur l'art de Lire a haute Voix*. Paris, 1802 [N].

Engel, Johann Jacob. *Ideen su Mimik*. Berlin: A. Mylius, 1785–86 [L,B,N].

————. *Practical Illustrations of Rhetorical Gesture and Action*. Adapted to the English Drama by Henry Siddons. London: Richard Phillips, 1807 [L,B]. Austin used a French translation.

Fénelon, Francois de Salignac de la Mothe (Archbishop of Cambrai). *Dialogues sur l'Eloquence*. Paris, 1718 [N]. English trans. Glasgow, 1760 [L,B]. English trans. W. S. Howell. Princeton, 1951 [L].

Fordyce, David Theodorus. *A Dialogue Concerning the Art of Preaching*. To which is added a sermon on the eloquence and an essay on the action of the Pulpit. London, 1745 [L,B].

Fortunatianus, Chirius. *Artis Rhetoricae Scholiae*. Venice, 1523 [B,N].

Gibbon, Edward. *An Essay on the Study of Literature* (written in French). London: Becket and De Hondt, 1764 [L,B,N].

Gildon, Charles. *The Life of Mr. Thomas Betterton*. London, 1710 [B]. London, 1761 [L].

Gros de Besplas, Joseph-Marie (Abbé). *Essai sur l'Eloquence de la Chaire*. Paris: Vallet la Chappelle, 1767 [N].

Harris, James. *Three Treatises. The first concerning Art. The second concerning Music, Painting, and Poetry*. London, 1744 [B].

Herder, Johann Gottfried Von. *Outline of a Philosophy of the History of Man.* English trans. T. Churchill. London: J. Johnson, 1800 [B,N].

Hill, Aaron. *The Art of Acting.* London: J. Osborn, 1746 [B,N].

Hippocrates. *Iacolii Afforismos Ypocratis.* Cremona, 1473 [B]. English trans., Elias Marks. New York, 1817 [L].

Hogarth, William. *The Analysis of Beauty.* London, 1753 [L,B].

Home, Henry (Lord Kames). *Elements of Criticism.* 2 vols. Edinburgh: A. Kincaid, 1762 [B].

Homer. *Homeri Ilias.* Florentiae: Philippi Iuntae, 1519 [N].

————. *Homeri Ilias, graece et latine.* London: Johannis and Pauli Knapton, 1754 [B]. Trans. Alexander Pope. London, 1715–20. 1796 edition [L,B].

Horace (Horatius Flaccus Quintus). *De Arte Poetica.* Milan, 1474 [B]. English trans. J. Bartlett. Cambridge, 1856 [L].

————. *Odes of Horace.* Trans. T. Hawkins. London, 1631 [B].

————. *Q. Horatii Flacci Epodon.* Strasburg, 1520 [N].

Hume, David. *Essays and Treatises on Several Subjects.* London, T. Cadeel, 1784 [B]. Edinburgh: Creech, 1817 [L].

Isocrates. *Isocratis Orationes et Epistolae.* Geneva, 1593 [B,N]. Greek edition, Milan, 1493 [B,N]. English trans. George Norlin. London: Heinemann. 1928–48 [L,B].

Lavater, Johann Casper. *Essays on Physiognomy: for the promotion of the Knowledge and Love of Mankind.* English trans. Thomas Holcroft. London: H. D. Symonds, 1804 [L,B].

Le Fáucheur, Michel. *Traité de l'action de l'orateur.* Revu, corrige et publie par Valentin Conrart. Paris: A. Courbé, 1657 [N]. 1676 edition [B]. Austin refers to this book as Conrart's book. See Howell's evaluation of Fáucheur, note 9.

Locke, John. *Essay Concerning Human Understanding.* London, 1690 [B].

————. *Some Thoughts Concerning Education.* London: Churchill, 1693 [L,B].

Lucas, Joannes. *Actio Oratoris, seu de gestu et voce.* 2 vols. Paris, 1675 [B,N].

Lucian of Samosota. *Luciani Laudatio Demothens.* Haganoae, 1533 [B].

Marmontel, Jean Francois. *Les Eléments de la Littérature.* 19 vols. Paris: Verdière, 1818–20 [L,B,N].

————. *Dictionnaire de Grammaire et de Littérature.* Liege, 1789 [N].

Massilon, Jean Baptiste. *Oeuvres de Massilon.* "Art of Preaching" from *Oeuvres.* London: St. John, 1805 [B].

Maury, Jean S. (Abbé and later Cardinal). *Principes de Eloquence pour la Chaire et le Barreau.* Paris: T. Warée, 1804 [L,B,N].

Petronius Arbiter. *Satyricon Petronii Arbitri.* Paris, 1585 [B,N]. English trans. M. Burnaby. London, 1694 [B]. New York: Century, 1929 [L].

Philostratus, Flavius (The Elder). *Imagines Heroica. Vitae Sophistarum.* Venetiis, 1535 [B,N]. English trans. Arthur Fairbanks. London: Heinemann, 1931 [L].

Pliny, Secundus. *Naturales Historia.* Venetiis: N. Jenson, 1472 [B,N]. English trans. Philemon Holland. London, 1601 [L,B].

Plutarch. *The Lives of the Noble Grecians and Romans.* English trans. T. North. London, 1579 [L,B].

Quintilian, Marcus Fabius. *Quintiliani Institutiones Oratoriae.* Rome, 1470 [N]. Coloniae, 1527 [B,N]. Geneva: Stoer, 1580 [B]. English trans. J. Patsall. London, 1774 [L,B].

Ricchieri, Ludovico (Coelius Rhodiginus). *Lectionum Antiquarium.* Basileae: J. Frohenius, 1517 [B,N]. 1550 edition [L].

Rollin, Charles. *Methods of Teaching and Studying the Belles Lettres or an Introduction to Language, Poetry, Rhetoric, History, Moral Philosophy, Physics, etc.* London: Bettesworth and Hitch, 1742 [L,B].

Sheridan, Thomas. *Course of Lectures on Elocution.* London: J. Dodsley, 1762 [B]. Providence, 1796 [L].

————. *Discourse Delivered in the Theatre at Oxford. . . . Being Introductory to His Course of Lectures on Elocution and the English Language.* London: A. Millar, 1759 [B].

————. *Lectures on the Art of Reading.* London: J. Dodsley, 1775 [L].

————. *A Rhetorical Grammar of the English Language.* London, 1780 [B]. Philadelphia, 1783 [L].

Spon, Jacob. *Recherche des Antiquités et Curiosités.* Lyon: T. Amaulry, 1673 [N]. 1676 edition [B]. 1683 edition [L,B].

Stanhope, Philip Dormer (Lord Chesterfield). *Letters written by the Earl of Chesterfield to his Son.* London: J. Dodsley, 1774 [N]. Philadelphia: T. Dobson, 1786 [L].

Steele, Joshua. *Prosodia Rationalis, or, An Essay toward Establishing the Melody and Measure of Speech to be Expressed and Perpetuated by Peculiar Symbols.* London: J. Almon, 1775 [L,B]. The 1779 edition added *Prosodia Rationalis* to the title.

Strebaeus, Jacobus Ludovicus. *In Omnes de Arte Rhetorica M. T. Ciceronis libros.* Paris, 1540 [B,N]. He also wrote commentaries on Quintilian, Seneca, and Xenophon.

Suetonius Tranquillus, Caius. *S. T. de grammaticus et rethoribus clarissimis libellus foeliciter incipit.* Veniis: N. Jenson, 1473 [N]. Florence, 1478 [B]. English trans. H. G. Bohn. London, 1855 [B].

Sulpicius, Joannes. *Quintiliani Institutiones cum Commento.* Pomponii: L. Vallensio, 1494 [B].

Tacitus, Publius Cornelius. *Dialogus de Oratoribus.* Parisiis: M. Vasconsani, 1539 [B].

————. *Dialogus an sui Seculi Oratores Antiquioribus.* Basileae, 1567 [N]. Ed. Charles E. Bennett. Boston: Ginn and Co., 1894 [L].

Valerius Maximus. *Factorum et Dictorum Memorabilium.* Venetiis, 1471 [L,B,N].

Vinci, da, Leonardo. *Trattato della Pittora de Lionardo da Vinci.* Parigi, 1651 [B].

Virgil (Virgilius Maro, Publius). *Omnia Opera.* Venetiis: B. Zannis, 1510 [B]. English trans. J. Ogilby. London, 1649 [B]. 1654 edition [L].

Vossius, Gerardus (Canon of Canterbury). *Ortoriarum Institutionum.* Frankfort on the Oder, 1616 [B].

Walker, John. *Elements of Elocution.* 2 vols. London, 1781 [L,B].

————. *Hints for Improvement in the Art of Reading.* London, 1783 [B].

————. *The Rhetorical Grammar.* London, 1785 [B]. 2nd edition, 1787 [L].

CHIRONOMIA;

OR A

TREATISE ON RHETORICAL DELIVERY:

COMPREHENDING MANY PRECEPTS, BOTH ANCIENT AND MODERN, FOR
THE PROPER REGULATION OF

THE VOICE, THE COUNTENANCE, AND GESTURE.

TOGETHER WITH AN

INVESTIGATION OF THE ELEMENTS OF GESTURE,

AND

A NEW METHOD FOR THE NOTATION THEREOF;

ILLUSTRATED BY MANY FIGURES.

BY THE REVEREND GILBERT AUSTIN, A. M.

Et certe quod facere oporteat, non indignandum est discere, cum præsertim hæc *Chironomia*,
quæ est (ut nomine ipso declaratur) *lex gestus*, et ab illis temporibus heroicis orta sit, et à summis Græciæ viris, et ab ipso etiam Socrate probata, à Platone quoque in parte civilium posita
virtutum, et à Chrysippo in præceptis de *liberorum educatione* compositis non omissa. *Quint.*

Non sum nescius, quantum susceperim negotii, qui motus corporis exprimere verbis, imitari
scriptura conatus sim voces. *Rhet. ad Herenn l.* 3.

LONDON:

PRINTED FOR T. CADELL AND W. DAVIES, IN THE STRAND;

BY W. BULMER, AND CO. CLEVELAND-ROW, ST. JAMES'S;

1806.

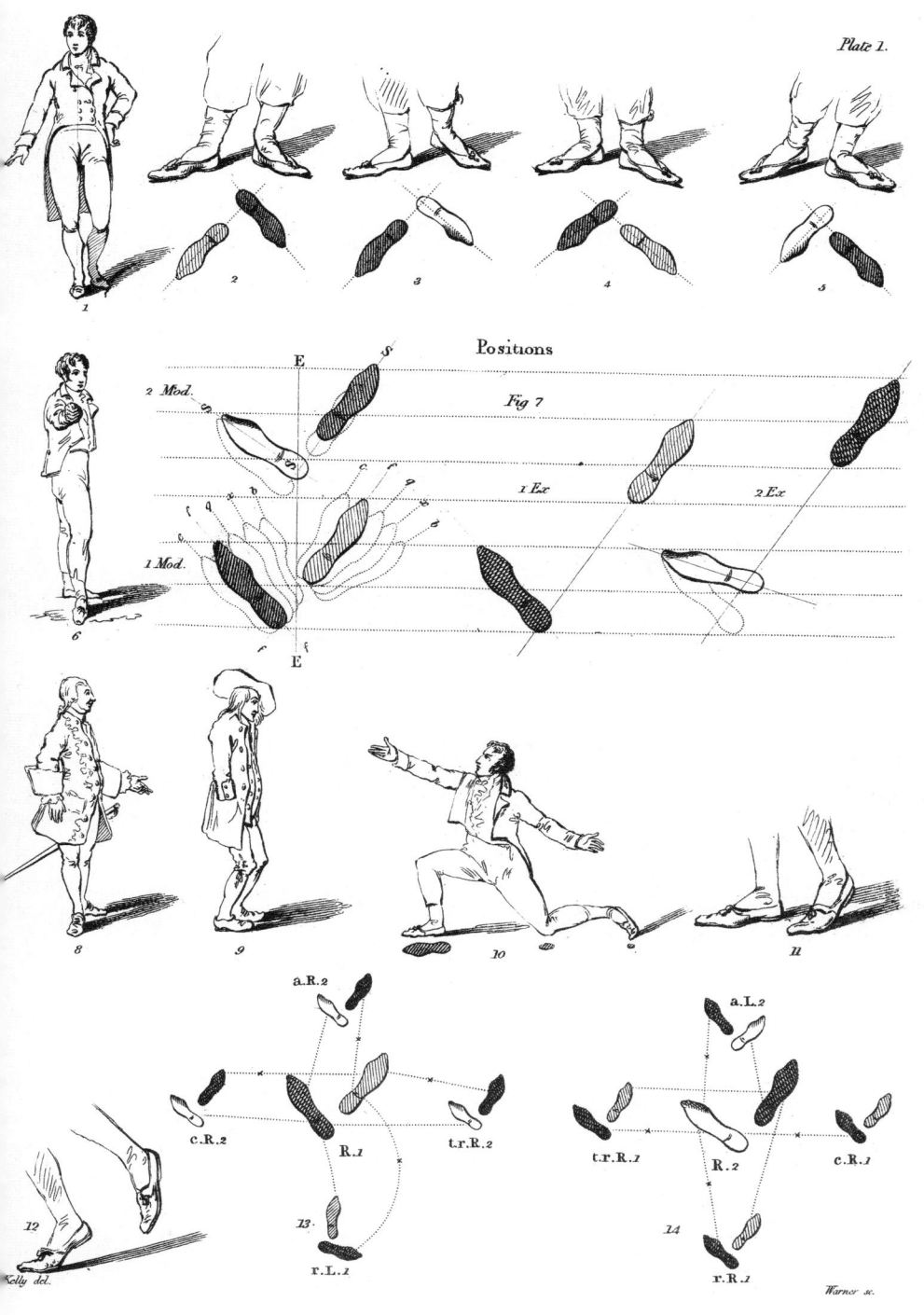

Plate 1.

Positions

Fig 7

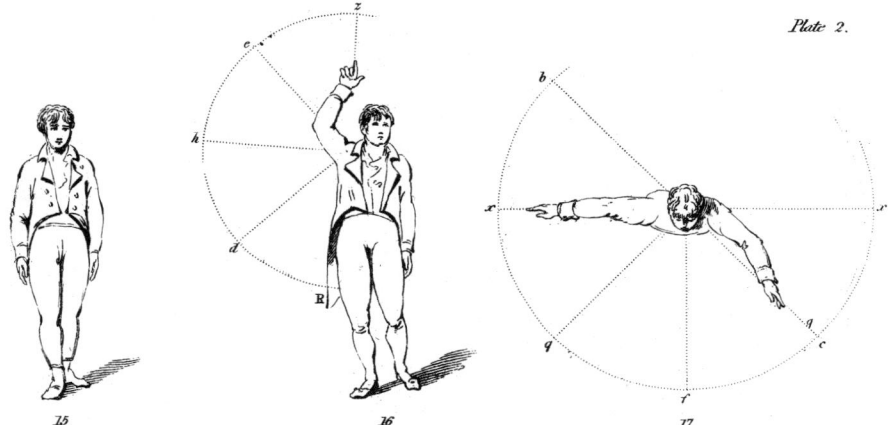

Plate 2.

15   16   17

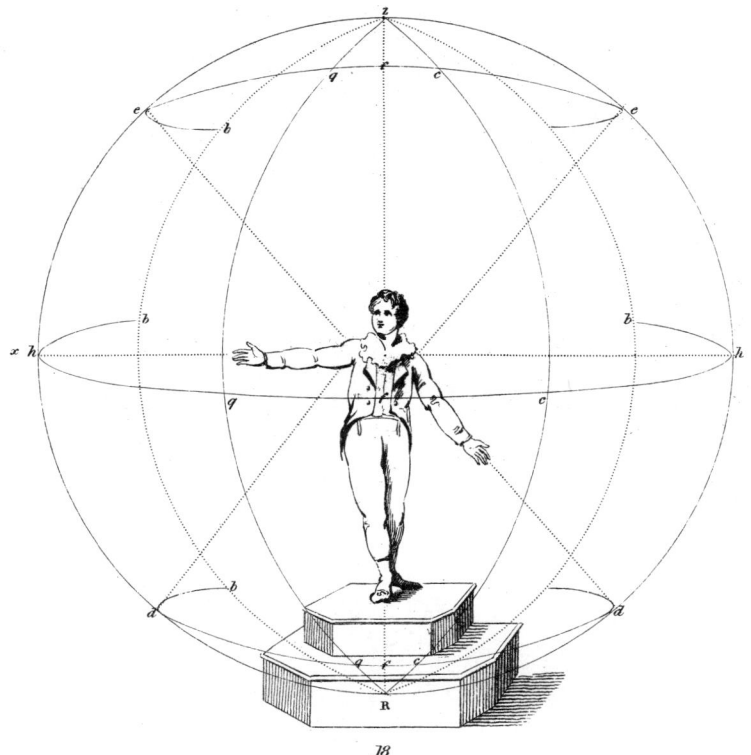

18

Kelly del.   *Warner sc.*

The Systematic Positions of the Arms.

Plate, 3.

Kelly del.

Warner sc.

Plate 4.

Plate 5.

Positions of the Hands used by ancient Orators.

from Quintilian l.11.c.3.

43

44

45

46

47

48

b

a

a

49

b

50

51

52

Kelly del.

Warner sc.

Plate 6.

Positions of the Hands used by ancient Orators.

from Quintilian l.11.c.3.

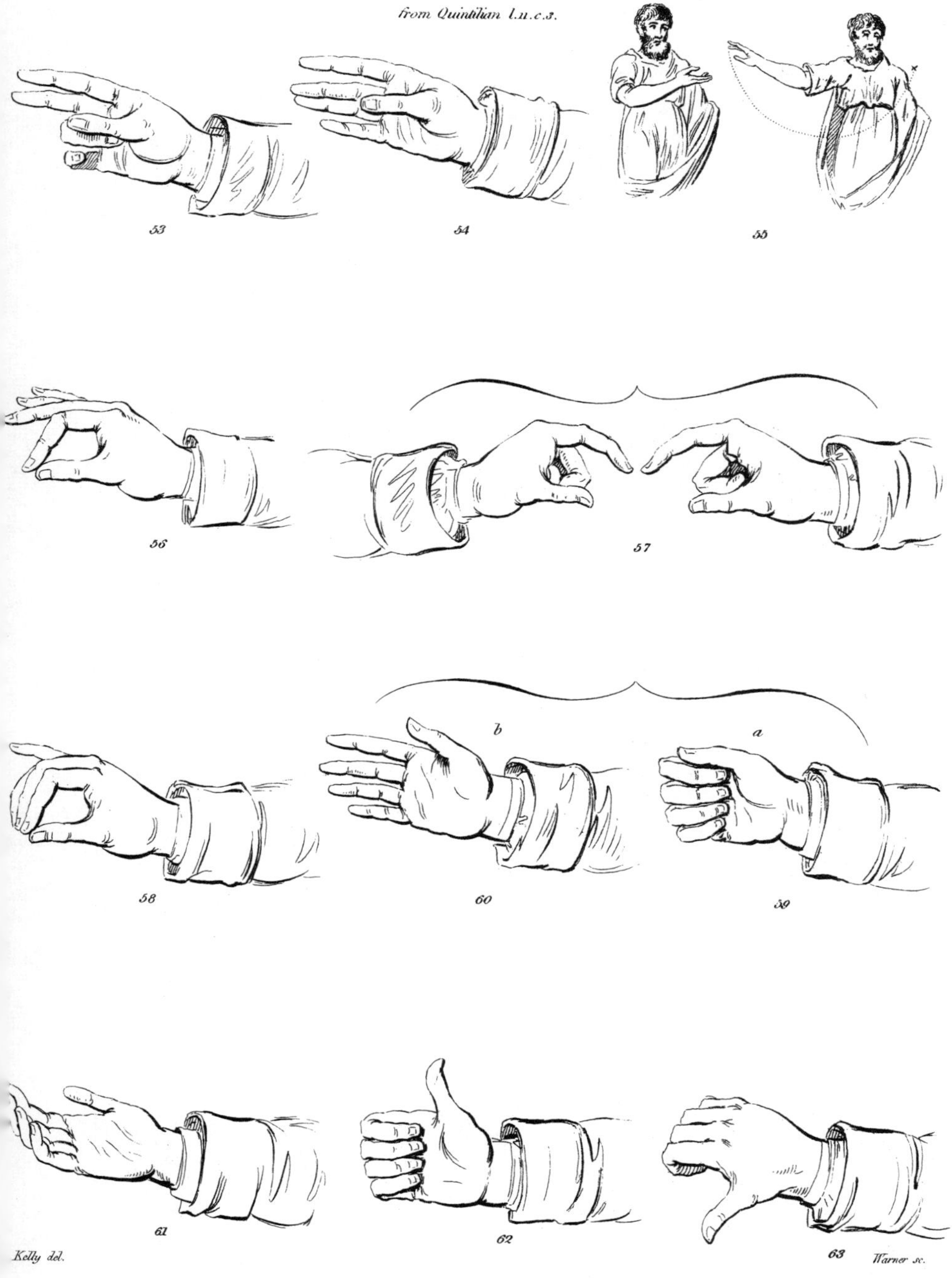

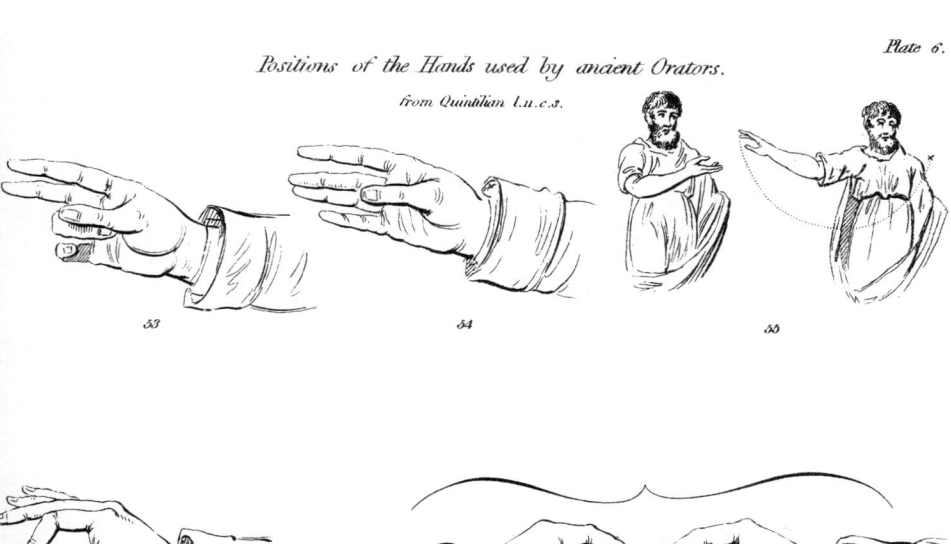

53   54   55

56   57

58   60   59

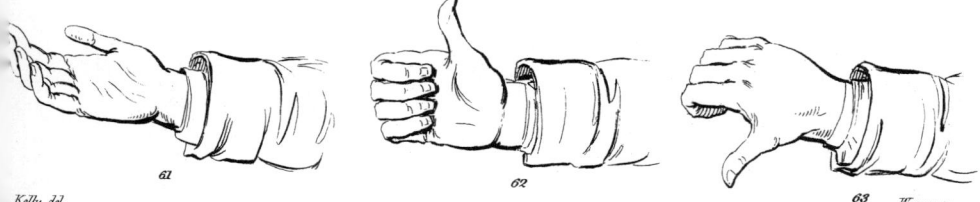

61   62   63

Kelly del.   Warner sc.

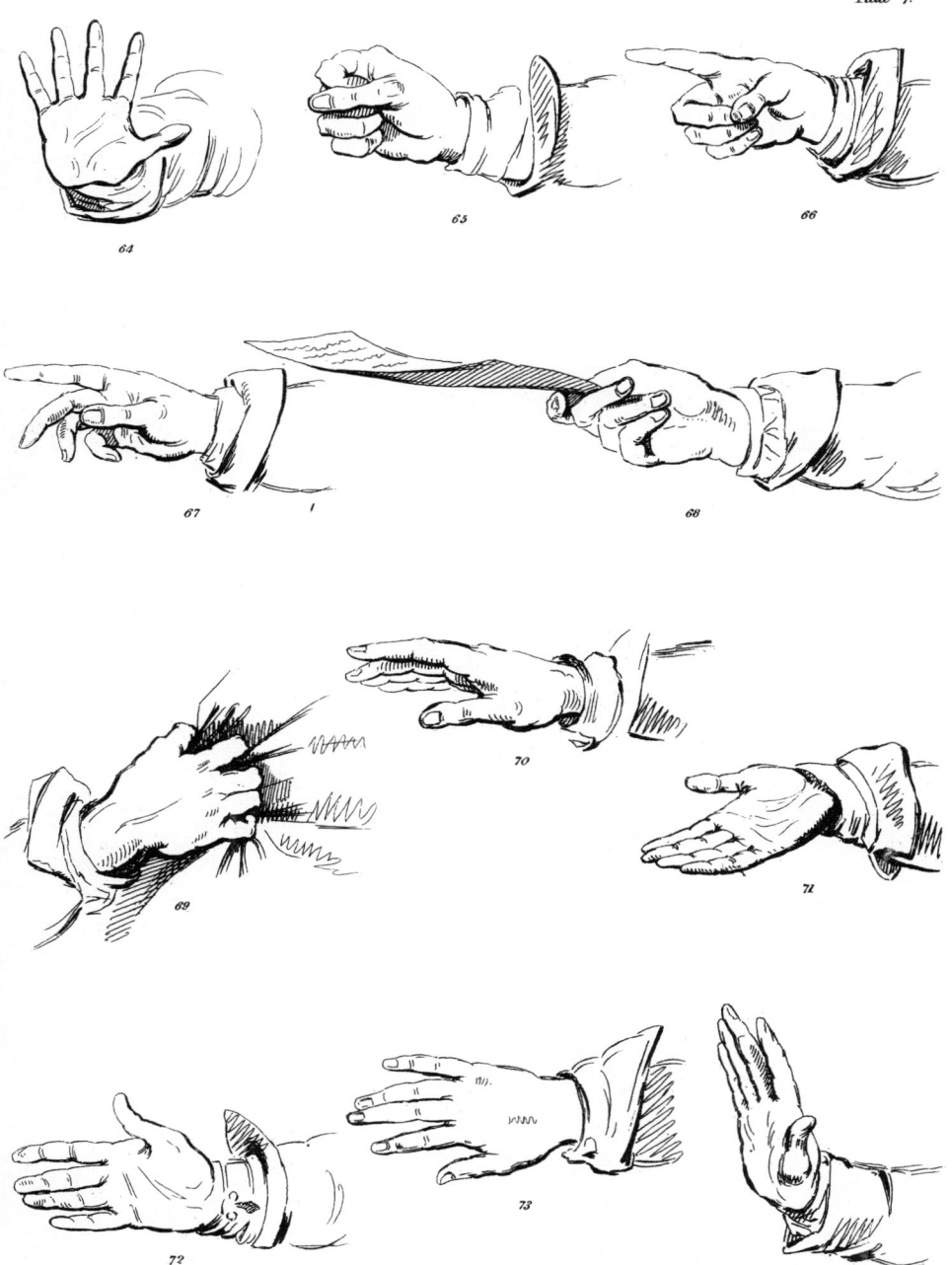

Plate 7.

64

65

66

67

68

69

70

71

72

73

74

Kelly del.

Warner sc.

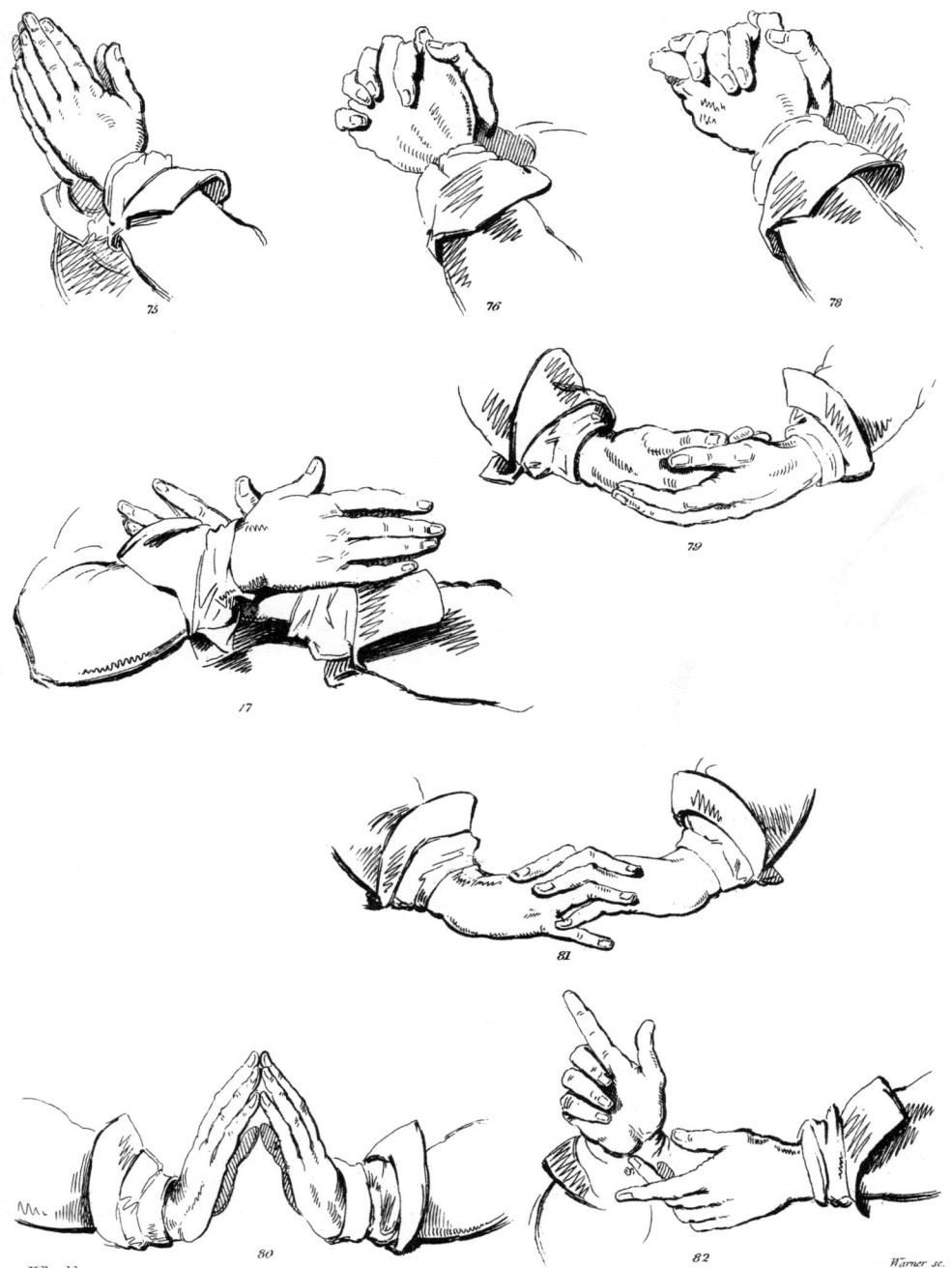

Plate. 8.

75

76

78

79

17

81

80

82

Kelly del.

Warner sc.

83   84   85   86

87   88   89   90

91   92   93   94

95   96   97   98

Kelly del.   Warner sc.

Complex Significant Gestures.

99   100   101   102

103   104   105   106

107   108   109   110

Kelly del.   Warner sc.

Complex Significant Gestures.

111 112 113 114

115 116 117 118

119 120 121 122

Kelly del. Warner sc.

TO THE

RIGHT HONOURABLE

FRANCIS WILLIAM

EARL OF CHARLEMONT,

ONE OF THE EARLIEST OF HIS PUPILS IN HIS AFFECTION
AND RESPECT,

THIS WORK IS INSCRIBED,

AS A

MEMORIAL OF HIS PRECEPTS ON AN IMPORTANT BRANCH OF

ORATORY,

AND AS AN

EXPRESSION OF HIS GRATITUDE FOR THE EARLY AND CONTINUED
PATRONAGE OF HIS LORDSHIP'S FAMILY,

BY

HIS LORDSHIP'S

FORMER PRECEPTOR, FAITHFUL FRIEND,

AND

MUCH OBLIGED HUMBLE SERVANT,

THE AUTHOR.

Woodville, near Dublin,
5th May, 1806.

PREFACE.

THE work here submitted to the judgment of the public will be found to be constructed of materials, some of which have been long in their possession, and some of which are new. As to the reception of the former, provided I shall be found to have selected and arranged them with any degree of judgment, I cannot doubt that it will be favourable; they have been always approved, however not always duly observed: as to the latter, I should hope, that not only their novelty[1] but also their

---

[1] As to the novelty of part of my work, I believe it to be new both in its plan and execution. I do not know, at least, of any writer who has undertaken to describe gesture by symbols. I shall, however, shelter myself under the modest declaration of the ancient critic: ἐγὼ γὲν ἐδεμιᾷ τοιαύτῃ περιτυχὼν ὅιδα γραφῇ, πολλὴν ζήτησιν αὐτῶν ποιησάμενος. ἃ μὲν δὴ διαβεβαιῦμαί γε, ὡς δὴ καὶ σαφῶς ἐιδώς· τάχα γὰρ ἂν ἔιέν τινες ἅι ἐμὲ διαλανθάνεσαι τοιαῦται γραφαί. . . . . . περὶ μὲν ἔν τέτων ὀυδὲν ἔχω, καθάπερ ἔφην, διαβεβαιῦσθαι. *Dion. Halicarnass. de Antiquis Orat.* p. 6. Edit. Oxon.

I have met with the following reference to books which I have not been able to procure; the reader may possibly possess or obtain them; in their object they bear some resemblance to my work, but most probably none in the execution.

Gesner's Isagoge.
Ille decor etiam pronuntiationem actionemque omnem dirigit unicè.

Habemus quidem de hoc quoque præcepta libris proposita: extat *Petri Francii Eloquentia exterior*, ubi non dedit modo præcepta, sed illa accommodavit etiam exemplis: addidit Ciceronis Orationes duas, pro Marcello, et Archia poeta; ostenditque, quomodo singula sint pronuncianda; quomodo, et ubi, movenda manus vel dextra, vel sinistra; temperanda vox; et hujus generis reliqua.——Ante eum jam simile quid tentatum est in Gallia a Conrarto: *Conrart Traité de l'Action de l'Orateur. Paris*, 1686. 12. Et nuper vir doctissimus

utility in an important department of literature may serve as their recommendation. In venturing thus to call the public attention to my speculations, I feel it my duty to anticipate every just and reasonable enquiry; and for this purpose I shall enter into a brief explanation of the origin, the progress, and the objects of the work.

The laborious duty of teaching declamation, as I have stated in another place, incited me first to devise some permanent marks, by means of which I might be enabled to record, and to communicate in writing, with brevity and precision, my own ideas as to the manner of delivery proper to be adopted on certain occasions. Having, as I conceive, fallen upon a fertile principle, as will be found explained in the work, I succeeded by considerable labour in the invention and arrangement of a notation applicable to my purposes; and proved its advantages by the test of my own experience. In the course of my investigation I was also induced, and, by means of the permanent marks, in some measure enabled to examine more minutely the various requisites for perfect rhetorical delivery. And no

---

Wernsdorfius Gedanensis Gymnasii professor, quum celebraret Gymnasium bisæculare Jubilæum, de eadem re egit in programmate suo: sed neque hic præcepta dari possunt satis universalia. (* Alias: optimum est exempla intueri bona et imitari.) Oportet videre, quid deceat. Et inter dicendum non semper cogitari potest de præceptis. Ille ipse decor naturalis, assuetudo, mentis ardor, inter dicendum, nobis non sentientibus dictat omnia. *Jo. Matthæi Gesneri prima lineæ Isagoges in Eruditionem universalem.* Leipsiæ, 1784. Vol. I. p. 331. Art. 383.

I do not altogether agree with the learned author in the latter part of this observation, my reasons will be seen in the work. He proceeds, after what is here quoted, to praise Mosheim for the eloquence of his orations, but says he failed in the graces of delivery. The example makes against his own observation.

longer limiting myself to my original intention of relieving merely my own labour, I extended my views and enquiries not only to the elementary principles of rhetorical action, but also to whatsoever appeared to me most intimately connected with the improvement and perfecting of public speaking in general. Upon these subjects I formed and completed a plan according to my own particular ideas; which, it was my intention, when properly digested, to lay before the public: but previous to this, I thought it incumbent on me to examine, as far as in my power, what had been done by others, who had laboured in the same enquiries; in order either to support my opinions by their authority, or to be prepared to vindicate them where any difference should appear irreconcileable with the principles, which I had adopted.

In the discharge of this duty to the public and myself, I have limited my researches only by the extent of my means of information: and although I have not been able to accomplish all that might perhaps be requisite to be done in this respect, I trust I shall be found to have done as much as will prove my diligence, and as may be necessary for the establishment of my general principles.

During my examination of modern writers, it has appeared to me, that, with little exception, they have neglected to pay due attention to the precepts and authority of the great and ancient masters; and that they have passed over in total silence the works of the older rhetoricians, as well as of some, who may be almost reckoned among the moderns, whose works contain much valuable instruction on the subject of delivery. All

immediately to my purpose, which I have found in those different authorities, I have produced, and placed before the reader's
eyes, as far as my reading and opportunities have led me to the
knowledge of them. For the copious extracts which I have
made from them for the ornament and support of my work, I
look with some confidence to the approbation of the liberal
scholar: and if any shall not (as in many instances I should
expect) confine himself to the actual specimens which I have
provided for him in these extracts, he will at least thank me
for stimulating him to indulge and satisfy his thirst at those per-
ennial sources, from which I have drawn, and to which I have
always made accurate references for his greater convenience.

In treating of public speaking in general, I have been obliged
to touch upon each principal species; as that of the senate, the
bar, the pulpit, and the stage. On the delivery of the preacher
I have ventured to speak the more freely, as lying within my
own more immediate province,·and belonging to my particular
profession. Of the other modes of public speaking I have treated
with greater reserve; yet as they may be reduced to common
principles, I have not hesitated to maintain certain opinions with
respect to all.

As to the arrangement of my materials, I have spared no
pains to dispose them in the most strictly methodical order;
and I have particularly laboured to render the new matter by
these means intelligible to the utmost of my power. How far I
may have sufficiently explained myself to the public at large, I
cannot altogether form a judgment: but if I may conjecture
from the opinions of a few friends whom I have consulted, and

also from the experience I have had in the instruction of youth; the whole plan of the notation (which I consider the only part of my work of apparent difficulty as to the comprehension), is sufficiently clear; may easily, I should think, be understood in an hour or two; and may instantly afterwards be put to the trial with the assistance of the tables and the plates. If I do not deceive myself in this expectation, I may hope the use of my notation may be considered to merit adoption by such public speakers as desire to improve, and wish to record either their own ideas or those of the most celebrated in their different modes of speaking.

The system of notation, as expressed in writing, however carefully explained, is also amply illustrated by numerous engraved figures. In the conduct of this part of the work nothing has been neglected in any respect conducive to the principal object, explanation. Figures have been given wherever necessary, and various contrivances have been devised for distinguishing to the eye the transitions and preparations of action: these are effected sometimes by separate figures, sometimes by dotted lines, expressing changes of position in the same figures, and sometimes by stars and dots, which shew the line of motion from a previous to a subsequent action. But notwithstanding the multitude of figures a proper regard to œconomy has been observed. The manner of the execution of the engraving, however light, is not unpleasing; and, though making no pretensions, will not discredit the artist. And the space which each figure occupies singly, as well as the size of the plates, has been reduced to the smallest dimensions, consistent with the necessary illustration. But this attention to the purchaser has

not been without its inconvenience. I have had the whole of
the plates more than three times delineated. The original
sketches, according to my first ideas of the work, were executed
by George Chinnery, Esq. now resident at Madras: but the
scale adopted was too large, and the manner too expensive, and,
when the whole of my system was arranged, many figures
proved redundant, whilst others were deficient; and as I could
not avail myself of the talents of this excellent artist for the
necessary additions and alterations, I have been obliged to
obtain the assistance of a young man of considerable merit,
who first altered and completed, and then reduced the whole
of the figures to their present form and size. It must be confessed, that this saving of expence to the publication has deprived it of a splendor which it would have derived from the
spirited designs first intended for it. I have to lament that the
figures of Mrs. Siddons in Plate XI. have also, from this cause,
lost considerably, and the more so because they are the contributions of elegant talents and private friendship. But I shall be
excused for having made every consideration give way to what
appears my duty to the public. I have for the same reasons
relinquished the ornament of a proposed frontispiece, which,
however, I may be permitted to describe below.[2]

---

[2] I had chosen for the frontispiece the figure of the Muse Polyhymnia, from an engraving
in the Galleria Giustiniana, Plate CXLVIII. The figure is beautiful, and the expression of
the countenance fine; she holds her robe with the right hand, and with the left points
upwards. A line from an epigram of Ausonius, and a couple also from the Greek, whence
he borrowed his, were to have been placed under, as follow:

Signat cuncta manu loquitur Polymnia gestu. *Aus. Ep. de novem Musis.*

Σιγῶ φθεγγομένης παλάμης θελξίφρονα παλμὸν,

Νεύματι φωνήεσσαν ἀπαγγέλλουσα σιωπήν.

Brodæi Anth. Græc. l. i. p. 139.

In speaking of the objects which I propose to myself in this work, I may be the more brief, because they will be found particularly explained hereafter: in this place something is also necessary to be said.

Although the ancient writers have left various and complete systems of rhetoric, as far as relates to the four first divisions, viz. invention, disposition, elocution, (that is, choice of language), and memory; and although modern writers have expounded, and detailed, and added to all these precepts, insomuch that in every language abundant instructions can be obtained in all that relates to these *four* divisions by every man who studies public speaking; and although within the British islands, in all these divisions, the public speakers have arrived at distinguished excellence; yet it is a fact, that we do not possess from the ancients, nor yet from the labours of our own countrymen, any sufficiently detailed and precise precepts for the *fifth* division of the art of rhetoric, namely, *rhetorical delivery*, called by the ancients *actio* and *pronunciatio*. Something more than we have attempted hitherto has been done abroad

---

I was, however, somewhat divided in my choice between this and another figure of Polyhymnia, which is said to be in the collection of the Queen of Sweden. She is sitting splendidly habited, holding her robe in her left hand, and pointing upwards with the right.

In the Iconologie of Cæsar Ripa, Paris, 1644, Part II. p. 74, Polyhymnia is thus described:

On la peint ayant des perles sur la teste, un robbe blanche, la main droite haussée en action de harranguer et en la gauche un rouleau où est ecrit le mot *suadere.*

La pierrerie et les perles, qu'elle a sur la teste, sont les marques de dons et des qualitez, qui enrichissent son esprit: car suivant les preceptes de la Rhétorique, elle employe l'invention, la disposition, la mémoire, l'élocution, et la prononciation, qui sont communes à ce bel art, faisant voir, comme dit Virgile:

Ou par son action, ou mesme par son geste
Ce quelle veut montrer et rendre manifeste.

by Mr. Engel and by others whose names and writings, except those quoted in the work, and the notice contained in a preceding note, are equally out of my reach. My object in this work is therefore to contribute my share of labour towards the completion of the rules for the better study and acquisition of rhetorical delivery, the *fifth*, and least cultivated, but if we are to believe ancient authorities, not the least important division of the art.

The rules which I have laid down are the best which I have been able to collect or to devise, however deficient or incomplete. But rules, even if perfect, cannot be expected to bestow genius where nature has denied it, nor yet to operate any absolute change upon the natural abilities of men:[3] true genius, whithersoever it turns, will always find out a sure and effectual passage for itself through every obstacle; it either creates rules for itself, or is above rules. But for the ordinary description of men, that is for the great majority, rules are not only useful, but perhaps indispensable, the better to bring forward and improve the talents which they may possess, and to afford the necessary support, and supply the necessary confidence to the diffident and reserved. And the total want of any regular system of such rules for rhetorical delivery appears to me to be the chief cause

---

[3] Nam si quantum de quaque dici potest, prosequamur, finis operis non reperietur. Illud tamen in primis testandum est, nihil præcepta atque artes valere, nisi adjuvante natura. Quapropter ei, cui deerit ingnium, non magis hæc scripta sunt, quam de agrorum cultu sterilibus terris. Sunt et alia ingenita quædam adjumenta, vox, latus patiens laboris, valetudo, constantia, decor: quæ si modica obtigerunt, possunt ratione ampliari: sed nonnunquam ita desunt, ut bona etiam ingenii studiique corrumpant: sicut et hæc ipsa sine doctore perito, studio pertinaci, scribendi, legendi, dicendi multa et continua exercitatione, per se nihil possunt. *Quint. Inst. Proem. l. i. ad finem.*

of the reproach of frigid indifference which is charged against our public speakers. If other more lively nations contrive to dispense with them altogether, and gesticulate naturally, if not with perfect grace, at least with sufficient expression; the speakers of our islands, as is evinced by fact, cannot with advantage depend solely on nature. But though in our temperate climate the people are less disposed to vivacity of manner, and are not easily excited; yet the cool, the solid, and the cultivated understanding of the British speaker, under the direction of rational principles, and roused into energy on great and interesting occasions, is capable, as well in action as in composition, of all that is graceful and persuasive, and even of all the energetic and irresistible powers of delivery. The fair hope and honourable ambition of assisting in the discovery and developement of those principles which may contribute to adorn and enforce our native eloquence, has encouraged me to proceed in my arduous undertaking; and, like other voyagers in unknown regions, to lay before the public the result of my labours for the advancement of this object. And if war, with its complicated interests, did not interfere to divert attention from these peaceful speculations, I should think it a favourable season for them, since the most liberal and enlightened persons in the different professions appear to be agreed upon the advantages and necessity of increased attention to rhetorical delivery. My chief efforts are directed to meet their opinions, and I look forward with considerable anxiety to the judgment which they shall pass on my endeavours.

By a few readers I hope to be received with some attention, and perhaps with a degree of partiality: those few either are, or have been my pupils, for whom this work was originally designed, who witnessed its progress, and shared in its labour; and who will recognize many precepts with which they must be familiar. It is with peculiar satisfaction that I indulge this hope, and that I look forward hereafter to extend, by means of this work, my communication with their ingenuous minds, at a period when, their understandings being more mature, they will be able to derive greater advantage from my instructions than they could in their boyish days: when perhaps they shall be anxious for information, when they shall have entered by profession or by rank upon the great theatres of public eloquence; when we shall be separated by time and place, and can no longer discuss together the various topics here considered. I seem to myself in these sheets to bequeath to the children of my affection a legacy which, if wisely used, may prove of some value, and which they cannot dissipate.

The title *Chironomia*, which I have adopted, will be vindicated from the affectation of modern fabrication, when it is recollected that it is a strictly classical term, and of the very earliest and highest authority, as will be seen by various proofs. And that it may also be properly applied in the extended sense in which I have used it; that is as the name of the whole art of gesture and delivery may, I conceive, be maintained on the authority of Cœlius Rhodoginus as quoted below.[4]

---

4 Et Glaucum de quo diximus, Græci scribunt fuisse ἐπιτηδειότερον τῷ χειρονομεῖν, hoc est Chironomiæ commodiorem: sed Fabius legem gestus interpretatur Chironomiam libro primo et manuum quidem ea proprie dicitur: verum per catechresin et ad alia membra relationem habet: nam legimus ἐχερονόμησε τοῖς σκέλεσιν ὁ Ἱπποκλείδης, id est, esticulatus est pedibus Hippoclides: unde accusatus invulgatum id jactatumque ingessit,

I avail myself here of the opportunity of making my acknow-
ledgments to Dr. John Kearney, the present Lord Bishop of
Ossory, late Provost of Trinity College Dublin, for his liberal
information, and for the communication of several rare books
from his valuable private library. And to the Right Honourable
George Knox, M. P. for Trinity College Dublin, &c. &c. I beg
to return my sincere thanks for his most judicious and important observations upon a considerable part of the manuscript.

ἒ φροντὶς Ἱπποκλείδη, non curæ est Hippoclidæ. Sed urbanius longe illud comici Anti-
phonis,

> Ὀυχ ὁρᾶς ὀρχώμενον ταῖς χερσὶ τὸν Βάκηλον ;

nonne vides manibus saltantem Bacelum ? At abusionem hoc genus mirari non decet ; ut
quæ sit vel frequentissima : ut cum chiropedas, manuum dicimus vincula, nam pedum
proprie peda est. Quod autem de Chironomia diximus, Galeni confirmatur authoritate :
Qui imbecilles sunt (inquit) cruribus, his superioribus partibus exercentur melius, Chiro-
nomiis, acrochirismis, disci jactu, halterum usu. *Ludov. Cælii Rhodogini Lec. Antiq. l.* xi.
p. 562.

GENERAL TABLE OF CONTENTS,

REFERRING TO THE PAGES IN WHICH THE CONTENTS
ARE DETAILED MORE AT LARGE.

GENERAL TABLE OF CONTENTS.

APPENDIX.

INTRODUCTION.

General Division of the Subject.—Of the Pains taken by the Ancients for the Acquisition of perfect rhetorical Delivery.

THE management of the voice, the expression of the countenance, and the gesture of the head, the body, and the limbs, constitute the external part of oratory; and relate to the personal talents and efforts of the public speaker, in like manner as the other divisions of rhetoric, invention, disposition, choice of words, and memory, relate to those of his understanding.

By the ancients the external part of oratory was called pronunciation or action; the former name derived from the voice, the latter from the gesture.[1] Cicero, in one place, says, action is, as it were, the language of the body; in another, that it is a species of corporal eloquence.[2,3] Under gesture he comprehends the

---

[1] Pronunciatio a plerisque actio dicitur, sed prius nomen a voce, sequens a gestu videtur accipere. Namque actionem Cicero alias quasi sermonem, alias eloquentiam quamdam corporis dicit. *Quint.* lib. xi. c. 3.

[2] Est enim actio quasi sermo corporis. *Cic. de Orat.* lib. iii, c. 59.

[3] Est enim actio quasi corporis quædam eloquentia. Cum constet e voce atque motu. . . . Dicerem etiam de gestu, cum quo junctus est vultus. *Cic. Orat.* xvii.

B

expression of the countenance. The above enumeration of the external parts of oratory appears to be sanctioned by Quintilian, in some places he makes three divisions, in others two.[4] We have also his authority, and shall adduce many others, for calling the art of gesture, to which this work is principally devoted, by the name of Chironomia. The modern name is Delivery, it has been frequenty called Elocution, particularly by late writers; but, as it appears, improperly. The term elocution is, by this acceptation, diverted from its original signification as established by the ancient rhetoricians. They used this term for the name of the third division of the art of rhetoric, which treats principally of the choice and arrangement of words.[5 6 7-8-9-10] It would therefore seem advise-able to restore it to its proper sense; particularly in our enquiries, which refer us often to the ancients, as the great masters of the

---

4 Affectus omnes languescant necesse est, nisi voce, vultu, totius prope habitu corporis inardescant. *Quint.* lib. xi. c. 3.

Cum sit autem actio ut dixi in duas divisa partes, vocem gestumque, quorum alter oculos, altera aures movet. *Quint.* ib.

5 Igitur quam Græci φράσιν vocant, Latine dicimus Elocutionem. Eam spectamus in verbis aut singulis aut conjunctis. *Quint.* lib. viii. c. 1.

6 Tertia rhetoricæ pars est elocutio, quæ verborum delectu et collocatione maxime constat. *Capperonius in Quint.* lib. x. c. 1.

7 Videamus nunc, quas res debeat habere elocutio commoda et perfecta. Quæ maxime admodum oratori accommodata est, tres res in se decet habere, elegantiam, compositionem, dignitatem. Elegantia est, quæ facit, ut unumquidque pure et aperte dici videatur. . . . . . . Compositio est verborum constructio, quæ facit omnes partes orationis æquabiliter perpolitas. . . . . . . Dignitas est, quæ reddit ornatam orationem varietate distinguens. *Rhet. ad Herenn.* lib. iv. c. 12.

8 Elocutio est, quæ arripit verba vel propria vel translata quæque nova facit veteraque componit. . . . . Pronunciatio vocis, motus, gestusque pro rerum et verborum dignitate moderatio. *Isidori de Arte Rhet.* p. 356. *Antiqui Rhetores.*

9 Elocutio est idoneorum verborum ad inventionem accommodata perceptio. *Cassiodorus,* ib. p. 336.

10 Elocutio oratoria est rerum inventarum et dispositarum, per verba sententiasque expositio ad persuadendum idonea. *Ger. Joan. Vossii Part. Orat.* lib. iv. c. 1.

art. To express what the Roman writers understood by *pronunciatio* and *actio*, we shall use the word Delivery, which is already established, in this sense, in our language.

That the ancients studied the art of delivery, with the most particular attention to every circumstance connected with it, cannot be doubted. They attached to it an importance almost equal to that of composition. The failure of Demosthenes himself, before he cultivated this art with sufficient care, and his extraordinary success afterwards, induced him to overvalue delivery, by giving it the preference to every other requisite which contributes to form the perfect orator. Plutarch relates, in his life of this great man, that he had failed in his first attempts at speaking in public, on account of his inattention to the art of delivery. Eunomius, on one occasion, endeavoured to encourage him to continue to make his utmost exertions, by assuring him that he approached the excellence of Pericles himself. On another occasion, when much cast down by a similar failure, he met the player Satyrus, his friend, and when he complained to him, that, notwithstanding his having laboured more than all the other orators, he could not succeed, whilst very wretched speakers were admired; Satyrus, in reply, desired him to pronounce for him some lines of Euripedes or Sophocles. When he had spoken them, Satyrus repeated them over again to Demosthenes, but with tones and gestures so appropriate, that they appeared to him to be altogether of superior excellence. " And being persuaded how much " of ornament and grace is added to the speech by the delivery, " he considered of little or no value the labour of any man who " neglected the pronunciation and the gesture suited to the

" words."" (This last sentence is interpreted literally.) Upon this he built for himself a subterraneous study (κατάγειον μελετητήριον), which Plutarch says was standing in his time, into which he descended every day to practise delivery (ὑπόκρισιν), and to modulate his voice. In this he often remained two or three months, with a part only of his head shaved, in order to put it out of his power to go abroad. After going through such labours as these, in order to acquire a just delivery, and having been in consequence crowned with the most complete success, it is not surprising that Demosthenes should have estimated this art even beyond its worth. Men are apt to set the highest value upon that which is of most difficult attainment. And the most difficult part of oratory, to Demosthenes, was probably the delivery, because he had natural impediments to surmount. But although Demosthenes may have been supposed for these reasons to have over-rated delivery, there can be nothing deduced either from its own nature, or from the anecdote which we have related, that does not prove it to be a very important part of the business of a public speaker.

---

[11] Πάλιν δὲ ποτε φάσιν ἐκπεσόντος αὐτῆ καὶ ἀπιόντος οἴκαδε συγκεκαλυμμένε καὶ βαρέως φέροντος, ὑπακολεθῆσαι Σάτυρον τὸν ὑποκριτὴν, ἐπιτήδειον ὄντα καὶ συνελθεῖν· ὀδυρεμένε δὲ τε Δημοσθένες πρὸς αὐτὸν, ὅτι πάντων φιλοπονώτατος ὢν τῶν λεγόντων, καὶ μικρε δέων καταναλωκέναι τὴν τε σώματος ἀκμὴν εἰς τετο, χάριν ἐκ ἔχει πρὸς τὸν δῆμον· ἀλλὰ κραιπαλῶντες ἄνθρωποι, ναῦται καὶ ἀμαθεῖς ἀκύονται, καὶ κατέχεσι τὸ βῆμα, παροξᾶται δ᾽ αὐτὸς· ἀληθῆ λέγεις, ὧ Δημόσθενες, φάναι τὸν Σάτυρον· ἀλλ᾽ ἐγὼ τὸ αἴτιον ἰασομαι ταχέως, ἄν μοι τῶν Εὐριπίδε τινὰ ῥήσεων ἢ Σοφοκλέες, ἐθελήσῃς εἰπεῖν ἀπὸ στόματος· εἰπόντος δὲ τε Δημοσθένες, μεταλαβόντα τὸν Σάτυρον ὕτω πλᾶσαι καὶ διεξελθεῖν ἕν ἤθει πρέποντι καὶ διαθέσει τὴν αὐτὴν ῥῆσιν, ὡς θ᾽ ὅλως ἑτέραν τω Δημοσθένει φανῆναι. πεισθέντα δ᾽ ὅσον ἐκ τῆς ὑποκρίσεως τῷ λόγῳ κόσμε καὶ χάριτος πρόσεςι μικρὸν ἡγήσασθαι καὶ τὸ μεδὲν εἶναι τὴν ἄσκησιν ἀμελε̃ντι τῆς προφορᾶς καὶ διαθέσεως τῶν λεγομένων. *Plut. in Vit. Demosth.*

It may therefore be fairly concluded, that to neglect all or any part of the labour which constitutes correct delivery; whether it be the due management of the voice, the expression of the countenance, or the appropriate gesture, is so far an injury to the cause in which the speaker is engaged, and so far deprives his composition of its just effect. Yet a strange prejudice has seemed to prevail against every effort to improve delivery. The voice is indeed so indispensable that some attention is given to its management. The countenance is left altogether to nature; and perhaps if feelings do exist, nature will be found to form it best. But gesture, unless some accidental and uncouth motions may be so called, is altogether reprobated. The origin of this prejudice may be traced to two sources; first, the injudicious use of gesture, that is the neglect or ignorance of its proper character, as suited to certain subjects and certain places. Thus, although the introduction of the gesture of the theatre into the pulpit is indecorous and offensive; yet to the pulpit belongs its own proper and becoming gesture. The second source of this prejudice may be found in the difficulty of determining the proper standard of gesture, and of suiting it to the particular case. All that the ancients have laboured on this business, or almost all, has died with them. Even modern speakers, if any succeed in this part of eloquence, can impart instruction only within a very limited space, and within a very limited time. Every man has to begin for himself; and hence few are willing to venture upon the labour of contriving a system, and choose rather to trust to the gesture suggested by the moment, than hazard the more dangerous exhibition of gestures imperfectly conceived, and which will consequently be imperfectly executed. Each public speaker therefore falls into a manner of his own, as it is called, which is pardoned as being *his way*, and which is in general most unimpressive and most ungraceful. If these gestures contribute in the warmer parts of an oration to give any force to the expression, nothing more can arise from them; they deduct from it amply by their wearisome sameness and iterated monotony. Some speakers, aware of this, do not venture upon any gesture of the limbs at all, but nod with their head, and labour with their body through the whole discourse. However excellent the compositions of our speakers may be, and many will be found to vie with the most perfect of the ancients, their delivery, it is to be feared, has advanced but little beyond that state in which it stood so long ago as Mr. Addison's time.

" Our preachers stand stock still in the pulpit, and will not so " much as move a finger, to set off the best sermons in the world. " We meet with the same speaking statues at our bars, and in all " public places of debate. Our words flow from us in a smooth " continued stream, without those strainings of the voice, motions " of the body, and majesty of the hand, which are so much cele- " brated in the orators of Greece and Rome. We talk of life and " death in cold blood, and keep our temper in a discourse which " turns upon every thing that is dear to us."[12]

Mr. Sheridan repeats this charge against the English preachers with even greater seriousness, and in many passages: I shall quote but one: " There is no emotion of the mind, which nature " does not make an effort to manifest by some of those signs " (tones, looks, and gestures), and therefore a total suppression " of those signs is of all other states apparently the most unna-

---

[12] Spect. No. 407.

" tural. And this, it is to be feared, is too much the state of the
" pulpit elocution in general in the church of England. On
" which account, there never was perhaps a religious sect upon
" earth, whose hearts were so little engaged in the act of public
" worship, as the members of that church. To be pleased, we
" must feel, and we are pleased with feeling. The Presbyterians
" are moved, the Methodists are moved; they go to their meet-
" ings and tabernacles with delight. The very Quakers are moved.
" Fantastical and extravagant as the language of their emotions
" is, yet still they are moved by it, and they love their form of
" worship for that reason; whilst much the greater part of the
" members of the English church are either banished from it
" through disgust, or reluctantly attend the service as a disagree-
" able duty."[13]

The Rev. James Fordyce has written expressly on the eloquence of the pulpit.[14] He is speaking of gesture, and in a note
makes the following observations: " I cannot forbear regretting
" here, that a matter of such vast importance to the art under
" consideration, should be so generally neglected or misunder-
" stood. There is a common apprehension prevails indeed, that
" a strict regard to these rules would be deemed theatrical; and
" the dread perhaps of incurring this imputation, is a restraint
" upon many. But is it not possible to attain a just and expressive
" manner, perfectly consistent with the gravity of the pulpit, and
" perfectly distinct from the more passionate, strong, and diver-
" sified action of the theatre? And is it not possible to hit off
" this manner so easily and naturally, as to leave no room for

---

[13] Sheridan's Lect. VII. p. 166.   [14] Printed at Glasgow, 1755.

" just reflection? An affair this, it must be owned, of the utmost
" delicacy; in which we shall probably often miscarry, and meet
" with abundance of censure at first. But still I imagine, that
" through the regulations of taste, the improvements of experi-
" ence, the corrections of friendship, the feelings of piety, and
" the gradual mellowings of time; such an elocution may be
" acquired, as is above delineated; and such as when acquired
" will make its way to the hearts of the hearers, through their
" ears and eyes, with a delight to both that is seldom felt; whilst,
" contrary to what is commonly practised, it will appear to the
" former the very language of nature, and present to the latter
" the lively image of the preacher's soul. Were a taste for this
" kind of elocution to take place, it is difficult to say how much
" the preaching art would gain by it. Pronunciation would be
" studied, an ear would be formed, the voice would be modu-
" lated, every feature of the face, every motion of the hands,
" every posture of the body would be brought under right
" management. A graceful and correct and animated expression
" in all these would be ambitiously sought after; mutual criti-
" cisms and friendly hints would be universally encouraged;
" light and direction would be borrowed from every quarter and
" from every age. The best models of antiquity would in a par-
" ticular manner be admired, surveyed, and imitated. The sing-
" song voice and the see-saw gestures, if I may be allowed to use
" those expressions, would of course be exploded; and in time
" nothing would be admitted, at least approved among per-
" formers, but what was decent, manly, and truly excellent in
" the kind. Even the people themselves would contract insen-
" sibly a growing relish for such a manner; and those preachers
" would at last be in chief repute with all, who followed nature,

" overlooked themselves, appeared totally absorbed in their sub-
" ject, and spoke with real propriety and pathos from the imme-
" diate impulse of truth and virtue."

The complaints against the English preachers and public
speakers for their inattention to delivery, however strong, are not
more so than those, which even our lively neighbours have urged
against their own speakers for similar inattention. Ludovicus
Cresollius, a Jesuit of Britany, who wrote a treatise upon the perfect action and pronunciation of an orator, published at Paris in
1620, gives the following description of the delivery of a public
speaker, whose style was polished and whose composition was
learned.

" When he turned himself to the left, he spoke a few words
" accompanied by a moderate gesture of the hand, then bending
" to the right, he acted the same part over again; then back
" again to the left, and presently to the right, almost at an equal
" and measured interval of time, he worked himself up to his
" usual gesture, and his one kind of movement; you could
" compare him only to the blindfolded Babylonian oxen going
" forward and returning back by the same path." He was so
disgusted, that he shut his eyes, but even so he could not get
over the disagreeable impression of the speaker's manner. He
concludes, " I therefore give judgment against and renounce all
" such kind of orators."[15] In another place he has made an enu-

---

[15] Cum se in sinistram convertisset, pauca verba fundebat cum modico manuum gestu;
tum reflectens se in dexteram, eodem plane modo agebat, iterum in sinistram, mox in dexteram pari prope et dimensa temporis intercapedine, statum illum ciebat gestum, et unius

C

meration of the most remarkable faults of bad speakers; it is so spirited and characteristic, particularly in his own language, that it merits to be set down at large. The translation is nearly as follows: " Some hold their heads immoveable, and turned to " one side, as if they were made of horn; others stare with " their eyes as horribly, as if they intended to frighten every " one; some are continually twisting their mouths and working " their chins, while they are speaking, as if, all the time, they " were cracking nuts; some like the apostate Julian, breathe in- " sult, express in their countenance contempt and impudence. " Others, as if they personated the fictitious heroes in tragedy, " gape enormously, and extend their jaws as widely as if they " were going to swallow up every body: above all, when they " bellow with fury, they scatter their foam about, and threaten " with contracted brow, and eyes like Saturn. These, as if they " were playing some game, are continually making motions with " their fingers, and, by the extraordinary working of their hands, " endeavour to form in the air, I may almost say, all the figures " of the mathematicians. Those, on the contrary, have hands " so ponderous and so fastened down by terror, that they could " more easily move beams of timber; others labour so with their " elbows, that it is evident, either that they had been formerly " shoemakers themselves, or had lived in no other society but " that of cobblers. Some are so unsteady in the motions of their " bodies, that they seem to be speaking out of a cock-boat; others " again are so unwieldy and uncouth in their motions, that you " would think them to be sacks of tow painted to look like men.

---

generis motionem, boves illos Babylonicos diceres, per eandem viam obductis luminibus euntes et redeuntes. . . . . Igitur totum illud genus hominum abjudico atque repudio. *Cresollius. Vac. Autum.*

" I have seen some who jumped on the platform and capered
" nearly in measure : men that exhibited the fullers' dance, and
" as the old poet says, expressed their wit with their feet. But
" who in a short compass is able to enumerate all the faults of
" gesture, and all the absurdities of bad delivery ?" [16]

Thus, if it afford any consolation, we find that other nations
also have cause to complain of deficiency and neglect in this
important branch of oratory. It has been said, and Mr. Addison
seems to have acquiesced in the justice of the charge, that it does
not suit the genius of our speakers to use gesture. [17] There may
possibly be nations whose livelier feelings incline them more to
gesticulation than is common among us, as there are also countries in which plants of excellent use to man grow spontaneously;

---

[16] Quidam rigidum caput et obstipum non magis movent, quam si essent cornei : alii tam
immaniter oculos aperiunt, ut terrere omnes velle videantur. Nonnulli quasi nucem perpetuo
frangerent, os et mentum in dicendo contorquent. Quidam instar perfidiosi Juliani ὕβριν πνέωσι,
vultu contumeliam, impudentiamque significant. Alii ut in tragedia fictam heroum personam acturi, ut cum Luciano dicam, παμμέγεθες χαίνωσι, vaste hiant velut faucibus excepturi
omnes ; præsertim cum irati boant, spumas agunt, striata fronte et Saturniis oculis minan-
tur. Hi velut in ludo, continuo micant digitis, et incredibili manuum agitatione prope
dicam omnes mathematicorum figuras in aere conantur effingere : illi contra tam ponderosas
habent manus et stupore defixas, ut celerius trabes moverent : alii cubitos ita ventilant,
facile ut appareat, aut sutores fuisse aliquando, aut cum cerdonibus assiduissime fuisse ver-
satos : quidam ita vaccillant toto corpore, quasi è lintre loquerentur, alii tam vasti sunt et
in motu corporis tam agrestes, ut stuppeos saccos putares in hominis effigiem depictos. Vidi
etiam qui exilirent in suggesto et prope ad numerum tripudiarent, qui fullonios saltus ede-
rent et ut vetus poeta loquitur, pedibus argutarentur. Sed quis breviter gestus omnia vitia,
et ineptæ pronunciationis, oratione percenceat ? *Cresoll. Vac. Aut.*

Vidi multos, quorum supercilia ad singulos vocis conatus allevarentur, aliorum constricta,
aliorum etiam dissidentia, cum altero in verticem tenderent, altero pene oculus ipse preme-
retur. *Quint. l. 1. c.* 11.

[17] I believe every one will agree with me in this, that we ought to lay aside all kinds of
gesture (which seems to be very suitable to the genius of our nation), or at least to make
use of such only as are graceful and expressive. *Spect.* No. 407.

these, by care and culture, are found to thrive also in colder countries, and by a little study we shall equal the most favoured nations. With respect to the delivery of an orator, in all its refinement and necessary circumstances, the fact appears to be, that it belongs to no particular people to the exclusion of others; and that it is not the gift of nature more than other high acquirements; but that it is the reward of arduous labour, under the guidance of consummate art. We admit the French to have more facility in learning this art than ourselves, the French allow the same superiority to the Italians, the Italians to the Greeks; but in truth the gift is not gratuitous to any people. Gracchus laboured incessantly, Cicero laboured incessantly, Hortensius laboured, Demosthenes, Æschines, Isocrates laboured; which of all the celebrated orators has not laboured? or which of them can be said to owe his fame merely to the gift of nature, as the indigenous produce of the soil from which he sprung? If a standard of comparison could be found, hardly would the British actors, whose excellence is chiefly confined to this one branch of eloquence, delivery, lose in comparison with either moderns or ancients of other nations; and what the talents, the industry, and the professional acquirements of our actors have accomplished, can we doubt would be accomplished with equal success by our orators, if they brought into action equal industry and equal professional learning? It is not because the British orators are incapable of the most consummate perfection in the art of delivery, that this perfection is hardly to be seen among them; but because perfection in this, as in all other arts, is a work of labour and of time. Whether the acquisition be worthy of that labour and time, is a question to be decided, either on the authority of the great models and masters of eloquence, or on the same ground as the value of eloquence itself, of which it makes an important and indispensable part. Either men should be limited in their communications (were this possible) to the relation of simple facts and to reasonings grounded on demonstration only,*—or if they are allowed to use persuasion for good purposes, or to guard themselves and their friends from evil machinations, they should avail themselves of all the arts, of which experience has proved the use; were it otherwise, they would be exposed to meet their enemy with unequal weapons. These weapons, whether offensive or defensive, are supplied by the art of rhetoric. This art has five[18] principal divisions, of which the first three are constantly used by all our public speakers; namely, invention, disposition, and the choice of language correct or ornamental, properly called Elocution; memory, the fourth, is frequently used. Why should the art be mutilated and deprived of the fifth, pronunciation, or delivery? It was a question which

---

[18] Artis rhetoricæ partes quinque sunt, inventio, dispositio, elocutio, memoria, pronunciatio. Inventio est excogitatio rerum verarum aut verisimilium, quæ causam probabilem reddant. Dispositio est rerum inventarum in ordinem distributio. Elocutio est idoneorum verborum ad inventionem eloquutio. Memoria est firma animi rerum ac verborum ad inventionem perceptio. Pronunciatio est ex rerum et verborum dignitate vocis et corporis moderatio. Primum est enim invenire quod dicas. Deinde quod inveneris disponere: tum quod disposueris verbis explicare. Quarto quod inveneris et disposueris et oratione vestieris memoria comprehendere. Ultimum ac *summum* quod memoria comprehenderis *pronuntiare. Alcuini de Arte Rhet. Dial.* p. 360.

This division is, according to the authority of Cicero: Cumque esset omnis oratoris vis, ac facultas in quinque partes distributa, ut deberet reperire primum, quid diceret; deinde inventa non solum ordine, sed etiam momento quodam, atque judicio dispensare atque disponere; tum ea denique vestire, atque ornare oratione; post memoria sepire; ed extremum agere cum dignitate et venustate. *De Orat. l. 1. c. 31.*

* Neither the high court of Parliament in Great Britain, nor the courts of justice in the empire, are constituted on the model of the celebrated court of Areopagus.

Plato discussed, whether rhetoric was not to be rejected as a dangerous weapon. He determined the contrary, upon the principle which allows the use of every dangerous weapon, that we may defend our rights, and oppose our adversaries.[19] But should we therefore turn our arms against our friends? The rhetoricians were banished from Rome at one period: this fact is asserted by Suetonius, who, in confirmation of it, quotes a curious decree of the senate, and also a declaration of the censors,[20] which took place about seventy years later: they were afterwards, however, not only admitted, but encouraged by the highest authority.

---

[19] Δεῖ μέντοι ὦ Σώκρατες, τῇ ῥητορικῇ χρῆσθαι, ὥσπερ τῇ ἄλλῃ πάσῃ ἀγωνίᾳ . καὶ γὰρ τῇ ἄλλῃ ἀγωνίᾳ ὂ τάτα ἕνεκα δεῖ πρὸς ἅπαντας χρῆσθαι ἀνθρώπους, ὅτι ἔμαθέ τις πυκτεύειν τε καὶ παγκρατιάζειν καὶ ἐν ὄχλοις μάχεσθαι, ὡς τε κρείτων εἶναι καὶ φίλων καὶ ἐχθρῶν· ὂ τάτα ἕνεκα τὰς φίλας δεῖ τύπ]ειν, ὂδε κεντεῖν τε καὶ ἀποκτιννύναι.

Neither is art or strength to be blamed, though some men pervert and use them to bad purposes.

Ὁι δὲ μεταςρέψαντες, χρῶνται τῇ ἰσχύϊ καὶ τῇ τέχνῃ ὂκ ὀρθῶς. ἔκουν ὅι διδάξαντες, πονηροὶ· ὂδε ἡ τέχνη, ὂτε ἀιτία, ὂτε πονηρὰ τάτε ἕνεκα ἐςιν· ἀλλ᾽ ὅι μὴ χρώμενοι, ὂιμαι, ὀρθῶς. ὁ ἀυτὸς δὴ λόγος καὶ περὶ τῆς ῥητορικῆς   *Plato in Gorgia.*

[20] Rhetorica quoque apud nos, perinde atque grammatica, sero recepta est, paullo etiam difficilius quippe quam constet nonnunquam etiam prohibitam exerceri. Quod ne cui dubium sit, vetus senatusconsultum, item censorium edictum subjiciam :* *Caio Fannio Strabone, Marco Valerio Messalla consulibus,* Marcus Pomponius prætor senatum consuluit. Quod verba facta sunt de philosophis et de rhetoribus, de ea re ita censuerunt, ut Marcus Pomponius prætor animadverteret, curaretque uti è republica fideque sua videretur; *uti Romæ ne essent.†* De iisdem interjecto tempore, Cnæus Domitius Ænobarbus, et Lucius Lucinius Crassus censores, ita edixerunt. *Renunciatum est nobis esse homines* qui novum genus disciplinæ instituerunt: ad quos juventus in ludos conveniat: eos sibi nomen imposuisse latinos Rhetoras : ibi homines adolescentulos totos dies desidere. Majores nostri, quæ Liberos suos discere, et quos in ludos itare vellent, instituerunt. Hæc nova, quæ præter consuetudinem ac morem majorum fiunt, neque placent, neque recta videntur. Quapropter et iis qui eos ludos habent, et eos qui eo venire consueverunt, videtur faciendum ut ostendamus nostram sententiam, *nobis non placere.*

Paullatim et ipsa utilis honestaque apparuit, multique eam præsidii causa, et gloriæ, appetiverunt. *Sueton. de Claris Rhet.*

* U. C. 592.   † U. C. 662.

The great advancement of the British islands in every department of literature and refinement, leaves no reason to apprehend any public or private violence of this kind. All the branches of rhetoric, if we except only the last, have been long cultivated with advantage. The neglect of it may probably be attributed with more reason to the want of approved living models for imitation, than to any supposed incapacity for, or rooted indisposition towards, this division of the art. The theatre indeed is in no want of living models of almost absolute perfection in the art of delivery, and accordingly stands perhaps unrivalled in the higher walks of the drama: and from the growing attention of the public to this subject, and the various attempts to form intelligible systems of delivery, all so favourably received; it may be expected, that in the progress of many improvements suggested by those who are engaged in these labours, and aided by the arts of engraving, so little known to the ancients, that correct delivery shall in a short time be as well understood, and as commonly practised, as correct composition: and that at the bar, in the pulpit, and in the senate, as many impressive and graceful speakers will be found in proportion, as in the theatres. If the authority of the ancient illustrious orators have any weight, we shall be the less inclined to shrink from the labour necessary for the acquisition of this excellence, when we recollect the incessant and extraordinary exertions, which they considered indispensable for the same object. All these labours (by some of the greatest orators esteemed the most important of any) have perished with their mortal remains; either through the difficulty of recording them, and the want of those aids which modern arts can supply, or from that fatality which deprived posterity of many of their valuable writings. Except what is briefly delivered in Cicero's works, and for this brevity he apologizes;[21] and what Quintilian has taught more at large, little has come down to us; but even that little will furnish an idea of the importance attached to the art. Quintilian has named his work Institutes of Oratory, and he has fully devoted it to this subject; but oratory in his sense, and under his management, takes a very wide range. It comprehends the whole of those studies which form the orator, beginning at the earliest period of education, and extending to the most perfect exercise of his public functions; it relates not only to the language, the composition, the memory, the action, but even to the means of aiding the invention; and it insists above all on the morality and virtues of the perfect orator. And whilst he shews that a liberal education contributes chiefly to the formation of the orator, he also insists that morality, science, and philosophy are so connected with eloquence, that he claims them by right, as forming absolutely a part of his plan.[22] Nay, he even requires ideal perfection itself.[23] Cicero

---

[21] Edidi quæ potui, non ut volui, sed ut me temporis angustiæ coegerunt. *Cic. de Oratore,* cap. 61.

[22] Oratorem autem instituimus illum perfectum, qui esse, nisi vir bonus, non potest. Ideoque non dicendi modo eximiam in eo facultatem, sed omnes animi virtutes exigimus. Neque enim hoc concesserim, rationem rectæ honestæque vitæ (ut quidam putaverunt) ad philosophos relegandum ; cum vir ille vere civilis, et publicarum privatarumque rerum administrationi accommodatus, qui regere consiliis urbes, fundare legibus, emendare judiciis possit, non alius sit profecto, quam orator. Quare, tametsi me fateor usurum quibusdam, quæ philosophorum libris continentur, tamen ea jure vereque contenderim esse operis nostri, proprieque ad artem oratoriam pertinere. *Quint. Proem.*

[23] Sit igitur orator vir talis, qualis vere sapiens appellari potest, nec moribus modo perfectus (nam id mea quidem opinione, quanquam sint qui dissentiant, satis non est) sed etiam scientia, et omni facultate dicendi; qualis adhuc fortasse nemo fuerit. Sed non ideo minus nobis ad summa tendendum est; quod fecerunt plerique veterum, qui etsi nondum quenquam sapientem repertum putabant, præcepta tamen sapientiæ tradiderunt. *Ibid.*

has declared himself to the same effect,[24] and these opinions, though disputed by a late noble Lord, will not be disregarded.[25] Indeed, in this view, the general classical education so long continued in our schools and universities, will be found to aim manifestly at the same very important object, the institution of an orator. The education of the British youth seems to have been modelled upon the very plan of Quinctilian. All the learning of the ancients is their study; they read their historians, their poets, their orators, their philosophers; they comment upon them, they commit them to memory, they write expressly in imitation of their most beautiful passages. And all this is associated with, and refined and enlightened by, a perfect system of morality unknown to the heathens; and this is the food of the ingenuous mind from the first dawn of reason to the last hours of old age. No wonder the compositions of our writers should be elegant and chaste. But why are not their orations eloquent? Nothing can be more favourable to eloquence than the peculiar

---

[24] Quamobrem, si quis universam, et propriam oratoris vim definire, complectique vult, is orator erit mea sententia, hoc tam gravi dignus nomine, qui, quæcumque res inciderit, quæ sit dictione explicanda, prudenter, et composite, et ornate, et memoriter dicat, cum quadam etiam actionis dignitate. Sin cuipiam nimis infinitum videtur, quod ita proposui, quacumque de re, licet hinc, quantum cuique videbitur, circumcidat, atque amputet : tamen illud tenebo, si, quæ cæteris in artibus aut studiis sita sunt, orator ignoret, tantumque ea teneat, quæ sint in disceptationibus, aut in usu forensi : tamen his de rebus ipsis si sit ei dicendum, cum cognoverit ab iis, qui tenent, quæ sint in quaque re, multo oratorem melius, quam ipsos illos, quorum eæ sunt artes, esse dicturum . . . . Hoc profecto efficiet, ut quamcunque rem a quoque cognoverit, de ea re multo dicat ornatius, quam ille ipse, unde cognorit. *Cicero de Orat. l. i. c.* 15.

[25] Tacitus agrees with Cicero. Itaque hercule in libris Ciceronis deprehendere licet, non geometriæ, non musicæ, non grammaticæ, non denique ullius ingenuæ artis scientiam ei defuisse. Ille dialecticæ subtilitatem, ille moralis partis utilitatem, ille rerum motus causasque cognovit; ita enim est, optimi viri, ita ex multa eruditione, ex pluribus artibus, et omnium rerum scientia exundat et exuberat illa admirabilis eloquentia; neque oratoris

circumstances and character of the inhabitants of the British islands. They possess a constitution the freest upon earth, which has been for ages maintained and improved by public discussion: their liberal religion enjoins by its ordinances frequent discourses upon the most elevated and interesting subjects; their taste is refined and discriminating, their genius is noble and ardent.[26] Eloquence of the highest character ought, therefore, it should seem, to be the abundant produce of such a soil. They require only attention to the single point of delivery to place their talents upon equal terms with all the excellence of antiquity. The want of this attention chills the ardour, and weakens the splendour of their compositions; whereas, the very purpose of animated delivery would warm and excite them. Demonstration suits but few of the questions which occur in human affairs, persuasion applies to all. The delivery and the composition mutually act upon and affect each other; where the delivery is to be cold, the compo-

---

vis et facultas, sicut ceterarum rerum, angustis et brevibus terminis cluditur : sed is est orator, qui de omni quæstione pulchre et ornate et ad persuadendum apte dicere, pro dignitate rerum, ad utilitatem temporum, cum voluptate audientium possit. Hæc sibi illi veteres persuadebant; ad hæc efficienda intelligebant opus esse, non ut rhetorum scholis declamarent, nec ut fictis nec ullo modo ad veritatem accedentibus controveisiis linguam modo et vocem exercerent; sed ut his artibus pectus implerent, in quibus de bonis ac malis, de honesto ac turpi, de justo et injusto disputatur. Hæc enim est oratori subjecta ad dicendum materia. *Dial. de Oratoribus, c.* 30, 31.

Tacitus, or the author of this dialogue, appears to have fully adopted the opinion of Cicero : against which may be weighed that of the noble Lord in modern times.

Cicero, in his book de Oratore, in order to raise the dignity of that profession, which he knew himself to be at the head of, asserts, that a complete orator must be a complete every thing, lawyer, philosopher, divine, &c. That would certainly be well, if it were possible; but man's life is not long enough, &c. &c. *Chesterfield's Letters.*

This statement of Cicero's opinions is not perfectly correct.

[26] ——————— natura sublimis et acer.

Nam spirat tragicum satis et feliciter audet. *Hor.*

sition must be dry and formal. Where it is to be animated and suited to the graces of eloquent delivery, the very language glows and burns as it is formed under the pen. But great indeed is the labour, and incessant, which is required to excite this flame.

The ancients began their toil early with the very first rudiments of education, and with the first spark of reason. All their care of youth was to form them for eloquence in all its branches. We shall pass over the other very important acquisitions so necessary for this purpose, and take a view only of those labours which they thought necessary for obtaining a just delivery. Quintilian directs that the voice of the young orators should be first modulated, by the practice of reading select passages from the best poets; making the proper distinction between the speeches (prosopopeiæ) and the narrative.[27] They were then, before they were put under the care of the rhetoricians, taught the first rudiments of delivery by the grammarians, who had extended their attention beyond their proper limits.[28] After this they were given

---

[27] Nec prosopopœias, ut quibusdam placet, ad comicum morem pronuntiari velim; esse tamen flexum quemdam, quo distinguantur ab iis, in quibus poeta persona sua utetur. *Quint*. lib. i. c. 8.

[28] Adjiciamus tamen eorum curæ quædam dicendi primordia, quibus ætates nondum rhetorem capientes instituant. Ib. lib. i. c. 9.

Rhetores utique nostri suas partes omiserunt et grammatici alienas occupaverunt. Nam et illi declamare modo, et scientiam declamandi ad facultatem tradere, officii sui ducunt. Ib. lib. ii. c. 1.

Veteres grammatici et rhetoricam docebant: ac multorum de utraque arte commentarii feruntur. . . . . . . Me quidem adolescentulo repeto quendam principem nomine, alternis diebus declamare, alternis disputare, nonnullis vero mane disserere, post meridiem, remoto pulpito, declamare solitum. Audiebam etiam memoria patrum, quosdam e grammaticis statim è ludo transiisse in forum, atque in numerum præstantissimorum patronorum receptos. Clari professores . . . . fere hi fuerunt. *Sueton. de illust. Gram.* c. 4.

into the management of approved players, who, under proper limitations, taught them the first rudiments of gesture and delivery; restraining the theatrical freedom within the more moderate bounds suited to the orator.[29] When capable of reading and understanding their spirit, they were instructed to pronounce by heart select orations with suitable gesture.[30] In order also to give freedom and grace to their gestures, the young orators frequented the palestræ; those schools in which the various gymnastic exercises were taught, of which dancing and the chironomia formed a part: these improved the person in ease and agility of motion. The palestræ are also recommended by Cicero, as essential in establishing manly and graceful gesture.[31]

---

[29] Dandum aliquid comœdo quoque, dum eatenus, qua pronuntiandi scientiam futurus orator desiderat. . . . . . Ne gestus quidem omnis ac motus a comœdis petendus est. Quanquam enim utrumque eorum ad quemdam modum præstare debet orator; plurimum tamen aberit a scenico, nec vultu, nec manu, nec excursionibus nimius. . . . . Debet etiam docere comœdus, quommodo narrandum, qua sit auctoritate suadendum, qua concitatione consurgat ira, qui flexus deceat miserationem. *Quint.* lib. i. c. 11.

[30] Ceterum, cum legere orationes oportebit, cum virtutes earum jam sentiet, tum mi diligens aliquis ac peritus assistat; neque solum lectione formet, verum etiam ediscere electa ex his cogat, et ea dicere stantem clare, et quemadmodum agere oportebit; ut protinus *pronunciatione* vocem et memoriam exerceat. *Quint.* lib. i. c. 11.

[31] Ne illos quidem reprehendendos putem, qui paulum, etiam palæstricis vacaverint. Non de his loquor, quibus pars vitæ in oleo, pars in vino consumitur; qui corporis cura mentem obruerunt (hos enim abesse ab eo quem instituimus quam longissime velim) sed nomen est ab iis, a quibus gestus motusque formantur; ut recta sint brachia, ne indoctæ rusticæve manus, ne status indecorus, ne qua in proferendis pedibus inscitia, ne caput oculique ab alia corporis inclinatione dissideant. *Ib.*

Horace distinguishes Mercury as the god of eloquence, attributing to him the two leading qualifications of fine delivery, the voice and graceful gesture; which he taught by the institution of the palæstra:

Mercuri facunde, nepos Atlantis,
Qui feros cultus hominum recentum
Voce formasti catus, et decoræ
          More *palaestrae.*   *Hor.* lib. i. ode 10.

Et certe quod facere oporteat non indignandum est discere; cum præsertim hæc *Chirono-*

When sufficiently advanced in knowledge and understanding to be capable of relishing the precepts of the rhetorician, whose office it was to give the last finishing to the delivery, and to teach the art of composition, the young orator was to be committed according to Quintilian[32] to his care: but with this especial caution, (so honourable to his judgment and virtue,) that the rhetorician should be a man of the purest morals. The morals of all the masters, he observes, should be strictly attended to, but those of the rhetorician more than any; because at the season when youth are committed to him, they are most susceptible of impressions, and because they continued usually under his instructions to an advanced period of life. Throughout all this celebrated work of this most justly celebrated orator and critic, the love of virtue breaks out so ardently on every occasion, as to prove it to be the genuine sentiment of his excellent and well regulated mind.

---

mia, (quæ est ut nomine ipso declaratur) lex gestus, et ab illis temporibus heroicis orta sit, et a summis Græciæ viris et ab ipso etiam Socrate probata,* a Platone quoque in parte civilium posita virtutum et a Chrysippo in præceptis de *liberorum educatione* compositis non omissa.—Nam Lacedemonios quidam etiam *saltationem* quamdam, tanquam ad bella quoque utilem, habuisse inter exercitationes accepimus. Neque id veteribus Romanis dedecori fuit. *Quint.* Ibid.

Subsequi debet gestus . . . . . . laterum inflexione hac forti ac virili, non ab scena et histrionibus, sed ab armis aut etiam a palæstra. *Cic. de Orat.* c. 59.

[32] Ergo cum ad eas in studiis vires pervenerit puer, ut quæ prima esse præcepta rhetorum diximus, mente consequi possit, tradendus ejus artis magistris erit. Quorum in primis inspici mores oportebit. Quod ego non idcirco potissimum in hac parte tractare sum aggressus, quia non in cæteris quoque doctoribus idem hoc examinandum quam diligentissime putem, sicut testatus sum in libro priore, sed quod magis necessariam ejus rei mentionem facit ætas ipsa discentium. Nam et adulti ferè pueri ad hos præceptores transferuntur, et apud eos juvenes etiam facti perseverant; ideoque major adhibenda tum cura est, ut et teneriores annos ab injuria sanctitas docentis custodiat, et ferociores a licentia gravitas deterreat. *Quint.* lib. ii. c. 2.

* (A Socrate probata) τᾶ τε σώματος αὐτὸς ἐκ ἠμέλει, τᾶς τε ἀμελᾶντας ἐκ ἠπήνει.

Yet not contented with the frequent incidental mention, in the course of the work, of the indispensable necessity, that he who aspired at the perfection of eloquence should be a truly good man, he employs a considerable portion of his last book in more particularly insisting on this, and in directing his studies and his sentiments accordingly. The first chapter of his 12th book begins thus: " Let then the orator whom we have educated, be " according to the definition of M. Cato, *a good man*, and *well* " *versed in speaking*. And truly the former part of his definition " is, agreeably to nature, the more important, and the greater, " that he be *a good man*."[33] To such authority we give respect almost amounting to veneration.

From other authorities we learn that it was the custom for the Roman youth to recite weekly, chosen passages from the poets, and also to write declamations on given subjects.[34] That it was

---

[33] Sit ergo nobis orator, quem instituimus, is, qui à M. Catone finitur, *vir bonus, dicendi peritus.* Verum id, quod ille posuit prius, etiam ipsa natura potius ac majus est, utique *vir bonus. Quint.* lib. xii. c. 1.

All writers are sensible of the necessity of moral character to the orator, in order to give just weight to what he delivers. Aristotle had long determined this point, and places it the first:

Τῶν δὲ διὰ τῦ λόγε πορισαμένων πίϛεων τριὰ ἔιδη ἐϛίν· αἱ μὲν γὰρ, ἐισὶν ἐν τῷ ἤϑει τῦ λέγονῖος· αἱ δε, ἐν τῷ τὸν ἀκροατὴν διαθεῖναί πως· αἱ δὲ, ἐν ἄυτῳ τῷ λόγῳ, διὰ τῦ δεικνύναι, ἤ φαίνεσϑαι δεικνύναι. Thus translated:

The credibility of an oration depends upon these circumstances: First, upon the moral character of the speaker. Secondly, upon the dispositions of the learner. And thirdly, upon the reasoning; on account of the demonstration it produces, or appears to produce. *Arist. Rhet. l.* i. *c.* 2.

[34]   Trojani belli scriptorem, maxime Lolli,
          Dum tu *declamas* Romæ.   *Hor.*

          Nil salit Arcadico juveni, cujus mihi *sexta*
          Quaque die miserum dirus caput Hannibal implet. *Juv.*

the custom among the higher classes, at their entertainments, to introduce their children during the desert, in order to amuse their company, by making them recite with suitable gesture the dialogues of Plato.[35] That they continued to a very late period to hear the instructions of celebrated rhetoricians, and even travelled for that purpose over Greece and Asia.[36] That they frequently employed a description of artists called Phonasci, whose sole business was to regulate the modulations of the voice, to manage it by peculiar regimen, and to administer remedies when it happened to be deranged.[37] That to the latest part of their

---

[35] Ἶσε γὰρ (ἔιπεν) ὅτι τῶν Πλάτωνος διαλόγων διηγηματικοί τινές εἰσιν, οἱ δὲ δραματικοί. τέτων ἔν τῶν δραματικῶν τὰς ἐλαφροτάτας ἐκδιδάσκονται παῖδες, ὥστε ἀπὸ ςόματος λέγειν. πρόσεςι δὲ ὑπόκρισις πρέπεσα τῷ ἤθει τῶν ὑποκειμένων προσώπων, καὶ φωνῆς πλάσμα καὶ σχῆμα, καὶ διαθέσεις ἑπόμεναι τοῖς λεγομένοις. *Plut. Sympos.* l. vii. p. 711. *Xyland.*

This, Plutarch says, was a custom lately introduced at Rome.

From a fragment at the latter end of the 9th Book of Plutarch's Symposion. P. 747, *Xyland.*

. . . πᾶσι νικητήριον ὀρχήσεως. ἀπεδείχθη δὲ κριτῆς μετὰ Μενίσκε τε παιδοτρίβε Λαμπρίας ὁ ἀδελφός. ὠρχήσατο γὰρ πιθανῶς τὴν πυῤῥίχην, καὶ χειρονομῶν ἐν ταῖς παλαίςραις ἐδόκει διαφέρειν τῶν παίδων.

[36] Doctores audiebant ex omni Græcia facile primos et dicendo mirabiles, ut Molonem Rhodium M. Tullius, ut Brutus Pammenem, ut Augustus Apollodorum, ut alii alios, qui non modo vim ingenii acuerunt ad uberem copiam orationis, verum etiam gestum vocemque limarent. Neque hoc contenti labore et studio, Græciam omnem atque Asiam, ut suadæ institores negotiosi, diligentissime, studiosissimeque lustrabant. *Cresoll. Prælusio.*

[37] Gracchi fistulam ὄργανον φωνάσκηκον ait fuisse Plutarchus. Octavius quoque Augustus dabat assidue Phonasco operam, idque fuerat eo labore consequutus, ut dulci omnia et proprio quodam oris sono pronunciaret. Galenus homo doctissimus et intelligens de se scribit, καὶ τὰς καλεμένας ὑπὸ τῶν φονασκῶν ἀναφονήσεις παρελάμβανον et quas Phonasci vocis excitationes, vociferationesque appellant assumebam. Nero princeps, qui summam curam vocis habuit et incredibilem diligentiam, nihil pene sine Phonasco, aut dicebat aut moliebatur. *Cressol. Vac. Aut. p.* 527.

Seneca speaking of Porcius Latro, mentions his neglect of his voice as an unusual

active lives, even whilst engaged in actual public business, and even during the period of their highest reputation, the Roman orators used to practise private declamation, in order to regulate their voice and action, and to keep themselves in a state of preparation for real business.[38]

It was owing to these indefatigable exertions, that ancient eloquence arrived at such perfection, as to be, even in the dead letter, the admiration and model of all posterity. How much greater would prove the delight arising from the beautiful compositions of the ancients, were their accomplished mode of delivery capable of being also recorded intelligibly? We know the value which they set upon this part of eloquence, and apparently with reason, since we also know that Hortensius in his lifetime rivalled Cicero himself, owing to the excellence of his delivery; even although his compositions were not only far

---

circumstance, and gives an idea of the manner of exercising the voice incidentally. Vox robusta, sed sordida lucubrationibus ... Nulla unquam illi cura vocis exercendæ fuit .... nil vocis causa facere: non illam per gradus paullatim ab imo usque ad summum perducere, non rursus a summa contentione a paribus intervallis descendere, non sudorem unctione discutere, non latus ambulatione reparare. *Senec. Proem. Cont.*

This practice was called by the Phonasci παιωνίζειν. And is alluded to by Cicero.

Suetonius in Nero, c. xxvi. gives the following account of his attention to his voice. Ac post hoc tantum abfuit a remittendo relaxandoque studio: ut conservandæ vocis gratia, neque milites unquam, nisi absens, aut alio verba pronunciante, appellaret: neque quidquam serio jocove egerit, nisi adstante Phonasco, qui moneret, parceret arteriis; ac sudarium ad os applicaret.

[38] Tam flagrans tamque eximium fuit studium, et ad bene dicendi laudem contentio, ut ipsi viri clarissimi, functi honoribus, insigni quadam et inaudita animi magnitudine præditi, sæpe declamarent. M. Tullius in foro diu curiaque spectatus, cum Rex quidem facundiæque antistes omnium confessione videretur, eam declamandi consuetudinem nulla die omisit. Cicero filius patria laude et exemplo commotus, quotidianam suam declamationem prædicat. *Cresoll. Vac. Aut.*

inferior, but probably below mediocrity, as Quintilian insinuates. But to arrive at this height of perfection requires a
degree of labour which modern public speakers do not think
proper to bestow.[39] Indeed false notions seem rather to prevail, which directly oppose all great advancement in eloquence.
The readiest speaker (among the youth at least who should

---

[39] Cicero l. xvi. ep. 21. Cicero's son writes an account of his occupations and society in
the country: Præterea declamitare Græce apud Cassium institui, Latine autem apud,
Bruttium exerceri volo . . . . . . De Gorgia autem quod mihi scribis, erat quidem ille in
quotidiana declamatione utilis. The extraordinary exertions, which Cicero made to improve
himself in oratory, even after having arisen to great celebrity, and whilst in a very delicate
state of health, may be seen in his work called Brutus de claris Oratoribus. Ed. Ol. p. 485, et
seq. Having mentioned his travelling to Athens, and the masters of rhetoric under whom
he studied, and also his going to Asia and to Rhodes, p. 486, he says, p. 487, sed omni
huic sermoni præpositum est, non ut ingenium, et eloquentiam meam perspicias, unde longe
absum, sed ut laborem et industriam.

Cicero ad præturam usque Græce declamavit: Latine vero senior quoque, et quidem
consulibus Hirtio et Pansa: quos discipulos et grandes prætextatos, vocabat. Cneium
Pompeium, quidam historici tradiderunt, sub ipsum civile bellum, quo facilius Caio Curioni
promptissimo juveni, causam Cæsaris defendenti contradiceret, repetisse declamandi consuetudinem. Marcum Antonium, item Augustum ne Mutinensi quidam bello omisisse.
Nero Cæsar et primo imperii anno, publice quoque bis antea declamavit, plerique autem
oratorum etiam declamationes ediderunt. Quare magno studio hominibus injecto, magna
etiam professorum ac doctorum profluxit copia, adeoque floruit; ut nonnulli ex infima
fortuna in ordinem senatorium, atque ad summos honores processerint. *Sueton. de claris.
Rhet.*

Suetonius's account of the studies of Augustus, will serve as an illustration of both this
and the former paragraph. Eloquentiam studiaque liberalia ab ætate prima et cupide,
et laboriosissime exercuit, Mutinensi bello in tanta mole rerum, et legisse, et scripsisse, et
declamasse quotidie traditur. Nam deinceps neque in senatu, neque apud populum, neque
apud milites locutus est unquam, nisi meditata et composita oratione: quamvis non deficeret
ad subita extemporali facultate. Ac ne periculum memoriæ adiret; aut in ediscendo tempus
absumeret; instituit recitare omnia. Sermones quoque cum singulis, etiam cum Livia sua
graviores, nonnisi in scriptis et e libello habebat, ("Something too much of this") ne plus
minusve loqueretur ex tempore: pronuntiabat dulci et proprio quodam oris sono: dabat-
que assidue Phonasco operam: sed nonnunquam infirmatis faucibus, præconis voce ad
populum concionatus est. *Sueton. in Aug.*

Octavo decimo anno publice declamavit (S. Severus imperator) *Ælii Spart. in Severo.*

E

be engaged in laborious study,) is held in the highest estimation; to be gifted with the ability of quick reply, and to pour
out an uninterrupted stream of language extempore, is the
summit of ambition. This sort of talent is considered as the peculiar mark of genius, whilst sound logic, correct rhetorical ornament, lucid order, and laborious research are thought to smell of
the lamp, and to be fit only for the drudgery of dulness. As to
delivery, that is supposed to be altogether the gift of nature, and
a modern orator would be ashamed to be discovered in the
practice of any thing conducing to improvement in this respect.[40]
Whilst such prejudices prevail, notwithstanding all the learning
and all the genius which heaven has lavished on these islands,
and under every circumstance favourable to the most exalted
eloquence; our public speakers will continue to be mere reasoners, or generally something less, and will ever fall short of
the orators of antiquity, whom they must be content to admire
at humble distance.

---

[40] Itaque jactent illi nostri repentini et tumultuarii oratores, quantum volent, naturæ
vim et gestuum facilitatem, quos ratio et effata magnorum sapientum, et experientia quotidiana refellit; ego prætium me operæ facturum putavi, si adolescentiam excitarem, ut in id
studium diligentissime incumberent, sine quo pulcherrimæ alioquin et elegantissimæ orationes, ut speciosum cadaver, in tenebris sine vita et motu abjiciuntur. *Cresol Prælus. ad
finem.*

Against this extemporary gesture we have also Quintilian's authority, to which we shall
more effectually appeal in another place.

CHAPTER I.

OF THE VOICE.

Advantages of a powerful voice—Quantity and quality—All voices in some degree capable of improvement—Articulation—Cicero's observations—Peculiar difficulty in acquiring a correct articulation of the English language — Impediments — Palliative cure — Dr. Darwin's opinions—Pronunciation and accent—Usage the standard—Provincial accent—Emphasis—Pauses and breathing—Management of the breath—Italian singers—Rhetorical pauses—Pitch or key—Great advantages of choosing the proper pitch—Manner of determining the pitch or key—Quantity of voice to be issued—Modulation—Variety and rate of utterance—Tones—their powerful effects, from Sheridan—And from Herder.

CHIRONOMIA.

CHAPTER I.

Of the Voice.

THE voice is the organ of eloquence, and has the entire dominion over one sense. All that language and tones can effect to influence the understanding, and to win the affections, depends on the power of the voice addressed to the ear. The countenance and the gesture, address their mute language to the eye. The very name of eloquence is derived from the exertions of the voice, and where the voice fails, eloquence ceases to have living existence, and may be found only in the dead letter. The qualities, and the management of the voice, are therefore of the highest importance to the public speaker; the former are principally the gift of nature; the latter chiefly depends on art.[1] The ancient

---

[1] Ac vocis quidem bonitas optanda est. Non est enim in nobis, sed tractatio atque usus in nobis. Ergo ille princeps variabit et mutabit; omnes sonorum, tum intendens, tum emittens, persequetur gradus. *Cic. Or. c.* 13.

orators, well aware of these circumstances, used every effort to improve the natural qualities of the voice, and exerted all their art in the management of it. Demosthenes is not less celebrated for his extraordinary and successful perseverance in labouring against the natural imperfections of his voice and utterance, than for his unrivalled eloquence.

That among us the same care is not bestowed upon the cultivation of the voice; may in some measure be owing to our comparative negligence of this, as well as of all other labours, which belong to the external part of oratory; and may also in some measure be attributed to the different situation, in which our public speakers are generally placed. The nature of the government of Greece and Rome, frequently obliged their public speakers to address themselves to the people at large, assembled in some open place, as in the Forum, and the Campus Martius at Rome, and in the Ἀγορὰ and Πνὺξ at Athens. It was requisite on these occasions, in order to be heard, that the voice should be powerful, and should be managed with the greatest judgment. Every thing made against the speaker, the open air, the great multitude, the unavoidable confusion. With us, the orator in general speaks in a room constructed for public deliberations, or for public devotion and instruction: where the enclosure, the disposition, and orderly attention of the hearers, are favourable to his efforts.

That loudness of voice gave extraordinary advantage to a popular orator in ancient times, we may easily imagine. All are not judges of fine composition, nor are all capable of estimating the just weight of argument. But on public occasions, men can be influenced only by what they hear:[2] and vociferation has these advantages, that it suffers nothing to be lost, and that by its apparent sincerity, it imposes on the vulgar understanding. Horace speaks of a certain Novius who had thus bawled himself into credit; which it would seem at Rome was not an uncommon thing:[3]

> But when two hundred waggons crowd the street,
> And three long funerals in procession meet,
> Beyond the fifes and horns his voice he raises,
> And sure such strength of lungs a wondrous praise is.   *Francis.*

The sound of a powerful human voice is imperious and awful; and we find it often used to terrify, as well as to convince. Homer attributes to the voice of his hero, this irresistible effect. Achilles upon the death of Patroclus, stands unarmed upon the rampart, and shouts dismay to the Trojans.[4]

> He stood and shouted: Pallas also rais'd
> A dreadful shout, and tumult infinite
> Excited throughout all the host of Troy.

> . . . .

---

[2] Neque enim tam refert, qualia sint, quæ intra nosmetipsos composuimus, quam quo modo efferantur; nam ita quisque, ut audit, movetur. *Quint. l.* 11. c. 3.

[3]   . . . . At hic, si plaustra ducenta,
        Concurrantque foro tria funera, magna sonabit,
        Cornua quod vincatque tubas; saltem tenet hoc nos.   *Hor. Sat. l.* i. 6.

Ἔνθα ϛὰς ἦυσ. ἀπάτερθε δὲ παλλὰς Ἀθήνη
Φθέγξατ'. ἀτὰρ Τρώεσσιν ἐν ἄσπετον ὦρσε κυδοιμὸν.

. . . .

Τρὶς μὲν ὑπὲρ τάφρȣ μεγάλ' ἴαχε δῖος Ἀχιλλεύς.
Τρὶς δ' ἐκκυκήθησαν Τρῶες κλειτοί τ' ἐπίκȣροι.   *Ilias.* xviii. 217.

> Thrice o'er the trench Achilles sent his voice
> Sonorous, and confusion at the sound
> Thrice seiz'd the Trojans and their fam'd allies.   *Cowp.*

The Grecian Stentor was so remarkable for this talent, that the goddess Juno is represented as condescending to borrow his form, and his voice, for her own purposes. But Homer did not reckon Stentor among his orators:[5]

> . . . . . . There white arm'd Juno stood,
> And in the form of Stentor, for his voice
> Of brass renown'd, audible as the roar
> Of fifty throats, the Grecians thus harrangued.   *Cowp.*

But the shout of Mars when wounded by Diomedes, as might be expected, was far beyond the power of mortal lungs; Homer represents it, as terrible as that of a whole army of men.

> [6]   . . . . . . Bellow'd brazen throated Mars
> Loud as nine thousand warriors, or as ten
> Join'd in close combat. Grecians, Trojans shook,
> Appall'd alike at the tremendous voice
> Of Mars, insatiable with deeds of blood.   *Cowp.*

---

[5]   Ἔνθα ςᾶς ἤυσε Θεὰ λευκώλενος Ἥρη,
      Στέντορι ἐισαμένη μεγαλήτορι χαλκεοφώνῳ,
      Ὃς τόσον ἀυδήσασχ᾽ ὅσον ἄλλοι πεντήκοντα.   *Ilias* v, 784.
Sed nunquam Homerus Stentorem inter oratores numeravit. *Caussinus, l.* ix, *p.* 557.
[6]   . . . . ὁ δ᾽ ἔϐραχε χάλκεος Ἄρης
      Ὅσσον τ᾽ ἐννεαχίλοι ἐπίαχον ἢ δεκάχιλοι
      Ἀνέρες, ἐν πολέμῳ ἔριδα ξυνάγοντες Ἄρηος.
      Τὼς δ᾽ ἄρ ὑπὸ τρόμος ἕιλεν Ἀχαιώς τε Τρῶάς τε
      Δείσαντας· τόσον ἔϐραχ᾽ Ἄρης ἄτος πολέμοιο.   *Ilias.* v. 859.

But the shout of Milton's rebel angels is still more magnificent and extraordinary than that of all Homer's heroes and gods :

> At which the universal host up sent
> A shout, that tore hell's concave, and beyond
> Frighted the reign of Chaos and old Night. *Paradise Lost, b.* 1, 541.

The voice is considered first as to its nature; secondly, as to the management of it. The nature of the voice is again divided into quantity and quality.[7]

In the quantity of the voice are considered,

The perfections.	*The opposite imperfections.*
The body or volume *(grandis plena)* -	Smallness, feebleness *(exigua, imbecilla.)*
The compass - - - - -	The narrow scale *(angusta.)*
The soundness and durability *(firmitas, puritas.)*	Weakness, liable to fail by exertion *(laterum infirmitas.*

In the quality of the voice,

Clearness *(clara.)* - - - - -	Indistinctness *(difficilis auditu.)*
Sweetness *(dulcis.)* - - - -	Harshness *(absona.)*
Evenness *(equalitas.)* - - - -	Broken, cracked *(discerpta.)*
Variety *(canora.)* - - - -	Monotony *(monotonia.)*
Flexibility *(flexibilis, mollitudo.)* - - -	Rigidity *(dura.)* [8]

The extract in the Appendix from Julius Pollux will furnish the ancient names of various other qualities of the voice.

" A good and sound voice (says Quintilian) is capable of " every exertion; but a bad and a weak voice in many respects " impedes the execution; as in the *crescendo* and in exclamation:

---

[7] In ea prima observatio est qualem habeas, secunda quomodo utaris. Natura vocis spectatur quantitate et qualitate. Quantitas simplicior est . . . . . *Quin. l.* xi. *c.* 3.

[8] The Latin words bear relation to the English, but are not meant as correct translation.

" and forces into faults, as the sinking of the pitch, and breaking
" the tenor of the delivery; it obliges the speaker to have
" recourse to a disgusting cant, in order to relieve the hoarseness
" of the throat, and the fatigue of the lungs. But we speak now
" of such a person only, for whom precept is not useless."[9]

That a voice decidedly imperfect can by any art be so improved as to answer every effort of oratory, is altogether hopeless.
In such a case, the person who is devoted to the study of
eloquence, had better turn all his talents to writing. But of
whatever description the powers or qualities of the voice may be,
provided it be moderately good, and that the ear be not
wholly depraved, they may be improved to great advantage by
due cultivation. The ancient Greek orators and tragedians,
carried their attention to the cultivation of their voice to such
extremes, that Cicero condemns their practice as indicating more
the drudgery of the theatre, than suiting the liberal study of
the public speaker. " What is so necessary to an orator, (says
" he,) as the voice? Yet would I never advise those who study
" public speaking to labour at their voice like the Greeks and the
" tragedians, who during several years practise to declaim in a
" sitting posture, and every day, before they speak in public,
" lie down and gradually elevate their voice, and after they
" have spoken, seat themselves and recover, and collect it in
" some manner, bringing it down from the highest tones to the

---

9 Bona enim firmaque ut volumus uti licet; mala vel imbecilla et inhibet multa, ut in-
surgere, exclamare : et aliqua cogit, ut summittere, deflectere et rasas fauces ac latus fatiga-
tum deformi cantico reficere. Sed nos de eo nunc loquimur, cui non frustra præcipitur.
Quint. lib. xi. c. 3.

" deepest. Should we proceed in this manner, our clients would
" be cast before we could practise our *Pean* and our *Munio* as
" often as the rules of art might require." [10]

And a little after he says ; " to carry this labour to such
" extremes would rather tend to deter than to encourage. You
" desire that each of us in our way should become a Roscius, and
" you have said that we do not afford as much pleasure when
" we succeed, as we excite disgust when we fail. But I do not
" think we are heard so fastidiously as the players. For I have
" often observed our speakers listened to most attentively, even
" when very hoarse : for the subject and the cause take sufficient
" hold of the hearer. Yet I have known Æsopus to have been
" hissed because he happened to be a little hoarse. The reason
" is that we expect from players nothing but the gratification of
" our ears, and if we are deprived of any part of this pleasure,
" we do not easily forgive them. But in eloquence many cir-
" cumstances interest us, and if the greater part be excellent,
" though all should not reach perfection, such as does, must of
" necessity appear admirable." [11]

---

[10] Quid est oratori tam necessarium, quam vox ? tamen me auctore nemo dicendi stu-
diosus, Græcorum more, et tragœdorum voci serviet, qui et annos complures sedentes
declamitant, et quotidie, antequam pronuntient, vocem cubantes sensim excitant, eandem-
que, cum egerunt, sedentes ab acutissimo sono usque ad gravissimum sonum recipiunt et
quasi quodammodo colligunt. Hoc nos si facere velimus, ante condemnentur ii, quorum
causas receperimus, quam toties, quoties præscribitur Pæanem* aut Munionem citaremus.
Cic. de Orat. lib. i. c. 59.

[11] Illud vero fuit horribile, quod mehercule vereor ne majorem vim ad deterrendum ha-
buerit, quam ad cohortandum. Voluisti enim in suo genere unumquemque nostrum quasi

*   Pæan—cantio quæ clara, exultanti, contentaque voce canitur.
        Munio—cantio quæ leni et remissiore voce edatur.   *Olivet.*

Though there are some methods by which the nature of the voice itself may be improved, yet it is to the management of the voice, such as it may be, which he possesses, that the orator should chiefly direct his attention. By due exertions in this way, though he may not absolutely improve the natural qualities of his voice, he will give them the highest effect of which they are capable. With certain management, few voices are so bad, as not to be rendered capable of discharging tolerably the functions of public speaking in our assemblies; and few perhaps are to be found so perfect as not to require some attention; or which may not derive benefit from the observation of some of the general rules for the proper management of that organ. These rules in the order of their importance, may be considered under the following heads:

1. Articulation. 2. Pronunciation and accent. 3. Emphasis. 4. Pauses. 5. Pitch. 6. Quantity. 7. Modulation and variety. 8. Tones.

ARTICULATION.

Articulation is obviously the first point in the management of the voice, and that of the most indispensable necessity; because any imperfection in this respect would obscure every other talent in

---

quendam esse Roscium; dixistique, non tam ea, quæ recta essent, probari, quam, quæ prava sunt, fastidiis adhærescere; quod ego non tam fastidiosè in nobis, quam in histrionibus, spectari puto. Itaque nos raucos sæpe attentissimè audiri video; tenet enim res ipsa atque causa; at Æsopum, si paullum irrauserit, explodi. A quibus enim nihil præter voluptatem aurium quæritur, in iis offenditur, simul atque imminuitur aliquid de voluptate. In eloquentia autem multa sunt, quæ teneant; quæ si omnia summa non sunt (et pleraque tamen magna sunt,) necesse est ea ipsa, quæ sunt, mirabilia videri. *Cic. de Orat.* lib. i. c. 16.

a public speaker."[12] It is thus defined in the Lectures on Elocution, by Mr. Sheridan, one of the best writers on the subject of public speaking, and one of the earliest who has successfully laboured at its reformation. " A good articulation consists in " giving every letter in a syllable its due proportion of sound, " according to the most approved custom of pronouncing it ; and " in making such a distinction between the syllables, of which " words are composed, that the ear shall, without difficulty, ac- " knowledge their number, and perceive at once to which syllable " each letter belongs. Where these points are not observed the " articulation is proportionally defective."

Correct articulation is the most important exercise of the voice and of the organs of speech. A public speaker, possessed of only a moderate voice, if he articulate correctly, will be better understood and heard with greater pleasure than one who vociferates without judgment. The voice of the latter may indeed extend to a considerable distance, but the sound is dissipated in confusion ; of the former voice not the smallest vibration is wasted, every stroke is perceived at the utmost distance to which it reaches ; and hence it has often the appearance of penetrating even farther than one which is loud, but badly articulated."[13]

---

[12] In primis vitia, si qua sint oris emendet : ut expressa sint verba ; ut suis quæque literæ sonis enuncientur : quarumdam enim vel exilitate, vel pinguedine nimia laboramus ; quasdam velut acriores parum efflamus et aliis non dissimilibus sed quasi hebetioribus permutamus. *Quint.* lib. i. *c.* 11.

[13] Est enim quædam (vox scil.) ad auditum accommodata, non magnitudine, sed proprietate, ad hoc velut tractabilis, utique habens omnes in se, qui desiderantur sonos, intentionesque, et toto (ut aiunt) organo instructa : cui aderit lateris firmitas, spiritus cum spatio pertinax, tum labori non facile cessurus. *Quint.* lib. xi. c. 3.

In just articulation, the words are not to be hurried over, nor precipitated syllable over syllable; nor as it were melted together into a mass of confusion: they should be neither abridged, nor prolonged; nor swallowed, nor forced, and, if I may so express myself, shot from the mouth; they should not be trailed nor drawled, nor let to slip out carelessly, so as to drop unfinished. They are to be delivered out from the lips, as beautiful coins newly issued from the mint, deeply and accurately impressed, perfectly finished, neatly struck by the proper organs, distinct, sharp, in due succession, and of due weight.[14]

Cicero considers good articulation not only to be conducive to the improvement of the voice in clearness, or strength and sweetness; but also seems to imply that it is the true criterion of the speaker's knowledge of his language. " Our organ of speech is " the voice, in which two qualities are required, that it be " strong, and that it be sweet: but we must allow that nature " alone can effectually bestow them both. Yet practice will " improve the one, and the imitation of those who speak dis- " tinctly and deliberately will improve the other. It was this " last circumstance alone, which obtained for the Catuli such " high literary reputation; they were indeed men of letters, but " not more so than others, and yet they were esteemed to be the " best speakers of the Latin language. Their tones were sweet; " their syllables, neither too strongly marked, nor smothered,

---

[14] Dilucida vero erit pronunciatio, primum, si verba tota exegerit, quorum pars devorari, pars destitui solet, plerisque extremas syllabas non proferentibus, dum priorum sono indulgent. *Quint.* lib. xi. c. 3.

" were neither affected nor indistinct. Their voice, without
" effort, was neither languid nor clamorous."[15]

The difficulty of acquiring a correct articulation being un-
usually great in the English language, the foundation must be
laid at that early age when the organs are most tractable.[16] This
difficulty arises sometimes from harsh combinations of consonants,
which occur even in single words; but more frequently from the
meeting of words in their arrangement in sentences. It often
happens that a word terminates with one or more consonants,
which require to be articulated by the organs, adjusted in such a
manner that they cannot be suddenly and easily changed, in
order to accommodate the articulation of the following words.
The ancient languages, particularly the Greek, allow of, or rather
require, many alterations of such letters, in order to prevent such
difficult and disagreeable collisions, and also to strengthen the
sound where an *hiatus* would otherwise take place, and in every
manner to facilitate the articulation. Several modern languages
have also their contrivances for this purpose, but the English language hardly admits any indulgence of this kind. In composition
therefore, attention ought to be paid to this circumstance, and as
far as smoothness of style is considered important, care should

---

[15] Sed cum orationis indicem, vocem habeamus, in voce autem duo sequamur ut clara sit,
ut suavis; utrumque omnino a natura petendum est: verum alterum exercitatio augebit,
(see former page, on quantity of the voice,) alterum imitatio *presse* loquentium et leniter.
Nihil aliud fuit in Catulis ut eos exquisito judicio putares uti literarum; quanquam erant
literati, sed et alii. Hi autem optime uti lingua Latina putabantur. Sonus erat dulcis, literæ
neque *expressæ* neque *oppressæ*, ne obscurum esset, aut putidum. Sine contentione vox, nec
languens nec canora. *Cic. de Off.* lib. i. 37.

[16] Hence the almost unconquerable imperfections in the utterance of those, who, in their
infancy, have been given up to the care of vulgar speakers.

be taken to avoid collisions of this nature. It is not to be desired, however, that this harshness should be altogether polished away, it forms the nerves of our language, and upon its judicious use, much of its vigour and variety depends."[17][18]

As connected with the subject of articulation, it appears necessary to say a few words concerning impediments of speech. Of these there are various descriptions, but the most difficult to get over is hesitation or stammering. Whether persons, who are subject in any great degree to this defect, can ever conquer it, may strongly be doubted; but supposing success possible, the constant vigilance, and the incessant efforts necessary, in difficult cases, are such as must effectually overcome the vigour of ordinary minds, and determine them rather to submit to their deficiency, than to the labour of correcting it. In cases where a small degree of hesitation occasionally breaks the fluent tenor of discourse; much may be done by due attention. If, in order to seek for a remedy, I might presume to offer an opinion upon the cause of this distressing defect, I should say that as persons of delicate habits are more generally subject to it; it proceeds

---

[17] Ποιεῖ δὲ καὶ δυσφωνία συνθέσεως ἐν πολλοῖς μέγεθος, οἷον τὸ, "Αἴας δ' ὁ μέγας αἰὲν ἐφ' Ἕκτορι χαλκοκορυςῆ." ἄλλως μὲν γὰρ ἴσως δυσήκοος ἡ τῶν γραμμάτων σύμπληξις. ὑπερβολὴ δ' ἐμφαίνεσα τὸ μέγεθος τᾶ ἥρωος. λειότης γὰρ καὶ τὸ εὐήκοον ἐ πάνυ ἐν μεγαλοπρεπείᾳ χώραν ἔχεσιν. *Demetrius Phalar. de Elocut.* sec. 48. Thus translated: But harshness in composition contributes in many instances to magnificence, as, Αἴας, &c. In some respects the collision of the letters may be unpleasing to the ear; but they have the advantage of strongly demonstrating the magnificence of the hero. For the polished style, and that which is agreeable to the ear, are seldom used in grand subjects.

[18] Superest compositio. Ea, quod ad juncturam, est vocalibus hiulca, consonantibus aspera. *Voss. part. Orat.* p. 300.

from a constitutional trepidation of the nerves : and I should therefore recommend, as the foundation of every hope of cure, such care of the health as may tend to strengthen the whole system. All excess should be avoided, particularly in the use of wine, tea, and coffee, which give a momentary stimulus, and leave behind increased debility. All personal irregularity ought to be still more carefully guarded against ; and then it may be hoped, that with the growing strength of the constitution, the defect may gradually diminish. That it is sometimes removed, we may judge from hence, that though we frequently meet young persons subject to hesitation, we do not, in proportionable numbers, meet grown people who labour under it in any great degree. And that it is owing principally to some nervous affection may be collected from observing, that whatever agitates the nerves, either increases or diminishes the complaint. The defect is aggravated by the fear of strangers, by surprise, by impatience, by anxiety ; it is moderated by familiar society, by indulgence, and by tranquillity. Since, therefore, in its distressing effects it is subject to all the variations of bodily health, it may also be presumed to be capable of being relieved by those means which contribute to establish the general health and vigour.

But much of the success in the combat against this defect will depend on the exertions made by the mind, and on the establishment of such habits as tend to counteract the weakness. A young person should therefore practise to speak with more than usual deliberation, and to practise frequently when alone those words and letters which he finds most difficult to enounce. He should also furnish his mind with a copious vocabulary of language ; and make himself as familiar as possible with all the synonymes,

G

so that if he finds himself unable to utter a particular word, he may readily substitute in its place some other of nearly the same import. The habit of running over synonymes will associate them in such a manner, that the idea of one word will readily bring the other into the recollection. It is one character of this impediment, that it is obstinate in struggling with the particular word which stops the current of discourse. But in such case, it appears to be the most adviseable method to divert it, if it can be done, into some other channel. Above all, a young person should be encouraged to exert the energy of his own mind, to assume a courageous command over himself, to check his trepidation with determined deliberation, and should he even fail, not to suffer himself to be disturbed, or to lose his temper, even when laughed at by his thoughtless young companions. If his hesitation be not extreme, these directions may be of some use, and palliate the evil in some degree, till time and strength shall perhaps nearly remove it.

The celebrated Doctor Darwin classes impediment of speech, under diseases of association. " Impediment of speech is owing " to the associations of the motions of the organs of speech being " interrupted or dissevered by ill employed sensation, or sensi- " tive motions, as by awe, bashfulness, ambition of shining, or " fear of not succeeding, and the person uses voluntary efforts in " vain to regain the broken associations.

" The broken association is generally between the first conso- " nant, and the succeeding vowel; as in endeavouring to pro- " nounce the word parable, the p is voluntarily repeated again " and again, but the remainder of the word does not follow,

" because the association between it and the next vowel is
" dissevered.

" The art of curing this defect, is to cause the stammerer to
" repeat the word, which he finds difficult to speak, eight or ten
" times without the initial letter, in a strong voice, or with an
" aspirate before it, as arable, harable; and at length to speak it
" very softly with the initial letter *p*, parable. This should be
" practised for weeks or months upon every word, which the
" stammerer hesitates in pronouncing. To this should be added
" much commerce with mankind, in order to acquire a careless-
" ness about the opinions of others."[9]

Hippocrates seems to consider this defect to arise from impatience of the organs, and the fullness of the mind, when the
ideas crowd upon each other without due arrangement. " The
" indistinctness of utterance (or rather impediment of speech)
" arises either from the affections of the mind, or from the
" hearing of external sounds. In the one case, before the sentence
" which should precede is completed, words foreign from it
" are introduced; in the other, before that which is conceived is
" fully expressed, intervening thoughts are charged upon it."[20]

Another very disagreeable imperfection of articulation, is the
guttural sound of the letter *r*; an imperfection which it was
formerly the fashion in France for *pétit maitres* to affect, and

---

[9] Darwin's Zoonomia, Vol. II. p. 505. Quarto.
[20] Ἀσαφίη δὲ γλώτῆς γίνεται, ἢ διὰ πάθος, ἢ διὰ τὰ ἔατα, πρὶν τε πρότερα ἐξαγῖεῖλαι,
ἔτερα ἐπιβαλεῖν, ἢ πρὶν διανενοημένον εἰπεῖν, ἔτερα ἐπιδιανοεῖσθαι. *Hippocrat. in Præcept.*

which they called *parler gras*. Such an affectation has never, I believe, disgraced our taste. The imperfection is best overcome by removing the articulation from the improper seat, the throat, to the proper organs, the tongue and the palate: and by practising to continue the sound of the letter in the proper place, or rather nearer to the teeth. This may be effected by forcing the breath between the palate and the tip of the tongue, and by causing the tongue to vibrate rapidly. And although this effort will produce an inarticulate sound, it will be an useful exercise. Words may then be practised, in which this letter occurs, in various combinations, slowly at first, till the proper method is acquired, and it should be a principal care to prevent the throat from interfering or being at all concerned in the articulation. In this, as in every other successful effort of persevering labour, the example of Demosthenes is encouraging, as he completely conquered this defect in his utterance.

The hissing of the letter *s*, that reproach to our language, is, as far as possible, to be moderated, both by attention to composition and enunciation, and should not be exaggerated, as some are found to do.

The letters *m* and *n* are also subject to be imperfectly sounded. Instead of passing the sound of *m*, when produced by closing the lips, entirely through the nose, it is stopped or resisted, apparently between the bony and cartilaginous part of the nose, and does not issue freely." This defect is called, by a contradictory

---

[21] This may be proved by holding the nose in the fingers and endeavouring to pronounce words in which those letters require to be sounded: such as *hummums,* (a German word,) *ninny,* *singing, ringing,* &c. when the sound will appear to be violently impeded in the place mentioned.

appellation, speaking through the nose, and is seldom difficult to remove. The sound of the letter *n*, when formed by pressing the upper part of the tongue against the palate, should also pass entirely through the nose, but more gently than that of *m*. In its general combinations imperfect articulation is not so disagreeable as when combined with the letter *g*: a combination very frequent in our language, and altogether offending the ear when not perfectly enounced. The words *ringing, singing,* sound as if the *n* was omitted, and are uttered most disagreeably, as if they were *riggig, siggig.* The defective articulation of both these letters may be successfully got over by attention and practice; except in cases where nature or accident may have denied the sounds a passage through the proper organ.

PRONUNCIATION AND ACCENT.

Pronunciation, in the modern acceptation of the term, is limited to the mode of enouncing certain words and syllables. Accent is understood, either to mean the stress laid on particular syllables, or in a more extended sense, the distinguishing tone or expression of voice with which whole sentences are delivered. The pronunciation of words and syllables relates to written language, and to the ordinary combinations of letters, and is generally regulated by the analogies of the language; but custom sometimes, with most arbitrary authority, contradicts those analogies, and determines according to the pleasure of the ear, in opposition to the artificial standard of written language. No sounds indeed can be irregular but with reference to such artificial standard, and the irregularity is truly not in the sound, but in the neglect of adjusting the orthography according to that sound, which the ear is pleased to adopt. But whatever may be the cause of the irregularity, every person who would speak or write a language with propriety, must submit to it. And hence it is that languages cannot in respect of their pronunciation be learned entirely from books, nor be judged with respect to their harmony from the dead letter. This knowledge is to be acquired only by conversing with correct speakers. Pronunciation (as does also the whole of language) varies with the modes and fashions of the times: it is sometimes so fluctuating in particular words, and high authorities are often so much at variance, that the most correct mode is hard to be determined.[22] Accent is also subject to the caprice of fashion. Ancient writers accented many words differently from the moderns: and not many years since the tide of innovation tended to throw the accent as far backwards as possible, even on words which by that alteration were rendered altogether difficult to pronounce. And it may be remembered that exertions were made to bring into vogue such uncouth accentuation, as *cómparative* and *ímperative;* and that they nearly succeeded. *Míscellany* is one of those words which has retained its new accent. It is incumbent on literary men to resist such innovations as violate the prosody, and destroy the harmony of the language, and render obsolete the measures of our best poets, which would otherwise remain as a fixed standard of both.

The effect of the accent on our syllables is either to lengthen or shorten their quantity. When the accent is placed on the vowel, the syllable is uniformly long, as *glóry, fáther*: when placed on the consonant, if it be a mute, the syllable will be

---

[22] Example—*Wind, important,* &c.

short as *bat'tle, hab'it.* If it be a liquid, the syllable will be long.[23]

But besides this literary accent, marked in written language, there is also an accent relating to the tones and expression of the living voice, and understood as the general song, or recitative in which whole sentences are delivered.[24] This is named the provincial accent. It is the peculiar song of each country and province, and according to the law of language established in every capital city, it is a stain of rusticity, and an object of censure: and must be guarded against or removed by every one who would not incur the penalty of being uncourtly.[25]

To err against the articulation, the pronunciation, or accenting of particular words, is altogether unpardonable, because every literary man may acquire sufficient information on this subject, partly from books, and partly from living authorities. But as to the general song or recitative of his speech, almost every man is compelled to fall into that of the majority of those with whom he converses; and whoever does not reside at the very court of London, Versailles, or Madrid, or live with the highest class of the persons who form it, must speak more or less with a

---

[23] Sheridan's Lectures, iii. p. 52.

[24] The recitative, song, accent, may be considered as something analogous to the *cantus obscurior*, which Cicero takes notice of in public speakers :

Est autem in dicendo etiam quidam cantus obscurior. . . . . · *Cic. Orat.* c. 18.

[25] Ita hæc (vox scil.) quoque emendata erit, id est, vitio carebit, si fuerit os facile, explanatum, jucundum, urbanum, id est, in quo nulla neque rusticitas, neque peregrinitas resonet. Non enim sine causa dicitur barbarum Græcumve. Nam sonis homines ut æra tinnitu dignoscimus. *Quint.* lib. xi. c. 3.

provincial accent. Even in London, the accent (in this sense of the term) of the citizen differs from that of the courtier; and every province in England has a peculiar accent of its own. Nor is this a peculiarity of the English language; in all countries there will be perceived a recitative, which distinguishes the nearest neighbours from each other, notwithstanding that they speak the same language, and speak it in the same idiom. But this unavoidable provincial accent, when not altogether the rude and exaggerated sound of rusticity, when free from the most offensive peculiarities, and from those violations of the established rules and analogies of the language, which disgrace any man of liberal appearance, meets with every indulgence. And whilst it is easily discovered that the person who speaks is either a native of North Britain, or Ireland, or of the counties on the East or West of England, (circumstances which in themselves bring neither honour nor disgrace,) it will be equally manifest whether the speaker use the language, and possess the manners of the gentleman, and of the man of letters, recognized as such, in the cultivated society of Europe at large.

The study of our own language is a very important branch of elegant knowledge, and no attention should be spared in order to improve in it as far as possible. But it appears to me, that a man of letters should set a higher value on every other power of his language, and be more solicitous to acquire any of them, in preference to that superficial cant, which strikes the ear as the tone of the court, and which is so commonly and so easily affected by the most illiterate. For this desirable object, the works of Dr. Johnson, Messrs. Sheridan, Nares, Walker, and other eminent orthoepists should be carefully studied; and the true sounds of the various combinations of the letters, according to the analogies of the language, be derived from the authorities of these masters, compared with the living authorities of the best speakers. To those who live with the court of London, this study is obviously unnecessary; but such is the rigid uniformity required in the use of the English language, that to all others it is indispensable, as no variety of dialect is tolerated: an easy severity, to be submitted to, and not to be complained of, and which is limited to the law of language only.

EMPHASIS.

In every sentence or expression of thought, there is generally some one word, which relates to the predominant idea in the speaker's mind, and which, in the utterance, is properly distinguished by a peculiar stress of the voice, called emphasis. " Emphasis (says Mr. Sheridan) discharges in sentences, the " same kind of office, that accent does in words . . . . As accent " dignifies the syllable on which it is laid, and makes it more " distinguished by the ear, than the rest; so emphasis ennobles " the word to which it belongs, and presents it in a stronger " light to the understanding . . . . The necessity of observing " propriety of emphasis is so great, that the true meaning of " words cannot be" (always) " conveyed without it. For the " same individual words, ranged in the same order, may have " several different meanings according to the placing of the " emphasis."

In writing, the emphatical words are marked by a dash underneath; in printing, they are expressed by different types, which are generally italics, but sometimes when more force is to

H

be marked, capitals are used. Emphasis in speaking should not be too studiously urged, as it gives an air of quaintness or affectation. Many dashes in writing, and frequent changes of character in printing, are attended with equally bad effects. They deform the page, defeat the end of distinction, and spread over it an air of pedantry, conceit, and curious minuteness. If the writing is well composed, the predominant ideas will start forward sufficiently of themselves without this artifice; and when the occasions really require it, they will be distinguished with greater effect.

PAUSES AND BREATHING.

The common pauses, necessary to be made according to the rules of punctuation, are so obvious; that a reader or speaker in public, must be very careless who offends against them. If such a violation, at any time, happen, the speaker betrays such ignorance of his subject, that he gives evidence against himself, proving that the composition which he delivers is not his own, and therefore he loses all influence with his hearers. The violation of pauses, in consequence of being run out of breath, is nearly as injurious and disgraceful to the public speaker. The lungs of all men are not equally capable of supporting the labour of exertion, but by due attention, and proper management, every one may avoid this inability, which is equally painful to the hearer and himself. Temperance and bodily exercise, strengthen the lungs; indolence and intemperance, injure them. Frequent repletion bloats the body and oppresses the lungs. The failure of the breath sometimes arises from the injudicious management of it, as when the speaker has given himself a habit of exhausting his lungs at the close of every sentence; nothing can be more injurious. The lungs must be kept inflated, like the bellows of an organ, and have a body of air always in reserve, so that the portion, which, in the delivery, is constantly giving out, must be imperceptibly, and constantly supplied. The speaker is not to put off this necessary supply till he arrive at a full period, and so run himself out of breath, if the sentence should be long; as any part of a sentence admitting a pause between its members,[26] though ever so slight, any place admitting a momentary suspension of the voice, suffices for the recovery of a small portion of the air which is thus expended.[27,28] This precept equally applies to singing as to public speaking, and it is considered as a point of the highest consequence in that art, to sustain the voice with equability; this can alone be effected by the management of the breath, and by seizing the proper opportunities for inspiration. In this beautiful point of art the singers of Italy excel all others; and it is the true secret of that unbroken flowing stream of voice, which is called the sostenuto, and which gives the power of swell and diminution of the volume; it regulates in effect the whole of their punctua-

---

[26] Mr. Walker very judiciously distinguishes those members in a sentence, between which a pause may be made, or the voice may be suspended.

[27] Spiritus quoque, nec crebrò receptus, concîdat sententiam, nec eo usque trahatur, donec deficiat. Nam et deformis est consumpti illius sonus, et respiratio sub aqua diu pressi similis, et receptus longior, et non opportunus, ut qui fiat, non ubi volumus, sed ubi necesse est. *Quint. Ins. Or.* xi. 3.

[28] Quintilian justly observes, also, that in some places pauses are to be made without taking breath, when a sentence consists of many members, the sense of which is presented separately to the imagination, and to which it is introduced—(circumductio) Sunt ali-quando, et sine respiratione quædam moræ etiam in periodis; ut in illa : *in cætu vero populi Romani, negotium publicum gerens, magister equitum, &c.* Multa membra h ibebat : sensus enim sunt alii atque alii; et sicut una circumductio est; ita paulum morandum in his intervallis, non interrumpendus est contextus. Ib.

tion, (if it may be so called,) and constitutes the inimitable expression of Italian song.

The ordinary pauses which are marked in writing, serve principally for grammatical discrimination. But in public speaking, pauses of a nature somewhat different are introduced; these may be termed rhetorical pauses, and require to be adjusted by correct judgment and feeling. They are placed either before or after important matter, in order to introduce or leave it impressed on the memory with stronger effect. By suspending the sense in an unusual manner and in an unexpected place, they arrest the attention. They break the uniform flow of delivery, and operate, by the sudden change from sound to silence, something in the manner in which Locke observes that " positive ideas are " produced from privative causes. The abatement of any former " motion must as necessarily produce a new sensation as the va- " riation or increase of it."[29]

But though the sound is to be interrupted in these pauses, the gesture and countenance must express that something further is to be expected. Rhetorical pauses thus contribute to the verisimilitude: the speaker appears full of his subject and rather to wait for the expression. He appears to take time for reflection, to exercise thought, to doubt, to resolve, to be alarmed. When he speaks after such pauses judiciously made, he seems to utter the persuasions of his mind at the moment, he seems to speak as nature dictates, and makes, on that account, the stronger impression. For among the most powerful means of influence which

[29] Essay on Human Understanding, lib. ii. c. 8.

oratory exerts, is the opinion which is entertained of the sincerity of the speaker. And of that we think we are able to judge, when we are, as it were, taken into consultation in his reasonings, and shewn the inmost feelings of his heart

On the stage, this power of persuading the audience of the feelings constitutes the great perfection of the actor. Every movement of the mind is manifest, and we enter into all the situation and interests of the man. Garrick was eminently great in this power over the minds of his audience. Among the arts by which he acquired it may be reckoned his advantageous use of these pauses, so finely recorded in the light and agreeable language of Sterne.

" —— And how did Garrick speak the soliloquy last night?
" —— Oh, against all rule, my lord——most ungrammatically !
" betwixt the substantive and the adjective, which should agree
" together in number, case, and gender, he made a breath
" thus —— stopping, as if the point wanted settling ;—and be-
" twixt the nominative case, which your lordship knows should
" govern the verb, he suspended his voice in the epilogue a
" dozen times, three seconds and three-fifths by a stop watch,
" my lord, each time—Admirable grammarian !—But in sus-
" pending his voice—was the sense suspended likewise? did no
" expression of attitude or countenance fill up the chasm?—was
" the eye silent? did you narrowly look?——I looked only at
" the stop watch, my lord.——Excellent observer."

The reading of verse requires certain pauses, which differ, in some measure, from the pauses used in reading of prose. The first is named, by Mr. Sheridan, the pause of suspension, or final pause, which takes place at the end of each line: in this pause there is not to be any inflexion of the voice.[30] The second is the " cesural pause, which divides the verse into equal or unequal " portions: upon the right management of which, the melody " and harmony of versification, in a great measure, depend. The " seats of the cesura most pleasing to the ear are either at the " end of the second foot, in the middle of the third, or at the " end of the third foot; but it may occasionally take place in all " parts of the line." Its place may be easily discovered by a good ear. Mr. Sheridan's rules for reciting verse are the following:

" 1. All the words should be pronounced exactly in the same " way as in prose.

" 2. The movement of the voice should be from accent to ac- " cent, laying no stress on the intermediate syllables.

" 3. There should be the same observation of emphasis, and " the same change of notes on the emphatic syllables, as in prose.

" 4. The pauses relative to the sense only," (which he calls sen- tential,) " are to be observed in the same manner as in prose; " but particular attention must be given to those two peculiar to " verse, the cesural and final, as before described, (which he calls) " musical pauses.

---

[30] See Home's El. of Criticism, ch. xviii. sect. 4. p. 78, &c. Dub. His observations appear to me better on this subject than Sheridan's.

" The usual fault of introducing sing-song notes, or a species
" of chanting, into poetical numbers, is disagreeable to every ear
" but that of the chanter himself. Such readers indeed seem ge-
" nerally in high raptures with their own music, for, according
" to the old observation, *haud cuiquam injucunda quæ cantat ipse,*
" No man's tune is unpleasing to himself. But they ought to
" consider that they are doing great injustice to the poet's music,
" when they substitute their own in its room. The tune of the
" poet can then only be heard, when his verses are recited with
" such notes of the voice as result from the sentiments; and
" a due proportion of time observed in the feet and pauses, the
" constituent parts of verse." [31].[32].[33]

---

[31] Sheridan's Rhet. Gram. prefixed to his Dictionary, Quarto, p. 57.

[32] There does not appear to be any necessity for attending particularly to this pause, as the harmony of the versification, and the very cadence of the line, render it inevitable. It seems to me more necessary to be guarded against than insisted upon, especially when the sense does not terminate with the line. In the French tragedy, the versification of which, from the uniform place of the cesural pause, is monotonous, the author and actor both seem to use every contrivance to avoid the disagreeable recurrence of the final pause. The author frequently makes the sense close in the middle of the line, and breaks a line between two interlocutors. The actor violates even full periods, and makes no pause till he has run into the beginning of the next sentence. This, at least, was formerly the manner of the French actors, and nothing could be attended with a more unpleasing effect. See Voltaire for examples.

[33] He is always considered as a good reader of rhymes, who in his recitation hardly suffers the hearer to perceive them. Why it should be requisite for the poet to produce, what it is a merit in the reader to conceal, I know not. It is something almost superfluous ; like the present (1794) fashion of dress, of wearing fine lace ruffles under the sleeve of a coat which very nearly covers them. The late Mr. Quin, whom I have heard recite, though not upon the stage, and Garrick also, who was consummate in the science of enunciation, would have turned away with disgust or pity from the repeater of verses, who let them know that they were such, by the mere rattling of the metrical faggot.

> He faggotted his notions as they fell,
> And if they rhym'd, and rattled, all was well. *Dryden.*

Preface to Jephson's Roman Portraits.

PITCH.

The voice in speaking, as in singing, is observed to move within a limited compass, above or below which it cannot reach without disagreeable straining. But the mode of moving within this compass is different in each; the musical tones are placed at considerable intervals which are passed by complete leaps; the speaking tones are at very small intervals, through which the voice slides by ascending or descending inflexions. Within the limits of the excursions of both, there are certain favourable stations which are preferred for the pitch or key note; from whence the intervals are calculated, and to which the modulations are referred. For these purposes the middle tones are evidently the most advantageous; as well because the voice has the command of the tones both above and below, within its compass; as that these tones are generally used in common discourse, and the organs must therefore be exceedingly strengthened in them by habitual exercise.[34] The principal efforts of the speaker should be directed to the improvement of this mean pitch of his voice: but as few voices are perfect in the extremes, some being deficient in the higher tones, whilst others are so in the deeper: Mr. Walker, in his Elements of Elocution, gives most judicious advice for the improvement of the imperfect tones. He recommends to those, whose voice is weak above, to practise impassioned speeches, and such as contain series of questions, which finish with the rising inflexion, and gradually

---

[34] The power of habit, in strengthening certain tones of the voice is observable, says Mr. Walker, in the powerful vociferation of those who cry certain commodities through the streets. *Walker, Elm. Eloc.*

excite the voice to its highest pitch. To those whose voice is weak below, he recommends the repetition of such passages as require to be delivered in a deep tone. He has for this exercise very properly selected the scene between King John and Hubert; for a guilty secret may well be supposed to be thus communicated. Guilt which is accompanied by fear sinks the voice; indignation and the bolder passions raise it.

Upon the proper pitching of the voice depends much of the ease of the speaker, and much also of the effect of his discourse. If he deliver his sentiments with facility, they are heard, so far, with pleasure; but if his efforts to make himself heard are attended with manifest pain, his audience will be impatient for his relief and for their own, whatever may be the merit of his discourse. He who shouts at the top of his voice is almost sure to break it; he destroys his own feelings, becomes a mere brawler, and stuns his audience. He who mutters below, soon wearies himself, becomes inaudible, and altogether oppresses his hearers. Thus each extreme is almost equally disadvantageous to the object of public speaking, but not equally irremediable.[35] All public speakers agree in the observation, that it is much easier to raise than to lower the pitch of a discourse; and therefore the high

---

[35] Neque gravissimus, ut in musica, sonus, nec acutissimus orationibus convenit. Nam et hic parum clarus, nimiumque plenus, nullum afferre animis motum potest; et ille prætenuis, et immodicæ claritatis, cum est ultra verum, tum neque pronunciatione flecti, neque diutius ferre intentionem potest. Nam vox ut nervi quo remissior, hoc et gravior et plenior: quo tensior, hoc tenuis et acuta magis est. Sic ima vim non habent, summa rumpi periclitatur. Mediis igitur utendum sonis; hique, cum augenda intentio est, excitandi; cum summittenda, sunt temperandi. Nam prima est observatio recte pronunciandi, equalitas, ne sermo subsultet imparibus spatiis ac sonis, miscens longa brevibus, gravia acutis, elata summissis; et inequalitate horum omnium, sicut pedum, claudicet. *Quin. l.* xi. *c.* 3.

I

extreme is most particularly to be guarded against. From the lower, unless the speaker be altogether exhausted, he may with less difficulty ascend. A change of key, where that is adviseable, must be conducted on the same principles by the speaker as by the musician. It takes place in music, in a new movement or division, and must in speaking, after a considerable pause: or if it is requisite to make the change before, it must not take place abruptly, but go through certain gradations, or, as it were, modulations; otherwise the sudden transition will offend in the extreme. The descending modulations are found to be much more difficult to the speaker than the ascending, (the cause I am not prepared to assign,) and therefore he should be more particularly careful not to remain long in that pitch, whence it may be beyond his ability to descend, without exposing his want of skill. He will therefore be cautious in the commencement of his discourse, and so construct the spirited parts, that they shall only occasionally run him into the high tones of his voice, but not detain him too long there. This precept will apply figuratively with equal advantage to his composition, which ought not to dwell very long on the vehement strain.[36]

In order that he may succeed in choosing the proper key or pitch of his voice, this important object to a public speaker, he

---

[36] The composers of Italian song observe this rule with great judgment and attention. The voice is made to slide gradually, or to make a run up to its very highest notes, from whence it is also made to descend speedily. This contrivance gives to the air, and to the performer, every advantage of brilliancy, without fatigue to the voice or pain to the hearer. It is worthy of imitation, but I am sorry to say, it is not always attended to by our composers: the upper parts of glees, which are sometimes executed by, if not intended for, female voices, particularly err against this rule; and are found to squeak perpetually within small limits, at the very extreme of the voice. This is a violation of the 3d rule for the preservation of the voice, chap. II. which see.

is advised to begin very low, and to ascend gradually, till he reach the pitch that suits the place, and his own powers best. Hence with great propriety, (exclusive of the suitable tone of prayer,) the preacher is accustomed to begin at the lowest tones of his voice; so as sometimes at first to be scarcely audible. Thus he feels, as it were, the room with his voice, and is better enabled to determine what key to adopt, which shall regulate the whole tenor of his discourse. For this purpose Mr. Sheridan recommends, that he should address himself to some person of the most distant in the audience, whom if he reach so as to be heard, he may be sure all the intermediate persons will hear him also. He gives also a caution that he should not raise his voice in pitch, but merely encrease it in quantity according to the distance. If a short sentence or two were to be delivered to a great assembly, this would undoubtedly be the best precept to ensure its being perfectly heard; but a long discourse begun in this way, notwithstanding the caution, is likely to run into the extreme pitch in height, and to become a clamorous din, which will destroy the feelings of both the speaker and the audience Mr. Walker agrees in this very just apprehension: and he accordingly advises to begin rather by addressing persons near; then to extend the attention and voice to others more distant, and frequently to change the address to persons in different situations. The discourse will thus obtain all the advantage of variety from the voice, and appear as if addressed to each individual.

The highest notes of the voice must, in the vehement parts of the discourse be frequently touched, and sometimes dwelt upon for some time. I have mentioned that in order to recover the proper pitch of the voice, a considerable pause should be made previous to beginning the next division of the discourse, which should also be so composed, as to admit of that proper rest and change of voice. Mr. Walker recommends, in order to acquire " the habit of lowering the pitch, to drop the voice at the end of " the sentence, and to commence the next sentence in the same " low key with which we concluded the former. This lowering " of the voice will be greatly facilitated if we begin the words we " wish to lower the voice upon, in a monotone or sameness of " sound, approaching to that produced by repeated striking the " same key of a harpsichord."

QUANTITY.

Loud and soft tones are altogether different from high and low, as those even but little acquainted with music can tell. *Piano* and *forte* have no relation to pitch or key, but to force and quantity, and when applied to the voice, they relate to the body or volume which the speaker or singer can give out. And this depends on the power of the lungs, and not upon the adjustment of the organs of articulation or song: that is, not upon the note being high or low. A voice is powerful according to the quantity it is able to issue, and is soft or loud according to the quantity which it actually does issue. The power of the voice is altogether a gift of nature, at least as far as other bodily powers are so. It may, like them, be improved by cultivation and exercise, but cannot be materially changed from natural feebleness to strength, nor the reverse. Whereas the pitch and management of the voice are altogether within the province of art. Thus experience demonstrates, that a voice which may not by nature be perfect and strong, shall, by due cultivation and art, be able to sustain greater efforts and to afford more pleasure to the hearer, than the uncultivated voice of a Stentor; which will break itself down by its own force.

MODULATION, VARIETY, AND RATE OF UTTERANCE.

The modulation of the voice is the proper management of its tones, so as to produce grateful melodies to the ear. Upon the modulation of the voice, depends that variety which is so pleasing, and so necessary to refresh and relieve the ear in a long oration. The opposite fault is monotony, which becomes at last so disagreeable, as to defeat altogether the success of a public speaker, (as far as to please is any part of his object,) by exciting the utmost impatience, and disgust in his audience. To the variety so grateful to the ear, not only change of tones is requisite, but also change of delivery. According to the subject, the rapidity of the utterance varies, as the time of the different movements in music. Narration proceeds equably, the pathetic slowly, instruction authoritatively, determination with vigour, and passion with rapidity; all of which are analogous to the *andante*, the *cantabile*, the *allegro*, the *presto*, and other musical expressions.

" The second observation (says Quintilian) on the true
" management of the voice, relates to variety, which alone con-
" stitutes eloquent delivery. And let it not be imagined, that
" the equability of the voice already recommended is inconsistent
" with variety; for unevenness is the fault opposite to equability,
" and the opposite of variety, is that monotony which consists in
" one unvaried form or tone of expression. The art of varying
" the tones of the voice, not only affords pleasure and relief to
" the hearer, but by the alternation of labour, relieves the speaker,

" As changes are grateful of posture and motions, of standing,
" walking, sitting and lying; and we cannot for a long time
" together submit to any one of them. The voice is to be
" adapted to the subject, and the feelings of the mind so as not
" to be at variance with the expressions: this is the great art.
" We should therefore guard against that uniformity of character
" called by the Greeks monotony; which is an unvarying effort
" of the lungs, and of the tones. But we should avoid not only
" shouting like madmen, but also that under voice in speak-
" ing which is deficient in emotion, and that low murmur which
" destroys all energy. Yet even in the same passages, and in
" the expressions of the same feelings, there must be in the voice
" certain nice changes according as the dignity of the language,
" the nature of the sentiments, the conclusion, the beginning or
" the transitions require. For painters who confine themselves
" even to one colour, nevertheless bring out some parts more
" strongly, and touch others more faintly; and this they are
" obliged to do, in order to preserve the just forms and lines of
" their figures." [37]

---

[37] Secunda (scil. observatio recte pronuntiandi) varietas est, quæ solum est pronunciatio. Ac ne quis pugnare inter se putet æqualitatem, et varietatem; cum illi virtuti contrarium sit vitium inæqualitas; huic, qui dicitur μονοειδὴς, quasi quidem unus aspectus. Ars porro variandi, cum gratiam praebet ac renovat aures, tum dicentem ipsa laboris mutatione reficit; standi, ambulandi, sedendi, jacendi vices sunt, nihilque eorum pati unum diu possumus. Illud vero maximum (sed id paullo post tractabimus) quod secundum rationem rerum, de quibus dicimus, animorumque habitus, conformanda vox est, ne ab oratione discordet. Vitemus igitur illam, quæ Græce μονοτονία vocatur, una quædam spiritus ac soni intentio: non solum ne dicamus omnia clamose, quod insanum est; aut intra loquendi modum, quod motu caret; aut summisso murmure, quo etiam debilitatur omnis intentio: sed ut in iisdem partibus, iisdemque affectibus sint tamen quædam non ita magnæ vocis declinationes, prout aut verborum dignitas, aut sententiarum natura, aut depositio, aut inceptio, aut transitus postulabit: ut qui singulis pinxerunt coloribus, alia tamen eminentiora, alia reductiora fecerunt, sine quo ne membris quidem suas lineas dedissent. *Quint, l.* xi. *c.* 3.

TONES.

The vital principle of the voice consists in those tones which express the emotions of the mind. And the language of ideas however correctly delivered, without the addition of this language of the passions, will prove cold and uninteresting. Upon this subject Mr. Sheridan has written with such happy ingenuity and elegance, that the reader is referred to him for the fullest gratification of his enquiries upon it. A few extracts from this work will suffice for the present topic, and serve to stimulate the reader's curiosity. " But as there are other things which pass " in the mind of man, besides ideas ; and he is not wholly made " up of intellect, but on the contrary, the passions, and the fancy " compose great part of his complicated frame ; as the operations " of these are attended with an infinite variety of emotions in the " mind, both in kind and degree; it is clear that unless there be " some means found, of manifesting those emotions, all that " passes in the mind of one man cannot be communicated to " another. Now as in order to know what another knows and, " in the same manner that he knows it, an exact transcript of the " ideas which pass in the mind of one man, must be made by " sensible marks, in the mind of another; so in order to feel " what another feels, the emotions which are in the mind of one " man, must also be communicated to that of another, by sensible " marks." These, Mr. Sheridan remarks, cannot possibly be words, which are merely signs of things and ideas perhaps exciting emotions, but not of emotions themselves. " Every one " will at once acknowledge, that the terms anger, fear, love, " hatred, pity, grief, will not excite in him the sensations of those " passions, and make him angry or afraid, compassionate or

" grieved; nor, should a man declare himself to be under the
" influence of any of those passions, in the most explicit and
" strong words that language can afford, would he in the least
" affect us, or gain any credit, if he used no signs but words. If
" any one should say in the same tone of voice, that he uses in
" delivering indifferent propositions from a cool understanding,
" 'Sure never any mortal was so overwhelmed with grief as I am at
" this present?" Or, ' My rage is rouzed to a pitch of frenzy, I can-
" not command it : avoid me, begone this moment, or I shall tear
" you to pieces.' Sure no one would feel any pity for the distress
" of the former, or any fear from the threats of the latter. We
" should either believe that he jested, or if he would be thought
" serious, we should be provoked to laughter at his absurdity. And
" why is this? Because he makes use of words only, as the signs
" of emotions, which it is impossible they can represent; and
" omits the use of the true signs of the passions, which are tones,
" looks, and gestures." Intellectual improvement in a high
degree, falls to the lot of few, says Mr. Sheridan, and is not
necessary for all. " But though it be not necessary to society
" that all men should know much, it is necessary that they should
" feel much, and have a mutual sympathy, in whatsoever affects
" their fellow creatures." Tones are the means for exciting this
sympathy, and are understood by all mankind, however differing in language. " That the whole energy or power of exciting
" analogous emotions in others, lies in the tones themselves (and
" not in the words) may be known from this, that whenever the
" force of these passions is extreme, words give place to inarticulate
" sounds : sighs, murmurings, in love; sobs, groans, and cries,
" in grief; half-choaked sounds in rage; and shrieks in terror,
" are then the only language heard."

This language of the passions is extended to all animals; those of the same species feel mutual sympathy; those of different species feel, if the prey of each other, mutual antipathy—man communicates with all. " The horse rejoices in the applauding " tones of his rider's voice, and trembles when he changes them " to those of anger. What blandishments do we see in the dog " when his master sooths him in kind notes; what fear, and even " shame, when he changes them to those of chiding? By those " the waggoner directs his team, and the herdsman his flock. " Even animals of the most savage nature, are not proof against " collective powers of the human voice; and shouts of multitudes " will put wild beasts to flight, who can bear without emotion " the roarings of the thunder."[38]

To this extract from Mr. Sheridan, I shall be excused for adding one of similar character from Herder, as translated by Mr. Churchill.

" It is singular that the ear should excite, and strengthen com-" passion so much more powerfully than the eye. The sigh of " a brute, the cry forced from him by bodily sufferance, bring " about him all his fellows, who, as often has been observed, " stand mournfully round the sufferer, and would willingly lend " him assistance. Man, too, at the sight of suffering, is more apt " to be impressed with fear and tremor, than with tender com-" passion: but no sooner does the voice of the sufferer reach " him, than the spell is dissolved, and he hastens to him, he is

---

[38] Sheridan's Course of Lectures on Elocution. *Lec.* vi.

K

" pierced to the heart. Is it that the sound converts the picture
" in the eye into a living being, and recalls, and concenters in
" one point our recollection of our own, and another's feelings?
" Or is there. as I am inclined to believe, a still deeper organic
" cause? Suffice it, that the fact is true, and it shews, that sound
" and language, are the principle sources of man's compassion.
" We sympathize less with a creature that cannot sigh; as it is
" destitute of lungs, more imperfect, and less resembling our-
" selves in its organization. Some who have been born deaf and
" dumb, have given the most horrible examples of want of com-
" passion and sympathy, with men and beasts; and instances
" enough may be observed among savage nations. Yet even
" among these the law of nature is perceivable. Fathers, who
" are compelled by hunger, and want, to sacrifice their children,
" devote them to death in the womb, before they have beheld
" their eyes, before they have heard the sound of their voices;
" and many infanticides have confessed, that nothing was so
" painful to them, nothing took such fast hold of their memory,
" as the first feeble voice, the suppliant cry, of their child."

CHAPTER II.

OF THE VOICE. GENERAL PRECEPTS.

Preservation of the voice, precepts for it—Improvement of the voice—Management—Story of a magpie from Plutarch, illustrating the silent preparation of the voice—Manner of adjusting the pitch—Series of tones—The stage whisper—Variety—Breathing—Echo—Estimation of the powers of the voice.

CHAPTER II.

Of the Voice.   General Precepts.

" THE nature of the voice (says Quintilian) is first to be con-
" sidered, the manner of using it next.   The nature of the voice
" is known by its quantity, and by its quality.   As to the
" quantity, it is easily estimated.   It is upon the whole, either
" powerful or feeble : but between these extremes, there are
" intermediate descriptions; and from the lowest to the highest,
" and contrariwise, there are many degrees.   The quality is
" subject to greater variation, for it is either clear or husky, full
" or small, smooth or rough, contracted or diffuse, harsh or
" flexible, distinct or confused: and all these qualities are affected
" by the strength or feebleness of the lungs."   " The manner of
" managing the voice is also very various."[1]

The general precepts which relate to the voice may be classed
under the following heads:

1. The preservation.[2]   2. The improvement.   3. The Management of the voice.

---

[1] In ea prima observatio est, qualem habeas; secunda, quomodo utaris.   Natura vocis
spectatur quantitate et qualitate.   Quantitas simplicior est.   In summa enim grandis aut
exigua est; sed inter has extremitates mediæ sunt species, et ab ima ad summum, ac retro,
multi sunt gradus.   Qualitas magis varia est; nam est et candida et fusca, et plena et exilis;
et lenis et aspera, et contracta et fusa, et dura et flexibilis, et clara et obtusa : spiritus etiam
longior breviorque. . . . . . . Utendi voce multiplex ratio.   *Quin. l.* 11, *c.* 3.

[2] Ad actionis autem usum atque laudem, maximam sine dubio partem vox obtinet; quæ
primum est optanda nobis; deinde quæcumque erit, ea tuenda.   *Cic. de Orat. l.* iii. *c.* 60.

These precepts may be collected from ancient and modern writers, and being brought here together in one view, will necessarily occasion some repetition.

THE PRESERVATION OF THE VOICE.

1. The first rule for the preservation of the voice, and which is equally supported by ancient authorities, and modern experience, is, that the public speaker should, if he " strive for the mastery," be habitually " temperate in all things ;"[3]—moderate in the use of wine, and in the indulgence of the table; and not given to any personal excess.[4] A bloated body, and an enfeebled constitution, are not only injurious to the voice, but render a man equally incapable of any other mental or bodily exertion.[5]

2. The voice should not be exerted after a full meal. This rule is a consequence of the first.[6]

3. The voice should not be urged beyond its strength; nor be strained to its utmost pitch without intermission: such mis-

---

[3] 1 Cor. ix. 25.

[4] Sed cura (vocis scil.) non eadem oratoribus, quæ Phonascis, convenit; tamen multa sunt utrisque communia, firmitas corporis, ne ad spadonum, et mulierum, et ægrorum exilitatem vox nostra tenuetur : quod ambulatio, unctio, veneris abstinentia, facilis ciborum digestio, id est frugalitas, præstat. *Quint. l.* xi. *c.* 3.

[5] Quin corpus onustum
Hesternis vitiis animum quoque prægravat una,
Atque adfigit humo, divinæ particulam auræ. *Hor.*

[6] Nam crudum quidem, aut saturum, aut ebrium, aut ejecto modo vomitu, quæ cavenda quidem monent, declamare neminem, qui sit mentis compos, puto. *Quint. Ib.*

Quare vocem deliciis non molliamus. *Ib.*

The players generally put off their principal meal till after the performance.

management would endanger its powers altogether; and it might break.[7] Frequent change of pitch is the best preservative.

The same rule holds in music. Well composed songs, and skilful singers, may sometimes, for brilliancy or effect, and to shew the compass of the voice, run up and touch the highest notes, or descend to the lowest, but they should by no means, in their modulations, dwell long on the extremes. High passion disregards this wholesome rule; but the orator will not be rash in its violation; nor should the composer of what is to be spoken, or sung, be remiss in his attention to it.[8]

4. At that period of youth when the voice begins to break, and to assume the manly tone, no violent exertion should be made; but the voice should be spared, until it becomes confirmed and established.[9] Neither, according to this rule, should the voice when hoarse, if it may be avoided, be exerted at any time.

5. Certain things are found injurious to the voice, and

---

[7] Vox autem ultra vires urgenda non est. Nam et suffocata sæpe et majore nisu minus clara est, et interim elisa in illum sonum erumpit, cui Græci κλωσμὸν nomen a gallorum immaturo cantu dederunt. *Quint. l.* xi. *c.* 3.

Nam ad vocem in dicendo tuendam nihil est utilius, quam crebra mutatio; nihil perniciosius, quam effusa sine intermissione contentio. *Cic. de Orat. l.* iii. *c.* 60.

[8] " In the furious resentment and indignation, which Posthumus expresses against him-
" self, for giving credit to the infidelity of Imogen, (as Mr. Walker justly observes,) the
" fury of the passion would be apt to carry the voice too high, but the poet has thrown in
" breaks and alterations in the passion, which give the speaker an opportunity of lowering,
" and altering his voice." *See the Observations at large. Elements of Eloc. p.* 312, *et seq.*

[9] Illud non sine causa est ab omnibus præceptum, ut parcatur maxime voci in illo a pueritia in adolescentiam transitu. *Quint. l.* xi. *c.* 3.

therefore to be avoided. Butter and nuts, are accounted so among singers, and also oranges and acid liquors. The ancients considered also all cold drinks to be injurious, and dry fruits, of which in the notes in the Apppendix, a fuller account will be given.[10]

6. Some things are found serviceable to the voice, and are used by modern singers. They may be equally advantageous to a public speaker. Warm mucilaginous and diluting drinks, in case of dryness of the fauces, or slight hoarsness, barley water and tea, preparations of sugar, sugar candy, barley sugar, and the various sorts of lozenges which modern ingenuity prepares so elegantly : a raw egg beat up is reckoned the best substance for immediately clearing the voice, and is preferred by the Italian singers.—The ancients made use of warm baths, and the exercise of walking, and both perhaps with advantage. The Phonasci used various things, which will be detailed in the Appendix. Their plasma or gargle, was probably a sort of mulled or medicated wine.—They confined themselves to a vegetable diet, and particularly valued for their virtues onions, leeks, and garlic, which last was much celebrated, and is still so, notwithstanding its offensive odour.

IMPROVEMENT OF THE VOICE.

1. The great means of the improving of the voice, as of all other improvement, is constant and daily practice.[11] The professional

---

[10] For an account of the Phonasci and their arts, see the Appendix.

[11] Jam confirmatæ, constitutæque vocis genus exercitationis optimum duco, quod est operi simillimum, dicere quotidie, sicut agimus. *Quint. l.* xi. *c.* 3.

exercise at the bar, the pulpit, the senate, and the stage, if properly attended to with a view to improvement, may suffice for the orator of our times."[12] But the ancients, even those who were in the highest real practice, exercised their voice besides in the daily practice of preparatory declamation. Their rule was, after proper bodily exercise, to begin at the lowest tones of their voices, and gradually to ascend to the highest, and thence again to descend gradually to the lowest. This was called *anaphonesis;* and sometimes the *pæan* and the *munio;* the former the exercise of the voice in the highest pitch, the latter in the lowest. They used to pronounce about 500 lines in this manner, and these were committed to memory, in order that the exertions of the voice might be the less embarrassed.

2. The second rule has been anticipated, which is bodily exercise.—The ancients recommend walking a certain space before breakfast; about a mile.—Riding on horseback we do not find recommended or practised as mere exercise.

3. In order to strengthen the voice,—Mr. Sheridan advises (Lec. 5) that any person who has fallen into a weak utterance,

---

[12] And this remark (the laborious profession of the stage) brings into my remembrance a great and general mistake among the players, at *rehearsal,* where it is their common practice to mutter over their parts inwardly, and keep *in* their voices, with a misimagined purpose of preserving them against their evening *acting.* Whereas the surest natural means of strengthening their delivery, would be to warm, dephlegm, and clarify the thorax and windpipe, by exerting (the more frequently the better) their fullest power of utterance; thereby to open and remove all hesitation, roughness, or obstruction, and to tune their voices, by effect of such continual exercise, into habitual mellowness, and ease of compass and inflexion; just from the same reason, that an active body is more strong and healthy, than a sedentary one. *Art of Acting, by A. Hill, p.* 32.

L

should daily practise to read, and repeat in a large room in the hearing of a friend. His friend should be placed at first, at such a distance as he may be able to reach in his usual manner; the distance is then gradually to be encreased, till he shall be so far from him, that he cannot be heard beyond him without straining. There should his friend hear the most part of his declamation. And through this practice should he proceed step by step daily; by which he may be enabled to unfold his organs, and regularly encrease the quantity and strength of his voice. Perhaps the same practice might more easily and effectually be made in the open air, as every speaker cannot conveniently obtain the use of a room of the requisite dimensions.

4. Mr. Walker's rules for strengthening the voice are excellent and practicable; they are his 4th, 5th, and 6th rules to which I beg to refer the reader. The general principle is this,—that in order to strengthen the higher tones of the voice, such passages should be practised as require the high tones. These are particularly a succession of questions ending with the rising inflexion. For the middle tones, passionate speeches requiring them should be practised; and for bringing down the voice, (which is apt to run wild, and not to be in our power when long continued above,)[13] the succeeding sentence is to be begun (if the subject admit), and delivered in a lower tone. His example for this last praxis is that of Posthumus already mentioned.

---

[13] Deinde quicquid dicunt, tanta voce tantaque contentione spiritus pronuntiant, ut ægrè postea submittere, et in exilem sonum deflectere possint. Sed vox semel incitata, quasi effrænus Numidarum equus ruit, et nulla moderatione temperatur. *Caussinus de Eloquentia sacrâ et profanâ, l.* ix. *c.* 4.

MANAGEMENT OF THE VOICE.

1. The first principles of the proper management of the voice depend on due attention to articulation, pronunciation, accent, emphasis, pauses, and tones, these have been already treated of in the former chapter. Quintilian, says it is useful to get by heart what is designed for the exercise of the voice.[14]

2. The actual practice of the various inflexions and pauses; of the pitch and the tones to be adopted, should take place previous to the public delivery of a written oration.

3. When time or opportunity do not permit this practice, the manner in which the voice should be managed in the different parts of the oration, should be considered and determined. This practice was not unknown to the ancients, it was called the silent preparation of the voice.[15] A celebrated actress of our times,

---

[14] Ediscere autem, quo exercearis, erit optimum (nam extempore dicenti avocatur cura vocis ille, qui ex rebus ipsis concipitur, affectus) et ediscere quam maxime varia, quæ et clamorem, et disputationem, et sermonem, et flexus habeant, ut simul in omnia paremur. *Quint. l.* xi. *c.* 3.

[15] Cresollius illustrates this subject by a story from Plutarch, which *he* declares he had heard attested by many both Romans and Greeks. A barber at Rome had a magpie which afforded him and the neighbourhood great amusement by its imitative garrulity and songs. It happened that the funeral of a wealthy citizen stopped in procession near the barber's shop, and a solemn concert of trumpets was performed. The magpie for three days after this remained in profound silence: so that his master thought he had been stunned by the noise of those brazen instruments, and feared that he had lost all his talents and his voice. But after his long silence, to the admiration of every one, he imitated with incredible elegance, and correctness, the sounds and the modulations of the whole concert. " So that the cause " of his three days silence, was the exercise and meditation within himself of his talent of " imitation, and his tuning and adapting his voice, like a musical instrument." This last sentence is literally translated from Plutarch. The passage in the original is as follows: Κουρευς γὰρ τις ἐργαϛήριον ἔχων Ῥώμη πρὸ τὰ τεμενους ὃ καλῶσιν Ἑλλήνων ἀγοϱὰν,

is said to prepare herself only by this sort of meditation; yet no voice can excel her's in pathos, variety, and effect.

4. The difficulty of pitching the voice is very considerable, particularly in a room or situation to which the speaker is not accustomed. And as it is found easier to ascend than to lower the pitch, it is a general rule that a speaker should begin rather under the ordinary pitch of his voice than above it.

5. As the middle pitch of the voice admits of ascending or descending freely, and is therefore favourable to ease and variety, and as the organs in this pitch are stronger from practice; every speaker should endeavour to deliver the principal part of his discourse in the middle pitch of his voice. This pitch to each voice will be found to be nearly that used in common discourse, when we address ourselves to each other, at the distance perhaps

---

Θαυμαστὸν τι χρῆμα πολυφώνε καὶ πολυφθόγγου κίτης ἔτρεφε, καὶ ἀνθρώπου ῥήματα καὶ Θηρείας φθόγγες ἀνταπεδίδε, καὶ ψόφους ὀργάνων, μηδενὸς ἀναγκάζοντος, ἀλλ' αὐτὴν ἐθίζεσα, καὶ φιλοτιμεμένη μηδὲν ἄρρητον ἀπολιπεῖν, μηδὲ ἀμίμητον· ἔτυχε δέ τις ἐκείνη τῶν πλησίων ἐκκομιζόμενος ὑπὸ σάλπιγξι πολλαῖς, καὶ γενομένης (ὥσπερ ἔιωθεν) κατὰ τὸν τόπον ἐπιςάσεως, εὐδοκιμῦντες ὁι σαλπιγκταὶ καὶ κελευόμενοι, πολὺν χρόνον ἐνδιέτριψαν· ἡ δὲ κίτα μετὰ τὴν ἡμέραν ἐκείνην ἄφθογγος ἦν καὶ ἄναυδος; ἐδὲ τὴν αὐτῆς ἐπὶ τοῖς ἀναγκαίοις πάθεσιν ἀφιεῖσα φωνήν· τοῖς ὂυν πρότερον αὐτῆς θαυμάζεσι τὴν φωνήν, τότε θαῦμα μεῖζον ἡ σιωπὴ παρεῖχε· κωφὸν ἀκρόαμα τοῖς συνήθως παροδεύεσι τὸν τόπον. ὑποψίαι δὲ φαρμάκων ἐπὶ τὲς ὁμοτέχνες ἦσαν. Ὁι δὲ πλείςοι τὰς σάλπιγγας εἴκαζον ἐκπλῆξαι τὴν ἀκοὴν, τῇ δ' ἀκοῇ συγκατεσθέσθαι τὴν φωνήν· ἦν δὲ ἐδέτερα τέτων, ἀλλ' ἄσκησις (ὡς ἔοικε) καὶ ἀναχώρησις εἰς ἑαυτὸ τὲ μιμητικὲ, καθάπερ ὄργανον ἐξαρτυομένε τὴν φωνὴν καὶ παρασκευάζοντος· ἄφνω γὰρ ἀῦθις ἧκε καὶ ἀνέλαμψεν, ἐδὲν τῶν συνήθων καὶ παλαιῶν μιμημάτων ἐκείνων ἀλλὰ τὰ μήλη τῶν σαλπίγων αὐταῖς περιόδοις φθεγγο- μένη, καὶ μεταβολὰς πάσας καὶ κρεμάτων δεξιοῦσα πάντας ῥυθμὲς. *Plut. de Solertia Animalium*

of 12 or 15 feet in ordinary rooms : at which time the voice is fully given out, but without effort.[16,17] Instead of the middle pitch, this manner of giving out the voice might possibly be named with advantage the ordinary pitch. This is a more intelligible appellation to the inexperienced speaker, and therefore he would fall into it without difficulty, and deliver himself naturally ; and not think it necessary to seek for some unpractised tones, which might lead him into error and affectation.

The tones of the speaking voice ascending from the lowest to the highest, may conveniently be considered in the following series :

1. A whisper—audible only by the nearest person.
2. The low speaking tone or mumur—suited to close conversation.
3. The ordinary pitch or middle—suited to general conversation.
4. The elevated pitch—used in earnest argument.
5. The extreme—used in violent passion.[18]

---

[16] In omni voce est quiddam medium, sed suum cuique voci. Hinc gradatim ascendere vocem utile et suave est. Nam a principio clamare, agreste quiddam est, et illud idem ad firmandum est vocem salutare. Deinde est quiddam contentionis extremum, quod tamen inferius est quam acutissimus clamor . . . . . . Est item contra quiddam in remissione gravissimum, quòque tanquam sonorum gradibus descenditur. Hæc varietas et hic per omnes sonos vocis cursus, et se tuebitur, et actioni afferret suavitatem. *Cic. de Orat. l.* iii. *c.* 61.

[17] Neque gravissimus ut in musica sonus nec acutissimus orationibus convenit. Nam vox, ut nervi, quo remissior, hoc et gravior et plenior: quo tensior hoc tenuis et acuta magis est. Sic ima vim non habet, summa rumpi periclitatur. Mediis igitur utendum sonis ; hique, cum augenda intentio est, excitandi ; cum summittenda, sunt temperandi. *Quint. l.* xi. *c.* 3.

[18] From the ordinary pitch to the extreme Cresollius reckons also two tones, as I have mentioned.

Viri quidem sapientes . . . tres vocis principes commutationes esse dicunt (vocant tonos,) et primam quidem eorum esse propriam, qui communi et familiari sermone utuntur; alteram paulo majorem aptam ad cohortandum, consolandum, exorandum, et quoties leniores motus

These different states or pitches of the voice are sensibly distinct and separated from each other. They may be subject to variation, according to the quantity of voice necessary to be issued; from that, which in each case is used in speaking to one individual, to the quantity necessary to be given out in addressing a multitude. The whisper must however be excepted which is limited to a small circle, but is also variable in quantity, and may be addressed with considerable force to several within its reach. As if children were to be checked for disturbing an invalid who was asleep: the voice would not venture upon a murmur, but the whisper would be encreased in force.

The whisper differs from the lowest speaking tones in this respect: that in the whisper, the voice is formed only within the mouth, of that quantity of air which is quietly supplied by the lungs as in breathing, and without bringing them or the throat into the action necessary for the utterance of the speaking voice. The lowest speaking tones require a sensible exertion of the lungs and throat; as may easily be proved by endeavouring to change from a whisper to the lowest murmur.[19]

---

ciendi sunt: tertiam deinque vehementam et contentam qualis in amplificationibus esse solet. Jam industria boni et studiosi oratoris in eo posita est, ut frequenti usu discat, a primo illo gradu ad secundum, ab hoc ad tertium, facile vocem et suaviter attollere, tum ab illo acutissimo sono cum licuerit revocare. Quod quam vim habeat tum ad fidem faciendam, tum ad reficiendos animos audientium, ingenuosus quilibet e corona percipit, et qui dicunt, si modo habeant decori sensum, et dignitatis, experiuntur. *Cresol. Vac. Aut.*

[19] The theatrical whisper, or speaking aside, differs essentially from the whisper in private conversation, as Mr. Walker very ingeniously shews. It is to be referred to the murmur increased in quantity; and delivered without change of inflexion in the monotone. " It is " no very difficult matter to be loud in a high tone of voice; but to be loud and forcible in " a low tone, requires great practice and management; this however may be facilitated by " pronouncing forcibly at first in a low monotone; a monotone, though in a low key, and

6. To study variety of tone in delivery is a most important point.[20] The opposite fault is monotony.[21] To variety may also be referred the government of the utterance with respect to rapidity or slowness. And also the various expressions necessary to be adopted in the different passions and emotions of the mind.[*]

[23][24][25][26][27]

7. The lungs are to be kept always to a certain degree inflated, so that the voice shall not at any time be run out of breath. And the air which is necessarily expended, must be gradually

---

" without force, is much more sonorous and audible, than when the voice slides up and down
" at almost every word, as it must do to be various. This tone is adopted by actors when
" they repeat passages aside. They are to give the idea of speaking to themselves, in such a
" manner as not to be heard by the person with them on the stage, and yet must necessarily
" be heard by the whole theatre. The monotone in a low key, answers both these purposes.
" It conveys the idea of being inaudible to the actors with them in the scene, by being in a
" lower tone than that used in the dialogue; and by being in a monotone becomes audible
" to the whole house. The monotone, therefore, becomes an excellent vehicle for such
" passages as require force and audibility in a low tone, and in the hands of a judicious
" reader or speaker, is a perpetual source of variety." *Walker's Elements of Elocution, p.* 309.

[20] Secunda, varietas est, quæ solum-est pronunciatio. See this passage quoted at large, and translated. Chap. I. note.

[21] Monotony is by some writers called flatness. " Of all faults that so frequently pass upon the vulgar, that of flatness will have the fewest admirers." *Colley Cibber's Life, p.* 61. *Dublin.*

[22] Many instances of the fine effect of variety in the voice may be recollected by those who have had the pleasure of seeing Mr. Kemble, particularly in Hamlet.

In his first soliloquy, he delivers in a very low tone *(sotto voce,)* these words,
" So loving to my mother
" That he permitted not the winds of heaven
" Visit her face too roughly."
Those immediately following:
—" Heav'n and earth."
" Must I remember,"—
he utters with a vehement burst of indignation and grief.

His address on the first appearance of the ghost, is throughout delivered in a pathetic and murmuring trepidation of voice. But when Horatio would prevent him from following according to his determination, he breaks out into an elevated and powerful pitch of voice with the finest effect, expressive at once of the most fixed resolution, and unshaken

and insensibly recovered at the proper times, and in the proper
places. And when by nature the breathing is short, it ought to

---

firmness of mind. This is particularly observable in the first line, and the first word. The
rest of the passage is beautifully touched with light and shade.

   Why—What should be the fear?
   I do not set my life at a pin's fee;
   And for my soul, what can it do to that,
   Being a thing immortal as itself?—
   It waves me forth again—I'll follow it.—

[23] B. Vous voudriez donc beaucoup d'inegalité dans la voix et dans le geste? A. C'est ce la
ce qui rend l'action si puissante et qui la faisoit mettre par Demosthène au-dessus de tout.
Plus l'action et la voix paroissent simples et familières dans les endroits où l'on ne fait qu'instruire, que raconter, que s'insinuer; plus preparent-elles de surprise et d'émotion pour les
endroits où elles s'éléveront à un enthousiasme soudain. C'est une espéce de musique:
toute la beauté consiste dans la varieté des tons, qui haussent, ou qui baissent selon les
choses, qu'ils doivent exprimer. *Fenelon Dialogues sur l'Eloquence. p.* 236.

[24] Tum intentis, tum remissis, tum elatis, tum inferioribus modis opus est, spatiis quoque
lentioribus aut citatioribus. *Quint. l.* xi. *c.* 3.

[25] Omnis enim motus animi suum quendam a natura habet vultum et sonum, et gestum:
totumque corpus hominis et ejus omnis vultus omnesque voces, ut nervi in fidibus, ita
sonant, ut a motu animi quoque sunt pulsæ. Nam voces ut chordæ sunt intentæ, quæ ad
quemque tactum respondeant, acuta, gravis; cita, tarda; magna parva: quas tamen inter
omnes est suo quæque in genere mediocris. Atque etiam illa sunt ab his delapsa plura
genera, lene, asperum; contractum, diffusum; continenti spiritu, intermisso; fractum, scis-
sum; flexo sono attenuatum, inflatum. Nullum enim horum similium generum, quod non
arte ac moderatione tractetur. Hi sunt actori, ut pictori, expositi ad variandum colores.
Aliud enim vocis genus iracundia sibi sumat: acutum, incitatum, crebro incidens ......
Aliud miseratio, ac mœror: flexibile, plenum, interruptum, flebili voce..... Aliud metus,
demissum et hesitans, et abjectum..... Aliud vis: contentum, vehemens, imminens quadam incitatione gravitatis.... Aliud voluptas effusum, lene, tenerum, hilaratum, ac remis-
sum..... Aliud molestia: sine commiseratione grave quiddam, et uno pressu ac sono ob-
ductum. *Cic. de Orat. l.* iii. *c.* 58.

[26] Dans certains endroits vifs, il faut parler plus vite, mais parler avec precipitation, et
ne pouvoir se retenir est un grand defaut. Il y a des choses qu'ils faut appuyer. Il en est
de l'action et de la voix comme des vers: il faut quelquefois une mésure courte et im-
peteueuse pour signifier ce qui est vif et ardent. Se servir toujours de la même action et
de la même mésure de voix, ce comme qui donneroit le même reméde à toutes sortes des
malades. *Fenelon. Dial. sur l'Eloquence, p.* 237.

[27] Promptum sit os non præceps: moderatum non lentum. *Quint.*

be strengthened by diligent practice; after the example of
Demosthenes.[28]

8. " In rooms where the quickly returning echo disturbs the
" speaker, he must lessen the quantity of his voice till the echo
" ceases to be perceptible.   And when he is disturbed by the slowly
" returning echo, he must take care to be much slower and dis-
" tinct in his utterance than usual, and to make his pauses longer.
" He is to attend to the returning sound, and not to begin after
" a pause till the sound is ceased."

9. " In enormous buildings, as old abbeys, cathedrals, and
" halls, in which the speaker has no more advantage than if he
" were in the open air; he should regulate his voice as he ought
" in the open air, and make himself audible as far as he can with-
" out straining."[29] These two last rules may apply to the management of a weak voice in rooms of any extent which it cannot
conveniently fill.

ESTIMATION OF THE POWERS OF THE VOICE.

1. The speaker discovers that his voice has filled the room by
the return of its sound to his own ear.

---

[28] Spiritus quoque nec crebro receptus concidat sententiam ; nec eo usque trahatur, donec
deficiat.   Nam et deformis est consumpti illius sonus et respiratio sub aqua diu pressi similis,
et receptus longior, et non opportunus : ut qui fiat non ubi volumus, sed ubi necesse est.
Quare longiorem dicturis periodum colligendus est spiritus ; ita tamen ut id neque diu,
neque cum sono faciamus, neque omnino ut manifestum sit: reliquis partibus optime inter
juncturas sermonis revocabitur.   Exercendus autem est, ut sit quam longissimus : quod
Demosthenes ut efficeret, scandens in adversum continuabat quam posset plurimos versus.
Quint. l. xi. *c.* 3.

[29] Sheridan's *Lectures,* 5. p. 113.

M

2. He will judge of the ability of his voice, by the degree of exertion necessary to enable him to fill a room of any particular size.[30]

3. And he may form a judgment concerning the opinion of his audience by the degree of their attention.

I have now gone over the principal circumstances to be attended to in the voice; that most important instrument of the public speaker; and have supported my opinions by many authorities ancient and modern; I refer the reader to the Appendix for the observations of Cresollius upon the voice, which are interesting, but too long for a note.

[30] Sheridan's Lectures, p. 111.

CHAPTER III.

OF THE COUNTENANCE.

*Herder's observations on the countenance—Observations from Lavater—
Cicero on the expression—Demosthenes—A modest expression becomes
an orator—Proper expression indicates the sincerity of the speaker—
Advantage of a fine countenance—The eyes principally mark the expression—Direction and influence of the eyes—Caution as to direction
of the eyes—Eloquence of the pulpit—Its proper character nearly described by Cicero—Extraordinary expression of the eye—Of looking
into the eyes—Tears of an orator—When proofs of weakness—Who
are subject to soft emotions according to Aristotle—Opinions of the
ancients relative to tears—Observations on the eyes by Pliny — by
Quintilian—On the eyebrows, forehead, cheeks, and mouth—Persons
celebrated for the graces of the mouth—Influence of moral habits on
the mouth—Causes of the changes in the mouth.*

CHAPTER III.

OF THE COUNTENANCE.

THE power of the countenance in oratory is ranked by Cicero, next to that of the voice. "To every thing which belongs to action, " (delivery,) nature has communicated a particular influence. " So that by it, the very illiterate, the vulgar, and even foreigners " ignorant of the language, are much affected. Mere words can " influence none but those who are associated in their sense, by " the use of the same language; and it often happens that acute " reasonings escape the notice of men who are not very acute. " But action, which is accompanied by the emotions of the mind, " affects every one. For the feelings of all men are excited by " emotions of the same kind, and they discover them in others " by the same indications, which they use to express them in " themselves."[1]

---

[1] Quare in hac nostra actione *secundum* vocem vultus valet. . . . Atque in iis omnibus, quæ sunt actionis, inest quædam vis a naturâ data. Quare etiam hac imperiti, hac vuigus, hac denique barbari maxime commoventur. Verba enim neminem movent, nisi eum, qui ejusdem linguæ societate conjunctus est; sententiæque sæpe acutæ, non acutorum hominum sensus prætervolant. Actio, quæ præ se motum animi fert, omnes movet: iisdem enim omnium animi motibus concitantur et eos iisdem notis, et in aliis agnoscunt, et in se ipsi indicant. *Cic. de Orat. l.* iii. *c.* 59.

And in another place, Vultus vero, qui *secundum* vocem plurimum potest, quantam affert tum dignitatem, tum venustatem? *Orat. c.* 18.

The great principle of oratory is to impress the auditors with a belief that the speaker delivers his own genuine sentiments, and that he endeavours to persuade others only from the full conviction of his own mind. And of this sincerity, the natural indications are his earnestness of manner manifested by the tones of his voice, the expression of his countenance, and the force of his gestures: of these all men are judges, and in these expressions of feeling, all participate; and hence it is that enthusiasm and absurdity succeed with the ignorant, whilst even the wise and the temperate, are cold in their attention to the most excellent instructions, and the strongest reasonings otherwise delivered.

To the power of the countenance Quintilian bears also strong testimony. By the countenance, he says, every feeling is expressed, " upon the countenance the hearers depend, and into it " they examine before the speaker opens his lips, the countenance " is the object of approbation or dislike, it gives a deeper " knowledge of the speaker's sentiments than his words, and " often says more than language can express."[2] And Pliny says, " to man alone is given a face, to other animals mouths or " beaks. They have indeed the forehead, but man alone can " use it to express his grief or his joy, his clemency or severity."[3] Lavater has quoted from Herder the following beautiful description of the human countenance. " Survey this soul beaming,

---

[2] Dominatur autem maxime vultus. Hoc supplices, hoc minaces, hoc blandi, hoc tristes, hoc hilares, hoc erecti, hoc summissi sumus: hoc pendent homines, hoc intuentur, hunc spectant etiam antequam dicamus: hoc quosdam amamus, hoc odimus, hoc plura intelligimus: hic est sæpe pro omnibus verbis. *Quint.*

[3] Facies homini tantum; cæteris os et rostra. Frons et aliis; sed homini tantum, tristitiæ hilaritatis, clementiæ, severitatis, index. *Plin. Nat. Hist. l.* xi. *c.* 37.

" this divine countenance, the thoughtful brow, the penetrating
" eye, the spirit-breathing lips, the deep intelligence of the as-
" sembled features. How they all conspiring speak! What
" harmony!—A single ray including all possible colours. The
" picture of the fair immeasurable mind within."[4]

Upon the subject of the countenance, although we are far from
intending physiognomical research, it will not be amiss to repeat
a few of the observations of Lavater, who had so attentively
studied all its powers. His distinction between physiognomy
and pathognomy, will be found worthy the attention of the
public speaker.

" Physiognomy (says Lavater) is the knowledge of the signs
" of the powers and inclinations of men. Pathognomy is the
" knowledge of the signs of the passions.

" Physiognomy therefore teaches the knowledge of the charac-
" ter at rest, and pathognomy, of the character in motion. All
" people read the countenance pathognomonically, (hence the
" expression of countenance necessary to the orator,) few indeed
" read it physiognomonically. Pathognomy has to combat the
" arts of dissimulation; physiognomy not."

Accounting why a tranquil countenance is an indication of
tranquillity of mind, he says; " when any passion is called into
" action, such passion is depicted by the motions of the muscles,
" and these motions are accompanied by a strong palpitation of

---

4 Lavater's Essays on Physiognomy, Vol. I. Ed. Holcroft.

" the heart. If the countenance be tranquil, it always denotes " tranquillity in the region of the heart and breast." Hence it appears that the orator who would move others, must appear to be moved himself: that is, he must express his emotions in his countenance and by his manner, otherwise his language will be contradicted by his looks; and his audience will be more inclined to believe them, which are the natural and sure indications of the inward mind, than his words, which may easily be feigned, and may differ much from his real sentiments.[5]

A failure in the due expression of the voice and countenance gives that frigid character to a public speaker, which however it may instruct, can never excite any interest.[6] It may perhaps suit public demonstrations in the abstract sciences, but is chilling and repulsive in a popular harangue. It may be proper for the solemnity of some judicial proceedings; and had formerly its

---

[5]　　Ut ridentibus arrident, ita flentibus adsunt
　　　　Humani vultus. Si vis me flere; dolendum est
　　　　Primum ipsi tibi: tunc tua me infortunia lædent
　　　　Telephe vel Peleu. Male si mandata loqueris,
　　　　Aut dormitabo aut ridebo. Tristia mœstum
　　　　Vultum verba decent; iratum, plena minarum;
　　　　Ludentem, lasciva; severum seria dictu.
　　　　Format enim natura prius nos intus ad omnem
　　　　Fortunarum habitum: juvat, aut impellit ad iram,
　　　　Aut ad humum mœrore gravi deducit et angit:
　　　　Post effert animi motus interprete lingua.
　　　　Si dicentis erunt fortunis absona dicta
　　　　Romani tollent equites peditesque cachinnum.　*Hor. de Arte Poet.* 101.

[6] Caussinus in his work de Eloquentia Sacra et Profana, speaking of frigid action, uses the following strong expressions and ludicrous image.

Aliorum longe dispar est ratio, qui adeo misere et frigide dicunt, ut ubi irasci, tonare ac fulgurare oporteat, non magis ardescant, quam *gallinæ madidæ,* et lectoris tono Thyesteas execrationes decurrant. *Causs. l. ix. c. 3.*

place in the celebrated court of the Areopagitæ, where causes were heard in the night, and the pleaders before whom were obliged to divest their speeches of every oratorical ornament, lest they should be supposed to influence the rigid justice of that high tribunal. However honest and however simple may be this manner of public speaking, it can never approach that wondrous eloquence which sways the councils of men, and moves all the passions of the soul: the power of which is beyond all strength, and the acquisition of which is more rare than that of the imperial purple.

Cicero, in his book, addressed to Brutus, concerning celebrated orators, having bestowed upon Callidius, an eminent orator of his own time, unqualified praise for his exquisite choice of words, and for the correctness of his composition, strongly illustrates by his example the importance of expression of voice and countenance, in which alone it appears he was deficient. " If he who " delivers himself in a pleasing manner has arrived at the summit " of excellence, we need not seek for a better model. But as we " have already observed, there appear to be three points, which " a public speaker should endeavour to accomplish. To instruct, " to please, and to move the passions. Two of these he possessed " eminently; his language illustrated his subject, and he arrested " the attention of his audience by the pleasure he afforded. He " did not merit the praise of the third point of eloquence, the " power of moving and exciting the passions; and this we have " stated to be most important. He had no vigour, no animation; " either he designedly restrained himself, because, in his opinion, " they appeared mad and intoxicated, whose language was more

N

" elevated, and whose action was more ardent; or that by nature
" he was not formed for such exertion, or that he had not given
" himself the habit, or that he had not powers for it. This one
" point, if possibly of no use, in him was wanting; if a necessary
" point, in it he was deficient. I remember, which may serve to
" illustrate this, when in his prosecution of Q. Gallius, he had
" charged him with a design to give him poison, which he dis-
" covered and had in his possession, and said that he would
" himself produce his handwriting, attestations, circumstantial
" proofs, and examinations in evidence of the fact; and when he
" had most accurately and precisely discussed the charge:—that
" in my answer to him, having advanced such arguments as the
" case admitted; I stated this very circumstance as one of my
" arguments against him, that even, whilst he declared, that he
" held in his hand the drug aimed against his life, and that he
" had evident proofs of the design to murder him, he had de-
" livered himself with such carelessness, such mildness, and with
" such indifference. Could you plead in this manner, Marcus
" Callidius, if you were not conscious of the falsehood of your
" charge? what? accustomed as you are to exert that eloquence
" which you possess in defending other men in their dangers,
" can you be regardless of your own? where is your indignation?
" Where is that ardour of spirit which is accustomed to excite
" the vociferation and the loud complaints even of the dullest
" speaker? what? no emotion of the mind—none of the body?
" not to strike your forehead nor your thigh? not even (but that
" is nothing,) to stamp with your foot? So far therefore, were
" you from inflaming our minds by such an accusation, that we
" could hardly refrain from sleep. Thus did we avail ourselves,

" it may be, either of the good sense or of the fault of this ex-
" cellent orator, as an argument to set his accusation aside." [7,8]

To this account of the opinion of the great Roman orator concerning the importance of expression of the voice and countenance, may be annexed with propriety, what Plutarch records
concerning the celebrated orator of Greece, on an occasion something similar.

" It is reported that a man came to him to request he would
" undertake his cause, stating that another had assaulted and

---

[7] Quod si est optimum suaviter dicere; nihil est quod melius hoc quærendum putes. Sed
cum a nobis paulò ante dictum sit, tria videri esse, quæ orator efficere deberet, ut doceret,
ut delectaret, ut moveret: duo summè tenuit, ut et rem illustraret disserendo, et animos
eorum, qui audirent, devinciret voluptate. Aberat tertia illa laus, qua permoveret, atque
incitaret animos, quam plurimum pollere diximus. Nec erat ulla vis, atque contentio: sive
consilio, quod eos, quorum altior oratio, actioque esset ardentior, furere et bacchari arbi-
traretur; sive quod natura non esset ita factus; sive quod non consuesset; sive quod non
posset. Hoc unum illi, si nihil utilitatis habebat, abfuit; si opus erat, defuit. Quin etiam
memini, cum in accusatione sua Q. Gallio crimini dedisset, sibi eum venenum paravisse,
idque à se esse deprehensum, seséque chirographa, testificationes, indicia, quæstiones, mani-
festam rem deferre diceret, deque eo crimine accuratè et exquisitè disputavisset. me in
respondendo, cum essem argumentatus, quantum res ferebat; hoc ipsum posuisse pro
argumento, quod ille, cum pestem capitis sui, cum indicia mortis se comperisse manifestò, et
manu tenere diceret, tam solutè egisset, tam leniter, tam oscitanter. Tu istuc, M. Callidi,
ni fingeres, sic ageres? præsertim cum ista eloquentia, alienorum hominum pericula defen-
dere acerrime soleas; tuum negligeres? ubi dolor? ubi ardor animi, qui etiam ex infantium
ingeniis elicere voces, et querelas solet? Nulla perturbatio animi, nulla corporis, frons non
percussa, non femur: pedis (quod minimum est) nulla supplosio. Itaque tantum abfuit,
ut inflammares nostros animos: somnum isto loco vix tenebamus. Sic nos summi oratoris
vel sanitate, vel vitio, pro argumento ad diluendum crimen usi sumus. *Cic. de Clar. Orat.
cap.* 80.

[8] Trajan was praised by Pliny for the opposite advantages in delivery. Quam inaffectata
veritas verborum? quæ asseveratio in voce? quæ affirmatio in vultu? quanta in oculis,
habitu, gestu, toto denique corpore fides? *Plin. Paneg. Traj. dictus.*

" struck him. I cannot, said Demosthenes, for you suffered no
" such injury, as you complain of. The man raised his voice, and
" exclaimed, What, Demosthenes, do you deny that I have suffered
" what I have said?—I believe you now, replied Demosthenes,
" for now I hear the voice of a man who has been insulted and
" injured.—So necessary to the credibility of their assertions did
" he consider the tones and action of those who spoke." [9]

It may be considered as an established point, that a public speaker should attend to the expression of his countenance as well as to that of his voice. The sort of expression to be adopted should be the next object of enquiry: and that in general will be such as suits best the nature of his subject, and the character of the feeling with which it should be accompanied. This general rule extends to every part of an oration. But as every public address should bespeak the attention and favour of the audience by due respect, and as the looks of the speaker precede his words, so it should be an established maxim (rarely to be violated) that an orator should temper with becoming modesty, that persuasion and confidence which his countenance should express of the justice and truth of what he recommends. [10]

---

[9] Λέγεται δ' ἀνθρώπου προσελθόντος δεομένε συνηγορίας, καὶ διεξιόντος ὡς ὑπὸ του λάβοι πληγὰς, Ἀλλὰ σὺ γε (φάναι τὸν Δημοσθένην) τέτων ὧν λέγεις ἐδὲν πέπονθας. ἐπιτείναντος δὲ τὴν φωνὴν τῦ ἀνθρώπυ, καὶ βοῶντος, Ἐγὼ Δημόσθενες ἐδὲν πέπονθα; Νὴ Δία (φάναι) νῦν ἀκέω φωνὴν ἀδικημένε καὶ πεπονθότος. ἕτως ᾤετο μέγα πρὸς πίςιν εἶναι τὸν τόνον, καὶ τὴν ὑπόκρισιν τῶν λεγόντων. *Plut. in Demosthene. Xyl. p.* 850.

[10] Homer's picture of Ulysses when he rose up to speak, is a portrait worthy the attention of every orator:

Ἀλλ', ὅτε δὴ πολύμητις ἀναίξειεν Ὀδυσσεὺς,
Στάσκεν, ὑπαὶ δὲ ἴδεσκε, κατὰ χθονὸς ὄμματα πήξας.

This sentiment of respect mingled with modest confidence, should pervade every part of a discourse intended to win over others to the opinion of the speaker. And in the forms in the courts of law, where the pleader is accustomed often to break the tenor of his argument by a respectful repetition of his address to the judges and the jury; and in parliament, where the orator in the same manner repeats his address to the speaker and to the house, it would seem that usage had provided for the proper manifestation of this respect. But in the opening of an oration it appears more particularly necessary to bespeak favour by the demeanour. Every circumstance that can indicate respect for the audience should be studied. The speaker should rise up in his place with modesty, and without bustle or affectation; he should not begin at once abruptly, but delay a short time before he

---

Σκῆπτρον δ' ἔτ' ὀπίσω ἔτε προπρηνὲς ἐνώμα,
Ἀλλ' ἀϛεμφὲς ἔχεσκεν, ἀΐδρει φωΐι ἐοικὼς.
Φαίης κεν, ζάκοτόν τινα ἔμμεναι, ἄφρονά θ' ἄυτως.
Ἀλλ', ὅτε δὴ ῥ' ὄπα τε μεγάλην ἐκϛήθεος ἵει,
Καὶ ἔπεα νιφάδεσσιν ἐοικότα χειμερίῃσιν,
Οὐκ ἂν ἔπειτ' Ὀδυσῆΐ γ' ἐρίσσειε βροτὸς ἄλλος·
Οὐ τότε γ' ὧδ' Ὀδυσῆος ἀγασσάμεθ' ἔιδος ἰδόντες.   *Ilias. 3.*

But when Ulysses rose, in thought profound,
His modest eyes he fixt upon the ground,
As one unskill'd or dumb, he seem'd to stand,
Nor rais'd his head, nor stretch'd his scepter'd hand;
But when he speaks what elocution flows !
Soft as the fleeces of descending snows,
The copious accents fall with easy art;
Melting they fall, and sink into the heart !
Wondering we hear, and fix'd in deep surprise;
Our ears refute the censure of our eyes.   *Pope.*

utters a word, as if to collect himself in the presence of those he respects. He should not stare about, but cast down his eyes, and compose his countenance: nor should he at once discharge the whole volume of his voice, but begin almost at the lowest pitch, and issue the smallest quantity; if he desire to silence every murmur, and to arrest all attention. These are the precepts of the greatest critics of ancient and modern days, and in this manner have the poets represented their hero to speak, whose eloquence and irresistible power of persuasion they have celebrated."[11][12][13]

---

[11] Ovid judiciously copies Homer in this part of the character of Ulysses:

    . . . . Donec Laertius heros
    Adstitit: atque oculos paulum tellure moratos
    Sustulit ad Proceres; expectatoque resolvit
    Ora sono: neque abest facundis gratia dictis.   *Metaph.* **13.**

[12] This passage has also obtained the approbation of the most able of critics, Quintilian. . . . . leniter consurgendum-. . . . paulum est commorandum . . . Etiam cum ad judicem nos converterimus, et consultus prætor permiserit dicere, non proùnus est erumpendum, sed danda brevis cogitationi mora. Mire enim auditurum dicturi cura delectat, et judex se ipse componit. Hoc precepit Homerus Ulyssis exemplo, quem stetisse oculis in terram defixis, immotoque sceptro, priusquam illam eloquentiæ procellam effunderet, dicit. *Quint. l.* xi. *c.* 3.

[13] A modern French writer of the name of DUBROCA, in a work entitled *Principes raisonnés sur l'art de lire à haute voix,* has many excellent observations on the externals of oratory, particularly in the 4th Section of his 24th Leçon. Des moyens de plaire aux yeux, ou de l'action exterieure du lecteur. From this work I shall be permitted to make a few extracts.

De la contenance et du maintien du Lecteur.

Soit assis ou debout, le lecteur conservera un maintien modeste; c'est un témoignage de déférence qu'il doit aux personnes qui l'écoutent et dont il va fixer les regards. . . . . . . En géneral, les yeux aiment à se porter sur une personne qui observe les regles de la convenance, tandis qu'on les detourne sans regret, et avec une sorte de dégoût, d'un lecteur qui, par des dehors suffisans, semble annoncer à l'assemblée le peu de prix qu'il attache à son attention. . . . . . . Après avoir donné à sa contenance le caractère de modestie et de fermeté qui convient à toute espéce d'ouvrages, le lecteur doit lui donner le caractère des choses qu'il se propose de déclamer ou de lire. . . . . . . Quand la contenance de l'orateur est exacte, elle doit faire aux yeux des auditeurs, un tel effet, que chacun y trouve l'expression anticipée des choses, qu'il doit dire.

. . . . On peut se passer rigoureusement de geste pour les exprimer, mais jamais d'émotion

If on ordinary occasions, and in the common business of life, modesty of countenance and manner be a commendable grace in a public speaker; such modesty is much more to be desired, or is rather indispensable, in the sacred orator. When he pours out the public prayers to God, when he reads and expounds his laws; he cannot fail to recollect, that he is himself equally obnoxious to their sanctions, and equally in need of mercy as his congregation; and that he kneels only as one among the supplicants, and that he stands up only as one among the guilty before his unerring Judge. Vanity and presumption in such a situation would be more than indecorous. Humility is the proper characteristic of a Christian minister. But this humility is not incompatible with earnestness of manner, nor with the just confidence which every public speaker should appear to have in the truth of what he delivers. It is the less necessary for a public speaker to be solicitous to give this expression to his delivery, because if he be truly in earnest, it cannot fail to manifest itself.

Expression of countenance, so important to the public speaker, will follow almost of course to all who sincerely deliver

---

extérieure ; et le contraste le plus étrange seroit celui qui offriroit, d'un côté, le tableau d'une passion vehemente et profonde, et de l'autre, celui d'une physionomie, où nulle alteration ne se feroit remarquer. Dans les lectures soutenues et oratoires, l'expression doit être marquée à grands traits sur le visage de l'orateur. Comme il addresse la parole à une assemblée souvent nombreuse, et que l'émotion doit parvenir à tous ceux qui la composent, il faut que le jeu de la physionomie ait des nuances plus prononcées et que l'expression ait un plus grand caractère. Bien des gens sentent la necessité de se conformer à cette regle, exagerent souvent l'expression, et finissent par grimacer horriblement ; c'èst un inconvenient qu'il faut éviter : le ridicule s'y attache, il vaudroit mieux n'exprimer qu'à demi les passions, que de tomber dans ce défaut.

their true sentiments. But far from this as well as from the other requisites of true eloquence will he be, whose heart is not engaged in the cause which he pleads. In vain does the apathy of rank and fashion deliver coldly and carelessly the law of his opinion; he may dictate to his creatures, but he cannot persuade. In vain does the pleader at the bar weary the judge and the jury in the cause which he only labours to think just. In vain does the preacher attempt to enforce with energy and pathos those heavenly precepts to which he reluctantly conforms his life. If an orator is truly good and sincere, the expression of his countenance will not disappoint the feelings of his heart.[14] Nature has done thus far for every man who can utter his sentiments at all; because it would be dangerous to the interests of society to leave

---

[14] Cresollius, Vac. Autumnales, has the following observations : volo imprimis oratorem in hoc eniti et studere ut in vultu honestatis humanique animi significationem adferat.

Xenophon was remarkable both for his eloquence and for his fine countenance. Καλὸν πάνυ καὶ πρᾷον ἰδέσθαι is the description of one of his hearers.

Pompey was also celebrated for his fine countenance. Is, si quando in forum descenderat ad agendum, in vultu ferebat tacitæ pignus honestatis et virtutis, quo prius quam loqueretur, jam prope judicibus ipsis et coronæ persuaserat. Id Plutarchus perspicuè illi tribuit τὴν ὄψιν ἐ μετρίως συνδημαγωγοῦσαν, καὶ προεντυγχάνουσαν αὐτῦ τῆς φωνῆς. Vultum non mediocriter gratiosam, quique illecebris hominum studia benevolentiamque pelliceret, atque adeò præveniret ejus orationem.

Porphyrius in Vita Plotini ait Philosophum ex Academia nobilem illo oris habitu atque luce prestitisse. Sic enim habet. Inter loquendum mens emicabat foras, lumen intimum ad vultum usque diffundens, et erat quidem amabilis aspectu, sed dum disputaret pulchrior admodum videbatur.

Pliny in his Panegyric to Trajan, describes his countenance thus : cujus lætissima facies et amabilis vultus, in omnium civium ore, oculis, animo sedet.

Faciem nemo fingere sibi potest, vultum potest.

Est enim ut scitis vultum inter faciemque differentia. Literatus Nonnius vultum ait esse voluntatem, quæ pro motu animi in facie ostenditur, faciem autem ipsam oris speciem. Hinc peritè scienterque Sallustius, *Prosus*, inquit, *in facie vultuque verecundia inerat.*

them doubtful or keep them oppressed by concealment, till art or cultivation should enable men to bring them to light." Art has little to do in this matter: the expression of the countenance is faithful, and that of the voice is also faithful; they are the universal language of all men, however rudely they may speak the language of convention. To the art of oratory belong only what are the objects of art, invention, arrangement, choice of words, graceful and impressive delivery, and other circumstances which are found to have conspicuous influence in deciding doubtful affairs.

A fine countenance, which above all things is to be desired by the orator, differs much from expression of countenance. The worst of men may have a sufficiently expressive countenance, but a fine countenance belongs to a good heart, and an improved understanding. This may also in some degree be acquired; and the means are, long habits of a virtuous life, and the cultivation of the benevolent dispositions. These in public will flash into the countenance and irradiate the looks of the orator: with an expression irresistible and almost divine. No assumed character of occasional benevolence or occasional virtue can imitate this fine habitual emanation of the good mind; the labour and affectation of the mere actor are manifest; and the audience will be more influenced by referring to the orator's life, when he utters generous and noble sentiments, than by his present looks and words, if discordant with his life.[16]

---

[15] See Home's Elements of Criticism on the external signs of the Passions.

[16]   Mene salis placidi vultum fluctusque quietos
          Ignorare jubes? mene huic confidere monstro?   *Virg.*

O

In theatrical representation of fictitious characters, in fictitious situations, some allowance is made by the audience, inasmuch as he who personates the hero is compelled to use the language already provided for him by the poet: and less reference is had to his private character, unless some manifest and glaring incongruity appear. And yet the rule will notwithstanding be found generally applicable in these cases also. And he whose life and habits best suit with generous and benevolent sentiments, will be found to express them best in his countenance and manner. Opinions somewhat different have been maintained, but not on any good foundation. A really worthy man may perhaps represent strongly the character of a villain, but the contrary will not hold, that a mean fellow should represent well the action of a hero, or that an unfeeling or a malicious mind should truly express the countenance of benevolence. The art of *feeling*, which is best learned from nature and from habit, is the true art which leads to just theatric expression. This is well expressed by the ingenious author of the Actor:

> The play'r's profession, ...
> Lies not in trick or attitude, or start,
> Nature's true knowledge is the only art,
> The strongfelt passion bolts into his face,
> The mind untouch'd, what is it but grimace!
> To this one standard make your just appeal,
> Here lies the golden secret, learn to FEEL;
> Or fool, or monarch, happy or distrest,
> No actor pleases that is not *possess'd*.

The true expression of countenance is well described in the following beautiful lines of the same poet:

> A single look more marks th' internal woe,
> Than all the windings of the lengthen'd oh!

Up to the face the quick sensation flies,
And darts it's meaning from the speaking eyes;
Love, transport, madness, anger, scorn, despair,
And all the passions, all the soul is there.   *Lloyd.*

To the expression of the countenance in oratory all the features contribute a share, but by far the greatest is derived from the eyes. For this we produce the authority of Cicero; for the general expression of the eyes we have first quoted the learned and eloquent Buffon." It is not thought necessary to translate the passage.

" But all depends on the countenance; over which the eyes " exercise absolute dominion. It was with reason therefore that " our old people did not praise even Roscius much, when he " acted in a mask. For all action is from the mind, and the " image of the mind is the countenance of which the eyes are " the index. The eyes are the only part of the body, which, how " various soever may be the emotions of the mind, can manifest " them by signs and expressions as various. But no person can

---

[17] Lorsque l'ame est tranquille, toutes les parties du visage sont dans un état de repos, leur proportion, leur union, leur ensemble marque encore assez la douce harmonie des pensées, et repondent au calme de l'intérieur ; mais lorsque l'ame est agitée, la face humaine devient un tableau vivant, où les passions sont rendues avec autant de delicatesse que d'énergie, où chaque mouvement de l'ame est exprimé par un trait, chaque action par un caractère, dont l'impression vive et prompte devance la volonté, nous décèle et rend au dehors par des signes pathétiques les images de nos secrettes agitations.

C'est surtout dans les yeux qu'elles se peignent et qu'on peut les reconnoitre ; l'œil appartient à l'ame plus qu'aucun autre organe, il semble y toucher et participer à tous ses mouvemens, il en exprime les passions les plus vives et les émotions les plus tumultueuses, comme les mouvemens les plus doux et les sentimens les plus délicats ; il les rend dans toute leur force, dans toute leur pureté tels qu'ils viennent de naître, ils les transmet par des traits rapides qui portent dans une autre ame le feu, l'action, l'image de celle dont ils partent, l'œil reçoit et réfléchit en même temps la lumière de la pensée et la chaleur du sentiment, c'est le sens de l'esprit, et la langue de l'intelligence. *Buffon, Hist. Nat. de l'Homme, p.* 520.

" give them the necessary expression who keeps his eyes fixed
" on the same object. Theophrastus said that a pleader of the
" name of Tauriscus used to speak as if he had his back turned
" on the audience, because in his delivery he pronounced with
" his eyes fixed on one particular object. The management of
" the eyes therefore is important. But the countenance in general
" is not to change its expression too frequently, lest we fall into
" affectation or absurdity. It is by the earnest looks or inatten-
" tion of the eyes, by their direction, and by their vivacity
" that we express the emotions of our minds suitably to the
" character of our discourse. For action is, as it were, the
" language of the body; for which reason it ought to be the
" more conformable to the thoughts: and nature has given eyes
" to us, as to the horse and the lion, the mane, the tail and the
" ears, to manifest the feelings of the mind."[8]

---

[18] Sed in ore sunt omnia. In eo autem ipso dominatus est omnis oculorum: quo melius nostri illi senes, qui personatum, ne Roscium quidem magnopere laudabant.* Animi est enim omnis actio: et imago animi vultus est, indices oculi. Nam hæc est una pars corporis, quæ, quot animi motus sunt, tot significationes et communicationes possit efficere:† neque vero est quisquam, qui, eadem contuens, efficiat. Theoprastus quidem Tauriscum quendam dixit actorem‡ aversum § solitum esse dicere, qui in agendo, contuens aliquid, pronunciaret. Quare oculorum est magna moderatio : nam oris non est nimium mutanda species, ne aut ad ineptias, aut ad pravitatem aliquam deferamur. Oculi sunt quorum intentione, tum remissione, tum conjectu, tum hilaritate, motus animorum significemus apte cum genere ipso orationis. Est enim actio quasi sermo corporis : quo magis menti congruens esse debet. Oculos autem natura nobis, ut equo et leoni, setas, caudam, aures, ad motus animorum declarandos dedit. *Cic. de Orat. l.* iii. *c. 59.*

　*　Persona est impedimento quo minus oculorum, narium, labrorum gestus et vultus appareat. *Strebœi Comment. Paris* 1562.

　† Quas ut efficiat respicienda sunt diversa ut cœlum, terra, oriens, occidens, judex, populus, circumjecta ædificia. *Strebœus.*

　‡ Actor erat causarum. *Strebœus.*

　§ Aversum, non toto corpore sed oculis, unum aliquid intuebatur et ab iis ad quos verba faciebat avertebat oculos, ut solent nonnulli rustici toto suo sermone aspicere cœlum, alii terram, alii manum. *Strebœus.*

As the principal object of every public speaker must be to obtain the attention of his audience ; so every circumstance which can contribute to this end must be considered important. In the external demeanour nothing will be found so effectually to attract attention, and to detain it, as the direction of the eyes.[19][20][21] It is well known that the eyes can influence persons at a distance ; and that they can select from a multitude a single individual, and turn their looks on him alone, though many lie in the same direction. The whole person seems to be in some measure affected by this influence of another's eyes, but the eyes themselves feel it with the most lively sensibility.[22] It is in the power of a

---

[19] Ce beau passage de Ciceron me rappelle ce que j'ai entendue d'un prédicateur Jesuite, appelé Teinturier, mediocre quant à l'élocution, mais qui faisoit plus d'effet en chaise que les hommes les plus éloquens ; *tant que j'aurois mes yeux,* disoit-il, *je ne les crains pas.* Œuvres de Marmontel, Tom. II. p. 286.

[20] Bourdaloue's action was very impressive, although he continually had his eyes shut when he was preaching. *Abbé Maury Princ. of Eloquence, Sec. 59.*

[21] Fenelon, in his Dialogues sur l'Eloquence, Tom. III. p. 241 ; seems also to remark concerning this fault in Bourdaloue's pronunciation:

. . . . Mais vous nous avez parlé des yeux, ont-ils leur éloquence ?

A. N'en doutez pas. Ciceron et tous les autres anciens l'assurent. Rien ne parle tant que le visage il exprime tout : mais, dans le visage, les yeux font le principal effet ; un seul regarde jetté bien à propos penetre dans le fond des cœurs.

B. Vous me faites souvenir que le predicateur dont nous parlions a d'ordinaire les yeux fermés : quand on le regarde de près cela choque.

A. Cest qu'on sent qu'il lui manque une des choses qui devroient animer son discours.

B. Mais pourquoi le fait-il ?

A. Il se hâte de prononcer, et il ferme les yeux, parceque sa mémoire travaille trop.

[22] The celebrated Dr. Moyes, who unfortunately lost his sight in early infancy, said he knew by the direction of the voice when any person who spoke turned his eyes upon him : but this is not sufficient to account in all cases for the influence I am inclined to attribute to the eyes, because by looking on another in perfect silence, you seem to attract their attention. Perhaps it may be said that the eyes being generally in constant motion, are naturally arrested upon those which are turned upon them. Whatever may be said on the subject, it does not interfere with the oratorical use of the eyes, which is my principal object.

public speaker to obtain the attention of any individual by turning his eyes upon him, though the matter of his discourse may not be particularly addressed or relating to that person. But if he direct his looks into the eyes of any one of his audience, he holds his attention irresistibly fixed. We seem to have the power, as it were, of touching each other by the sense of sight, and to be endued with something of that fascination of the eye which is attributed to other animals, and which the serpent is particularly said to possess. Not only is every one conscious when he is looked upon himself, but he even perceives when others are looked upon. The line of the direction of the axis of the eye, however invisible and imaginary, seems as if in effect it could be seen, and that in every instance throughout a great assembly, crossing and radiating in a thousand directions from the centre of every orb of sight.[23] And if in such an assembly any individual should be conspicuous from his situation or appearance, he glories, and is seen to glory in the contemplation of every eye.[24] If another be remarkable for any thing unusual, and which affords no ground of pride, he is oppressed by the weight of eyes which are turned upon him. Hence bashfulness casts down the curtains of the eyes, and cannot bear to raise them lest it should encounter the glance of curiosity in that most tender organ: whilst it feels painfully enough the gazing eye which wanders over its whole person.[25]

---

[23] Hence also may be supposed to arise the uneasiness felt from conversing with persons who squint much. The mind is distracted in attempting to address persons labouring under such a defect.

[24] Gaude quod spectant oculi te mille loquentem. *Hor.*

[25] Vidi quosdam adolescentes non sat peritos, nec paratos ad dicendum, qui quasi in pariete legerent ita semper cum unum in locum oculos haberent conversos. Quin et reperti

However these circumstances may be accounted for, the public speaker will judiciously take care to avail himself of them in a proper manner. He will therefore turn his eyes upon the eyes of his audience, and in the more important and earnest passages, he will look into the very pupils of their eyes. But in the practice of this direction of the eyes, which is of such advantage towards obtaining attention, he will be most cautious not to appear to fix on any particular person as the object of invective, or as the subject and example of the vices he may condemn; unless unhappily in public debate such severity should be absolutely necessary.[26] In the pulpit it can never be necessary, and is never admissible. From Cicero it may be permitted to borrow a beautiful passage which may serve to illustrate the qualities of the eloquence of the pulpit. He is speaking of Xenophon and Plato : " Their discourses had neither the nerves

---

sunt, qui non secus quam si animus sub tegulis habitaret; tabulatum et laquearia contueantur. . . . .

[26] Est enim oratori omni cura studioque providendum, ne dum vitia reprehenduntur, aut dicuntur ea, quæ nemo sibi dicta velit agnoscere, in aliquem certum intueatur, quem conjectu oculorum designari cæteri putent. Hoc Homerus (l. 1.) δενδίλλειν ἐς ἑκαςον dixit loquens de Nestore. Horatio est

. . . . Distorquere oculos putans.

Distorquens oculos ut me eriperet.

Tertulliano, *acie figere.* Plaut in Asin. *Neque ille ulli homini nutet, nictet, annuat* . . . . . Hic audiendum foret sapiens illud admonitum D. Augustini, *oculi nostri etsi jaciuntur in aliquem, figantur in neminem* . . . . Nec mihi fere minus reprehendendi illi videntur, qui non quidem in uno aliquo diutius hærent; sed in cœtu et circumfusâ coronâ quasi unum aliquem deposcerent, ita singulos tacitis luminibus designant et studiosi circumspiciunt, aquilæ non dissimiles, quæ ab aere prædam oculis investigari solet acuteque deligere. Talem describit Menelaum poeta Græcus in omnem partem intuentem, si forte in ea frequentia quæ objecebatur Antilochum animadverteret.

Πάντοσε παπταίνων ὡς ἀετὸς ὃν ῥὰ τὲ φάσιν
Ὀξύτατον δέρκεσθαι ὑπϖρανίων πετεεινῶν. *Il.*

Ludov. Cresol. Vac. Autum.

" nor the stings of the orator or pleader. They converse with
" the learned, whose minds they wish rather to compose, than to
" irritate. Therefore they discourse on subjects of calm enquiry,
" not of turbulent disputation; in order to instruct, not for cap-
" tious argument. You find in them nothing angry, nothing
" insidious, nothing cruel, nothing marvellous, nothing artful.
" They appear untainted altogether like a chaste and modest
" virgin. Therefore these writings are called rather discourses
" than orations. For though every conversation is a discourse,
" yet the conversations of an orator alone are distinguished by
" this name." [27,28] If the language and matter of a discourse from
the pulpit should be divested of every thing like acrimonious
personality, not less so in the delivery should the minister of the
Gospel guard against fixing on the individual the odium which
his duty requires him to charge against the general sin. And if
in a discourse composed in his closet he should illustrate by a
" strong picture the danger of some particular sin, and when he
comes to deliver it, he should suspect that any person is present
who may be supposed strongly to resemble his picture, or to be

---

[27] Horum oratio neque nervos, neque aculeos oratorios, ac forenses habet. Loquuntur
cum doctis, quorum sedare animos malunt, quam incitare. Sic de rebus placatis, ac
minime turbulentis, docendi causa, non capiendi loquuntur. . . . . . . Nihil iratum habet,
nihil invidum, nihil atrox, nihil mirabile, nihil astutum : casta, verecunda, virgo incorrupta
quodam modo. Itaque sermo potius, quam oratio dicitur. Quanquam enim omnis locutio
oratio est, tamen unius oratoris locutio hoc proprio signata nomine est. *Cic. Orat. c.* 19.

[28] Atque his detractis vitiis, facile quivis intelligat quæ sit illa oculorum moderatio
honestissimo oratori quærenda. Existet enim gravitas atque humanitas singulari modestia
illuminata, quæ veluti muta ipsius commendatio omnium animos et benevolentiam conciliet.
Illius compositi intuitus, quanta sit vis declaravit, qui omnium elegantissime potuit magnus
Chrysostomus, ait enim impurissimos et flagitiosissimos homines αἰσχύνεσθαι καὶ ἐριθριᾷν
καὶ τῆς οἰκείας ἐνδιδέναι μανίας, ὅταν πρὸς αὐτὴν ἴδωσιν ἀκριβῶς, pudefieri et erubescere
ac furorem suum remittere, si in eum vultum accurate intueantur. *Ludov. Cresol. Vac. Aut.*

the very original, it will become him either to alter and soften the features, so that it shall no longer be a resemblance of the individual; or even to weaken the force of his argument by leaving out the passage altogether, rather than offend, when his duty calls upon him to instruct. Illustration from example, is perhaps the most useful part of the preacher's discourse; and in forming the example his recollection must be turned on individual experience. But if one or two individuals alone furnish him with the reflections, which he is led to make, he must take care that they are not notoriously belonging to his own congregation; the characters must be sought distant in time or place, and touch those who hear him only in the general resemblance of human frailty. He must not proceed, as the painter did, who, representing the torments of hell-fire, introduced the portrait of his private enemy among the damned.

If it be surprising that the direction of the axis of vision (as it may be called) of every eye is capable of being traced by any observer as exactly as if a radiant and visible line was drawn from each; not less surprising is the power of judging by the expression of another's eye, when it is, that it exercises no speculation, even though the axis be in the direction of a particular object. This singular expression may be termed bending the eye on vacuity or vacancy; in which case distinct vision is not intended, but the focus falls short of the objects in the line of the axis of the eye. Persons in deep thought often look in this manner, with their eyes perfectly open, directed towards some objects and yet manifestly not seeing them, but void of speculation, as those who walk in their sleep. Of this expression, every beholder is sensible, it gives the appearance of abstracted meditation and inward

P

retirement. The short-sighted eye, however near to the description, is distinguished easily from the eye bent on vacuity—in the
vacant eye the peculiar expression is observed, in the short-sighted
eye the peculiar conformation. They who unfortunately labour
under cataracts (even before their malady is otherwise perceived)
are easily distinguished by the erring and undecided motion of
the axis of vision.

As much of the mind is discovered by the countenance, and
particularly through the windows of the eyes; so all men
examine the countenance and look into the eyes of those from
whom they have any expectations, or with whom they are to
have any important intercourse or dealings.[29,30] Nay the very
domestic animals learn thus to read the human countenance, and

---

[29] L'ame parle le plus souvent, et de la manière la plus facile et la plus claire par les
parties dont les muscles sont les plus mobiles; donc elle s'expliquera le plus souvent par les
traits du visage, et principalement par les yeux ; mais ce ne sera que rarement qu'elle em-
ploiera les changements dans les attitudes caracteristiques de tout le corps. La première
espéce de ces expressions, savoir celles des yeux, s'opére avec tant de facilité et si spontané-
ment en ne laissant, pour ainsi dire, aucun intervalle entre le sentiment et son effet, que le
sang froid le plus réfléchi et l'art le plus exercé à masquer les pensées secretes, n'en peuvent
pas arreter l'explosion, quoiqu'ils maitrisent tout le reste du corps. L'homme, qui veut
cacher les affections de son ame, doit sur tout prendre garde de ne pas se laisser fixer dans
les yeux; il ne doit pas moins veiller avec soin sur les muscles qui avoisinent la bouche, qui
lors des certains mouvemens intérieurs se maitrisent très-difficilement. " Si les hommes,"
dit Leibnitz, " vouloient examiner davantage avec une veritable esprit observateur les signes
extérieurs de leurs passions, le talent de se contrefaire deviendroit un art moins facile." Cependant l'ame conserve toujours quelque pouvoir sur les muscles; mais elle n'en a aucun
sur le sang, dit Descartes ; et par cette raison la rougeur où la pâleur subite dépendent peu
où presque point de notre volonté. *Engel Idées sur le Geste, Lettre* 6.

[30] The observations of Mr. Engel are very ingenious and founded in nature, the external
signs, he mentions, are no doubt the effects of internal emotion, the difficulty lies in determining the species of emotion. Blushing and paleness may as well arise from the pain felt
on a false charge, as from the consciousness of guilt ; too much care cannot be taken in
discriminating, for obvious reasons.

the dog is found to look for his surest and most intelligible instructions into his master's eyes. To look fairly in the face or rather into the eyes of those who are objects of respect, bespeaks, in youth especially, a candid and ingenuous mind: as on the contrary an habitual down look, as it is vulgarly called, and averted or unsteady eyes, are universally understood to indicate the opposite character. The reserve and dark consciousness of an unworthy heart do not willingly expose themselves to be penetrated by the beam of a searching eye. But this is altogether different from the occasional downcast bashfulness of modesty, which as soon as it is encouraged to look up, becomes enlightened with candour and intelligence."[31]

To the eyes, among their other powerful expression, belongs the affecting effusion of tears. By some it has been doubted, whether the orator should at any time give way to this proof of his feelings, as it may be considered rather as a mark of weakness than of sensibility, and is in danger of exciting derision rather than commiseration. Quintilian, speaking of the difficulty and hazard in attempting to move the audience to tears, says what is equally applicable to the tears of the speaker himself. " This advice is principally to be attended to, that no " speaker except one of the highest talents shall presume to " attempt at moving the audience to tears. For as this affection " is by far the most powerful when it succeeds, so, if it fail, it " chills those feelings, which the feeble orator had better have " trusted to the silent reflection of the judges. For the counten- " ance and the voice, and the very appearance of the agitated

---

[31] Hence, says Aristotle, the proverb—That modesty dwells in the eyes. ὅθεν καὶ ἡ παροιμία, " τὸ ἐν ὀφθαλμοῖς εἶναι αἰδῶ." *Arist. Rhet. l. i. c. 8.*

" criminal, become ludicrous to all, whom they do not affect.
" Let the pleader therefore measure and diligently estimate his
" own powers, and judge how far he is able to sustain the weight
" of such an attempt. It will admit no medium, and must pro-
" duce either tears or derision."[32]

If the speaker be himself moved to tears, it should appear evidently to the audience that the cause of his emotion is of weight sufficient so to disturb him; and then he is not only pardoned, but the effect on the hearers is powerful. Among the adequate causes for this affection of the speaker, may be reckoned the following: when an oration is to be pronounced upon the death of some great and good man, particularly if he is one by whom the speaker has been honoured and befriended, it cannot be charged against him as unmanly weakness, if he drop a tear over his memory.—When manly firmness must be supposed to give way, under the irremediable loss of what is most dear; tears are allowed to speak the anguish of the heart. The warlike Richmond in Shakspeare's Richard III. is not lowered in the estimation of the audience, by his effusion of tears on hearing of the murder of his family by the tyrant.—The tear of humanity is also a bright gem in the eye of the judge who pronounces the awful sentence of the law upon a criminal, who might have been expected to fulfil better

---

[32] Illud præcipue monendum, ne quis nisi summis ingenii viribus ad movendas lachrymas aggredi audeat. Nam ut est longe vehementissimus hic, cum invaluit, affectus; ita, si nihil efficit, tepet; quem melius infirmus actor tacitis judicum cogitationibus reliquisset. Nam et vultus, et vox, et* ipsa illa excitati rei facies, ludibrio etiam plerumque sunt hominibus, quos non permoverunt. Quare metiatur ac diligenter æstimet vires suas actor; et quantum onus subiturus sit, intelligat. Nihil habet ista res medium, sed aut lachrymas meretur, aut risum. *Quint. l.* vi. *c.* 1.

* What a proof of barbarism !

hopes.—His feeling is vindicated by the highest authority. When our Lord approached Jerusalem, and contemplated the miseries impending on this devoted city, he wept over it, and broke into that beautiful exclamation which at once shewed his patriotic love for his country, his prophetic spirit, and his deep affliction for the guilt and misery of his people.—On another occasion, under the terror and feeling of his own personal sufferings, with the most exalted magnanimity he forbid even the spectators to weep on his account. " Weep not for me, but weep for your-
" selves and for your children."

To weep on every tender emotion is weakness; a whining orator quickly fails to move aught but derision. It is therefore a judicious rule of Cicero's on this point, that the lamentation should be as brief as possible. " But when you have touched
" the feelings, says he, you must not dwell long on the cause of
" distress. Since as the rhetorician Apollonius says, " *nothing*
" *dries sooner than a tear.*" [33,34,35]

---

[33] Commotis autem animis, in conquestione morari non oportebit. Quemadmodum enim dixit Rhetor Apollonius, *lachryma nihil citius arescit. Cic de Inv. Rhet. l. 1.*

[34] The author ad Herennium repeats the same precept. Commiserationem brevem esse oportet. *Nihil* enim lachrymâ citius arescit. *Rhet. ad Heren. l. ii. c. 31.*

[35] Cresollius says, that it is allowable in some cases to sigh. He thus distinguishes them :

Duplex genus suspirii, placidum unum et quietum, alterum vehemens, turbidum et concitatum crebro anhelitu et singultu. Prius illud initiis convenit, ubi dolor mœrentis animi significatur; posterius autem in augendo et amplificando luctu et dolore, in explicanda misera et funesta calamitate, in incendendis auditorum animis, et miseratione commovendis adhiberi potest.

Thus he thinks St. Paul pronounced these words : Infelix ego homo ! quis me liberabit de corpore mortis hujus? *Cresol. Vac. Autumnales, p.* 250.

The observations of Aristotle upon the characters and situation of persons easily affected, and those not to be moved, are short and worthy of attention: they may be here inserted with advantage.

" It is evident that a man likely to feel commiseration may
" be classed under some of the following descriptions: One who
" thinks himself liable to misfortune, either in his own person,
" or in that of some person dear to him: or one who thinks him-
" self in danger either of such a misfortune as has been described
" in the definition, or of a similar one, or of something ap-
" proaching to it. For this reason, neither they who are alto-
" gether undone are disposed to pity; for they do not think they
" can suffer any thing worse, their sufferings are over. Nor
" they who consider themselves very fortunate; they are apt
" rather to be insolent. For since they think that all good fortune
" belongs to them, they must evidently suppose themselves not
" subject to any reverse, for such a persuasion forms a part of
" their happiness.—But they are apt to pity, who having already
" felt misfortune, but who have got over it, suppose themselves
" still liable to suffer from it. And they also who are advanced
" in life, both on account of their observations and experience.—
" The feeble in constitution, and the timid still in a greater
" degree.—The learned, because they form a just estimate of
" life.—They who have parents, or children, or wives, for these
" are a part of themselves, and may be subject to the evils men-
" tioned.—And they who are not under the influence of vehement
" passions, as anger and valour (for such persons are careless of the
" future), or of any insolent feeling (for neither do they think them-

" selves subject to misfortune); but those who are intermediate
" between these. Nor they again who are under strong influence of
" fear, for men when they are terrified feel no commiseration, as
" they are occupied with their own apprehensions.——They feel
" for others who entertain a good opinion of mankind, but he
" who does not think well of any one, considers of course, that
" all deserve to suffer. Upon the whole, if a man recollect, that
" similar misfortunes have befallen himself or any of those dear to
" him; or when he apprehends, that they may befal either him-
" self or his own relations; then we have observed that a man
" so circumstanced is open to the feelings of commiseration." [36]

Thus the unfeeling, according to the account of this venerable
author, are the ruined, the fortunate; the impassioned; the
valiant (under the immediate action of courage); the proud; the
terrified; and the misanthropical.

---

[36] 2. Δῆλον γὰρ ὅτι ἀνάγκη τὸν μέλλοντα ἐλεήσειν ὑπάρχειν τοιᾶτον· ὅιον, οἰήσεσθαι
παθεῖν ἄν τι κακὸν, ἢ αὐτὸν, ἢ τῶν αὐτᾶ τινὰ, καὶ τοιᾶτον κακὸν, ὅιον ἔιρηται ἐν τῷ ὅρῳ
ἢ ὅμοιον, ἢ παραπλήσιον· διὸ, ᾆτε οἱ παντελῶς ἀπολωλότες ἐλεᾶσιν (ᾀδὲν γὰρ ἄν ἔτι
παθεῖν ὅιονται· πεπόνθασι γὰρ·) ᾆτε οἱ ὑπερευδαιμονεῖν οἰόμενοι, ἀλλ' ὑβρίζᾀσιν· ἐι γὰρ
ἅπαντα ὅιονται ὑπάρχειν τἀγαθὰ, δῆλον ὅτι καὶ τὸ μὴ ἐνδέχεσθαι παθεῖν τι κακὸν. καὶ
γὰρ τᾶτο τῶν ἀγαθῶν. 3. Εἰσὶ δὲ τοιᾶτοι, ὅιοι νομίζειν παθεῖν ἄν· ὅιτε πεπονθότες ἤδε
καὶ διαπεφευγότες. 4. Καὶ οἱ πρεσβύτεροι, καὶ διὰ τὸ φρονεῖν, καὶ δι' ἐμπειρίαν. 5. Καὶ
οἱ ἀσθενεῖς· καὶ οἱ δειλότεροι μᾶλλον. 6. Καὶ οἱ πεπαιδευμένοι· εὐλόγιςοι γάρ. 7. Καὶ
ὅις ὑπάρχᾀσι γονεῖς, ἢ τέκνα, ἢ γυναῖκες· αὐτᾲ γὰρ ταῦτα, καὶ ὅια παθεῖν τὰ ειρημένα.
8. Καὶ οἱ μήτε ἐν ἀνδρίας πάθει ὄντες, ὅιον ἐν ὀργῇ καὶ θάρρει· (ἀλόγιςα γὰρ τᾶ ἐσομένᾳ
ταῦτα·) μήτ' ἐν ὑβρισικῇ διαθέσει· (καὶ γὰρ ᾆτοι ἀλόγιςοι τᾶ πείσεσθαί τι·) ἀλλ' οἱ
μεταξὺ τᾲτων· μήτ' ἄν φοβᾲμενοι σφόδρα· ᾆ γὰρ ἐλεᾶσιν οἱ ἐκπεπληγμένοι διὰ τὸ εἶναι
πρὸς τὸ ὀικείῳ πάθει· 9. Κᾲν ὅιωνταί τινας εἶναι ἐπιεικεῖς· ὁ γὰρ μεδένα ὀιόμενος,
παντας ὀισεται ἀξίας εἶναι κακᾷ. 10. Ὅλως δὴ, ὅταν ἔχῃ ὅυτως, ὡς· ἀναμνησθῆναι
τοιαῦτα συμβεβηκότα ἢ αὐτῷ ἢ τῶν αὐτᾲ, ἢ ἐλπίσαι γενέσθαι ἢ αὐτῷ, ἢ τῶν αὐτᾲ· ὡς
μὲν ἄν ἔχοντες ἐλεᾶσιν, ἔιρηται. *Aristot. Rhetor. l. ii. c. 10.*

The feeling are those, who have themselves suffered, but have got over their misfortunes; those advanced in life; those of delicate constitution; the timid; those connected by dear relations; the worthy, who think well of mankind; and they who think themselves liable to similar misfortunes.

From these last, tears may be drawn for the afflictions of others, and in their eyes the orator may find grace, when he manifests his own feelings in the same manner:[37] but from the others he has little to expect in the way of impression or indulgence, and if they withold derision, he need look for no other favour. And it is worthy of his observation, that in every audience these characters are pretty equally mixed, and that ridicule or disgust are more easily caught and communicated than the finer feelings.[38]

---

[37]   Sunt lachrymæ rerum et mentem mortalia tangunt. *Virg.*
The effect of the orator's painting is like that of the pictures which Æneas contemplated in Dido's palace, and the sympathy of his audience is his greatest glory.

[38] Extraordinary circumstances are however sometimes able to move the hardest hearts, as the deluded Othello confesses :

. . . . Whose subdu'd eyes,
Albeit unused to the melting mood,
Drop tears as fast as the Arabian trees
Their medicinal gum.

Jaffier is always in tears, and loses in estimation for his weakness.—Yet Pierre himself is moved in the last sad scene :

Jaff. Tears ! amazement ! tears !
I never saw thee melted thus before.

In Othello's character after his last fatal act, the paroxysm of jealousy is over, his cruel injustice has debased him, he is lowered and softened after his fever. All is according to the poet of nature. The pride of Pierre is wrung to tears by the ignominious death prepared for him. This too may be in nature. Milton says of Orpheus, that he

Drew iron tears down Pluto's cheek
And made hell grant what love did seek.

But these cases are rare, and more rare are the talents of the orator who on ordinary occasions can move such hearts as Aristotle has pronounced to be unfeeling.

On these accounts he will restrain himself as much as possible, and not suffer his pathetic imagination to get the better of him, except on the most justifiable occasions; and then he will be brief. If he burst out for a moment, he will stifle his emotion and quickly recover his voice, and speak his feelings with firmness, even though the silent tear obscure his eyes, and trickle down his manly cheek. Precepts are unnecessary on this head for the public speaker, who is not apt thus to be moved; unless we except this caution, that he never venture to assume the affectation of emotion, which would be incongruous and offensive.

That tears were not thought unworthy of an orator we may prove from the practice of the ancient orators, and from the approbation of antiquity. Indeed if the sincerity of the orator can have any weight, what can evince it more, or what stronger evidence can he give of his own feelings? Ludovicus Cresollius, to whose labours we are already so much indebted for information, and from whom we shall borrow much more, has collected many instances of the unrestrained indulgence and efficacy of the tears of the ancient orators, and with a few of these we shall close what we have to say on this subject.

" The most celebrated orators (says Cresollius) used formerly
" to shed tears in their pleadings. Demosthenes, the light of
" Greece, made this such an established and regular custom, that
" he seemed by it alone to gain his causes, and to raise the
" trophies of his victorious eloquence in the theatre of Athens.
" . . . . Dinarchus being engaged in a capital cause at the oppo-
" site side, warns the judges not to suffer themselves to be carried

" away by the lamentations and the tears of Demosthenes. And
" Æschines engaged in the same manner against him, says, this
" man sheds tears with greater facility than others laugh. . . . . .
" The poet Ion, declares concerning himself to the divine Plato,
" as a thing to be boasted of, and to be published with deserved
" triumph, that, when he spoke of any thing affecting, his eyes
" were filled with tears. . . . . . To some this may perhaps appear
" to belong to a weaker mind, than that which a wise, a grave, and
" a magnanimous man ought to possess. But it is not so: for if
" it were, we should not find recorded in their history or the
" writings of their poets, the tears and the grief of heroes. . . . . .
" Thus we see that the luminaries of antiquity wept at times
" profusely; Xerxes, Alexander the Great, Scipio Africanus,
" Marcellus, the very stoic and austere Cato, Titus Vespasianus,
" and others innumerable have been known to weep. Virgil
" says of Æneas, thus he speaks in tears. Ulysses is said to have
" wept on the death of his faithful dog. It was a common ob-
" servation in Greece, that worthy men are easily moved and
" prone to tears. The stern Manes alone, void of humane affec-
" tions, are incapable of weeping, and are not touched by tears.
" . . . . But those rare and precious drops should not be wantonly
" shed, lest tragedy should seem to be introduced in trifles."[39]

---

[39] Clarissimi oratores olim in judiciis fleverunt. Græciæ lumen Demosthenes tam id
habebat consuetum et solenne, ut eo uno causas eripere et Attico in theatro victricia
linguæ trophæa collocare videretur . . . . Dinarchus, in judicio capitis adversus
Demosthenem, monet judices ne ejus lamentis et comploratione moveantur, μὴ οὖν ἄχθεσθαι
αὐτῶ κλαίοντος καὶ ὀδυρομένω. Æschines in eundem ait οὗτος κλαίει μὲν ῥᾷον ἢ ἄλλοι
γελῶσιν, facilius, inquit, hic plorat, quam alii rident. . . . . Ion poeta hoc apud divinum
Platonem de se profitetur, ut gloriandum et merita prædicatione ferendum, ἐγὼ γάρ, inquit,

The eyes are so conspicuous, so beautiful, and so inestimable an organ of sense, that it is not wonderful that whoever has written concerning them, should express themselves in the most animated language. The poets have not alone indulged themselves in celebrating the eyes in every possible light, but even the gravest philosophers in speaking of them have suddenly elevated their language, and filled their descriptions with rhetorical figure. I have already quoted a long and beautiful passage from Cicero, and have reserved to this place the observations of Pliny and Quintilian on the eyes, that I may give them together with what they say concerning the other features which form that wonderful assemblage, the human countenance, and concerning the management and nature of which it is now time to speak. I shall however be excused for first transcribing from Lavater a spirited passage which he quotes from *Daumer Dissertatio de Oculiloquio.* " The images of our secret agitations are " particularly painted in the eyes. The eye appertains more to " the soul than any other organ; seems affected by, and to parti- " cipate in all its emotions; expresses sensations the most lively,

---

ὅταν ἐλεεινόν τι λέγω, δακρύων ἐμπίμπλανταί μв ὄφθαλμοι, cum ego aliquid miserabile loquor, lachrymis mihi complentur oculi . . . . Forte quibusdam mollioris hoc animi esse videatur, quam ut in virum sapientem et gravem atque magnanimum cadere possit. At non ita est nam alioqui neque in monumentis annalium, neque in scriptis poetarum heroum fletus doloremque videremus . . . . Itaque videmus lumina antiquitatis ubertim aliquando flevisse, Xerxem, Alexandrum Magnum, Scipionem Africanum, Marcellum, Stoicum etiam et austerum Catonem, Titum Vespasianum, innumerabiles alios . . . . Æneas . . . Sic fatur lachrymans. . . . . . Ulyssem mortuo cani illachrymasse ferunt. . . . . . E Græcia commune dictum ἀγαθοὶ δ' ἀριδάκρυες ἄνδρες, viri probi in lachrymas proni sunt et faciles. Tantum rigidi Manes humanitatis expertes flere non possunt et miseratione non capiuntur. . . . . . . nec ea rara temerè usurpanda, ne tragedia in nugis induci videatur. *Ludov. Cresol. Vacationes Autumnales, p.* 178.

" passions the most tumultuous, feelings the most delightful, and
" sentiments the most delicate. It explains them in all their
" force, in all their purity, as they take birth, and transmits
" them by traits so rapid, as to infuse into other minds the fire,
" the activity, the very image with which themselves are in-
" spired. The eye at once receives and reflects the intelligence
" of thought, and the warmth of sensibility; it is the sense of
" the mind, the tongue of the understanding," [40] The brief and
beautiful language of our Lord, is still superior to this splendid
passage.—" The light of the body is the eye;" and this is introduced not for the shew, but only to illustrate the most interesting
instructions which follow, " therefore when thine eye is single,
" thy whole body also is full of light: but when thine eye is
" evil, thy body also is full of darkness. Take heed therefore,
" that the light which is in thee be not darkness." [41]

The passage from Pliny seems particularly written in that
poetical spirit from which the gravest cannot refrain when
speaking of the eyes. Some observations on the other features
also are worthy the attention of a speaker who studies the countenance.

" The face is given to man alone, to other animals mouths or
" beaks. They have the forehead, it is true, but in man alone it
" serves to indicate grief or joy, clemency or severity. On the
" rising of the forehead are placed the brows of men, which are

---

[40] Lavater, by Holcroft, Vol. III. p. 175.

[41] Luke ii. 34, 35. Single ($\dot{\alpha}\pi\lambda\tilde{o}\upsilon\varsigma$ simplex) clear, pure, unobstructed. Beware lest the
light, the principle, which you have set up for your guide through life, should prove erroneous.

" capable both of moving together, and alternately; and by them
" the mind is partly made known; as in refusing and assenting.
" The haughty spirit above all is indicated by the brows."[42]
" Pride is conceived in another place, but here she sits upon her
" throne. Born in the heart, she mounts up here, and hence
" impends over the countenance. She finds in the whole body
" no place more elevated, none more abrupt where she may fix
" her solitary abode.

" Beneath are placed the eyes, the most precious part of the
" body, which by their sensibility of light distinguish life from
" death. . . . . . They are found to give indications of the mind
" more strongly than any other part, in all animals, particularly in
" man. In him they discover moderation, clemency, compas-
" sion, hatred, love, sorrow, joy. Their expression also is most
" various, they are savage, fierce, flaming, serious, oblique, dis-
" torted, submissive, insinuating. The soul assuredly inhabits
" the eyes. They burn, they strain, they swim, they twinkle.
" From them drops the tear of compassion : and when we kiss
" them, we seem to touch the very soul. From them weeping
" rivers bedew the countenance. Whence is drawn that mois-
" ture, in grief so abundant, and so quickly furnished; or where
" at other times does it remain? the sense of seeing is in the
" mind, perception is in the mind : the eyes, like appropriate
" vessels, receive and transmit to it the visible particles. It is

---

[42] Après les yeux, les parties du visage qui contribuent le plus à marquer la physionomie, sont les sourcils; comme ils sont d'une nature différente des autres parties, ils sont
plus apparens par ce contraste, et frappent plus qu'aucun autre trait : les sourcils sont une
ombre dans le tableau, qui en relève les couleurs et les formes. *Buffon Hist. Nat. De
l'Homme, p.* 524.

" for this reason that profound thought seems to deprive of
" sight, because the sense is withdrawn and turned inwards."[43]

This passage of Pliny, though highly eloquent, is not perhaps
so well suited to the practice of the orator as the following one
of Quintilian, who wrote expressly for his instruction. He is
speaking of those monstrous and unnatural masks which the
ancients used in their dramatic representations, and which the
good sense and better taste of modern times has wholly rejected.

" The father, who is always a principle character, and appears
" sometimes angry, and sometimes calm, has one eyebrow of his
" mask raised up, and the other composed, and it is customary,
" particularly for the Latin actors, to shew that side which is suit-
" able to the part which they act. But in the countenance the eyes
" have the greatest power, for the very soul emanates through
" them, so that exclusive of their motion, they brighten when
" cheerful, and are overcast with a sort of cloud in sadness.

---

[43] Facies homini tantum: cæteris os, aut rostra. Frons et aliis; sed homini tantum tristitiæ hilaritatis, clementiæ severitatis, index. In ascensu ejus supercilia homini, et pariter et alterne mobilia, et in iis pars animi. Negamus, annuimus. Hæc maxime indicant fastum. Superbia aliubi conceptaculum, sed hic sedem habet. In corde nascitur, huc subit, hinc pendet. Nihil altius abruptiusque invenit in corpore, ubi solitaria esset. Subjacent oculi, pars corporis pretiosissima, et qui lucis usu vitam distinguant à morte. . . . . . . Neque ex ulla parte majora animi indicia cunctis animalibus, sed homini maxime, id est moderationis, clementiæ, misericordiæ, odii, amoris, tristitiæ, lætitiæ. Contuitu quoque, multiformes, truces, torvi, flagrantes, graves, transversi, limi, summissi, blandi. Profectò in oculis animus inhabitat. Ardent intenduntur, humectant, connivent. Hinc illæ misericordiæ lachrymæ. Hos cum osculamur, animum ipsum videmur attingere. Hinc fletus, et rigantes ora rivi. Quis ille humor est, in dolore tam fœcundus et paratus ? aut ubi reliquo tempore ? Animo autem videmus, animo cernimus : oculi, ceu vasa quædam, visibilem ejus partem accipiunt, atque transmittunt. Sic magna cogitatio obcœcat, abducto intus visu. *Plinii Natur. Hist. l.* xi. *c.* 38.

" Nature has also supplied them with tears to indicate the feel-
" ings, which gush out in sorrow, and trickle down the cheeks
" in joy.   By their motion they become attentive, remiss, proud,
" savage, mild, austere, expressions which they give as circum-
" stances require.   But they must sometimes look harsh and
" strained, or languid and dull, or stupified, or wanton and
" moving, or swimming, and suffused as it were with pleasure,
" and glancing oblique (and if I may use the expression) like
" the eyes of Venus, or as if they were asking or giving a promise
" of something.   But who, except an absolute dunce or a fool,
" would keep them covered or closed when he speaks?

" And in order to bring about all these various expressions,
" the eyelids and the cheeks lend assistance by their auxiliary
" service.   The eyebrows also contribute much.   For they give
" the form to the eyes in a certain degree, and altogether
" govern the forehead.   By them the forehead is contracted,
" raised, or lowered; and accordingly, as any circumstance parti-
" cularly affects it, the blood, which is accelerated by the feeling
" of the mind, when it reaches the skin delicate with modesty, i
" diffused in blushes: and when it suddenly retires through fea
" it entirely forsakes the forehead, which it leaves pale and col
" When the blood is temperate, the forehead appears like th
" serene sky.   It is a fault in the eyebrows, either to be altogeth
" immoveable, or to move too much, or to be at variance
" being unequally raised, (as I have just instanced in the con
" mask,) or to be formed in any manner different from what
" have mentioned.   For anger is manifested by the contract
" of the brows, sorrow by their depression, and cheerfulness

" their relaxation, and in granting and refusing they are drawn
" down or raised up.

" It is seldom proper to manifest our feelings by the nostrils
" or the lips, though they are sometimes used to express derision,
" contempt, and pride. It is indelicate to turn up the nostrils,
" (as Horace calls it,) or to inflate or move them, or to disturb
" them with the fingers, and with sudden violence to force the
" breath through them, or to spread them out too often, and to
" press them flat with the palm of the hand; and even the
" frequent blowing of the nose is condemned, and not without
" reason.

" It is wrong to thrust out the lips, to separate them, to press
" them together, and to stretch them, to expose the teeth, to
" draw them aside almost to the ears, to fold them over each
" other with a sort of self sufficiency, to let them hang down, or
" to make the voice issue only from one side of the mouth. To
" lick or bite the lips is also disgusting, and even in articulation
" their motion should be moderate; for we should speak with
" the mouth more than with the lips." 44

---

44 Pater ille cujus præcipuæ partes sunt, quia interim concitatus, interim lenis est, altero
erecto, altero composito est supercilio: atque id ostendere maxime Latinis actoribus moris
est, quod cum iis, quas agunt, partibus congruat. Sed in ipso vultu plurimum valent oculi,
per quos maxime animus emanat, ut citra motum quoque et hilaritate enitescant et tristitia
quoddam nubilum ducant. Quinetiam lachrymas his natura mentis indices dedit : quæ aut
erumpunt dolore aut lætitia manant. Motu vero intenti, remissi, superbi, torvi, mites,
asperi fiunt : quæ, ut actus poposcerit, fingentur. Rigidi vero et extenti, aut languidi et
torpentes, aut stupentes, aut lascivi et mobiles, aut natantes et quadam voluptate suffusi, aut
limi, et (ut sic dicam) venerei aut poscentes aliquid, pollicentesve nonnunquam esse debe-
bunt. Nam opertos compressosve eos in dicendo quis, nisi plane rudis aut stultus, habeat ?

The latter part of this extract from Quintilian contains an enumeration of the principal faults practised by the lips, that is by the exterior part of the mouth: and these are both numerous and offensive. The mouth, of which we are now to treat, is next to the eyes, or even in preference to the eyes themselves, the most important part of the countenance: it is so in whatever way we consider it, whether in the variety and precision of which it is capable, or in the interest which it excites, whether by the language and tones which issue from it, or from its expression and character as it strikes the beholder. " How," says Cresollius, " must the dignity and composition of that most honoured mouth " avail to detain the attention of the auditor. The mouth is the " vestibule of the soul, the door of eloquence, and the place in " which the thoughts hold their high debates; and that part of " the man is placed in an elevated situation obvious to the sight, " most pregnant in its use."[45]

Et ad hæc omnia exprimenda in palpebris etiam et in genis est quoddam deserviens his ministerium. Multum et superciliis agitur. Nam et oculos formant aliquatenus, et fronti imperant. His contrahitur, attollitur, dimittitur: ut una res in ea plus valeat, sanguis ille, qui mentis habitu movetur, et, cum infirmam verecundia cutem accipit, effunditur in ruborem; cum metu refugit, abit omnis et pallore frigescit; temperatus medium quoddam serenum efficit. Vitium in superciliis, si aut immota sunt omnino, aut nimium mobilia, aut inæqualitate (ut modo de persona comica dixeram) dissident, aut contra id, quod dicimus, finguntur. Ira enim contractis, tristitia deductis, hilaritas remissis ostenditur. Annuendi quoque et renuendi ratione demittuntur, aut allevantur. Naribus labrisque non fere quidquam decenter ostendimus; tametsi derisus, contemptus, fastidium significari solet. Nam et *corrugare nares* (ut Horatius ait) et inflare et movere et digito inquietare, et impulsu subito spiritum excutere, et diducere sæpius, et plana manu resupinare indecorum est: cum emunctio etiam frequentior non sine causa reprehendatur. Labra et porriguntur male et scinduntur, et adstringuntur, et diducuntur, et dentes nudant, et in latus ac pene ad aurem trahuntur, et velut quodam fastidio replicantur et pendent et vocem tantum altera parte dimittunt. Lambere quoque ea et mordere deforme est: cum etiam in efficiendis verbis modicus eorum esse debeat motus. Ore enim magis, quam labris, loquendum est. *Quint.* *l.* xi. *c.* 3.

[45] Quantum oris honestissimi dignitas et compositio valeat in dicendo ad tenendum

R

The mouth is the seat of grace and sweetness; smiles and good temper play around it; composure calms it, and discretion keeps the door of its lips.[46]

It is more particularly important to attend to the mouth, than even to the eyes themselves. The eyes at all times can assume the character suited to the expression of the moment. But the mouth being one of the softest features is soonest changed, and if it once lose its character of sweetness, it changes perhaps for ever. How few mouths which have been beautiful in youth (the season of happiness and smiles,) are preserved beyond that period: whilst the eyes are often found to retain their lustre, or to flash occasionally with their early brightness even in advanced life. Every bad habit defaces the soft beauty of the mouth, and leaves indelible on it the traces of their injury. The stains of intemperance discolour it, ill nature wrinkles it, envy deforms, and voluptuousness bloats it. The impressions of sorrow upon it are easily traced, the injuries which it suffers from ill-

---

auditorem. . . . Cum sit os animi vestibulum et orationis janua, et cogitationum comitium eaque pars hominis loco celsa, visu prompta, usu fœcunda. *Cresol. Vac. Aut.*

[46] La bouche et les lévres sont après les yeux les parties du visage qui ont le plus de mouvement et d'expression; les passions influent sur ces mouvemens, la bouche en marque les différens caractères par les différentes formes qu'elle prend; l'organe de la voix anime encore cette partie et la rend plus vivant que tous les autres; la couleur vermeille des lévres, la blancheur de l'émail des dents, tranchent avec tant d'avantage sur les autres couleurs du visage, qu'elles paroissent en faire le point de vue principal; on fixe en effet les yeux sur la bouche d'un homme qui parle, et on les y arrête plus long temps que sur toutes les autres parties; chaque mot, chaque articulation, chaque son produisent des mouvemens différens dans les lévres: quelque varies et quelque rapides que soient ces mouvemens, on pourroit les distinguer tous les uns des autres; on a vu des sourds en connoitre si parfaitement les différences et les nuances successives, qu'ils entendoient ce qu'on disoit en voyant comme on le disoit. *Buffon Hist. Nat. de l'Homme p.* 527.

health are manifest, and accident may often deform its symmetry. It is sweetened by benevolence, confirmed by wisdom, chizzeled by taste, and composed by discretion: and these traces if habitually fixed last unaltered in its soft forms, throughout every varying stage of life. We should therefore labour in our own persons, and watch those of the youthful under our control, to form if possible this distinguished and pliant feature to decorum and grace,[47] lest it assume an ungracious form irretrievably.

But whatever may be that beauty and expression of the mouth which prepossesses in favour of an orator, a gracious mouth is to be desired on another very important account, which is for the advantage of more perfect articulation and delivery. An ill-formed, uncouth, underhung, or gaping mouth, can never finish perfectly and correctly the articulation of words, nor deliver them out with that winning and irresistible grace which delights the ear as well as the eye of every hearer. The authors of the fantastic tales of the fairies describe this talent very impressively, as the gift of dropping at every word pearls and diamonds from the lips.[48] A near approach to this imaginary gift, is made in real life by those who acquire the most perfect eloquence: who

---

[47] Ovid in his fable of Narcissus makes him admire particularly the graces of his own mouth :

. . . . decusque
Oris . . . . . .

[48] The eloquence of Nestor is represented to be of this delightful character :

. . . . τοῖσι δὲ Νέςωρ
Ἡδυεπὴς ἀνόρεσε, λιγὺς Πυλίων ἀγορητὴς,
Τᾶ καὶ ἀπὸ γλώσσης μέλιτος γλυκίων ῥέεν αὐδὴ.

join to correct and finished enunciation, the graces of a refined taste, and the riches of a cultivated mind. On their lips sit persuasion and delight, and the words which fall from them precious and brilliant, may well be compared to the brightest gems.

These acquisitions are not indeed equally within the reach of all; but it is shameful to be the last in the race of honour.[49] No attention should therefore be spared in order to guard against bad habits, nor should any labour be thought too heavy which may correct defects. To these points must be added the careful improvement of the mind, and the regulation of the finer affections, for by these combined means, even uncouth forms will be rendered agreeable, and the beauty or grace bestowed by nature will be preserved even to old age.

Cresollius gives us the names of persons celebrated for the graces of the mouth.

" Damasius speaking of Asclepiadotus (a celebrated physi- " cian), a man of extraordinary genius and learning, says, his " mouth and his whole countenance were the habitation of the " graces themselves."

" Alcibiades had such a prepossessing mouth and language, " that none could resist his eloquence."

---

49   Non jam prima peto Mnestheus : neque vincere certo :
            (Quanquam ô) sed superent, quibus hoc, Neptune, dedisti.
            Extremos pudeat rediisse : hoc vincite cives,
            Et prohibete nefas.   *Virg. Æn.* 5.

" T. Pomponius Atticus, when a boy, had such docility of dis-
" position, and such sweetness of the mouth and voice, that he
" not only learned most rapidly whatever he was taught, but
" pronounced declamations most admirably. For this talent he
" was celebrated among his equals, and shone with such a
" splendor as his noble schoolfellows could hardly bear:—he
" therefore excited the emulation of all by his diligence, among
" whom were Torquatus, C. Marius the younger, and M. Cicero.
" And those he attached to himself by such strict friendship,
" that through life no man was ever more dear to them." [50]

Pliny, in speaking of persons who happened to resemble
Pompey in a singular manner, is led incidentally to bear the
most striking testimony to the graces of his mouth, and the
beauty of his countenance. " One Vibidius a plebeian, and
" Publicius who had even been freed from slavery; resembled
" Pompey the Great with a likeness almost indistinguishable,
" they had the very probity of his mouth, and all the dignity of
" his admirable forehead." [51,52]

---

[50] Damasius de Asclepiadoto præstabili ingenio et doctrina viro aiebat τὸ ϛόμα ἀυτᾶ, καὶ τὸ ἄλλο πρόσωπον, ὁικητήριον εἶναι ἀυτῶν τῶν χαρίτων. Os ejus et reliquam faciem domicilium fuisse gratiarum. *Photius.*

Alcibiadi olim tanta erat commendatio oris atque orationis, ut nemo ei dicendo posset resistere. *Æmil. Prob. in Alcib.*

T. Pomponio Attico erat autem in puero, præter docilitatem ingenii, summa suavitas oris ac vocis, ut non solum celeriter arriperet quæ tradebantur, sed etiam excellenter pronuntiaret; qua ex re in pueritia nobilis inter æquales ferebatur, clariusque explendesce-bat, quam generosi condiscipuli animo æquo ferre possent; itaque incitabat omnes suo studio, quo in numero fuerunt L. Torquatus, C. Marius filius, M. Cicero, quos consuetudine sua sic sibi devinxit, ut nemo iis perpetuo fuit carior. *Corn. Nep. in Attico.*

[51] Magno Pompeio Vibius quidam e plebe, et Publicius etiam servitute liberatus,

The observations which Cresollius makes on Pompey's mouth are in his usual spirit, and are worthy of being presented to the English reader.

" His mouth of probity, he (Pliny) has so named, in my
" judgment, because it was distinctly marked with integrity,
" formed of some diviner clay, not by the hasty art of Prome-
" theus, but by the dedalean and perfect hand of nature, tinged
" with the colours of the graces, harmoniously sculptured in
" every line, pencilled with the respected border of modesty as
" with a list of purple: not distorted, not vast and rustic, not
" gaping like the wide-mouthed ape, nor bloated like the Moor,
" nor frightened in savage horror, nor deformed with any other
" blemish; but perfect and gracious, and worthy to be shewn
" from its superior situation. A mouth of this character is
" formed in the primitive and native lineaments of those
" men, who are born to every excellence and gifted most boun-
" tifully by the artificer of all things; it is afterwards preserved
" by wisdom and discretion; and they who vigilantly guard their
" generously composed and perfect nature, cannot fail to possess
" that rectitude and probity of the mouth, thus adorned with
" every expression of integrity: and which therefore the wisest
" men advise not to be changed by the smallest alteration." [53,54]

---

indiscretâ prope specie fuere similes, illud os probum reddentes, ipsumque honorem eximiæ frontis. *Plin. Hist. Nat. l.* vii. *c.* 12.

    52 Plutarch is already quoted in this chapter as celebrating the fine countenance of Pompey.

    53 Os probum meo judicio nominavit, honestate insignitum, diviniori quodam luto, non Promethei subito artificio, sed dædalâ naturæ manu factum, gratiæ coloribus tinctum, undique numerose tornatum, modestiæ honoro limbo, ut tenui purpura litum; non tortum

That moral habits are capable of altering the fine expressions of the countenance, as Cresollius seems in the latter part of this passage to imply, can hardly be doubted. The character of the entire countenance, is under the dominion of those habits. And beauty is often (and perhaps better) attributed to the mind, and dispositions beaming through the countenance, than to symmetry of features and fine colouring. The most beautiful face soon ceases to please, if unworthy passions habitually deform its expression. Of this truth many sad examples may be found among an unhappy class of females, who too easily seduce unwary youth by their beauty and their practised smiles, but who again soon lose their conquests by the vicious manners and unworthy sentiments which debase them. Whilst homely features when illuminated by habitual virtues, benevolence and candour, and fidelity, when tinged with modesty, and adorned by grace and taste, find true admirers, and grow almost into genuine beauty. It is thus that husbands often (for sometimes other passions interfere) find beauty in their excellent though not handsome wives. And this will also serve to account for that happy illusion, if such it be, which fills the fond parent with the persuasion of the beauty of her amiable but absolutely

---

non vastum et agreste, non simiæ rictu, non tumore Mauro, non horrore barbarico, non alio vitio deformatum : denique perfectum et decens et ostendi è superioie loco dignum. Hujusmodi os primis quidem et nativis lineamentis, in iis hominibus effingitur, qui ad omnem excellentiam nati sunt, et a rerum omnium opifice liberalissime subornati, judicio deinde prudentiaque retinetur, quique naturam tuentur suam ingenue compositam et perfectam, non possunt non habere os rectum, os probum, et specie honestatis illuminatum, unde quam minime id esse mutandum viri sapientes admonent. *Lud. Cres. Vac. Aut.*

[54] A print of General Washington after a picture by Stewart, gives me a strong idea of the *os probum.*

ugly child; and will also explain why it is that children are never offended at any want of beauty in their good and affectionate parents. Mutual good offices, mutual benevolence, habitual faith, and love and respect enlightening the countenance, impress on the eyes of each, and communicate to the imagination the idea of a real and lasting beauty, superior to form and colour, and beyond the power of the fatal injuries of time itself.

Lavater has quoted from Gellert, the following lines, and has accompanied them by the following observations on a beautiful youth changed by vicious habits. The translation is that of Mr. Holcroft.

> His morn of youth how wondrous fair!
>   How beauteous was his bloom!
> But ah! he stray'd from virtuous paths,
>   And pangs his life consume.
> His wasted form, his livid eye,
>   His haggard aspect pale,
> Of many a hidden hideous vice
>   Recount the fearful tale.

" I have known (he continues) handsome and good young " men, who in a few years, by debauchery and excess, have been " totally altered. They were still generally termed handsome, " and so indeed they were, but good God! how different was " their present from their former beauty? . . . . .

His mode of accounting for this, and such changes in the character of the countenance, is philosophical and just.

" Dissimilar passions have not similar expressions, neither
" have similar passions dissimilar expressions. . . . . . The result
" of this will be, the passions of the mind produce their ac-
" cordant effects on the countenance. . . . . Each frequently re-
" peated change, form, and state of the countenance, impresses at
" length a durable trait on the soft and flexible parts of the face.
" The stronger the change, and the oftener it is repeated, the
" stronger, deeper, and more indelible is the trait. We shall
" hereafter shew, that the like impression is made in early youth,
" even on the bony parts. An agreeable change by constant
" repetitions makes an impression on, and adds a feature of
" durable beauty to the countenance. A disagreeable change by
" constant repetition makes an impression on, and adds, a
" feature of durable deformity to the countenance. A number of
" such like beautiful changes, when combined, if not counter-
" acted, impart beauty to the face, and many deformed changes
" impart deformity."

S

CHAPTER IV.

OF GESTURE IN GENERAL.

Objections to the use of gesture examined—Theatrical gesture not to be affected by the orator—A knowledge of the principles of gesture does not lead to incessant gesture——Nature uncultivated does not suggest proper gesture—Awkward gestures—Whether gesture is contrary to the genius of the British people—Modern public speakers in manner strongly resemble Scaurus and Rutilius—Oratory, having been brought to perfection by the ancients, not limited by the usages of the best modern speakers—Delivery highly estimated by the ancients—The precepts which have come down to us not sufficient on this subject—Ancient authorities for the necessity of correct and animated delivery—Isocrates—Demosthenes—Cicero—Quintilian—D. Halicarnassus—Pliny—Valerius Maximus—Opinions of Aristotle—Earlier writers after the revival of letters—Causinus—Cresollius—Talæus—Sulpitius Victor.—Modern writers; Rollin—Lord Chesterfield—Dr. Darwin—Maury—Edmund Burke.

CHAPTER IV.

Of Gesture in General.

THE third division of the external part of oratory, or of delivery, is gesture. Under gesture is comprehended the action and position of all the parts of the body; of the head, the shoulders, the body or trunk; of the arms, hands, and fingers; of the lower limbs, and of the feet.

Of the importance of the due management of the voice, which constitutes the first division of delivery, no public speaker seems to entertain any doubt. Every man's experience quickly convinces him both of the necessity of making himself audible by issuing a sufficient quantity of voice, and also of so managing his voice as to accomplish this object with the greatest facility, and with the least possible inconvenience to himself. As to the countenance, the generality of public speakers do also give it something of the expression suited to their subject; and if their feelings be at any time awakened, they seldom fail to manifest them with sufficient evidence, both in their countenance and in the tones of their voice. There are some indeed who seem to think monotony of voice and inflexibility of countenance equally suited to their dignity and indifference; and who are never either moved themselves, nor attempt to move others. But, as to the use of the third division of delivery, gesture, the majority in this country seem to have altogether decided against its expediency and use; except so far as they may be forced upon something like it, by the immediate and irresistible impulse of their feelings.

Therefore, before we enter fully into the consideration of this part of our subject, it will be necessary, in some degree, to combat this prejudice.[1]

Among men of liberal education, and such as are even in the habit of public speaking, who admit the necessity of diligent study for acquiring all the literary parts of oratory; language, invention and arrangement; many are found to question the use, if not to deride the study and practice of gesture.

A man is not, they say, to introduce into the courts, or to exhibit in the pulpit, the gestures of the theatre : nor is he to run the hazard, by the trifling affectation of the schools, of turning into ridicule the real business of life. It is not the genius of the people of Great Britain to gesticulate; they are a grave people. To saw the air perpetually is absurd; and where gesture may be necessary, if a man is moved, nature will teach him enough to enforce what he has to say. It is not the custom therefore of our best speakers to use much gesture, nor to study very carefully the gesture, which they may use.[2]

---

[1] Under the article *action* in the new Cyclopedia other objections to its use are stated, to which the reader is referred. The writer does not appear altogether decided in his opinion. See also the objections of Mr. Barrow to oratorical action. *Essay on Educa. c. 23.*

[2] Venimus ad summum fortunæ. Pingimus atque
Psallimus et luctamur Achivis doctius unctis. *Hor.*

Such are the principal objections urged against the study of gesture; and it will be allowed they are stated with sufficient force. They shall be answered briefly, and in order.

1. As the theatre affords the only correct models of delivery with which we are acquainted,[3] so there appears reason to apprehend the introduction of its gesture into places which it does not suit. The gravity of the courts of law, the dignity of Parliament, and the modesty of the pulpit, would be much offended by the licentiousness of theatrical gesture. Yet so far as every kind of gesture is to be performed by the same beings, furnished with the same faculties, and for the same purposes, that is, in order to enforce, to illustrate, and to adorn their discourses, the principles of all, if truly investigated, must be referred to the same source. And the advocate, the senator, and the preacher, will have in the principles of their action much in common with the actor, but they will differ also much from him in their manner, and not a little from each other also. To distinguish the character of the delivery belonging to each profession, to discriminate their peculiar manner, force, and expression, and if possible to mark the limits of each distinctly, lest they should indecorously break in upon the bounds of each other, is the proper object of a system of gesture, and one of its most arduous labours.

A system which is designed to suit the various exigences of public speakers of every description, must of necessity be

---

[3] With Quintilian, therefore, we agree, who says, Dandum aliquid comœdo.

extensive, and its details must be minute. With these details young persons should be acquainted, and they should be exercised in them, as far as is practicable, in order to give them the necessary command of voice, countenance and gesture. In the system here presented, the powers and actions of the human body are attempted to be exhibited in a point of view affording (it may be almost said) an infinity of combinations, all capable of being distinctly and briefly noted. From this variety the speaker will bring into actual use, such parts only as may suit the particular situation, in which he may be placed. He is not advised to be intemperate on account of the profusion set before him, much the contrary; he has the opportunity of selection, and will make it according to his taste and judgment, such as it may be; which it is not in the power of any system altogether to correct, and which it is hoped this system will not pervert. The detail may appear tedious to the impatient, and unnecessary to those who think lightly of it : but without the most minute detail a system can be of little use. It is therefore hoped that the minutiæ into which this enquiry leads, may not be considered as an attempt to impose a trifling affectation of gesture, but merely as a necessary developement of the parts of the plan.

Though according to the system, gesture may be varied almost to infinity, it is not proposed that the speaker's gesture should be incessant; nothing could so completely defeat every expectation of the advantage arising from gesture. In many parts of an oration little gesture should be used; in many the speaker should be almost unmoved; and very few passages admit of vehement gesticulation. It is not necessary always to saw the air, far from it.—But it is necessary to consider and to judge *when* the air is to be divided by the arm of the orator; when he is to move his head, his body, and his limbs; and *how* he is to do all this with effect, with propriety, and with grace. And instead of adding much to his action, he who studies it the most carefully, will only be inclined to alter it for the better, or perhaps in many places to retrench it altogether. The art of gesture however culti vated, is not to be used for incessant flourishing; as well might the steps and bounds in dancing be adopted on all occasions, instead of the simple movement of walking: and our art may serve the same excellent purpose to the awkward gesticulator for which the father sent his clownish son to the dancing school, that he might learn to stand still. An observation of Cicero applies to our present purpose; those, he says, who have learned at the Palæstra, are distinguished even in other exercises by their grace and agility; they who have learned to dance elegantly are also easily distinguished in all their motions from the untaught, even when they are not dancing. And the gesture also of the well instructed speaker, even in its most trivial movements, is altogether different from neglected rudeness.

That nature without cultivation should suggest on the moment to every man all the gesture necessary to enforce his feelings, and to illustrate and grace his sentiments, cannot be maintained by any analogy from the assistance afforded by nature in the other parts of oratory, nor is it found agreeable to fact. All the strong passions of the mind

T

do indeed communicate themselves so suddenly and irresistibly to the body, that vehement gesticulations can hardly
be avoided: and these are no doubt natural. Thus anger
threatens, affright starts, joy laughs and dances. But nature
does not by any means suggest (except it may be to some
chosen few) the most dignified or graceful expressions of
those various passions, as may be sufficiently observed in
the untutored extravagance and uncouth motions of the
vulgar; in the gesticulations of mirth in their dances, and of
anger in their quarrels. These, though they may be perfectly
intelligible, and strongly energetic, degrade the person who
uses them from all pretensions to the character of liberality
of mind, or of enlightened eloquence, and are more likely
to excite in the cultivated spectator, laughter or disgust, than
the kindred passion of the gesticulator. So fastidious is the
taste with respect to oratory. And if a public speaker, conscious of his own deficiency, should be contented to relinquish
the honour of aspiring to the name of an orator, he must
carefully guard himself against manifesting any emotion of
the mind, and limit his efforts to dry expositions and frigid
reasonings. For should he at any time be moved, and be
betrayed into vehemence, he is undone; he has abandoned
his place of security, and has ventured upon the enchanted
ground of the orator (for to him belongs all the region of
the dignified and strong passions), where he is incapable of
governing himself; he falls into undignified gesticulations, and
into absurd distortions; and instead of inspiring others with
his feelings, he will frequently become ridiculous, and be
laughed at himself. Well aware of this danger, such speakers
are often found carefully to restrain themselves, and to stand

unmoved; using no gesture at all,[4] but seeming to speak like the face in the picture in the ludicrous French farce of the *Tableau Parlant.* Others more bold, but equally uninstructed, and without study, fall into some uncouth gesture, as a vehement stroke of the right arm, and stamping of the foot, or balancing of the body, which they repeat invariably whenever they are moved. These iterations of awkward gesture are disgusting at first, but at last are entirely overlooked, and stand for nothing; they are pardoned as the peculiar manner of the man, provided he is found to possess the other essential requisites expected in one who undertakes to instruct the public, or to maintain an interesting argument. And this description will be found applicable to many of our most celebrated public speakers: but this is far short of the praise of consummate eloquence, or even of that degree of it, which, with due attention and labour, such speakers might have attained.

As to the objection that the genius of our speakers does not dispose them to gesture, much has been already said on that subject in the Introduction to this work. It is very possible, and perhaps may be very true, that there are people who possess more vivacity than we do, and who are more prone to express themselves by gestures. Our neighbours the French, are reckoned such with respect to us, and are like ourselves with respect to their more lively neighbours, the Italians. And again, the ancient inhabitants of Italy, the Romans, held the Greeks to be more disposed to gesticulate than themselves. And

---

[4] See a passage of Cresollius quoted in the Introduction.

yet Cicero himself, as he tells us, was excited to no small degree
of vehemence in his oration for Aquilius. He precipitated
himself on his client, whose breast he tore open in order to
expose to the judges, the scars of those wounds, which he had
received in the service of his country, and by which he
desired to commend him to their favour.[5] In sacred writ the
Jews, particularly their prophets, are recorded to have been
in the habit of using the most violent gestures to express their
indignation or their grief. They tore their garments, and
covered their heads with ashes, and wore sackcloth next their
skin. The genius of our people does not indeed lead them
into any such extravagancies, but are they therefore to be
absolutely immoveable and void of every expression of feeling? may there not be also some kind of gesture suited to the
gravity of our manners, and the nature of our habits, that
shall not shock by affectation, nor yet suffer admirable compositions to languish and chill the hearer for want of being
delivered with proper energy? may there not be something
of gesture and expression adopted which shall give due
dignity and effect to noble sentiments conceived in the
spirit of ancient eloquence, and expressed in language not
less vigorous than that of Greece and Rome? May not some
advantageous change be made from awkward rusticity to

---

[5] Quem enim ego consulem fuisse (M. Aquilium sc.) imperatorem ornatum a senatu,
ovantem in capitolium ascendisse meminissem, hunc cum afflictum, debilitatum, mœrentem,
in summum discrimen adductum viderem, non prius sum conatus misericordiam aliis com-
movere, quam misericordia sum ipse captus. Sensi equidem tum magnopere moveri judices,
cum excitavi mœstum ac sordidatum senem, et cum ista feci, quæ tu, Crasse, laudas, non
arte, de qua quid loquar nescio, sed motu magno animi, ac dolore, ut disciderem tunicam,
ut cicatrices ostenderem, cum C. Marius mœrorem orationis meæ præsens ac sedens
multum lacrymis suis adjuvaret. *Cic. de Orat. l. ii.*

manly grace; and instead of defacing the beauty of our compositions, by negligence and frigid indifference in action;
should we not invent some new and more efficacious exertions
for striking deeply the impressions of our native eloquence?

Among the examples of antiquity, our public speakers seem
to have particularly and almost exclusively selected for their
imitation, the two Roman orators Scaurus and Rutilius, out of
the many, whom Cicero so judiciously characterizes in his work
on celebrated orators: a work, which, on account of its admirable criticism on the almost living portraits, (particularly of the
great men of his own time,) which he has sketched with the
hand of a master, ought to be perpetually studied by all who
devote themselves to speaking in public.

" I shall here be allowed to speak briefly concerning Scaurus
" and Rutilius, neither of whom obtained the reputation of a
" great orator, though they had each been employed in many
" causes. They were men, who in some respects deserved to be
" well spoken of, for although they were not of the first rate
" talents, their industry was praiseworthy. Not that they were
" altogether wanting in ability, but they were deficient in orato-
" rical ability. For it is of little consequence that you prepare
" what is to be spoken, unless you are able to deliver your
" speech with freedom and grace. Nor is even that sufficient,
" unless, what is spoken be delivered by the voice, by the
" countenance, and by the gesture in such a manner as to give it
" a higher relish. Why should I not mention learning as also
" necessary? Without which, even if a man happen occasionally
" to speak well by his natural talents, his success must be

" considered accidental, because he cannot always be in a state
" of preparation. Scaurus in his speaking possessed the dignity
" and natural authority of a wise and upright man; so that
" when he spoke for his client, you would not think he was
" pleading a cause, but that he was giving testimony. This
" kind of speaking seemed little suited to the business of an
" advocate, but for delivering his opinion in the senate, of
" which he was the first in rank, it was excellent. For it ex-
" pressed not only wisdom, but what was more important in
" the matter, integrity. This he possessed from nature alone,
" he could not possibly have acquired it by study. Though
" even for this, as you know, there are precepts. . . . .

" But Rutilius practised a certain grave and severe style of
" speaking; yet both of them were vehement and warm by
" nature. For when they stood together as candidates for the
" consulship, not only he who lost the election charged the
" successful candidate with undue influence, but Scaurus also,
" when he was acquitted, retorted the charge on Rutilius.

" Rutilius was a man of great labour and industry, which
" was the more proper, because he laid himself out for the
" important business of giving opinions in law. His orations
" are jejune; his law arguments are excellent; he was a man of
" learning, and acquainted with the Greek literature; he was a
" hearer of Panætius, and was almost a perfect stoic. The style
" of speaking of this sect, is subtile and full of art, but meagre,
" and not sufficiently accommodated to influence a popular
" assembly. The confidence of self-opinion, which is peculiar
" to this sect of philosophers, was strongly rooted in Rutilius:

" so that when he was brought to trial on this charge, of which
" he was most innocent (and we know this trial took place when
" the republic was altogether convulsed), though there were at
" that time two most eloquent speakers of consular rank, L.
" Crassus, and M. Antony, he did not choose to employ either
" of them. He pleaded his own cause himself. C. Cotta, indeed,
" spoke some little for him, as he was his sister's son, and
" he spoke in an oratorical manner too, although he was
" at that time very young. Q Mucius also spoke for him, in
" his usual accurate and polished manner : but by no means
" with that vigour and copiousness, which a trial of that kind,
" and the magnitude of such a cause required."

" Thus we reckon Rutilius among the orators of the stoics,
" and Scaurus among the ancients. Yet let us give some praise
" to both ; because by their means, even these different styles of
" speaking in our city were honoured with the name of oratory.
" It is my wish, that as on the stage, so in the courts, not those
" only should be applauded who make use of rapid and difficult
" gestures, but those also who are called quiet speakers (statarii)
" who assume a simple and unaffected truth in their action."[6]

---

[6] De Scauro et Rutilio breviter licet dicere, quorum neuter summi oratoris habuit
laudem, et uterque in multis causis versatus erat. In quibusdam laudandis viris, etiamsi
maximi ingenii non essent, probabilis tamen industria : quanquam iis quidem non omnino
ingenium, sed oratorium ingenium defuit. Neque enim refert videre, quid dicendum sit,
nisi id queas solutè et suaviter dicere. Ne id quidem satis est, nisi id, quod dicitur, sit
voce, vultu, motuque conditius. Quid dicam opus esse doctrina? sine qua etiam si quid
bene dicitur adjuvante natura, tamen id, quia fortuitò fit, semper paratum esse non potest.
In Scauri oratione, sapientis hominis et recti, gravitas summa, et naturalis quædam inerat
auctoritas, non ut causam, sed testimonium dicere putares, cum pro reo diceret. Hoc
dicendi genus ad patrocinia mediocriter aptum videbatur ; ad senatoriam vero sententiam,
cujus erat ille princeps, vel maximè. Significabat enim non prudentiam solum, sed, quod

It is evident from this characteristic scetch of those two Roman orators, that Cicero is far from holding them up as general examples for imitation. He speaks of them with all possible indulgence, as being the best in their own class of orators, and he therefore solicits for them some degree of praise. But their manner is far different from his idea of a perfect orator, as we shall have abundant occasion to evince.[7] This style of speaking must however be admitted to have its use: thus it is well suited to law arguments, or the stating of cases, which relate to property in our courts; it is proper in the situation among us

---

maximè rem continebat, fidem. Habebat hoc à natura ipsa, quod a doctrina non facile posset: quanquam hujus quoque ipsius rei, quemadmodum scis, præcepta sunt. . . . . . .
. . . .
  Rutilius autem in quodam tristi et severo genere dicendi versatus est, et uterque naturâ vehemens et acer. Itaque cum una consulatum petivissent, non ille solum, qui repulsum tulerat, accusavit ambitus designatum competitorem, sed Scaurus etiam absolutus Rutilium in judicum vocavit: multâque operâ multâque industriâ Rutilius fuit, quæ erat propterea gratior, quod idem magnum munus de jure respondendi sustinebat. Sunt ejus orationes jejunæ; multa præclara de jure: doctus vir, et Græcis literis eruditus, Panætii auditor, prope perfectus in Stoicis, quorum peracutum et artis plenum orationis genus, sed tamen exile, nec satis populari assensioni accommodatum. Itaque illa, quæ propria est hujus disciplinæ, philosophorum de se ipsorum opinio, firma in hoc viro, et stabilis inventa est; qui cum innocentissimus in judicium vocatus esset, (quo judicio convulsum penitus scimus esse rempublicam) cum essent eo tempore eloquentissimi viri L. Crassus et M. Antonius consulares, eorum adhibere neutrum voluit. Dixit ipse pro sese, et pauca C. Cotta, quod sororis erat filius, et is quidem tamen, ut orator, quanquam erat admodum adolescens, sed Q. Mucius enucleatè ille quidem, et politè, ut solebat, nequaquam autem ea vi atque copia, quam genus illud judicii et magnitudo causæ postulabat. Habemus igitur in Stoicis oratoribus Rutilium, Scaurum in antiquis. Utrumque tamen laudemus, quoniam per illos ne hæc quidem in civitate genera hac oratoria laude caruerunt. Volo etiam, ut in scena, sic etiam in foro, non eos modò laudari, qui celeri motu et difficili utantur, sed eos etiam, quos *statarios* appellant, quorum sit illa simplex in agendo veritas, non molesta *Cic. de Clar. Orat. c.* 29, 30.

  7 The Stoics in general, with the exception of Cato, were good reasoners, but bad orators. Ut omnes fere Stoici prudentissimi in disserendo sint et id arte faciant, sintque architecti pene verborum; idem traducti à disputando ad dicendum, inopes reperiantur; unum excipio Catonem. *Cic. Orat. c.* 31

similar to that in which it became Scaurus, that is for the purpose of delivering mere opinions in parliament, or calculations
in finance, and such *routine* business. This style too, may often
be found to suit the pulpit in discourses wherein the doctrinal
points of Christianity are discussed and explained, and in delivering arguments upon its evidences, where fidelity and precision
are chiefly required and in general in all the parts of every
discourse which turn upon mere reasoning. But the frigid
speaker must relinquish all the more arduous and noble objects
of eloquence.

It is not, say they who object to gesture, the custom of our
best speakers to use much gesture, or to study very carefully
that which they use. To argue against the advantage arising
from gesture in oratory, by referring to the practice or even to
the success of our public speakers, who neglect or despise its
aid, is not just. Their talents and their progress are to be judged
not according to the general mediocrity of either the public
taste, or of the ordinary acquirements in eloquence, but according to laws established long since, and during the highest and
most splendid demonstrations of human genius. Oratory is no
new art of merely modern invention, it has been long since
brought to perfection, and its models are to be sought in the
writings and opinions of those great masters who excelled in all
its branches. The ignorance or neglect of all, or any of its laws,
does by no means set them aside; nay, if we could imagine so
dismal a catastrophe to take place, as that all those works were
lost for ever, and that the world was sunk in universal barbarism; before men could emerge from their darkness, and be re-
instated in all the elegant refinements of life; before oratory

U

could be again re-established in her empire over the human heart, all her laws as we have them at this moment must be reinvented nearly without variation, or human nature itself must be changed, because they are all founded in the original principles, feelings, and relations of cultivated men.

This dismal catastrophe did once indeed nearly befal mankind, but not entirely; the light of men was for a while obscured, but the precious models of antiquity, in all the high attainments of human genius, were fortunately preserved, and are now so multiplied and dispersed by the art of printing, that we have no just ground to apprehend any similar misfortune while the world endures.

We may boast that we have excelled the ancients in many of the arts of life; but in oratory, which is perhaps the highest of all, we must still admit their superiority. Something in the nature of our different governments is assigned as the cause of this, and this difference has its weight against modern eloquence: but much more might have been done; our free constitution affords as many grand occasions for eloquence, as even Rome or Greece; and in the discharge of the duty of the preacher, a field of oratory is opened more splendid, and more interesting, than any in which either Demosthenes or Cicero ever expatiated. An additional reason for our deficiency, and one perhaps as true, will be found in our partial and imperfect application to the principles of the art of oratory. If studied at all, (for sometimes we have seen young men expect to become great orators by the sole inspiration of natural genius, and a confident assurance,) it is studied only in the writings of the ancients, which must necessarily be deficient in the living principle, delivery. As to the precious remains of the compositions of the ancient orators, they have been often, and happily emulated by our public speakers: and this is no doubt a proof of sufficient advancement in the most valuable part of oratory. But this is not the whole of oratory, and the error lies in estimating it as such. It is only the dead letter, the spirit of the art is lost. That consisted in the living delivery; and it has disappeared together with the voice, the countenance, and the action of the orator who gave it life. This portion of the art we are apt to think the ancient orators estimated beyond its just value, because we avail ourselves little of its potent influence: yet who shall pronounce it to have been in their management less important than they said? and perhaps it is a proposition containing a simple truth: that what is said, is of less consequence than how it is said. We collect our information of the importance which the ancients attached to delivery more from the occasional expression of their opinions, than from their actual and precise instructions. They all incidentally speak of delivery as the highest point in eloquence, but few give express instructions upon the subject. Cicero has said something upon it, valuable indeed, as every thing must be from him, but extremely short; to Quintilian we are indebted for the most extensive, and the best treatise which antiquity has left us; he has devoted nearly a whole book of his Institutes to the subject of delivery, and has given many excellent precepts; but even from him we cannot recover the lost knowledge of the whole of this art. Whether the difficulty of conveying instructions intelligibly on all the minutiæ of this subject prevented the ancients from treating of it so largely as the other parts of oratory; whether their works are lost (if such there were) which treated of it, or whether they might not rather have considered it as more properly to be learned by practice from the numerous professors of it, the rhetoricians, and also the players; or whatever was the cause of the loss or omission, the state of oratory in our country is injured and mutilated by the want of this branch of the art. And if the public speakers of Great Britain would adequately emulate the perfection of the ancient models of eloquence, they must endeavour to acquire the whole comprehension of their art. By their industry and ingenuity, they must recover what is lost of the art of delivery; and though the effort may be attended with considerable difficulty, there is no reason to despair; as we see, though rare indeed, instances of complete success in the profession of the theatre, which depends solely on delivery; and the models of which, as Roscius and Œsopus, are as transitory and irrecoverably lost to them, as Demosthenes and Cicero, in their action, are to us. The orator who has successfully imitated the best compositions of the ancient models, should not stop short of perfection. The sculptor who should copy exactly, or even excel the truth and symmetry of the ancient *Torso*, (were it possible for him,) would unquestionably give proof of his abilities in the most difficult and important power of his art: but would he rest contented with his progress, would he limit all his exertions to the mutilated, however admirable, trunk; and be not rather stimulated by his partial success to endeavour to execute an entire human figure, with all the beauty and dignity of the head, and with all its perfect limbs and finished graces? the *Torso* is the dead letter of oratory, the delivery the head and limbs.

As the necessity of correct and animated delivery towards the perfection of oratory, is an argument which very materially concerns this work; I have reserved for this place the principal ancient authorities as they have occurred to me, and also some modern authorities, upon which it may be maintained. They may, thus viewed together, contribute to illustrate and enforce each other; and their weight will become more sensible, when estimated in the mass. The opinions of those who have excelled in the whole art of oratory should be considered as decisive, as to the particular importance of any of its component parts. And next to their opinions should be respected those of the learned rhetoricians and critics, who were also themselves celebrated orators, and whose labours contributed much to raise eloquence to that height of perfection, to which it formely arrived. They studied all the springs and movements of the human mind, and the powers of the human body, and knew all their efficacy when moved or exerted for this object. They lived in the society of the most consummate orators, they imparted to them their instructions and advice, they observed their successful efforts, and knew how to appreciate their attainments, and they committed their precepts and opinions, so formed to writing, whilst the sound of their eloquent voices was still vibrating in their ears, and whilst the energy, the majesty, and the grace of their action was still almost depicted in their eyes.

As, at this distance of time, we cannot always obtain direct proofs of what is here advanced from the different authors themselves; we must be satisfied with such evidence as the nature of the case will admit; and will be allowed to collect the opinions of the original authors, from critics or historians of credibility, who have written since their times : and who had no doubt open to them sources of information altogether lost to us.

The opinion of Isocrates, one of the earliest orators who obtained celebrity in Athens, whose works have come down to us, may on this subject be learned from his own words. As a writer, Isocrates was considered to be polished even to a fault; but if it had been his opinion that composition alone was necessary to an orator, he would not have apologized to Philip of Macedon, in the following manner, for the deficiency and pro- bable inefficacy of a written oration which he had sent to him in his old age. " I think I shall lay before you something which " you will allow to be proper and expedient for you. And yet " I am not ignorant, how much in their efficacy to persuade, " discourses, which are delivered by the orator, differ from those " which are merely read. And that, when discourses are so " delivered, all consider the occasions to be important and " pressing; and that the others are written only for ostentation, " or in the hope of gain. And their judgment in these respects " is not amiss. For when an oration is deprived of the influence " of the speaker, and of his voice, and of that variety of action, " which takes place in rhetorical delivery ; and loses the " effect of the occasion, and the zeal which the immediate " occasion inspires ; and has no auxiliary to contend on its side, " and to aid its persuasion; but when stripped of all those cir- " cumstances, it is left deserted and naked ; and is then read " by some person who manifests no expression of feeling or " sentiment, but reads, as if he was going over a calculation of " numbers ; the discourse in my opinion is likely to appear to

" every one who hears it a dull composition. This may pro-
" bably prove very injurious to that which I now present to you,
" and lower it in your estimation.[8]

The commentator observes, that this oration was sent by
Isocrates to Philip to persuade him to conciliate the cities of
Greece, and to turn his arms against Persia. Isocrates was at
that time very old, he did not succeed with Philip, and both he
and Philip died shortly after. But, says the commentator, his
son Alexander read this oration, and was by it excited to make
war upon Darius Ochus.[9]

As to his manner of study, or his opinions concerning his art,
Demosthenes himself has said little which has come down to us;
and the most we know of him, immediately from those of his
own age, we learn from the reproaches of his contemporary and
rival Æschines. He charged him with labouring at writing out
his orations, and reproached him with affectation in his gestures,

---

[8] Οἶμαι γὰρ ἐρεῖν τι τῶν δεόντων, καὶ τῶν σοὶ συμφερόντων. καί τοι μ᾿ ἒ λέληθεν, ὅσον διαφέρεσι τῶν λόγων εἰς τὸ πείθειν, οἱ λεγόμενοι τῶν ἀναγινωσκομένων. οὐδ᾿ ὅτι πάντες ὑπειλήφασι, τοὺς μὲν περὶ σπουδαίων πραγμάτων, καὶ κατεπειγόντων ῥετορεύεσθαι, τὰς δὲ πρὸς ἐπίδειξιν, καὶ πρὸς ἐργολαβίαν γεγράφθαι. καὶ ταῦτ᾿ ἒ κακῶς ἐγνώκασιν. ἐπειδὰν γὰρ ὁ λόγος ἀποςερηθῇ τῆς τε δόξης τἒ λέγοντος, καὶ τῆς φωνῆς, καὶ τῶν μεταβολῶν τῶν ἐν ταῖς ῥητορείαις γιγνομένων, ἔτι δὲ καὶ τῶν καιρῶν, καὶ τῆς σπεδῆς τῆς περὶ τὴν πρᾶξιν, καὶ μηδὲν ᾖ τὸ. συναγωνιζόμενον, καὶ συμπεῖθον, ἀλλὰ τῶν μεν προειρημένων ἁπάντων ἔρημος γένηται, καὶ γυμνός, ἀναγινώσκη δὲ τις αὐτὸν ἀπιθάνως, καὶ μηδὲν ἦθος ἐνσημαινόμενος, ἀλλ᾿ ὥσπερ ἀπαριθμῶν, εἰκότως οἶμαι φαῦλος εἶναι δοκόιῃ τοῖς ἀκούουσιν. ἅπερ καὶ τόν νῦν ἔτι δεικνύμενον μάλις᾿ ἂν βλάψειεν, καὶ φαυλότερον φαίνεσθαι ποιήσειεν. Isocratis ad Philip. Oratio, Suasoriarum Secunda.

[9] Philostratus says, that he succeeded in obtaining the favour of Philip towards the Athenians. τόν τε γὰρ Φίλιππον, ἐν οἷς πρὸς αὐτὸν ἔγραφεν, Αθηναίοις δήπε διωρθᾶτο. *Philos. de Vit. Soph. Isocrates.*

from which he said he had justly got an opprobrious nick-name. But the malice and spleen of a rival enemy, whatever might have been its ebullitions in the anger of debate changed into admiration when the irritation was over; as may be recollected in the answer which Æschines made to the people of Rhodes. But the celebrity of Demosthenes, in all the requisites of a consummate orator, does not depend alone on the justice of his rival. History has furnished abundant proofs of his indefatigable exertions, more especially in the delivery of his orations, and has also recorded in strong terms the importance he attached to it: and of the various authors who have recorded his fame, not one has omitted the mention of these circumstances. Though Lucian is not the first in order yet he has collected together into a very small compass, so many particulars concerning the industry of this great orator, that I am induced to quote him previous to older writers. He says that love is of two kinds, the one sensual, the other intellectual; and that Demosthenes was smitten with this last. " This love was let " down from heaven by a golden chain, not by fires, or arrows " inflicting the pain of wounds difficult to cure, but enamour- " ing of its beauty the uncontaminated and pure intellect; " exciting by a discreet madness of the soul, as says the tragic " poet, those who are near to Jupiter, and who are associated " with the gods. To this love all was easy, the tonsure, the " cave, the mirror, the sword, the conquering of impediments, " the learning at a late period of life the art of gesture, the " strengthening his memory, the contempt of tumult, the " adding of nights to laborious days. Who is there, that " knows not, how great an orator Demosthenes came forth " after these exertions; enriching his eloquence by thoughts

" and expressions, establishing the credit of his arguments
" by the evidence of his feelings, splendid in his copiousness,
" vehement in his impetuosity, exquisite in his choice of words
" and sentiments, inexhaustible in the variety of his figures?"
it is not surprising after all this that, as Lucian tells us, " Pythias
" should say that the orations of Demosthenes smelled of the
" lamp."[10]

The favourable report of Cicero, concerning Demosthenes,
serves the double purpose of affording the strongest testimony
to these facts relating to this great orator, and of proving what
were Cicero's own private opinions on the points which are
the subject of our enquiry. *Laudari a laudato* is the highest
glory of human praise, and even if Cicero stood single in his
high commendation of Demosthenes, Cicero's single voice
would establish his fame for ever. " But to return," says he, " to
" the first principle, which we have laid down, let our orator
" be a man, as Crassus has defined him, who is able to speak

---

[10] .... τὴν δ' οὐρανία χρυσῆς τινος σειρᾶς ἕλξιν, οὐ πυρὶ καὶ τόξοις ἐντιθεῖσαν
δυσαλθεῖς νόσους τραυμάτων, ἀλλ' ἐπὶ τὴν αὐτῆ τῆ κάλλης ἄχραντόν τε καὶ καθαρὰν
ἰδέαν ἐξορμῶσαν, μανίᾳ σώφρονι τῶν ψυχῶν, ὅσαι Ζηνὸς ἐγγὺς, καὶ θεῶν αἰχίσποροι, φησὶν
ὁ τραγικὸς. ἔρωτι δὴ πάντα πόριμα, κηρὰ σπήλαιον, κάτοπτρον, ξίφος, γλῶτlαν διαρθῶσαι,
μετελθεῖν ὀψὲ τῆς ἡλικίας ὑπόκρισιν, μνήμην ἀκριβῶσαι, θορύβου καταφρονῆσαι, συνάψαι
νύκτας ἐπιπόναις ἡμέραις. ἐξ ὧν τίς οὐκ οἶδεν ὁποῖος ὁ Δημοσθένης, ἔφη, σοι τὴν ῥητορικὴν
ἐγένετο; ταῖς μὲν ἐννοίαις, καὶ τοῖς ὀνόμασι, καταπυκνῶν τὸν λόγον, ταῖς δὲ διαθέσεσιν
ἐξακριβῶν τὰς πιθανότητας; λαμπρὸς μὲν τῷ μεγέθει, σφοδρὸς δὲ τῷ πνεύματι, σωφρο-
νέστατος δὲ τὴν τῶν ὀνομάτων καὶ νοημάτων ἐγκράτειαν, ποικιλώτατος δ' ἐναλλαγαῖς σχημά-
των. . . . .

Πυθέα δὲ ὁ κρότος τῶν Δημοσθενικῶν λόγων ἀπόζειν ἐφαίνετο τῆ νυκτερινῆ λύχνη. *Lucian.*
Demosth. Encom.

X

" so as to persuade.　And let him be confined to that business,
" which is the common and forensic practice in cities; and,
" having relinquished all other pursuits, however great and
" laudable, let him be oppressed, as I may say, day and night
" by this single occupation.　And let him imitate him, to
" whom unquestionably the highest powers of oratory are
" attributed, Demosthenes the Athenian.　In him, was said in
" the first place to have been such zeal and labour, that by
" his diligence and industry, he overcame his natural impedi-
" ments, and though his articulation had been so imperfect,
" that he could not pronounce the first letter of the art of
" rhetoric which he studied, he became so perfect by practising
" in private, that no person was reckoned to speak more dis-
" tinctly than him.　In the next place, though his lungs were
" naturally weak, he acquired such power by managing his
" breath, that in one uninterrupted continuation of speaking
" (as his own writings declare) he could twice raise his voice
" to the highest pitch, and twice sink it to the lowest.　And
" we have also this tradition of him, that he was accustomed,
" with pebbles in his mouth, to pronounce a great number of
" verses in his loudest voice, and in one breath, and that not
" standing in the same place, but whilst he was walking or
" ascending a high hill."'" Cicero, farther, on in the same

---

¹¹ Ergo ut ad primum illud revertar, sit orator nobis is, qui, ut Crassus descripsit, ac-
commodatè ad persuadendum possit dicere.　Is autem concludatur in ea, quæ sunt in usu
civitatum vulgari, ac forensi: remotisque cæteris studiis, quamvis ea sint ampla atque
præclara, in hoc uno opere, ut ita dicam, noctes et dies urgeatur: imiteturque illum, cui
sine dubio summa vis dicendi conceditur, Atheniensem Demosthenem, in quo tantum
studium fuisse tantusque labor dicitur, ut primum impedimenta naturæ diligentia industria-
que superarit: cumque ita balbus esset, ut ejus ipsius artis, cui studeret, primam literam
non posset dicere, perfecit meditando, ut nemo planius eo locutus putaretur.　Deinde cum

work, illustrates the advantage of action by a well known story of the report of Æschines concerning Demosthenes. He has just finished his account of the necessary parts of oratorical composition, and thus proceeds. " But all these things have their " effect, just in proportion as they are delivered. Delivery, I " say, bears absolute sway in oratory. Without this the great- " est orator cannot be reckoned in the number of the perfect: " whilst a moderate speaker, is possessed of this, often excels " the best. When Demosthenes was asked, what was the first " requisite in speaking, he answered, that delivery was the " first, that it was the second, and that it was the third. For " which reason, what Æschines said appears to me the more " just. On account of the disgrace he suffered in the judgment " which was passed upon him, he had retired from Athens, " and had gone to live at Rhodes; where it is said, that at the " request of the Rhodians he read the oration which he pro- " nounced against Ctesiphon and Demosthenes: when it was " finished, they requested of him, that, on the next day, he " would read that also, which had been delivered against him " by Demosthenes for Ctesiphon. When he had read it with " the sweetest and most powerful voice, and had excited " general admiration of its excellence; How much greater, said " he, would your admiration have been, if you had heard " Demosthenes himself? by this he sufficiently shewed, how

---

spiritus ejus esset angustior, tantum continenda anima in dicendo est assecutus, ut una continuatione verborum (id quod ejus scripta declarant) binæ ei contentiones vocis, et remissiones continerentur. Qui etiam (ut memoriæ proditum est) conjectis in os calculis, summa voce versus multos uno spiritu pronuntiare consuescebat: neque is consistens in loco, sed inambulans, atque ascensu ingrediens arduo. *Cic. de Orat. l. i c.* 61.

[12] See also Plutarch in Vita Demosth.

" important he must have considered the power of delivery,
" since he esteemed the same oration to be altogether dif-
" ferent, when delivered by another speaker." [13,14,15,16]

The observations of Valerius Maximus on this story are so
strong, and so much to our purpose, that I am induced to give
a translation of them also : " What, said he, if you had heard
" Demosthenes himself? he who was himself so great an orator,
' and who had been so recently his bitter adversary, admired
" the force and ardour of his enemy's delivery so much, that
" he acknowledged himself to be unequal even to read what
" he had written. He had experienced the irresistible light-
" ning of his eyes, had been borne down by the terror of his
" countenance, and had felt impressed on every word the

---

[13] Sed hæ ipsa omnia perinde sunt, ut aguntur. Actio inquam in dicendo una dominatur.
Sine hac summus orator esse in numero nullo potest : mediocris, hac instructus, summos
sæpe superare. Huic primas dedisse Demosthenes dicitur, cum rogaretur, quid in dicendo
esset primum ; huic secundas, huic tertias. Quo mihi melius etiam illud ab Æschine dictum
videri solet, qui cum propter ignominiam judicii cessisset Athenis, et se Rhodium contulisset, rogatus à Rhodiis, legisse fertur orationem illam egregiam, quam in Ctesiphontem
contra Demosthenem dixerat : quâ perlecta, petitum est ab eo postridie, ut legeret illum
etiam, quæ erat contra a Demosthene pro Ctesiphonte edita : quam cum suavissima et
maxima voce legisset, admirantibus omnibus, quanto, inquit, magis admiraremini, si
audissetis ipsum? ex quo satis significavit, quantum esset in actione, qui orationem eandem,
aliam esse putaret, actore mutato. *Cic. de Orat. l.* iii. *c.* 56.

[14] For the same story and similar reflections, see also *Quint. l.* xi. *c.* 3.

[15] See also *C. Plin. Epist. l.* ii. *ep.* 3, in which he advises Nepos to come and hear
Isæus, illustrating by this story of Æschines the impossibility of deriving equal advantage
from reading the works of orators. In this Epistle also he speaks of the astonishing labour
of Isæus, and of his admirable eloquence. He declaimed on imaginary subjects with all the
fire of youth, though past sixty. " Multo magis (ut vulgo dicitur) viva vox afficit. Nam
licet acriora sint, quæ legas, altius tamen in animo sedent, quæ pronuntiatio, vultus, habitus,
gestus etiam dicentis adfigit." After this passage, follows the abovementioned story.

[16] See also Philostrat. *Vit. Soph. in Æschine.*

" sound of his voice, together with his most energetic gestures,
" Therefore, although nothing can be added to his orations.
" yet in Demosthenes is wanting a great part of Demosthenes;
" since he must be read and cannot be heard."[17] In the preface to this chapter, his observations merit the attention of
the public speaker. " The ornaments of eloquence consist
" in correct delivery, and in suitable gesture of the body.
" And he who arms himself with these, assaults his hearers in
" three ways. He invades their understandings by his elo-
" quence, he delivers up their ears to be charmed by his voice,
" and their eyes to be charmed by his gesture.[18]

The examples which Valerius Maximus adduces (in his
manner) to support these opinions, are those of Demosthenes
and Æschines already mentioned, that of Cicero himself, that
of C. Gracchus and of Hortensius. Both Cicero and Quintilian
celebrate C. Gracchus for his delivery as well as for every
other perfection of eloquence. In the passage, immediately
after that just quoted from Cicero, he proceeds thus: " What
" power of delivery did not Gracchus display, as you Catulus
" remember better, in that passage so celebrated when I was

---

[17] Valerius Maximus, *l.* viii. *c.* 10, adds the following reasons for the observations of
Æschines. Quid si, inquit, ipsum audissetis? tantus orator et modo tam infestus adversarius,
sic inimici vim ardoremque dicendi suspexit; ut se scriptorum ejus parum idoneum lectorem
esse diceret: expertus acerrimum oculorum vigorem, terribile vultus pondus, accommodatum singulis verbis sonum vocis, efficacissimos corporis motus. Ergo etsi operi illius adjici
nihil potest, tamen in Demosthene magna pars Demosthenis abest: quod legitur potius
quam auditur.

[18] Eloquentiæ autem ornamenta in pronunciatione apta et convenienti motu corporis
consistunt: quibus cum se instruxit, tribus modis homines aggreditur, animos eorum ipsa
invadendo, horum alteri aures, alteri oculos permulcendos tradendo. *Val. Max. l.* viii. *c.* 10.

" a boy.—Wretched that I am, whither shall I betake myself?
" whither shall I turn? to the Capitol? ah! it streams with
" my brother's blood. To my own home? there to witness the
" misery, the tears, and the desolation of my mother?—these
" words he pronounced with such expression of his eyes, his
" voice, and his gesture, that even his enemies could not re-
" frain from tears. This I the more particularly mention to the
" greater number, because the orators, who are actors of the
" reality itself, have entirely relinquished this style of speaking,
" and the players who are only the imitators of the reality have
" taken possession of it." [19.20]

In another passage of another work, Cicero has also ably recommended attention to delivery. " Action is, as it were, a kind of
" eloquence of the body, as it consists of the voice and gesture.
" The inflexions of the voice are as various, as those emotions
" which are excited principally by the voice. Therefore the
" perfect orator, whom we have just now been describing, ac-
" cordingly as he wishes to appear affected himself, and to
" move the feelings of his audience, will employ suitable tones
" of his voice: concerning which I would say more, if this was

---

[19] Quid fuit in Graccho, quem tu, Catule, melius, meministi, quod me puero tantopere
ferretur.—*Quo me miser conferam ? quo vertam ? in Capitoliumne ? at fratris sanguine redundat. An domum? matremne ut miseram, lamentantemque videam, et abjectam ?* Quæ sic
ab illo acta esse constabat, oculis, voce, gestu, inimici ut lachrymas tenere non possent.
Hæc eo dico pluribus, quod genus hoc totum oratores, qui sunt veritatis ipsius actores, re_
liquerunt, imitatores autem veritatis histriones occupaverunt. *Cic. de Orat.* 3, 56.

[20] Gracchus was certainly a great favourite of Cicero; at least his introduction of him
among his celebrated orators implies great admiration.

Sed ecce in manibus vir, et præstantissimo ingenio, et flagranti studio, et doctus a puero,
C. Gracchus. The rest of his character as to his talents does not fall off, nor as to the
expression of Cicero's feelings.

" the place for giving precepts upon it, or if you required them.
" I would also speak upon gesture with which is connected ex-
" pression of the countenance. It is hardly possible to express·
" of how great consequence is the manner in which the orator
" avails himself of all these. For even indifferent speakers, by
" the dignity of their action, have frequently reaped the fruits
" of eloquence; whilst those, whose language is that of an orator,
" often, on account of the awkwardness of their action, have
" been reckoned indifferent speakers. So that it was not without
" reason, that Demosthenes assigned to action the first, the
" second, and the third place. For if eloquence cannot sub-
" sist without action, and if without eloquence action has such
" influence, certainly its importance is very great to a public
" speaker." [21]

In Cicero's time, Hortensius, his rival orator and his friend,
was one of the most brilliant examples of the success attending
delivery, though not supported by the highest oratorical talents
in other respects. Cicero indeed allows him great merit in
his choice of language, in memory, and in correctness. But
other writers do not speak so favourably of him, except as to

---

[21] Est enim actio quasi corporis quædam eloquentia, cum constet voce atque motu. Vocis mutationes totidem sunt, quot animorum, qui maxime voce commoventur. Itaque ille perfectus, quem jamdudum nostra indicat oratio, utcumque se affectum videri, et animum audientis moveri volet, ita certum vocis admovebit sonum : de quo plura dicerem, si hoc præcipiendi tempus esset, aut si tu hoc quæreres. Dicerem etiam de gestu, cum quo junctus est vultus. Quibus omnibus dici vix potest, quantum intersit, quemadmodum utatur orator. Nam et infantes, actionis dignitate, eloquentiæ sæpe fructum tulerunt ; et diserti, deformitate agendi, multi infantes putati sunt : ut jam non sine causa Demosthenes tribuerit, et primas, et secundus, et tertias actioni. Si enim eloquentia nulla sine hac ; hæc autem sine eloquentia tanta est ; certe plurimum in dicendo potest. *Cic. Orat. c. 17.*

his delivery, so that Cicero perhaps was restrained by his delicacy, from a very strict criticism upon his friend. Of his delivery, for which he was most celebrated, he says: " His voice " was full and sweet. His action and his gestures had even more " of art, than was sufficient for an orator." [22]

Valerius Maximus, in his admiration of Hortensius, vindicates Cicero's criticism, and mentions a singular proof of the merit of his delivery in the attention of the great actors of his time. " But Q. Hortensius, persuaded that very much depended " upon the graceful movements of the body, bestowed perhaps " more attention in bringing these to perfection, than even on " the study of eloquence itself. So that you could not determine " whether the people crowded more eagerly to hear him or to " see him. Such an ornament to his oratory was his appearance, " and such to his appearance were his words. And it is a fact " ascertained, that Æsopus and Roscius, men the most eminent in " the dramatic art, when he pleaded a cause, frequently stood " in the circle of his hearers in order that they might introduce " upon the stage the gestures learned in the forum." [23]

Quintilian's observations upon Hortensius at once vindicate

---

[22] Vox canora et suavis. Motus et gestus etiam plus artis habebat, quam erat oratori satis. *Cic. de Cl. Orat. c.* 88.

[23] Q. autem Hortensius plurimum in corporis decoro motu credens, penè plus studii in eodem elaborando, quam in ipsa eloquentia affectanda impendit. Itaque nescires, utrum cupidius ad audiendum eum, an ad spectandum concurreretur : sic verbis oratoriis aspectus et rursus aspectui verba serviebant. Itaque constat, Æsopum et Roscium ludicræ artis peritissimos viros, illo causas agente, in coronâ frequenter astitisse, ut foro petitos gestus in scenam referrent. *Val. Max. l.* viii. *c.* 10.

Cicero, and prove the great importance of delivery. They merit to be recited at large.

" Action even in itself has wonderful effect and power in
" oratory. For what we compose within our own thoughts, is
" not of so much consequence as the manner in which it
" is made known to others: since according to the expression
" of what he hears, so a man is affected. Therefore no proof
" which is merely advanced by the orator, can be so firm, as
" not to lose its strength, unless it be enforced by the earnest
" ness of the speaker. All the affections of necessity must
" languish, if they be not excited by the voice, by the counten-
" ance, and by the whole demeanor of the body. And after we
" have done all this, happy shall we be, if even so, the judge
" shall catch the flame from us: to move him by supine care-
" lessness is hopeless, nay our indifference is likely to prejudice
" him against us. We may derive on this subject instruction
" from the players; who add so many graces even to the best of
" the poets, that we are much more delighted in hearing the
" same passages recited by them, than in reading them ourselves;
" and even for the most wretched they obtain a hearing, so that
" pieces which never have admission into libraries are often
" seen upon the stage. But if delivery can produce such an
" effect as to excite anger, tears, and solicitude in subjects which
" we know to be fictitious and vain, how much more powerful
" must it be, when we are persuaded in reality? nay, I venture
" to pronounce that even an indifferent oration, recommended
" by the force of action, would have more effect than the best,
" if destitute of this enforcement. Demosthenes, as we are told,
" being asked, what in the whole labour of oratory was of the
" first importance, gave the palm to delivery; and to the same

Y

" gave the second and the third place, till the man ceased to
" ask him: so that he would appear to have esteemed it not
" merely the principal, but the single requisite. For this reason
" he himself studied so diligently under the player Andronicus;
" and Æschines, not unjustly, said to the people of Rhodes when
" they were in admiration of an oration of his; what if you had
" heard himself? Cicero thinks that delivery alone has the
" dominion in oratory: and he says that Cn. Lentulus obtained
" higher estimation by this than by his eloquence: and that by
" this also C. Gracchus, when he was deploring the murder
" of his brother, drew tears from the whole Roman people.
" Anthony and Crassus were remarkable for their powerful
" delivery; but above all Q. Hortensius; of which this is a
" proof, that, although he was long reckoned the first of orators,
" and was for some time the rival of Cicero, and latterly whilst
" he lived was esteemed the next to him, his writings fall far
" short of his celebrity; so that it appears, there was something
" that captivated in his speaking, which we cannot find in read-
" ing his orations. And unquestionably since mere words have
" in themselves a powerful efficacy, and since the voice adds to
" what is said, its own influence, and since gesture and emotions
" have also their peculiar significancy, something perfect must
" necessarily be produced when all are combined together. Yet
" there are some who consider that rude action, such as the force
" of every feeling produces, to be the most energetic, and alone
" worthy of a man. But these are perhaps the same, who are
" accustomed to disapprove in speaking, as affected and unna-
" tural, care, and art, and polish, and whatever is the result of
" study: or who, as Cicero says, was the manner of Cotta, by a
" rusticity in their language, and even in their very voice, affect

" to imitate antiquity. But let them enjoy their persuasion, who
" think, that to be born, is sufficient to make a man an orator:
" they will pardon our labour, who think, that nothing can
" arrive at perfection, unless when nature is assisted by careful
" cultivation. But to this I assent not unwillingly, that from
" nature we derive the principal requisites. For he certainly
" will not be able to deliver himself well, who either cannot
" depend on his memory for what he has written, or if any
" unexpected point should require to be spoken to, who is de-
" ficient in ready facility; nor he whom incurable defects in ut-
" terance oppose. Nay even the deformity of the body may be
" such as no art can correct; nor can even the voice itself, unless
" liberally bestowed by nature, be exerted in delivery to the
" best advantage." [24]

---

[24] Habet autem res ipsa miram quamdam in orationibus vim ac potestatem. Neque enim tam refert, qualia sint, quæ intra nosmetipsos composuimus; quam quo modo efferantur, nam, ita ut quisque audit, movetur. Quare neque probatio ulla, quæ modo venit ab oratore, tam firma est, ut non perdat vires suas, nisi adjuvetur asseveratione dicentis. Affectus omnes languescant necesse est, nisi voce, vultu, totius prope habitu corporis inardescant. Nam cum hæc omnia fecerimus, felices, si tamen nostrum illum ignem judex conceperit: nedum eum supini securique moveamus, ac non et ipse nostra oscitatione solvatur. Documento sunt vel scenici actores, qui et optimis poetarum tantum adjiciunt gratiæ, ut nos infinite magis eadem illa audita, quam lecta, delectent, et vilissimis etiam quibusdam impetrent aures, ut, quibus nullus est in bibliothecis locus, sit etiam frequens in theatris. Quod si in rebus, quas fictas esse scimus et inanes, tantum pronunciatio potest, ut iram, lachrymas, sollicitudinem afferat, quanto plus valeat necesse est, ubi et credimus? equidem vel mediocrem orationem, commendatam viribus actionis, affirmaverim plus habituram esse momenti, quam optimam eadem illa destitutam. Siquidem et Demosthenes, quid esset in toto dicendi opere primum, interrogatus, pronuntiationi palmam dedit, eidemque secundum ac tertium locum, donec ab eo quæri desineret; ut eam videri posset non præcipuam, sed solam judicasse. Ideoque ipse tam diligenter apud Andronicum hypocritem studuit, ut admirantibus ejus orationem Rhodiis, non immerito Æschines dixisse videatur: *quid si ipsum audissetis?* Et M. Cicero *unam in dicendo actionem dominari* putat.* Hac Cn.

* *Cic. de Clar. Orat.*

The order of priority in time has not been observed in quoting Quintilian previous to Dionysius Halicarnassus. But Quintilian's observations are so connected with those of Cicero, that they illustrate each other by being placed together. D. Halicarnassus flourished immediately after Cicero, and is allowed to have been one of the most acute and excellent critics.

" I have often wondered what the men who heard him
" speak in this manner have felt, when we, so far removed
" from those times, and who have no concern in those affairs, are
" so subdued and conquered, and go whithersoever the oration
" leads us. How greatly in those days must the Athenians and
" the other Grecians have been influenced by this man in those
" contests which were real and their own; whilst he himself
" delivered his own compositions with that native dignity, which-

---

Lentulum plus opinionis consecutum, quam eloquentia tradit. Eadem C. Gracchum in deflenda fratris nece, totius populi Romani lacrimas concitasse: Antonium et Crassum multum valuisse, plurimum vero Q. Hortensium. Cujus rei fides est, quod ejus scripta tantum intra famam sunt, qui diu princeps oratorum, aliquando æmulus Ciceronis existimatus est, novissime, quoad vixit, secundus : ut appareat, placuisse aliquid eo dicente, quod legentes non invenimus. Et Hercle cum valeant multum verba per se et vox proprium vim adjiciat rebus, et gestus motusque significet aliquid, profecto perfectum quiddam fieri, cum omnia coierint necesse est. Sunt tamen qui rudem illam, et qualem impetus cujusque animi tulit, actionem judicant fortiorem, et solam viris dignam : sed non alii fere, quam qui etiam in dicendo curam, et artem, et nitorem, et quicquid studio paratur, ut affectata et parum naturalia solent improbare, vel qui verborum atque ipsius etiam soni rusticitate, ut L. Cottam dicit Cicero fecisse, imitationem antiquitatis affectant. Verum illi persuasione sua fruantur, qui hominibus, ut sint oratores, satis putant nasci : nostro labori dent veniam, qui nihil credimus esse perfectum, nisi ubi natura cura juvetur. In hoc igitur non contumaciter consentio, primas partes esse naturæ. Nam certe bene pronuntiare non poterit, cui aut in scriptis memoria, aut in iis, quæ subito dicenda erunt, facilitas prompta defuerit; nec si inemendabilia oris incommoda obstabunt. Corporis etiam potest esse aliqua tanta deformitas, ut nulla arte vincatur. Sed ne vox quidem, nisi liberalis, actionem habere optimam potest. *Quint. Inst. l.* xi. *c.* 3.

" he possessed, exhibiting his free sentiments, and his presence of
" mind; adorning every thing, and adding to its energy by
" appropriate gestures, of which, as all confess, he was the
" greatest master? and this may be seen in those orations of
" his, to which we have just referred. These cannot possibly
" be run over as an entertaining subject for reading, but the
" very composition suggests how they ought to be pronounced;
" now in a strain of irony, now with indignation, now with re-
" proaches: again terrifying and soothing, restraining and ex-
" citing, and demonstrating every thing that requires to be done
" in the delivery of the sentiments."[25] Farther on in examining
one of the orations of this great man, he uses expressions nearly
similar, but even stronger.—" Does he not exclaim here, and
" instruct how this passage should be spoken, and do we not
" almost hear his voice? again he says, speak this passage ele-
" gantly, that pronounce rapidly, that deliberately. Here omit
" the connection, there join what follows. In these words con-
" dole, in these express contempt. With these terrify, with

---

[25] Καὶ δὴ ποτε καὶ ἐνεθυμήθην τί ποτε τοὺς τότε ἀνθρώπους ἀκούοντας αὐτῦ λέγοντος
ταῦτα, πάσχειν εἰκὸς ἦν. ὅπου γὰρ ἡμεῖς, οἱ τοσῦτον ἀπηρτημένοι τοῖς χρόνοις, καὶ
ἐθὲν πρὸς τὰ πράγματα πεπονθότες, οὕτως ὑπαγόμεθα καὶ κρατύμεθα, καὶ ὅποι ποτ'
ἂν ἡμᾶς ὁ λόγος ἄγῃ πορευόμεθα· πῶς τότε Ἀθηναῖοί τε καὶ οἱ ἄλλοι Ἕλληνες ἤγοντο
ὑπὸ τῦ ἀνδρὸς ἐπὶ τῶν ἀληθινῶν τε καὶ ἰδίων ἀγώνων, αὐτῦ λέγοντος ἐκείνᾳ τὰ ἑαυτῦ μετὰ
τῆς ἀξιώσεως ἧς εἶχε τὴν αὐτοπάθειαν, καὶ τὸ παράσημα τῆς ψυχῆς ἀποδεικνυμένᾳ,
κοσμῦντος ἅπαντα καὶ χρηματίζοντος τῇ πρεπούσῃ ὑποκρίσει, ἧς δεινότατος ἀσκητὴς
ἐγένετο, ὡς ἅπαντες τε ὁμολογοῦσι, καὶ ἐξ αὐτῶν ἰδεῖν ἔςι τῶν λόγων ὧν ἄρτι προηνεγκάμην,
ὃυς ἐκ ἔνι τῷ βυλομένῳ ἐν ἡδονῇ ὡς ἀνάγνωμα διελθεῖν, ἀλλ' αὐτοὶ διδάσκυσι πῶς αὐτὰς
ὑποκρίνεσθαι δεῖ, νῦν μὲν εἰρωνευόμενον, νῦν δ' ἀγανακτῦντα, νῦν δὲ νεμεσῶντα· δεδιττό-
μενον ἇυ καὶ θεραπεύοντα, καὶ νουθετῦντα, καὶ παρορμῶντα, καὶ πάνθ' ἃ βύλεται ποιεῖν
ἡ λέξις, ἀποδεικνύμενον ἐπὶ τῆς προφορᾶς. D. Halicarnass. Demosthenes. p. 177. Edit.
Sylburg.

" those reproach, with those give honour."[26] This passage, on account of its similarity to the former, I have in some degree displaced. It should follow that, which begins in this manner;
" One subject I have hitherto omitted, that which relates to
" gesture, with which he adorned his elocution, a virtue neces-
" sary in public speaking, particularly on political subjects.
" For where it is present, there is then also room for other excel_
" lencies; but where it is wanting, there is no use in any one
" of them. But we may form a judgment of the power which
" this principle has, by observing how great the difference is
" between certain actors both of tragedy and comedy. For in
" performing the same characters, they do not all affect us in
" the same manner; but with some we are both disgusted, and,
" as if we suffered some injury from them, by their representing
" falsely and corrupting the sense of the pieces, we are abso-
" lutely offended. This excellence, I say, is altogether necessary
" in forensic orations, if they are to have the decided characters
" of truth and spirit; of which, (as of all other perfections)
" this man had the strongest perception. Perceiving that the
" nature of this virtue was two-fold, he exerted himself ardently
" in both parts: and thus with no small labour, he acquired both
" the expression of the voice, and the gestures of the body,
" which he found necessary to possess most eminently. For
" by nature, he had no facility in acquiring these, as Deme-
" trius Phalareus says, and all others who have written his

---

[26] ἃ καταβοᾷ, καὶ διδάσκει πῶς αὐτὰ δεῖ λέγεσθαι, μόνον οὐ φωνὴν ἀφιέντα· ἐνταῦθα ἀςεῖον ἦχον· ταῦτα ἐσπευσμένως εἰπὲ, ταῦτ' ἀναβεβλημένως· δευρὶ δ' ἀπόλιπε τὸ συνεχὲς, ἐνταυθοῖ σύναψον τὰ ἑξῆς· τέτοις συνάλγησον, τέτων καταφρόνησον· ταυτα ἐκδειματώθητι, ταῦτα διάσυρον, ταῦτα αὔξησον; D. Halicar. Demosth.

" life. But it may be said, what have all these things to
" do with the beauty of his composition? the composition
" then is carefully constructed with a view to them, being full
" of the gentler as well as of the stronger passions, and indi-
" cating with what kind of action it ought to be delivered. So
" that they who read this orator, should take especial care
" that every passage be spoken in the same manner as he
" designed. For the very style informs those who have a soul
" to be moved, with what action and expression it should be
" pronounced." Here he quotes from the orations of Demosthenes, suitable passages to illustrate what he has advanced,
and then makes these observations : " Is it not necessary that
" these passages should be pronounced with extreme indigna-
" tion and commiseration? but what are the tones of anger and
" lamentation, what are the proper emphases, and what are
" the expressions of the countenance and the gestures of the
" hands; which they use who in reality are affected by these
" feelings? for it would be altogether weak to abandon nature
" and to look for any other teacher of gesture." [27]

---

[27] Εἷς ἔτι μοι καταλείπεται λόγος, ὁ περὶ τῆς ὑποκρίσεως, ὡς κεκόσμηκε τὴν λέξιν ἀνήρ,
ἀναῖκαίας ἀρετῆς ὅσης περὶ λόγες, καὶ μάλιϛα τῆς πολιτικῆς· ἧς παρέσης μὲν, καὶ ταῖς
ἄλλαις ἀρεταῖς γίνεται χώρα καὶ τότε· ἀπέσης δὲ ὅτιᾶν ὄφελος οὐδ' ἐκείνων ἐδεμίας.
τεκμήραιτο δ' ἄν τις ἡλίκην ἰσχὺν τᾶτο τὸ ϛοχεῖον ἔχει, καταμαθὼν ὅσον ἀλλήλων
ἀλλάῖϛσιν οἱ τραγῳδίας τὲ καὶ κωμῳδίας ὑποκρινόμενοι· τὰ γὰρ αὐτὰ ποιήματα
λέγοντες, οὐχ ὡσαύτως ἡμᾶς κηλῦσιν ἅπαντες, ἀλλ' ἐνίοις τε ἀχθόμεθα, καὶ ὥσπερ
ἀδικέμενοί τι, καθυποκρινομένοις, καὶ διαφθείρεσι τὰς βελήσεις τῶν ποιημάτων, καλε-
παίνομεν. ταύτης δὴ φημι τῆς ἀρετῆς πάνυ δεῖν τοῖς ἐναγωνίοις λόγοις, ἐ μέλλεσιν ἕξειν
πολὺ τὸ ἀληθινὸν καὶ ἔμψυχον. ἧς πλείσην ὥσπερ καὶ τῶν ἄλλων, πρόνοιαν ἔσχεν
ὄντος ὁ ἀνήρ. διῖλὴν δὲ τὴν φύσιν αὐτῆς ἔσαν ὁρῶν, περὶ ἄμφω τὰ μέρη σφόδρα ἐσπάδασε.
καὶ γὰρ τὰ πάθη τὰ τῆς φωνῆς, καὶ τὰ σχήματα τᾶ σώματος, οἷς κράτιϛα ἕξειν

The conclusion of this able critic's observations on the writings and gesture of the great orator is this:

" To me it appears not possible for a man, who possesses only
" the soul of an irrational animal, or whose nature is rather
" that of a stone, sluggish, dull of perception, immoveable and
" unfeeling, to deliver the composition of Demosthenes. Far
" from it indeed. Since the spirit, the most exquisite perfection
" of it is lost, and it will differ nothing from a body beautiful
" indeed, but motionless and dead." [28]

ἔμελλεν, ἃ μικρῷ πόνῳ κατειργάσατο· καί τοι φύσει πρὸς ταῦτα οὐ πάνυ εὐτυχεῖ χρησάμενος, ὡς Δημήτριος ὁ Φαληρεὺς φησὶ καὶ οἱ ἄλλοι πάντες οἱ τὸν βίον αὐτῶ συγγράψαντες. τί δὴ ταῦτα πρὸς τὴν λέξιν αὐτῶ συντείνει; φαίη τις ἄν. ἡ λέξις μὲν οὖν, εἴποιμ᾽ ἄν, οἰκείως κατασκεύασαι πρὸς ταῦτα, μηςὴ πολλῶν ἔσα ᾽ηθῶν, καὶ παθῶν, καὶ διδάσκασα οἵας ὑποκρίσεως αὐτῇ δεῖ. ὥςε τὰς ἀναγινώσκοντας τὸν ῥήτορα τῆτον, ἐπιμελῶς χρὴ παρατηρεῖν ἵνα τῆτον ἕκαςα λέγηται τὸν τρόπον, ᾧ ἐκεῖνος ἐβάλετο. αὐτὴ γὰρ ἡ λέξις διδάσκει τὰς ἔχοντας ψυχὴν εὐκίνητον, μεθ᾽ οἵας τῆς ὑποκρίσεως ἐκφέρεσθαι δεήσει. . . . . ὀυ δι᾽ ὀργῆς γοῦν ταῦτα ὑπερβαλλύσης καὶ οἴκτα λέγεσθαι προσήκει; τίνες ἂν εἰσιν ὀργῆς καὶ ὀλοφυρμῦ τόνοι, καὶ ἐγκλίσεις, καὶ σχηματισμοὶ προσώπα, καὶ φοραὶ χειρῶν, ἅς οἱ κατ᾽ ἀλήθειαν ταῦτα πεπονθότες ἐπιτελοῦσι;* πάνυ γὰρ ἔυηθες ἄλλο τι ζητεῖν ὑποκρίσεως διδασκάλιον, ἀφέντας τὴν ἀλήθειαν.

[28] ἐμοὶ μὲν δοκεῖ, ἐκ ἔνεςιν ἀλόγε ζώα ψυχὴν ἔχοντα, μᾶλλον δὲ λίθε φύσιν νωθρὰν, ἀναίσθητον, ἀκίνητον, ἀπαθῆ, τὴν Δημοσθένους προφέρεσθαι λέξιν. πολλᾶ γε καὶ δεῖ.

* That the practice of gesture is founded in nature, and must be derived originally, from the natural expression of the passions, is unquestionable. The object of art in the study of gesture is to correct and to embellish nature, in this as in most other instances, by rejecting awkward and rude gestures, and by adopting those which are most graceful and dignified. Therefore the truth of the observation of the ancient critic is fully admitted; but taking it in this obvious sense, it cannot be considered to favour their opinions who would leave gesture to nature without cultivation. If that might be ventured among the polished Greeks, that *natio comœda,* it would not produce any thing very accomplished in our stiff and cold climate.

To modern feelings, which are accustomed to be excited by variety of illustration, and by variety of example, it may seem tedious to have the name of Demosthenes repeated and iterated, and echoed from one to another, again and again, for a series of ages: and what is more, to have the same story told over again in this place. It may fairly be replied, that no example so completely in all its parts recommends the study of eloquence, and encourages the undertaking of the necessary labours by the exhibition of such splendid success, and such victorious perseverance. Cicero himself dwells on the example of Demosthenes, induced equally by his judgment, and by his modesty; and has so closely followed it as to have rivalled his model in all his excellence, and antecedently in almost all his labours. The example of Demosthenes has therefore been, and ever will continue to be, the polar star of all who pursue the glory of eloquence, through every toil and every difficulty: so long as literature shall continue to hold him up to stimulate and to enlighten mankind. The repetition of his great great name should not cause any disgust, but every circumstance should be considered worthy of investigation, and of being recorded, which in him contributes to the perfection of the history of eloquence. " Let us then imitate Demosthenes (exclaims Cicero) " gracious gods! what else, I beseech you, do we attempt, or " what more do we wish? yet still we shall never reach his " perfection." [29]

ἐπὶ τὸ κάλλιϛον αὐτῆς ἀγαθὸν ἀπολεῖται, τὸ πνεῦμα, καὶ ꙗδὲν διοίσει σωματος καλꙗ μὲν, ἀκινήτꙋ δὲ καὶ νεκρꙋ. *D. Halicar. Demosth.*

[29] Demosthenem igitur imitemur. O dii boni! quid, quæso, nos aliud agimus, aut quid aliud optamus? at non assequimur. *Cic. de Clar. Orat. c. 84.*

Z

Against this body of evidence in proof of the importance of that ornament of eloquence, gesture, which is now particularly treated of, it must not be dissembled, that high authority may in some degree be opposed. The great Aristotle, who was contemporary with Demosthenes and Æschines, in his Rhetoric speaks slightingly of gesture; but that is the less to be wondered at, as composition, in the view he is taking of it, falls under similar condemnation. He holds it more proper to banish all art from public speaking, and merely to treat of matter of fact. To account for this prepossession of Aristotle against oratory, it will be recollected that it was an art which grew up almost to perfection in his own times, and that he himself did not cultivate it, being engaged in various and profound philosophical speculations. He was awakened to its importance by the glory of Demosthenes, and is said to have been induced to turn his thoughts to the composition of his rhetoric by a degree of jealousy of that glory. The following extract will shew that perfect oratory was rather a recent art in the times of Aristotle, and bears also strong impressions of his dislike, to every thing except simple and rigid demonstration, of which he was himself the great master.

" Our first enquiry, as it is naturally suggested, to be made
" first, has been, what those things are, which tend to per-
" suasion. The second, how to express them in proper language:
" and the third, which has undoubtedly very great influence,
" but has not yet been distinctly treated, all that relates to
" delivery. For action has been but recently applied to tragic
" and epic poetry: as the poets themselves formerly delivered
" and acted their own dramatic compositions." In speaking of

this action he mentions only the management of the voice, but evidently intends the whole of theatrical action. He then proceeds thus : " They, who excel in this art, carry off almost all " the prizes in the contests; and as in the drama, the actors " are now esteemed even more than the poets themselves; so " also is delivery preferred in the political contests, on account " of the corruption of public principle. No system has yet " been composed on the subject of delivery. For even the " art of elocution itself *(choice of language)* has but lately " appeared. And if properly understood, attention to language " is a light matter, but as the whole business of rhetoric relates " to opinion, and is more a matter of necessity than of right, it " must be attended to. For in public speaking this alone " is right, that a man should neither seek to offend nor to " please. For justice requires, that the debate should be " concerning facts, so that every thing, except proof, is su- " perfluous. Yet has it great influence, as has been ob- " served on account of the vicious judgment of the hearer. " Attention to style is in some degree necessary in every kind " of instruction; for in conveying information it makes a " difference whether a man speak in one manner or in another : " however not a great deal, for all this relates chiefly to the " imagination and to the hearer. Geometry, not having any " such relation, is not taught in this manner. When this art " *(style)* is brought to perfection, it will have the same effect " in oratory, as the art of acting has in theatrical representa- " tions. Some inconsiderable attempts have been made to " treat on this subject, as those of Thrasymachus in his work " on the Pathetic. The talent for theatrical delivery is a gift " of nature, and belongs little to art; but style depends

" much on art. For which reason prizes are given also to
" those who have acquired it, as to those orators who excel in
" delivery."[30]

As it appears to have been Aristotle's opinion that delivery
is not a subject for instruction, but that it is altogether a natural
talent, he says no more about it, but proceeds, to give rules
for those parts of rhetoric, which relate to language, and were
comprehended under the name of elocution.

The author of the Rhetoric addressed to Herennius, who,
though not of such high authority as some have supposed,

---

[30] Τὸ μὲν ἓν πρῶτον, ἐζητήθη κατὰ φύσιν, ὅπερ πέφυκε πρῶτον, αὐτὰ τὰ πράγματα
ἐκ τίνων ἔχει τὸ πιθανόν· δεύτερον δὲ, τὸ ταῦτα τῇ λέξει διαθέσθαι· τρίτον δὲ τούτων, ὃ
δύναμιν μὲν ἔχει μεγίστην, ἔπω δ' ἐπικεχείρηται τὰ περὶ τὴν ὑπόκρισιν. Καὶ γὰρ εἰς τὴν
τραγικὴν, καὶ ῥαψῳδίαν ὀψὲ παρῆλθεν· ὑπεκρίνοντο γὰρ αὐτοὶ τραγῳδίας οἱ ποιηταὶ τὸ
πρῶτον.
. . . . Τὰ μὲν ἓν ἄθλα, σχεδὸν ἐκ τῶν ἀγώνων ἤτοι λαμβάνουσι· καὶ καθάπερ
ἐκεῖ μεῖζον δύνανται νῦν τῶν ποιητῶν οἱ ὑποκριταὶ, καὶ κατὰ τᾶς πολιτικᾶς ἀγῶνας, διὰ
τὴν μοχθηρίαν τῶν πολιτειῶν· ἔπω δὲ σύγκειται τέχνη περὶ αὐτῶν. Ἐπεὶ καὶ τὸ περὶ
τὴν λέξιν ὀψὲ προῆλθε. Καὶ δοκεῖ φορτικὸν εἶναι, καλῶς ὑπολαμβανόμενον· ἀλλ' ὅλης
ὅσης πρὸς δόξαν τῆς πραγματείας τῆς περὶ ῥητορικὴν, ἐκ ὀρθῶς ἔχοντος, ἀλλ' ὡς ἀκαλκαίᾳ
τὴν ἐπιμέλειαν ποιητέον· ἐπεὶ τόγε δίκαιον μηδὲν πλείω ζητεῖν περὶ τὸν λόγον, ἢ ὡς μήτε
λυπεῖν, μήτε εὐφραίνειν· δίκαιον γὰρ αὐτοῖς ἀγωνίζεσθαι τοῖς πράγμασιν, ὥστε τἄλλα
ἔξω τᾶ ἀποδεῖξαι, περίεργά ἐστιν· ἀλλ' ὅμως μέγα δύναται, καθάπερ εἴρηται, διὰ τὴν τᾶ
ἀκροατᾶ μοχθηρίαν· Τὸ μὲν οὖν τῆς λέξεως ἔχει τι μικρὸν ἀναγκαῖον ἐν πάσῃ διδασκαλίᾳ·
διαφέρει γὰρ τὶ πρὸς τὸ δηλῶσαι, ὡδὶ, ἢ ὡδὶ εἰπεῖν· ὲ μέντοι τοσοῦτον ἀλλ' ἅπαντα
φαντασίᾳ ταῦτά ἐστι, καὶ πρὸς τὸν ἀκροατήν· διὸ οὐδεὶς ὕτω γεωμετρεῖν διδάσκει. Ἐκείνη
μὲν ἓν ὅταν ἔλθῃ, ταὐτὸ ποιήσει τῇ ὑποκριτικῇ· ἐγκεχειρήκασι δὲ ἐπ' ὀλίγον περὶ αὐτῆς
εἰπεῖν τινες, ὅιον Θρασύμαχος ἐν τοῖς ἐλέοις. Καὶ ἔστι φύσεως τὸ ὑποκριτικὸν εἶναι, καὶ
ἀτεχνότερον· περὶ δὲ τὴν λέξιν ἔντεχνον· Διὸ καὶ τοῖς τοῦτο δυναμένοις γίνεται πάλιν
ἆθλα, καθάπερ ἐν τοῖς κατὰ τὴν ὑπόκρισιν ῥήτορσιν· *Arist. Rhet. l. iii. c.* 1.

lived in the age of Cicero, seems justly offended at the extraordinary and unreasonable power attributed to delivery: and wishes to assign its proper place in the art of oratory. With his judicious observations few will altogether disagree; but it will be observed, that having professed his intention to write copiously on this subject, he says less than many who went before him, and is obliged to get off by acknowledging the difficulty of fulfilling his promise. This, it is hoped, will be admitted as some apology for the imperfections of the present work.

" Many have said, that of all things, the most useful to an " orator, is delivery; and that it is the most powerful mean " of persuasion. But we cannot readily admit that any one of " five requisites, should have greater power than the other " four; nor can we boldly assert that the advantage of de- " livery is extraordinarily great. For then should we say, that " the invention of suitable arguments, the choice of appropriate " words, and the judicious arrangement of the parts of the sub- " ject, together with the exact recollection of all these, without " just delivery, would have no more influence, than delivery " would have alone and without their assistance. Therefore " since no one has written critically on this subject, (for all " have been of opinion that it is hardly possible to write " intelligibly on the voice, the countenance, and the gesture, " as these subjects belong merely to the cognizance of the " senses) and because it is very important that this part of " rhetoric should be illustrated for the purposes of the orator, " it will be advantageous to consider the whole of the subject

" in no careless manner. Delivery is then divided into the
" management of the voice and the gestures of the body."[31]

Having given first a treatise on the voice pretty much at
large, he then devotes to gesture a single short chapter, in
which are, no doubt, useful observations: but which he seems
in haste to dispatch, however necessary he has considered it.
He concludes with this remark.

" I am not ignorant how difficult a task I have undertaken
" in attempting to express by words the motions of the body,
" and to describe the voice by writing. But I was neither
" confident, that on these subjects, I could write with sufficient
" clearness, nor even if I should fail in some measure, did I
" think what I have written, would be without its use; because
" I have wished here rather to mention merely what is neces-
" sary, and shall leave the rest to practice. It should however
" be well understood that correct delivery is attended with
" this advantage, that what is spoken appears to come from
" the heart."[32]

---

[31] Pronunciationem multi maxime utilem oratori dixerunt esse, et ad persuadendum
plurimum valere. Nos quidem unum de quinque rebus plurimum posse non facile dixeri-
mus ; nec egregiè magnam esse utilitatem in pronuntiatione, audacter confirmaverimus.
Nam commodæ inventiones, et concinnæ verborum elocutiones, et partium causæ artifi-
ciosæ dispositiones, et horum omnium diligens memoria, sine pronuntiatione, non plus,
quam sine his rebus pronuntiatio sola valere poterit. Quare quia nemo de ea re diligenter
scripsit (nam omnes vix posse putarunt de voce, et vultu, et gestu dilucide scribi, cum hæ
res ad sensus nostros pertinerent) et quia magnopere ea pars a nobis ad dicendum compa-
randa est, non negligenter videtur tota res consideranda. Dividitur igitur pronuntiatio in
vocis figuram, et corporis motum. *Rhet. ad Herenn. l.* iii. *c.* 11.

[32] Non sum nescius, quantum susceperim negotii, qui motus corporis exprimere verbis,

Of the writers comparatively modern with respect to those now quoted, who have treated of the subject of delivery in their rhetorical works, the most learned and copious are Caussinus and Cresollius: particularly the latter, who has written a large treatise expressly upon this subject. These authors were both of the order of Jesuits, and wrote about the same period.

Cressolius's book was published at Paris in 1620: under the whimsical title (for which he gives his reason) of *Vacationes Autumales sive de perfecta Oratoris, Actione, et Pronuntiatione.* Caussinus treats of eloquence more at large, and his work seems to have been in high estimation; the title is, *De Eloquentia sacra et profana*; many editions of it have been published at Lyons. From these I have already quoted much, and I shall be obliged to them for much more. All the other old rhetoricians treat in some degree upon this subject, and I have derived valuable observations from them, from Alcuinus, Talæus, Curius Fortunatianus, Vossius, Erasmus and others. Among the modern writers, which are in the hands of every one, some of those who have spoken most particularly on the subject of delivery, are Fenelon, Rollin, Marmontel, Condillac, and Maury, among the French; and among our own writers, Addison, Fordyce, Sheridan, Burke, Blair, Walker, and others.

---

imitari scriptura conatus sim voces. Verum nec hoc confisus sum posse fieri, ut de his rebus satis commode scribi posset ; nec, si id fieri non posset, hoc, quod feci fore utile putabam, propterea quod hîc admonere voluimus, quod operteret, reliqua trademus exercitationi. Hoc scire tamen oportet, pronuntiationem bonam id perficere, ut res ex animo agi videatur. *Rhet. ad Herenn. l.* iii. *c.* 15.

Caussinus having instituted a comparison of Demosthenes and Cicero in their different oratorical talents, decides in favour of Cicero. And speaking of their action, he thus laments its irreparable loss. " The orations of Demosthenes and Cicero which " are extant committed to writing, afford in many respects op- " portunity to judge of their manner of delivery : but their " action, which has perished along with themselves, has left a " subject of regret to all. " If they could have expressed this " in their writings, we might, after searching into the monu- " ments of antiquity, be less in the dark." [33] And again in the introduction to his 9th book, which is particularly devoted to delivery, he says :

" It is principally by the practice of speaking that graceful " action is usually acquired, the force of which is very great, " and most efficacious in the power of persuasion. For action is " a kind of eloquence of the body, by which the mind abound- " ing in the finest sentiments flows out upon the body, and " impresses upon it a noble image of itself. As light therefore " proceeds from the sun, so does action proceed from the inmost " recesses of the mind. Nay the mind displays itself by action " as if in a mirror ; and makes itself known externally, by the " countenance, by the eyes, by the hands, and by the voice, the " most excellent organ of eloquence. And since the internal

---

[33] Demosthenis quidem et Ciceronis orationes, quæ literis extant consignatæ, multis judicium, actio, quæ cum ipsis interiit, omnibus desiderium reliquit : quam si exaratis eloquentiæ monumentis imprimere potuissent, minus laboraremus. *Caussin. l.* i. *c.* 67.

" feelings are not easily disclosed to the conception of the
" multitude, who are accustomed to estimate every thing by the
" eyes: and since on the contrary whatever is seen and heard,
" when transmitted through the senses affects the feelings most
" powerfully, it has always been observed, that those speakers
" who excelled in action, carried (as they say) every point. And
" therefore it was not without reason that Demosthenes recog-
" nised it as the first, if not the single excellence in oratory."[34]

An. Talæus, in his Rhetoric, published at Basle in 1569, speaking of the importance of action, repeats many of the arguments
already quoted from Cicero and Quintilian, and concludes with
these observations. " But of this most important art we are in
" want of the proper masters, the phonascus, the actor, the
" fencer, the teacher of the palæstra.—And we want also De-
" mosthenes and Cicero, that is, the true orators, after whose
" example, the learner of eloquence should be exercised.
" Therefore so much the greater industry is requisite on this
" subject, because those living masters are no more, and can
" hardly be recognized from their faint portraits depicted in
" their writings."[35]

---

[34] In eloquentiæ potissimum exercitatione conformari solet actio, cujus vis maxima est
et ad omne momentum persuasionis efficacissima. Est enim corporis quædam eloquentia,
qua fit, ut animus optimis sensibus affluens in corpus emanet, eique sui generosam speciem
imprimat. Ut igitur lumen a sole, sic ab intima mente profluit actio; imo mens ipsa in
actione se prodit, quasi in speculo: et per vultum, per oculos, per manus, per vocem,
optimum eloquentiæ instrumentum, in exteriora sese diffundit: cumque ea quæ interiora sunt
minus patant multitudinis ingeniis quæ omnia ex oculis metiri solent: contra, quæ videntur
et audiuntur, vehementius animos per sensum transfusa percellant, evenit, ut qui actione
floruerint oratores, omne (quod aiunt) punctum semper retulerint: nec immerito eandem
eloquentiæ primariam et penè unam virtutem agnovit Demosthenes. *Caussinus. l.* ix. *proem.*

[35] Artis tamen hujus tantæ magistri nobis desunt, phonascus, scenicus histrio, lanista,

Sulpitius Victor, as quoted below,[36] is of opinion that delivery should be carefully studied, lest the whole labour of composition should be lost. But I hasten to conclude this chapter on the general necessity of attention to gesture, and shall only make one extract from Rollin, whose learning and judgment are acknowledged, and who, as he declares himself, had paid great attention to this subject: and another from the Abbé Maury, who has recently published a treatise upon eloquence.

" The answer of Demosthenes as to what he judged to hold
" the first place in eloquence, is known to all the world; and it
" proves that this great man considered delivery not only as
" the most important quality in an orator, but in a certain sense
" as that which alone was necessary. It is in effect the quality
" which is least able to conceal its own deficiences, and which
" is most capable of concealing all others: and we often observe
" that an indifferent discourse, supported by all the force, and
" by all the graces of action, produces greater effect, than the
" most excellent composition which is stripped of these orna-
" ments." [37]

---

palæstricus, Demosthenes et Cicero, id est, verus orator, cujus exemplo eloquentiæ discipulus exerceatur. Itaque tanto majore industria hic opus est, quia magistri illi vivi nusquam sunt, tantumque picti in libris vix apparent. *Andom. Talæi. Rhet. Basil* 1569, *p.* 57.

[36] Nam pronunciatio artis quidem quodammodo non est, magnam tamen et nimirum maximam vim obtinet. Nam cum omnia fecerimus, nisi illa, quæ recte disposita sunt, apte et cum decoro fuerint pronunciata, omnis labor prorsus peribit. Itaque etsi magnam istius partem vel negat natura vel tribuit, danda tamen opera est, ut in pronuntiando et vox, et vultus, et gestus, et cætera adhibeantur, ejusmodi; quare labor in comenda oratione adhibitus non pereat. *Sulpitius Victor Inst. Orat. p.* 247.

[37] La réponse de Demosthène sur ce qu'il jugeoit tenir le premier rang dans l'éloquence, est connue de tout le monde; et elle montre que ce grand homme regardoit la pronunciation, non seulement comme la plus importante qualité de l'orateur, mais en un certain sens

" These are specimens, which would be no discredit to the
" writings of Demosthenes. (Says the Abbé Maury, speaking of
" certain eloquent passages of Lord Bolingbroke and of Mr. Fox.)
" But a sublime idea does not constitute a discourse; a beautiful
" detached passage does not comprehend the art of eloquence.

" Even until the present period, the value of English orators
" is restrained within narrow bounds. *Famous islanders! it is*
" *not genius, it is the genius of oratory, that you want,* we
" may say to you, as Cicero did formerly to some of his con-
" temporaries.[38]

" The human mind owes an unceasing debt of gratitude for
" your sublime discoveries on light, on gravitation, on electri-
" city, on the aberration of the stars; but let not your pride
" be wounded, if we contest the pre-eminence with your orators.
" Eloquence, the usual companion of liberty, is a stranger in
" your country. Do not affect a false and barbarous contempt
" of gifts, which nature hath denied you. Turn your attention
" to the models of antiquity, and to the examples of Greece and
" Rome. Add to the glory of the good actions, which are so
" common in your country, the merit, perhaps, no less honour-
" able, of knowing how to celebrate them." [39,40]

---

comme l'unique. En effet c'est cette qualité dont le défaut peut le moins se couvrir, et qui
est le plus capable de couvrir les autres : et l'on voit souvent qu'un discours mediocre,
soutenu de toute la force et de tous les agrémens de l'action, fait plus d'effet, que le plus
beau discours qui en est dénué. *Rollin Belles Lettres. Vol. II, p.* 628.

[38] Illis non ingenium, sed oratorium ingenium deficit. *Cic. Brut.* 110.

[39] See notes in Maury from Hume, Knox, and Blair.

If what Messrs. Hume, Knox and Blair, have said (as stated in the notes of Mr. Lake's
translation of the Abby Maury, which I quote) relative to the state of English oratory be

The eloquent and learned Dr. Darwin, in the passages cited below, admits the full effects of oratorical action, particularly in the last line.[41,42] In the former passage he mentions the association between the gestures and the passion. This is an

---

correct, the eloquence of composition itself is indeed very low. It is not certainly want of genius to which this deficiency should be attributed, for the sparks of genius are emitted whenever the sleeping embers are stirred, nay they burst often into a transitory blaze as the Abbé himself has proved. The want of application is alone the cause of deficiency in oratory of the most exalted kind in the British Isles. After the ordinary course of education is finished, all is left to the *routine* of public practice; it would be reckoned a shame to be found to study even the composition in private, much more the manner of delivery. And if an accidental passage should betray a taste for eloquence, it must be supposed the result of genius, and of the happy inspiration and effusion of the moment: and as to gesture, to be thought to study that, would subject to the extreme of ridicule.

[40] " I know a young man (says Lord Chesterfield), who being just elected a member of " parliament, was laughed at for being discovered, through the keyhole of his chamber door, " speaking to himself in the glass, and forming his looks and gestures. I could not join in " that laugh, but on the contrary thought him much wiser than those that laughed at him; " for he knew the importance of those little graces in a public assembly, and they did not." *Chesterfield's Letters by Gregory, p.* 296.

[41]   When strong desires or soft sensations move
       Th' astonish'd intellect to rage or love;
       Associate tribes of fibrous motions rise,
       Flush the red cheek, or light the laughing eyes.
       Whence ever active imitation finds
       Th' ideal trains that pass in kindred minds;
       Her mimic arts associate thoughts excite,
       And the first language enters at the sight.
                     Darwin's Temple of Nature, Can. iii. *l.* 319.

[42]   Association's mystic pow'r combines,
       Internal passion with external signs,
       From these dumb gestures first th' exchange began,
       Of viewless thought in bird, and beast, and man:
       And still the stage by mimic art displays
       Historic pantomime in modern days;
       And hence the enthusiast orator affords
       Force to the feebler eloquence of words.   *Ib. l.* 358.

important fact for the attention of the orator, who is often obliged to assume, and also to inspire the feelings he has assumed. The note of Dr. Darwin upon the passage is more particularly worthy of attention in this place. " And the first language, " line 342. There are two ways by which we become ac- " quainted with the passions of others: first by having ob- " served the effects of them, as of fear or anger on our own " bodies, we know at sight when others are under the influence " of these affections. So children, long before they can speak, " or understand the language of their parents, may be frigh- " tened by an angry countenance, or soothed by smiles and " blandishments. Secondly. When we put ourselves into the " attitude that any passion naturally occasions, we soon in some " degree acquire the passion; hence when those that scold " indulge themselves in loud oaths and violent actions of the " arms, they encrease their anger by the mode of expressing " themselves: and on the contrary, the counterfeited smile of " pleasure in disagreeable company soon brings along with it a " portion of the reality, as is well illustrated by Mr. Burke. " (Essay on the Sublime and Beautiful.)" [43]

The constraint which virtue or good manners lays upon the external and uncontrolled expression of our passions, operates much, no doubt, to keep them within proper bounds. Hence the prepossessing exterior of persons bred at courts, where all must be guarded with propriety. The passage alluded to by Dr. Darwin in Mr. Burke's treatise on the sublime, appears to be

---

[43] Hence public speakers who use gesture not only seem in earnest, but actually become so, even though at first they might have been indifferent.

the following, with which, as being much to the purpose, this long list of authorities shall conclude.

" It appears very clearly to me from this, and from many " other examples, that when the body is disposed by any means " whatsoever, to such emotions as it would acquire by the means " of a certain passion, it will of itself excite something very like " that passion in the mind.

" To this purpose Mr. Spon, in his *Récherches d'Antiquité*, gives " us a curious story of the celebrated physiognomist Campanella; " this man, it seems, had not only made very accurate observa- " tions on human faces, but was very expert in mimicking such, " as were any way remarkable.⁴⁴ When he had a mind to pene- " trate into the inclinations of those he had to deal with, he " composed his face, his gesture, and his whole body as nearly " as he could into the exact similitude of the person he intended " to examine; and then carefully observed what turn of mind he " seemed to acquire by this change. So that, says my author, " he was able to enter into the dispositions and thoughts of " people, as effectually as if he had been changed into the very " men. I have often observed that on mimicking the looks and " gestures, of angry or placid, or frightened or daring men, I

---

⁴⁴ These observations are very favourable to the particular object of this chapter. The orator has but to assume the aspect and gestures which he ought, and he will both become in earnest himself, and persuade others.

On this principle, the bragging and swaggering fellow who is at heart a coward, must be indeed a wretched one who cannot work himself up to valour by his words and gestures. And he must be possessed of true courage who can calmly proceed to any extremities which brave men encounter. In battle the attitude of the soldier may contribute to his steadiness, and it is not without reason that savage nations shout on the onset.

" have involuntarily found my mind turned to that passion
" whose appearance I have endeavoured to imitate; nay, I am
" convinced it is hard to avoid it; though one strove to separate
" the passion from its corresponding gestures. Our minds and
" bodies are so closely, and intimately connected, that one is
" incapable of pain or pleasure without the other. Campanella,
" of whom we have been speaking, could so abstract his atten-
" tion from any sufferings of his body, that he was able to
" endure the rack itself without much pain;[45] and in lesser
" pains, every body must have observed, that when we can
" employ our attention on any thing else, the pain has been
" for a time suspended; on the other hand, if by any means
" the body is indisposed to perform such gestures, or to be
" stimulated into such emotions, as any passion usually produces
" in it, that passion itself never can arise, though its cause
" should be never so strongly in action; though it should be
" merely mental, and immediately affecting none of the senses.
" As an opiate, or spirituous liquors, shall suspend the operation
" of grief, or fear, or anger, in spite of all our efforts to the con-
" trary; and this by inducing in the body a disposition contrary
" to that which it receives from these passions."[46]

---

[45] The tortures sustained by the American Indians without betraying the external symp-
toms of pain, may perhaps be accounted for by such efforts of the mind.

[46] Burke's Sublime and Beautiful. *Part.* iv. *sec.* 3, 4.

CHAPTER V.

OF READING.

*Of public speaking in general—Different modes of public speaking—
Reading the simplest and most useful—Its divisions—The intelligible
reader—Acquirements necessary for him, and offices suited to his
talent—The correct reader—His acquirements and offices—The impressive reader—His acquirements and public reading—Reading of
the Liturgy and of the holy Scriptures—Frequent repetition of the
church service—Its effects on the feelings of the reader—The efforts
necessary to be made and persevered in by a minister of the Gospel—
The rhetorical reader—Requisites for him—The value of accomplished
reading—Of dramatic reading—Private dramatic readers—Public
dramatic readers—Of dramatic reading in which the characters are
distributed among several persons in private company—Reading of
history—Of epic poetry—Of novels—Reflections on this last species of
writing.*

CHAPTER V.

Of Reading.

HAVING treated in general of the three great divisions of the external part of oratory, the voice, the countenance and gesture; and having maintained their importance both by argument, and by authority; I proceed to enquire under what circumstances, and in what degree, they should be brought into exercise by the public speaker. This will appear best, by considering the general objects and modes of public speaking.

The general objects of public speaking are, instruction, persuasion, or entertainment. These objects are sometimes kept distinct, sometimes they are combined in various proportions.

In their various modes of exercise, these objects will obtain their ends, that is succeed in influencing the hearer in the degree proposed, not only by the interesting matter which may be presented to him, but also by the manner in which it is presented. The manner is called the delivery. And the advantages of good delivery are such, as to conceal in *some degree* the blemishes of the composition, or the matter delivered, and to add lustre to its beauties: insomuch that a *good* composition well delivered, shall, with any popular audience, succeed better

in its object (as we have already proved from high authorities),
whether that be instruction, persuasion or entertainment, than a
superior composition not delivered so well. The following
among many reasons may be assigned for this.

First, because the majority are incapable of appreciating the
matter of a discourse, separately from the manner; and secondly,
because the manner has naturally considerable influence, in proportion to the degree of persuasion which it impresses on the
hearer, of the sincerity of the speaker.

The modes adopted in public speaking are, Reading, Recitation,
Declamation, Oratory, and Acting. Of which the three first are
often practised for the purpose of exercise or preparation, as
well as on real occasions.

Of these different modes of public speaking, I shall first treat
briefly, and then proceed to the detail of a system of gesture.

Reading, if not the simplest mode of public speaking, is,
among cultivated nations, the most useful and the easiest.
Because any man can in this mode, deliver the sentiments of the
wisest of all ages and nations, in language already prepared and
approved: and the public speaker has, on ordinary occasions,
only to pronounce *intelligibly*, what he has before him; or, if he
would perfectly discharge his office on higher occasions, *impressively*. But it may be proper to speak more particularly of
reading in all its degrees, in order to distinguish more accurately
the characteristics of the different species.

Reading considered as to its purpose and manner, admits a general, though very unequal division, into silent reading, and reading aloud. The silent reader has arrived at all necessary perfection, when his talent is sufficiently *apprehensive;* that is, when he understands all the characters and symbols used by the author, whose work he reads, and when he comprehends with facility his language and his opinions.

In reading aloud there is greater scope and variety. Of this the lowest species, as to the requisite acquirements, may evidently be considered that, in which a man sometimes reads aloud to himself. The object of this reading may be only to impress the subject on the reader's own memory, or to obtain a more distinct perception of his author's style and matter by clothing them in words, or to exercise himself in the pronunciation of the language, or in the music of the lines, or possibly to prepare for a public exhibition. For any of these purposes the reader, if he would not confirm himself in bad habits, should have a competent knowledge of the prosody, and of the pronunciation of the language in which he reads.[1] But he may

---

[1] Whoever reads a perfect or finished composition, whatever be the language, whatever the subject, should read it, even if alone, both audibly and distinctly. In a composition of this character, not only precise words are admitted, but words metaphorical and ornamental. And farther, as every sentence contains a latent harmony, so is that harmony derived from the rythm of its constituent parts.

A composition like this, should (as I said before) be read both distinctly and audibly; with due regard to stops and pauses; with occasional elevations and depressions of the voice, and whatever else constitutes just and accurate pronunciation. He who, despising or neglecting, or knowing nothing of all this, reads a work of such character as he would read a sessions paper, will not only miss many beauties of the style, but will probably miss (which is worse) a large proportion of the sense. *Harris's advice to readers, Eleg. Ex. Prose,* p. 383.

proceed very rapidly, and in many respects very carelessly. This sort of reading is sometimes introduced upon the stage in an exaggerated manner, and with good effect. As when an actor is supposed to read a letter as it were to himself. He mutters over a part of what he reads, and articulates distinctly only the principle words and phrases.

But reading aloud, is more generally for the purpose of communicating exactly to others the subject, and the language of the writing which is read: and this may be effected variously according to the particular object in view, and the particular style of the writing. From the particular objects or the combination of them arise different kinds of reading; which may be described under the following names, beginning from that which requires the lowest effort of the talents of delivery, and proceeding to that which requires the highest. The scale of reading will then be disposed thus: 1. Intelligible. 2. Correct. 3. Impressive. 4. Rhetorical. 5. Dramatic. 6. Epic.

The lowest degree of reading aloud for the information of others, which can be admitted as useful to the public, is that which is named *intelligible* reading.

To a reader of this class the following are the only requisites, good articulation, proper attention to pauses, and accents, and sufficient effort of voice to render himself audible to all concerned in the matter.

If a reader, either from deficiency of utterance, want of comprehension of the language or characters of the writing, or from inability of voice, cannot reach this small but necessary excellence, he should relinquish the task altogether. And yet to the disgrace of our progress in these first rudiments of oratory, it must be admitted that such readers are sometimes to be met. The lower orders of persons engaged in the courts of law are sometimes found thus grossly illiterate, and incapable of enouncing intelligibly what even themselves have written: It is seldom now, that a more sacred place is profaned by such indecent ignorance. The intelligible reader, according to the description above given, is qualified to read and compare common law writings, to hold the office of a clerk in public business, as in the parliament house, to read advertisements and articles of intelligence in the public prints, and to discharge such like humble literary employments.

To the articulation, pauses, accents and effort of voice, necessary to render a reader fully intelligible; the *correct* reader must add something more; the additional requisites for him are, proper emphasis, purity of pronunciation, and suitable demeanor. The correct reader must evince his own just conception of what he reads, by applying proper emphases, which serve as touches of light in a picture to bring forward the principal objects. He must study purity of pronunciation that he may not offend, and distract the attention of his hearers, by diverting it from his subject and turning it upon himself.[a] Upon this principle, it is necessary, that he be most careful not to offend by affectation; which even in a greater degree than provincial vulgarity itself, disturbs the attention from the

---

[a] Nihil potest intrare in affectum, quod in aure velut quodam vestibulo statim offendit. *Quint.*

proper objects of public speaking, persuasion and instruction. The one is often pardoned where sincerity and good sense appear; the other perpetually disgusts, by obtruding self as the prominent and distinguished figure, however important may be the subject. As a consequence it follows, that the correct reader should demean himself with modesty, decorum, and simplicity.

In this manner of reading, public documents are properly delivered in parliament, and calculations of finance are read. In this manner also, the prayers and service of the church are often delivered; and some appear to think it all that is requisite for the solemnity of public worship. It must be admitted that many parts of the service should be delivered in this manner *only*, and that if the whole be so delivered, it cannot offend. But the merely correct reader is dry and cold in manner, and in many parts of the Liturgy passages occur which admit or rather require more warmth, to give them their just effect.

How cold must the reader be, who does not deliver with due earnestness the supplications in the beginning of the litany, and encrease in feeling as well as in fervor of manner with the iteration of the petition so solemnly repeated, " have mercy " upon us miserable sinners? " how can a minister deliver without strong sensations and suitable expression of countenance, more particularly, the close of the solemn adjuration to our Lord? " By thine agony and bloody sweat; by thy cross ard passion, by thy precious death and burial," or fail to mark the change into consolation and triumph on these words, " By thy glorious resurrection and ascension, and by the coming of the holy Ghost, " and again fall back into the humility of supplication, " Good Lord deliver us?" and must he not assume both the tones and countenance of authority, when he pronounces in high solemnity the Commandments of God from the sacred table, from the very altar and holy place, and removed to the utmost distance, as if to separate him from the congregation?

The reading of divine service is usually limited to the above mentioned qualifications and efforts on the part of our ministers : and the style extends from the merely *intelligible* to *correct* reading.

But the *impressive* reader will be found to discharge more perfectly the office of reading the Liturgy and the Scriptures. In addition to the requisites already stated as necessary to the correct reader, the impressive reader must possess the following : expression of the voice, expression of countenance, direction of the eye, variety of manner as to rapidity of delivery, and rhetorical pauses. In delivering the prayers, expression of the voice, with which is almost necessarily connected expression of the countenance, are required of the reader (as has been observed), in order to excite both in his hearers and in himself a proper feeling and interest. And in reading the Scriptures, he must also awaken their attention to important and affecting matter, by directing his eyes upon them, by rhetorical pauses, and by varying the rapidity of his delivery according to the subject.

Thus impressive reading comprehends two entire divisions of the art of delivery, the modulations of the voice, and the expression of the countenance; of gesture, the third division, it partakes but little.

C c

Within the whole range, through which the exercise of this valuable talent, the art of reading, is extended, impressive reading will be found no where so requisite as in delivering the service of the established church. The Liturgy, so often repeated, stands much in need of the reader's exertions, to keep his congregation alive to the many excellencies of this admirable composition; and what is more important, to engage them at the same time to a due communication in its sentiments: so that instead of oscitancy and inattention on either part, the minister and the congregation shall mutually sympathize in the repetition and hearing of those petitions, confessions, and thanksgivings of which it consists.

The reading of the Scriptures must be considered as even more interesting than the Liturgy itself, and is also more difficult. Their composition is of that original and various character, which demands every effort on his part, who is called upon to deliver them for the instruction of others. Hardly is there a chapter, which does not contain something, which requires the most impressive reading; as remonstrance, threatening, command, encouragement, sublime description, awful judgments. The narrative is interrupted by frequent and often unexpected transitions; by bold and unusual figures; and by precepts of most extensive application, and most admirable use.

In the narrative, the reader should deliver himself with a suitable simplicity and gravity of demeanour. In the transitions, which are often rapid, he should manifest a quick conception, and by rhetorical pauses and suitable changes of voice, express and render intelligible the new matter or change of scene. In the figurative and sublime which every where abound, his voice should be sonorous, and his countenance expressive of the elevation of his subject. In the precepts he should deliver himself with judgment and discretion; and when he repeats the words and precepts, as recorded, of our Lord himself, with more distinguished mildness mingled with dignified authority. Such reading would be a perpetual and luminous commentary on the sacred writings; and would convey more solid information than the most learned and brilliant sermons.[3] But who can enumerate the various interests, which those sacred books are calculated to awaken?

---

[3] Examples of passages of Scripture requiring particular expression on the part of the reader.

A pause of suspension with due expression of countenance should precede this short passage which contains more than a long declamation against the infatuation of the Jews:

Now Barabbas was a *robber. John,* chap. xviii. ver. 40.
Pathos.
O Jerusalem, Jerusalem, thou that killest the prophets, and stonest them which are sent unto thee:
How often would I have gathered thy children together, even as a hen gathereth her chickens under her wings, and ye would not.
Pronouncing of Judgment with Commiseration.
Behold, your house is left unto you desolate. *Matt.* chap. xxiii. ver. 37, 38.
Authority.
Thou hast answered right: this *do,* and thou shalt live. *Luke,* chap. x. ver. 28.
Prayer and Resignation.
O my father, if it be possible, let this cup pass from me: nevertheless, not as I will, but as thou wilt.
Moderated Surprise and gentle Remonstrance.
And he cometh unto the disciples and findeth them *asleep,* and saith unto Peter, *What,* could ye not watch with me *one hour ?*
Warning and indulgent Apology.
Watch and pray, that ye enter not into temptation: the *spirit* indeed is willing, but the *flesh* is weak. *Matt.* chap. xxvi. 39, 40, 41.
But this 26th Chapter of St. Matthew requires, to do justice to all its interesting events,

and all of these, if possible, should be so deeply entered into, that he who reads, should, by every expression of voice and countenance, deliver them, as if he felt in his heart the force of their sacred truth. Such is the description of truly impressive reading, and such are the writings, which above all others, require reading of this kind. But however it were to be wished that the Scriptures should be always read in this manner, it is not to be expected that we shall often meet such desirable perfection. Two circumstances principally oppose it. *First*, the necessary and frequent repetition of the service blunts the feelings of those who by constant practice might otherwise be expected to improve daily. And this impediment is of a degree of difficulty, not easily conceived, except by those who have so laboured. Hence the reader of the service falls into an habitual train, which admits of no future improvement, and which it is almost impossible to change, or in any wise to correct. To those already established in their manner, advice comes too late; but to those who are beginning their ministry, it may not be altogether useless to offer a few precepts. In the commencement of his public reading of the service of the church, whilst his feelings are still alive, and whilst he is still docile, before he has absolutely

---

all its important passages, and all its variety of sentiment, more than ordinary talents, and more than ordinary feelings on the part of the reader.

In the Proverbs will be found examples of antithesis and of instruction; and in various passages of the Old Testament of authority, terror, and admiration. Some occur, in which the reader must express disapprobation, as the falsehood of Jacob; and some require the expression of affection, as the meeting of Joseph and his brethren; and some of absolute horror, as the treacherous murder of Sisera; but this is not the place for extensive enquiries on this subject: let it suffice that examples may be found in the Scriptures requiring, and surely meriting, the exertion of all the powers of the most accomplished reader.

adopted any particular manner; a young man should make every possible effort to understand thoroughly what he reads, and to practise correct delivery; he should particularly read Sheridan on the Liturgy, and in private exercise himself in the manner recommended by that judicious reader and critic; and at all times obtain if possible the observations and judgment of a learned and candid friend upon his performance.[4]

He must also attentively hear the best readers, compare their different manners, and finally adopt that which he shall determine to be the best. The deep study of his own language, and the weighing of every syllable according to the authorities of the most celebrated orthoepists and public speakers, is particularly necessary. He must examine, and correct where deficient, his own articulation, his accent, his voice and all his powers; he must think no labour too minute, nor to arduous which may tend to his improvement and perfection.[5] By these means he will improve and advance truly towards perfection; and keep long alive both his own feelings and those of his hearers: and should they even grow dull, by frequent repetition; the good habits he has acquired will, if not renew them, still carry him through in the discharge of his duty so as to benefit his hearers, which is the main object, and impress upon his reading the characters of propriety, of feeling, and of devotion.

---

4 If he is commended as a good reader after a little pains, let him not rest upon his trophies, let his rising reputation operate only as an encouragement towards his obtaining a higher and juster title by greater labour.

5 And above all, he should keep up as long as possible the habit of improvement, to which his mind should be always open, instead of indulging the idea, almost at any period, of his having acquired a manner sufficiently correct.

And these characters will not altogether forsake his reading, even in the moments of absence, when the best men's thoughts wander from the immediate and important subject which ought to occupy them solely.[6]

They who read the Service of the church only at considerable intervals, or occasionally, will not have the same reason to complain of blunted feelings, or of distraction, as those, who labour daily and often in the day; their attention will be kept alive by the comparative novelty of their situation, and their sensibility will happily recover its tone by rest; so that on such occasions men ought to make, and in general also, are found to make their best exertions.

The frequent repetition of the same form is then one reason why the Service of the church is not always read impressively as it ought. A second reason for this is want of talents in the reader. It is not every man, who has received a liberal education, and who is appointed to the ministry, who, even after his utmost efforts, is capable of becoming an impressive reader. To read with attention, with seriousness, and with propriety, is in the power of every diligent and well informed man; but a fine voice capable of every variety of modulation, and a fine ear capable of distinguishing every change, together with a correct and cultivated taste to regulate every inflexion,

---

[6] If at certain times the reader (such is the imperfection of man) cannot excite his feelings so as to accord fully with his duty, nor altogether guard himself from those wanderings, it will be consolatory if he think himself but the organ for other men's service, and do his utmost. But he will seriously endeavour, he will carefully recall his thoughts, and habitually excite his attention, so that his insensibility shall not overcome him, and that his wanderings shall be as short and as rare as possible.

to moderate its force, and govern its rapidity according as the subject demands, are gifts not bestowed on many. But above all, the feelings of lively intelligence and sensibility to every changing sentiment, and such expression of the eye and countenance as shall convey them warm from the reader's understanding and heart, to the hearts and the understandings of the hearers, are gifts bestowed only on a few. Yet are these endowments necessary for those who aspire to the praise of impressive reading. But though the rarity of these gifts, and the difficulty of the necessary attainments may be admitted in mitigation of the censure, to which those public readers of the Scripture might otherwise be liable, whose manner is uninteresting : yet it must be acknowledged, that with all allowance made for human infirmity and deficiency, much more in general might be done: and also, that young readers are often culpably negligent, and often get rid of their labour along with their apprehensions ; that few bring their talents to as high a degree of cultivation as they are capable of attaining for the discharge of this serious and important duty ; and that nearer approaches to perfection might be made by those who possess many of the requisite endowments, were they not too soon tired of learning, and carried off by bad example and by indolence. And to some of these causes shall we be obliged in general to attribute the cold, dry, uniform, and monotonous strain in which the Scriptures are too often delivered in our churches.

If to the impressive style of reading be added such a degree of acquaintance with subject as that it shall be nearly committed to memory, and that it be also accompanied with gesture to a certain degree, and more decided expression of the eyes and countenance, it constitutes a more forcible style, which may be termed *rhetorical reading*. This style of reading is adapted to popular discourses from the pulpit, which if intended to be so delivered should be composed in all the forms of a regular oration. In our churches correct reading suits a discourse on evidences, impressive reading an exhortation, and rhetorical reading those subjects which call for the higher exertions of pulpit eloquence, as funeral orations, great public occasions, and the solicitation of alms for useful charities.[7]

Public reading, within these limits, will be found, if not capable of all the brilliancy that can be desired, yet to possess the most solid advantages; the conveying of instruction in the surest manner. What is read in public, is presumed to have been composed at leisure; to have been maturely considered, digested, and arranged in all its arguments. It carries with it all the weight which can be attached to the opinions or talents of the reader, if the composition be his own; and if he read an approved and known book, the propriety of his manner illustrates the subject as a valuable commentary, and his energy impresses it effectually on his hearers. To read well, must therefore be esteemed a very high attainment in public speaking; and no labour should be thought too arduous for its acquirement by those who are likely to be called upon in any situation to read in public; that is, by any men of liberal education, or of rank in life above the lowest vulgar; all of

---

[7] But such subjects suit even better the freedom of oratory unincumbered by notes. In our church rhetorical reading generally takes this place.

whom will probably on some occasion be obliged to exhibit this talent.[8]

The good reader possesses the solid and substantial part of public speaking; but he may also add considerably the ornamental parts, and in his own writings practise successfully to persuade and captivate, as well as to convince: which he may effect not only by rhetorical composition, but by rhetorical delivery. And these exertions will be required on the most important occasions, that is for the advancement of the eloquence of the pulpit, where the subjects, above all others, are capable of every species of argument and illustration, not only by reasoning and proof; but also by the ornaments of figurative language and suitable delivery: so as not only to convince, but also to interest and delight the hearer.

Reading in private is seldom carried farther than that description named *impressive.* But in the reading of a play, when one person goes through the whole drama, a manner is almost necessarily adopted which may be called *dramatic* reading. In this style of reading the voice, the countenance, and the

---

[8] De toutes les magies de l'art, la plus difficile en effet est de repandre sur ce qui est généralement connu les graces et les attraits de la nouveauté : il n'y a point d'objet de lecture ou de debit, qui exige autant d'habilité, que celui où il ne s'agit, ni de donner aux hommes une instruction nouvelle, ni de les convaincre d'une vérité qu'ils ignorent; mais de leur présenter des choses dont ils sont déjà instruits et convaincus, sous des couleurs capables de faire, sur leur esprit et sur leur cœur, une impression profonde. C'est par cette raison, sans doute, que quoiqu'il y ait un grand nombre de prédicateurs passables, on en voit si peu atteindre à un certain dégré de perfection. Que leur manque-t-il ? cet art de bien lire, ou de s'énoncer, qui rajeunit les vérités les plus rebattues, qui donne une couleur agréable aux choses les plus triviales, et qui jette de l'intérêt jusque sur les idées les plus simples.

Dubroca, Principes sur l'Art de Lire, p. 404.

D d

delivery, as to rapidity or slowness, force or feebleness are nearly suited to the character which is supposed at any time to speak; and even provincial and foreign accents are also in some degree imitated:[9] moderate gesture of the hand is used, accompanied now and then by the head, in passages requiring particular discrimination. But the efforts of the reader in mere private and family society seldom go farther.[10] [11] In the reading of plays in this style, the names of the characters are sometimes read in a sort of dry under voice before the passages they are supposed to speak: but this awkward expedient should not be used except to prevent ambiguity; as where there are many interlocutors in the dialogue of manners and ages not strongly contrasted; on the entrance of a new character; or when any one speaks after a considerable interval. A person of taste and judgment will feel when he may divest his reading of this incumbrance, and will know when he ought to submit to it.

The talent for dramatic reading in its highest excellence is very rare. It includes not only all the requisites for correct, impressive, and dramatic reading of the ordinary kind, which is sufficient for the mere presenting the scenes of a play to a domestic circle; but the fine dramatic reader must be possessed

---

9 Quod faciunt actores comici, qui nec ita prorsus ut nos vulgo loquimur pronuntiant, quod esset sine arte: nec procul tamen a natura recedunt quo vitio periret imitatio; sed morem communis hujus sermonis decore quodam scenico exornant. *Quin. l.* ii. *c.* 10.

10 Ne gestus quidem omnis ac motus a comœdis petendus est. Quanquam enim utrumque eorum ad quemdam modum præstare debet orator; plurimum tamen aberit a scenico, nec vultu, nec manu, nec excursionibus nimius. *Quin. l.* i. *c.* 11.

11 Adeo in illis quoque (comœdis scil.) est aliqua vitiosa imitatio, quorum ars omnis constat imitatione. *Quint. l.* xi. *c.* 3,

of the quickest conception, and of an eye which intuitively com·prehends the whole dialogue at a glance, of a versatility of manner capable of adapting itself to every character, and such a power of modulation of the voice as shall also present each changing character to the hearer within the bounds of decorous imitation, without naming him, which would often break the interest of the scene; and above all he must possess a true and lively feeling of the situation and interest of every person in the drama. Private reading of this degree of excellence is very rare, even in public it is seldom to be obtained.[12] In public an exhibition of dramatic readings by an ingenious foreigner has been for many years favourably received. He performs generally sitting, with a book before him, but appears not to require its assistance: he reads, or delivers the whole piece himself, and speaks in the character of the different persons with surprising ability and versatility of manner. His gestures, his voice and countenance change with every character often as successfully as rapidly. He does not name the persons, but then his performance is an absolute imitation of each, which is not to be looked for in private dramatic reading.[13] In one circumstance alone he appears not to give his performance the full effect of which, with his talents, it seems capable: he seldom turns his eye upon the audience even, in the soliloquies.

Another species of dramatic reading has of late years been

---

[12] I have never been so fortunate as to hear in private any reader who approaches my ideas of excellence so nearly as the Hon. F. H. H———

[13] This gentleman will be recognized to be Mons. Texier; I have never heard him read tragedy, and do not know whether he does read it in public. But his manner appears to me better suited to comedy. And the French tragedy also appears to me altogether too heavy for such exhibition.

practised in private companies assembled for the purpose. It differs from that just mentioned, by limiting each individual to the reading of the part of a single character. In this entertainment, as on the stage, the characters of the drama are distributed among the readers according to their supposed talents; and each being furnished with a separate book, either the whole play, or certain select scenes from one or more, are read by the performers sitting round a table, whilst others of the company serve as the audience. The reading is performed by each in his best and most characteristic manner, the part allotted to each is often nearly committed to memory, and such gestures are used as can be conveniently executed in a sitting posture. Higher efforts are here required in order to keep the auditors alive to the interest of the scene, thus divided and stript of all that aids delusion, and mutilated of its complete action. On these occasions favourite scenes are often performed in a part of the room considered as a stage, by such of the party, as wish to exhibit higher dramatic powers, and temporary arrangements of screens are made accordingly; sometimes dresses are assumed or modified the more nearly to approach theatrical exhibition: but reading ceases here.

History, which is the most improving subject of private reading, in the mere narrative parts requires no greater efforts on the part of the reader than the style which is termed correct. But in those lively descriptions of places, situations, and great actions which rhetoricians name hypotoposes, impressive reading is altogether necessary; and in the speeches or prosopopœias which sometimes occur, rhetorical reading should in some measure be introduced.

The same circumstances occur more frequently, and more heightened in epic poetry: and therefore, as well as on account of the lofty measure, and elevated language, an epic poem requires of the reader a more dignified and exalted strain, and a manner almost constantly sustained above the ordinary level. Descriptions in such poetry abound more, and are more highly ornamented than in the most interesting history; similes and other poetical figures are introduced in all their grandeur and beauty; battles are described with the most terrible and striking precision, and speeches are delivered with all the ornaments, and all the powers of eloquence. Thus every thing sublime and beautiful, awful and pathetic, being assembled in an epic poem as in a tragedy, the reader must be all awake if he would deliver either with just effect; he must be filled with his subject, governed by taste and judgment, alive to feeling, and inspired like the poet himself with a degree of enthusiasm.

Novels, or modern fictitious biography, are so frequently the subject of private readings, and influence so much the taste of young people, that they demand some notice. Perhaps it would be well if this species of writing were still unknown: in its best form, and in its most innocent preparations, it is found to retain certain relaxing and sedative qualities, injurious to the vigour of the mind; and to have an influence upon it altogether different from those more solid studies of which Cicero says; " Other studies do not suit all times, or all ages or places; " but these are the food proper for the nourishment of youth, " they are the delight of old age; they adorn prosperity, and " supply refuge and consolation in adversity: they afford

" pleasure in private, and give no embarrassment in public;
" they are our companions throughout the night; they travel
" with us abroad, they follow us into our retirement in the
" country."[4] But it is not to be expected that the rapid
progress of extreme refinement which has pervaded every art
and enjoyment of life in Europe, should fail to shed its softness
also upon our literature.　And if this soft learning was never
corrupted, or served only for the amusement of a leisure hour,
instead of engrossing every hour in amusement, we should
have less reason to complain.　Some of those compositions
may be esteemed valuable additions to our stock of amusing
literature, and we may apply to such the former part of the
passage just quoted from Cicero, who is speaking of other
writings, and knew of none of this species.[5]　In reading these
works aloud to the private circle, custom, arising from the
eager desire of unravelling the story, has determined that the
mere narrative should be read with unusual rapidity.　The
interesting scenes demand impressive reading, and many of
the scenes, which are constructed like those in a regular
drama, require to be read in a similar manner.

---

[4] Nam cætera neque temporum sunt, neque ætatum omnium, neque locorum: hæc
studia adolescentiam alunt, senectutem oblectant, secundas res ornant, adversis perfugium ac
solatium præbent, delectant domi, non impediunt foris, pernoctant nobiscum, perigrinantur,
rusticantur. *Cic. pro Archia Poeta.*

[5] Quod si non hic tantus fructus ostenderetur et si ex his studiis delectatio sola peteretur: tamen ut opinor, hanc animi remissionem, humanissimam ac liberalissimam judicaretis. *ib.*

CHAPTER VI.

OF RECITATION AND DECLAMATION.

How recitation differs from declamation—The purposes for which recitation is practised—Declamation practised by the ancients—By Cicero —By Quintilian—By Seneca—Modern declamation—Speaking societies—Historical society of the University of Dublin—Its origin and present state—Declamation at schools.

CHAPTER VI.

Of Recitation and Declamation.

If the public speaker desire to give to the composition, which he delivers, more interest than it can derive from mere reading; or rather desire to give it the highest interest of which it is capable; he must commit it perfectly to memory, and adorn and enforce it with all the aids of the various modulations of the voice, expression of the countenance, and suitable gesture. So that, even though he should deliver the sentiments of another person, he must appear altogether to adopt and feel, and recommend them as his own. When the composition thus delivered is poetical, this mode of public speaking is called recitation. When it is argumentative, and pronounced or composed on an imaginary occasion, for the purpose of exercising the speaker's rhetorical talents, it is called declamation. And when the speaker delivers in this manner a composition of his own on a real occasion, it is oratory: for the acquiring of the external art of which, recitation and declamation are chiefly practised. They are sometimes also practised as exercises for theatrical exhibition. For either purpose they are important.[1]

---

[1] That sort of recitation of certain passages in plays which is used before a manager by a young actor in order to recommend himself; is merely a part of his business. And that which is practised in private companies by persons vain of their theatrical talents, and which is vulgarly called *spouting*, is not considered as meriting to be classed as a separate division of public speaking. This last sort of exhibition is seldom more than the wretched imitations practised by vanity, ignorance, and idleness.

Recitation, as not implying the composition of the speaker, may be considered according to the order of the requisite acquirements in the place immediately after rhetorical reading; to all the requisites for which, recitation must add perfect memory and suitable gesture. In the different modes of reading, except in the instance of a person standing up to read a part in a play, the performer has been considered as using only the gestures of the head, of the body, and of the arms and hands: the lower limbs are either unmoved or concealed.[2] In recitation and all the other modes of public speaking, the whole person is, or may be, exhibited, and every part takes its share in the gesture. Recitation is properly the rhetorical delivery of poetical compositions and pieces of imagination, by a performer standing separate from the company. In its first degrees, recitation is practised in private, as a rhetorical exercise by young persons; in its more perfect degrees, it is exhibited in public, as a very high species of dramatic entertainment. The great variety in poetical composition, and works of imagination, must afford equal variety for the modes of recitation. The simplest subjects are narratives and fables in which Quintilian tells us the Roman youth were first exercised; and the most difficult are Lyric Odes. These last are therefore selected for public entertainment by those who are considered competent to the task of delivering them with effect, which is indeed a task not a little arduous.[3]

---

[2] An old gentleman who was fond of dramatic readings, and had a good voice, but an uncouth person, used to say, " legs had nothing to do in the business."

[3] Martial with his usual point ridicules bad reciters :

Quem recitas, meus est, ô Fidentine, libellus ;

Sed, male cum recitas, incipit esse tuus. *Epig.* 39, *l.* i.

Declamation, which is properly a prose exercise composed by the speaker on some imaginary subject or occasion, on account of the requisite ability in composition as well as in the exercise of all the arts of delivery, may be considered as next in order above recitation. The ancient Roman orators bestowed extraordinary attention upon the composition and practice of declamation.[4] Cicero continued this exercise many years after he had arrived at the highest eminence as an orator, and after his example the most celebrated of the Roman orators followed the same plan, as has already been fully explained. The practice of declamation began however soon to fall into merited discredit, owing to the extravagant and unnatural imaginations of the Rhetoricians. They exhausted their talents in devising the most improbable and intricate cases as subjects to exercise the declamatory talents of their pupils, so that good sense became disgusted, and declamations were neglected. In order to be convinced of this, it is necessary only to look into the subjects of Seneca's declamations, or even into those of the elegant and correct Quintilian, whose high reputation does not depend on this part of his works.[5][6]

Though the practice of declamation either in the manner of

---

[4] *Sueton. de Claris Orator. c.* i. Already quoted.

[5] Sint ergo et ipsæ materiæ, quæ fingentur, quam simillimæ veritati: et declamatio in quantum maxime potest, imitetur eas actiones, in quarum exercitationem reperta est. Nam *magos* et *pestilentiam* et *responsa* et *sæviores tragicis novercas*, aliaque magis adhuc fabulosa frustra inter sponsiones et interdicta quæremus. *Quint. l.* ii. *c.* 10.

[6] Et ideo ego adolescentulos existimo in scholis stultissimos fieri, quia nihil ex iis, quæ in usu habemus, aut audiunt aut vident: sed piratas cum catenis in littore stantes, et tyrannos edicta scribentes, quibus imperent filiis, ut patrum suorum capita præcidant; sed responsa in pestilentia data, ut virgines tres aut plures immolentur. *Petron. Satyr. c.* i.

Cicero, or according to that of the rhetoricians, has not been expressly adopted in modern times, something similar may be found among us. The speaking societies set up at various times in London and in Dublin, and perhaps in other cities, have had the practice of declamation for their object. Imaginary subjects have been discussed and debated with all the interest of real occasion, and with all the efforts of declamation; and not unfrequently with considerable powers of eloquence. These societies operated as incentives to oratory, and awakened the love of eloquence, if they did not teach it. But of such societies we now hear no more : they are extinct along with the occasions which gave rise to them, as the fashion of the times in those days, or the interest of some individual proprietor of public rooms who thus wished to attract a crowd to his house ; and the danger of such meetings in the present days is a sufficient reason for discouraging them, so that we hear of no celebrated public places of this kind now.

One voluntary institution formed in those times, and for the same objects, the exercise of declamation, has survived. But it was formed in a high situation, and under higher auspices, and with truly classical objects, for the improvement of liberal youth in a great seminary of learning. This I trust will long survive and adorn my country with rising eloquence and classical taste; this institution is the Historical Society of the University of Dublin. It owed its existence originally to the spirit of a few of the students, one of whom is now at the head of the University. Perhaps the fashion of the day influenced them ; but the fostering care and discerning judgment of the heads of the University cherished, and encouraged the institution, and about the year 1770 they gave them laws and regulations, and appropriated, within the walls, for their meetings, elegant and commodious apartments fitted up like a little senate-house. From hence have issued the greater number of all the eloquent men who have since that period adorned our courts of law, our pulpits, and our parliament. From that period the Historical Society flourished till the late civil convulsions in our unfortunate country rendered it necessary, in order to curb the licentious spirit which had begun to manifest itself even among the pupils of the University, to put a stop to the meetings for a time, and to revise the laws. The Historical Society was opened again under stricter regulations in the year 1795, and it is at this day flourishing in all the acquirements of classic knowledge, classic eloquence, morality, loyalty, and religion; a nursery of oratory, learning, and taste; and an honour to the parent University.

In our schools debates on questions of ancient history are conducted under the direction of the masters, and the talents of boys are early exercised in composition and declamation; and chosen passages are also recited frequently from the most celebrated poets. So that in modern education nothing is neglected which can contribute to form the orator; and nothing in fact is wanting to make him perfect, except his own labours and exertions after the period of education is ended both at school and at the university. Here commences certainly the most arduous part of the labour of a public speaker, but here, most unaccountably, labour often is relinquished.

CHAPTER VII.

OF ORATORY.

CHAPTER VII.

Of Oratory.

ORATORY, which is public speaking on real and interesting occasions, is the most splendid object of all literary exertion, and the highest scope of all the study and practice of the art. To oratory belongs whatever the perfection of composition can produce, as well as all which the perfection of delivery can externally recommend and enforce. Oratory is the power of reasoning united to the various arts of persuasion, presented by external grace, and by the whole energy of the human powers.[1] Reasoning

---

[1] The power of eloquence is represented, as Lucian tells us, by the Gallic Hercules. This strong old man held his audience by chains of gold, and amber issuing from his lips and attached to their ears. Raphael has given a fine sketch of this subject, which is published in one of the volumes of the Orleans Gallery.

Καίτοι τὸ παραδοξότατον ἐδέπω ἔφην τῆς εἰκόνος. ὁ γὰρ δὲ γέρων Ἡρακλῆς ἐκεῖνος ἀνθρώπων πάμπολύ τι πλῆθος ἕλκει ἐκ τῶν ὤτων ἅπαντας δεδεμένες. δεσμὰ δὲ εἰσιν οἱ σειραὶ λεπταὶ χρυσῆ καὶ ἠλέκτρα εἰργασμέναι, ὅρμοις ἐοικυῖαι τοῖς καλλίςοις. Καὶ ὅμως ἀφ' ἕτως ἀσθενῶν ἀγόμενοι, ἔτε δρασμὸν βαλεύεσι, δυνάμενοι ἂν εὐμαρῶς, ἔτε ὅλως ἀντιτείνεσιν. . . . ἀλλὰ φαιδροὶ ἕπονται καὶ γεγηθότες. . . . . . εἰ δὲ γέρων πεποίηται, μὴ θαυμάσῃς· μόνος γὰρ ὁ λόγος ἐν γήρᾳ φιλεῖ ἐντελῆ ἐπδείκνυσθαι τὴν ἀκμὴν, ἔιγε ἀληθῆ ὑμῶν οἱ ποιηταὶ λέγεσιν.

Ὅτι μὲν αἱ τῶν ὁπλοτέρων φρένες ἠερέθονται.

Τὸ δὲ γῆρας ἔχει τι λέξαι τῶν νέων σοφώτερον.　　*Luc. Hercules.*

Lucian here quotes Hom. Il. Γ. 108, but not correctly. He adds, that the Gallic Hercules is represented as advanced in years, because eloquence does not arrive at perfection in early life.

divested of rhetorical composition and of rhetorical delivery becomes strict demonstration. Such reasoning is found in logic, mathematics, evidences of facts, and law arguments. Reasoning in this sense is distinct from oratory: both indeed alike aim at bringing over other men to their opinions, but by different means. Reasoning appeals to the understanding alone; oratory deals with the passions also. Reasoning proceeds directly to the truth, and exhibits it in the simplest language. Oratory chooses the most favourable view of the subject, engages the attention of the hearer by the detail of circumstances, interests him by the colouring which he gives them, delights him by ornament, and, having won his favourable attention, appeals at once to his understanding and to his heart. When the subject admits of demonstration; reasoning is the most powerful, it is irresistible: but when strict demonstration cannot be had, oratory has then the advantage. And since in a very few of the most interesting enquiries which occupy the attention of men, strict demonstration can be obtained, so the demand for the talents of the orator is frequent and indispensable in the business of life. Reasoning is therefore applied principally to philosophical research, and to objects of science: oratory to the interests of men, and to objects admitting choice. It is an advantage which oratory possesses above reasoning, that oratory constantly avails itself of reasoning, where it can be applied; but strict reasoning does not condescend to call in the aid of oratory.

The public speakers of Great Britain have long been celebrated as excellent reasoners; their orators have been few. For this various reasons have been assigned; the truest perhaps may be indolence with respect to the requisite labour, and inattention to the high value of eloquence: as to natural inability, every idea of such an impediment is to be rejected as no less false, than unworthy of a learned and illustrious people. An extreme attachment to every thing which bears the appearance of demonstration may also in part account for the paucity of orators among us. Accurate reasoners affect to despise the assistance of oratory, and to consider truth and reason, when fairly presented, sufficient to make their own way. If sophistry could never delude under the pretence of demonstration, and if men were constituted without passions, reason would indeed be sufficiently powerful; but the passions hold such a dangerous correspondence with the understanding, that mere reason cannot always vindicate the truth: therefore the aid of eloquence is required in order to expose their treachery: and it were well for mankind if the triple alliance of reason, truth, and eloquence, proved always victorious.

Our public speakers, it has been often remarked, content themselves with reasoning well; and, owing to some of the causes mentioned, indolence, inattention, and the want of splendid examples, aim at no higher excellence, and stop short of eloquence. The true foundation of oratory, no doubt, is sound logic; but then it should be remembered that it is only the foundation; and, that, to complete the plan, the superstructure, with all its accommodations, and with all its ornaments, is wanting. To be an orator is more difficult than to be a reasoner, and demands in addition many other talents and perfections both natural and acquired. The consummate orator is therefore rare, and a wonder in every age and in every country :[2,3,4] And perhaps Demosthenes in Athens, and Cicero in Rome, were the only perfect orators (if even they reached perfection) whom the world has yet seen. But there are many degrees of excellence far below theirs, and below perfection, by reaching any of which, a public speaker may acquire considerable fame and honour. The high degrees of excellence, should a man aspire to them, can be attained only by those whom nature has endowed with great abilities, and who attempt perfection itself. For this object long and laborious exertion must be made, but the very effort will bring its adequate reward in every stage, and will carry the aspiring mind further and further beyond the dull boundaries of mediocrity, and place him within the regions of honourable excellence.

Among the many who have taken this view both of the subject of eloquence in general and of national eloquence, perhaps the authority of none will be admitted with greater deference than that of Mr. Hume.

---

[2] Vere mihi hoc videor esse dicturus, ex omnibus iis, qui in harum artium studiis liberalissimis sint, doctrinisque versati, minimam copiam poetarum egregiorum extitisse; atque in hoc ipso numero, in quo perrarò exoritur aliquis excellens, si diligenter et ex nostrorum et ex Græcorum copia comparare voles, multo tamen pauciores oratores, quam poëtæ boni reperientur. *Cic. de Orat. l.* i. *c.* 4.

[3] Ac mihi quidem sæpenumero in summos homines ac summis ingeniis præditis intuenti, quærendum esse visum est, quid esset, cur plures in omnibus artibus, quam in dicendo admirabiles extitissent. . . . . . . sic facillime, quanta oratorum sit, semperque fuerit, paucitas, judicabit. *Cic. de Orat. l.* 1. *c.* 2.

[4] Non quæritur mobilitas linguæ, non celeritas verborum, non denique ea, quæ nobis non possumus fingere, facies, vultus, sonus. In oratore autem acumen dialectorum, sententiæ philosophorum, verba propè poetarum, memoria jurisconsultorum, vox tragœdorum, gestus penè summorum actorum est requirendus. *Cic. de Orat. l.* i. *c.* 28.

" In ancient times," says this acute philosopher and learned writer, " no work of genius was thought to require so great parts " and capacity, as the speaking in public; and some eminent " writers have pronounced the talents, even of a great poet or " philosopher, to be of an inferior nature to those, which are " requisite for such an undertaking. Greece and Rome pro- " duced, each of them, but one accomplished orator; and what- " ever praises the other celebrated speakers might merit, they " were still esteemed much inferior to these great models of " eloquence. . . . .

. . . . " Of all the polite and learned nations, England alone " possesses a popular government, or admits into the legisla- " ture such numerous assemblies as can be supposed to lie " under the dominion of eloquence. But what has England to " boast of in this particular? in enumerating the great men " who have done honour to our country, we exult in our poets " and philosophers; but what orators are ever mentioned? or " where are the monuments of their genius to be met with? " there are found indeed in our histories, the names of several " who directed the resolutions of our Parliament: but neither " themselves nor others have taken the pains to preserve their " speeches; and the authority which they possessed seems to " have been owing to their experience, wisdom, or power, more " than to their talents for oratory. At present there are above " half a dozen speakers in the two houses, who, in the judg- " ment of the public, have reached very near the same pitch of " eloquence; and no man pretends to give any one the pre- " ference above the rest. This seems to me a certain proof that " none of them have attained much beyond a mediocrity in their

" art, and that the species of eloquence, which they aspire to, gives
" no exercise to the sublimer faculties of the mind, but may be
" reached by ordinary talents, and a slight application. A
" hundred cabinet-makers in London can work a table or chair
" equally well, but no one poet can write verses with such
" spirit and elegance as Mr. Pope.

" We are told that when Demosthenes was to plead, all
" ingenious men flocked to Athens from the most remote parts
" of Greece, as to the most celebrated spectacle of the world.[5]
" At London you may see men sauntering in the court of re-
" quests, while the most important debates are carrying on in
" the two houses; and many do not think themselves suffi-
" ciently compensated for the losing of their dinners, by all
" the eloquence of our most celebrated speakers."[6]

It has been already observed, and it may here be permitted
to repeat the observation, that the manner, in which a composition is intended to be delivered, influences altogether the spirit
of it. When it is to be read merely as a dry dissertation (which,
among us is not unfrequent), the writer does not attempt any
thing like rhetorical expression, or eloquent arrangement. Far
from it; if even a figure or a brilliant thought should occur to
him, he rejects it as not of a piece, or in the language of Sterne,

---

[5] Ne illud quidem intelligunt, non modo ita memoriæ proditum esse, sed ita necesse
fuisse, cum Demosthenes dicturus esset, ut concursus, audiendi causa, ex tota Græcia fierent.
At cum isti Attici dicunt, non modo à corona (quod est ipsum miserabile) sed etiam ab
advocatis relinquuntur. *Cic. de Claris Orat.*

[6] Hume's Essays, 13.

as " intended for another man;" and if in his researches on his subject, he meets with any thing beautiful as well as illus- trative, he strips it of its ornaments, and clothes it in the plain garb of household labour. He blushes to introduce a figure too elegant to be reckoned of his society, and which he knows not how to present as he ought. To be able to write with spirit a rhetorical composition, which a man is to pronounce himself, he must also feel his own ability to deliver it with spirit.[7] And therefore the ignorance or neglect of rhetorical delivery must be considered as one great impediment to the progress of eloquence.

Another impediment to eloquence, as being an impediment to just and graceful delivery; may be reckoned the local posi- tion of our public speakers. The great schools of oratory from whence our most celebrated speakers proceed to the grand council of the nation, the houses of parliament; are the bar and the pulpit. The local position of a public speaker at the bar, is most unfavourable for the general practice of gesture, crowded as he is, and embarrassed by benches and desks, and placed below the judge and the jury, whom he is principally to address. The local situation of the preacher is not much better; he is enclosed nearly as high as his breast, and bolstered up with cushions in a narrow pulpit, from which he generally reads his discourse, with his face almost close to his book, whilst

---

[7] Omnium sententiarum gravitate, omnium verborum ponderibus est utendum. Accedat oportet actio varia, vehemens, plena animi, plena spiritûs, plena doloris, plena veritatis, *Cic. de Orat. l.* ii. *c.* 17.

little more than his head and shoulders can be seen. Such a place of confinement is not favourable for the graces or energies of delivery. In the houses of parliament indeed, such as think proper, have sufficient opportunity to stand forth, and to bring into effect every power of oratory. But the habits of those, from whom most might be expected, are already formed by the bar or the pulpit; and they make little efforts to adorn or to enforce their arguments; except when it happens, that the speaker becomes so animated by the earnestness of his ardor, that gesture is irresistible, and he is compelled to call in its assistance, in order to enable him to discharge the full feelings of his mind. Then he repeats again and again some one energetic, and it may be awkward gesture, with which his auditors soon become familiar, then weary, and disgusted; and which at last is altogether disregarded; or if at any time thought upon, is pardoned as his manner. But this is sorry praise in that art, to which Demosthenes gave the first place in oratory !

How far, or whether at all, any regular practice of gesture may hereafter be thought worthy of attention at the bar or in Parliament, I do not even conjecture. Most of the business of the bar, and much also of the business of Parliament, depends upon circumstances, with which oratory has, or ought to have, little concern. Facts, evidences, law, rights, and logical deductions, are the general enquiries of the barrister: and when he is borne out by the force of these, it is of little consequence to his client how he manages his cause. Because, although his arrangement may not be good, though his language be incorrect and vulgar, and his delivery uncouth and barbarous;[8] if he produce such matter he will be heard with attention, the judge will sift the wheat from the chaff, and he must succeed. But neither does the weight of evidence always lie in one scale, nor are the courts of justice always restricted to mere legal investigation. Occasions occur, not unfrequently, both there and in Parliament, wherein all that is valuable to men in this life, may depend on the powers of the orator: on such occasions, the rude and vulgar speaker is cautiously passed over, and eloquence is purchased as the pearl of price.[9]

The low and immediate interests of men engage their attention in many cases so deeply, that it is of little consequence in what manner they are discussed or recommended; the appetite

---

[8] Marmontel is of opinion, that the great truths of religion have sufficient influence when simply delivered, as have the important matters relative to property or to the state. But though this may be true as he states it, there is reason to fear, that not every audience, among *us at least,* is so docile and obedient to the preacher; among sectaries such a preacher is favourably heard.

Mais dans un discours où la religion annonce des vérités terribles; dans un conseil national, où s'agitent les grands intérêts de l'état; dans un barreau, où devant les juges, esclaves de la loi, on plaide pour l'honneur, pour la fortune, ou pour la vie d'un citoyen; les accessoires cédent au fond; la forme extérieure de l'éloquence, le style, l'élocution, l'action de l'orateur ne sont plus de la même importance; et celui qui a le talent d'instruire, de prouver, d'émouvoir, n'a plus besoin des dons de plaire. Peutêtre même un air austere, inculte, et negligé est-il ce qui convient le mieux à un orateur des communes, comme à un bon missionaire; et partout, même sous les plus belles formes de la diction et de l'action, le premier attribut de l'éloquence et le plus essentiel, c'est l'air de la verité. Rien n'est persuasif que ce qui paroit naturel. *Marmontel Elémens de Littérature; art. Orateur. p.* 146.

9 Nam quid ego de actione ipsa plura dicam? quæ motu corporis, quæ gestu, quæ vultu, quæ vocis conformatione, ac varietate moderanda est: quæ sola per se ipsa quanta sit, histrionum lævis ars et scena declarat: in qua cum omnes in oris et vocis et motus moderatione elaborent, quis ignorat, quam pauci sint fuerintque, quos æquo animo spectare possimus? *Cic. de Orat. l.* i. *c.* 5.

G g

is too keen to be fastidious; and the cloud must indeed be dense through which each man cannot see his own interests distinctly.[10][11] It is not so with respect to the higher, but more remote interests of men. They must be judiciously presented, or they disgust. The preacher who has to address the higher classes will be deserted if he deliver wholesome truths in a homely style. His composition must be correct, and his delivery must not offend by vulgarity, else he fails almost completely in the object of his labour. But if he possess talents and industry, what a field of eloquence is open before him! the universal and most important interests of mankind! far beyond those for which the thunder of Demosthenes rolled in Athens, far beyond those for which Cicero shook the senate-house in Rome. It is for him to rouse his auditors to a valiant resistance of the most formidable slavery, of the tyranny which is set up within a man's own bosom: and to exhort his hearers to maintain the liberty, the life, and the hopes of the whole human race for ever. These subjects of the preacher, in all their connections, and in all their divisions, form such themes for eloquence as never can be exhausted, and as can never fail to meet an audience deeply interested in the discussion, wherever mankind are to be found.

---

[10] Sæpe ex me requiris, Juste Fabi, cur cum priora sæcula tot eminentium oratorum ingeniis gloriaque effloruerint, nostra potissimum ætas, deserta, ac laude eloquentiæ orbata, vix nomen ipsum oratoris retineat: neque enim ita appellamus nisi antiquos; horum autem temporum, diserti, causidici et advocati et patroni et quidvis potius quam oratores vocantur. *Tacitus Dial. de Causis Cor. Eloq.*

[11] Tumque ego hac eadem opinione adductus, scripsi etiam illud . . . disertos me cognosse nonnullos, eloquentem adhuc neminem: quod eum statuebam disertum, qui posset satis acute atque dilucide apud mediocres homines ex communi quadam hominum opinione dicere: eloquentem vero, qui mirabilius et magnificentius augere posset atque ornare quæ vellet, omnesque omnium rerum quæ ad dicendum pertinuerent, fontes animo ac memoria contineret. *Cic. de Orat. l. i. c. 21.*

But luxury and prosperity indispose the mind for such enquiries, and render fastidious those who stand most in need of them. So long as health and prosperity endure, what can rouse them? the voice of eloquence alone. This is the field of eloquence, which merits the highest cultivation, and which has produced the most excellent fruit. In this great field, eloquence has already been brought almost to such perfection as may be said to vie with all that has been heard in Greece and Rome: and to this perfection could I wish it were carried again, and that in these countries. The first of those great Christian orators was John the Patriarch of Constantinople, emphatically and justly sirnamed Chrysostom, a man learned in all the precious literature of antiquity, and educated by the most celebrated rhetorician, Libanius of Antioch, whose Christian eloquence is enriched by all the vigour and taste of philosophical and classic elegance. What a model! and yet how little is he read! [12]—Basil and Gregory, his contemporaries, emulated his eloquence. For a long period the cruel acrimony of controversy banished pure and Christian oratory; nor did it revive till the splendid æra of Lewis XIV. in France. The learned Bossuet Bishop of Meaux, Bourdaloue, and Massillon, and we may add Flechier, excelled in pulpit eloquence, and in Holland among the reformed, Saurin. [13]

To them Great Britain has to compare the manly vigour, the correct reasoning, and the pure gospel excellence of many

---

[12] Whole pages from Chrysostom might at this day be introduced in our pulpits with the best possible effect, particularly the last division of his subject, in which he makes the *moral application.* (ηθικα.)

[13] See Abbé Maury upon Eloquence, who in the present age is himself a most eloquent preacher.

of her preachers; but little of eloquence. Her time is not yet arrived; no great pulpit orator among her many learned and pious divines has been celebrated in Great Britain. One has appeared in Ireland. That he is a great orator, the manner in which he is attended will alone evince. He, to use the emphatical expression of our great Parliamentary orator,[14] " has broken in upon the slumbers of the pulpit;" he is truly an extraordinary preacher, but yet cannot be esteemed a model for general imitation. His genius is too much *sui generis,* ardent and uncontrolled; his manner zealous and decided, and his doctrine rigid. But his composition is excellent, his arrangement luminous, his invention happy, his style pure and admirably varied, often most simple, and often magnificent; his

---

[14] Volo hoc oratori contingat, ut cum auditum sit eum esse dicturum, locus in subselliis occupetur, compleatur tribunal, gratiosi scribæ sint in dando et cedendo loco, corona multiplex, judex erectus: cum surgit is, qui dicturus sit, significetur à corona silentium, deinde crebræ assensiones, multæ admirationes: risus, cum velit; cum velit, fletus : ut, qui hæc procul videat, etiamsi, quid agatur, nesciat: at placere tamen et in scena esse Roscium intelligat. Hæc cui contingant, eum scito Attice dicere, ut de Pericle audivimus, ut de Hyperide, ut de Æschine, de ipso quidem Demosthene maxime. *Cic. de Clar. Orat. c.* 84.

All these circumstances, and others stronger than these (perhaps owing to the greater rarity of perfect orators among us), attend the great preacher alluded to. They crowd to hear him who on no other occasion appear within the walls of a church, men of the world who have other pursuits, and men of profession who have not time, physicians, lawyers, actors. The pressure of the crowd is immense. Guards are obliged to be stationed without to keep off from our largest churches the overflowing curiosity which cannot contribute adequately to the great charities for which he generally preaches. The parishioners resign their pews to the officers appointed to accommodate often the Lord Lieutenant and the court, at all times the high nobility of both sexes, archbishops and bishops, the great judges, the great law officers, the great Parliamentary orators, the clergy, and all who wish to be instructed or to be moved and delighted by his eloquence. The sums collected always exceed any thing known on similar occasions.

If this man be not a great orator, Cicero was mistaken.

[15] Since that was written, the Imperial Parliament has passed an honourable judgment upon the talents of our Irish parliamentary orator.

figures are always just, and frequently sublime. His memory is perfect, his fluency uninterrupted, his voice well managed, his action though not altogether graceful, yet various and highly energetic. The eloquence of the pulpit has never among us been carried to such perfection, nor have we heard of any preacher in Great Britain to be compared with him in this respect.*

The peculiar character of the church of England does not encourage the preacher to assume to himself that sort of authority with which the Roman Catholic considers himself invested, and deprives him of many topics which are to the other fruitful in eloquence.[16] The English preacher addresses his equals on subjects equally important to all, with a tempered sobriety of discussion, which influences the understanding, but does not excite the feelings. A sermon, with us, is an appeal to the equal reason of our hearers, and to their equal information; the Scriptures and their interpretation are open to all alike, and we invite them to draw at the source.'[17][18] And so great is the

---

* Our great preacher has been removed to a better world since the above tribute was paid to his extraordinary talents. It might be improved, but I leave it as originally written. November 19th, 1805.

[16] He is also deprived of many of those topics which are to the other fruitful in eloquence.† Except in express discourses on evidences, the peculiar doctrines of the Gospel are referred to with modesty and reserve, and its sanctions are looked upon with awe. The language upon these subjects is chastened and restrained, and were it on them to be dogmatic, to break out into any attempt at the sublime, it would rather create disgust. The controversial discourses long persisted in, have also given a cast rather of dialectics than of eloquence to many of the earlier pulpit compositions of the church of England. This is charged to our account, but need be so no longer; those questions are at rest.

[17] Not so the French preachers; they broadly and directly undertake proofs of all those

† Such are fasting, pennance, virginity, martyrdom, and all the opinions which lead to seclusion from the common duties of life, the high-wrought enthusiam that shuts up in the cloister, and drives into the desert, which makes of men more than men, and affords topics for enflaming the imagination upon ideal perfection.

beauty and moral excellence of many of the best discourses
of our English preachers, that if the alternative were to be
chosen, either of writing in the manner of the best French
preachers, or of adhering to the style of the best among our
own, we ought not to hesitate a moment to determine not to
make any change.   But we are not put to this alternative; it is
possible to unite the excellence of both manners, if we choose to
undertake the necessary labour.   All that is most desirable in
pulpit eloquence might be acquired by our preachers, by a little
addition to the zeal and ardour of their manner," and by

---

doctrines which are most controverted, in such a manner as to overturn the faith of those
they address, if they can reason at all.

Let any man accustomed to the good sense and strict reasoning of the English divines,
and the unassuming sobriety of their discussion, the dropping word that penetrates the
hardest heart, look into any of the celebrated French preachers, particularly Bourdaloue
upon the mysteries which he talks of much, or any other doctrine which he undertakes to
prove, and he will probably rest contented with the manner of his own church.

[18] The French composition in sermons turns upon quaint deductions from the mysteries
of the Christian Religion, and upon severe and rigid doctrines built upon hard interpretations of Scripture; on these grounds they are most offensive to an English reader.   Where
their preachers take the broad and true grounds of the morality of the Gospel, they are
often highly and truly eloquent; they always write in the form of orations.

The English preachers, instead of the form of an oration, almost universally confine
themselves to that of a dissertation.   If the subject be argumentative, it is dry ; if doctrinal,
it turns upon evidences ; if upon morals, it is well enforced, sometimes, floridly and poeti-
cally, but seldom rhetorically : it has every excellence except this.

The French preachers on their mysterious doctrines are miserable reasoners, borrowing
their best arguments from the authority of the fathers, and their other arguments from con-
ceits and forced interpretations.

[19] I should have read it ten times better, sir, answered Trim, but that my heart was so
full.—That was the very reason, Trim, replied my father, which has made thee read the
sermon as well as thou hast done ; and if the clergy of our church, continued my father,
addressing himself to *Dr. Slop*, would take part in what they deliver, as deeply as this poor
fellow hath done,—as their compositions are fine,—[I deny it, quoth Dr. Slop]—I maintain
it,—that the eloquence of our pulpits, with such subjects to inflame it, would be a model
for the whole world :—But, alas ! continued my father, and I own it, sir, with sorrow, that,
like French politicians in this respect, what they gain in the cabinet they lose in the field.—

due attention to rhetorical composition, and rhetorical delivery.[20] Both must go together: and both united to truth and
good sense, would be attended with every desirable effect. They
would awaken the inattentive, stimulate the fastidious, engage
the public feelings, and take away from our churches the reproach of coldness and languor.[21] How powerful this ardor is
to excite others, may be observed in the zeal with which sectaries are attended who have often nothing else to recommend
their discourses. The timid, the feeble, and the ignorant may
be addressed in the language of terror: but a people whose
minds are cultivated with all that knowledge and art can give,
a nation of philosophers, requires to be influenced in another
manner; they must be convinced by reason and evidence;
they must be persuaded by an appeal to those feelings which
are originally wrought into the texture of the human breast;

'Twere a pity, quoth my uncle, that this should be lost. I like the sermon wen, replied my
father,—'tis dramatic,—and there is something in that way of writing, when skilfully
managed, which catches the attention.—We preach much in that way with us, said Dr.
Slop.—I know that very well, said my father,—but in a tone and manner, which disgusted
Dr. Slop full as much as his assent, simply, could have pleased him.—*Tristram Shandy*,
c. 17, *Vol. II. p.* 212.

[20] Une observation assez singuliere, c'est que le commun des auditeurs regarde encore plus
le predicateur qu'il ne l'écoute : les yeux ont leur maniere d'entendre, et fatiguent moins
que l'ouie. Il importe donc *de peindre la parole et de parler aux yeux. Besplas. Eloquence
de la Chaire, p.* 345.

[21]
   In point of sermons, 'tis confest
   Our English clergy make the best ;
   But this appears, we must confess,
   Not from the pulpit but the press.
   They manage with disjointed skill,
   The matter well, the manner ill ;
   And, what seems paradox at first,
   They make the best, and preach the worst.   *Byrom*

and they must be excited by the taste of high wrought composition, and by that just and magnificent eloquence which
adorns the truth, and is capable of charming the ear of refinement itself."[22]

The paucity of orators in the fertile and magnificent field of
religious discourses, particularly in Great Britain and Ireland,
induces enquiry into the probable causes. Want of talents
cannot be among those causes, because no where are higher
talents to be found. Neither can they be owing to deficiency
in learning and taste, for it may with truth be asserted that
Great Britain is the foremost in literature of all the nations
upon earth: of which the works of learning that daily issue from
the press give incontrovertible proof. The want of example, is
the principal cause; and consequently the difficulty of breaking
away from the beaten path, in favour of which, habit is pre-
judiced. But more of this deficiency in eloquence is to be
attributed to the custom of reading the sermons, which has
obtained exclusively in the church of England.[23] The compo-

---

[22] Tria autem præstare debet pronunciatio: conciliet, persuadeat, moveat; quibus
natura cohæret, ut etiam delectet. Conciliatio fere aut commendatione morum, (qui nescio
quomodo ex voce etiam atque actione pellucent) aut orationis suavitate constat. Persua-
dendi vis asseveratione, quæ interim plus ipsis probationibus valet. *An ista* (inquit Callido
Cicero) *si vera essent sic a te dicerentur?* et, *tantum abest, ut inflammares nostros animos,
somnum isto loco vix tenebamus.* Fiducia igitur appareat et constantia, utique si auctoritas
subest. Movendi autem ratio aut in representandis est, aut imitandis affectibus. *Quint.
l.* xi. *c.* 3.

[23] Pliny the younger had been desired by his friend Cerealis to read an oration of his
before some of his friends. He is aware of the disadvantages, and thus represents them,
l. ii. *ep.* 19. *Cereali suo.*

Neque enim me præterit, actiones, quæ recitantur, impetum, omnem calorem ac prope
nomen suum perdere. . . . . ad hoc, dicentis gestus, incessus, discursus etiam,

sition is suited to the talent of reading, which is not always highly improved, and the reading again is suited to the composition. Thus they mutually influence each other, and fashion has bound up in chains of ice, the warmth and the eloquence of our country. We do not always hear a sermon read impressively, but seldom indeed delivered rhetorically. To relinquish altogether the custom of reading sermons, would perhaps be on the whole an injurious innovation; even were it practicable. Reading is well calculated for examining the evidences of religion, for the discussion of moral duties, and for the explanation of difficult passages in Scripture. But without attempting any alteration in this so long established mode, it might be possible, were a change made only in the form of the pulpit, to bring about a most advantageous improvement to the style of preaching: so as to place the reading of a discourse almost upon the footing of equal advantage with the delivery of it from memory.

The pulpit, in its present form (as has been already observed), is most unfavourable for delivery.[24] If then, instead of such a mass of buildings as is seen to encumber our churches—the clerk's desk, surmounted by the reading desk, and that by a towering

---

omnibusque motibus animi consentaneus vigor corpris. Unde accidit ut hi qui *sedentes* agunt, quamvis illis maxima ex parte supersint eadem quæ stantibus, tamen hoc quod sedent quasi debilitentur et deprimantur. Recitantium vero præcipua pronunciationis adjumenta, oculi, manus, præpediuntur, quo minus mirum est, si auditorum intentio languescit, nullis extrinsecus aut blandimentis capta aut aculeis excitata.

This whole passage, particularly the latter part, is a complete description of the English preacher, in ordinary.

[24]   Parte ferox, ardensque oculis, et sibila colla
        Arduus attollens ; pars vulnere clauda retentat
        Nexantem nodos, seque in sua membra plicantem.   *Æn.* 5, 277.

H h

pulpit, and that again with the sounding board, together with its cushions, its staircase, and all its apparatus accommodated only for repose,—if these were totally removed, and in their place a platform were erected of convenient size and height, the preacher might stand on that, and deliver thence his discourse with grace, and with effect.[25] This situation, which at first appears novel, differs little from that of the reader at the communion table, whose position has always a grand and decorous effect: because no close panels cut off the half of his person; but the whole is seen with all possible advantage.[26]

The platform should have either rails at the back, and steps at the three sides next the congregation to give the position an air of safety and gradual elevation, or if it were preferred, might have the steps at the back, and a low rail enclosing the three sides.[27] Upon this platform should the preacher stand

---

[25] As the preacher, even according to our custom, stands in delivering his discourse, there does not appear to be any necessity for a system of cushions to induce him to loll upon, nor, as he is clothed to the feet, for any enclosure to conceal his lower limbs, nor yet is any support necessary for his writing, which is never too heavy to be held in the hand.

[26] Sterne's picture of Trim is highly suitable for the character he has employed to read; but St Paul's, by Raphael, is much more becoming to the preacher.

[27] Marmontel approves of the form of the pulpits as they are used in France and in England. He thinks they restrain the extravagance of the preachers of his country: for a contrary reason I should prefer the form of the ancient tribune, or that of the pulpits of Italy, in order to give more freedom to the action of our preachers, who are disposed to be too tame and cold.

C'est peutêtre une raison pour nous de ne pas regretter l'espace de la tribune ancienne et celui des chaires d'Italie. On voit par un mot de Ciceron que les orateurs de son temps abusoient quelquefois de la liberté de leurs movemens: *rarus incessus*, recommandoit il, *nec ita longus. excursio moderata, eaque rara. Orat.*

On dit que les prédicateurs d'Italie auroient souvent besoin de la même leçon. En France, la forme de nos chaires, et la situation de nos avocats au barreau, ne laisse que l'action du buste: c'en est assez pour les orateurs eloquens, et c'en est beaucoup trop encore pour les mauvais *déclamateurs. Elémens de Littérature, artic. Declamation Oratoire, p.* 290.

(as St. Paul is so finely represented in the Cartoons of Raphael); he might hold his sermon in his left hand, and with his right in general make his gestures. Sometimes he might use both, sometimes use with fine effect his hand and sermon. And if the preacher should prefer to pronounce his discourse without notes, he would in this situation, and clad in the decent and graceful robes which are the proper habit of our ministers, be enabled to practise with advantage every power of delivery, and every dignified and suitable gesture.[28,29]

The platform should be raised about as high as the breasts of the congregation, and not be placed at such a giddy elevation as should give the idea of danger, nor boxed up, as if some juggling were to be performed within. It should be railed like the communion table, and be in all respects similar, only raised somewhat higher, and enclosing a smaller space. The furniture should be a chair for the preacher to sit in before or after

---

[28] Mr. Sheridan very freely condemns the form of the pulpit. *Art of Speaking, p.* 42. *Edit. Dub.*

The clergy have one considerable apology from the awkwardness of the place they speak from. A pulpit is, by its very make, necessarily destructive of all grace of attitude. What could even a Tully do in a tub, just big enough for him to stand in, immersed up to the arm pits, pillowing his chin upon its cushion, as Milton describes the sun upon the orient wave? but it is hardly to be expected, that this, or any other impropriety in sacred matters, of which there are many greater, should be altered. Errors in them, become, by long establishment, sacred. And I doubt not, but some of the narrower part of the clergy, as well as of the people, would think any other form of a pulpit, than the present, though much fitter for exhibiting the speaker to an advantage, an innovation likely to prove dangerous to religion, and, which is worse, to the church.

[29] An observation in the Dialogus de Oratoribus attributed to Tacitus, applies to our pulpits and to the bar. Quantum virium detraxisse orationi auditoria et tabularia credimus, in quibus jam fere plurimæ causæ explicantur? nam quomodo nobiles equos cursus et spatia probant; sic est aliquis oratorum campus, per quem nisi liberi et soluti ferantur, debilitatur ac frangitur eloquentia. *Dial. de Orat. c.* 39.

the sermon, and a cushion to kneel upon, with a small moveable reading desk or oratory holding a prayer book. A moveable or suspended branch would be necessary, if a discourse were to be delivered in the evening.

CHAPTER VIII.

ACTING.

Difference between the actor and the orator in the character sustained by each, and in the mode of action—Comparative rank of actors—The opera—The serious opera compared with tragedy—Causes of the imperfections in the construction and execution of the opera—Ideal perfection of the opera—Its general degree of perfection—The necessity and effects of fine acting in the opera.

CHAPTER VIII.

Of Acting.

As the different modes of public speaking, hitherto treated of, have been discriminated each from the former by some additional requisites; so, however evidently distinct acting may be from them all, it will not be improper, in order to carry on the uniformity of this plan, to examine acting also in the same view.

Acting is distinguished from oratory, both by the subject, the character of the speaker, and the manner. The actor is seldom supposed to deliver his own composition, so that his merit is generally considered separately from that of the part, which he sustains. But this just judgment is sometimes defeated by the illusion, which in the common eyes, identifies him with his part; because the actor appears as the very person represented by the dramatic writer. The orator, on the contrary, appears always in his own character. The actor's manner must be a close representation of the character he assumes, even as far as the very dress; he must imitate nature exactly, and in some cases exaggerate, in order to give the portrait more force. The orator, however various may be the tones of his voice, the expression of his countenance, and his gesture; and however various and strong the circumstances, he may have to represent, must guard himself against imitation; the limits allowed to such indulgence are very narrow; and if he transgress them in the smallest degree, he loses at once his dignity and his credit with his audience. The actor traverses the whole stage; as he is moved by passion, or by the circumstances of the scene. The orator is limited in the movement of his lower limbs, at most, to an occasional, single, step in advancing or retiring, or perhaps merely to a change of position of the feet.[1,2,3] The gesture of the actor is unrestrained, except that he is forbidden by the great master to " overstep the modesty of nature." But the liberty of the theatre would be licentiousness in the orator, and he is to guard himself carefully against it.[4] Although his action is required to be various and graceful, it is never to degenerate into triviality or affectation; and although it should be energectic, it should never transgress by extravagance: nor should he for a moment forget the importance of his subject, the solemnity of the place in which he speaks, the respect due to his audience, and the dignity of his own character.[5] Affectation altogether defeats

---

[1] Quintilian allows to his orator some degree of walking, differing from Cicero.

Procursio opportuna, brevis, moderata, rara. Conveniens etiam ambulatio quædam, propter immodicas laudationum moras: quanquam Cicero rarum incessum neque ita longam probat. Discursare vero, et, quod Domitius Afer de Sura Manlio dixit, *satagere*, ineptissimum: urbaneque Flavius Virginius interrogavit de quodam suo antisophista, *quot millia passuum declamasset. Quint. l.* xi. *c.* 3, &c. *vide infra.*

[2] The platform proposed instead of the pulpit should therefore not be large; lest the preacher should become liable to incur the reproach of the sophist. Quot millia passuum declamasset.

[3] Idemque motu sic utetur, nihil ut supersit in gestu. Status erectus et celsus: rarus incessus, nec ita longus: excursio moderata, eaque rara. *Cic. Orat.* 18.

[4] Dandum aliquid comœdo. . . . . Ne gestus quidem omnis ac motus a comœdis petendus est. Quanquam enim utrumque eorum ad quemdam modum præstare debet orator; plurimum tamen aberit a scenico, nec vultu, nec manu, nec excursionibus nimius. *Quin. l.* i. *c.* 11.

[5] Dans l'hypothese théâtrale, l'acteur est le personage même qui est malheureux,

the objects of the orator; by disgusting his audience; extra-vagance renders him ridiculous, and weakness gives him over to contempt. He loses all influence with his audience, who appears to have lost himself: for the power of self-government is indispensable to those who would govern the opinions of others. Even when an orator is moved to tears, there must appear adequate cause for such emotion, and the continuance must be only momentary, if he wish to escape the charge of imbecillity and its consequences, as has been already observed. And sincerity itself, that first of qualifications in an orator, loses all its influence, and becomes absolutely ridiculous unless ac-companied with a dignified self-possession. - This happens when

---

souffrant, tourmenté de telle passion : l'orateur, au contraire, n'est le plus souvent que l'ami, le confident, le temoin, le solliciteur, le defenseur de celui qui souffre. Alors il doit y avoir entre sa déclamation et celle de l'acteur la même différence que la nature a mise entre patir et compatir : or on sent bien que la compassion est une passion affoiblie ; ce n'est qu'un reflet de douleur. Celui qui fera la peinture d'une situation cruelle et désolante, l'exprimera des plus vives couleurs : l'expression de la parole n'a pour lui d'autres bornes que celles de la verité, que celles mêmes de la vraisemblance. Mais quant à la déclamation, elle doit se reduire, dans l'orateur, à ce qu'un tiers peut éprouver d'un malheur qui n'est pas le sien.

Supposé même que l'orateur plaide sa propre cause, ou qu'en parlant pour un autre que lui, il ne laisse pas d'exprimer la passion que lui est propre, comme l'indignation, la pitié, la douleur, encore ne doit il pas se livrer aux mêmes mouvemens que l'acteur du théâtre. Son premier soin doit être de conserver, soit dans la tribune, soit dans la chaire, soit au barreau, son caractere de dignité, de bienséance, d'organe de la verité, d'homme qui ne vient pas seulement émouvoir ou son auditoire ou son juge, mais l'instruire, et lui presenter l'honnête, l'utile, ou le juste. Il faut donc que dans les mouvemens les plus passionnés on s'ap-perçoive qu'il se possede dans tout son integrité. Ce qu'on voit dans les peroraisons de Cice-ron, où le douleur même qui lui arrache les larmes, est decente et majesteueuse: c'est qu'on voit dans les invectives de Demosthene, où, après apostrophe soudaine, rapide, et violente, il reprend de sang froid le fil de son récit, ou la chaine de son raisonnement; semblable à un sanglier qui d'un coup de defense éventre un dogue, et poursuit son chemin. Un orateur qui s'abandonne et qui s'égare, comme on en voit souvent, perd ses droits à la confiance; car on n'en doit aucune au désordre des passions. *Marmontel, Elémens de Littérature, Tom. II. p. 287.*

I i

an orator is carried beyond the bounds of manly indignation, and falls into the feeble vehemence of passion; or when he melts into tears without sufficient ground for such emotion.

To the actor the same precautions are not so necessary. If he conceive the character truly, he may represent it strongly, and he is limited by no restraint except the bounds of decency and of nature.

The dignity of the player's art consists in his ability to represent and sustain the higher and nobler passions and characters. For these reasons the tragic actor, who represents justly the manners and the feelings of a hero, has always been esteemed high in the rank of public speakers. The powers, the acquisitions and the taste of the man, who can adequately support such a character, must be rare and admirable, and he is classed next to the great orators. The actor, who performs the superior characters in common life, and who is therefore named the genteel comedian, ranks next to the tragedian.[6] The inferior actors hold a situation respectable according as their talents approach the highest cast, and descend in estimation as they verge towards vulgarity and buffoonery.

The opera, which adds the powers of music to the grandest

---

[6] Aristotle has given to tragedy the highest rank as to composition: but to comedy the reverse. What moderns name genteel comedy was not known in his day.

Ἐπεὶ δὲ μίμησίς ἐςιν ἡ Τραγῳδία βελτιόνων, ἡμᾶς δεῖ μιμεῖσθαι τὰς ἀγάθας εἰχονογράφας. *Arist. Poet. c. 14.*

Ἡ δὲ Κωμῳδία ἐςὶν ὥσπερ εἴπομεν, μίμησις φαυλοτέρων μὲν, ὰ μέντοι κατὰ πᾶσαν κακίαν, ἀλλὰ τᾶ αἰσχρᾶ ἐςὶ τὸ γελοῖον μάριον. *Arist. Poet. c. 5.*

tragic subjects, in order to awaken pity and terror, their peculiar feelings, according to the great philosopher, is the utmost effort of dramatic illusion.[7][8] And, were not the difficulties almost insurmountable, which impede its perfect execution, the opera would rank above tragedy itself. Along with all the requisites of the most perfect tragic actor, the first singer in the serious opera should be also possessed of the most exquisite taste and skill in music, together with all that nature can bestow upon the organ of the voice, and with all that art can give to bring it to perfection.[9] The rarity of such talents and acquirements is the first difficulty which opposes the perfection of the serious opera. But if this may be occasionally got over, others arise from the nature of the opera itself. The principal of these is the narrow limits to which the dialogue is restricted on account

---

[7] Οὐ μόνον τελείας ἐςὶ πράξεως ἡ μίμησις, (Τραγῳδία) ἀλλὰ καὶ φοβερῶν καὶ ἐλεεινῶν. *Arist. Poet. c. 9.*

[8] The manner of conducting the music of an opera gives it the power of great variety of expression. The ordinary course of the dialogue is carried on in recitativo, aided by various modulation according to the change of expression necessary to the subject. Where the expression requires stronger force, the recitativo accompanied is introduced with great effect. And where the highest effect is intended to impress a passion with irresistible and repeated force, the modulation of song is produced with all its pathos of cantabile or brilliancy of bravoura to excite the hearer, and to support the feelings of the performer.

[9] The theory of the perfection of the opera above all other dramatic entertainments is thus given by Count Algarotti:

Di tutti i modi, che, per creare nelle anime gentili il diletto, furono immaginati dall'uomo, forse il più ingegnoso e compito si è l'opera in musica. Niuna cosa nella formazione di essa fu lasciata indietro, niuno ingrediente, niun mezzo, onde arrivar si potesse al proposto fine. E ben si può asserire, che quanto di più attrattivo ha la poesia, quanto ha la musica, e la mimica, l'arte del ballo, e la pittura, tutto si collega nell'opera felicemente insieme ad allettare i sentimenti, ad ammaliare il cuore, e fare un dolce inganno alla mente. Se non che egli avviene dell'opera come degli ordigni della meccanica, che quanto più riescono composti, tanto più ancora si trovano a guastarsi soggetti. E però non sarebbe maraviglia, se cotesto ingegnoso ordigno, fatto di tanti pezzi, com' egli è, non sempre rispondesse al fin suo, ancorchè, a ben unire e congregare insieme ogni suo pezzo, venisse posta da coloro, che il governano, tutta la diligenza, e tutto lo studio. *Saggio sopra l'Opera in Musica, p.* 257, *Livorno.*

of the necessary prolongation of the music. Hence the sentiments of the interlocutors are necessarily curtailed, and do not admit of that variety of expression and of imagery which brings them with such vivacity to the feelings and understanding in tragedy: but for all this they principally depend on the vague and doubtful expression of the music. They are abridged in the expression of language, which is comprehensive and applicable to every complicated feeling of the passions, and they are dilated in the expression of the music, which is limited to the obscure and dubious representation of few sensations. Love and pity, sorrow and joy, terror and valour, are perhaps the principal passions to which musical expression can give considerable additional force. But even in the language chosen for these subjects, many words must be rejected, lest they should impede the execution of the music. In the Italian language, the best suited to musical expression of any known, and under the hand of the greatest poet of his age, the number of fine and sonorous words, which Metastasio was obliged constantly to reject from his dramas, amounted to many thousands.[10] Yet no want of power of expression is perceived. His scenes are only too much abridged, and under all this unnatural constraint, the fire and vigour of genuine poetry breaks out in every scene.

But the combinations of difficulty against the general excellence of the opera are wonderfully encreased by the necessity of the addition of musical composition, as well as of musical execution. So that the performer must equal the tragic actor in his art, as well as sustain the part of an admirable and accom-

---

[10] Baretti, in his preface to the Works of Metastasio, Genova 1772, says, that of 44,000 radical words of which the Italian language consists, the poet was restricted to the use of fewer than 7,000.

plished singer. And the composer of the music must in his ideas and execution rival the talents of the most excellent poet. This combination of difficulty must, in order to the absolute perfection of the opera, be supposed also to be got over in all its subordinate parts. The orchestra should be excellent, the dancers admirable, the dresses and decorations superb, and every person performing a character in the piece should be found capable of sustaining fully its musical and dramatic force. Were a serious opera thus composed, and thus represented; it would, to the lovers of the drama, and to the intelligent in music, afford, no doubt, the highest gratification. But such an entertainment is not calculated for the general ear, and in its best perfection, on account of the abridgment of the dialogue, must fall short of the deep and various interest which the merely recited tragedy is capable of inspiring. The union of all those talents, which we have mentioned, and their bearing thus upon a single point condensed into a focus, is a hopeless imagination; and therefore the opera will always rank below the dignity of tragedy. The utmost that can be expected, is that the ear shall sometimes, at the opera, be delighted with fine music executed by fine singers, moderately skilled in the habits of acting, and accompanied by a fine band, with the addition, to delight the eye, of splendid dresses, dances, and decorations. The poetry, the sublimest part of tragedy, merges in this apparatus, and ceases to be an object of regard. All interest in the progress of the action is lost on account of the difficulty of comprehending the dialogue delivered in recitative; " which is

---

[11]   Le vrai recitatif, sans appareil frivole
                Doit marcher, doit voler, ainsi que la parole.
                Pour lier l'action ce langage est formé,
                Et veut être chanté, bien moins que déclamé.   *D'Orat sur l'Opera.*

not intelligible even to native Italians, being too often articulated badly, of which a celebrated critic complains.[12] To this we must add the carelessness and even clamour of the audience, which is not chargeable on the nature of the opera itself; but upon the frequent repetition of the same entertainment till all become weary of it, when afterwards the favourite airs of the favourite singers appear alone to arrest the attention. So that in an opera there appear only certain brilliant points by which the attention of the audience can be excited, all the rest seems as if calculated to induce conversation, or contrived in order to prolong the occasions of polite intercourse.[13] In the entertain-

---

[12] La buona composizion musica per altro, avutosi riguardo all' effetto che dee produrre, non è il tutto; questo dipende in gran parte anche dal modo, con che ella viene eseguita da' cantori. E potrebbe assai facilmente intervenire, che un buon compositore fosse un buon capitano alla testa di un cattivo esercito: con la differenza che il capitano buono può far buoni i soldati; ma il maestro di musica non può lusingarsi di tanto co' suoi virtuosi. A' più di loro non è mai caduto in pensiero quanto sarebbe prima di ogni altra cosa necessario, che imparassero à ben pronunziare la propria lingua, a bene articolare, e farsi intendere, e a non iscambiare, come è lor vezzo, un vocabolo con l' altro. Niente vi ha di più sconcio di quella loro comune pratica di mangiarsi le finali, e nel tenero lor palato dimezzar le parole. Tanto che se uno non ha dinanzi gli occhi il libretto dell'opera, non ricevi per gli orecchi impressione alcuna distinta di quanto e' cinguettano. *Algarotti Saggio sopra l'Opera,* p. 287.

[13] Ed ecco per avventura la principal sorgente di quella noia sovrana, che signoreggia alla rappresentazione delle nostre opere Contro alla quale si suole cercare il rimedio di quel parlottar continuo, del far visite, del cenare, e insino a quel rimedio, che bene spesso è peggiore del male medesimo, il giuoco. *Algarotti sopra l'Opera,* p. 291.

The complaint of the Count relates principally to the inattention of the Italian audience. The English are remarkably attentive to the performance, and the music is never drowned by the clamour which is so distressing and offensive abroad, and which was equally complained of in former days:

Garganum mugire putes nemus, aut mare Tuscum,
Tanto cum strepitu ludi spectantur et artes.

If the language of the piece should be supposed to influence the attention by rendering more apparent the conduct of the drama or otherwise, we should look for effects the reverse of what are found, and an English audience might be supposed to behave with inattention and indecorum at an Italian opera; but the fact is, that the behaviour is to be

ment accordingly, the favourite airs and the dances, and perhaps the dresses, the decorations, and the leader of the band, are alone objects of criticism or of recollection. The poet is always forgotten, and the actor in general is disregarded. But these scattered gratifications, and fragments, as it were, of absolute magnificence, which are usually the amount of the pleasures arising from the opera, are only the parts of the disjointed materials of the most perfect of the dramatic entertainments; for that such it is in its ideal perfection will readily be admitted, since the addition of exquisite music to exquisite poetry and acting, when that is to be obtained, must constitute the highest species of the delights of the drama. But for this, an audience with learned ears is as necessary, as the excellence of the performance, which is thrown away upon the gross organs, and the ignorance of the vulgar.

The effect of fine acting in the opera may be conceived from the favour which has been most deservedly obtained by the Grassini. In whatever rank the public estimation may place her as a singer, it will not be thought too much to say that she ranks still higher as an actress. So that, even within hearing of the most enchanting voice of perhaps the finest singer in Europe, she justly wins attention and admiration.[14] If, according to Aristotle, pity and terror are the constituent passions of tragedy, the opera of Proserpina may be considered as a truly tragic drama, in which the Grassini finely represents all the feelings

---

accounted for by the manners and character of the different people, and that the drama is entirely overlooked by both. Such are the actual effects of the opera. How different from the theory!

[14] Is it necessary to say, that Mrs. Billington is here alluded to?

suited to the different situations of the heroine. Her musical recitation (for such it may properly be called) of the song, *O Giove onnipotente,* may be selected among many instances of the display of her talents, as one of the most distinguished. It affords an opportunity for great variety, grace, and expression in gesture, of which she most happily avails herself; [15] and consequently by a necessary sympathy of taste, adds all these most charming characters to her song.[16]

---

[15] Vim illam manuum et præstantiam doctus à Græcia vidit Meletius, qui ne quidem musicum ullum eximium esse putavit et probatum, sine manuum gestu atque præsidio. Etenim musicus, inquit, dum cantu utitur, manus gesticulationem ad vocis sonum accommodat, et vicissim quæ manu figurat eadem vocalibus instrumentis emodulando perspicua reddit. Sed et in choris psallentes, et χοϱῦ διδάσκαλοι, nisi manuum gesticulationes psalmorum tono accommodent, quæ comitari psallentes ipsos videatur, de se ridendum spectaculum præbent. *Cresol. Vac. Aut.*

[16] D'Orat, in his poem on the Opera, says, that the singer cannot be excused from the exhibition of the highest expression of countenance and gesture, as well as of musical and vocal excellence: in proof of which he gives the example of a celebrated singer, Mademoiselle Arnould, whom in a note he calls, la seule actrice de l'opera :

> Ses regards tour-à-tour altiers, sombres, touchans,
> Peignoient les passions, mieux encore que les chants.
> Dans tous ses mouvemens respiroit le delire,
> Son geste et son visage accompagnoit sa lyre ;
> Et de son action l'éloquente chaleur
> Transmettoit à ses sons la flâme de son cœur.
> L'organe le plus beau, privé de cette flame,
> Forme un stérile bruit, qui ne va point à l'ame.
>
> . . . .
>
> A l'ame seule alors il faut que j'applaudisse ;
> La Chanteuse s'éclipse, et fait place à l'Actrice.
>
> . . . .
>
> Telle est du grand talent la puissante féerie,
> Il rend tout vraisemblable, il donne à tout la vie,
> Il embrase la scene, et, pour donner des loix,
> Apeine a-t-il besoin du secours de la voix.   *D'Orat, sur l'Opera.*

CHAPTER IX.

OF THE ANCIENT PANTOMIMES.

The pantomimic art not properly connected with rhetorical delivery— The gestures of an orator very different from those of the pantomime —The rise of the ancient pantomimes—Account from Athenæus— Anecdotes of their art from Macrobius—From Suetonius—From Lucian—Observations of Mr. Gibbon—Division of gesture and recitation in the ancient drama—modern pantomimes—Ancient theatrical masks.

K k

CHAPTER IX.

Of the Ancient Pantomimes.

IF the art of gesture be worthy of cultivation, it would appear that it should be cultivated in its highest perfection, and that its perfection must consist in its power of communicating the thoughts independant of language. In this view the pantomimic art should be the sole object for the investigation and acquisition of those who study the art of gesture; for the pantomimes express entire dramas without the aid of words. Their art, however extraordinary, forms hardly any portion of the proper subject of our present enquiry; which relates to the gesture suited to the illustration and enforcement of language, not to the gesture which supersedes its use, and which in its purposes and manner of application is altogether different. In order to express his sentiments by mute action, the pantomime is obliged to avail himself of every natural and imagined connection between thought and gesture; he is of necessity confined to the representation of the most ordinary feelings and situations, such as love, hatred, jealousy, terror, pity, courage, fear, the objects of which are easily made known, and the expression of which is understood by all. If the pantomime wish in the conduct of his fable to go beyond the bounds of these expressions, he is forced upon many awkward expedients, and obliged to invent a language of signs which is attended with the same inconvenience as every other language, that is, it is understood only so far as communicated to, admitted and studied by others.[1,2,3,4] The gestures of the orator, on the contrary, are restrained within very narrow bounds as to imitation, and few of them comparatively are significant; by far the greatest number being so uncertain in their use as to be

---

[1] Nous avons dit ci-dessus que l'art du geste étoit composé de gestes naturels et de gestes d'institution. On peut bien croire, que les pantomimes se servoient des uns et des autres, et qu'ils n'avoient pas encore trop de moyens pour se faire entendre. *Dubos, Réflexions, Tom. III. p.* 262.

[2] Modern pantomimes when obliged to express what would require very peculiar gestures of institution, supply themselves with a scroll, upon which is written the nature of the situations of the dramatic characters. In the same manner Apollonius Tyanæus, when under the vow of Pythagorean silence, was forced upon the awkward expedient of writing what he might have better spoken.

The ancients used to have a sort of cryers to announce the plot of their pantomimes; this is done by us by means of printed bills and descriptions.

[3] Primis temporibus saltante pantomimo, præco pronuntiabat populis Carthaginis quod saltator vellet intelligi. Quod adhuc multi meminerunt senes, quorum relatu hæc solemus audire. Quod ideo credendum est, quia nunc quoque si quis talium nugarum imperitus intraverit nisi ei dicatur ab altero quid illi motus significent, frustra intentus est. *St. August. de Doct. Chr. l.* ii. Quoted by Dubos, *p.* 263.

[4] Le pantomime des tems modernes n'a aucun avantage sur celui des anciens; car lorsque renonçant à des actions communes et connues, il prétend exécuter des sujets à intrigue de sa propre invention, il se trouve dans l'alternative ou de peindre par des signes aussi expressifs qu'il lui est possible de les créer, en laissant au hasard ce que leur signification vague et incertaine permettra aux spectateurs de saisir, ou d'appeller à son secours l'interprete qui doit expliquer par la parole ce que le geste, la mine, et l'attitude ne peuvent exprimer complettement. M. Noverre rejette absolument ce dernier moyen. . . . . il compare ceux qui en ont besoin à ces tableaux des premiers tems de la peinture, dans lequels les peintres se servoient des rouleaux de papier qui sortoient de la bouche des figures, et sur lesquels l'action, l'expression, et la situation de chaque personnage se trouvoient écrites. *Idées sur le Geste, Lettre* 30.

The rule for forming a pantomime from a known subject, according to the celebrated M. Noverre, is this:

" Resserrez l'action, retranchez tout dialogue tranquille, rapprochez les incidens, ré-" unissez tous les tableaux épars, et vous réussirez." *Lettres sur la Dance, p.* 63.

This is no doubt a good recipe for making a pantomime, but the detail of the composition exhibits the medicine in no very favourable point of view.

equally suited to a great variety of sentiments, as we shall more particularly explain hereafter. But although the pantomimic art is remote from the main object of this work, it would be deemed perhaps a blameable omission to pass over in total silence, a subject still in some measure connected with it, and which boasts of classic origin. I shall therefore give a slight sketch of the rise and progress of this art, referring those who wish for full information to the original authors, and among the moderns particularly to the *Réflexions critiques sur la Poesie et sur la Peinture* of the late ingenious and learned Abbé Dubos, whom I shall freely quote.

According to Athenæus, the poet Eschylus was the first inventor not only of the dresses, but of theatrical gesture,[5] and Telestes the author of the pantomimic art: he was a dancer employed by Eschylus, and " so great an artist was he, that " when he represented the seven kings before Thebes, he " rendered every circumstance manifest by his gestures in " dancing."[6][7]

From Greece, or rather from Egypt, this art was brought to

---

[5] Καὶ ᾿Αισχύλος δὲ ἀ μόνον ἐξεῦρε τὴν τῆς ςολῆς εὐπρέπειαν καὶ σεμνότητα, ἣν ζηλώσαντες ὅι ἱεροφάνται καὶ δαδᾶχοι ἀμφιέννυνται, ἀλλὰ καὶ πολλὰ σχήματα ὀρχηςικὰ αὐτὸς ἐξευρίσκων ἀνεδίδε τοῖς χορευταῖς. *Athen. Causab. l. i. p.* 21.

[6] . . . . Τελεςὴς ὁ ᾿Αισχύλε ὀρχηςής ἄτως ἦν τεχνίτης, ὥς τε ἐν τῷ ὀρχεῖσθαι τὰς ἑπτὰ ἐπὶ Θήβας φανερὰ ποιῆσαι τὰ πράγματα δὶ ὀρχήσεως. *Athen. Causab. p.* 22.

[7] Suivant Athénée Thelestes avoit été l'inventeur de cette espece du jeu muet, ou de danse sans saults et sans pas élevés, et laquelle nous appellerons ici le plus souvent l'art du geste. Nous ne ferons en cela que lui donner le même nom, que lui donnoient souvent les anciens. Ils l'appelloient souvent *chironomie*, et ce mot traduit littéralement signifie la regle de la main. *Dubos Réflex. critiques, Tom. III. p.* 211.

Rome, or perhaps there invented by an Egyptian: and in the time of Augustus it appears not only to have delighted all the spectators of ordinary rank, but to have engaged also the attention of Mæcenas, and even of Augustus himself. "Bathyl- " lus of Alexandria was the first who introduced the pan- " tomimic dance." His contemporary and rival was Pylades, and all Rome was split into parties respecting the merit of these two celebrated actors. " The action of Pylades was magnificent, " pathetic and affecting, that of Bathyllus was more sprightly."[8] Athenæus says, that in his own time, (he died A. D. 194,) " a " certain *dancing philosopher* (a mixture of occupation which " excites a smile in a modern reader) was named Memphis, as " a mark of respect for his skill in gesture, from one of the " most ancient and royal cities; which Bacchylides calls

" The tranquil Memphis:"

" for he has shewn us what the Pythagorean philosophy " can do, by exhibiting in silence every thing with stronger " evidence than they could who profess to teach the arts of " language."[9,10]

---

[8] Τῆς δὲ κατὰ τᾶτον ὀρχήσεως τῆς τραγικῆς καλυμένης, πρῶτος εἰσηγητὴς γέγονε Βάθυλλος ὁ Ἀλεξανδρεὺς. . . . .

Bathyllus is said here to have introduced the tragic dance, and below, his style is described as comic, probably because he succeeded best in that style.

. . . ἦν δὲ ἡ Πυλάδε ὄρχησις ὀγκώδης παθητική τε καὶ πολύκοπος. ἡ δὲ Βαθύλ- λειος, ἱλαρωτέρα.   *Athen. Deip. Caus. l.* i.

[9] Τὸν ἐφ᾽ ἡμῶν φησὶ φιλόσοφον ὀρχηστὴν, Μέμφιν ἐκάλεσαν· ἀπαρχαΐζοντες τὴν διὰ τᾶ σώματος αὐτᾶ κίνησιν, τῆ τῶν πόλεων ἀρχαιοτέρα καὶ βασιλικωτέρα· περὶ ἧς Βακχυλίδης φησὶ,   Τὴν αχείμαντόν τε Μέμφιν . . . . .

ὄντος τὴν Πυθαγόρειον φιλοσοφίαν ἐπιδείκνυσιν ἥτις ἐςὶ, μετὰ σιωπῆς πάνθ᾽ ἡμῖν ἐμφανί- ζων σαφέστερον, ἢ οἱ τὰς τῶν λόγων τέχνας ἐπαγγελλόμενοι διδάσκειν. *Athen. Deip. l.* i.

Macrobius has preserved some anecdotes of the pantomimes who flourished in the times of Augustus, which give considerable information relative to their style of acting, as well as to the interest and the parties which they excited, the manner in which they behaved, and the treatment they experienced from Augustus. He mentions Pylades and Hylas as the two great competitors; the commentators are inclined to consider this Hylas as Bathyllus already mentioned, but he might have been, as Macrobius says, the pupil of Pylades.

" Since I have been led to speak of the theatre, I cannot pass " unnoticed Pylades the pantomime, who was celebrated in his " art in the times of Augustus, and so perfectly instructed his " disciple Hylas, that he contended with himself almost upon " an equality. The people were divided in their partiality " to each. Hylas had to perform a scene in which he was to " represent this passage, *Agamemnon the Great*, and he described " him by his gestures as a tall and large man. Pylades could " not bear this, but exclaimed from the pit, *You make him a huge* " *but not a great man.* The audience then compelled him to

---

[10] Even philosophers themselves were carried away by their admiration of the pantomimes. Athenæus says, that Socrates was fond of practising the Memphic saltation. Lucian wrote an express treatise to vindicate their art and utility, but that is less surprising than that the grave Seneca should have confessed that he had an absolute passion for the representation of the pantomimes. Plutarch records a curious analogy which Simonides considered to subsist among the fine arts, painting, poetry, and dancing, or pantomime gesture.

Καὶ ὅλως ἔφη μεταθέσιν τὸ Σιμονίδειον ἀπὸ τῆς ζωγραφίας ἐπι τὴν ὄρχησιν σιωπῶσαν, καὶ φθεγγομένην ὄρχησιν δὲ πάλιν, τὴν ποίησιν. ὅθεν εἶπεν ὅτε γραφικὴν εἶναι ποιητικῆς, ὅτε ποιητικὴν γραφῆς, ἔδε χρῶνται τὸ παράπαν ἀλλήλαις. Ὀρχηστικὴ δὲ καὶ ποιητικῇ κοινωνία πᾶσα καὶ μέθεξις ἀλλήλων ἔσι. *Plut. Symp. l.* viii. *p.* 748.

" perform the scene himself, and when he came to the passage
" which he had found fault with, he represented a man immersed
" in thought; because he conceived that nothing was so becom-
" ing a great general as to be occupied in thinking for all. Hylas
" was performing the part of Œdipus: and Pylades corrected
" the negligence of his action by crying out, *Thou seest.* When
" he appeared in the character of Hercules the mad, and when
" some found fault with his demeanour as unsuitable to a panto-
" mime, he pulled off his mask, and thus retorted upon those
" who derided him, *Fools! I am acting a madman.* In this piece
" he even cast arrows among the audience. When, by the com-
" mand of Augustus, he performed the same character in his
" palace, he both drew his bow and shot his arrows, nor was
" Cæsar offended on finding himself treated by Pylades in the
" same manner as the Roman people. As he was reckoned to
" have introduced novelty and grace, instead of the rude dance
" which was formerly practised; Augustns asked him what
" contributed most to the perfection of dancing; he answered,
" the sound of the flutes and of the instruments, and the ap-
" plauses of the spectators. When, on account of a popular
" tumult, caused by a contention between him and Hylas, he
" experienced an angry remonstrance from Augustus, What,
" prince, said he, are you displeased? you had better suffer
" them to occupy their minds about us." [11,12]

---

[11] Sed quia semel ingressus sum scenam loquendo, nec Pylades histrio nobis omittendus est, qui clarus in opere suo fuit temporibus Augusti, et Hylam discipulum usque ad æqualitatis contentionem eruditum provexit. Populus deinde inter utriusque suffragia divisus est, et cum canticum quoddam saltaret Hylas, cujus clausula erat;

τὸν μέγαν Ἀγαμέμνονα,

This extract, which I have given at large, fully demonstrates the futility of the efforts of the ancient pantomimes to express in mute action sentiments beyond the ordinary character of the passions, and leaves us nothing to regret, as if the art had been among those that are lost. The enthusiasm of the Roman people was nothing greater than modern Europe has felt on the revival of these pantomimic shews, nor does the self-sufficiency of Pylades outstrip that of some of the moderns. Their audacity, however, and their profligacy, brought upon them more than once the punishment they deserved. Augustus, mild as he was, with great justice banished Pylades for pointing to one of the audience in an opprobrious manner: and ordered Hylas to be scourged even in his own palace, to which he fled

---

sublimem ingentemque Hylas velut metiebatur. Non tulit Pylades, et exclamavit è cavea

Σὺ μακρὸν ἃ μέγαν ποιεῖς.

tunc populus eum coegit idem saltare canticum, cumque ad locum venisset, quem reprehenderat, expressit cogitantem, nihil magis ratus magno duci convenire quam pro omnibus cogitare. Saltabat Hylas Oedipodem: et Pylades hac voce securitatem saltantis castigavit; σὺ βλέπεις. Cum in Herculem Furentem prodiisset et nonnullis incessum histrioni convenientem non servari videretur, deposita persona ridentes increpuit

Μωροὶ, μαινόμενον ὀρχῆμαι.

Hac fabula et sagittas jecit in populum. Eandem personam cum jussu Augusti in triclinio ageret; et intendit arcum et spicula misit. Nec indignatus est Cæsar eodem se loco Pyladi, quo populum Romanum fuisse. Hic quia ferebatur mutasse rudis illius saltationis ritum quæ apud majores viguit, et venustam induxisse novitatem interrogatus ab Augusto quæ saltationi contulisset respondit; αὐλῶν συρίγγων τ᾽ ἐνοπὴν, ὁμαδὸν τ᾽ ἀνθρώπων. Idem cum propter populi seditionem pro contentione inter se Hylamque habita concitatam indignationem excepisset Augusti, respondit: καὶ ἀχαριςεῖς βασιλεῦ ; ἔασον αὐτὲς περὶ ἡμᾶς ἀσχολεῖσθαι. *Macrob. Sat. l.* ii. *c.* 7.

[12] The Abbé Dubos makes a reflection on this passage, which I quote. L'émulation étoit si grande entre Pylade et Bathylle un autre pantomime, qu' Auguste, à qui elle donnoit quelquefois de l'embarras, crut qu'il devoit en parler au Pylade et l'exhorter à bien vivre avec son concurrent que Mécenas protégeoit. Pylade* se contenta de lui répondre que ce

* Dion. *l.* 54.

for refuge from the prætor.[13.14.15.16] In the reign of Tiberius, Tacitus informs us that popular disturbances arose from the contests of the pantomimes;[17] at first he passed over the

---

qui pouvoit arriver de mieux à l'Empereur, c'étoit que le peuple s'occupât de Bathylle et de Pylade. On croit bien qu'Auguste ne trouva point à propos de repliquer à cette réponse.

[13] Hylam pantomimum, querente prætore, in atrio domus suæ, nemine excluso, flagellis verberaverit: et Pyladem urbe atque Italia submoverit quod spectatorem a quo exsibilabatur, demonstrasset digito, conspicuumque fecisset. *Suet. in August. c.* 45.

[14] Ludos Augustales tunc primum cœpta turbavit discordia, ex certamine histrionum. Indulserat ei ludicro Augustus dum Mæcenati obtemperat effuso in amorem Bathylli neque ipse abhorrebat talibus studiis et civile rebatur misceri voluptatibus vulgi. Alia Tiberio morum via : sed populum per tot annos molliter habitum, nondum audebat ad duriora vertere. *Taciti Annal. l.* i. *c.* 54.

[15] The following proof of modest confidence in his own talents and superiority, is well known to have been given by a celebrated dancer. As he was going to make his *entrée*, he addressed his companions, the other dancers, who pressed round to admire him : *Faites place, canaille, pour le Dieu de danse.* But, what is more extraordinary, it does not appear that his insolence at the time gave offence; such was the worship which he obtained. It will be found generally true, that the lower an art is in which any man excels all others, the higher is his pride of superiority. For to arrive at excellence in any thing is the labour of a whole life ; and when a man is ignorant of every thing but his own art, whatever that may be, and obtains admiration for his acquirements, he is apt to think he has arrived at the summit of human glory. After all, perhaps, he is right, and that to excell in any thing, is to be great. It is only the pride of philosophy and literature that would say otherwise.

The dancing and music of an opera, which appear alone to be the objects of popular attention and applause, seem also to the performers to be alone of importance: the fable and the poetry, are considered merely as a vehicle for them. This is another bar to the perfection of the opera. I remember to have heard two distinguished dancers condemning very loudly the late celebrated Marmontel for having at the rehearsal of a new piece, which he had just produced at the opera, presumed to interfere and give his directions as to some points in the conduct of it. And they seemed only to repeat the general sentiment of the performers, who were of opinion, that a poet had no right to interfere after committing his piece into their hands ; and that his talent was, comparatively with theirs, of no estimation.

[16] Apulius in the 10th book of his Metamorphosis, or Asinus Aureus, gives a detailed account of the performance of the fable of the Judgment of Paris by the pantomimes. They who choose to refer to it will think they are reading a description of a modern serious opera ballet.

[17] They were banished from Italy by Tiberius. Pulsi tum histriones Italia. *Tac. An.* 4,

irregularities of the people, but he afterwards restrained them by very strict laws, the very terms of which, prove the absolute necessity for them. " Against the wantonness of their " partizans many resolutions were passed, of which these are " the most remarkable. That no senator should enter the " habitations of the pantomimes: that the Roman knights " should not collect about them when they appeared abroad : " that they should not go to see them any where but at the " theatres; and that the pretors should have the power of " punishing by exile the improper behaviour of the spectators " towards them."[18]

Under the succeeding reigns, the pantomimes seem to have become the peculiar objects not only of imperial favour, but of imperial imitation. " Caligula was so carried away by his " passion for music, and pantomimic action, that even at the " public exhibitions he could not refrain from joining in the " recitative with the tragedian, and openly imitating the " gesture of the actor, as if either approving of or correcting " it. Nor does it appear that on the day on which he fell, " he appointed a festival for the night for any other reason; " but in order that the licentiousness of such a time might

---

14. They were again expelled from Rome under Nero, and some other Emperors. Domitian expelled them, and Nerva, though one of the wisest Emperors, recalled them. Neque enim a te minore concentu ut tolleres pantomimos quam a patre tuo ut restitueret, exactum est, says Pliny the younger in speaking to Trajan. *Plin. Paneg. c.* 46.

[18] . . . Adversus lasciviam fautorum multa decernuntur: ex quis maxime insignia. " Ne domos pantomimorum senator introiret: ne egredientis in publicum, equites Romani cingerent: aut alibi quam in theatris spectarentur: et spectantium immodestiam exsilio multandi potestas praetoribus fieret. *Tac. An. l.* i. *c.* 77.

" excuse his determination to make his appearance on the
" stage. He exercised himself in the practice of pantomimic
" dance sometimes also on other nights. On one occasion he
" ordered three men of consular dignity to be brought to the
" palace in the middle of the night, and placed them on the
" highest part of the stage, and whilst they were agitated with
" various terrors, and fearing even for their lives, he suddenly
" sprang out, and accompanied by a loud concert of trumpets
" and other instruments, performed the gestures of a soliloquy,
" and disappeared." [19]

Nero was devoted to all the exhibitions of the theatre; he
made his first appearance on the stage at Naples,[20] according to
Tacitus, and contended afterwards publicly on the theatre at
Rome for the prize in music.[21] And purposed, as Suetonius
says, near the close of his life, to display his theatrical talents
in various other ways; among the rest, he was to perform the
character of Turnus from Virgil. This historian insinuates

---

[19] Canendi ac saltandi voluptate ita efferebatur, ut ne publicis quidem spectaculis temperaret, quo minus et tragœdo pronuntianti concineret* et gestum† histrionis quasi laudans vel corrigens palam effingeret Nec alia de causa videtur eo die, quo periit, pervigilium indixisse, quam ut initium in scenam prodeundi licentia temporis auspicaretur. Saltabat autem nonnunquam etiam noctu : et quondam tres consulares secunda vigilia in palatium accitos, multaque et extrema metuentes super pulpitum collocavit : deinde repente magno tibiarum et scabellorum crepitu, cum palla tunicaque talari prosiluit, ac desaltato cantico abiit. *Sueton. Calig. c.* 54.

[20] Non tamen Romæ incipere ausus, Neapolim, quasi Græcum urbem, delegit. *Tac. An.* 15, 33.

[21] . . . Ingreditur theatrum, cunctis citharæ legibus obtemperans. *Tac. An. l.* 16, 4.

* The ancient dramatic entertainments were accompanied throughout with music, which though not perhaps the same as the modern recitative, may yet be most nearly translated by that word.

† The actor who performed the gestures.

that through envy of the rival talents of the player Paris, he had him murdered.[22]

In the reign of Nero flourished a celebrated pantomime, of whom Lucian relates the following anecdotes. He had often solicited the cynic Demetrius, who was in the habit of speaking of the pantomimes with contempt, to be present at his performance, and to forbear his reproaches till he should have seen him. He at last prevailed on the philosopher to visit the theatre, were he saw him perform admirably many dances on various fabulous subjects. Demetrius at last could contain his approbation no longer, but shouted out with a loud voice, this extraordinary tribute of applause. " Man, I not only see, " but I hear what you do; for to me, you appear to speak with " your hands.[23] Immediately after this follows another testimony of the talents of the pantomimes. A barbarian prince of Pontus having come to Rome to do homage to the Emperor Nero, had been brought to visit the theatre, where he was much delighted by the pantomimes. On his departure the Emperor desired him to ask him for some present as a mark of his favour. The barbarian begged he might have the principal dancer: and upon being asked why he made such an

---

[22] Sub exitu quidem vitæ palam voverat si sibi incolumis status permansisset, proditurum se partæ victoriæ ludis, etiam hydraulam et choraulam et utricularium, ac novissimo die histrionem, saltaturumque Virgilii Turnum. Et sunt qui tradant Paridem histrionem occisum ab eo, quasi gravem adversarium. *Sueton. Nero, c.* 54.

[23] Ὥϛε τὸν Δημήτριον ὑπερησθέντα τοῖς γιγνομένοις, τῦτον ἔπαινον ἀποδῦναι τὸν μέγιϛον τῷ ὀρχηϛῇ. ἀνέκραγε γὰρ καὶ μγάλη τῇ φωνῇ ἀνεφθέγξατο, Ἀκώω ἄνθρωπε ἃ ποιεῖς, ἐχ᾽ ὁρω μόνον, ἀλλά μοι δοκεῖς ταῖς χερσὶν αὐταῖς λαλεῖν. *Lucian. de Saltatione,* p. 516. *Bourdalottii.*

odd request; he replied that he had many neighbours who spoke such various and discordant languages, that he found it difficult to obtain any interpreter who could understand them, or explain his commands; but that if he had the dancer, he could by his assistance easily make himself intelligible to all.[24]

The extraordinary perfection to which this art was brought, and the passion which the Romans had for it, maintained its reputation and practice for a long series of years.[25] " The " tragic and comic muse of the Romans, (says the eloquent " author of the Decline and Fall of the Roman Empire,) who " seldom aspired beyond the imitation of Attic genius, had " been almost totally silent since the fall of the republic; and

---

[24] Τὸν ὀρχησὴν, ἔφε, δὲς, τα μέγιςα ευφραινεῖς. τῶ δὲ Νέρωνος ἐρομένου, τί ἄν σοι χρήσιμος γένοιτο ἐκεῖ; Προςοίκας, ἔφη, βαρβάρας ἔχω, οὐχ' ὁμογλώτlας, καὶ ἑρμηνέων οὐ ῥάδιον ἐυπορεῖν πρὸς αὐτάς. ἤν ἄν τινος δέωμαι, διανεύων ὄυτος ἕκαςά μοι ἑρμηνεύσει.

[25] Marmontel in his Elémens de Litérature, article Pantomimes, gives the following among the reasons which he assigns for the passion of the Romans for their exhibitions.

Les Romains n'étoient pas un peuple sensibile comme les Grecs aux plaisirs de l'esprit et de l'ame : leurs mœurs austeres ou dissolues, selon les temps, n'eurent jamais la delicatesse des mœurs attiques: il leur falloit des spectacles faits pour les yeux. Or la pantomime parle aux yeux un langage plus passionné que celui de la parole; elle est plus vehemente que l'éloquence même, et aucune langue n'est en état d'en égaler la force et la chaleur. Dans la pantomime tout est action, rien ne languit; l'attention n'est point fatiguée: en se livrant au plaisir d'être émue, on peut s'épargner presque la peine de penser; ou s'il se presente des idées, elles sont vagues comme les songes. La parole retarde et refroidit l'action; elle préoccupe l'acteur, et rend son art plus difficile. Le pantomime est tout.à l'expression du geste; ses mouvemens ne lui sont point tracés; la passion seule est son guide. L'acteur est continuellement le copiste du poete; le pantomime est original : l'un est asservi au sentiment et à la pensée d'autrui, l'autre se livre et s'abandonne aux mouvemens de son ame. Il doit donc y avoir entre l'action du comédien et celle du pantomime, la différence et la distance de l'esclavage à la liberté.

" their place was unworthily occupied by licentious farce,
" effeminate music and splendid pageantry. The pantomimes
" maintained their reputation from the age of Augustus to the
" sixth century, expressed, without words the various fables
" of the gods and heroes of antiquity, and the perfection of
" their art, which sometimes disarmed the gravity of the
" philosopher, always excited the applause and wonder of the
" people. The vast and magnificent theatres of Rome were
" filled by three thousand female dancers, and by three thousand
" singers, with the masters of the respective chorusses. Such
" was the popular favour which they enjoyed, that in a time of
" scarcity, when all strangers were banished from the city,
" the merit of contributing to the public pleasures exempted
" them from a law, which was strictly executed against the
" professors of the liberal arts." [27] [28] [29]

The attachment of the Romans to gesticulation, which, from
the historian Livy, appears to have been of high antiquity,

---

[26] Cassiodorus who, lived under the Emperor Theodoric A. D. 514, speaks of the talents
of the pantomimes in these strong terms : orchestrarum loquacissimæ manus, linguosi digiti,
silentium clamosum, expositio tacita, quam musa Polymnia reperisse narratur ostendens
homines posse sine oris afflatu velle suum declarare. *Cassiod. Variar. l. iv. ep. 5.*

[27] Gibbons Decline and Fall, *c.* xxxi.

[28] Ammianus, *l.* xiv. *c.* 6. He complains (says Mr. Gibbon) with decent indignation,
that the streets of Rome were filled with crowds of females, who might have given children
to the state, but whose only occupation was to curl and dress their hair, and, jactari volubilibus gyris, dum exprimunt innumera simulacra, quæ finxere fabulæ theatrales.

The passage at large to which Mr. Gibbon alludes in Ammianus Marcellinus is this :

[29] Postremo ad id indignitatis est ventum, ut cum peregrini ob formidatum non ita dudum
alimentorum inopiam pellerentur ab urbe præcipites, sectatoribus disciplinarum liberalium
impendio paucis sine respiratione ulla extrusis, tenerentur mimarum asseclæ veri, quique id

probably gave rise to a practice which to our ideas appears little less than absurd: and to which as connected with the subject before us, it seems proper to advert: this was the custom of dividing between two persons the recitation, and the gesture of the same piece. Accident, as it appears, first excited this strange taste.

" A few years afterwards, Livius (Andronicus the Poet), who
" first relinquished the satires and ventured to construct a play
" with a regular plot, and who was himself, as all in those days
" were, the actor of his own compositions, is said, when he had
" become hoarse by being frequently required to repeat a
" favourite passage, to have obtained permission to get a boy
" to sing to the music, and then to have acted what was sung
" with considerably greater spirit, because he was not impeded
" by the exertion of his voice. Hence arose the custom of
" singing in the soliloquies to the gesture of the actors, who
" used their voice only in the dialogue." [30.31.32]

---

simularent ad tempus ; et tria millia saltatricum ne interpellata quidem, cum choris toti-demque remanerent magistris. Et licet quocunque oculos flexeris, fœminas adfatim multas spectare cirratas, quibus si nupsissent per ætatem ter jam nixus poterat suppetere libero-rum, adusque tædium pedibus pavimenta terentes, jactari volubilibus gyris, dum exprimunt innumera simulacra, quæ finxere fabulæ theatrales. *Ammian. l. 14. p. 26. Lugd.*

[30] Livius post aliquot annos, qui ab saturis ausus est primus argumento fabulam serere (idem scilicet, id quod omnes tum erant, suorum carminum auctor) dicitur, quum sæpius revocatus vocem obtudisset, venia petita puerum ad canendum ante tibicinem quum statuisset, canticum egisse aliquanto magis vigenti motu, quia nihil vocis usus impediebat. Inde ad manum cantari histrionibus cœptum, diverbiaque tantum ipsorum voci relicta. *Tit. Livii Hist.*

[31] Πάλαι μὲν γὰρ αὐτοὶ καὶ ᾖδον καὶ ὠρχῦντο· ἔιτ' ἐπειδὰν κινυμένων τὸ ἄσθμα τὴν ᾠδὴν ἐπετάραττεν, ἄμεινον ἔδοξεν ἄλλυς αὐτοῖς ὑπᾴδειν. *Luc. de Saltatione.*

The ingenious Abbé Dubos has laboured earnestly to maintain the reasonableness and the good effect of this strange practice. He has among other comparisons by which he defends it, referred to the exhibition of puppet-shews: the passage I have quoted.[33] I do not recollect that he has mentioned a reason for its not appearing to the Romans as absurd as it must to us, and which seems to me more probable than any he has offered. The Roman actors performed their parts in monstrous masks which destroyed all expression of the countenance, and therefore provided the sounds were heard, and that the gestures accompanied them regularly, they might as well be supposed to issue from the mask as if they had done so in reality.

It is hardly necessary to speak of those performances in England which are called Pantomimes, and which are executed

---

Formerly the same actors both sung and danced. But when the short breathing in consequence of the exertion distressed their voice, they thought it better that the accompaniment of singing should be performed by different persons.

[32] The Abbé Dubos gives the following passage (from Isidore. Orig. *l.* xviii. *c.* 44.) in proof of the division of the gesture and the recitation. Ibi enim poetæ, comœdi et tragœdi, ad certamen conscendebant, iisque canentibus, alii gestus edebant.

For the same purpose he adduces the four first lines of the epigram following: in which *cantor* in the 4th line means the reciter, and *ipse* the saltator or the actor himself. The other four lines are added from Rosinus :

> Ingressus scenam populum saltator adorat,
>> Solerti spondens prodere verba manu :
> Nam cum grata chorus diffudit cantica dulcis
>> Quæ resonat cantor motibus ipse probat.
> Pugnat, ludit, amat, bacchatur, vertitur, adstat
>> Illustrat verum cuncta decore replet,
> Tot linguæ, quot membra viro ; mirabilis est ars,
>> Quæ facit articulos, voce silente loqui.

[34] In the fine collection of antique statues of the late Mr. Townley, there is a figure, probably of a *Davus*, in a mask ; the head is in most perfect preservation. The figure, is about 18 inches high, and repaired in other parts rather rudely.

without speaking. They serve to exhibit variety of machinery, the activity of the Harlequin, the grimace of the other characters, and to excite laughter by their folly; but are below criticism as dramatic exhibitions. They seem to be borrowed from the grotesque characters of the Italian comedy, dressed out in the English taste for the marvellous, the supernatural, and for ingenious contrivance.

The Roman custom of wearing masks[34] appears to modern ideas little less injurious to just dramatic effect, than the division of the gesture and the declamation. The usual excuse for this practice is founded on the vast magnitude of the ancient theatres, where the expression of the natural countenance must have been lost to the great majority of the spectators: and which therefore induced them to adopt the expedient of strongly marked and often hideous masks. But perhaps it may be better accounted for from the paucity and uniformity of the characters introduced in the ancient drama; a careful father, a profligate son, a parasite, and a cunning slave, were always the principal persons.[35] Similar circumstances admit

---

[33] Les Marionettes, où la déclamation est partagée, nous amusent, quoique l'action n'y soit exécutée que par une espéce d'automate. Il ne faut pas dire que ce spectacle puérile nous divertit, parceque le ridicule de l'exécution s'y trouve parfaitement bien assortie avec le ridicule du sujet. L'Opera des Bamboches, de l'invention de la Grille, &c. qui fût établi à Paris vers l'an 1674, attira tout le monde durant deux hyvers; et ce spectacle étoit un opera ordinaire, avec la différence que la partie de l'action s'exécutoit par une grande Marionette, qui faisoit sur le théatre les gestes convenables aux récits que chantoit un musicien, dont la voix sortoit par une ouverture ménagée dans le plancher de la scéne. J'ai vu en Italie des opera représentés de cette maniere, et personne ne les trouvoit un spectacle ridicule. *Dubos Réflexions critiques, Tom.* III. *p.* 244.

[35] 　　. . . . . . Adspice, Plautus
　　　Quo pacto partes tutetur amantis ephebi,
　　　Ut patris attenti, lenonis insidiosi:
　　　Quantus sit Dorsennus edacibus in Parasitis.　　　*Hor. Ep.* 1, 2.

the continuation of the custom of wearing masks in the Italian comedy. Harlequin, Scapin, and Pantaloon, in whatever different situations they appear, are still the same identical personages, and so are the other characters, with little variation. Hence it seems possible with very little incongruity to perform (if they could be heard out) half a dozen Italian comedies of this species as a single drama.

CHAPTER X.

OF NOTATION OF GESTURE.

The want of a method of notation one cause of the neglect of the art of gesture—Why more neglected by orators than by actors—Invention of notation of gesture attended by many difficulties—Analogy to musical notation—General description of gesture in words affords but inadequate ideas of it—Particular description altogether tedious— The want of some means of recording the gesture of the ancient orators to be lamented— The same to be said of our own great Orators and players—Portraits do not adequately supply this want—Origin of this attempt to produce a notation of gesture—Conjectures as to the manner in which were delivered certain passages of Cicero, Demosthenes, and Gracchus, which are remarked as having derived much of their effect from fine action—This art may be of use to the historical painter— More so to the actor—The want of such an art the subject of frequent complaint—Examples from Betterton—Lloyd—Sheridan.

CHAPTER X.

Of Notation of Gesture.

ONE of the reasons which may be assigned for the neglect of cultivating the art of gesture, is the want of a copious and simple language for expressing its different modifications with brevity and perspicuity. Some modern authors speak of the hope or possibility of supplying this want.[1,2,3,4] The ancient

---

[1] S'il étoit possible de tracer les figures des gestes sur le papier, comme on présente nettement dans des exemples les figures des pensées et des mots, vous verriez qu'il n'existe pas un seule affection de l'ame, ni par conséquent une seule figure dans le discours à laquelle ne réponde un geste particulier. . . . . Quant aux régles pour se former au geste, peu d'auteurs ont entrepris de les présenter avec un certain détail: après avoir exposé quelques principes généraux, ils se sont arrêtés là ; et par cette conduit ils semblent avoir fait l'aveu de leur impuissance pour traiter avec succès, et dans toute son étendue, cette partie si essentielle de l'action oratoire. Est-il étonnant qu'ils aient senti d'avance toutes les difficultés de leur entreprise, et qu'ils aient cédé à l'embarras de l'effectuer? le geste est comme le jeu de la physionomie, susceptible d'autant de nuances que les passions ont de dégrés de chaleur ou de mouvemens opposés; pour l'assujettir à des régles de détail, il faudroit pouvoir embrasser toutes les diverses modifications du cœur humain, et encore, après avoir fait cette opération sur un seul individu, il faudroit la répéter sour tous ; car chaque homme ayant sa manière de sentir, il deviendroit nécessaire d'établir des régles particulières pour chaque individu, ce qui est impracticable et au-dessus des forces humaines. On a donc eu raison de se borner, en traitant du geste, à des principes généraux, et d'abandonner les régles de détail au gout particulier de chaque individu et à l'influence de ses émotions personelles. *Dubroca l'Art de Lire à haute Voix. Leçon 25.*

M. Dubroca expresses the difficulty of forming a system of gesture with sufficient force. But in the latter observations he has failed to perceive, that in the various gestures of different men, there is sufficient similarity to give ground for the general classification, and naming of gestures.

[2] Action is a sort of language which perhaps one time or other may come to be taught

systems or classes of gesture do not appear to have related to this view.[5] This desideratum operates with more sensible effect against the improvement of the orator, than that of the player. The orator obtains his chief estimation from his ingenuity and force of reasoning, and therefore he applies with the vigour of his ability principally to composition; delivery among us has not yet obtained the estimation due to its importance, and if at all, it is imperfectly and partially studied. But the player must exert himself in all the art of delivery, because

---

by a kind of grammar rules; but at present it is only got by rote, and imitation. *Hogarth, Analysis of Beauty, p.* 139.

[3] Mr. Engel speaks of Lessing, a German author, who had proposed to write upon the art of gesture, this he considers evidently most difficult, as appears by his expressions.

Au passage cité de Lessing. . . je puis en opposer un autre tiré d'un de ses ouvrages antérieurs, qui prouve de la manière la plus convaincante *qu'il a été persuadé de la possibilité de former un art du geste;* qu'il doit même en avoir esquissé le plan. *Idées sur le Geste. Lettre* 1.

[4] In the same letter Engel says, Lessing was to call his work *Eloquence du Geste,* and laments his early death, which prevented its execution; he says of him, qu'il même en avoit déjà redigé le plan, si non sur le papier, du moins dans sa tête (car Lessing n'a jamais promis une chose dont l'exécution lui paroissoit douteuse), ne devoit pas envisager comme impossible l'exécution d'un pareil ouvrage.

[5] The ancients possessed, no doubt, a regular system of gesture, of which nothing more than the names of different divisions or classes has reached us. For these names and their use we are obliged to Athenæus. The class of gesture suited to comedy was called Cordax, the class suited to tragedy Eumelia, and that suited to satire Sicinnis, from the inventor Sicinnus a barbarian. Bathyllus from these three classes formed a fourth suited to the pantomime, which he called the Italic.

Τᾶτον τὸν Βάθυλλον φησὶν Αριϛόνικος καὶ Πυλάδης ᾗ ἐϛὶ καὶ σύγγραμμα περὶ ὀρχήσεως, τὴν Ιταλικὴν ὄρχησιν συϛήσασθαι ἐκ τῆς κωμικῆς ἢ ἐκαλεῖτο Κόρδαξ· καὶ τῆς τραγικῆς ἢ ἐκαλεῖτο Ἐμμέλεια· καὶ τῆς σατυρικῆς ἢ ἐλέγετο Σίκιννις. . . . ἧς εὑρητὴς Σίκιννός τις βάρβαρος. *Athen. Deip. l.* i. *p.* 20.

This system of gesture appears to have been accommodated to the music of dramatic performances alone, and we do not read of any particular system of gesture belonging to oratory. The orators we know borrowed from the theatre, but did not use such licentious gesture.

his fame and fortune depend solely on this art. He obtains instructions therefore, the best in his power; he hears and attends to the traditions of the green-room relative to the deportment of the great players who had been celebrated before his time; he listens to the advice of his seniors, he imitates his superiors, he struggles against his own imperfections and awkwardness, and all this for cogent reasons, because if he does not conquer them, he will be laughed at, and sink in reputation and in fortune.[6] To all this he adds his own private study and meditation, and after a few years he improves and advances in his profession. His first failures only cause him to redouble his efforts; and almost the dullest of men, if they persevere, arrive on the stage at last to some degree of useful and respectable talent. The orator in our country has no person to instruct him in gesture, he sees few models, which are worthy of imitation; if he has a taste for the theatre, and if he attempt to borrow from it, he runs the hazard of introducing indecorous gesture; and if he should fail in his ideas and execution at his first setting out, he generally relinquishes his ambitious attempts in disgust, and falls into some restrained and habitual gestures, or into the torpor of absolute inaction. The orators, whether of the bar, the senate, or the pulpit, from their literary habits and their knowledge of the value of delivery, as celebrated in those classical authors so familiar to them in our country, it is to be presumed,

---

[6] Histrio si paullum se movit extra numerum, aut si versus pronuntiatus est syllaba una brevior, aut longior, exsibilatur et exploditur. *Cic. Parad.* 3, 2.

The same disgrace would happen to an actor in modern times if he violated accent or pronunciation: our gesture not being so strictly regulated as that of the ancients, which kept exact time with the music, a greater degree of latitude is allowed in this respect: but still absurdity or awkwardness do not pass uncensured.

would not indolently give up the attempt at improvement in rhetorical delivery, were they enabled to obtain sufficient information from literary enquiry and private practice.[7,8,9] But it has been the misfortune of this art, that to display it fully and intelligibly is most difficult, for it has hitherto been unfurnished with appropriate written language. And we labour under the same difficulties now as to the rules for gesture, as we should with respect to the laws of rhetorical composition, could we imagine that to this hour the languages in which Demosthenes and Cicero once spoke, had never yet been committed to writing.

To produce a language of symbols so simple and so perfect as to render it possible with facility to represent every action of an orator throughout his speech, or of an actor throughout the whole drama, and to record them for posterity, and for

---

[7] The notation of gesture possessed by the ancients perhaps related more to the music than to the style of action: and yet this must be mere conjecture, for we are left totally in the dark on this subject.

[8] The Abbé Condillac seems to be of opinion that the ancients did write some notation of gesture.

De là nous voyons que leurs (les Grecs et les Romains) gestes pouvoient être assez marqués pour être appreciés. Nous n'aurons donc plus de peine à comprendre qu'ils leur aient préscrits des régles et qu'ils aient trouvé le sécret de les écrire en notes. *Tom. I. p.* 304, § 31.

But in the next section this notation seems to refer to music.

§ 32. Les gestes étant reduits en art et notes, il fut facile de les asservir au mouvement et à la mesure de la déclamation ; c'est que firent les Grecs et les Romains.

[9] The Abbé Dubos seems also to refer this notation to the connection of the declamation with the music.

Dans les titres qui sont à la tête des comédies de Terence, on voit avec le nom de l'auteur du poeme et le nom du chef de la troupe des comédiens qui les avoient représentés, le nom de celui qui en avoit faite la déclamation, en Latin. *Qui fecerat modos.*—The teachers of this musical declamation were called by Quintilian *artifices pronuntiandi. Réflexions critiques, Tom.* III. *p.* 140.

repetition and practice, as well as common language is recorded; if considered merely as an accession to the means of communicating our ideas by writing, may not be deemed unworthy of attention; and, to all concerned in public speaking, that is, to all men of liberal education, may possibly be esteemed useful. An attempt at such a language is here presented to the public. But although it is the result of considerable labour, it is readily acknowledged to be imperfect: and it will claim indulgence more perhaps for the intention than for the execution. To bring it to perfection will require the united labours and ingenuity of many; yet even in the present state it is hoped it may prove not altogether uninteresting.[10][11][12]

---

[10] Farther on, the learned Abbé mentions an invention of a Mons. Feuillée, which approaches nearer to this here presented to the public, than any thing antiquity has left us. I have never seen the work of Mons. Feuillée; it is named Chorégraphie, being on the art of dancing, p. 150. . . . La déclamation notée ne seroit autre chose que les tons et les mouvemens de la prononciation écrites en notes. . . . . . Quant au moyen d'écrire en notes la déclamation, il ne sçauroit être aussi difficile. . . qu'il l'étoit de trouver l'art d'écrire en notes les pas et les figures d'une entrée de ballet dansée par huit personnes. . . . Cependant, Feuillée est venu à bout de trouver cet art, et sa note enseigne même aux danseurs comment ils doivent porter leurs bras. Sa Corégraphie a été publiée en 1606.

[11] In another place, Abbé Dubos mentions his difficulties in conceiving the manner in which the ancients expressed the various gestures by notation, but the observation implies that he understood, that they were supposed to have had a method of such expression.

Comment, dira-t-on, les anciens avoient-ils pu venir à bout de rédiger ces méthodes par écrit, et de trouver des notes et des caractères qui exprimassent toutes les attitudes et tous les mouvemens du corps? je n'en sçai rien, mais la Corégraphie de Feuillée, dont j'ai déjà parlé, montre suffisamment que la chose étoit possible. Il n'est pas plus difficile d'apprendre par des notes quels gestes il faut faire, que d'apprendre par des notes quels pas, quelles figures, il faut former. C'est qu'enseigne très-bien le livre de Feuillée.

[12] The learned Abbé Barthelemi, in the notes of his Voyage of Anacharsis, chap. 70, denies with much appearance of reason, that the whole of the ancient drama was accompanied by music: and seems to have had no idea of what the Abbé Dubos imagines as to notation of gesture.

Mons. Duclos considers the notation of declamation to have been the writing by musical notes of the inflexions of the voice, and the variety of its expression. Academie des

The language of gesture bears more analogy to that of music than to the language of general ideas : and therefore it is named the notation of gesture. As the notation of musical sounds records the melodies and happy harmony of sounds which in their nature endure but for a moment, so the notation of gesture records the beautiful, the dignified, the graceful or expressive actions of the body, by which the emotions of the mind are manifested on great and interesting occasions, and which in themselves are no less transitory. And these gestures are not merely transitory, but they are also important. For in order to conceive the entire effect of what has been said, it is necessary that we should be as well acquainted with the manner, as with the words. To present to the mind correct ideas of the manner in which important matter has been delivered, ordinary language is altogether inadequate, because it is furnished only with general terms, and cannot enter into particulars. He spoke, nobly, firmly, calmly ; he used the gestures of a graceful speaker, of a dignified orator, of a theatrical hero; these and such observations are of the same indefinite import, with respect to the detail of the delivery, as the language and sentiments so described would be without the record of the very words and of the structure of the sentences. As if an oration should be said to have been well and elegantly composed, to have been correct, ingenious and argumentative: from such description, as little could be known of the arguments and ornaments, as from

---

Inscriptions et de Belles Lettres, Tom. XXI. p. 199. A little farther on, he gives an account of the attempt to adjust to musical notes the inflexions of the voice of the Chinese man Arcadio Hoang, who was at Paris ; p. 202. This has been most ingeniously and perfectly done by Mr. Steel in his Prosodia Rationalis, who has accomplished, it appears to me, the most difficult of problems, *si vis similem pingere, pinge sonum.*

the general description could be understood any thing of the gesture or expression. The matter of an oration may be correctly and perfectly detailed in written language, but the description of the manner has been hitherto nearly limited to general terms only. I have said *nearly*, because sometimes particular gestures have been described, but the number of words necessary for any such description is so very great, that to particularize the gestures used in a few sentences would occupy in common language almost as much room as a long oration. So that we have but few examples of such attempts, and those who have given them have been soon tired of their task: whilst others, very willing to undertake it, upon a short trial, have complained of the labour, and relinquished it, expressing their admiration of the difficulty and tediousness of description.[13][14]

All the other parts of rhetorical delivery are either not subject to the same difficulty of description, or having been more

---

[13] In a work printed at Paris 1796 entitled Recueil de Pieces intéressantes concernant les Antiquités, les beaux Arts, &c. Tome troisième; there is a translation from the German into French of a treatise upon gesture. Idées sur le Geste et l'Action théâtrale par M. T. T. Engel de l'Academie Royale des Sciences de Berlin, &c.

In the 401st page of this volume, the author having described a particular Italian gesture, which takes him up an octavo page, concludes with this reflection : il est singulier que cette pantomime soit si aisée à comprendre, et que cependant son explication offre tant de difficultés. In the next page he describes another gesture which takes him up nearly as much room. Yet both of these could be perfectly expressed in a very few symbolic letters.

[14] Quant à l'attitude et aux mouvemens du corps, Ciceron en dit peu de chose qui nous convienne. . . . . Et en effet, il est difficile de prescrire autre chose à l'orateur à l'égard du geste, si ce n'est de le modérer, et de se souvenir que, dans les mouvemens les plus passionnés, il n'est pas un comédien. *Marmontel, Elémens de Litérature, art. Déclamation (Rhétorique), p.* 287.

attended to are better understood. Precepts for the management of the voice abound, and are very intelligible; and the
countenance is so interesting as to have been the object of examination, and of description, in almost all its possible varieties
of expression. But gesture has been uncultivated down to our
times; or if the ancients wrote any particular instructions relative to it, little has reached us, and the field is almost open.

If any thing effectual can be done towards establishing a
language, or notation of gesture, the orator will not alone derive
advantage from it; other arts will obtain their share. The
painter, above all, will profit by it: his art depends eminently
upon the knowledge of gesture: but in the present state of this
knowledge, he works principally from recollection, or fancy,
and fails to represent truly the action of the character he de-
lineates. He perhaps finds in a portrait the record of the
countenance of the great man, whom he wishes to paint, as he
appeared on some great occasion; but he is obliged to trust to
his own imagination for his deportment and gesture; and he
does not always choose well, much less according to the truth.
Roscius and Æsopus are long departed: they once enchanted
Rome, the seat of arts and empire; but of the characters of
their excellence we have no memorial, except in vague and
general terms.

Roscius contended once with Cicero in a playful trial
of the variety of his art of gesture against the variety of
Cicero's expression in words of the same idea. It is a pity
Cicero did not preserve the memory, as he might, of his
own part. As to the part of Roscius, in this contest, it
could not be recorded, without using many more words than

Cicero or he might have been inclined to bestow on such a trifle. But neither have the inimitable gestures of Roscius and Æsopus, in their most interesting scenes, been handed down to us, for the same reason; nor even of Cicero himself, in those orations which have filled all ages with admiration. Garrick is gone, and some of us have seen him; and an attitude of his is preserved by the pencil of Hogarth; and something, perhaps correctly like, of the same sort, by Sir Joshua Reynolds. Uncertain and fading traditions have in their frail keeping all the rest of the action of this great man; and the knowledge of his manner will be soon obliterated, together with that of Betterton's. Kemble still exhibits the majesty of the drama, the perfection and the glory of art, so finished, that every look is a commentary, every tone an illustration, every gesture a model for the statuary, and a study for the painter. His art is the last polish of the most perfect mirror, which represents every object according to the truth and dignity of nature, and is itself unseen." His sister is, with respect to him, as Eve, in Milton, is described, with respect to Adam, all that is beautiful in grace and dignity, yet looking up to him." The fame of these illustrious dramatic characters will go down to posterity, and their portraits will be handed down to posterity; for the artists have not been careless of the

---

[15] Ars est celare artem.

[16] What is here said of Mr. Kemble, will be allowed to apply justly to the happy exertion of his powers in his principal characters. Under such circumstances he has only one equal, his sister, Mrs. Siddons :

> Not spirits, yet to heav'nly spirits bright,
> Little inferior ; whom my thoughts pursue
> With wonder, and could love, so lively shines
> In them divine resemblance, and such grace
> The hand that form'd them on their shape hath pour'd. *Milton.*

honour, which the happy representation of such interesting and celebrated features must bestow on their pencils."[17] Nor have they altogether neglected to record some of the prominent splendors of their theatrical action: and perhaps on account of the improvement in the artists of the present day, more of their portraits, and of their attitudes, have been preserved, than of any former celebrated actors. But such representations do not give an idea of their manner, connected with the whole of the scene: they serve, to the traveller in the darkness, only as flashes of lightning, which shew him for a moment the surrounding objects, but are of little use to guide him: the dim light of a lamp would be to him of more advantage, which should, however faintly, illustrate every step. Some art, or invention is wanting, that may keep pace with the public speaker, and represent with fidelity his manner of delivery, and his gestures, accompanying his words in all their various transitions and mutual relations."[18]

For the purpose of making a step towards the accomplishment of this object, an attempt is here, with due respect, pre-

---

[17] The portrait of Mr. Kemble, by Lawrence, is, independantly of the happiest resemblance, an exquisite specimen of art: that of Mrs. Siddons seems to have been an earlier production. I mean those in Mr. Kemble's house.

[18] Marmontel, speaking of the sources from whence a great actor should derive his information in his art, mentions four principal:

La première est l'éducation. Baron avoit coutume de dire qu' *un comédien devroit avoir été nourri sur les génoux des reines :* expression peu mesurée, mais bien sentie.

La seconde seroit l'example d'un acteur consommé ; mais ces modeles sont rares, et l'on neglige trop la tradition, qui seul pourroit les perpétuer.

Kemble never saw Garrick play. Mrs. Siddons played with him the last year of his performing. Whatever he has achieved in the theatrical art, he owes to his own genius and labours alone. In the third requisite mentioned by Marmontel, as perhaps in the last, he stands unrivalled.

La troisième (mais celle-ci regarde l'action, dont nous parlerons dans la suite) c'est l'étude

sented to the public: and it is hoped that, in an inventive and learned age, it may obtain a favourable reception, as in some degree adding to the stock of knowledge, by extending the powers of writing to the easy comprehension of ideas, which had hitherto been found either to elude its hold, or had proved too cumbrous for the convenience of general use. The original idea of this attempt was suggested by the labour of teaching declamation in the usual manner. During this labour,[19] which for many years has constituted a part of his duty in his grammar school, the author, having often found that he forgot on a following day his own mode of instructing on a former, wished to be able to invent some permanent marks, in order to establish more uniformity in his instructions, for the ease both of himself and of his pupils. The expression of the voice, and of the countenance, were not liable to much variation, as to the mode of instruction, as the sentiments always sufficiently pointed them

---

des monumens de l'antiquité. Celui qui se distingue le plus aujourd' hui dans la partie de l'action théâtrale, et qui soutient le mieux par sa figure l'illusion du merveilleux sur notre scene lyrique, M. Chassé, doit la fierté de ses attitudes, la noblesse de son geste, et le bon goût de ses vetemens aux chef-d'œuvres de sculpture et de peinture qu'il a savamment observés. (Il y a long temps que ceci est écrit). This parenthesis, in the work, is apparently introduced by the editor ; long time though it may be since Marmontel wrote it for another, it may serve as a portrait of Kemble at this day.

La quatrième enfin, la plus féconde, et la plus négligée, c'est l'étude des originaux et l'on n'en voit guere que dans les livres. Le monde est l'école d'un comédien, théâtre immense, où tous les états, toutes les passions, tous les caractères sont en jeu. Mais comme la plupart des ces modéles manquent de noblesse et de correction, l'imitateur peut s'y meprendre, s'il n'est d'ailleurs éclairé dans son choix. Il ne suffit pas donc qu'il peigne d'après la nature, il faut encore que l'étude approfondie des belles proportions et des grands principes du dessein l'ait mis en état de la corriger.

L'étude de l'histoire et des ouvrages d'imagination, est pour lui ce qu'elle est pour le peintre et pour le sculpteur. *Marmontel Elém. de Littérature, art. Déclam. théâtrale.*

[19] Tu declamare doces, O ferrea pectora, Vecti.   *Juv.*

O o

out : but the great difficulty lay in ascertaining, and marking the suitable gesture ; and that for these obvious reasons ; because a language of gesture was wanting, and because gesture may be infinitely varied, and yet perhaps be equally just. To leave the pupil to choose for himself in this variety would but distract him, and instead of giving him freedom and grace would deprive him of both. On his commencement as a public speaker (which cannot be too early), it is necessary to teach him every thing, and to regulate by rules every possible circumstance in his delivery ; his articulation, accent, emphasis, pauses, tones, voice, countenance, and along with all, his gesture. After sufficient practice and instruction, he will regulate his own manner according to the suggestions of his judgment and taste.[20]

---

[20] The advantage of rules, and also the inconvenience at the commencement, are so sensibly stated by Mr. Engel, that I shall transcribe the passage at large.

Tant que la regle est presente au souvenir du disciple ; tant que sa mémoire la lui rappelle sans cesse, et que timide et incertain dans l'application qu'il doit en faire, il craint toujours de commettre des fautes ; aussi long-temps sans doute l'exécution restera très-imparfaite, et même au-dessous de ce quelle seroit, s'il ne suivoit que l'impulsion d'un heureux instinct. Aussi l'habilité de l'exécution s'acquiert-elle plus tard par l'étude et la connoissance approfondie des régles, que par le tact que donnent les idées confuses du sentiment ; cependant on y parviendra toujours : la régle qui s'offroit d'abord avec clarté à l'esprit, se transformera d'elle-même en idée, et se confondra avec le sentiment qui au besoin se présentera avec plus de promptitude et de facilité. L'ame par l'attention qu'elle doit donner à la regle, ne perdra plus rien de sa force, parceque cette attention ne sera plus nécessaire ; l'exécution deviendra aussi facile, elle aura autant de vivacité et de souplesse que celle du simple élève de la nature ; mais il y aura plus de fermeté, plus d'effet, et plus d'adresse à surmonter les obstacles. Je ne disconviens pas qu'un homme doué du sentiment musical, et d'une heureuse mémoire, qui veut retrouver sans papier noté sur le clavecin les morceaux de musique qu'il a dans la tête, et qui se sert de ses mains suivant l'impulsion de la nature ou le besoin du moment, ne parvienne pas plutôt et avec moins de peine à une grande habilité dans l'exécution, que celui qui doit apprendre auparavant à lire la note et à se familiariser avec le doigter de Bach. Examiner à la vue de chaque note sa place et sa valeur, se ressouvenir sans cesse des clefs du-dessus et de la basse, apprécier la durée des tons,

The difficulty of confining within reasonable limits the particular precepts on gesture, and not any want of importance in the art, has hitherto perhaps obliged writers on delivery to restrict their observations to general precepts, as Cicero and Quintilian, and also the older rhetoricians have done; and perhaps may be the reason why many of the best modern writers, have almost relinquished every attempt to give instructions on this point. In some of the most celebrated rhetorical treatises now in use, the instructions with respect to gesture are altogether trifling, and never descend into particular instances. As to the voice and countenance, a sufficient number of useful and particular illustrations for their management are to be found; but as to gesture, not a single page is given either in ancient or modern writer, in which the appropriate gesture, suited to the whole passage is attempted to be described, in all its preparations, action and transitions. Quintilian alone has left to us a literary curiosity in his conjectures concerning the particular gestures, which Demosthenes used in the commencement of his oration for Ctesiphon, and those with which Cicero began his oration for Archias.[21]

The system of gesture here presented to the public, however imperfect, as a first attempt, it must necessarily be, is the result

---

&c. se demander en frappant chaque touche, quel doigt il faut employer, enfin s'occuper d'objets sans cesse variés, et dont chacun partage l'attention, c'est sans contredit un travail très-pénible, qui doit rendre l'exécution fort imparfaite. Mais lorsqu'après de peines opiniâtres, l'habilité s'obtient enfin (ce qui ne manque presque jamais d'arriver) alors l'élève devient dans son art un maitre consommé, qui sait vaincre sur son instrument toutes les difficultés possibles, d'une manière aussi facile que sûre et précise ; avantage auquel l'homme guidé seulement par son instinct naturel, ne pourra jamais prétendre. Il en est de même de tous les arts; comment donc celui du geste seul, *si nous l'avions*, seroit-il une exception à la régle ? *Engel Idées sur le Geste, Lettre* 2.

[21] Est et ille verecundæ orationi aptissimus, quo quatuor primis leviter in summum coëuntibus digitis, non procul ab ore aut pectore fertur ad nos manus, et deinde prona ac

of considerable labour and reflection ; and in one respect, that for which it was originally intended, that is to shorten and relieve the labour of teaching declamation, it has had its utility fairly put to proof. This to many persons engaged in the various toil of education, will, it is hoped, be found not uninteresting.

Among its higher objects may be reckoned, its uses as a record from whence the historical painter may derive the materials of truth, and from whence the orator and the actor may not only obtain the instructions of the great men who have preceded them in the same career; but by which also, they may secure unalterably their own improvements for the advancement of their art, and for the benefit of posterity. To these advantages must be added the extension of the powers of writing, and of the sphere of knowledge and literary enjoyment; by which, in his closet, the lover of the drama may almost contemplate by this aid to his imagination, the actual performance of the most eminent actors, and by which the admirer of oratory may almost see as well as hear the wonderful effects of eloquence.

---

paullulum prolata laxantur. Hoc modo coepisse Demosthenem credo in illo pro Ctesiphonte timido summissoque principio: sic formatam Ciceronis manum, cum diceret,

l. br—— ———phf——
Si quid est in me ingenii, judices, quod sentio quam sit exiguum.
The passage from Demosthenes' Oration is this :

l. br——
Πρῶτον μεν, ὦ ἄνδρες Ἀθηναῖοι, τοῖς θεοῖς εὔχομαι πᾶσι καὶ πάσαις, ὅσην εὔνοιαν ἔχων
———phf——
ἐγὼ διατελῶ τῇ τε πόλει καὶ πᾶσιν ὑμῖν, ταυσαύτην ὑπάρξαι μοι παρ' ὑμῶν εἰς τ·ḗον·
·τὸν ἀγῶνα·

This short passage requires more gesture than Quintilian has mentioned.
Of the celebrated passage from C. Gracchus, Quintilian says, Plus enim affectus in his junctæ exhibent manus. *Quint. l.* xi, *c.* 3.

Had the ancients possessed the art of notation of their delivery, such was the unwearied diligence of their great orators Demosthenes and Cicero, that we should, most probably, at this day be in possession of their manner of delivery as well as of the matter of their orations; and not be limited to conjecture relative to a single sentence of each on the great occasions which called forth their powers. Both Quintilian and Cicero speak with admiration of the impressive delivery of the younger Gracchus, who " by his looks, his voice, and his gestures," drew " tears from the whole Roman people, and " made his very " enemies to weep." How interesting would prove the record, if any such were in existence, which should describe in language at large, or in symbols intelligibly, the captivating expression of this great orator, or the grace and energy of Demosthenes and Cicero?[23]

The notation of gesture above all would prove interesting to the historical painter. A scene of Shakspeare, or a passage of Milton so noted after the manner of a great actor or a great master of recitation; or an oration so noted as delivered by an

---

[22] This passage, already quoted, is here repeated:

Quo me miser conferam ? quo vertam ? in capitoliumne ? at fratris sanguine redundat. An domum ? matremne ut miseram lamentantemque videam, et abjectam ! quæ sic ab illo acta esse constabat oculis, voce, gestu, inimici ut lacrymas tenere non possent. *Cic. de. Orat. l. iii. c. 56.* What a character of eloquence is the following from the hand of Cicero?

Sed ecce in manibus vir, et præstantissimo ingenio et flagranti studio, et doctus a puero, C. Gracchus. *Brut. 33.*

[23] Caussinus thus laments the loss of the action of the great orators. Demosthenis quidem et Ciceronis orationes, quæ literis extant consignatæ, multis judicium, actio quæ cum ipsis interiit, omnibus desiderium reliquit: quam si exaratis eloquentiæ monumentis imprimere potuissent, minus laboraremus. *Causs. de Eloquentia. Cap. 67.*

admired speaker, would prove an incessant study of truth and nature combined with imagination. If the historical painter would hand down to posterity truth instead of fiction, and so stamp a double value on the productions of his pencil, he would represent the actual manner of gesture of the speakers concerned in the great events, which he celebrates. He would pourtray not only their dignified looks; but might sometimes mark even their awkward energies, and so bring into the contemplation of posterity the whole identity of the scene. Or if such strict truth of representation might not accord with the grander aims of his art, he might so far embellish its homely simplicity, as still to preserve the general congruity with the character of truth. The enquiry on great occasions is naturally not only what has been said, and by whom, but also how it has been said. And when the art of recording gesture and expression shall have arrived at the perfection of which it is capable, the record of the manner will be as capable of being truly represented, as the record of the words. Neither is this limited to the powers of the pencil, for without calling on the pencil, such gestures, and such expressions may be correctly and abundantly conveyed to the imagination by their proper symbols or letters.

But from this notation, the dramatic art is of all others most likely to derive improvement. If great actors would themselves note their most successful efforts, and mark their ideas of the conduct of favourite scenes, or of all the scenes in their principal characters, these would go down to posterity as memorials of their acquirements in their art, and as models for the improvement of posterity. And the aspiring actor would not be obliged as at present, almost before he can emerge from obscurity, to invent for himself an entire system of action. He might light, his talents at the perpetually burning lamps of the dead, and proceed at once by their guidance towards the highest honours of the drama. Nor would the transitory blaze of his fame continue to be the subject of just and inevitable regret both to the actor and his historian, as well as the theme of every poet's elegiac lamentations.[24]

In the life of Colley Cibber, the author, speaking of the celebrated Betterton, is led into reflections exactly to the present purpose. " How Shakespear wrote, all men who have a " taste for nature may read, and know; but with what higher " rapture would he still be read, could they conceive how " Betterton played him! then might they know, the one was " born alone to speak, what the other only, knew to write! " pity it is, that the momentary beauties flowing from an har- " monious elocution, cannot like those of poetry, be their own " record! that the animated graces of the player, can live no " longer, than the instant breath and motion that presents them ; " or at best can but faintly glimmer through the memory, or " imperfect attestation of a few surviving spectators. Could " *how Betterton* spoke be as easily known as what he spoke ; " then might you see the muse of Shakespear in her triumph,

---

[24] Combien il seroit à desirer qu'il existât un dépôt où seroient consignés les grands effets de la déclamation théâtrale, et où chaque acteur reconnu pour modele, iroit, après avoir recueilli les justes applaudissements du public, tracer lui-même l'histoire de son ame, de ses intentions et de ses moyens, au moment où il a excité le plus grand enthusiasme ! c'est dans cet dépôt, dévenu proprieté exclusive du théâtre pour lequel il seroit fait, que les jeunes acteurs pourroient puiser l'idée de ces mouvemens sublimes, qui transportent toute une assemblée, et sont le triomphe de la belle déclamation. *Dubroca, l'Art de Lire.* Leçon 37.

" with all her beauties in their best array, rising into real life
" and charming her beholders. But alas! since all this is so
" far out of the reach of description, how shall I shew you
" Betterton?"[25]

The close of Lloyd's Actor, is a pathetic complaint of the
transitory nature of the player's fame which cannot be recorded :
and which it is one object of this system in some degree to preserve from oblivion.[26]

> " Yet, hapless Artist! though thy skill can raise
> The bursting peal of universal praise,
> Though at thy beck applause delighted stands,
> And lifts, Briareus like, her hundred hands,
> Know, fame awards thee but a partial breath!
> Not all thy talents brave the stroke of death.
> Poets to ages yet unborn appeal,
> And latest times th' eternal nature feel.
> Though blended here the praise of bard and play'r,
> While more than half becomes the actor's share,
> Relentless death untwists the mingled fame ;
> And sinks the player in the poet's name.
> The pliant muscles of the various face,
> The mien that gave each sentence strength and grace,

---

[25] Life of Colley Cibber, p. 60. Dublin.

[26] The French writers complain justly of the same irremediable privation in the removal
of their great actors from the scene.

On vit alors (in the time of Baron et le Couvreur) ce que la scène tragique a jamais
réunis de plus parfait, les ouvrages de Corneille et de Racine représentés par des acteurs
dignes d'eux. En suivant le progrès et les vicissitudes de la déclamation théâtrale, j'essaye
de d·nner un idée des talens qu'elle a signalées, convaincu que les principes de l'art ne sont
jamais mieux sentis que par l'étude des modèles. Corneille et Racine nous restent ; Baron
et le Couvreur ne sont plus : leurs leçons n'étoient écrites que dans le souvenir de leurs ad-
mirateurs ; leur exemple s'est évanoui avec eux. *Marmontel Elém. Lit. art. Déclam.*

The tuneful voice, the eye that spoke the mind
Are gone, nor leave a single trace behind."

The author of the verses to the Memory of Mr. Garrick, spoken
as a monody by Mrs. Yates, has fallen into the same sentiments,
and has more fully developed them.[27] After speaking of the
security of the fame of the painter, the sculptor, and the poet, he
laments the short-lived remembrance of the actor, in these
beautiful lines :

" Such is their meed, their honours thus secure,
Whose hearts yield objects, and whose works endure.
The actor only shrinks from time's award;
Feeble tradition is his memory's guard;
By whose faint breath his merit must abide,
Unvouch'd by proof, to substance unallied!
Even matchless Garrick's art, to heav'n resign'd,
No fix'd effect, no model leaves behind.
The grace of action, the adapted mien,
Faithful as nature to the varied scene ;
Th' expressive glance, whose subtle comment draws
Entranc'd attention, and a mute applause;
Gesture that marks, with force and feeling fraught,
A sense in silence, and a will in thought;
Harmonious speech, whose pure and liquid tone,
Gives verse a music, scarce confess'd its own;
As light from gems assumes a brighter ray,
And cloth'd with orient hues, transcends the day !
Passion's wild break, and frown that awes the sense,
And ev'ry charm of gentle eloquence,
All perishable !—like th' electric fire,
But strike the frame, and, as they strike, expire:
Incense too pure a bodied flame to bear,
Its fragrance charms the sense, and blends with air.

---

[27] Said to be R. B. Sheridan, Esq.

P p

Where then, while sunk in cold decay he lies,
And pale eclipse for ever veils those eyes !
Where is the blest memorial that ensures
Our Garrick's fame—whose is the trust ?—'tis yours."[28]

---

[28] Mr. Steele, in his *Prosodia Rationalis,* has most ingeniously and perfectly recorded in certain passages Garrick's manner of delivery as to the modulation of his voice. From the present system of notation combined with that, and aided by the arts of painting and engraving, permanent monuments and valuable models of the transitory excellence of delivery might be preserved for entertainment or improvement.

CHAPTER XI.

OF THE POSITION OF THE FEET AND LOWER LIMBS.

The similarity of gestures affords opportunity for classification — Every part of the human body contributes to the perfection of gesture— Enumeration of the parts most necessary to be considered—The position of the standing figure should be manly and decorous—The positions of the feet and their notation—Moderate and extended positions—Equilibrium of the body and limbs—Changes of position—Walking and running—Steps with the notation.

CHAPTER XI.

Of the Position of the Feet and lower Limbs.

The variety of gestures, of which the human figure is capable, in all the motions, positions, and combinations of the head, the body, and the limbs, may almost be accounted infinite.¹ In this great variety there appears however a similarity and relation among many gestures, which affords opportunity for classification and nomenclature: so that however unattempted hitherto in this view, the art of gesture and its notation (that is the representation of any gesture by appropriate symbols) seems capable of being reduced to a regular system. In a first attempt many difficulties are to be encountered, which united efforts may hereafter remove, should the art be thought worthy of cultivation; and many imperfections and omissions must be expected, which future attention, and the suggestions of judicious critics may supply. The candid reader will give all just indulgence to the novelty and difficulty of this attempt.

. . . . . . Comely and in act
Rais'd, as of some great matter to begin.
As when of old some orator renown'd
In Athens or free Rome, where eloquence
Flourish'd, since mute, to some great cause address'd,
Stood in himself collected, while each past
Motion, each act, won audience ere the tongue. *Milton, Book* ix. *p.* 668.

The parts of the human figure which are brought into action in gesture, cannot, in truth, be considered separate: for every muscle, every nerve, over which men can exercise voluntary action, contributes in some measure to the perfection of gesture.[2] We may however enumerate and class in relation to them for convenience, the most distinguished parts of the body which effect the principal gestures. These are: 1 The head. 2 The shoulders. 3 The trunk or body. 4 The arms. 5 The hands and fingers. 6 The lower limbs and knees. 7 The feet.

We begin, as it were, with the foundation of the building, and shall first consider the positions and motions of the feet and lower limbs; since without the stability and ease of these, no grace or dignity can consist in the standing figure.

As the object of the orator is to persuade, and as prejudice against his person or manners may greatly impede him, and may be easily conceived by the fastidious or light minded, whom it is often important to influence and gain over; he must recommend himself by every attention to his external de-

---

[2] Pride braces the nerves and muscles, and valour in a higher degree. Submission relaxes them, and fear relaxes them still more. If the nerves and muscles assume the degree of tension suited to any passion, the mind will sympathize with the bodily action. And if the mind is affected by a particular passion either involuntary or by choice, as when actors endeavour to conceive it strongly; the muscular action and nervous sensibility excite to the expression of gesture: such is the effect of their mutual sympathy. Hence strong feelings seldom fail to shew themselves in gesture, unless some stronger feelings operate to suppress them, as fear or a sense of decorum, and hence fine or forcible gestures without a correspondent elevation or energy of feeling are most incongruous. *See on this, Burke, Darwin, Engel.*

portment, which may be deemed correct and proper;[3] and guard against every species of inelegance that may prove disadvantageous. He must therefore, even in his position as he stands, prefer manly dignity and grace, to awkward rusticity, or rude strength. Rude strength may suit him who wishes to terrify or to insult; but this is rarely the purpose of a public speaker. Grace and decorum win favour; and this is the general object. Rude strength stands indeed with stability, but without grace. Of this description is the portrait of Henry the VIII. mentioned by Hogarth, presented full in front, the arms a kimbo, and supporting his weight equally on both feet.[4] Before a person standing in this manner can change his place, he must make an awkward effort to poise his weight on either leg, in order that he may advance or retire with the other. The gracefulness of motion in the human form, or perhaps in any other, consists in the facility and security with which it is executed. And the grace of any positions (except such as are manifestly designed for repose), consists in the apparent facility with which they can be varied. Hence in the standing figure, the position is graceful when the weight of the body is principally supported on one leg, whilst the other is so placed as to be ready to relieve it promptly and without effort. And as the legs are

---

[3] A reasonable attention to dress becomes the orator, as far as the fashion of the age and country admits; it should be regulated on the maxims of Quintilian.

Cultus non est proprius oratoris aliquis, sed magis more conspicitur. Quare sit, ut in omnibus honestis debet esse, splendidus et virilis. Nam et toga et calceus et capillus, tam nimia cura, quam negligentia, sunt reprehendenda. Est aliquid in amictu, quod ipsum aliquatenus temporum conditione mutatum est. *Quint. l. xi. c. 3, p.* 1030, *edit. Bur.*

After this passage follow very minute directions for the adjustment of the dress of the orator as then worn.

[4] Analysis of Beauty, p. 20 and 137.

formed for a mutual share of labour and of honour, so their alternation in position and in motion is agreeable and graceful. A man may indeed stand very firmly on both legs, and it is in his power in moving to leap or spring with both feet together; but though they may both be practised on occasion, yet the continuance of the one is ungraceful, and of the other would be ridiculous.

The body must then be supported, if grace be consulted, on either limb, like the Apollo, the Antinous, or other beautiful and well executed statues. The foot, which at any instant sustains the principal weight, must be so placed, that a perpendicular line let fall from the hole of the neck shall pass through the heel of that foot.[5.6.7] Of course the centre of gravity of the body is for the time in that line, whilst the other foot assists

---

[5] Leonardo da Vinci in his treatise on painting, calls this hole or hollow of the neck *the middle point between the shoulders,* and in another passage, *the little well of the neck.*

P. 23, edit. fol. Paris, 1651, speaking of the position of the figure when resting on one leg, he observes that the parts of the body on the same side are contracted, and that this middle point is placed over the foot on which the figure rests.

E questo abbassamento nasce, perchè la figura che posa sopra un piede, quel piede si fà centro del sopraposto peso: essendo così, il mezzo delle spalle vi si drizza di sopra, uscendo fuori della sua linea perpendicolare, la qual linea passa per i mezzi superficiali del corpo: e questa linea più si viene a torcere la sua superiore estremità, sopra il piede che posa. See Fig. 1.

[6] And p. 54. *Dell' Attitudine, cap.* 192.

La fontanella della gola cade sopra il piede, e gittando un braccio inanzi, la fontanella esce di essi piedi, e se la gamba getta in dietro, la fontanella và inanzi, e così si rimuta in ogni attitudine.

[7] And. p. 62, cap. 209.

Se la figura posa sopra uno de' suoi piedi, la spalla di quel lato che posa sia sempre più bassa che l'altra, e la fontanella della gola sarà sopra il mezzo della gamba che posa. Il medesimo accaderà per qualunque linea noi vedremo essa figura essendo senza braccia sportanti non molto fuori della figura.

merely for the purpose of keeping the body balanced in this position, and of preventing it from tottering.

The positions of the feet are the following, which are symbolically expressed by the notation annexed, which is to be written under the word where the speaker is to assume such position.[8][9]
10·11·12

---

[8] I must confess myself in this description of the positions of the feet to be involved in great difficulty. Quintilian, and after him Cresollius, Vossius, and others, condemn the advancing of the right foot, and also the using of gesture with the hand, which corresponds with the foot advanced. One danger manifestly attends the neglect of this caution, and that is, lest the orator in the earnestness of his discourse should be inclined to work himself round into the attitude of a fencer, as in Fig. 6, which would be altogether faulty, and would be in great measure prevented by his standing in the position L. 1. The orator must always present himself in front *æquo pectore* to his audience: but provided he does so, I cannot discover any impropriety in the positions and the corresponding action which the great critic and his followers condemn. The most celebrated players use either hand and all positions freely, and that without appearing to violate either grace or decorum. But the reader will determine for himself: the possibility of such positions, as I have stated, will be admitted easily, the speaker will apply them as he shall think proper. Quintilian's observations are these:

In pedibus observantur status et incessus. Prolato dextro stare, et eamdem manum ac pedem proferre, deforme est. In dextrum incumbere interim datur, sed æquo pectore: qui tamen comicus magis, quam oratorius gestus est. Male etiam in sinistrum pedem insistentium dexter aut attollitur, aut summis digitis suspenditur. Varicare supra modum, et in stando deforme est. *Quin. l.* xi. *c.* 3.

[9] And further on in the same book Quintilian repeats his precepts; which more nearly accord with my idea. Status sit rectus, æqui et diducti paullum pedes, vel procedens minimo momento sinister. *Quint. l.* xi. *c.* 3.

[10] Vossius repeats the former observation of Quintilian, and adds a reason which does not appear conclusive.

Ne pes dexter porrigatur, sed sinister, quia vitiosum est eundem proferre pedem et manum. *J. Ger. Voss. Ins. Orat. p.* 61.

[11] Igitur hoc sit primum in monitis nostris, pedes ut æquos esse oportere, paululumque diductos, vel minimo momento sinistrum procedere. *Cresoll. p.* 391.

[12] Nonnulli in dextrum pedem incumbunt, quod interdum concedendum esse putat Fabius, modo id fiat æquo pectore, nam in alterum latus incumbere, sic ut animdverti à corona id facile queat, omnino vitiosum. *Cresol.*

This last passage seems to relate to the faulty position in Fig. 6.

Q q

The first position of the right foot, noted R. 1.

The upper part of the figure represents the elevation of the position, the lower the plan.

Fig. 2, and 7. In this position the right foot (advanced before the left about the breadth of the narrowest part of the foot) forms with the left foot an angle of about 75 degrees, as may be seen in the plan. The lines which form this angle passing through the length of each foot, meet its vertex under the heel of the left. The principal weight of the body is sustained by the left foot, the plan of which is deeply shadowed, the right foot rests lightly, but in its whole extent upon the ground, and is faintly shadowed.[3]

The second position of the right foot, noted R. 2

Fig. 3 and 7. In this position, the right foot sliding forwards about half the breadth of the foot, receives the principal weight of the body, the left heel being raised, and turning as far inwards towards the right, and the ball of the left great toe only lightly

---

[3] Fig. 7. This is a more correct plan of the feet than that annexed to the elevations. In both positions the right foot advances about half its own length, as may be seen by comparing it with the equidistant parallel lines. In the first position, the line (f f) passing through the centre of the feet makes an angle of about 75 degrees, and in the second position, the lines (S S) make an angle of about 90 degrees. These angles are nearly bisected by the line (E e) which goes to the eye of the person addressed. In the first position the lines (c f q x b) annexed to the dotted prints of both the feet, mark the manner in which they are shifted, without altering their own angle according as the gesture is directed. Those are the symbolical letters which will be explained in their place. In the plan the gesture is supposed to be directed forwards. This plate may be supposed to be reversed for the first and second positions of the left foot.

touching the ground to keep the body from tottering. The left heel, and all the rest of that foot is raised entirely from the ground. In the figure the right foot is deeply shadowed, and the part of the left which touches the ground is shadowed faintly. The part of the left which does not touch the ground is not shadowed in the plan. The angle formed by lines drawn through the length of the feet in this position is nearly equal to a right angle, or 90 degrees. In this position, if the feet are very near together, the entire sole of the left foot may lightly touch the ground: but when the feet are separated about their own length or more, the left touches only near the great toe; the knee is bent, and the inside of the leg is presented to view, as in Fig. 84, 86, &c.

The first position of the left foot, noted L. 1.

Fig. 4. This position of the left is in all respects analogous to the first position of the right. The left foot is advanced, and the body is principally supported on the right. The shadowing of the plan is similar to that in the first position of the right, and for the same purposes.

The second position of the left foot, noted L. 2.

Fig. 5. This position of the left is in all respects analogous to the second position of the right; and in the figure it is represented in the same manner, only reversed.

Besides the four positions above mentioned, there are two others which may be called positions in front. The heels are placed nearly together at the distance of about half the breadth of the foot, and the body is supported alternately on the right and left foot, whilst the toes of the other lightly touch the ground. The angle formed by the feet in these positions, is somewhat greater than a right angle. In other respects they are similar to the ordinary positions.

The right position in front, noted **F. R.** is when the body is supported on the right foot.

The left position in front, noted **F. L.** is when the body is supported on the left foot.

The position in front is used, when persons are addressed alternately on either side, whilst the auditors are in front; as on the stage. It is not graceful, and should not often be used: it is too stiff and formal, like the military figure, and presents the body with too much uniformity and flatness. This appears to be the position condemned by Quintilian. " The swing also of those, " who balance their body to the right side and left upon the " alternate feet, is very ungraceful."" Connected with these positions which express the moderate state of the feet, are marked the same positions in the extended state. These differ from the moderate, principally in the greater separation of the feet; the 2d position extended, enlarges the angle a few degrees by drawing up the heel of the retired foot nearer to that of the advanced foot. Fig. 39 and 99. The first extended position is

---

[14] Est et illa indecora in dextrum ac laevum latus vacillatio alternis pedibus insistentium. *Quin. l.* xi. *c.* 3.

made when a person retires in any degree of alarm, and the second when they advance with boldness, as may be observed in many figures, particularly in Fig. 38 and 106. The contracted position is not marked in the ichnography of fig. 7, as it may be easily understood by supposing the heels to be brought close together. Hogarth's dancing-master, fig. 8, seems, as well as the clown from Engel, fig. 9, to be standing equally supported on both feet, a position not elsewhere exemplified, as not being graceful.

In the various positions of the feet, care is to be taken that the grace which is aimed at be attended with simplicity. The position of the orator is equally removed from the awkwardness of the rustic with toes turned in and knees bent, and from the affectation of the dancing-master, constrained and prepared for springing agility, and for conceited display. Fig. 8 and 9.

The orator is to adopt such attitudes and positions only, as consist with manly and simple grace. The toes are to be moderately turned outwards, but not to be constrained; the limbs are to be disposed so as to support the body with ease, and to change with facility. The sustaining foot is to be planted firmly; the leg and thigh braced, but not contracted; and the knee straightened; (contraction suits the spring necessary for the dancer, and bent knees belong to feebleness or timidity), the other foot and limb must press lightly, and be held relaxed so as to be ready for immediate change and action."⁵

---

¹⁵ Genua recta, sic tamen, ut non extendantur. *Quint.*

The trunk of the body is to be well balanced, and sustained erect upon the supporting limb, except in such attitudes as particularly require its inclination: as veneration, supplication, &c. The breast should in general be so presented, that a line drawn from the eye of the person addressed, should be nearly perpendicular to a line drawn across the speaker's shoulders. That is, whatever his position may be, he should present himself as Quintilian expresses it, *æquo pectore*, Fig. 10, 1, 93, &c, and never in the fencer's attitude Fig. 6. In every change of attitude the equilibrium, and at the same time the grace of the body, is maintained, by so extending the limbs in contrary directions as to bring the centre of gravity and the line of direction over the supporting limb. In kneeling, prostration, and bending forwards, as well in order to preserve grace as to maintain equilibrium, the limbs not immediately advanced are extended behind.[16] Fig. 10.

In changing the positions of the feet, the motions are to be made with the utmost simplicity; and free from the parade and sweep of dancing. The speaker must advance, retire, or change, almost imperceptibly; except only when particular energy requires that he should stamp with his foot, that he should start back, or advance with marked decision. The general rule for the time of change in the position of the feet, is, that it should take place after the first gesture or preparation of the changing hand,

---

[16] La figura che senza moto sopra li suoi piedi si sostiene, darà di se eguali pese opposti intorno al centro del suo sostentacolo. Dico che se la figura senza moto sarà posata sopra li suoi piedi, che s'ella getta un braccio inanzi al suo petto, ch'ella debba gettar tanto peso naturale in dietro, quanta ne getta del naturale et accidentale inanzi: e quel medesimo dico di ciascuna parte che sporta fuori del suo tutto oltre al solito. *Leonardo da Vinci, c.* 214. *p.* 64. *fol.*

and coincide with the second or the finishing gesture; and it is particularly to be observed that the changes should not be too frequent. Frequent change gives the idea of anxiety or instability, which are unfavourable to an orator.[17]

In changing the positions of the feet the person advances, (noted *a.*) retires, (*r.*) traverses, (*tr.*) starts, (*st.*) stamps, (*sp.*) Running or leaping are seldom used, even on the stage, and are not here noticed.[18]

If more steps than one are to be expressed (as in the business of the theatre), the number may be introduced in a parenthesis after the letter marking the step, and then the position follows which

---

[17] Cresollius gives directions on this subject with his usual judgment and humour : Quidam perpetuo commutant statum quasi pedes indignentur unum alteri præponi et dedecus sibi esse putent, si in postremis hæreant. Igitur ad singulas periodos, ingrata penitus insuavi et inepta vicissitudine modo hunc modo illum anteponunt. Fateor ego quidem non modo commutationem esse aliquando opportunum, verum etiam et necessarium, ne veluti clavo trabali affixus in eodem vestigio orator putetur. . . . . Sic dicentis illam inconstantem levitatem indecoram et repudiandam judico. Itaque pueri olim a pædagogis studiosissime docebantur μὴ ἴσχειν τὼ πόδε ἐπαλλὰξ, ut pedes non alternarent, ut meminit Aristides, Platon. 1. . . . . Nonnulli in dextrum pedem incumbunt quod interdum concedendum esse putat Fabius, modo id fiat æquo pectore, nam in alternum latus incumbere, sic ut animadverti à corona id facile queat, omnino vitiosum.

[18] It may not be amiss here to observe the difference in the position of the feet in walking and in running. Fig. 11. In walking, the advanced foot is firmly planted sometime before the following foot is lifted off the ground, and both are actually for an instant on the ground together; the advanced foot placed steadily, and the following foot just in action, leaving the ground. In running, the feet touch the ground alternately, and sometimes the body and both feet together are raised into the air. Fig. 12. Hence appears the greater security of walking, and hence it is that no rapidity of walking can become running, nor can any slow running become walking. If this speculation be carried to four-footed animals, it will be found that in walking one foot only is raised from the ground, the other three are in different states of stability on the ground, one just in action, another just resting, and the third firmly placed. In trotting, the alternate feet are completely raised and planted ; in gallopping, the fore feet and the hind alternate; and in ambling or pacing, the fore and hind foot at one side alternates with the fore and hind foot of the other.

finishes the movement, as *a* (2.) R. 2. means advance two steps to the 2d position of the right. In private declamations or recitations on a platform or rostrum, these figures are not necessary: as a single step in advancing or retiring is sufficient.

Changes of position or steps are considered to be executed only by the foot on which the body is not supported, for that foot alone is free. Should it be required to move the foot which supports the body, (suppose the left foot in the first position of the right fig. 2.) two motions are necessary, in the first the position must be changed to R. 2. fig. 3, so as to throw the weight of the body on the right foot, then the left may be moved as required.

According to this principle it will be found that from each original position, four steps may be made. The plan in the original position is in the centre, and drawn larger, the plan of the steps made from that original position is represented smaller. The line of motions of the feet is represented by a dotted line nearly of the form which each foot should trace; the line of the free or first moving foot is marked with a star. In the figures it will be observed, that from each position four steps may be made, in advance, retiring, traversing, and across. In advancing and traversing, each step finishes on the 2d position of the advancing foot, and in retiring from the first position, the step finishes on the 1st of the contrary foot; but from the second, it finishes on the first of the same foot. Fig. 13 and 14.

In crossing from the first position, the foot passes before and finishes on the 2d position, and from the second position it passes behind the planted foot, and finishes on the first.

The steps from the two positions of the left are similar, and do not require to be explained by another figure.

CHAPTER XII.

OF POSITIONS, MOTIONS, AND ELEVATIONS OF THE ARMS.

The motions of the arm in the vertical and transverse direction the foundation of this system of notation—The place of the spectator's eye with respect to the circles imagined for the uses of notation. The angles formed by the different intervals of gestures—Enumeration and notation of the systematic positions, motions, and elevations of the arm—The great variety of gesture arising from combinations of the simple or systematic positions—These combinations encreased by the energy of the action considered in a threefold degree—Particular positions of the arms arising from other relations and circumstances.

CHAPTER XII.

Of Positions, Motions, and Elevations of the Arms.

Lᴇᴛ a person stand in some one of the positions mentioned in the former chapter; his arms and hands hanging unconstrained, and at rest. Fig. 15.

If from this position either arm be raised as high as it can be, the extremity of the fingers will sweep, in the vertical direction, a semicircle terminating in the zenith, in which are marked five principal points, R d h e Z at the interval of about 45 degrees each. Fig. 16. The centre of this is the shoulder, and the radius, a line compounded of both parts of the arm, of the wrist, and of the hand. If in the transverse direction, the arm be extended across the body as far as convenience will permit, and then swept horizontally round and outwards, without turning the back; Fg. 17. in this case also, the extremity of the fingers will describe a curve which may be estimated as a semicircle, and in this also are marked five principal points, c f q x b at similar intervals; upon these observations is built the present system of gesture. In order to explain which, the following diagram is necessary.

Fig. 18. Let a sphere be described according to the stereographic projection, consisting of the primitive circle (Z h R h),

the right circle (Z R), and two oblique circles (Z q R and Z C R),
in an angle of 45 degrees at each side between the right and
primitive circles. These circles are in the hemisphere next the
eye. In the other hemisphere let two other oblique circles
Z b R and Z b R; be described also at 45 degrees distant from the
primitive circle. In the figure these circles are distinguished by
dotted lines, and, lest they should be confounded with the other
oblique circles, are placed nearer to the primitive. All these
circles are intersected by three others; by one great circle (h f h)
passing through the projecting point, and here called the
horizontal circle, and by two lesser circles (c f e and d f d) parallel
to it above and below at the distance of 45 degrees.

The human figure being supposed to be so placed within
this sphere, that the centre of the breast shall coincide with
its centre, and that the diameter of the horizontal circle perpendicular to a radius drawn to the projecting point, shall pass
through the shoulders, the positions and motions of the arms
are referred to, and determined by these circles and their
intersections.

It must be observed that the eye of the spectator, or of the
person addressed among the spectators, or on the stage among
the interlocutors, is always supposed to be in the plane of the
right circle (Z f R), and nearly in the point (f).

It will also be observed, that in speaking of angles and elevations determined by degrees, mathematical precision is not
intended, and is not necessary: it is sufficient for the present
purpose, that the position described should be nearly in the
angle or direction mentioned.

The circles fig. 18. which are strongly marked, relate to the right hand, the faint circles to the left. The right circle and the oblique circles at each side of it serve for both hands, but the names of the oblique circles as applied to one hand, are reversed when applied to the other. That marked (q) for the right becomes (c) for the left, and the contrary. In the figure the circles are marked only for the right hand, to prevent confusion.

The positions of the arm are thus determined and noted:

First, in the Vertical Direction.

Fig. 15.   When the arm hangs down at rest, it is noted   R

19 to 23.   When directed downwards within 45 degrees of the Nadir nearly   -   -   -   -   *d*

24 to 28.   When directed towards the horizon nearly   –   *h*

29 to 33.   When elevated between the horizon and zenith   *e*

30.   When pointing to the zenith   -   *   -   -   Z

Second, in the Transverse Direction.

19. 24. 29.   When the arm is extended as far as convenient across the body, 45 degrees beyond the right circle (Z f R.)   -   -   -   -   -   *c*

20. 25. 30.   When directed in the plane of the right circle, and of the spectator's eye   -   -   -   -   *f*

21. 26. 31.   When directed nearly 45 degrees obliquely from this   -   -   -   -   -   -   *q*

22. 27. 32.   When in the primitive circle and at right angles with the line from the spectator's eye, and extended in the plan of the speaker's breast   -   *x*

23. 28. 33.   When behind this, nearly 45 degrees backwards   *b*

Fig. 16, 17. From the combination of these 3 vertical and 5 transverse positions, (exclusive of those at rest (R), and pointing to the zenith (Z), in both of which the transverse positions meet and unite with the vertical), the 15 fundamental or systematic positions are formed. In the plate of these systematic positions of the arms, the upper line of figures will be observed all to direct the arm downwards, but to different points in the transverse circle: the second line move the arm in the horizon: and the third move it in the elevated lesser circle parallel to the horizon. If they are taken in the vertical direction, those in the first column of three point across, the second forwards, the third oblique, the fouth extended, the fifth backwards. And these differents directions combined produce the 15 systematic positions, as has been mentioned.

1st Line.

Fig.	No.						Noted
19.	1.	Directs the arm downwards across	-	-	$d\,c$
20.	2.	-	-	downwards forwards	-	-	$d\,f$
21.	3.	-	-	downwards oblique	-	-	$d\,q$
22.	4.	-	-	downwards extended	-	-	$d\,x$
23.	5.	-	-	downwards backwards	-	-	$d\,b$

2d Line.

24.	1.	-	-	horizontal across	-	-	$h\,c$
25	2.	-	-	horizontal forwards	-	-	$h\,f$
26.	3.	-	-	horizontal oblique	-	-	$h\,q$
27.	4.	-	-	horizontal extended	-	-	$h\,x$
28.	5.	-	-	horizontal backwards	-	-	$h\,b$

3d *Line.*

Fig.	No.							Noted
29.	1.	Directs the arm elevated across		-	-	-		*e c*
30.	2.	-	-	elevated forwards	-			*e f*
31.	3.	-	•	elevated oblique	-	-		*eq*
32.	4.	•		elevated extended	-		-	*ex*
33.	5.	-	•	elevated backwards	•		-	*eb*

Such are the simple positions of the whole arm, which, with the latitude allowed, will be found sufficient to represent most of the ordinary gestures. By the latitude allowed, is meant that deflexion from the accurate point by which the position is named: since it is sufficient, as has been already mentioned, that a position in order to obtain the name, should be nearly directed to the proper point.

Fig. 34, 35, 36. The colloquial elevations of the arm are less bold than those described in the systematic gestures. In the horizontal elevation, instead of being raised to the height of the shoulder, the fore arm points about so high as the middle of the breast; in the elevated position, the hand is not raised much above the eyes, and in the position downwards, it is held but little below the waist. The transverse positions are more nearly like those of the systematic figures, but less marked. In delineating the systematic positions, the boldest and most decided action has been chosen which is suited, as will appear hereafter, to the epic style, (see Chap. xix), because the different positions are in this style most strongly discriminated. The colloquial positions and elevations are similar but more tame; and in them the distinctive character is that the joint of the

S s

elbow is bended, and that the upper arm is held closer to the side. Quintilian's rule seems to apply to this style of gesture, and not to the boldness of the epic.'

The great variety, which the systematic or fundamental positions afford will appear more evidently, by considering that the 15 positions contained in Plate III. from fig. 19 to 33 inclusive, are first to be considered as 45, because they can be performed either by the right hand, by the left, or by both hands.

The 45 systematic, positions, in another view, will again be multiplied by 3 and produce 135. It is to be observed, that the degree of energy proceeding from the sentiment of desire or aversion with which a passage is delivered influences much the character of the gesture, in the same manner that it does the tones and expression of the voice; the language still remaining unaltered. If the passage to be delivered, may properly be illustrated by the arm in the position horizontal extended (*h x*), the degree of that extension will vary with the spirit of the passage. Fig. 37. If an object is simply pointed to in the horizon, the arm will be moderately extended, forming a small angle at the shoulder, the elbow, and the wrist. Fig. 38. If the object is highly interesting, and supposed to be in the same situation, as if a general pointed to those troops which he required to be instantly sustained, the arm stretches to the utmost, the wrist is thrown up, and the fingers down, whilst

---

' Tolli autem manum artifices supra oculos, demitti infra pectus vetant. *Quint.* B. 1023.

See the Chapter on Classification of Gesture.

The pulpit was probably constructed on this principle.

the whole body is projected forwards; the arm in this position is considered still to be horizontal extended as the last, but in the extreme degree, and is marked with an additional *x* as *h x x*. If the object in the same situation as before be supposed something producing disappointment or horror, the arm is contracted, and the whole person recoils. Fig. 39. Yet this also is considered horizontal extended; *horizontal* because the hand is directed towards the horizon, and *extended* because the arm continues in the same plane as in the former gestures; but with respect to the character of this gesture, it differs, and in order to express it by the symbolic letters, a *c* is added (*h x c*), which are read horizontal, extended, contracted.[2] The moderate degree is marked only by the two first letters. It will be observed that the hand is always directed accurately to the proper point, and that the variation arising from the force or energy of the action relates to the arm principally.[3] The hands will be particularly spoken of in the next chapter.

---

[2] In order to do away the absurdity which sometimes appears in the expression, when the symbols of notation are enounced in words: the reader will take into consideration and be pleased to admit what hereafter will be fully explained, that the terms having a different reference or value according to their place are not at all contradictory. The English language, not furnishing a sufficient variety of terms equally significant for this new application, forces upon the apparent incongruity. In the management of the symbolic letters there is some analogy to the disposal of the arabic numerals, in which each is of value according to its place, though expressed by the same name Thus each symbol in the sum 3333, is known to be of different value. *Horizontal, extended, contracted*, in the language of notation of gesture will not therefore appear an absurd expression, when it is considered that the word *extended*, placed as it is in this notation, does not relate to tension of the muscles, but only to the position of the arm in a certain plane in the transverse direction. But this will be easily understood farther on.

[3] Animal life displays itself through all the body and especially through all the animal parts, yet does it act most conspicuously in the arm from the shoulder to the ends of the fingers. *Lavater ed. Holcroft. Vol. I. p.* 15.

Thus there may be reckoned 135 systematic or fundamental positions of the arms, to which if we add the two Z and R, and multiply the former 2 by 3, in order to express the moderate, extended, and contracted states of the arm, we have four more, in all 139 fundamental positions. The number of these positions is adverted to, merely in order to shew how fruitful the system is in its very opening, not for the purpose of calculating its extent. For when to the combinations arising from these positions, are added the various positions of the hands and other circumstances necessary to be taken into the account, it will appear that the possible changes capable of distinct notation may be esteemed infinite. From these a few in proportion will suffice for any purpose, and from these every one may choose such as may suit himself best.

But besides these systematic gestures, however copious, there are some in general use which do not exactly fall under them, and therefore require to be separately detailed.

These particular positions of the arms are named from the manner of holding or resting them on the body: and may admit of considerable variety ; but the description of the following will suffice to explain the class, in which they are to be reckoned.

Fig. 40. The arms are said to be *folded* or *encumbered* when they are crossed and enclose each other, the fingers of the left hand holding the upper right arm, and the right hand passing under the upper left arm. (*en*).[4]

---

[4] With arms encumbred thus. *Hamlet.*

Fig. 41. *A kimbo,* when the hands are rested on the hips, and the elbows are stuck out at either or both sides.(*k*)

Fig. 42. *Reposed,* when the elbows are nearly resting on the hips, and one hand holds the wrist of the other.(Rp)   This is a female position (posées).

CHAPTER XIII.

OF THE POSITIONS AND MOTIONS OF THE HANDS.

The motions of the hands perhaps innumerable—Their expressions according to Quintilian—According to Vossius—According to Cresollius—Story of Apollonius Rhodius from Philostratus—Importance attached by the ancients to the disposition of the fingers—Passage from Quintilian with the translation illustrated by figures—Observations on Quintilian by Cresollius—Positions of the hands divided into four different classes together with the notation—Motions of the hands and notation.

CHAPTER XIII.

Of the Positions and Motions of the Hands.

THE positions and motions of the hands are so numerous, and may be so exceedingly varied by minute changes, that it would perhaps prove impossible, and would certainly be a very useless labour, to attempt to describe them all. The efforts of the ancient pantomimes, who digested the motions of the body, and particularly those of the hands, into a sort of language, were very extraordinary; and were probably more so in this respect, than those of modern dancers, whose attention is chiefly engaged by the lower limbs. But at present I shall forbear to enter into any discussion on this subject, I have now to enquire only into a few of those positions and motions of the hands which may suit the public speaker, and may perhaps be of some use to the actor who applies gesture only to illustrate the sentiments which he delivers, and not as an independant language. Quintilian considers the gesture of the hands of such importance for illustration and enforcement, that after a long and eloquent enumeration of their powers, he even attributes to them the faculty of universal language.

" Without the aid of the hands, action would be mutilated
" and void of energy, but it is hardly possible, since they are
" almost as copious as words themselves, to enumerate the

T t

" variety of motions of which they are capable. The action
" of the other parts of the body assists the speaker, but the
" hands (I could almost say) speak themselves. By them do
" we not demand, promise, call, dismiss, threaten, supplicate,
" express abhorrence and terror, question, and deny? do we
" not by them express joy and sorrow, doubt, confession,
" repentance, measure, quantity, number and time? do they
" not also encourage, supplicate, restrain, convict admire,
" respect? and in pointing out places and persons do they not
" discharge the office of adverbs and of pronouns? so that in
" the great diversity of languages, which obtain among all
" kingdoms and nations, theirs appears to me the universal
" language of all mankind." [1]

Vossius follows the opinion of Quintilian almost in the same
words. " The hands" he says " not only assist the speaker, but
" seem almost themselves to speak." [2] But Cresollius in his
ardent manner goes far beyond the correct criticism and
tempered warmth of Quintilian. The very contents or title
of the chapter in which he treats of the hands, are in this spirit :

---

[1] Manus vero, sine quibus trunca esset actio ac debilis, vix dici potest, quot motus
habeant, cum pene ipsam verborum copiam persequantur. Nam ceteræ partes loquentem
adjuvant, hæ (prope est ut dicam) ipsæ loquuntur. An non his poscimus? pollicemur?
vocamus? dimittimus? minamur? supplicamus? abominamur? timemus? interrogamus?
negamus? gaudium, tristitiam, dubitationem, confessionem, pœnitentiam, modum, copiam,
num;rum, tempus, ostendimus? non eædem concitant? supplicant? inhibent? probant?
admirantur? verecundantur? non in demonstrandis locis atque personis adverbiorum atque
pronominum obtinent vicem? ut in tanta per omnes gentes nationesque linguæ diversitate
hic mihi omnium hominum communis sermo videatur. *Quint. l.* xi. *c.* 3.

[2] Manus non modo loquentem adjuvant, sed ipsæ pene loqui videntur. *Voss. Inst.
Orat.*

—" The hand, the admirable contrivance of the divine
" artist.—The minister of reason and wisdom.—Without the
" hand no eloquence.

. . . " Man, I say, full of wisdom and divinity could have
" appeared nothing superior to a naked trunk or a block, had
" he not been adorned with this interpreter and messenger of
" his thoughts.

" The celebrated Physician Cous, called the practice of the
gestures of the hand the most excellent lesson in eloquence.

" The brother of St. Basil said, that had men been formed
" without hands, they would never have been endowed with
" an articulate voice.

" Among the wise men of Egypt, the inventors of the sacred
" hieroglyphics, their designation of language, was by the
" symbol of a hand placed under a tongue.

> " Contention, play, love, revels change and rest,
> " And truth and grace are by the hand express'd.

" Every thing, it must be confessed, depends on the hand ; it
" gives strength and colouring to eloquence, and adds force and
" nerves to the riches of thought, which, otherwise languid,
" creeping on the ground, and deficient in vigour, would lose
" all estimation."

" Hence we see how it came to pass, that among the inter-
" preters of dreams, the hand signifies language, because the

" gestures of the hands are requisite to be used along with
" language, as Artemidorus says. He has even declared in
" those works of his which remain, that if a public speaker
" should dream that he had many hands, he might expect the
" most fortunate events of profit and honour from his studies
" in oratory. In my judgment, therefore, the hand may pro-
" perly be called a second tongue, because nature has adapted
" it by the most wonderful contrivance for illustrating the art
" of persuasion."

" Since then nature has furnished us with two instruments
" for the purpose of bringing into light and expressing the
" silent affections of the mind, language and the hand ; it has
" been the opinion of learned and intelligent men, that the
" former would be maimed and nearly useless without the
" latter; whereas the hand, without the aid of language, has
" produced many and wonderful effects."[a]

---

[a] The contents of Cresollius's 9th chapter are in the following strong expressions :

Manus divinæ mentis opificium mirabile, rationis et sapientiæ ministra. Sine manu
eloquentia nulla. à doctis ea ponitur inter præcipua recitantium adjumenta.

. . . . Homo inquam plenus consilii et divinitatis, truncus modo atque stipes videri
potuisset, nisi hoc mentis interprete atque internuncio fuisset ornatus. . . . . . . Cous
medicorum omnium coryphæus manuum usum esse dixit κάλλιςον διδασκαλεῖον, optimum
dicendi magistrum. Clarissimus D. Basilii frater. . . . . negat futuram in nobis ἔναρθρον
φωνὴν articulatam quasi vocem εἰ μὴ παρῆσαν αἱ χεῖρες τῷ σώματι, nisi in corpore
manus extitissent. Itaque Sapientes apud Egyptios, qui sacras notas adinvenerunt, sermonem innuentes, γλῶσσαν καὶ χεῖρα ὑποκάτω, linguam subtusque manum pingebant.
(Horus in Hyeroglyph.)

Vates anonymus de manu,

       Pugnat, ludit, amat, bacchatur, vertitur, astat,
         Illustrat verum, cuncta decore replet.

. . . . Nimirum fatendum est in manu sita esse omnia : hæc vim et colorem addit

Cresollius, after this passage, refers, as an example of the extraordinary effects of the eloquence of the hand, to the stories told by Philostratus concerning Apollonius Tyanæus during the period of his Pythagorean silence.—How he quieted many seditious cities by his looks and gestures alone; and above all, how he obliged certain monopolists of Aspendium in Pamphylia, to sell out their corn to the starving people, and so saved their governor, whom they were going to put to death: and all this without speaking a single word: Philostratus indeed allows that in the last instance, he wrote a pretty strong sentence for the consideration of Aspendian monopolists.[5] Whatever effects the

---

eloquentiæ, hæc dictioni robur et lacertos adjungit, quæ alioqui languida et humi repens et defecta viribus obsolesceret. . . . . . .

. . . . . Hinc factum fuisse videmus, ut manus quoque apud Onirocritas sermonem significet, quod una cum sermone, manuum quoque motus requireretur, ut ait Artemidorus, (*l. i. c.* 45.) qui etiam monumentis suis prodidit, oratori in agendis causis nobili et honoris studioso felicissimos eventus portendi, qui se plures manus habere somniaverit. Manum proinde linguam veluti alteram jure quispiam meo judicio nominaret, quam natura maximo quasi artificio fabricata sit ad suadam illuminandam. . . . . *p.* 289.

. . . . . Quare cum duo nobis instrumenta natura concesserit ad tacitas animorum affectiones in lucem et cognitionem expromendas, sermonem atque manum: docti homines et polito judicio præditi existimaverunt, illum sine hac mancum esse ac prope inutilem : manum autem sine copia orationis multa et eximia præstitisse. *Ib.*

4 Caussinus speaks of the hand in the same manner.

Membrorum omnium totius humani corporis, manus ut habilissima et in omnem partem motu facillima ; ita etiam ut multiplicis habitus artifex et variæ significationis est index. *De Eloq. Sac. et Prof. l.* ix.

5 Philostratus de Vita Apollonii Tyanensis. *l. i. c.* 16. *Edit. Olearii, p.* 19.

Τιμῶν δὲ τὸ τῆς σιωπῆς δόγμα, γράφει ἐς γραμματεῖον ἐπίπληξιν, καὶ δίδωσιν ἀναγνῶναι τῷ ἄρχοντι. ἡ δὲ ἐπίπληξις, ὧδε εἶχεν. Ἀπολλώνιος σιτοκαπήλοις Ἀσπευ-δίων. ἡ γῆ πάντων μήτηρ, δικαία γάρ. ὑμεῖς δὲ ἄδικοι ὄντες, πεποίησθε αὐτῶν αὐτὴν μόνων μητέρα. καὶ εἰ μὴ παύσεσθε, οὐκ ἐάσω ὑμᾶς ἐπ᾿ αὐτῆς ἑστάναι. Ταῦτα δείσαντες ἐνέπλησαν τὴν ἀγορὰν σίτᾳ, καὶ ἀνεβίω ἡ πόλις.　But reverencing his obligation to silence, he wrote a remonstrance on a tablet, and gave it to the prefect to read. The remonstrance was in these terms : " Apollonius to the monopolists of Aspendium, The earth is the

the countenance and the gestures of the hand may have towards
obtaining the attention of an angry mob, to what a grave
personage might have to say; and we have high poetical
authorities for this much; [6][7][8][9] neither experience nor poetry
authorize us to attribute much greater effects to dumb shew
words must be added.

Having supported on sufficient authorities the general importance to the orator of attention to the gestures of the hand; I
proceed now to enter upon the detail of some of the most usual
and necessary of its positions and motions. The ancient Roman
critics and orators attributed considerable importance to the
manner of disposing the fingers in delivery: [10][11][12][13] attributing

---

" mother of all, and she is just. But you in your injustice have made her the mother of
" yourselves alone; and if you do not desist, I will not suffer you to stand alive upon her."
Through fear of this they filled the market with corn, and the city recovered its strength.

[6]   Ac veluti magno in populo cum sæpe coorta est
          Seditio, sævitque animis ignobile vulgus;
          Jamque faces et saxa volant, furor arma ministrat:
          Tum, pietate gravem ac meritis si forte virum quem
          Conspexere, silent, arrectisque auribus astant:
          Ille regit dictis animos, et pectora mulcet.   *Virg. Æn.* 1.

[7]   Fert animus calidæ fecisse silentia turbæ
     Majestate manus.   *Per. Sat.* 4.
[8]   . . . . . Qui postquam voce manuque
     Murmura compressit, tenuere silentia cuncti,
     Substitit et clamor pressus gravitate regentis.   *Met. l.* i.
[9]   . . . . tumultum
     Composuit vultu, dextraque silentia fecit.   *Lucanus.*

[10] Seneca implies thus much in this exclamation :
          O digitum multum significantem !   *Senec. l.* iii. *cont.*

[11] Cresollius thus explains the præcept of Cicero. *Nullæ argutiæ digitorum.*—Sunt
veto digitorum celeres quædam et subtiles motiones, quales præstigiatorum esse consueverunt qui fucum faciunt, oculosque illudunt. Hinc manus argutæ furum dictæ, quæ celeriter

to each particular disposition of them a significancy or suitableness for certain expressions, of which we do not always see the force. We may be allowed to conjecture from the gesticulations of the fingers used by the modern Italians in common discourse, that the value of these dispositions has been handed down to and admitted by them. As matter perhaps rather of curiosity than of absolute use, yet immediately connected with my subject, I shall report what Quintilian has said upon the fingers: and then shall borrow from him what appears most suitable to my purpose.

Fig. 43. " It is a very common gesture to bend down the
" middle finger to the thumb, and to extend the other three.
" This gesture is suited to the opening of an oration; and is
" moderately extended with gentle motion towards either side,
" at the same time the head and shoulders sensibly accompany
" the direction of the hand. In narration this gesture should be
" decided and then a little more advanced; in reproach or argu-
" ment, it should be sharp and earnest. For it is extended farther
" and more boldly in these parts of the discourse. But it is a
" vicious custom to push it so far towards one side, as if aiming

emicant et è conspectu modo abripiuntur, modo emergunt et in omnem partem cientur. *Cresoll. Vac. Aut.*

¹² Suetonius de Tiberio Cæsare ita memorat, vix unquam loquebatur sine molli quadam digitorum gesticulatione. *Suet. c. 68. Cresol. Vac. Aut.*

¹³ Cresollius thus describes certain awkward gestures of the hands : Novi senatorem unum è curia, virum amplissimum, judicio vere magno et exacto, sed qui externam actionem non opere magno curet. Vix sententiam potest unquam dicere quin sinistram manum alterius manus digitis fricet obiter atque scabat, seu prurigine titillante, seu consuetudine illiciente, seu fixa in gravibus negotiis mente, quæ proinde minus cogitet de externis. Nonnunquam vero lævam manum ad pectus applicatam et quietam leviter alia et subinde quatit manu. Aliquando terit utramque manum, ut fieri ab aliis solet, qui inter utramque volam crebra manuum agitatione terere aliquid atque imminuere volunt : quod ipse tamen rarius facit atque lentius. *Cresoll. Vac. Aut. p. 364.*

" at the left shoulder; though some stretch their arm across
" even in a more faulty manner, and gesticulate with their
" elbow.

Fig. 44. " The two middle fingers are also contracted under
" the thumb. This gesture is still more vehement than the
" former, and is not suited to the exordium or to the narration.

Fig 45 and 66. " But when the three last are bended in-
" wards and are pressed down by the thumb, then that finger
" is extended, which, as Cicero says, Crassus used to such
" advantage. This gesture is used in reproach and indication
" from which last it has its name, (index.) And, when the
" hand is raised and turned towards the shoulder, it affirms
" by a small inclination. When turned towards the earth and
" pointing as it were downwards, it is urgent; sometimes it
" stands for a number.

Fig. 46 and 47. " This finger also when its upper joint is
" lightly held at both sides, whilst the other two fingers (but
" the little one less so), are moderately bended, is proper for
" disputation

Fig. 48. " But they seem to dispute with more eagerness
" who rather hold the middle joint, contracting the last fingers
" the more in proportion as the first go down.

Fig. 49. " That gesture is also well suited to a modest
" oration, in which, lightly collecting together at their points
" the four first fingers, the hand is brought near to the lips or

" to the breast, and then gradually extended prone with the
" fingers relaxed. In this manner, I conceive that Demosthenes
" began in the timid and submissive exordium for Ctesiphon:
" and that Cicero held his hand in this manner when he said:
" If, O judges, any abilities are possessed by me, which I feel to
" be so inconsiderable.

Fig. 50. " The hand also, the fingers being more freely
" turned upwards, is collected towards the lips, and then ex-
" tended a little more widely in the contrary direction, seeming,
" as it were, to carry forth the words along with it.

Fig. 51. " Sometimes we extend two fingers more distinctly,
" but without pressing the thumb inwards (towards the palm);
" the last fingers however are a little turned in, yet without
" much extending the upper fingers.

Fig. 52. " The two last fingers sometimes press the palm of
" the hand near the ball of the thumb, which is joined itself
" to the first fingers at the middle joint.

Fig. 53. " Sometimes the fourth finger is inclined obliquely.

Fig. 54. " Sometimes the four fingers being rather relaxed
" than extended, and the thumb inclined inwards, we put our
" hand into a convenient position for demonstrating or distin-
" guishing at the sides, when it is turned supine to the left and
" prone on the right side.

" These are modest gestures,—when the hand moderately
U u

" expanded in the manner of those who are making a vow, is
" moved within a small interval, the shoulders accompanying
" its motion. This suits remarkably those who speak but a few
" words, and with timidity.

Fig. 55 and 93. " A gesture suited to admiration is this.
" The hand is held nearly supine, and the fingers are collected
" from the smallest; in the returning sweep, they are extended,
" and the hand is turned into another position.

" In questioning, we do not compose our gesture after any
" single manner: the position of the hand, for the most part, is
" to be changed, however disposed before.

Fig. 56. " The fore finger of the right hand joining the
" middle of its nail to the extremity of its own thumb, and
" moderately extending the rest of the fingers, is graceful in
" approving in narration and in discrimination.

Fig. 57. " Not unlike which, but with the three fingers com-
" pressed, is that gesture, now very much used by the Greeks,
" and even with both hands, as often as by their gestures they
" strike their enthymemas like pushing horns together

" The hand moved gently promises and assents, when more
" rapidly it encourages, and sometimes praises.

Fig 59 and 60. " And that gesture which urges on the
" words, contracting and opening the hand with alternate and
" rapid motion, is rather admitted by common usage than ac-
" cording to art

Fig. 61. " The hollowed and opened hand raised above the
" shoulder, with some degree of motion, as if encouraging, is a
" gesture nearly adopted from the foreign schools.

" The tremulous hand is theatrical.

" To collect the fingers and approach them to the mouth,
" why it displeases some people I know not. For we use this
" gesture both when we express moderate admiration, and
" sometimes sudden indignation, or fear or deprecation.

" And we move towards our breast our hand clinched as the
" indication of repentance or of indignation; at which time
" it is not improper even to force the voice through the teeth.
" *How shall I conduct myself at this moment? what shall I do?*

Fig. 62. " To point out any thing with the thumb averted,
" is rather permitted, than becoming to an orator." [14]

---

[14] Est autem gestus ille maxime communis, quo medius digitus in pollicem contrahitur
explicitis tribus, et principiis utilis cum leni in utramque partem motu modice prolatus,
simul capite atque humeris sensim ad id, quo manus feratur, obsecundantibus; et in
narrando certus, sed tum paullo productior: et in exprobrando et arguendo acer atque
instans. Longius enim partibus his et liberius exseritur. Vitiose vero idem sinistrum quasi
humerum petens in latus agi solet : quanquam adhuc pejus aliqui transversum brachium
proferunt et cubito pronuntiant. Fig. 43.

Duo quoque medii sub pollicem veniunt: et est hic adhuc priore gestus instantior,
principio et narrationi non accommodatus. Fig. 44.

At cum tres contracti pollice premuntur, tum digitus ille, quo usum optime Crassum
Cicero dicit, explicari solet. Is in exprobrando et indicando (unde ei nomen est) valet : et
adlevata ac spectante humerum manu pallum inclinatus affirmat : * versus in terram et
quasi pronus urget, aliquando pro numero est. Fig. 45.

* Hinc Constantia in nummis depingitur indicem attollens. Vid. ad Tabul. Arschol. tab.
19, n. 12. ALMEL. *Burman.*

Polyhymnia is also represented as using this gesture. Statue Antiche et Moderne, No. 117.

These passages of Quintilian I have given with such interpretation as they appear best to admit, and have accompanied

---

Idem summo articulo utrimque leviter apprehenso, duobus mod ce curvatis, minus tamen minimo aptus ad disputandum est. Fig. 46.

Acrius tamen argumentari videntur, qui medium articulum potius tenent: tanto con-tractioribus ultimis digitis, quanto priores descenderunt. Fig. 47.

The two last positions of the fingers represented by Fig. 46 and 47, instead of being confined to one hand as there represented, may relate to both. In which supposition the fore finger and thumb of the right hand may be understood to hold, in the first instance, the first joint of the fore-finger of the left, and in the next the second joint; the learned reader will determine for himself. Fig. 48.

Est et ille verecundæ orationi aptissimus, quo quatuor primis leviter in summum coeuntibus digitis, non procul ab ore aut pectore fertur ad nos manus, et deinde prona ac paullulum prolata laxatur. Hoc modo coepisse Demosthenem credo in illo pro Ctesiphonte timido summissoque principio: sic formatam Ciceronis manum, cum diceret, *si quid est in me ingenii judices, quod sentio quam sit exiguum*. Fig. 49.

Eadem aliquatenus liberius deorsum spectantibus digitis colligitur in os et fusius paullo in diversum resolvitur, ut quodammodo sermonem ipsum proferre videatur. Fig. 50.

Binos interdum digitos distinguimus, sed non inserto pollice, paullum tamen inferioribus intra spectantibus, sed ne illis quidem tensis, qui supra sunt. Fig. 51.

Duo interim extremi palmam circa ima pollicis premunt, ipse prioribus ad medios articulos jungitur: Fig. 52.

Interim quartus oblique reponitur. Fig. 53.

Interim quatuor remissis magis quam tensis, pollice intus inclinato, habilem in latus demonstrando aut distinguendo, quæ dicimus, manum facimus, cum supina in sinistrum latus, prona in alterum fertur. Fig. 54.

Sunt et illi breves gestus,† cum manus leviter pandata, qualis voventium est, parvis intervallis, et subassentientibus humeris movetur, maxime apta parce et quasi timide loquentibus.

Est admirationi conveniens ille gestus, quo manus modice supinata, ac per singulos à minimo collecta digitos, redeunte flexu simul explicatur atque convertitur. Fig. 55 and 93.

Nec uno modo interrogantes gestum componimus: plerumque tamen vertentes manum, utcunque composita est.

Pollici proximus digitus,‡ mediumque, qua dexter est, unguem pollici summo suo jungens, remissis ceteris, est et approbantibus, et narrantibus, et distinguentibus decorus. Fig. 56.

† Short gestures move *parvis intervallis*, through a small space, and are therefore modest or moderate.—Bold or free gestures move through a larger space.

‡ This passage appears to be corrupt. The explanation which I have given is supported by the Abbé Gedoyn, and apparently by Cresollius. See note 15.

them with figures, in order to render my interpretation une-
quivocal." Some of them are sufficiently obvious, but others,
particularly those to which Fig. 56 and 57 refer, are extremely difficult to understand; the text is perhaps corrupted,
which, although the commentators have admitted, they have
studiously avoided to elucidate; presenting, in the place of
rational emendation or conjecture, only a mass of various read
ings equally unintelligible. Caussinus has merely transcribed
these gestures, without making any observation; and Cresollius
has very plainly charged Quintilian with perplexity.[16] The

Cui non dissimilis, sed compressis tribus digitis, quo nunc Græci plurimum utuntur,
etiam utraque manu quoties enthymemata sua gestu velut cornu tundunt cæsim. Fig. 57
and 58.

Manus lenior promittit et assentatur, citatior hortatur, interim laudat.

Est et ille urgentis orationem gestus vulgaris magis, quam ex arte, qui contrahit alterno
celerique motu et explicat manum. Fig. 59 and 60.

Est et illa cava et rara et supra humeri altitudinem elata cum quodam motu velut
hortatrix manus, à peregrinis scholis jam prope recepta. Fig. 61.

Tremula scenica est.

Digitos cum summi coierunt, ad os referre, cur quibusdam displicuerit, nescio. Nam id et
leviter admirantes, et interim subita indignatione, velut pavescentes et deprecantes facimus.

Quin compressam etiam manum in signum pœnitentiæ vel iræ pectori admovemus, ubi
vox vel inter dentes expressa non dedecet. *Quid nunc agam ? quid faciam ?*

Averso pollice demonstrare aliquid, receptum magis puto, quam oratori decorum.
Fig. 62. *Quint. Inst. Orat. l.* xi. *c.* 3. *p.* 1018, *&c. Burm.*

[15] Fig. 56. Represents the position which the Romans called *premere pollicem.*

Fig. 63. Represents that position which they called *vertere pollicem. See Juvencus' notes
on Horace, l.* i. *ep.* 18. In which he explains the latter position with no great delicacy.

[16] The following passages from Cresollius will serve as a good commentary on Quintilian,
and as a vindication of what I have said.

Quidam explicata manu pronuntiant, hi prona, illi supina ; contrahunt alii et pugnum
faciunt : pollicem quidam cum indice conjungunt, non nemo cum ceteris digitis : quot
denique sunt oratores, tot modos in dicendo varios et discrepantes animadverti. Scio
veteres quiddam in ea re præcepisse, quæ cum æque vobis nota sint, malim audire a vobis
quid sequi possim quam opinionem meam forte repudiandam proponere. Ea de re verum
ait Juventius (one of the speakers in this dialogue of Cresollius). *Legi Fabium, eumque
perplexè in multis loquentem* et explicantem ea, quæ non satis in hodiernam agendi rationem
conveniant, nisi me ratio fugit. *Cresol. p.* 241.

plates, an auxiliary which the ancients wanted, will explain my conception of Quintilian's meaning, which may hereafter be amended where it is erroneous, by abler critics.

Several of these dispositions of the fingers are commonly retained by our speakers, but without attaching to them any particular significancy. Either they are natural gestures or imitations of which the origin is not remembered or regarded, as many of our apparently original actions are. Some of the gestures described from Quintilian are hardly ever used among us; of this kind sufficient examples will be discovered by inspecting the plate.

The state of the extension of the fingers, and partly of their position, depends much upon the mood of the speaker.

When the speaker is calm and unmoved, they are relaxed, and assume their different dispositions without force; as the greater number from Quintilian are represented.[7] When the speaker is excited, they are extended or contracted with energy:

Jam vero de certa conformatione digitorum quæritur, non displicent modi illi duo, quos tu, Victor, è Fulgentio, Apuleio, Fabio, modò protulisti, ut nimirum duobus aut tribus digitis protensis, cum pollice medius copulatur: vel ut minimis duobus complicitis, exporriguntur alii, qui modus Apuleianus est, et veterum statuarum, quæ dicentium similitudinem referunt. Sed illa mihi ratio longe omnium pulcherrima, et maxime ingenuosis animis congruens videtur, cum summus index pollici adjungitur aliis tribus explicitis, idque vel extenso brachio in anticam, quod fortiori dictioni convenit, vel inflexo modice brachio, elataque manu ante pectus, quem gestum viris elegantissimis placere etiamnum scio et iis qui audiunt nimium quantum probari. *Cresoll. p.* 344.

[7] Brachii moderata projectio remissis humeris, atque explicantibus se in proferenda manu digitis continuos et decurrentes locos maxime decet. At cum speciosius quid uberiusque dicendum est, ut illud, *saxa atque solitudines voci respondent,* expatiatur in latus, et ipsa quodammodo se cum gestu fundit oratio. *Quint. l.* xi. *c.* 3, *p.* 1017.

such are Fig. 59 and 60 from Quintilian. Fig. 47, which ac_
cording to him is an argumentative gesture, appears to be only
a contracted and eager state of Fig 52. And Fig. 52 and 53
bear the same relation to Fig. 51. Of the degrees of energy in
the same gesture, which form very important differences,
Quintilian has taken little notice. Some of the most remarkably
energetic positions of the hand he has omitted, as that of the
fingers extended in horror, of which Hogarth's Garrick, in the
tent scene in Richard, affords a fine example. The gestures of
both hands in combination, he has but slightly noticed, and yet
they are capable of great variety and expression. These shall
be observed in their place.

I shall now proceed to describe, according to my own ideas,
and give the notation of several gestures and motions of the
hand and arm which appear most necessary for the public
speaker.

The positions of the hand are determined by four different
circumstances. 1. By the disposition of the fingers. 2. By the
manner in which the palm is presented. 3. By the combined
disposition of both hands. 4. By the part of the body on which
they are occasionally placed.

1 The disposition of the fingers

Fig. 54. *The natural state,*" in the notation marked (*n*)

** The hands of the Venus de Medici are in the natural state.

The hand, when unconstrained in its natural and relaxed state, either hanging down at rest or raised moderately up, has all the fingers a little bended inwards towards the palm; the middle and third fingers lightly touch, the point of the middle finger resting partly on the nail of the third. The fore finger is separated from the middle finger, and less bended, and the little finger separated from the third, and more bended. The extremity of the thumb bends a little outwards, and in its general length and disposition, is nearly parallel with the fore finger. When raised *horizontal*, the hand is held obliquely between the positions *inwards* and *supine*. This position of the hand is recommended by Cresollius to be adopted by the public speaker, and for his opinion he adduces the authority of Hippocrates and Galen.[19] But it is not at all necessary that a speaker should confine himself to any one position; variety demands the contrary: if however he should limit himself, this position merits the preference.

Fig. 64.   *Extended* in the notation marked (*x*).[20]

---

[19] Hippocrates (says Cresollius) is of opinion that the hand cannot be long held supine without pain; in this Galen agrees with him: it is pretty obvious; they decided therefore in favour of the prone position. Cous took his choice of a position between prone and supine, and Cresollius also.

Atque hunc ego statum et conformationem tenendum esse puto oratori, cum soluta et passa manu pronuntiat, ut non pronam habeat penitus, vel omnino supinam, sed medio quodam modo, qui ut maximè de medicorum sententia naturalis, sic facillimus mihi videtur et modestiæ conveniens.

[20] It will be observed that the symbolic letters chosen for the notation of a particular gesture are not always the initial letters, because the names of many of the gestures begin with the same letter. It becomes necessary therefore to choose some remarkable letter in the word, thus *x* is used for *extended*, and *l* for *collected*: which may be easily remembered. Of the many names of gestures which begin with the same letter, the gesture most used is marked by the initial letter.

The fingers in this state, whatever may be the general position of the hand, are separated from each other with energy in proportion to the excitation of the speaker.

Fig. 65.   *Clinched*, in the notation marked (*c*), *pugnum.*

The fingers in this disposition are firmly closed, and press their extremities upon the palm, the thumb aids the pressure, and is lapped particularly over the middle finger.

Fig. 49 and 50.   *Collected* (*l*).   When the points of all the fingers are gently inclined towards or touch the point of the thumb.

Fig. 61.   *Hollow* (*w*).   When the palm is held nearly supine, and the fingers turn inwards without touching *(cava manu).*

Fig. 45, 66 and 67.   *The index* (*i*).   Pointing with the fore finger, and sometimes also with the middle finger extended, the other fingers turned inwards and contracted with force according to the energy of the speaker.

Fig. 68, 46 and 47.   *Holding* (*h*).   The finger and thumb are pressed together, either the fore or middle finger or both, the other fingers are contracted or extended according to the energy.   Fig. 56, (*presso pollice*).

Fig. 62 and 63.   *Thumb* (*m*).   Pointing with the thumb, the fingers are clasped down, and the thumb extended.   When turned down (*verso pollice*, fig. 63).

Fig. 69. *Grasping* (*g*). The fingers and thumb seizing the garments or tearing the hair (*uncis digitis*).

The second class of the positions of the hands depends on the manner in which the palm is presented.

Fig. 70 and 49. The hand is *prone* (*p*) when the palm is turned downwards.

Fig. 71. *Supine* (*s*). When the palm is turned upwards.

Fig. 72. *Inwards* (*n*). When the palm is turned towards the breast, and the hand is held on the edge, the thumb erect.

Fig. 73. *Outwards* (*o*). When the palm is turned from the body and towards the object, the thumb downwards, the hand held on the edge.

Fig. 64 and 74. *Vertical* (*v*). When the plane of the palm is perpendicular to the horizon, the fingers pointing up-wards.

The third class of the positions of the hands arises from the combined disposition of both hands. Of this class a few only are noticed, which are most in use among public speakers: others may be supplied at pleasure as occasion may require. For the notation of each of these positions, it is found necessary to use two symbolic letters: but this will not occasion any confusion, as the two small letters with a capital (B) signifying that both hands are considered, is all that, in general, it is necessary to express in the notation.[21,22]

Both hands (B) may be considered as,

Fig. 75. *Applied* (*ap*), when the palms are pressed together, and the fingers and thumbs of each are mutually laid against each other.

Fig. 76. *Clasped* (*cl*). When the fingers are all inserted between each other and the hands pressed close together, particularly at the balls of the thumbs and at the fleshy muscle under the little fingers, in its whole length to the wrists.

Fig. 77. *Crossed* (*cr*). When one hand is laid on the breast and the other is laid over it crosswise.

Fig. 78. *Folded* (*fl*). When the fingers of one hand at the second joint are all laid between the thumb and fore finger of the other, and are clasped down on its back: whilst its fingers fold the former from the lowest knuckle of the little finger to

---

[21] Motionum in manibus differentiæ quædam à doctis numerantur, est enim manuum connixio, consertio, compectinatio, agitatio, commutatio, complosio, dejectio, elatio, jactatio, adductio, compressio, dilatatio, aliique modi in humana vitâ consueti, quibus quando et quomodo oratori sit utendum, consilii fuerit atque prudentiæ. *Cresoll.*

[22] Cresollius also mentions another combination which he calls subjectio manuum. Veteres manum manui subjiciebant, quod illis χεὶρ καταπρηνῆς χείρι dicebatur, cum manui manus substernebatur, inquit Julius Scaliger (l. ii. poet. c. 18.) This gesture is used to express great and growing heights, as the piling of huge masses, the poetic mountains; then one hand is raised prone alternately above the other. . . . . hic tamen cavendum ne mimica nimis sit manuum commotio, *p.* 314.

the wrist, the thumbs crossing each other nearly at the middle joint.

Fig. 79. *Inclosed* (*in*). When the knuckles at the middle joint of one hand moderately bended are received within the palm of the other, the fingers of which stretch along the back of the inclosed hand nearly to its wrist, the thumbs crossing, or rather laid at length over each other.

Fig. 80. *Touching* (*tc*). When the points of the fingers of each hand are brought lightly into contact.

Fig. 81. *Wringing* (*wr*). When both hands are first clasped together and elevated, then depressed and separated at the wrists without disengaging the fingers.

Fig. 82. *Enumerating* (*en*). When the index of the right hand is laid successively upon the index or the different fingers of the left. If the number of divisions be more than four, the enumeration begins from the thumb. Sometimes the finger and thumb of the right hand, hold the finger of the left which represents the division : but this is not approved by Quintilian.[23] Fig. 48.

The fourth class of the positions of the hands arises from the

---

[23] Dextera imprimis numeros, argumenta, partes et variorum membrorum distributionem in digitis lævæ manus solet ponere. *Quint. l.* iv. c. *ult.* says this was the action of Hortensius.—Fit autem id vulgo hac ratione, ut dextræ index singulos lævæ digitos ordine designet, leviterque attingat ; qui non ita retinentes sunt honestatis et decori, summos digitos premunt etiam et manu complectuntur. Cicero, Cresollius says, used this action on the words Scientiam rei militaris, virtutem, auctoritatem, felicitatem. Pro. Lege Man. *Cresoll. Vac. Aut.*

part of the body on which they are occasionally placed. The symbolic letter by which these are noted is a capital, and is substituted in the place of those two small letters in the systematic table, which represent the position of the arm in the vertical and transverse direction.

The parts of the body or head most remarkable in this respect are:

Fig. 83, 84, 85, 86, 87. The breast noted (B).[24] The eyes (E). The lips (L). The forehead (F). The chin (C).

Besides the particular positions of the arms and hands, which have now been treated of, their motions require to be considered. Because a position of the hand and arm together, observed at the moment after the gesture is made, will be of very different character, according to the manner in which it has been made.[25] And not only the effect of the gesture will depend upon the sort of motion by which the arm arrived at a particular position; but its force will be determined by the force of the motion with which it commenced, and the distance through which the arm has moved from the commencement to the termination of the gesture.

---

[24] Manu pectus tangere in dicendo, meo quidem judicio sine ulla reprehensione fierit, cum de nobis est sermo, et placida leni quasi flumine fertur oratio. Quo gestu Ciceronem fuisse usum putat Fabius cum illa diceret; si quid in me ingenii judices, &c. *Ib.*

[25] This may be worthy the attention of painters, in order that the gesture they give their figures may have the full effect which they design. The gesture of Oliver Cromwell in the House of Commons, as represented in West's picture, is very happy in this respect. The air of the head, and all the character of the standing figure, seem to indicate his having raised his finger with authority; he has just laid it down *horizontal* with a scornful *noting*. This will be more clearly understood after the system has been developed.

The motions of the hands and arms together are therefore considered; *first*, as to their direction, and *secondly*, as to their manner of moving. The energy is not here taken into account.

The symbols for the notation of these motions are the 4th and 5th small letters, should so many be necessary.

Fig. 88. In the direction of the motion, gestures are considered as 1. Ascending (*a*). 2. Descending (*d*). 3. To the right (*r*). 4. To the left (*l*). 5. Forwards (*f*). 6. Backwards (*b*). 7. Revolving (*v*). This last is disapproved by Quintilian.[26] The figures illustrating the notation of the Miser and Plutus, afford many examples of the direction of motion. The stars, connected with the hand by dots, shew the various points from which the motion of the gestures has commenced.

As to the manner of the motion, gesture may be considered as:

Fig. 89. *Noting* (*n*). When the hand, in whatever posision, is first drawn back and raised, and then advanced, and with a gentle stroke depressed.

Fig. 90. *Projecting or pushing* (*p*). When the arm is first retracted and then thrust forwards in the drection in which the hand points.

---

[26] Sed cum omnis motus sex partes habeat, septimusque sit ille, qui in se redit, orbis, vitiosa est una circumversio: reliqui, ante nos, et dextra lævaque, et sursum et deorsum aliquid ostendunt: in posteriora gestus non dirigitur. Interim tamen velut rejici solet. *Quint. l.* xi. *c.* 3.

Fig. 91. *Waving* (*w*). When the fingers are first pointed downwards, and then by a smart motion of the elbow and wrist, the hand is flung upwards into a vertical position.

Fig. 92. The *flourish* (*fl*). Describes a circular movement above the head.

Fig. 93. The *sweep* (*sw*). Describes a curved movement descending from the opposite shoulder, and rising with velocity to the utmost extent of the arm, or the reverse; changing the position of the hand from supine to vertical in the first case, and from vertical to supine in the latter. The sweep is sometimes doubled by returning the arm back again through the same arch.[27]

Beckoning (*bk*). When with the fore finger or the whole hand the palm turned inwards, a motion is made inwards towards the breast.

Repressing (*rp*). The reverse of the preceding gesture, when the fore finger or the whole hand, the palm turned outwards, makes a motion in opposition to the person addressed. The motions in these two last gestures are often repeated.

---

[27] Kemble used the double sweep with fine effect on these words :
. . . . The play's the thing
Will catch the conscience of the king.   *Hamlet.*
Quintilian seems in these words to describe the sweep :
Est admirationi conveniens ille gestus. . . . . redeunte flexu simul explicatur atque convertitur. *See Fig. 55.*

Advancing (*ad*). When the hand being first moved downwards and backwards in order to obtain greater space for action, is then moved regularly forwards and raised as high as the horizontal position, a step being at the same time made in advance to aid the action, as in the figure in the Miser and Plutus. No. 4.

Springing. (*sp*). When the hand having nearly arrived at the intended limit of the gesture, flies suddenly up to it by a quick motion of the wrist; like the blade of a pocket knife, when it suddenly and decidedly snaps into its proper situation by the recoil of the spring.

Fig. 94. *Striking* (*st*). When the whole fore arm and the hand along with it descend from a higher elevation rapidly, and with a degree of force like a stroke which is arrested, when it has struck what it is aimed against.

Fig. 95. *Recoiling* (*rc*). When after a stroke as in the former gesture, the arm and hand return back to the position from whence they proceeded.

Throwing (*th*). When the arm, by the force of the gesture, is flung as it were in the direction of the person addressed.

Clinching (*cl*). When the hand being held forth *prone* or *supine*, and the arm moderately extended, the hand is suddenly

---

²⁸ Nonnunquam resilit vel negantibus nobis vel admirantibus. *Quint. Bur.* p. 1021.

clinched, and the arm raised and contracted in a position of threatening or contempt; as in Fig. 26 of the Miser and Plutus; or in Fig. 95. Supposing the dotted lines to have been the first position of the arm, and supposing both hands to be clinched in the position represented.

Collecting (*ll*). When the arm from an extended position sweeps inwards.

Shaking (*sh*). When a tremulous motion is made by the arm and hand.

Pressing (*pr*). When the hand already laid on some part, the effort of pressing is marked by raising the elbow and contracting the fingers.

Many other gestures may be named and marked by proper notation, as occasion may require: these will suffice as a specimen of some of the most usual in this class. If, with what has been already explained concerning the elevation and transverse positions of the arm, the different classes of gestures of the hand now explained be combined, the result will be a very comprehensive system of gesture, capable of recording distinctly most of the necessary circumstances observable in the positions and motions of the arms and hands.

Y y

CHAPTER XIV.

OF THE HEAD, THE EYES, THE SHOULDERS AND THE BODY.

Quintilian's directions respecting the positions and motions of the head—Observations of Cresollius—The most usual positions of the head and expressions of the eyes with the notation—Motions of the body from Quintilian.

CHAPTER XIV.

Of the Head, the Eyes, the Shoulders, and the Body.

UPON the subject of the positions and motions of the head, the best instructions are to be derived from Quintilian.

" As the head gives the chief grace to the person, so does it
" principally contribute to the expression of grace in delivery.
" It must be held in an erect and natural position. For when
" hung down it expresses humility, when turned upwards
" arrogance, when inclined to one side it expresses languor;
" and when stiff and rigid it indicates a degree of barbarity in
" the mind. Its movements should be suited to the character
" of the delivery, they should accord with the gesture, and fall
" in with the action of the hands,[1] and the motions of the body.
" The eyes are always to be directed as the gesture points;
" except when we have occasion to condemn, to refuse, or to
" require any object to be removed; on which occasions we
" should at the same moment express aversion in our counten-
" ance, and reject by our gesture, as in these passages :

> " . . . . Banish, ye gods, this monster from the earth."
> " . . . . I hold myself not worthy of such honour."

---

[1] The according motions of the hand and head are of the following nature. When the hand approaches the head, the head bends forwards to meet it; when the hand moves from the head, the head is, in general, held back or averted. In submission when the hands are *prone* and the arms descend, it bends downwards and accords with the movement of the hands and arms. *Fig.* 100, 101, *&c.*

" The head is capable of many appropriate expressions.
" For besides those motions, which by a nod signify assent, or
" rejection, or approbation; there are other motions of the head
" known and common to all, which express modesty, doubt,
" admiration and indignation. But to use the gesture of the
" head alone unaccompanied by any other gesture, even on the
" stage, is considered faulty. It is also a fault to shake or nod
" the head too frequently; but to toss it violently or to agitate
" the hair by rolling it about, is the action of a madman." [2,3]

---

[2] Præcipuum vero in actione, sicut in corpore ipso, caput est, cum ad illum, de quo dixi, decorem, tum etiam ad significationem decoris. Illa sunt, ut sit primo rectum, et secundum naturam. Nam et dejecto humilitas et supino arrogantia et in latus inclinato languor, et præduro et rigente barbaria quædam mentis ostenditur. Tum accipiat aptos ex ipsa actione motus, ut cum gestu concordet et manibus ac lateribus obsequatur. Aspectus enim semper eodem vertitur, quo gestus, exceptis quæ aut damnare aut non concedere, aut à nobis removere oportebit: ut idem illud vultu videamur aversari, manu repellere:

> . . . . Dii talem terris avertite pestem.
> . . . . Haud equidem tali me dignor honore.

Significat vero plurimis modis. Nam præter annuendi, renuendi, confirmandique motus, sunt et verecundiæ et dubitationis et admirationis, et indignationis noti et communes omnibus. Solo tamen eo facere gestum scenici quoque doctores vitiosum putaverunt. Etiam frequens ejus nutus non earet vitio: adeo jactare id, et comas excutientem rotare, fanaticum est. *Quint. l.* xi. *c.* 3.

[3] The observations of Cresollius upon the positions and action of the head will be found also worthy of attention: they supply a good commentary on Quintilian.

Sententia (Platonis scil.) hæc fuit, totum hominem in capite vultuque esse. Sed perspicue Philosophiæ dux et magister in problematis, θειοτάτην τῶν περὶ ἡμᾶς κεφαλὴν omnium partium divinissimum esse caput asseruit.

Sit igitur in monitis meis hoc primum, ut caput sit erectum, et statum habeat naturalem. . . . . quod sit veluti in medio positum inter extrema vitiosa. . . . Vis hujus præceptionis hæc est, eam capitis adhibendam esse moderationem ut neque nimium deprimatur, nec plus justo attollatur. . . . . Quæ naturæ compositio est et decori splendor ut eleganter et ingeniose animadvertit Sanctus Gregorius Nyssenus (de Opif. hom.) Caput, inquit, super humeros positum, non compressum, non humile et abjectum, ἀλλ᾽ ἐρείσματι ἀξωλόγῳ τῷ αὐχένι ἐπίκειται. Sed decore specioseque firmatum collo insidet. . . . . . .

Ut vitiosa capitis elatio superbientis animi arrogantiam et inanem insolentiam arguit, ita

The most usual motions and positions of the head may according to this great critic be enumerated as follow.　In the

---

nimia ejus demissio odiosam humilitatem significat; (ut ait Quint. l. xi. c. 3.) Sunt vero quidam qui partem in anteriorem proni et aliquantulum demisso vultu, sic in ea positione hærent, nunquam ut cervicem attollant, ne si quidem de rebus cœlestibus et altissimo beatorum domicilio sit agendum.　In quibus contenti sunt duntaxat oculos, qua ratione possunt erigere, eosque distortissimos, cum horrore nonnunquam intuentium, quod in quibusdam ego animadverti: caput autem non commutant magis, quam si corneum sit aut æneum.

De tollendo capite p. 108.　Attolli debet sed moderate, sic ut cum manu lateribusque consentiat, cum divinitas omnia è cœlo tuens describitur et res humanas providentissime gubernans, cum beatæ mentes ad nos superne devolantes, cum immortalium divorum cœtus, qui ævo perpetuo fruuntur; cum sol, luna, splendor stelliferi globi, signorum ortus obitusque, cum tonitrua, cum aeris prodigia, ut flammiferæ et crinitæ stellæ, ut præliantes inter se acies, ut lapsus divinitus ignis ad hominum scelus puniendum, ut alia de quibus historiæ prodiderunt, cum denique de iis dicitur, quæ excitatam altitudinem habent et exaggeratam, nosque vehementer exsuperant, ut montes, ut colossi, ut insanæ substructiones ædificiorum, et similia quæ facile animadverti possunt.　Sed hi gestus breviter celeriterque fiunt, nisi forte longiori orationi, is qui dicit, Deum optimum maximum, cœlitesve alloquatur, ut cum Cicero extrema Verrina, Jovem, Minervam, Apollinem, Dianam, Mercurium, et reliquam veterum geniorum turbam affatur.

In descriptions of triumphant circumstances, and in panegyrics, he allows the head to be held up: it is to be hung down on the contrary occasions, *p.* 118.

Magnopere id cavendum ne caput unquam penitus in tergum reflectatur.　Nam quæ a tergo sunt, ut exempli gratia, si quis anticam orientem solem posuerit et notare velit occidentem, id potius modica ipsius capitis atque manus in latus revocatione, quam perfecta conversione et inconsiderato illo motu significari solet.　At hæc quidem rudimenta sunt actionis, quæ a parvis pueris opinor tenentur.

Sed ecce tibi aliud genus hominum. . . . . in gestu parcos, an nimis in motu religiosos, qui una manuum actione contenti, caput non magis movent, quam si ænei sint, aut homines fœnei, aut stipites hæreant.

　　　　Rhetoris hæc Rufi statua est.　Si saxea Rufus.
　　　　Cur id ais? semper saxeus ipse fuit.　　　　　　*Auson. Epig.* 51.
　　　　Ῥήτωρ ἦν ἐικὼν, ὁ δὲ ῥήτωρ ἔικονος ἐικὼν.　　　　　*Anthol.*

Debet igitur esse motus in capite, qui sit cum partium reliquarum actione congruens.

Verum enimvero an solo capite fieri gestus possit, quærunt magistri.　Id perspicue vitiosum pronunciat Quintilianus, quod nescio an universum doctis hominibus probetur; si de tota id oratione intelligit subscriptorem me habet, et sententiæ adstipulatorem suæ. Sed quis nescit oratorem aliquando, sine ullo manuum gestu capite annuere? . . . . . Hic gestus decet eos maxime, qui consilio, virtute, sapenitia, magnam sibi apud alios auctoritatem.

notation, the head and eyes may, without confusion, be considered together.

The Head.	Looks of the Eyes or positions of the Head.
I. inclined.	F. forwards.
E. erect.	A. averted.
AS. assenting.	D. downwards.
DN. denying.	U. upwards.
SH. shaking.	R. around.
TS. tossing.	V. vacuity; or
S. aside.	vacancy.[4]

The last look of the eyes, named vacuity, is observed, when the eye is directed towards an object, but without speculation, the focus evidently not being adjusted to the distance, but falling short, when the eye appears (most wonderfully) to the spectators not to see any object distinctly.[5]

For the motions of the body or trunk, th best instructions will also be found in Quintilian.

" The sides should bear their part in the gesture. The motion

---

pepererunt, quorum capitis commotio non leve pondus et momentum adjungit orationi; quare in sacris admonitis et concionibus ad rem quasi in animis hominum defingendam utilis adhiberi videmus. . . . . Caput etiam moderate agitare ii solent qui rem improbant, qui negant, qui fieri non posse, aut esse minus honestum significant; in quo senilis, aut maturæ jam ætatis effigies cernitur, quæ plurima tacita significatione et non modo verbis, animi notiones in hominum cognitionem efferre solet.

4 *Queen.* Alas! how is it with you?
           That you do bend your eye on vacancy,
           And with the incorporeal air do hold discourse?   *Hamlet.*

5   Turn inwards, eyes, so shall you still behold her.
           . . . . Oh! dull mechanic sense
           Not seeing of election but necessity,
           Not what thou would'st but must, a star, a toad.

" also of the whole body contributes much to the effect in
" delivery : so much that Cicero is of opinion that more can be
" done by its gesture, than even by the hands themselves.
" Thus he says in his work *De Oratore*. No affected motions
" of the fingers, no measured cadence of their articulations.
" Let the gesture rather regulate itself by the movements of
" the whole trunk, and by the manly inflexion of the sides." [6]

The gestures of the arms and hands are not therefore to be
so executed, as if they proceeded from the trunk as from a rigid
log : but are to be always supported by the accompaniment of
the body. Not by affected and ridiculous contortions, but by
the manly and free exertions of the muscles of the body, the
general consent of which is indispensable for the production of
graceful motion. The raising up or shrugging of the shoulders
in order to express indifference or contempt is merely theatrical,
and should be sparingly used even on the stage. Quintilian
condemns it altogether in an orator. " Some people raise up
" their shoulders in speaking, but this is a fault in gesture.
" Demosthenes, in order to cure himself of it, used to stand in
" a narrow pulpit, and practised to speak with a spear hanging
" over his shoulder; in such a manner, that if in the heat of

---

[6] . . . . Latera cum gestu consentiant. Facit enim aliquid et totius corporis motus : adeo
ut Cicero plus illo agi, quam manibus ipsis putet. Ita enim dicit in Oratore ; *Nullæ
argutiæ digitorum, non ad numerum articulus cadens, trunco magis toto se ipse moderans et
virili laterum flexione.* Quint.

The words of Cicero which Quintilian seems here to quote from memory are, Laterum
inflexione hac forti ac virili. . . . . Manus autem minus arguta, digitis subsequens verba
non exprimens. *De Orat. l.* iii. *c.* 59.

Z z

" delivery, he failed to avoid this fault, he should be corrected
" by hurting himself against the point." [7]

The positions of the body might also be enumerated and be
subjected to the rules of notation, but this would be unnecessary, as they are always sufficiently understood, being the
accompaniment of the gestures and motions of the head, the
arms and the hands.

---

[7] Reprehendenda est et illa frequens et concitata in utrumque partem nutatio, quam in
Curione patre irrisit et Junius, quærens quis in lintre loqueretur. . . . . . .

. . . . . Jactantnr et humeri : quod vitium Demosthenes ita dicitur emendasse, ut, cum
in angusto quodam pulpito stans diceret, hasta humero dependens immineret : ut, si calore
dicendi vitare id excidisset, offensatione illa commoneretur. *Quint. l.* xi. *c.* 3.

CHAPTER XV.

APPLICATION OF THE SYMBOLS, AND SYMBOLIC LETTERS.

Difficulties which occurred in adjusting the application of the symbolic letters—Why letters have in general been preferred to symbols of any other kind—The contrivances for varying the signification of the same symbolic letter—Of the sets of letters—General rules relative to the symbolic letters—Symbols expressing various relations and connections —Of marking the positions of the feet—Symbols for the voice—Systematic arrangement of the symbolic letters—Alphabetical table and arrangement—Illustration of the method of notation applied to a part of Gay's fable of the Miser and Plutus.

CHAPTER XV.

Application of Symbols, and Symbolic Letters.

Having appropriated to the gestures of the various parts of the body, symbolic letters, in such a manner as to be intelligible and distinct in their separate use, I now proceed to explain their application when combined together. In order to do this more effectually, it is necessary to give a short account of the difficulties which occurred in this system of notation of gesture, and of the manner in which they have been got over.

The language by which the vast variety of different gestures might be clearly expressed, appeared extremely limited; so much so, that it became a question, whether it would not be necessary in such an undertaking, to invent many new names, the better to discriminate their minute and undefined differences. But this was considered as likely to prove so offensive an embarrassment, that it was determined to try every contrivance which might extend the resources of the ordinary language, and give variety to the common terms, by placing them in new situations; strictly avoiding the introduction of any word not already established in the language. The object of this, was both to guard against offence, and, by the use of common words, to facilitate the acquisition of the art of notation. In the same view, letters have in general been preferred to symbols, as their application is more easily understood and retained in memory.

The names applicable to gestures, which the English language affords, have been found more copious than was expected, but still they are few in comparison to the wide application for which they are required on this occasion, and are besides embarrassed by a great difficulty, which without various contrivances, almost renders them useless for the purposes of notation ; because in this art a single letter, or two at most, could be allotted for the designation of any one name. The difficulty arises from this circumstance, that many of the best words relating to gesture in our language, begin with the same letter, as may be seen in the table annexed. The consequence of this was, the necessity of resorting to expedients which would not otherwise have been submitted to. One of these was, the being obliged often to reject a more expressive and appropriate name, in order to bestow its initial letter upon some other name recurring more frequently or more necessary in another place.

When many names beginning with the same letter are necessarily retained, several contrivances are resorted to in order to distinguish them from each other; one is marked by a capital and another by a small letter: and again, instead of the initial letter, some letter in the name is adopted as its symbol, sufficiently remarkable, so as to be easily associated with it and remembered: thus *x* is used for *extended*, and *q* for *oblique:* And lastly, two letters are used to designate certain names. These two are varied also, sometimes being both of them small letters, and sometimes consisting of a capital before a small letter.'

But these *literary* contrivances, though they very considerably extended the notation, were not sufficient. It was therefore necessary to add some other device. That which has been chosen is the *local* signification which is given to the symbolic letters. This consists in disposing the names into different classes according to certain analogies, and assigning a particular place in the combinations of the different letters to each class. This expedient opened a fertile field, and rendered practicable, what before had seemed almost impossible.

Thus the most complicated gestures, are those which relate to the combined positions and motions of the arms and hands together; yet these are expressed with sufficient accuracy in all their movements, by four, or fewer symbolic letters for each movement. They are for this purpose divided into four classes,

---

' The words commencing with the letter *a* which relate to gesture are very numerous, and such as are retained are necessarily discriminated by those various contrivances. A, averted, *a,* ascending, *c,* across, *ap,* applied, *ad,* advancing, *as,* assenting *ad,* admiration.

the symbolic letters of which, always preserve their own place as to priority or succession, and derive their signification from their place, as the Arabic numerals do their value. The four letters, or three first taken together, are called a set of letters. In a set, as *phſd*—or *seqn*—

The first letter relates to the position of the hand.
The second to the elevation of the arm.
The third to the transverse situation of the arm.
The fourth to the motion or force of the gesture.

This last letter is often omitted. Thus *phſd* is to be read, *prone horizontal forward descending.* *Prone* is the position of the hand; *horizontal* is the elevation of the arm; *forward* the position of the arm in the transverse direction. And *descending* means, that in arriving to that position, the arm descended from a higher elevation.—*seqn* is read, *supine elevated oblique noting.* *Supine*, the hand; *elevated*, the arm as to elevation; *oblique*, the arm in the transverse direction; *noting*, the motion or action of the hand andarm; as may be seen in the explanatory arrangement of the symbols.

As both hands and both arms are equally capable of executing any gesture, the letters and sets of letters relate to both indifferently. But they are thus distinguished. When there are two sets of small letters, the first denotes the gestures of the right hand and arm, the second those of the left. In this case, the two sets are separated by a short dash between, as *phq—pdb, prone horizontal oblique* the right hand, and *prone downwards backwards* the left.

When only a single set of three, four, or five small letters is marked, the gesture of one hand only is expressed; that of the other, is supposed to be easily supplied according to the rules of accompaniment. A short dash is always marked with each set of small letters: if this dash follow the letters, they denote the gesture of the right hand only; if the dash precede the letters, they denote the gestures of the left hand only. Thus *p h q*—denotes only t e gesture of th e right hand and arm as before, and—*p d b* the gesture of the left.

When a long dash follows the small letters connecting them to other small letters, or to a single one farther on, a change of gesture is marked, which is to take place on the word over which such letter or letters are placed: and the commencement or termination of the dash is conveniently used to mark the commencement or termination of the particular gesture.

When after the set of small letters a dash, and then a dotted line of connection is marked, extending to another set of small letters marked with a contrary dash, it is to be understood, that the gesture made by the first hand is to be followed and supported by another gesture made by the other hand, which is to take place where the second set of letters is marked. This is called *alternate* gesture, and noted *al.*

The positions of the head, and the looks of the eyes, are marked with their symbolic capital letters towards the beginning of the sentence, and considerably separated from the symbolic letters relating to the hands and arms: both in

3 A

order to prevent confusion by their interference, and because the expression of the countenance should precede the gesture of the hands.

The positions of the feet and the steps are marked below the line, and under the word where they should take place. This should generally be a short time after the gesture of the hands and arms, except in vehement passion, where they all seem to move together. The order in succession of the gestures of the different parts is, first, the eyes and countenance, second, the head, hand, and body, and last the feet.

In the arrangement of the symbolic letters, several pairs are assigned for the expression of particular passions. But this is not necessary, except at the pleasure of the person who makes the notation, as all the gestures suited to those passions may be expressed in detail. It would be perhaps still better to note in the margin the general sentiment or passion, according to the manner of Sheridan. See his Art of Reading.

The symbols relating to the voice may be used as occasion requires, and written in the margin. They are chiefly borrowed from the very ingenious work, *Prosodia Rationalis*, by Steele.

In order to illustrate the use of the symbolic letters, some short passages of poetry are annexed and numbered, so as to answer to the references This method will be found more advantageous than the exemplification by single lines, as the whole connections and transitions of the gestures may be comprehended better. The manner of delivery is such as occurred, and might have been varied in a thousand ways: it is to be considered as an example, merely for illustrating the system. See the notation of part of the Fable of the Miser and Plutus at the end of this Chapter.

Synoptical arrangement of the Symbolic Letters.[*]

Letters written above the Line on which the Gesture is noted, relating to the Hands, the Fingers, and Arms.

The Hands.

FIRST, *small letter.*

Noting the manner of presenting the Palm.

p. prone.   *f.* forwards.[3]
s. supine.   *b.* backwards.
n. inwards or natural.   *v.* vertical.
o. outwards.

Noting the disposition of the Fingers.

i. index.   *x.* extended.
n. natural or inwards   *h.* holding.
e. clinched.   *m.* thumb.
l. collected.   *w.* hollow.
g. grasping.

Elevation of the Arms.

SECOND, *small letter.*

and two Capital letters.

d. downwards.   **Z.** zenith.
h. horizontal.   **R.** rest.
e. elevated.

---

[*] The order of this *synoptical arrangement of the symbolic letters* will be found to depart, in a small degree from that pursued in the investigation of the principles of the notation of gesture. This has been adopted for the convenience of practice, the symbolic letters being here placed as nearly as possible in the order of their most frequent use. But each class of symbols of gesture is preserved distinct, and may be easily referred to for explanation under their respective heads in Chapters 11, 12, 13 and 14.

[3] *Forwards.* The palm presented forwards, the fingers pointing down.
Backwards. The palm turned backwards, the fingers pointing down.

Position of the Arms in the transverse Direction

THIRD, *small letter.*

c. across.

f. forward.

q. oblique.

x. extended.

b. backwards.

For motions of the Hands and Arms, and force of Gesture.

FOURTH and FIFTH, *small letters.*

Force of Motion or Energy.

x. extreme.   *c.* contracted.   *m.* moderate.

Direction of Motion.[4]

a. ascending.

d. descending.

r. right.

l. left.

f. forwards.

b. backwards.

v. revolving.

Manner of Motion.

n. noting.

p. projecting or pushing.

w. waving.

fl. flourish.

sw. sweep.

bk. beckoning.

rp. repressing.

ad. advancing.

sp. springing.

st. striking.

pr. pressing.

rc. recoiling.

sh. shaking.

th. throwing.

cl. clinching.

ll. collecting.

Head and Eyes.

Capitals placed at the commencement of Sentences.

Head.

I. inclined.

E. erect.

As. assenting.

Dn. denying.

Sh. shaking.

Ts. tossing.

S. aside.

Looks of the Eyes and Position of the Head.

F. forwards.

A. averted.

D. downwards.

U. upwards.

R. round.

V. vacancy.

---

4 See observation XXV. at the end of this Chapter.

Letters below the Line for the Feet.

POSITIONS *of the Feet.* Capitals and Numerals.

F.	1.	front 1st position.		L.	1.	left 1st position.
F.	2.	front 2d position.		L.	2.	left 2d position.
R.	1.	right 1st position.		K.		kneeling.
R.	2.	right 2d position.		S.		aside.

x. extended—the feet separated widely.

STEPS, *small letters.*

a.	advance.		*st.*	start.
r.	retire.		*sp.*	stamp.
tr.	traverse.		*sk.*	shock.
c.	cross.			

Capitals substituted for the Second and Third small Letters, and relating to particular Parts on which the Hands may be Placed.

E.	eyes.	F.	forhead.
N.	nose.	C.	chin.
L.	lips.	*br.*	breast (small letters.)

A capital B. *preceding and joined to a set of small Letters signifies that both Hands or both Arms perform the same Gesture.*

B. both hands or both arms.

The manner of combining the fingers of both Hands is noted by two small Letters preceded by a capital B. *These Letters are substituted for the whole set relating to both Hands.*

B.	*ap.*	both applied.		*in.*	inclosing.
	cl.	clasped.		*wr.*	wringing.
	cr.	crossed.		*tc.*	touching.
	fl.	folded.		*nu.*	enumerating.

The Combinations of both Arms.

en.	encumbered or folded.	*km.*	a kimbo.
rp.	reposed.		(either one or both B).

Significant Gestures and Expressions of Countenance which may be Noted in the Margin, after the manner of Mr. Sheridan.

Ap.	appealing.	*Av.*	aversion.
At.	attention.	*Cm.*	commanding.
Vn.	veneration.	*Ad.*	admiration.
Ls.	listening.	*Hr.*	horror.
Lm.	lamentation.	*Gr.*	grief.
Dp.	deprecation.	*Fr.*	fear.
Pr.	pride.	*En.*	encouraging, and many others at
Sh.	shame.		pleasure.

Alphabetical Arrangement of Symbolic Letters.

	Above the Line. Hands, Arms, Body and Head.							Below the Line Feet.		
	Small Letters relating to the Hand and Arm.				Capital B and double small Letters. Both Arms and both Hands.	Capitals for particular Parts.	Capitals for Head and Eyes.	Small Letters Steps.	Capitals Positions.	Capitals and small; significant Gestures.
	1. Hand.	2. Elevation of the Arm.	3. Transverse Position of the Arm.	4 and 5. Motion and Force.						
A	- - -	- - -	- - -	ascending alternate	applied	- - -	{ assenting { averted	advance	- - -	appealing attention admiration aversion
B	backwards	- - -	backwards	backwards beckoning	both	breast		- - -	both	
C	clinched	- - -	across	collecting contracted clinching	crossed clasped	Chin	- - -	cross	- - -	commanding
D	- - -	downwards	- - -	descending	- - -	- - -	{ downwards { denying			deprecation declaration
E	- - -	elevated	- - -	- - -	encumbered	Eyes	erect	- - -	- - -	encouragement.
F	forwards	- - -	forwards	forwards flourish	folded	Forehead	Forward		front	fear
G	grasping	- - -	- - -	grasping	- - -				- - -	Grief
H	holding	horizontal	- - -						- - -	Horror
I	index	- - -	- - -	inwards	inclosed	- - -	inclined			
K	- - -			- - -	a kimbo	- - -	- - -		kneeling	{ Lamentation { Listenng
L	collected	- - -	- - -	left	- - -	Lips	- - -		left	
M	thumb	- - -	- - -	moderate						
N	natural inwards	- - -	- - -	noting	enumerating	Nose				
O	outwards	- - -	- - -	outwards						
P	prone	- - -	- - -	{ pushing { pressing	- - -	- - -	- - -		- - -	Pride
Q	- - -	- - -	oblique	- - -	- - -	- - -	- - -	- - -	oblique	
R	- - -	Rest	- - -	{ right recoiling repressing rejecting	reposed	- - -	round	retire	right	
S	supine		- - -	{ sweep springing, striking shaking	- - -	- - -	{ shaking { aside	{ start { stamp { shock	side	shame
T	- - -		- - -	{ touching { throwing	- - -	- - -	Tossing	traverse	- - -	threatning
U	- - -				- - -	- - -	Uwpards			
V	Vertical	- - -	- - -	revolving	- - -	- - -	Vacancy	- - -	- - -	Veneration
W	hollow	- - -	- - -	waving	wringing					
X	extended	- - -	extended	extreme						
Z		- - -	Zenith							

Symbols for Noting the Force and Rapidity or Interruption of the Voice in Delivery.

The symbols are to be marked in the margin near the commencement of the passage which they are to influence.

		Symbols.
Piano		≡
Uniform loudness, or forte . . .		⋀⋀⋀
Crescendo (as in music) . . .		<
Diminuendo (as in music) . . .		>
Rapid		◡ ◡ ◡
Slow		– – –
Suspension of the voice, the break or dash ⎫ after a word . . . . ⎭		– —
Long pause, or new paragraph . . .		‖
Whisper or monotone		———

Compound Symbols.

Piano and slow		≡ ⸱
Piano and quick		◡ ◡ ◡
Loud and slow		⋀⋀⋀
Loud and quick		◡ ◡ ◡ ⋀⋀⋀
Monotonous or whisper slow . . .		≡≡≡
Monotone or whisper quick . . .		◡ ◡ ◡

Compare with page 24 of Steele's *Prosodia Rationalis.*

IT is requested to be understood that the various passages, which are marked with the notation, are intended merely to illustrate the foregoing system : and that among the innumerable methods of possible delivery, that which is chosen and represented is to be considered as one method only, how far soever removed from the best. It is one property of this system of notation, that whilst it furnishes the means of recording each persons ideas of gesture, it does not presume to dictate. It is a language, which may be used to express every variety of opinion.

In the portion of Gay's fable of the Miser and Plutus, which is doubly illustrated both by engraved figures and by notation, it has been found necessary to omit in the notation some circumstances, in order to express nothing more than what is seen in the figures, and in others for the same reason to be redundant. Thus the retired hand and also the feet are sometimes noted oftener than absolutely necessary, and some transitions are of necessity omitted. It is hoped, however, that the great pains and attention bestowed upon these illustrations will suffice for the purpose of conveying to the reader a tolerably accurate knowledge of the manner of using the notation.

For the greater convenience and precision each figure is numbered in the Plate, and referred to accordingly in the following notation.

The perpendicular line—divides the portions of writing which refer to each numeral and figure.

THE MISER AND PLUTUS.

GAY.

1. 2. THE wind was high, the window shakes;

3. With sudden start the miser wakes!

4. Along the silent room he stalks;

5. 6. Looks back, and trembles as he walks!

7. Each lock and ev'ry bolt he tries,

8. In ev'ry creek and corner pries;

9. Then opes his chest with treasure stor'd,

10. And stands in rapture o'er his hoard:

11. But now with sudden qualms possest,

12. He wrings his hands, he beats his breast.

13. By conscience stung he wildly stares;

14. And thus his guilty soul declares.

15. Had the deep earth her stores confin'd,

16. This heart had known sweet peace of mind,

3 B

17. 18.   But virtue's soid ! | Good Gods ! what price |
vhf—vhx U   Bsef sp ————————a
aR2

19.   Can recompense the pangs of vice ? |
F—R

20.   O bane of good ! seducing cheat ! |
D   Bsdf d ———————————n
rR1

21. 22.   Can man, weak man, | thy power defeat ? |
Bvhf————vef   shf st—sdq

23.   Gold banish'd honour from the mind, |
seb sw — sdq
rL1

24.   And only left the name behind ; |
br—R

25.   Gold sow'd the world with ev'ry ill ; |
Bphc ——————·x

26.   Gold taught the murd'rer's sword to kill : |
ceb sh — cdq
L1x

27.   'T was gold instructed coward hearts |
shf sh — sdq
aR2x

28.   In treach'ry's more pernicious arts. |
Bvhf rj
rR1

29.   Who can recount the mischiefs o'er ? |
seq — sdq
R2

30.   Virtue resides on earth no more ! |
Bpdf d

* * * * * * * * * * * * * * *

Observations on the Notation.

No. I.   The direction of motion expressed by the 4th small letter *r*, means that from the position in which both hands are presented *vhf*, they should move both towards the right and stop at the position *oblique* as noted by *q*, connected by a dash to the position mentioned.

No. II.   The 4th small letter *n* signifies noting. See manner of motion in the synoptical table, and Chap. XIII.

The little stars in each subsequent figure of the Plate shew the place of the position of the hands in each former figure; and the dotted lines connecting them with the hands, shew the lines of transition from one gesture to another, with their different connections and accompaniments. The gestures which require extraordinary preparation, are also distinguished by these dotted lines, and are seen chiefly in Fig. 2, 4, 15, 23, and 25. For the meaning of the terms preparation, transition, and accompaniment of gesture, see Chapter XVIII.

No. XII. The position of the hands at first is, *both folded horizontal forwards* as expressed in the notation *Bfl. hf.* At the *a* connected by the dash, which signifies *ascending*, the hands are raised up, and at the next notation *Bfl. br.* they are forcibly withdrawn back on the breast.

No. XXI. This position begins *horizontal* as first noted *Bvhf*, and ends *elevated* as in the figure; *Bvhf*, but the *B* is omitted over the word *weak*, being understood by the connect-dash.

No. XXV. The *third small letter* relating to the transverse direction of the arm is often placed alone, but connected by a dash with a preceding set of letters, as already observed No. I. In such case it is to be understood that the position of the hands remains as before, and that the transverse direction only of the arm is changed. Here each arm passes through the whole semicircle from the position *across* to *extended*.

The *fourth and fifth small letters* also, which relate to *direction and manner of motion*, are also often separated, in this manner, from the position, to which they belong, in order that the place of the motion or action may be the more distinctly marked. See observation XII, and also No. 9, 15, 20, in which *n* is thus separated to point out the particular syllable on which the action of *noting* falls.

The action of the hands and arms, at No. 15 and 20, is the same, but the general effect is altered by the difference of the positions of the feet. In the preparation for these gestures the palms of both hands are so raised, as almost to touch the forehead; then both arms descend gradually, and when a little below the *horizontal elevation* the wrists make that particular motion called *noting*, on the respective words *stores* and *cheat*.

No. XXVI. The position of the *Left* 1st. *extended*. To make this position *extended*, the left foot is advanced and touches the ground only at the toes, the body is at the same time thrown back, and sinks a little, bending the right knee. It is to be observed that the lower the sustaining knee is bended in the first position of either foot, the greater degree of extension is given to that position.

No. XXVIII. This gesture *Bvhf rj*, that is *both vertical, horizontal, forwards, rejecting,* is thus made. Both hands are drawn backwards nearly to the mouth in the vertical position, the eyes at this time look forwards, the hands are then pushed forwards, whilst at the same time the head is averted, and the feet retire in a greater or lesser degree in proportion to the disgust or abhorrence to be expressed. See Fig. 101, 102, in which this same gesture is represented in its commencement and termination, but in another position or point of view. The figure 101 however uses only one hand.

The symbols for the voice are not noted in this fable; they may be introduced at pleasure, and are obvious in their use when required.

CHAPTER XVI.

THE STROKE AND TIME OF GESTURE.

Advantages of the structure of the arm and hand—The distinguished place and powers of the hand—The stroke of the gesture—Gives precision to gesture—The gesture of the arms of dancers merely for display—Unmeaning gestures—Analogies observed in the voice and the gesture—The time of the gestures—Whether gesture should accompany, precede, or follow the words—The natural order.

CHAPTER XVI.

The Stroke and Time of Gesture.

THE arm, the hand, and the fingers united in one flexible
line of several joints, which combine together their mutual
action, form the grand instrument of gesture, or as Cicero calls
it, " the weapon of the orator." The centre of motion of this
compound line, is the shoulder, which does not move all
together in the manner of an inflexible line; but each separate
joint becomes often a new centre of motion for the portion
between it and the extremity. Accordingly, in directing the
gesture towards any particular point, the upper arm first
arrives at its proper position, then the fore arm, turning on the
joint of the elbow, and lastly the hand moving on the joint of
the wrist: [1] and in some cases there is a fourth motion of the

---

[1] M. Engel, in his Letters upon Gesture says, a certain German writer, Mr. Loewe,
quotes *Riccoboni's Art du Théatre,* in which he gives rules for the motions of the arm, and
which appear to him too minute. To me they appear very correct.
(See similar instructions of Mr. Rollin in a note, chap. 18.)

Lorsqu'on veut lever un bras, il faut que la partie supérieure, c'est-à-dire, celle de
l'épaule au coude, se detache du corps la première, et qu'elle entraine les deux autres pour
ne se mouvoir que successivement et sans trop de précipitation. La main ne doit donc
agir que la dernière; elle doit être tournée en bas jusqu'à ce que l'avant bras l'ait portée à
la hauteur de la coude; alors elle se tourne en haut, tandis que le bras continue son
mouvement, jusqu'au point où il doit s'arrêter. *Idées sur le Geste, Lettre* 7 Though Mr.
Loewe disapproves of this precision of instruction, I cannot. I would add to this observation of Riccoboni (whose work I have not seen, that the *stroke* of the gesture is made at this
point, where the hand arrests its motion, either in ascending or in descending.

fingers from the knuckles next the palm, as in the gesture Fig.
49 and 50 from Quintilian; in which the last motion is the
expanding of the collected fingers. The other joints of the
fingers have in this case also their peculiar motions, but they
are so inconsiderable, that however contributing to grace, they
do not require to be particularly noticed in this place.

The construction of the arm and hand together, in the
adjustment of the number and nature of the joints, is such as to
allow almost as much variety of motion as if they formed a
pliant chain, whilst at the same time they possess as much
firmness and decision as if they consisted of an inflexible line,
or were an instrument with a single joint, like a flail. The
admirable variety of the motions of the hand, depends partly
on the power of the fore arm, which can turn at the wrist nearly
a complete revolution, and partly upon the joint of the wrist
itself, which is capable of moving both upwards and downwards, and also to either side, with equal facility.

This compound instrument, the upper arm, the fore arm, and
the hand with the fingers, in gesticulation seldom continues
long, either in one direct line or in any particular flexure, but
changes every moment the angles formed by the different joints;
adding at once grace and variety to the motions. The farther
any portion of the compound line formed by those parts is
from the centre of motion, the greater space does it pass
through. The least motion therefore is that made by the
upper arm, and the greatest of course, that made by the hand;
so that from this circumstance alone its gestures must be conspicuous. But in performing the different gestures, the hand

has not only the advantage of being placed at the extremity of the line farthest from the centre of motion; but by means of the joint at the wrist it can reserve to itself the power of springing with encreased velocity as from a new centre on its approach to the point, to which its gesture is directed. In this manner the hand often finishes its gesture and marks its complete termination. This action is termed the *stroke* of the gesture; and should be marked by different degrees of force according to the energy of the sentiment expressed; being sometimes in high passion distinguished by a strong percussion, and again in the more moderate state of the speaker's feelings being distinguished, merely by a turn of the hand, by a change of position or elevation of the arm, or by a momentary arrestation of the motion of the gesture in its transitions : but whenever gesture is used, the stroke in its proper force is indispensably required to mark it with precision.

The stroke of the gesture is analogous to the impression of the voice, made on those words, which it would illustrate or enforce ; it is used for the same purposes and should fall precisely on the same place, that is, on the accented syllable of the emphatical word ; so that the emphatical force of the voice and the stroke of the gesture co operate in order to present the idea in the most lively and distinguished manner, as well to the eye as to the ear of the hearer. The stroke of the gesture is to the eye, what the emphasis and inflexions of the voice are to the ear, and it is capable of equal force and variety.

When gesture is used and not marked by the precision of the stroke in the proper places, the arms seem to wander about

3 G

in quest of some uncertain object, like a person groping in the dark; and the action is of that faulty kind, which is called *sawing* the air; which though suitable for some particular expressions (as doubt or general rejection of means proposed), is very offensive when frequently and injudiciously used. Even graceful motions, as they may sometimes be seen, particularly among singers on the stage, unmarked by the precision of the stroke of the gesture, lose much of their force and effect; and their soft flowing quickly ceases to afford pleasure. Gesture used for the mere display of the person without reference to any other particular or decided meaning in its movements and changes, very soon disgusts. The gesture of a serious dancer in a *pas seul*, by its vanity and affectation soon fatigues all, who are not enamoured either of the dancer or of the art. It is perhaps in order to do away this incongruity that ballets are invented and accommodated to some story, so as to create an interest in the gestures of the dancers by their imagined situation, and to give them the variety arising from the passions they are supposed to feel as love, jealousy, hope, fear, disappointment and joy. But all the unmeaning and unmarked motions of public speakers whether on the stage or elsewhere, are attended with the same ill effect, as a mouthing and canting tone of declamation, which lays no emphasis with just discrimination, but swells and falls with a vain affectation of feeling, and with absolute deficiency both of taste and judgment.

There are also other points of analogy in the management of the voice and gesture, which merit consideration. In the simple and narrative parts of a discourse, there is little effort or variety of expression in the voice; it barely slides up and down within the small interval which limits its modulation.

Under the same circumstances the gesture, if any be used, is tame and simple; but, in the more impassioned parts, they are both equally exerted: the voice is elevated and varied, and the gesture becomes more bold and frequent. The gesture also in many instances nearly imitates the manner of the inflexions of the voice. When the voice rises, the gesture seems also naturally to ascend, and when the voice makes the falling inflexion, or lowers its tones, the gesture follows it by a corresponding descent; and in the level and monotonous pronunciation of the voice, the gesture seems to observe a similar limitation, by moving rather in the horizontal direction without varying its elevation. And in general, the gesture will be found to follow the voice implicitly, as nearly as possible, by marking for the eye every idea, which that distinguishes for the ear, and by reserving its most forcible action for that word or syllable which the voice marks by the strongest emphasis.

The writers upon gesture, in general desire that it should accompany the words, that is, that it should neither precede nor follow them. This rule, if applied to the calmer parts of a discourse, will be found very nearly correct. But if the speaker be warmed or excited, some difference of time, however small, will take place between the gesture and the language. [2.3.4.5.6] The order of the different actions or movements of the

. . . . . ut de gestu prius dicam : qui et ipse voci consentit, et animo cum ea simul paret. *Quint. B. p.* 1012.

speaker will be best determined by investigating the rise and progress of the ideas which he has to recommend to his audience.

A public speaker is supposed to have made, either from previous study at home, or from the rapid glance of the moment, some arrangement of the topics upon which his argument is to be maintained. These cannot all be produced at once; they not only appear to the hearers to arise in the speaker's mind in succession, but they actually do so, even when he pronounces a premeditated, or reads a written discourse. If his manner of speaking be confined to mere dry dissertation, he will proceed coldly and uniformly throughout; but if his argument be maintained by rhetorical ornament and illustration; and if he appeal to the passions of his audience, he will himself be

---

[3] Les maitres de l'art avertissent que le geste de la main doit commencer et finir avec le sens; parcequ' autrement il faudroit qu'il précédât la parole ou qu'il durat encore après. Or l'un et l'autre seroient vicieux.

This is a translation of a passage from Quintilian, which will be found at large *c.* 19 *note. Rollin Belles Lettres.*

[4] Le geste suit naturellement la voix. *Ib.*

[5] Comme le geste *suit la parole*, ce que j'ai dit de l'une peut s'appliquer à l'autre. *Marmontel, Élémens de Littérature, article Declamation théâtrale.*

[6] Le geste au théâtre doit toujours *précéder la parole* : on sent bien plutôt que la parole ne peut le dire : et le geste est beaucoup plus preste qu'elle : il faut des momens à la parole pour se former, et pour frapper l'oreille ; le geste que la sensibilité rend agile, part toujours au moment même où l'ame éprouve le sentiment.

Dubroca, art de Lire à haute Voix, agrees in this principle and borrows it. *Encyclopedie Paris, art. Geste, Déclamation.*

These contradictory sentiments in the two last extracts which appear in the Encyclopedie, and are I believe the work of the same Mr. Marmontel, are reconciled by referring to the calm or vehement parts of the discourse. As to gesture following the words, it seldom takes place, except with persons under the influence of intoxication or insanity, who are apt to gesticulate after they have ceased to speak.

excited, and the interest he feels, however rapidly he may proceed, will discover itself at each different period in the following order. The thought which arises in his mind will instantly be seen in his countenance, and first in his eyes, which it will brighten or suffuse, then suitable gestures follow, and last the words find utterance. The countenance and gesture are the language of nature, words are derived from art, and are more tardy in their expression; sometimes in high passion they cannot at all find their way, till the voice first breaks out into those tones and interjections, which appear to be the only language of nature belonging to the voice.[7.8.9]

In this view of the subject, the difficulty of reconciling authors to each other, and even to themselves, is got over: and the order of the combined expressions of the signs of a public speaker will be thus: In calm discourse the words and gestures are nearly contemporaneous: and in high passion

---

[7] From attending to these circumstances, the reason of the absurdity of using gesture without feeling will be manifest; unless the assumption of the looks and gestures suited to the sentiments excite the feelings, which they sometimes do, the performances must be miserable acting. This is well expressed by M. Marmontel in the passage following that just cited: what he says of the actor equally applies to the orator.

L'acteur qui ne sent point et qui voit des gestes dans les autres, croit les égaler au moins par des mouvemens des bras, par des marches en avant, et par des froids réculemens en arrière; par ces tours oisifs enfin toujours gauches au théâtre, qui refroidissent l'action et rendent l'acteur insupportable. Jamais dans ces automates fatiguans l'ame ne fait agir les mouvemens; elle reste enseveli dans un assoupissement profond: la routine et la mémoire sont les chevilles ouvrieres de la machine qui agit et qui parle.

[8] Baron avoit le geste du rôle qu'il jouoit: voilà la seule bonne manière de les adopter sur le théâtre aux différens mouvemens du caractere et de la passion.

[9] Je ne vois qu'une figure rude qui marche d'un pas apprêté, qui remue au hazard deux grands bras d'un mouvement monotone de pendule agité; mon attention cesse; le froid me gagne; le charme a disparu. *Paris. Encyclop. art Geste (Chant du Théâtre.)*

the order is. 1. The eyes. 2. The countenance in general. 3. The gestures. 4. Language. But the interval between each is extremely limited.[10]

---

[10] Quando il moto dell' huomo è causato mediante l'obbietto o tale obbietto nasce immediatè o nò : se nasce immediatè, quel che si muove torce prima all' obbietto il senso più necessario, ch' è l'occhio, lasciando star li piedi al primo luogo, e solo muove le coscie insieme con i fianchi e ginocchi verso quella parte dove si volta l'occhio, e così in tali accidenti si farà gran discorso. *Leonardo da Vinci, cap.* 247. *p.* 71. *fol.*

CHAPTER XVII.

OF THE CLASSIFICATION OF GESTURE.

Gesture considered in four general points of view—Principal and subordinate gesture—Significant and not significant gesture—Qualities of gesture—Proportion of qualities entering into the different styles of public speaking—Of the advanced and retired hand—Greatest number of gestures not significant—Classes of gestures of this kind—Examples illustrating these different classes—These classes not described by the ancients—Of the gestures suited to the different parts of an oration from Quintilian—Of the gesture of the left hand—Why the ancients seldom used the left hand in gesture—Influence of fashions—Opinions of Cresollius on the gestures of the left hand—The right has the precedence, but does not preclude the occasional gestures of the left—Occasions when the left hand properly assumes the principal gesture—When it may not—Of advancing the corresponding hand and foot—Ancient statues.

CHAPTER XVII.

Of the Classification of Gesture.

GESTURE, as has been already observed, when considered in a general view, relates to all the combined efforts, motions, and expressions of every part of the body. Among the parts of the body the head and countenance hold the principal rank, and next the hands, on account of the variety of their motions and their distinguished effects. The motions of the features of the face, though sometimes included under the name of gesture, more frequently claim for themselves, at least among the moderns, the peculiar name of expression of the countenance; and are properly considered as forming a distinct class of motions. The expression of the countenance, which is the very reflection of the soul in the face, and the most vivid bodily image of the sentiments of the mind, has always been so interesting to mankind in society, that all its modifications and smallest changes, have been classed and discriminated by every observer at all times; and are so well understood as to require no illustration in a work like this. The countenance has engaged the attention and illustrations not only of the poets and painters, but also of the philosophers in every age. And though physiognomy, as this science is named by the latter, may still afford ample employment to ingenious investigation, it demands only an incidental notice in this work. But the

3 D

gestures of the limbs, and particularly of the arms and hands, however an important subject of investigation to certain descriptions of men, have not been treated of with the attention which they merit.[1] This wide field is yet almost unexplored by moderns, and little, of what antiquity has discovered in it, has come down to our times: so that our enquiries are as if without a guide in an unknown region.

Gesture then is here understood to relate only to the motions of the whole head, of the body, and of the limbs. Something on the detail of the particular motions of each has been already explained in the preceding chapters of this work: the object at present is the general classification of them.

Gesture may be considered under *four* general points of view. 1. With respect to the instrument or manner by which it is performed. 2. The signification of the gesture. 3. The quality of the gesture. 4. As suited to the style or character of the matter delivered. These general divisions are thus subdivided:

I. Gesture referred to the instrument or manner of performance is subdivided into, 1. *Principal*, performed by the advanced or more elevated hand and arm. 2. *Subordinate*, performed by the hand and arm more retired and more depressed.

---

[1] The investigation of gesture appears to have attracted more attention in Germany than elsewhere, as I judge not only from the ingenious observations of Mr. Engel, but also from his references to other writers. I shall quote largely from the French translation of his work. Those he speaks of, as Lessing, Riccoboni, Sulzer, Loewe, &c. I have not seen.

II. Gesture with reference to its signification, is considered as
1. *significant*, and 2. *not significant;* these are subdivided.

Significant gestures:
    1. Natural.
    2. Instituted.
Gestures not significant:
    1. Commencing.
    2. Discriminating
    3. Auxiliary, or Alternate.
    4. Suspended, or Preparatory.
    5. Emphatical, which are also terminating gestures.

III. Gesture is considered to be capable of the following
general
Qualities :
    1. Magnificence.
    2. Boldness.
    3. Variety.
    4. Energy.
    5. Simplicity
    6. Grace.
    7. Propriety.
    8. Precision.

IV. Gesture, as to the proportion of those qualities requisite
in the delivery, may be suited to the
Style of speaking :
    1. Epic.
    2. Rhetorical.
    3. Colloquial.

These divisions, with their subdivisions, will be considered nearly in order. The two last divisions will be spoken of in Chapter XX.

First. Gesture with reference to the instrument or manner of performance.

The gestures of the arms and hands, may be performed by each separately, or by both together, each using similar or dissimilar actions. Thus the arms and hands may mutually imitate the positions of each other, or the hands only may imitate each other, whilst the arms are differently elevated or differently directed. Both arms and hands may perform the same gesture, or exactly imitate each other, when the body of the speaker is presented towards the person addressed precisely in front, Fig. 96 : but if the body be not so presented; the gestures will not be exactly similar, Fig. 97 ; and as such a position and gestures are not graceful, they are not frequently used. The body is generally presented a little obliquely, and one hand is usually advanced before the other and elevated differently : under this view the gesture may be first considered.

The advancement of one hand before the other is a manifest assumption of precedence, as is also in general its higher elevation. The advanced hand is therefore said to perform the *principal gesture:* and upon examination we find that in fact it does so.

For the retired hand only occasionally imitates the gesture of the advanced hand, and then its action is performed with less energy and authority. In general, the elevation of the retired arm is a whole position lower, and the gesture of the hand, though always imitative, is more moderate and reserved. For these reasons the action of the retired hand is named the *subordinate gesture.*

Thus on the advancement or retirement of the hand, the first general class of gestures is founded. The next class of gestures is derived from the established usage of certain gestures for indicating certain persons, feelings, or expressions: in arranging these there is no great difficulty, as many have been described by Quintilian and other rhetoricians and critics of good authority. Indeed this class comprehends nearly all that has hitherto been done, (as far as my information extends) on the subject of gesture: all of this class are named *significant gestures.*[2] Thus the index finger extended towards them points out persons or things, the hand laid on the breast refers to the feelings of the speaker, the finger laid on the lips signifies an injunction of silence, and many others. For them a particular chapter is reserved.

But by far the greatest number of gestures are too vague to

---

[2] The ancients divided the gestures proper for the different species of dramatic entertainments first into three classes, and afterwards added a fourth. That description called *Emmelia* was appropriated to tragedy, *Cordax* to comedy, and *Sicinnis* to dramatic satire. Bathyllus, added to these another description of gesture called the *Italic,* composed from the tragic and comic together. It is probable that the ancients possessed some kind of notation for recording these gestures, but nothing of it has reached our times. Athenæus notices these divisions of gesture.

Τᾶτον τὸν Βάθυλλον φήσιν . . . . . τὸν Ιταλικὴν ὄρχησιν συςήσασθαι ἐκ τῆς Κωμικῆς ἣ ἐκαλεῖται Κόρδαξ· καὶ τῆς Τραγικῆς ἣ ἐκαλεῖται Ἐμμέλεια· καὶ σατυρικῆς ἣ ἐλέγετο Σίκιννις. *Athen. l. i. c.* 17.

be compredended within this description; they do not mark any particular sentiment; but are rather used to denote a sort of general relation in the expressions, and derive their significancy from the time and manner of their application, from the place in which they are used, and from their various combinations. Some are used at the beginning of a sentence, merely as an indication of commencement in action as well as speech; some are used for description, some for explaining, extending, or limiting, and some for the enforcing of the predominant idea; some for suspending the attention previous to the more decided gestures, and some for marking the termination of the sense and the final result of the reasoning These and various other kinds of gestures may be observed as circumstances arise to cause them; and they might be divided into very numerous classes: but the perplexity of such a division will be avoided, and the present purpose will be sufficiently answered by limiting them to five classes. 1. Commencing gestures. 2. Discriminating. 3. Auxiliary. 4. Suspended. 5 Emphatical

1. Commencing gestures begin the discourse or division, by simply raising the hand from rest; and that in general not higher than the downward or horizontal position of the arm.*

2. Discriminating gestures comprehend all those, which serve the purpose of indicating persons or objects; or which are used for explaining, extending, limiting, or modifying the

---

* Dextera cum jam incipiendum erit, paulum prolata ultra sinum gestu quam modestissimo, velut expectans quando incipiendum sit. *Quint.*

predominant idea; or in question and answer, when made without vehemence. They are performed in the intermediate degrees of the range of the gesture, with moderate force and at small intervals, and are frequently confined in colloquial action to the motions of the head.

3. Auxiliary or alternate gestures serve to aid or enforce the gesture of the advanced hand. They are thus performed: after the advanced hand has made its gesture on the emphatical word, instead of passing to another gesture on the next emphatical word, it remains in the attitude of the last stroke, till the retired hand is brought up in aid of it, either by a similar gesture or by a more decided one; which gives at once variety and extraordinary energy to passages admitting such gestures: they are used of course with great advantage in high passion:[3] but are also frequent in description, where they are executed more tamely.

4. Suspended or preparatory gestures elevate the arm preparatory to the stroke which is to fall on the emphatical word; or contract or bend it for the purpose of a forcible projection

---

[3] Of the first kind of auxiliary gesture in which the retired hand is brought up with a different gesture, I noted a short passage in the Grecian Daughter, by Mrs. Siddons. The left hand here performed the principal gesture. The passage is, if I recollect, at the end of Act III. I noted it on the spot.

—phf . . . : . . veb —
I   obey
r.L.ı

This attitude was inimitably grand, and the effect was admirable.
The notation of the auxiliary gesture is connected by dots as above. Of the second kind, the following line of Milton may serve as an example; both hands perform the same gesture.

vhf sp— . . . . . —vhf sp   Bnef Bsdf st
Awake,   arise, or be for ever fall'n
Emph.   aux.   susp. Emph.

unbending or stroke of the arm. Suspended gestures are so named because they hold the attention in suspense by the elevation of the arm on some less important word preceding, and because they are also expected to lead to some emphatical gesture on a more important word. It will be observed, thatnot only those gestures, which are elevated high in preparation for a descending stroke, are named suspended, but also all such as seem preparatory to others, and so hold the expectation in suspense. Of this kind, as already mentioned, are the gestures in which the arm is contracted, withdraw nor bended in order that it may the more forcibly thrust, advance, or unbend itself on the stroke of a succeeding gesture.

5. Emphatical gestures mark with force words opposed to or compared with each other, and more particularly the word which expresses the predominant idea. Their stroke is generally arrested on the horizontal elevation, but sometimes they are directed to the highest point of the range of the gesture, and sometimes also to the lowest. Emphatical gestures when directed to the highest point serve often as suspended or previous gestures to the next emphatical gesture: and when made at the close of a sentence or division of a subject they serve as closing or terminating gestures, because when the last important idea is marked, no other gesture should be added to weaken its effect ; the arm then falls to rest.

In Gray's Elegy, examples of these different gestures may be found ; but as the descriptive abounds, the discriminating gestures will be the most numerous. In Brutus's harangue, on the contrary, the gestures will principally be the suspended and the emphatical suited to the vehemence of the speaker's manner, which seeks no ornament, but hastens to produce the main impression on his hearers by the most direct method. Mark Antony's speech by the same great author on the same occasion, is constructed very differently, it abounds in subtle discrimination, and requires every variety of gesture as well as of voice, and countenance, and manner.[4]

As a sentence is an epitome of a complete composition, and consists of a beginning, a middle, and a conclusion: so among single sentences illustrations of all these different kinds of gesture may be found. And moral sentences will be found more easily, which may furnish such illustration, because they contain much within a narrow compass, as comprehending the moral conclusions of long experience. First let a simple sentence of this kind be taken and marked for the gesture of the right hand.

---

4 It is not a little singular, if Shakspeare was as illiterate as is reported, that he has given to Antony almost the very species of eloquence which Cicero describes him to have possessed: so that it is questionable whether the real could have equalled the imagined Antony of our great Poet.

Sed cum hæc magna in Antonio, tum actio singularis: quæ si partienda est in gestum atque vocem ; gestus erat non verba exprimens, sed cum sententiis congruens. Manus, humeri, latera, supplosio pedis, status, incessus, omnisque motus cum verbis, sententiisque consentiens: vox permanens, verum subrauca natura : sed hoc vitium huic uni in bonum vertebat. Habebat enim flebile quiddam in conquestionibus, aptumque cum ad fidem faciendam, tum ad misericordiam commovendam : ut verum videretur in hoc illud, quod Demosthenem ferunt ei, qui quæsivisset quid primum esset in dicendo, actionem ; quid secundum, idem ; et idem tertium respondisse. Nulla res magis penetrat in animos, eosque fingit, format, flectit: talesque oratores videri facit, quales ipsi se videri volunt. *Cic. de clar. Orat. c.* 38.

Comparing him with L. Crassus a little afterwards, he adds other circumstances which it would almost appear that Shakspeare had in view—chap. xxxix. Nam, ut Antonius conjectura movenda, aut sedanda suspicione, aut excitanda, incredibilem vim habebat; sic &c.; and then he proceeds in his comparison of Crassus with him.

shf——   ncf—— shf st—   R
No man is wise at all times.
com.   susp.   emph. ter.

The first is a commencing gesture, the second a suspended gesture, the third emphatical, and as it is the last, it is also a terminating gesture, and the arm falls to rest. If this sentence were pronounced in a public assembly, with the gesture as noted, and accompanied with the proper motion of the head and body, and that a person, without being near enough to hear, should observe the speaker attentively with his eye: he would appear to him to have performed, what may be termed, a regular *period* of gesture, by the commencement, the suspension, and the emphatical close of the action. If the sentence be rendered more complex by the introduction of other members, discriminating gestures will be introduced.

shf——   ief——   ihf n——
It is an old observation, but not therefore the less true, that
com.   dis   dis
shq——   nef —— shf st —— R
no man is wise at all times.
dis   sus   emp and ter

The beautiful reply of St. Paul to Agrippa, entering as such, at once into the subject abruptly without exordium, has no commencing gesture.

Bsef sp   Bshf p ———— q ——
I would to God, that not only thou, but also all that hear
emp.   emp.   dis
———— x   veq——·   —— a ——   br ——
me this day, were both almost and altogether, such as I am,
dis   dis   dis   emp.
Bnef   Bshf sh   R
except these bonds.
susp.   emp. and ter.

The different classes of gesture described in this chapter seem to be sufficiently comprehensive, as they include most of the principal relations under which gesture in general may be viewed. The *principal* and *subordinate gestures* relate to the advanced and to the retired hand: the *significant gestures* to general usage, which has bestowed upon them a peculiar signification: and the five last classes just now described sufficiently comprehend those numerous gestures which however vague in themselves, derive force and perhaps significancy from their occasional situations and connection. The ancient rhetoricians, as has been already observed, have supplied many examples of significant gestures: and they have also given rules for the principal and subordinate gestures which will immediately come under consideration. They have besides described with sufficient accuracy, the characters of the gestures proper to be used in the different parts of an oration. But they have not touched upon the four classes described last, except in some degree upon the first, which relates to commencing gestures, and which are directed to be performed with modesty. These classes differ from all the others, because they may be used in any part of an oration, and belong to every character of style and speaking, and are as it were the elements and roots of gesture, which by their combinations produce its whole power of language and expression. These elements are the component parts of every style of delivery, whether tame or vehement, argumentative or diffuse, ardent or indifferent, cold, or pathetic, and the enquiry into their application is conceived to open a clearer view into the nature of gesture, and to be associated advantageously with the knowledge of the ancient precepts.

Quintilian among the ancients has delivered the most regular system of precepts on this subject; they are indeed very short, and treat more of the voice than of action, but are valuable as far as they go and are the foundation, with not very considerable additions, of all that the older rhetoricians after him, as well as the moderns, have delivered and repeated. Cresollius has indeed enlarged considerably upon Quintilian's precepts, and although he has implicitly followed him, is an able commentator. Henischius has given a brief but methodical treatise, built also upon Quintilian's authority, from which some extracts will be found in an Appendix.

" A gentle manner of delivery most generally suits the " commencement of an oration. For nothing is more gracious " or conciliating than modesty : but not however at all times. " For the exordium is not always spoken in the same manner; " as I have already observed. In general, both moderation " of voice is becoming, and modest gesture, the robe adjusted " on the shoulder, a gentle inclination of the body to either " side, and the eyes directed towards the object pointed to by " the gesture.

" The narration will require the hand to be extended more " boldly, the robe falling from the shoulder, the gesture " marked, the tones of the voice nearly those of common " conversation, except that they should be louder; some " passages require simplicity of tones; the affections, whether " vehement or tender, require peculiar expression of the voice.

" The action is most various and diversified in the proofs.—

" The proposition, the division, the questioning, and the
" answering of objections, approach very near to conversation.
" And yet the proposition admits of some diversity of manner,
" for we pronounce it sometimes in the style of derision, some-
" times of imitation.

" Argument, in general, when subtle, sharp, and vehement,
" requires gesture suited to its expressions, such as unites
" strength and rapidity. In some parts the sentiments are to
" be urged with rapidity, and the delivery requires more
" frequent gesture.

" Digressions are to be delivered in a manner for the most
" part gentle, harmonious and flowing : as the rape of Proserpine,
" the description of Sicily, and the praise of Pompey. Nor is
" it surprising that there should be less of vehemence in those
" topics, which are unconnected with the question.

" Imitation may be made in a moderate degree, where the
" different objects are marked with disapprobation, *I imagined*
" *I saw some coming in, others going out, some reeling with wine.*
" In such passages a degree of gesture not at variance with the
" voice is allowed, by which a sort of slight mimickry is made
" at either side, but confined to the motions of the hands,
" without any movement of the body." [5]

---

[5] Prooemio frequentissime lenis convenit pronunciatio. Nihil est enim ad conciliandum
gratius verecundia : non tamen semper. Nec enim uno modo dicuntur exordia, ut docui.
Plerumque tamen et vox temperata, ac gestus modestus, et sedens humero toga, et
laterum lenis in utramque partem motus, eodem spectantibus oculis decebit.
Narratio magis prolatam manum, amictum recidentem, gestum distinctum, vocem

These few are all the precepts which Quintilian has delivered for the gestures suited to the different parts of an oration, the remainder relate almost solely to the modulations and management of the voice: and on these, as has been said, are built the precepts of the succeeding rhetoricians.

It has been observed that the *principal gesture* is performed by the advanced hand, and the *subordinate gesture* by the retired hand. The observation and general rule is derived from the practice of modern speakers: the best of whom use either the right or the left hand indiscriminately for the principal gesture, as occasion may require. As this practice is altogether at variance with the opinions and rules of the ancient critics and rhetoricians, it will be proper to enquire how far we are justifiable in our departure from their great authority.

" The left hand, says Quintilian, can never with propriety

---

sermoni proximam, ac tantum apertiorem; sonum simplicem frequentissime postulabit . . . . . . Aliud in eadem poscunt affectus, vel concitati . . . . . vel flebiles . . . .

Maxime varia et multiplex actio est probationum. Nam et proponere, partiri, interrogare, sermoni sunt proxima, et contradictionem sumere. Nam ea quoque diversa propositio est. Sed hæc tamen aliquando irridentes, aliquando imitantes pronuntiamus.

Argumentatio plerumque agilior, et acrior et instantior, consentientem orationi postulat etiam gestum, id est fortem celeritatem. Instandum quibusdam in partibus et densanda oratio.

Egressiones fere lenes, et dulces, et remissæ, ut raptus Proserpinæ, Siciliæ descriptio, Cn. Pompeii laus. Neque est mirum, minus habere contentionis ea, quæ sunt extra quæstionem.

Mollior nonnunquam cum reprehensione diversæ partis imitatio, *videbar videre alios intrantes, alios autem exeuntes, quosdam ex vino vaccillantes.* Ubi non dissidens a voce permittitur gestus, quo fit in utramque partem tenera quædam, sed intra manus tamen, et sine motu laterum, translatio. *Quint. B.* 1036.

" perform gesture alone: but frequently acts in support of the
" right." In this opinion the older rhetoricians all agree.[6.7]
The consideration of the dress of the ancients, which differed
so essentially from that of the moderns, may be sufficient to
account for the difference of their customs. The form of the
ancient dress obliged the speaker, if not totally to disuse his left
hand, at least to restrain its action very considerably.[8.9] Fig. 98.
The right arm was bare above the elbow, and the shoulder,

---

[6] Manus sinistra nunquam sola gestum recte facit; dextræ se frequenter accommodat,
sive in digitos argumenta digerimus, sive aversis in sinistrum palmis abominamur, sive
objicimus adversas, sive in latus utramque distendimus, sive satisfacientes, aut supplicantes.
Quint. B. 1023.

The examples adduced to shew when the left hand is to be used in aid of the right,
are so many instances of *significant gestures;* more will be given when these gestures are
specially treated of.

[7] Non sinistræ, quod est malæ educationis indicium, sed dextræ motu loqui oportebit.
Henischius.

[8] Sinistrum brachium eousque allevandum est, ut quasi normalem illum angulum faciat,
Super quod ora ex toga duplex æqualiter sedeat. *Quin. l.* xi. iii. *p.* 1031.

[9] It was formerly the custom among the Greeks to keep the hand within the outer
garment. Fabius superioris ævi lumina priscos illos Italiæ proceres nullos sinus habuisse
dicit in toga, quorum proinde in dicendo brachium necesse fuit, ut Græcorum, veste
contineri. Senioris in hanc rem Senecæ, (l. 5. cont.) animadversio perillustris. Apud
patres, inquit, nostros qui forensia stipendia auspicabantur nefas putabatur brachium extra
togam exerere. . . . . . nunc quidem manu in sinu collocata penitusque abdita pronuntiare, esset hominis communi judicio inepti et expertis humanitatis. . . . . . referunt
Cleonem primum turbulentum Athenis oratorem ἐν τῷ δημιγορεῖν διασπάσαι τὸ ἱμάτιον
pallium in dicendo aperuisse. . . . . .

Æschines (in Dinarchum), reproaching Demosthenes for his action, says Solon's statue
was sculptured with the hands concealed, Demosthenes answered that the statue was
executed 240 years after Solon, and that Æschines had imitated the frigid position of the
statue, but not the virtue of the legislator. That he ought not to speak without extending
his hand from his robe, but that he ought to have kept his hand within when on his
embassy; intimating his corruption in holding it out to Philip. Οὐ λέγειν εἴσω τὴν
χεῖρα ἔχοντα δεῖ, ἀλλα πρεσβεύειν τὴν χεῖρα ἔχοντα, σὺ δὲ προτείνας, &c. *Cresoll. Vac.*
Aut.

and the rest of the upper arm were covered only with the short and wide sleeve of the inner clothing or tunic. . The robe or toga had one extreme fastened to the left shoulder, its ample folds were carried under the right arm, and reached down to the middle of the leg, and from thence swept round again to the left shoulder. To make it sit in this manner the better it was rounded in some degree; but it covered the whole person before and hid the inner clothing, except so far as it might be discovered by the left hand which was passed under the lowest border of the robe, and collected it in folds over the arm in the angle formed at the elbow. These folds concealed half and more of the left fore arm, and more of it did not usually appear than the hand and a little beyond the wrist.

When the left hand of a speaker was so encumbered it is not surprising, except when under such vehement feelings as that he could not moderate his gestures, that he forbore to use it, for he must otherwise derange his dress altogether. Accordingly we find Quintilian giving directions, for the management of this cumbrous robe. Having described particularly the dress becoming an orator, he says, " But this " attention to the adjustment of the dress belongs only to the " commencement of an oration. Even at the beginning of the " narration the folds (sinus) fall with propriety from the " shoulder of themselves. . . . . When a considerable portion of " the oration is exhausted, and whilst fortune favours, almost " every thing is allowable, perspiration itself, and fatigue, and a " greater negligence of adjustment, and the robe loosened, and " as it were falling down on every side. . . . . But if at the

" commencement or when only a small progress is made in the
" oration, the robe should fall down, not to adjust it again. is alto-
" gether a proof of negligence, or indolence, or even of igno-
" rance of the propriety of dress." [10] These instructions shew in
a stronger light, than perhaps more direct evidence could afford,
the extreme inconvenience of the Roman toga, and the difficulty or almost impossibility in such a dress of using the left
hand to any good purpose in gesticulation; so that it must
have been a proof of awkwardness to attempt it, and must
hence have fallen into disrepute, and disuse." Fashions
though often derived from slight circumstances, are still desir-
ous of supporting themselves on rational grounds. And those
which afforded to the ancient Romans objections against the
gestures of the left hand, may be opposed with equally just
reasons by the moderns, whose dress leaves either hand equally
free." Why Cresollius has laboured so much to disparage the
use of the left hand in the principal gesture, can perhaps be

---

[10] Sed hæc amictus observatio, dum incipimus: procedente vero actu, jam pene ab
initio narrationis, sinus ab humero rectè velut sponte delabitur. . . . . Cum vero magna
pars est exhausta orationis, utique afflante fortuna, pene omnia decent, sudor ipse et
fatigatio, et negligentior amictus, et soluta ac velut labens undique toga. . . . . At si
incipientibus aut paullum progressis decidat toga, non reponere eam, prorsus negligentis
aut pigri aut quommodo debeat amiciri, nescientis est. *Quint. B.* 1032.

[11] Factum hinc est, ut sinistra idonea fraudibus et apta furto existimetur. Nam cum
vulgo sit abdita, cum posita veluti in obscuro, et sinu togæ pallioque involuta, fit plerumque
nec opinantibus hominibus, ut nihil agens et devota quieti, agat tamen et humani aliquid
patiatur, dum nihil alienum a se putat. Buccinator fabularum poeta dicto illustri rem ita
prodidit. (*Ovid. Met. l.* xiii.) . . . . . natæque ad furta sinistræ. . . . Plautus *furtificam
laevam* dicit. See more offensive epithets of the left hand. *Cresol. Vac. Aut. p.* 306.

[12] Est aliquid in amictu, quod ipsum aliquatenus temporum conditione mutatum est.
Nam veteribus nulli sinus, perquam breves post illos fuerunt. Itaque etiam gestu necesse
est usos esse in principiis eos alio, quorum brachium, sicut Græcorum, veste continebatur.
Quint. B. p. 1030.

3 F

best accounted for by the prejudice of opinion, and by his attachment to the customs of antiquity, in which he was deeply learned. But it is not very uncommon even now for rhetori- cians to maintain the same opinion, so that what Cresollius has said is the less to be wondered at. Such is the effect of pre- judice and the dominion of prescription, even when the reasons on which it has been supported have ceased to exist. In the nature of their formation there can be discovered no reason why either hand should not be equally used for every pur- pose.[13] The construction and natural abilities of both hands are equal, and the habit of using the one in preference to the other, alone confers upon it its strength and dignity. If the right has from these causes become the better hand, it may be proper that in gesticulation also it should have its prece- dence, but no more.[14,15] Precedence does not exclude the use of the left altogether, even from the occasional performance of the principal gesture. And for the propriety of this occasional advancement of the left hand we can produce from the grand

---

[13] The following passages from Cresollius seem rather to prove the contrary of what he intends ; as he objects to the use of the left hand.

In hoc orator complurium opificum studio artificioque discrepat quod utramque illi manum sine discrimine ad opus et machinationem suam accommodent, Hippocrates me- dicum monet ἔργα πάντα ἀσκέειν ἀμφοτέρησιν ἅμα, ad opera omnia utramque manum adhibere ; sunt enim, inquit similes. Plato vellet omnes pueros institui περιδεξίας. Aristo- teles cives omnes; ἀμφιδεξίας esse oportere; hominem quoque ait, μόνον ἀμφιδεξίον γίνεσθαι τῶν ἄλλων ζώων ; (l. ii. de Hist. An. c. 1.) inter omnes animantes solum utraque manu dexterum nasci. *Cresoll. Vac. Aut.*

[14] Plato vero de manibus cum loqueretur, eo ingenio, quo divina atque humana com- prehendit, asseruit τὴν φύσιν ἑκατέρων τῶν μελῶν σχεδὸν ἰσορροπῶσαν, parem dextræ atque sinistræ vim a natura fuisse concessam, hominis autem consuetudine tantum fieri, ut illa potior esse videatur, hæc infirmior. *Ib.*

[15] Aristotelis axioma notum est τὸ ἀριστερὸν πεφυκὸς ἀκολᾰθεῖν τῷ δεξιῷ ita compara- tum est a natura, ut lævæ dextris obsecundent. *Ib.*

source of noble and dignified gesture, our own tragic drama, authorities not inferior in perfection and in art to those which Rome formerly derived from her celebrated Roscius. It cannot be supposed that any thing is here alluded to inferior to the consummate art and dignity of Mr. Kemble, and the native grace and majesty of his incomparable sister. Their practice, which is on this point classical and incontrovertible, authorises the use of the left hand, and that not unfrequently for the principal gesture.

The occasions, on which the left hand may be used thus, as derived from their practice, and under proper limitations applicable to other modes of public speaking, are nearly the following.[16,17] 1. When the persons addressed are on the left side, the left hand naturally performs the principal gesture, in

---

[16] Nam et dexter pes à læva judicis sedenti proferendus est, et ex altera parte multi gestus necesse est in sinistrum eant, ut ad judicem spectent. *Quint. l.* xi. *p.* 1029.

[17] Cresollius allows the left hand to be on some occasions used equally with the right, as in antitheses and comparisons.

Ex æquo læva gestum exhibet cum dextra, in contrapositis, cum dissimilia inter se conferuntur, tum enim per vices manus utraque partes suas agit. Quomodo illa pronuntiavit orator. Ex hac enim parte pudor pugnat, illinc petulantia; hinc pudicitia, illinc stuprum; hinc fides, illinc fraudatio; hinc pietas, illinc scelus, &c. Geminum illud est e. b. verrina. Conferte hanc pacem cum illo bello: hujus prætoris adventum, cum illius exercitu invicto; hujus libidines, cum illius continentia; ab illo qui cepit conditas, ab hoc qui constitutas accepit, captas dicetis Syracusas. Huc refertur oppositorum significatio; ut illi ad orientem positi sunt, isti ad occidentem. Divertunt illi ad lævam, hi ad dexteram. Quanquam hæc quidem ultima solius dexteræ commutata motione sæpe a doctis hominibus designentur. *Cresoll. Vac. Aut.*

Læva manus adhibenda est in votis et precationibus, cum summum rerum omnium parentem Deum vel coelites alloquimur, cum templa, tropæa, monumenta et similia compellamus, utraque enim manus tum extendi solet. Hujusmodi sunt illa pro Milone; Vos enim jam Albani tumuli atque luci, vos, inquam, imploro atque obtestor, vosque Albanorum obrutæ aræ sacrorum populi Romani sociæ et æquales, &c. Similia illa Gracchi; Quo me, miser conferam? &c.

Præterea vero utraque manu utimur, cum rerum immensitatem, cum infinitum prope

order to avoid the awkwardness of gesticulating much across
the body. 2. The necessary discrimination of objects opposed
to each other, requires the left hand alternately to assume the
principal gesture. This Cresollius himself has allowed. 3. The
advantage of variety. 4. The power of giving not only variety
but force by occasionally elevating and bestowing, as it were,
upon the retired hand all the spirit and authority of the
gesture. This species of gesture is confined to the highest
strain of tragedy. And the effect of such a change, as introduced sometimes by those great tragedians, is altogether astonishing, and causes a revolution of feeling that surprises and
awakens in the most extraordinary manner, impressing the idea
of uncommon majesty, or rather sublimity of character.[18]
Though it appears from these observations that the moderns
have restored the left hand to its use and dignity, by investing
it occasionally with the authority of the principal gesture; it
must be obvious that some gestures are appropriated by custom
to the right hand alone, upon which the left should never
intrude. On the stage, except in ridicule, the left never
brandishes a sword,—neither does it threaten or command
with propriety—nor imitate the manner of writing, nor take
the lead in salutation. On all such occasions the right hand
claims the precedency, and also in much the greater number of

---

numerum, cum Spatia longe et latè patentia designamus, quale istud Pompeiana Marci
Tullii; Testes vero jam omnes oræ atque omnes exteræ gentes ac nationes, denique maria
omnia tum universa, tum in singulis oris omnes sinus atque portus, &c. *Ib.*

[18] Some examples of dignified attitudes of this kind may be seen in Fig. 120 from Mrs.
Siddons in Imogen, and in Fig. 121 from her Lady Randolph : another has been already
given in this Chapter from the same great actress in the Grecian Daughter, as noted on the
words " I obey." Fig. 102 may afford an example of an attitude of horror of this kind, in
which although the left is the advanced hand, the right by its elevation assumes the principal gesture.

energetic gestures, but in most ordinary cases it freely allows the left to participate.

But it is not only in the use of the left hand, that modern speakers differ from the ancients (or rather from the precepts of the ancient critics, for if we may judge by the remains of their arts, their practice seems to have sometimes been at variance with their rules), they also violate constantly another precept not less rigorously enjoined by Quintilian and his followers, by speaking with the corresponding hand and foot advanced.[19] And yet if the natural emotions are considered as affording any just foundation for the manner of gesture, we shall be inclined to give the preference, on this ground, to modern custom.[20] It will be observed that in the more vehement

---

[19] Prolato dextro stare, et eamdem manum ac pedem proferre, deforme est. In dextrum incumbere interim datur, sed æquo pectore: qui tamen comicus magis, quam oratorius gestus est. *Quint. B.* 1026.

[20] The following figures in different publications from antique statues, prove that it was not considered altogether ungraceful to advance the corresponding hand and foot, otherwise the statuaries would not have left upon record examples of bad taste, the positions of which being once determined were irremediable.

Musæum Florentinum, Tom. III.

		Notation of the Gesture.
Plate 45.	Dei præstitis signum ex ære - - - -	sdq—R ———— R 2
	This figure manifestly speaks to the right side inclining his body together with his gesture; same hand and foot advanced.	
81.	Haruspex; same hand and foot advanced " -	ncq—R ———— R 2
83.	Vir consularis ; same " " " -	idq—hhf ———— R.2
90.	Virgo Vestalis ; same " " " -	pdx—hhf ———— R.2

The greater number of the statues in this Collection are in different positions, and ad-

passions of whatsoever kind, the corresponding hand and foot advance together. Those passions which incline us to advance towards their object, as love, desire, anger, or revenge, naturally cause the corresponding hand and foot to advance together with the head and body; for thus the nearest approach is made to the object. And when passions of the contrary nature, as aversion and terror, affect the man, still the corresponding leg and arm are advanced, as if the better to guard the body and head which are thrown back. In such cases it would produce unnatural distortion to advance the contrary or alternate hand and foot. When strong and mixed emotions are to be expressed, then the hand and foot may be thus at variance, as in the figure from Engle, which expresses surprise well marked by the retiring of the body and of the right foot; and joy, by the advancing of the head and both arms. Fig. 110. Under tranquil circumstances, as when the speaker delivers the narration, or reasons calmly, the advanced hand and foot may alternate with

---

vance the alternate hand and foot. The favourite position of the feet is L. 2. But the above examples are exceptions, with many others suiting my purpose.

Statue Antiche e Moderne, No. 4933, Bib. Fagelliana.

Notation of Gesture.

			phq—idf
Plate 92. Severus; corresponding hand and foot - - -			R. 2

Galleria Giustiniana No. 4940, Bib. Fagelliana.

148. Polyhymnia, an example of the left hand performing the } principal gesture, and also of the advancing of the cor- } responding hand and foot. }   hhc—iex / L. 2

It is unnecessary to multiply examples which abound in publications of this kind. It may be possible that the figures are reversed in the plates, but unless those only which make in support of the opinion here advanced were so changed (and that is by no means probable), the greater number would support it by being considered to be also reversed. But there is every reason to suppose the figures are printed so as to give the true positions of the statues, because the right hands of most are represented as performing the principal gesture.

sufficient grace and propriety. Indeed perhaps such position is most proper, as presenting the body more exactly in front towards the persons addressed. And it was probably such circumstances alone which Quintilian had in view when he pronounced his opinion, and which most other rhetoricians have followed; namely, that it is unbecoming to stand with the corresponding hand and foot advanced. This explanation will serve to reconcile the apparent deviation of the moderns from the ancient practice. But in the more vehement parts of an oration when the body is almost projected forwards, or when the speaker starts back, his figure would be distorted, if the corresponding arm and leg were not advanced together.

CHAPTER XVIII.

OF THE PREPARATION, TRANSITION, AND ACCOMPANIMENT OF GESTURE.

Of the line in which the hand moves in gesture—Preparations made for gestures of different kinds—Of the connection of gestures—Of the transition of gesture—The character of gesture affected by the manner of transition—Illustration from West's picture of Oliver Cromwell—Transition of the principal gesture from one hand to the other—When the right hand should resign the principal gesture to the left—Subordinate gesture analogous to accompaniment in music—Illustrations—Accompaniment of the head, the body, and lower limbs—Examples—Of letting the hands fall to rest—Termination of gesture—Illustrations of termination.

CHAPTER XVIII.

Of the Preparation, Transition, and Accompaniment of Gesture.

THE gesture of a public speaker is essentially different from the motions of a soldier performing the manual exercise. In the latter, the object is to effect a change of position within as narrow a space and in as short a time as possible. But confined and sudden motions do not suit an orator, except when perhaps the vehemence of passion urges him to the most rapid expression. Persuasion, which is his particular office, reaches the mind slowly, and is insinuated by circumlocution not of words only, but it may almost be said, of gesture also. In the transition from gesture to gesture, his hand and arm do not therefore precipitate towards the intended position by the shortest possible line, but move in the calmer parts of the oration in a sort of waving line, or one returning upon itself, somewhat in this manner:

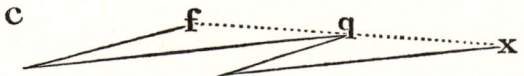

Let *f* represent the position of the arm and hand *forwards*, and let the place of the next gesture be *q oblique*, and of a third be *x extended*. The hand does not move in the dotted lines, directly from *f* to *q*, and to *x*, but from *f* goes back almost to *c across*, in order that it may traverse the greater space; and then proceeds towards *q* with an accelerated motion for the stroke of the gesture, when near that point. In the same manner and for the same purpose it returns back almost to *f* before it proceeds to *x*. The ascending and descending gestures are performed in the same manner under similar circumstances as may be seen in the figure: in which *z* is the zenith and R the point of rest, and where the hand in ascending and descending is represented as making returning inflexions at the principal points, *d h* and *e*.

The line of preparation sometimes assumes a different form, partaking in the transverse direction something of the ascending and descending motions, or of the sweep, thus :

It will also occasionally follow other curves. But whatever the form of this indirect line may be, it is used as a preparation for the gesture to which it leads: and the extent of the return or the depth of the sweep or indentation is determined by the character of the sentiments delivered. The more magnificent they are the greater is this parade, and the nearer to ordinary discourse the less it is: familiar conversation is entirely divested of it, and gesture, if any be made, is sharp, dry, and direct. The preparation made by those different curves does not suit every species of gesture; it is adapted almost solely to that kind, which is termed *discriminating*. Another kind of preparation is made for *emphatical gestures*. They are generally preceded by a suspended gesture, which serves the double purpose of marking some less important word, and of preparing for the stroke of the most emphatical gesture. It will be re-collected that contracted and retracting gestures are reckoned among the suspended gestures, as being made previous to some forcible effort, and are therefore preparatory to the gestures which ensue.

In order to illustrate what is here advanced : let it be sup-posed that the emphatical gesture requires a strong percussion of the arm descending forwards, as *shf st*,—the preparation for this is the suspended or preparatory gesture *nef bn*—as in the fol-lowing passage from Brutus' speech in Shakspeare's Julius Cæsar :

        nef bn—   shf st—
    " Hear me for my cause."
        ‾‾‾‾‾   ‾‾‾‾‾   ‾‾‾‾‾
        Susp.   ———   Emph.

An example of a preparatory contracted gesture :

        vhf rt—   vhf rj—
    " I hate the drum's discordant sound."   *Langhorne*

A gesture *across* may also be used as a preparation for rejection, which passes rapidly to the extended position.

            ohc————————————x rj—
    " Who's here so base that would be a bondman?"
                                            Shakspeare.

Another example of a previous contracted gesture :

        Bvhf rj————p   ——— ——x
    " To hear the roar she sends through all her gates."
                                            Cowper.

In the last passage from Cowper, the suspended or previous gesture *Bvhf rj* contains all the letters belonging to the notation of the subsequent emphatical gesture, except the last *p* which belongs to the 4th place. This new letter only is expressed, and is joined by a long dash or mark of connection to the preceding gesture: another line of connection joining this last letter to the letter *x* signifies, that both hands continuing in the same position, viz. *vertical*, the arms are to be extended. The gestures marked at large on this line would be as follow:

Bvhf rj————Bvhf p ————————Bvh x
" To hear the roar she sends through all her gates."

But the former method is preferred, as abridging the trouble of notation, and marking more distinctly the connection of the gestures.

The connection of gesture is therefore the relation which one gesture bears to another, that is the observation and notation of the different circumstances in which they agree, and of those in which they differ. Thus the gestures noted in the line above agree, first in being common to both hands (B), and then in the position of each hand, *v vertical*, and also in the elevation of both arms *h horizontal*. So that it is unnecessary to repeat those circumstances in which they agree, as the connecting dash expresses them with greater clearness and brevity.[1]

The connection of gesture in the vertical direction, when

---

[1] Il y a melodie dans les gestes, lorsqu'ils sont unis et liés entre eux ; car, dans le geste qui se fait actuellement, il doit y avoir un reste de celui qui a précédé et une naissance de celui qui va suivre. *Dubroca l'Art de lire, Leçon* 25.

the hand without altering its position merely ascends by short intervals in order to mark a succession of discriminating gestures is noted by the usual connecting dash and an *a* over the word where the hand ascends.

phf ———— a
I mourn the pride

————a————— —————————nef—R   shf st—
And avarice that make man a wolf to man.   *Cowper.*

But this passsage would perhaps answer better with the auxiliary gesture thus :

Bphf a   vef— . . .
I mourn the pride

. . . . —vef   Bnef bn——Bshf st
And avarice that make man a wolf to man.

The transition of gesture relates to the manner of arriving at a gesture, and to the changes of gesture ; and signifies either the particular changes of the position of the hand and arm, or the general change of the principal gesture from one hand to the other.

A gesture may have a very different character and effect according to the manner in which the hand arrives at its destined point. It may ascend, descend, move towards the right or towards the left, and may also make the stroke with various degrees of energy and in various manners; and these motions constitute in each an absolutely different gesture, though, after the moment of the stroke, which a painter might choose to represent, the hand and arm of each should be in the same precise position. Fig. 88, and Plate 12 passim. The character of the other parts of the figure, if well delineated, may serve to aid the imagination and judgment in this respect. West's Oliver Cromwell, represented in the House of Commons in the attitude E. $\frac{\text{phfx}-}{\text{R 1}}$ The head erect and thrown back, the right hand and position of the feet as in the notation, seems as if he had just pronounced these words: (I speak only from recollection, not being in possession of the print.)

pef sp—   phf st—

" Away with that bauble,"

Sus   emp. and ter.

and to have just struck the last emphatical and terminating gesture; which must have been prepared by the suspended gesture *pef sp*—it would be tame if it proceeded from any other preparation, and the spirit of the figure forbids that supposition. As however the emphatical gestures are liable to ambiguity on account of the various transitions which might be supposed to bring them to their stroke; painters more frequently choose to represent the suspended gestures, which give an idea of action and greater interest to their principal figures. St. Paul in the Cartoons lifts up his hands in a grand suspended gesture of oratorical action, and in the representation of battles, the pistol is presented and the sword uplifted ready to fall: In West's General Wolf, the gesture of every figure is completed with fine propriety, and all the figures are at rest except the distant officer who hastens with the news of victory. Many more examples will suggest themselves to those who possess or have opportunities of viewing fine pictures. It is here enough to direct the attention to this agreeable contemplation

But the transition of gesture particularly relates to the change of the principal gesture from one hand to the other: which may be regulated in some measure according to the following principles. So long as there subsists a strict connection between the sentiments, uninterrupted by any considerable pause or change of persons, no transition can take place in this last sense; the same hand, which began, continues to perform the principal gesture. And the variety which it is always desireable to produce, must not be attempted by the change of the principal gesture: it must arise alone from the graceful and well regulated action of the advanced hand, supported by the combined assistance or accompaniment of the other. Neither should the positions of the feet change too freely from right to left, but they may vary in advancing, and retiring, or change from the first to the second position alternately as occasion may require. If the passage to be pronounced be of considerable length, the right hand should by all means perform the principal gesture throughout the whole of it. For the left, though, among modern speakers, allowed to take its place occasionally, according to certain rules, by no means arrives at an equality of honour. The right always continues the better hand both from long prescription and the ability arising from use. The soliloquy of Hamlet is entirely delivered without changing the principal gesture at any time from the right hand. But certain circumstances admit with advantage, and even require a change.

The right hand resigns the principal gesture to the left, when the person addressed is situated at the left side of the speaker. This takes place frequently on the stage, when the

3 H

actor stands on that side which lies towards the left hand of
the spectator. It takes place in Parliament, when the chair,
which Parliamentary order requires to be principally addressed, is at the left of him who delivers his opinion. The
gesticulating constantly with the right hand across the body
would be attended with an awkward effect, exclusive of the
indecorum of obliging the orator nearly to turn his back upon
the House. In such cases, the matter is best compounded by
addressing the chair in general with the left hand, and by
using the right in delivering those arguments to the members
of the house which are designed to influence their opinions.
The Parliamentary speaker will thus, as he ought, direct his
attention to the whole assembly as well as pay proper respect
to the chair; and will comprehend within the range of his
influence, every person within an entire semicircle or more
from his left hand to his right extended in a right line; or
even occasionally directed backwards to the benches behind
him.

The preacher being obliged to address himself to every
individual assembled in the church, should as much as possible
extend his attention to all, and must of course in leaning or
turning round to the left side, often find it necessary, if he use
any, to make the principal gesture with his left hand. The
barrister, though he may choose his place in front of the judges,
may not at the same time be able to accommodate his place
equally to the jury, as they may happen to be situated on his
left hand. Under such circumstances, it appears decorous that
he should rather address the judges with the gesture of the
right hand, and reserve the gesture of the left for the jury.

These are the principal local situations which admit the gestures of the left hand.

The circumstances in the oration or matter of the composition delivered which admit or require the gestures of the left hand, are now to be considered. In the narrative parts of an oration where different persons or things are to be described as variously disposed, or in the recitation of descriptive poetry, when a picture as it were, is to be represented by the speaker, consisting of many natural objects in different parts of a landscape, of which Gray's Elegy in a country church yard, or Milton's Penseroso, will afford many examples, the right hand having first pointed out those persons or objects supposed to lie adjacent to itself, may yield to the left the arrangement and ordering of those other parts which may be imagined to be at its own side. This interchange judiciously regulated, produces a pleasing variety in the gesture; and if the speaker possess the imagination of a painter, his disposition and colouring will produce the most distinct and vivid picture.

Variety, which is a most important object to be kept in view by a public speaker, allows with advantage an interchange of the principal gesture, even when the subject may be of a more abstruse and demonstrative nature. When there is any opposition or antithesis among the ideas, or even in the structure of sentences; or where a new argument is introduced after the discussion of a former is ended, as at a new division or a new paragraph, there may be a change of the principle gesture. But it will be a point of judgment and taste in the speaker not to carry this balancing or alternation of gesture to an affected extreme, and not even in allowable cases to indulge in it over much; nor will he prolong too far the principal action permitted to the left hand, which he will always feel to be the weaker, and recollect to be admitted into the foremost place, rather by courtesy, than of right; and which he will therefore require to use its distinction with discretion.[2]

In the changes made from one hand to the other, the transition should be managed with ease and simplicity. As soon as the advanced hand has made the stroke of its last emphatical gesture, it should fall quietly to rest, whilst at the same time the hand which is in its turn to assume the principal action commences its preparation for the ensuing gesture. It will be observed that a commencing or discriminating gesture as a modest beginning suits its first entrance into authority. An emphatical gesture immediately after one from the other hand would be violent and outrageous; something like the gesticulations of those little wooden figures set up to frighten birds from corn or fruit; which have the arms fixed on an axis in such a manner that they are alternately raised and depressed with equal vehemence, according as they are blown about by the wind. An obvious exception to this rule will occur, as necessarily taking place on the stage in very sudden affections or alarms: thus

---

[2] Certain gestures are appropriated by custom to the right hand, and should never be made by the left. On the stage, the sword or pistol are never held in the left hand, except in ridiculously low comedy. The right hand claims to itself the principal gesture in threatning, in exercising the authority of command, in salutation, and in the representation of habits confined to it by custom, as the gesture of writing, of presenting a musket, or of carving at table. The class of gestures in which the left hand chiefly partakes, are discriminating gestures.

when Hamlet starts at his father's ghost he changes at once the entire position of both hands and feet. Mr. Kemble, before this event, standing in the quiet position of familiar observation with his face towards the spectators, suddenly turns aside into this strong attitude. $\frac{Bvhf}{st.L1.\ x}$ In the same passage the attitude of Mrs. Siddons was $\frac{nhx-vhf}{st.\ L1.\ x}$, in which the left hand assumes also the principal gesture, and the right is thrown out from it *extended*, with fine effect. But oratory is not liable to surprise of this nature; therefore with respect to it the rule is absolute. When the orator finds it necessary to change the position of the feet, so as to advance that which was before retired, the general rule is that he should effect it imperceptibly, and not commence the change till after the hand has begun its change of action. Sometimes, however, in vehement passages the orator is allowed by the highest authority to advance suddenly, and even to stamp with his foot.

The subordinate gesture already mentioned as performed by the retired hand will be found to bear a close analogy to accompaniment in music. It is seldom inactive, sometimes imitates exactly and with considerable spirit, but in general performs an under part supporting and adorning, but by no means moving in the same manner as the superior hand. A little observation will suffice for acquiring a general knowledge of the accompaniment of gesture; and after attentively practising for some time, the inferior hand will as easily fall into a suitable accompaniment of the principal gesture, as in ordinary melodies the left hand of a performer on a keyed instrument will strike correctly the fundamental bass.

The accompanying gesture either exactly imitates the principal, and the arms are held parallel and equally advanced; or the
imitation is as near as the position of the body will allow, and
both point in the same direction (in the notation marked B),
though one may happen to be directed across the body whilst
the other is oblique; the figures reconcile this seeming incongruity which is principally in the names. Fig. 96, 97, 110. The
general rule for accompaniment of gesture in calm and moderate speaking, when both hands do not perform the same
gesture, is that the retired arm should be about one interval
less raised than the advanced arm, and that in the transverse
position it should be distant from it not less than two intervals,
or a right angle nearly, and sometimes more. Thus the first
set of letters or the right hand being considered to perform the
principal gesture, the accompaniment is expressed in the
second set for the left hand *sef—shx* Fig. 30, and *vhf—pdb* Fig. 25.
prin.   ac.   prin.   ac.

When the force of the expression is strong, the accompanying
hand is equally elevated with the principal, thus in this degree
of force the gestures are thus, *vhf—vhx*. It is not necessary to
prin.   ac.

dwell on these observations, a little attention will furnish
abundance. These circumstances afford convenient opportunities for abridging the notation. When both hands perform the
same or nearly the same gesture, a capital B preceding one
set of letters suffices for both hands, as *B vhf*. And when
the accompanying gesture follows the general rule, and has
nothing remarkably distinguishing it, the gesture of the principal hand only is noted, the accompaniment is easily understood, and will follow of course to the well practised speaker.[3]

---

[3] Mr. Engel observing that all the muscles and every part of the body should co-ope-
rate in expressing the feelings by gesture, relates this anecdote of Garrick:

If the right hand only be marked a set of small letters is followed by a short dash thus, *ihq*—. If the left hand only be marked as performing the principal gesture, the short dash precedes the set of small letters as —*ihq* : this has been already noticed.

But besides the motions of the subordinate gesture, other very important accompaniments are to be attended to ; as those of the lower limbs, of the body and of the head: otherwise the performance will be rigid and absurd like that of a puppet. Indeed not only those more-prominent and distinguished parts must accompany the voice and principal action of the speaker, but every muscle of the body, and every expression of the countenance must join in harmony with those gestures, in order to impress upon them the characters of nature and truth. There is no gesture or change of gesture which is not meant to enforce or to illustrate some new circumstance, which either calls into action muscles before at rest, or into a change of action those already in exertion. And this impression and influence extends not only to those muscles which are most strong and distinguished, but even to the most delicate fibres of the human frame, such as those which adjust the expression of the mouth, of the nostrils, of the brows, and

---

Garrick doit avoir dit un jour à un comédien François, qui lui demandoit son avis sur la maniere dont il avoit joué dans une piece. " Vous avez rempli le rôle d'ivrogne avec beaucoup de vérité, et, ce qui est très-difficile à réunir dans des pareilles rôles, avec beaucoup de grace. Mais permettez moi de faire une petite observation critique, c'est que votre pied gauche étoit trop à jeun. *Idées sur le Geste, Lettre* 24.

The influence of intoxication should have been represented by the French actor as extended to every part, as would have taken place in reality.

of that wondrous organ the eye.[4]   An example may be here
given of some of the stronger changes of the head, body, and
lower limbs which accompany certain principal gestures.[5,6]   If
the right hand be forcibly withdrawn so that the inside of the
upper arm shall press the side and the right be presented *vhfc*,
the left will *vdqc*, the feet will naturally retire and be *r R.1.x.*

---

[4] Il ne suffit pas que l'harmonie la plus parfaite existe entre tous les membres du corps
et entre tous les traits du visage, pour rendre l'expression d'un sentiment; mais il faut
aussi que cette harmonie soit proportionnée au degré de force et de vivacité de ce sentiment. Si le desir se manifeste trop par le jeu des bras, et trop peu par le mouvement des
pieds; si l'effroi ne fait pas ouvrir assez la bouche et les yeux ? tandis que le corps est presque
renversé, et que les bras, élevés avec rapidité, restent immobiles; si la colere ne fait pas
froncer assez la front et laisse appercevoir la tranquillité sur les levres, tandis que les pieds
frappent la terre avec fureur, &c.; l'illusion et tout effet quelconque cessent subitement
pour celui qui s'appercevoit ce defaut de l'harmonie, et l'acteur se retrouve devant ses yeux,
tandis qu'il ne devroit voir que le personnage. Vous devez avoir remarqué nombre d'exemples de pareilles incoherences dans l'expression, principalement sur ces visages où brillent
trop tous les charmes de la jeunssse. Il y a des fronts qui ne se rident jamais, des lèvres
qui ne sauroient s'abbatre, et des yeux qui ne peuvent sortir de leurs orbites; en un mot,
il y a des Physionnomies pleines et arrondies, sur lesquelles certaines affections se peignent
avec des traits si légers et si imperceptibles à quelque distance, qu'on ne croit en reconnoitre
tout au plus que les premiers symptomes où une nuance tres-fugitive; et lorsqu'en pareils
cas le jeu du reste du corps exprime toute la véhémence de l'affection, il en resulte un effet
fort désagréable, du moins, à mon avis, de maniere que j'aimerois mieux voir l'expression
totalement manquée. *Engel, Idée sur le Geste, Lettre 24.*

The above rule is changed in representing Hypocrisy.

[5] Le siege du jeu des gestes n'est fixé pas dans telle membre, ou telle partie du corps en
particulier. L'ame exerce sur tous les muscles un pouvoir égal et dans nombre de ses
operations, et de ses passions elle agit sur tous en general. Vous savez que chaque membre
et chaque muscle parle dans la figure du Laocoon. *Ideés sur le Geste, Lettre 6.*

[6] Shortly after the above follows this note of the French translator, on the expression of
the countenance.

Cela nous rappelle le bon mot d'une femme d'esprit, qui disoit, " il est bien hardi, ce
coquin là : il osera regarder en face un homme qui tent le pinceau." C'étoit sans doute
aussi par les moyens des yeux que le célèbre la Tour prétendoit lire dans l'ame de ceux
qu'il peignoit. " Ils croient, disoit-il, que je ne saisis que les traits de leur visage ; mais je
descends au fond d'eux mêmes et je les remporte tout entiers."

the left will *vdqc*, the feet will naturally retire and be *r R.*1.*x*. And the body at the same time will be thrown backwards and the head averted, whilst the whole countenance will express aversion or horror, Fig. 99, and 39. The gesture of the right *phf ad* will be accompanied and noted thus : $F \frac{\text{phf ad}-\text{pdq}}{\text{a.R2.}}$, which signifies that the head, and consequently the body leans forwards, and that the eyes are turned earnestly in the same direction ; which evident desire of inspecting the object more nearly is also accompanied by an advanced step of the right foot, the principal gesture being performed by the right hand. The gesture of the left might have been omitted in the notation; as it could hardly be avoided under the circumstances mentioned. Again it will be observed, that if the hand in its gestures at any time approach the head, the head bends towards the hand, and if the hand presents its palm and pushes, as it were, an object away in disgust, the head accompanies the action not only by retiring back, but by averting the countenance. And the motions expressing this aversion are, first the approaching of the back of the hand towards the face, the eye directed and the head bending towards the hand and the object, and then the pushing forwards of the palm of the hand, and the throwing back and averting of the head at the same time; in notation thus, $F. \frac{\text{vhf c}-}{\text{aR2}}$ Fig. 100, and then $A \frac{\text{vhq p}-}{\text{rR.1.x}}$ Fig. 101. The feet also partake in these movements.

After the stroke of the emphatical gesture, if the speaker have completely closed his sentiments on a particular part of his subject, or if he have finished his oration, both hands fall to rest in a manner suiting his own character, and the last expressions which he has delivered. This falling of the hands to rest is named the close and termination of gesture. Quintilian and the rhetoricians require the concluding gesture to be made at the right hand;[7,8,9] and for a good reason: because, supposing the principal gesture to be made only with the right hand, if the emphatical and closing gesture is made towards the left or *across*, another gesture will be required before the hand can be brought into the position *oblique*, from which the arm falls with that kind of relaxation which indicates that its exertions are, for the present, completely finished. If the arm were thus abandoned when in the position across, it would be apt to swing or vibrate for some time like a pendulum before it settled at the point of rest, or be forcibly stopped there, either of which circumstances would not accord with the impression intended by a terminating gesture, or mark it with proper decision. And it is contrary to the correct simplicity of gesture to mark any single word or idea with more than a single emphatical stroke, any appendix of gesture after this, would only weaken its force, or render it ridiculous. Intoxication and insanity are observed to continue their gesticulations,

---

7 Optime autem manus à sinistra parte incipit, in dextra deponitur: sed ut deponi, non ut ferire videatur; quanquam et in fine interim cadit, ut cito tamen redeat. *Quint. l.* xi. *c.* 3. *p.* 1021.

8 To this Cresollius adds after the words non ut ferire videatur, nisi forte in graviori contentione, ubi justa iracundia locum habet. *Vac. Aut.*

9 M. Rollin gives nearly the same directions, but more enlarged. Le mouvement des mains suit naturellement la voix et doit s'y conformer. Dans le geste periodique et ordinaire on doit porter la main droite de gauche à droit en commençant devant soi, et finissant à côté, les doigts de la main étant un peu élevés au dessus du poignet, ouverts et en liberté, étendant le bras de toute sa longeur, sans lever le coude aussi haut que l'épaule, mais le tenant toujours detaché, et eloigné du corps et observant que c'est par le mouvement du coude que doit ordinairement commencer le geste. (See also note from Engel 1. ch. 16.) Après cela on porte la main gauche de droit à gauche avec les mêmes proportions qu'on aura gardées pour la main droite. Il faut suspendre et soutenir le bras après chaque geste

and to reiterate the same after they have ceased to speak; but the decorum of public speaking ought not to be betrayed into any intemperance bearing the most remote similitude to the manner of such unhappy or vicious derangement. The rule of Quintilian should therefore be carefully observed; and it may be rendered more general according to our modern customs by saying, that the emphatical and terminating gestures should not be made across.

The termination of gesture, or rather the emphatical gesture which terminates, is generally made about the horizontal elevation, but sometimes may also be made downwards or elevated according to the sentiment. The horizontal termination suits decision, and instruction; the downward disapprobation and condemnation; the elevated pride, high passion, and devotion.

In the observations made on the action of a public speaker, he has been supposed to stand free from incumbrance, whether arising from the pressure of a crowd or from that of the enclosure of a narrow pulpit. In this latter situation, the terminating fall of the arm cannot always be effected, at least in a proper manner; the hand is often arrested by the cushion, which impedes as much the gesture of the preacher as the crowded courts do that of the barrister. One half of the semicircle in which the vertical action of the arm is performed, is completely

---

à côté de soi jusqu'à ce que la periode finisse; et lorsqu'elle est finie, les deux mains doivent tomber negligemment sur la chaire, si c'est là qu'on parle, et jamais en dedans; ou tout de leur long sur la personne, si on parle debout sans apuis, ou sur les deux genoux, si on parle assis sur une chaise; il y a mille manieres de varier ces gestes, que l'usage seul et l'exercice peuvent apprendre. *Rollin, Belles Lettres.*

cut off from each. The remedy for this mutilation to the preacher is to raise himself on a high stool, and to lower or remove the cushion; awkward expedients both; another I have seen resorted to by a Sectary, but not to be recommended; he stretched his body as far forwards over the pulpit as he could, and gesticulated with his right arm by striking the pannells on the outside, and swinging and brandishing it from the shoulder, whilst he rested his right side nearly on the cushion. Greece, the native soil of manly eloquence, and true taste, was not the inventress of the pulpit.

The termination of gesture, as has been said, takes place only when both arms fall to rest. So long as either appears in action, though the other may rest, there is no proper pause or break in the thoughts; they are supposed still to continue, though the action varies according as circumstances may require. Many examples may be given of this proper termination of gesture. Such is the pause which takes place after the short exordium of Brutus's harangue to the Romans in Shakspeare's Julius Cæsar, ending thus:

" Awake your senses, that you may the better judge."

Milton's Penseroso, if recited, requires the closing termination after those lines which dismiss all cheerful ideas, ending:

The fickle pensioners of Morpheus' train.

It may also be applied at the end of the different scenes which he seeks for the indulgence of his pensive mood. After the first stanza of Gray's Elegy in the country church yard, which is a sort of preface to the contemplations which follow, the

arms may fall to rest in recitation: and also at the close of
each completed description. But where the description, though
the sense is sufficiently complete, is not absolutely finished,
because in the next stanza other objects are presented as existing in a different part of the landscape, the discrimination is
advantageously made, by what may be termed the *semipause* or
semitermination of gesture; this, in effect, is no more than the
change of the principal gesture to a different hand, by which
the former falls to rest, as has been already mentioned. The
second stanza of the same poem, and the beginning of the
third will afford an example.

> Save where the beetle wheels his droning flight
> phf p—R
> And drowsy tinklings lull the distant folds;
> aR2
>
> —ieq n—
> 3 Save that from yonder ivy mantled tow'r
> rL1
> —veq   U   —seb n
> The moping owl does to the moon complain.

The principal gesture in the second stanza is represented as
performed by the right hand. The new objects in the third
stanza may be represented in another part of the picture, and
are described by the gestures of the left hand; whilst the right
falls to rest in the close of the second. In the third, the right
hand not being noted accompanies the left according to the
rules of accompaniment. The position of the feet is also
changed in this stanza.

CHAPTER XIX

OF THE FREQUENCY, MODERATION, AND INTERMISSION OF GESTURE.

Gesture should be used with moderation—Sometimes intermitted altogether —The frequency determined by the number and novelty of ideas— Periods of gesture—Quintilian's directions as to frequency of gesture —The best rule for regulating gesture—Gesture should not be used unless for illustration or enforcement—An English audience prepossessed in favour of quiet dissertation—But acute in judgment when excited—Premeditated gestures to be moderated in actual delivery, if the feelings are not sufficient for their perfect execution—A public speaker should always be able to govern his feelings, and restrain them within proper bounds.

CHAPTER XIX.

Of the Frequency, Moderation, and Intermission of Gesture.

As gesture is used for the illustration or enforcement of language, it should be limited in its application to such words and passages only as admit, or rather require, such illustration or enforcement. That is, gesture should not be used by a public speaker on every word, where it is possible to apply it without manifest impropriety; but it should rather be reserved for such passages as require to be rendered more prominent than the others, and to be coloured higher. A judicious speaker will therefore reserve his gesture, at least the force and ornament of it, for those parts of his discourse for which he also reserves the brilliancy of language and thought. As words of themselves when composed and delivered with propriety, are fully intelligible for every purpose of argument, instruction, and information; in those divisions of a discourse, therefore, which treat of such topics, gesture may be well spared, and if any is used it ought to be the most moderate and unostentatious.[1] The simple and occasional inclination of the head, the

---

[1] The character of the discourses delivered from our pulpits in general is such, that gesture is rather properly to be omitted. They are no more than quiet dissertations. Sermons admitting rhetorical delivery must be composed, as has been already observed, in rhetorical spirit.

A portico supported on Corinthian columns would be a very incongruous entrance into a simple, neat cottage.

direction of the eyes, and the noting of the hand and similar quiet discriminating gestures are altogether sufficient, and sometimes perhaps even more than necessary. It will be evident hence, that if an entire discourse is composed in this character, the gesture, in no part, should trangress this moderation. In many parts absolute intermission of gesture is advantageous, in such compositions; as in the commencement, and at the beginning or opening of arguments ; afterwards, when the argument is brought more nearly to a conclusion, a little of gesture will give it more force, and relieve the monotony of a mere dry demonstration, should the spirit of the composition admit such addition.[2,3]

---

[2] The general advantage of moderation in gesture is thus well described by Cresollius. In hac re, ut in omnibus, medium consequi et auream mediocritatem, pulchrum æstimo, et considerato homine dignissimum. Debet enim esse actio plena dignitatis, liberalis animi index, qualis eorum hominum esse dicitur a Xenophonte, qui enthei amoris vi afflantur, qui, inquit, τὰ σχήματα εἰς τὸ ἐλευθεριώτατον ἄγεσι, gestus ad speciem quendam maxime liberalem conformant. Est autem ea species actionis in moderatione quadam posita, sic ut absit illa fervida incompositaque temeritas, nimiumque audax manuum jactatio, et hæc contra rusticana timiditas et impolita, quæ necessarium motum solet infringere. *Cresol. Vac. Aut.*

[3] Sed malim ego quidem oratorem verecundiæ et ingenuæ timiditati propiorem, quam impudentiæ, quod in timidis cautio quædam reperitur a vitiositate abhorrens. Quare cum probro Cleanthi daretur quod esset timidior, Est ita, inquit, sed eam ipsam ob causam, ὀλίγα ἁμαρτάνω, pauca pecco. Si quando res jucunditatis habet plurimum, gestus potest esse liberior, ut in narrationibus, quæ ad animos exhilarandos adferuntur, ut in fabellis, quas vel Æsopus, vel Hesiodus primus excogitavit. . . . . De Demos bene inveni Plutarcho (ejus vit.) Populo quidem ἤρεκε θαυμασῶς, mirum in modum actio ejus probabatur, eruditi autem humilem putabant ejus gestum καὶ ἀγενὲς τὸ πλάσμα καὶ μαλακὸν, et degenerem et mollem, quod Demetrius Phalareus existimat. Quare illi contumeliæ loco objecit Æschines, quod in dicendo consuevisset ταρατεύεσθαι τῷ σχήματι, in gestu quædam veluti portenta exhibere. A. Gellius dicit, manus argutæ Demosthenis. M. Tullius eundem (Demosth.) significat tam arguto et celeri manuum gestu fuisse ut oculos intuentium perstringeret. Illa quoque in gestu mediocritas Tyrtamo defuit, illi sophorum

In discourses, or particular parts of discourses, admitting freer gesture, the frequency of it will be determined, in general, by the number, the novelty, and the discrimination of ideas. In every well constructed sentence some new idea is advanced, which may be marked by a suitable gesture ; and possibly the various limitations and modifications of it will also admit of a similar distinction.   And the new gesture will be forcible according to the importance of the new idea or modification introduced, and will fall upon the accented syllable of the word which contains it.   Thus each separate clause or member of a sentence may admit a distinct gesture on the principal word ; and as each epithet or adjective is a new quality added to the principal name, and each adverb has the same effect on the principal action expressed by the verb, a new gesture may be made on each.   But for this purpose, unless the word be important or emphatical, a turn of the hand, a small motion in the transverse direction or in the elevation of the arm, or a small inclination of the head, are sufficient, or any of those intermediate gestures termed discriminating gestures.

In a sentence where each word is important, if gesture be used, each should be marked with a gesture.   Sentences of this kind are generally moral observations, which condense in a short compass valuable information, and should therefore be strongly enforced and marked with precision.   The indispensable

---

in dicendo suavissimo, quem Aristoteles διὰ τὸ τῆς φράσεως θεσπέσιον à divinitate loquendi Theophrastum indigitavit; eum autem ὐδεμίας ἀπέχεσθαι κινήσεως, ἀ δὲ σχήματος τινος, nullum gestum nec corporis motionem prætermisisse, in sapientum convivio scribit Athenæus *lib.* i. *Cresol. Vac. Aut.*

requisite for the proper production of the desired effect, is that
the sentence be delivered most distinctly and deliberately : if
it be so, the gestures will have good effect, but if hurried on
rapidly, the gestures confuse the sentiment, and may even cast
a degree of ridicule upon it : as may be found, by pronouncing
the following serious observation with different degrees of
rapidity and gravity.

shf—   nef—   shfst
Man is born to trouble.
com.   susp.   emp. and ter.

This is a period of gesture, (as already spoken of in Chap.
XVII.), and consists of a regular commencing, suspended, and
emphatical and terminating gesture, as marked. But neither
the emphatical gesture in a sentence, nor the force of the voice,
are always found to fall on those words which are the principal
in a gramatical sense; the nouns and verbs. The gesture falls
rather on the word which modifies each; on the adjective
which expresses the quality of the noun, or on the adverb
which has a similar effect upon the action or assertion of the
verb. The noun and the verb are, in such cases, considered
only as the simple idea, the distinguishing character of which
arises from the quality annexed, which with the noun or verb
together, form a new compound idea, and as it were a new
compound word. This disposition to unite and coalesce produces the wonderful combinations in language, which render a
few terms capable of expressing a boundless infinity of ideas.
On these qualifying words the principal emphasis is laid both
of voice and gesture. Thus :

A *wise* son maketh a *glad* father.

In this sentence it is evident that the nouns, son and father, connected with the verb without the adjectives, would not only fail to make the same sense as the compound terms, but would make nonsense; therefore are these qualities of distinguished value in their place, and both the stress of the voice, and the stroke of the gesture should fall on them in delivery. The verb when standing by itself is an important word, and requires the emphasis and action; but, if qualified by an adverb, transfers also its rights like the noun. Of both cases the following affords an example

That thou *doest*, do *quickly*.

What is here advanced will derive some support from a passage of Quintilian; and contribute to illustrate some part of it, which appears obscure.

" Here the old masters have judiciously observed, that the " action of the hand should begin and close with the sense." This appears to signify that the commencement of the motion, or as it is named in this treatise, the preparation of the gesture, should take place at the beginning of the clause; leading to the emphatical word; and that the stroke of the gesture should be made on that word, and the hand then fall to rest. " For other- " wise the gesture will precede the voice or follow it, both of " which are improper." In the calm parts of a discourse, the gesture should certainly be regulated by this rule of Quintilian; but in the ardent passages the order is rather this, the feelings of the mind are first disclosed by the countenance, then by the gesture, and lastly expressed in words which, however short the interval, being artificial are not supplied so rapidly, as the other natural and often involuntary signs. " They have fallen

" into too subtile refinement on this subject, who require,
" between each interval of action, three words : which neither
" is, nor can be attended to ; but they have fixed upon it as a
" kind of mean regulation between too great rapidity and the
" opposite tediousness ; and they have some reason. For the
" hand ought neither to be long inactive, nor, (as many are
" found to do), disturb the argument by continual gesticula-
" tion. There is another fault, which speakers more frequently
" fall into, and is not so easily corrected. In discourse certain
" obscure cadences occur, a sort of measured feet, upon which
" many mark their gestures. As suppose one motion on these
" words.—*A new charge:* another, *C. Cæsar:* a third, *and before*
" *this day :* a fourth, *unheard of :* again, *my kinsman :* and again,
" *Quintus Tubero has brought before you.* From whence arises
" this vicious manner, that young men when they write,
" adjusting their thoughts to the gesture, compose in such a
" manner as to accommodate the falling of the hand. And
" from hence also proceeds another fault, that the gesture,
" which at the end of a sentence should terminate at the right
" side often closes at the left. It is a better method, as in every
" discourse there are certain short divisions, at which, if neces-
" sary, the speaker may take breath, to make his gestures fall
" on these. As in the former example ; *A new charge, C. Cæsar ;*
" this passage has a sort of close in itself, because a conjunction
" follows ; then this, *and before this day unheard of,* is suffi-
" ciently limited. To these divisions the hand is to be accom-
" modated, and that whilst the action is beginning and in
" preparation. But when the ardor of the speaker hurries it
" on, the frequency of the gesture encreases with the rapidity
" of the delivery. It will be proper in some places that the

" pronunciation be accelerated, in others that it be retarded.
" In some cases, we run over the subject, we condense, we
" overflow, we hurry on; but in these we urge, we inculcate,
" we impress our sentiments." [4]

If the passage, which Quintilian has here chosen from Cicero
to illustrate the proper frequency of gesture, were noted according to this system it might stand thus. Each passage is
numbered according to Quintilian, to shew where a new gesture
is to take place. " A new charge, C. Cæsar, and before this day
shf— nef— pefa—

1 2 3

unheard of, my kinsman, Quintus Tubero has brought before
phf st— ihq— shfn—

4 5 6

" you." The four first gestures appear evidently too frequent,
as Quintilian observes, and he would have them reduced to

---

4 Hic veteres artifices illud recte adjecerunt, *ut manus cum sensu et inciperet et depone-*
retur. Alioqui enim aut ante vocem erit gestus, aut post vocem, quod est utrumque
deforme. In illo lapsi nimia subtilitate sunt, quod intervallum motus tria verba esse
voluerunt: quod nec observatur, nec fieri potest ; sed illi quasi mensuram tarditatis celeri-
tatisque aliquam esse voluerunt, nec immerito, ne aut diu otiosa esset manus, aut (quod
multi faciunt) actionem continuo motu conciderent. Aliud est, quod et fit frequentius et
magis fallit. Sunt quaedam latentes sermonis percussiones, et quasi aliqui pedes, ad quos
plurimorum gestus cadit, ut sit unus motus, *Novum crimen:* alter, *C. Cæsar:* tertius,
Et ante hanc diem: quartus, *inauditum:* deinde, *Propinquus meus:* et, *ad te Quintus*
Tubero detulit. Unde id quoque fluit vitium, ut juvenes, cum scribunt, gestu præmo-
dulati cogitationem sic componant, quomodo casura manus est. Inde et illud vitium,
ut gestus, qui in fine dexter esse debet, in sinistrum frequenter desinat. Melius illud,
cum sint in sermone omni brevia quædam membra, ad quæ, si necesse sit, recipere
spiritum liceat, ad hæc gestum disponere : ut puta, *novum crimen, C. Cæsar,* habet per se
finem quemdam suum, quia sequitur conjunctio : deinde, *et ante hunc diem inauditum,*
satis circumscriptum est. Ad hæc commodanda manus est, idque dum erit prima et composita actio. At ubi jam calor eam concitaverit, etiam gestus cum ipsa orationis celeritate
crebescet. Aliis locis citata, aliis pressa conveniet pronunciatio. Illa transcurrimus, con-
gerimus, abundamus, festinamus : hac instamus, inculcamus, infigimus. *Quint. B.* 1022.

shfp—

two; perhaps thus, " A new charge, C. Cæsar, and before this
'1
nef sp
" day unheard of, &c. Something of this kind seems to be what
2
Quintilian requires; the manner of the gesture may be varied
as shall be thought most suitable, by those who are disposed
to make the enquiry. But he allows only two gestures, that is
perhaps two gestures marked with decision on this passage, for
in whatever manner they may be varied, the preparations will
amount to almost as much as the small discriminating gestures
2 and 3, which are noted in the first manner. The art of
managing gesture to the best advantage appears, according to
my conception, to be this; to contrive so, that the discriminating gestures shall serve as preparations for the more emphatical gestures. The discriminating gestures, it will be recollected,
are made by a slight turn of the hand, or a small variation in
the transverse direction or in elevation. When the gestures
are managed in this way, I should be inclined to prefer the
action as noted in the first manner: provided they are made
with due deliberation In the second gesture marked *nef*—
which is followed by another marked also *elevated* and *ascending*,
the hand should not be raised very high, in order to allow the
next gesture to be raised higher without straining. This observation applies generally to all similar passages. It has been
already said that the points noted in the elevation and transverse
direction are not to be considered as mathematically strict.
And there is also a latitude allowed according to the energy
of the speaker. The same notation applied to a vehement
passage is understood to require the arm to be raised higher
than when it is applied to one of the contrary character. One

observation more must be made on this passage of Quintilian, the passage *idque dum erit prima et composita actio* is translated, whilst the action is beginning and in preparation. If this be not admitted as the sense, I must relinquish it as obscure beyond my reach: but I am inclined to think it is the true interpretation; if prepossession in favour of system may not have led me astray.

From the observations made on this subject it appears that a judicious speaker will often intermit his gesture altogether, that he will restrain its frequency, and use it only when absolutely necessary to illustrate or to enforce his sentiments.[5,6] Gesture will be recollected to hold the place of high seasoning and ornament, and it must be managed with discretion lest it should defeat it own purposes and create disgust or disapprobation. It will also be recollected by the judicious speaker that our prepossessions in general are not in favour of gesture; and that nothing less than the most evident correctness, spirit, and chastity of manner can obtain approbation, or in spite of prejudice afford delight. It is not for want of judgment or through any deficiency in taste that a British audience do not

---

[5] En effet, il n'est point naturel de remuer toujours les bras en parlant : il faut remuer les bras parcequ'on est animé ; mais il ne faudroit pas, pour paroitre animé, remuer les bras. Il y a des choses même qu'il faut dire tranquillement sans se remuer. *Fenelon, Dial. sur l'Eloquence. Paris,* 1787, *Tom. III.* p. 231.

[6] Mr. Charles Gildon, the writer of the life of Betterton, seems to be of opinion that there should not be any intermission of gesture ; his rule for the hands is sometimes repeated, but seems not a little erroneous, if we look to other writers :

You must never let either of your hands hang down as if lame or dead ; for that is very disagreeable to the eye, and argues no passion in the imagination. In short, your hands must always be in view of your eyes. *Betterton's Life, p.* 77.

require of a public speaker the gesture which is the last refinement and polish of eloquence; custom alone, and a certain habitual gravity of character, disposes our people to listen with patience to long and tedious dissertation, delivered with good sense but without grace. Whole assemblies attend with complacency, and absorb with tranquillity, and weigh with judgment the public reasonings of public speakers. Many prefer the quiet information thus obtained to any efforts of oratory. When at any time excited from their tranquillity by attempts at eloquence, they are at first rather disturbed than pleased; and are apt to judge of the innovation with severity, joined to all the critical skill which learning and refined taste unite. If the speaker prove truly eloquent, and truly elegant and judicious, he is sure of most liberal and solid approbation. But he must be discreet, and not hazard too much till he finds himself possessed of his audience and filled with his subject.[7] He will be quiet and guarded in the commencement of his discourse, (and particularly in the commencement of his practice of this art,) he will restrain his gestures in the calm and reasoning passages, and reserve its force and brilliancy for the appropriate expression of his most earnest feelings and boldest thoughts.[8,9] His transitions from the placid and tranquil

---

[7] L'abbatement de la douleur permet peu de gestes ; la reflexion profonde n'en veut aucun ; le sentiment demande une action simple comme lui ; l'indignation, le mépris, la fierté, la menace, la fureur concentrée n'ont besoin que de l'expression des yeux et du visage : un régard, un mouvement de tête, voilà leur action naturelle : le geste ne feroit que l'affoiblir. Que ceux qui reprochent à un acteur de negliger le geste dans les rôles pathétiques de pére ou dans les rôles majesteueux de Rois, apprennent que la dignité n'a point ce qu'ils appellent des bras. *Marmontel, Elémens de Littérature, Tom. II. p.* 330.

[8] Il faut que son corps ait du mouvement quand ses paroles en ont : et que son corps demeure tranquille quand ses paroles n'ont rien que de doux et de simple. *Fenelon, Dial. sur l'Eloquence.*

[9] Vous voudriez donc beucoup d'inégalité dans la voix et dans le geste ? A. C'est la ce

narrative, to the parts which are most highly wrought, and which require his utmost exertions, will be gradual and just, and free from sudden extravagance. As he warms, his gesture will commence; and when he glows, it will be more vehement, and also more frequent.[10][11][12] A public speaker sometimes delivers his sentiments from the impression of the moment ; when these are ardent and generous, nothing further is to be wished, than that he may have been well practised and instructed beforehand in all the powers of language, as well as in all the external arts of eloquence. Words of fire will then be supplied, and lightnings will flash as splendid as irresistible; and voice, countenance, and gesture will be such as expression, force, and gracefulness demand. But this is a felicity not to be expected always, even by the most consummate orators. The matter and the manner of the oration are

---

qui rend l'action si puissante, et qui la faisoit mettre par Demosthéne au-dessus de tout. Plus l'action et la voix paroissent simple et familiéres dans les endroits où l'on ne fait qu'instruire, que raconter, que s'insinuer ; plus préparent-elles de surprise et d'émotion pour les endroits où elles s'éleveront à un enthousiasme soudain. C'est une espece de musique ; toute la béauté consiste dans la variété des tons ; qui haussent ou qui baissent selon les choses qu'ils doivent exprimer. *Fenelon, Dial. sur l'Eloq.*

[10] Dans certains endroits vifs, il faut parler plus vite ; mais parler avec précipitation, et ne pouvoir se reténir est un grand défaut. Il y a des choses qu'il faut appuyer : il en est de l'action et de la voix comme des vers : il faut quelquefois une mesure courte et impétueuse pour signifier ce qui est vif et ardent. Se servir toujours de la même action et de la même mesure de voix, c'est comme qui donneroit le même remede à toutes sortes de malades. *Ib.*

[11] La plupart de ces déclamateurs sont pour le geste comme pour la voix : leur voix a, une monotonie perpétuelle et leur geste une uniformité qui n'est ni moins ennuyeuse, ni moins éloignée de la nature, ni moins contraire au fruit qu'on pourroit attendre de l'action. *Ib.*

[12] Mais ce que je trouve le moins naturelle en ce prédicateur, c'est qu'il donne à ses bras un mouvement continuel, pendant qu'il n'y a ni mouvement ni figure dans ses paroles. *Ib.*

both generally composed in the closet, it would be presumption and disrespect to a great assembly should it be otherwise: and the example of the greatest orators proves that it can be attended with no imputation against our talents: for we have still remaining for our instruction what Demosthenes and Cicero had thus composed. A prudent speaker, who has meditated his oration and his delivery, will perhaps not always find his feelings on the actual exertion to answer his premeditations. In such an event his care should be that his action shall not overpass the degree of feeling with which he is actually affected. If he cannot excite himself to the degree he proposed or expected during the composition of his discourse, he will not allow his purposed style of gesture to overpower the force and expression of his voice; otherwise it will prove cold and artificial. The voice, which is the true test of the feelings, should regulate the whole external demeanor; and if it be languid or uninterested, notwithstanding the speaker's efforts, he will accommodate it from his ready store with gesture and manner of such sort, as shall be rather below than above the feelings which he can reach. By such management gesture will not fail to please even those who are not used to this great addition to a popular discourse.

The knowledge of the extreme bounds also to which decorum should allow a speaker to proceed according to his situation ought to be familiar to his imagination. So that even in the " tempest and whirlwind of his passion" he shall be still in possession of himself, and never abandon himself to undue extravagance. All that energy, brilliancy, or pathos can require, may, in the pulpit, in parliament, and at the bar be kept within such bounds, as shall better produce the intended effect, than the most licentious indulgence. Even on the stage itself, where more is permitted, if our great Poet may be considered as authority, temperance should be strictly observed. If it should be transgressed wantonly and audaciously, the outrage is sure to produce derision instead of applause.

CHAPTER XX.

OF THE QUALITIES OF GESTURE SUITED TO MODES OF PUBLIC SPEAKING.

Analogy of gesture and language—Ordinary gesture suited to common subjects—Graceful gesture suited to subjects more elevated— The difference consists principally in the preparation and manner of extending the arm—Gesture suited to different modes of public speaking— The epic—The rhetorical—The colloquial—Qualities of gesture— Magnificence — Boldness — Energy—Variety—Simplicity—Grace— Propriety—Precision—With their opposite imperfections—In what proportions these qualities enter into the different modes of public speaking—Whether an orator may with advantage take for his models the gestures of the theatre—When public speakers should use gesture most freely.

CHAPTER XX.

Of the Analogy of Gesture and Language ; of the Qualities of Gesture, and of the Gesture suited to different Modes of Public Speaking.

GESTURE is in itself capable of being used as the sign of ideas, and therefore of being substituted for language. The excellence of the art of the ancient pantomimes, and that also of the modern pantomimic dances evinces this power of gesture. And it will occur to the recollection of most people, that they who by the privation of the sense of hearing are precluded from the imitation of articulate sounds, which are the great medium of rational communication, can usually maintain a very strict intercourse of mind with their near intimates by the use of gestures alone. Language and gesture have also these circumstances in common ; that in order to express vulgar feelings, and the common wants of nature, a few and rude words, and a few rude gestures are equally sufficient :[1] but if by language we would represent sentiments above those which relate to the most ordinary wants and desires, a great variety is required in the meaning, disposition, connections, and relations both of language and of gesture.

---

[1] Apud agrestes ferosque homines pauca sunt verba, dura, et vix juncta, quæ necessitati tantum sufficiant. *Sup. Dial. de Orat. Tacit. c.* 13.

Language in this respect has much the advantage of gesture, and is a more highly cultivated and more perfect vehicle of thought: but gesture is not altogether deficient in powers of expression, and in contrivances in some degree similar. Another resemblance between language and gesture may be found in the style of each, as suited to the different modes of expression. The language of poetry, and the gesture suited to express elevated ideas equally differ from the colloquial and ordinary. But this difference, if we except the English, and a few rich languages, which possess also a distinct language of poetry, is in general more in the arrangement and in the splendour of the thoughts, than in the matter. The gesture of the tragedian is in all essential points the same as that of the social circle, and performed by the same organs and instruments; by the voice, the countenance, the limbs, the body, and head. And it will be recollected that in private there is nothing different from the gesture of other men in that of distinguished actors. Wherein does their action in private life differ from that which astonishes and delights on the stage, and wherein does their language differ? in the splendor and parade more than in the mere sense, or the absolute object, supposing the circumstances similar; that is either equally interesting to the individual, or equally indifferent. The language of poetry in the high flights of passion and grandeur is adorned and enforced by its figures, by its pomp, by its circumlocutions. The language of gesture imitates that of poetry, it has its graces, its preparations, its grand transitions, and its accompaniments. Strip poetry of its figures, its swell, its circumlocutions, and its measure, and it becomes mere prose, the plain and downright expression of thought, Strip gesture of its graces, and all its superfluous ornamental movement, and it becomes the short and sharp action of ordinary however earnest dialogue. The graces of language, to use a figure, consist in the manner of leading the mind about in order to present the object in the most favourable point of view. The graces of gesture, to use less of figure, depend on the flowing or bold preparations which lead to the decisive and impressive action. The ornament of language consists in the grateful variety of ideas presented to the mind, and tending to the principal object of the poet. The graces of other arts, as gardening and architecture, depend on the same principle; and not less so the graces of gesture; sudden turns, short passages, confined limits, dead stops, and impassable fences, may indeed answer the conveniencies of common life, but more of pomp and circumstance, and display is suited to the grand and majestic style of princely residence.

The grace of movement consists as we have seen according to Hogarth in the inflexion of the lines in which it moves. And these lines must not be either too much or too little bended; the line of beauty will be transgressed by either extreme. Indentations too deep, and flourishes too much extended, fall into quaintness, or run out into bombast and wild extravagance, whilst the want of a certain degree of deflexion from the direct line, degenerates into stiff and cold formality. True elegance of gesture follows the graceful mean. So far the principals of Hogarth. But the parallel between the line of beauty in drawing, and the line of grace in gesture, does not entirely hold. There is in gesture a latitude allowable, which when occasion requires overpasses the forms of grace, and on the one hand enters within the confines of the grand and magnificent, and on the other, with great propriety, and with equal grace, the circumstances being considered, retrenches from its flowing, and brings it nearer to the unaffected simplicity of truth and common life. This latitude, as to the parade or conciseness of gesture, gives occasion for distinguishing its grace rather by its suitableness to the style of speaking, which it is to accompany, and to adorn or enforce, than by the precise inflexion to which the lines in drawing may properly be confined. Those different modes of public speaking, to each of which a different style of gesture may be suitable, however numerous, may be reduced to three principal, admitting different subdivisions according to the accuracy of discrimination. 1. The epic. 2. The rhetorical. 3. The colloquial.[a]

1. The epic or tragic style of delivery requires every natural and acquired power on the part of the speaker: and in its perfect execution is implied every excellence of the highest class. Among the vast numbers who have devoted themselves to the cultivation of eloquence at large, or even of those who limit their attention to delivery alone, as on the theatre, nature has gifted only a chosen few with the rare endowments which are necessary for a consummate tragedian. And of those few, who, in the grand requisites have been distinguished, hardly do we hear of any, who in all respects have been absolutely perfect. The eye and ear of criticism are too acute to let pass small imperfections of the most highly accomplished in the wonderfully difficult art of delivery, or of the most highly

---

[a] The ancient division of the kinds of gesture related solely to theatrical performances. Cordax was the gesture for comedy, Emmelia for tragedy, Sicinnis for satire, and Italique for pantomime. See *Athenæus, l.* 1. already quoted.

gifted in natural advantages. Since nature is too œconomical to lavish her treasures all on one, we are the more disposed to hold in admiration those who approach nearest to perfection. Where dignity and beauty of person, expression of countenance, and powers of voice are given; talents and taste perhaps are wanting; and where all these are united; perhaps industry and learning are denied, and indolence or love of pleasure defeats the noblest endowments.

In order to the better understanding of the characteristic difference in each style of gesture, it will be of advantage to enumerate the different qualities which constitute the perfection of gesture, together with their opposite imperfections. These may be considered as reducible to the following : 1. Magnificence. 2. Boldness. 3. Energy. 4. Variety. 5. Simplicity. 6. Grace. 7. Propriety. 8. Precision.

1. Magnificence of gesture.—This consists in the ample space through which the arm and hand are made to move : and it is effected by detaching the upper arm completely from the body, and unfolding the whole oratorical weapon. The centre of its motion is the shoulder. In magnificent gesture the action is flowing and unconstrained, the preparations are made in some graceful curve, the transitions are easy and the accompaniments are correct, and in all respects illustrative of the principal action. The motions of the head are free, and the inflexions of the body manly and dignified. The action of the lower limbs is decided, and a considerable space is traversed with firmness and with force.

The opposite imperfections are short, and dry, and mean gestures, constrained motions, rigidity of the joints, and stiffness of the body with short steps and doubtful or timid movements.

2. Boldness of gesture.—This consists in that elevated courage and self confidence which ventures to hazard any action productive of a grand or striking effect however unusual. In this sort of gesture, unexpected positions, elevations and transitions surprise at once by their novelty and grace, and thus illustrate or enforce their ideas with irresistible effect.

The opposite imperfection is *tameness* ; which hazards nothing, is timid and doubtful of its own powers, and produces no great effect.

3. Energy of gesture.—This consists in the firmness and decision of the whole action: and in the support which the voice receives from the precision of the stroke of the gesture which aids its emphasis.

The opposite imperfections are feebleness and indecision.

4. Variety of gesture.—This consists in the ability of readily adapting suitable and different gestures to each sentiment and situation; so as to avoid recurring too frequently to one favourite gesture or set of gestures.[3,4,5]

---

[3] Variety of gesture is so essential, that even the most appropriate gestures must be

The opposite imperfections are sameness, barrenness, and monotony of gesture analogous to that of the voice.

5. Simplicity of gesture.—This consists in such a character of gesture as appears the natural result of the situation and sentiments; which is neither carried beyond the just extent of the feeling through affectation of variety, nor falls short of it through meanness or false shame.

The opposite imperfection is affectation.[6]

6. Grace of gesture.—This is the result of all other perfections, arising from a dignified self-possession of mind; and the power of personal exertion practised into facility after the best models, and according to the truest taste. To the more particular investigation of this quality a Chapter is devoted.

---

avoided if they recur too often. Nothing is so injurious or disgusts so soon as barrenness of manner: the gesture had better be intermitted, or even be in some measure wrong, than monotonous.

Et quoniam generatim quædam hic mouenda mihi videbantur hoc addo, similitudinem gestus esse omni mente et provisione vitandam. Nam quemadmodum in voce μονοτονία, sic motus in omnibus fere similis et manuum per eandem veluti lineam circumductiones fugiendæ sunt oratori: meliusque esset efferri aliquando audaciusque moveri, quam eandem veluti cramben obtrudere. Nihil peccat, nisi quod nihil peccat aiebat olim Plinius; quod sic explicavit; Debet enim orator erigi, attolli, interdum etiam effervescere, efferri et sæpe accedere ad præceps, quæ omnia æque in actionem et stylum conveniunt. *Cresoll. Vac. Aut.*

4 Variare orationem magnopere oportebit nam omnibus in rebus similitudo satietatis est mater. *Cic. de Invent. l.* i. 76.

5 Un jeu uniforme et continuel des bras tel qu'on le remarque dans un écolier qui recite ou declame ses exercices de classe, est aussi fatiguant et aussi insipide pour l'œil qu'une monotonie éternelle de ton peut l'être pour une oreille délicate. *Engel, Idées sur le Geste.*

6 Longissime fugienda mollis actio, qualem in Tityo Cicero dicit fuisse, unde etiam saltationis quoddam genus *Tityus* sit appellatum. *Quint.*

The opposite imperfections are awkwardness, vulgarity, and rusticity.

7. Propriety of gesture, called also truth of gesture, or natural gesture.[7,8] This consists in the judicious use of the

---

[7] The gesture of Massillon was remarkable for propriety, though in other respects not a model for imitation.

A l'égard de l'action, cette partie si essentielle à l'orateur, ce ne fut pas d'abord par cette endroit qu'il se fit admirer. Le gout du tems n'étoit pas le sien. Il ne pouvoit souffrir qu'au lieu de cette air naturel qui porte avec soi la conviction, l'on prit un certain air emprunté et un ton de déclamateur, qui faisant regarder les ministeres de Jesus Christ comme des gens qui ne montent en chaire que pour jouer un personnage, ôte presque toute la force et tout croyance à leurs discours. . . . . Au reste, il seroit fort difficile de faire comprendre à ceux qui ne l'ont point entendu, ce que c'étoit que son action. Elle lui étoit tellement propre, qu'on peut assurer que comme il n'eut point de modele à suivre, il n'a point formé d'éleve qui l'ait imité.

On le voyoit arriver dans la chaire comme un homme, qui vient de mediter profondement un sujet. Dès qu'il paroît, son air recueilli et pénétré annonce déjà la grandeur et l'importance des verités dont il va vous entretenir. Il n'a pas ouverte sa bouche et l'auditoire est saisi. Il parle enfin, mais ce n'est pas comme un orateur qui vient débiter avec art un discours dont il a chargé sa mémoire. Tout coule de source. Il parle de l'abondance du cœur, ne pouvant contenir au dedans de lui les verités dont il est plein. Une feu intérieur le devore ; il faut qu'il lui ouvre une issue, et qu'il le laisse éclater au dehors. Aussi rien en lui qui ne soit animé ; tout parle, tout persuade, tout remue, tout attendrit, tout porte dans l'ame la conviction et le sentiment ; et cela n'étoit point du tout un effet de l'art dans le pere Massillon ; c'étoit un talent naturel qu'il lui faisoit exprimer et dire les choses avec force et vivacité parcequ'il les sentoit de même.

Il faisoit donc proprement consister tout le merite de l'action à paroitre bien pénétré lui même des vérités dont il vouloit convaincre ses auditeurs. Jamais personne n'a porté ce talent plus loin que le P. Massillon ; c'est le témoignage que le public en a rendu, et l'éloge qu'en ont fait toutes les personnes de gout. Seroit-il permis de rapporter à ce sujet un trait remarquable par la singularité, et qui nous échappe ? L'acteur le plus parfait qu'ait eu le théâtre François voulut l'entendre ; il fut frappé du vrai qu'il trouva dans sa manière de prononcer, et dit à un autre acteur, qui l'avoit accompagné. Mon ami, voilà un orateur : et nous ne sommes que des comédiens. *Preface des Sermons de Massillon.*

[8] The sophist Polemon who presided at the Olympic games celebrated at Smyrna, disqualified one of the public speakers for having been guilty of a solecism in gesture ; this consisted in his looking and pointing downwards when he addressed Jupiter, and looking upwards when he addressed the earth. ἀγωνίζε δὲ τραγῳδίαις, ἐν τοῖς κατὰ τὴν Σμύρναν Ὀλυμπίοις, τὸ ὦ Ζεῦ εἰς τὴν γῆν δείξαντος· τὸ δὲ, ὦ γᾶ εἰς τὸν ἐρανὸν ἀνασχόντος,

gestures best suited to illustrate or to express the sentiment. Appropriate gestures are generally founded in some natural connection of the sentiment with the gesture; significant gestures are strictly connected with the sentiments.

The opposite imperfections are false, contradictory, or unsuitable gestures: such as produce solecism in gesture.

8. Precision of gesture or correctness.—Arises from the just preparation, the due force, and the correct timing of the action: when the preparation is neither too much abridged and dry, nor too pompously displayed; when the stroke of the gesture is made with such a degree of force as suits the character of the sentiment and speaker; and when it is correctly marked on the precise syllable to be enforced   Precision of gesture gives the same effect to action, as neatness of articulation gives to speech.

The opposite imperfections are the indecision uncertainty, and incorrectness, arising from vague and sawing gestures, which far from illustrating, render dubious the sense of the sentiments, which they accompany, and distract the spectator.

Epic gesture requires to be attended with all these qualities

---

προκαθήμενος τῶν Ολυμπίων ὁ Πολέμων ἐξέωσεν αὐτὸν τῶν ἄθλων, εἰπὼν, ἔτος τῇ χειρὶ ἐσολόικισε.   *Philostratus in Polemon.*

Vossius repeats this story, with observations.

Variat tum vultus tum gestus pro rei natura, ut diximus, conformanda est ipsa actio, ne rideamur cum rhetore illo, quem Philostratus scripsit, cum dixisset ὦ Ζεῦ! in terram conjecisse vultum; cum addidisset ὦ γῆ! oculos in cœlum sustulisse, cum rerum natura contrarium dictet.   *J. Ger. Vossius. Inst. Orat.*

in perfection: to it belong magnificence, boldness, energy, variety, simplicity, grace, propriety, and precision. The compositions requiring epic gesture in the delivery are tragedy, epic poetry, lyric odes, and sublime description.

Rhetorical gesture requires principally energy, variety, simplicity and precision. Grace is desirable. Magnificence is rarely wanting, but may sometimes have place. Appropriate or significant gestures are seldom to be used, yet propriety in a limited sense should be observed. Boldness of gesture is inadmissible.[9]

Colloquial gesture, when concerned in the higher scenes of polite life requires principally simplicity and grace. Precision will follow of course. It may occasionally demand something of energy and variety. Propriety is not necessary except in the most limited sense, nor in any respect either magnificence or boldness. Common and vulgar manners neither attain nor even aim at any of these perfections of gesture.

Colloquial gesture, which is at the opposite extreme from epic, differs from it essentially in the manner of action of the arm. Instead of unfolding the whole oratorical weapon, as in tragedy, in description, and sometimes in the more vehement passages

---

9 The orator not being, as the player is, subjected to any unexpected circumstances, is not at liberty to express his surprise or any other similar passion by bold gestures.

Among the different classes of gestures enumerated in Chapter XVII. those which suit best the usual objects of the orator are the commencing, the discriminating, the suspended, and the emphatical; and the qualities suited to those gestures are principally, as here stated, energy, variety, simplicity, precision and grace.

in oratory, the upper arm in colloquial gesture is barely detached from the side; and the elbow, instead of the shoulder, becomes the principal centre of motion; hence the action must be shorter and less flowing in every respect. This kind of gesture is generally used by persons who deliver either orations or lectures in a sitting posture; the arm is seldom extended altogether, and the action is made short and sharp by the hand, the fingers and wrist, with the assistance of the fore arm almost alone. Fig. 34, 35, 36. Neither is the action frequent; it takes place only on the most important passages, and during the others remains at rest; resigning to the head to mark ordinary emphasis by a moderate nod or inclination, and depending principally on the countenance, the direction of the eyes, and the modulation of the voice for the general effect.[10][11]

Perhaps much of the characteristic difference in the styles of gesture will be found in the manner of sustaining the action, something analogous to the flight of birds, if it may be permitted

---

[10] The Figures 34, 35, and 36, with the arm in the downward, horizontal, and elevated positions, shew the limited range of colloquial gesture compared with the bolder gestures which are exemplified in most of the other figures; and particularly in the two following, which shew the horizontal position. Fig. 37, 38. The reason of using chiefly those gestures for illustrating this work is on account of their greater precision and distinctness, and also on account of their greater difficulty of execution : if a speaker is able to execute gracefully the grand gestures, he will find no difficulty in performing the colloquial. It is easy to retrench in this respect; one of the greatest difficulties to the young speaker is the acquisition of such freedom, as to detach his elbows completely from his sides.

[11] The colloquial gestures are very nearly described by Cresollius, he directs them to be used in the tranquil parts of an oration.

Cum ergo erit orationis lenitas, remotis illis tragediis, et asperiori contentione, illa decebit brachii compositio, quæ normalem veluti angulum, in cubito facit demisso, elevata modice manu, et decori modestia conformata. *Cresol. Vac. Aut.*

to draw from thence an illustration. The transition from gesture to gesture with the arms long displayed and seldom falling to rest, is analogous to the soaring and graceful flight of certain greater birds, whose extended wings do not close for a considerable time, though they vary their movements, and change their rapidity. The flight of the hawk, and the soaring of the eagle, whose motions are both powerful and swift, and magnificiently sustained, and boldly terminated, present the image of high tragic and epic gesture; which takes place, when the actor is engaged in grand and terrific scenes, or when he recites the sublime poetry of lyric odes. The sailing and fine variety of motion, with the changing lustre of the great seafowl, is the gesture of recitation in magnificent and beautiful descriptions of nature. The orator seems to fly on the wings of the dove, " rapid, strong, and light." For a time he ascends in towering elevation, but does not long hover among the clouds, he rather descends to adorn the more interesting domestic scene. The colloquial gesture in all its variety will find illustration among the different domestic birds. Some using their wings gracefully, but rarely, some seldom using them at all, and some distinguished by frequent resting after short, and rapid flight, which seems to be resorted to only as the most direct and speedy way by which they can reach their object, and is seemingly divested of all idea of pleasure or grace in the action.

From the observations made upon the different classes of gesture (Chap. XVII.), and their qualities in this chapter, we shall be able without much difficulty to determine a question which has long been agitated. That is, whether an orator can with advantage take for his models the gestures of the theatre.[12] The action of the theatre supplies the most perfect models, because in its highest performance, tragedy, all the

---

[12] Mr. Engel's opinions on this subject are extremely interesting, and particularly worthy the attention of the clerical reader.

Je terminerai cette suite de remarques isolées, en y en ajoutant encore une qu'à la verité vos observations n'ont pas fait naître, mais qui, comme je m'en flatte, ne vous déplaira pas. On a demandé si l'orateur sacré pouvoit se former d'après l'acteur, et s'il lui étoit permis d'en imiter le ton et le geste ? il n'y a pas longtems même qu'on a beaucoup débattu cette question. J'y répondrai qu'il le peut et qu'il ne le peut pas, tout comme on le voudra. Il ne le peut pas, en tant que les pensées et le caractère de la plupart de rôles ne peuvent être aucunement d'accord avec les pensées et le caractere de l'orateur sacré; et secondement, parce que le drame et le sermon diffèrent trop entr'eux pour que l'action qui convient à l'un puisse être propre à l'autre. Les personnages du drame debitent des pensées qui doivent leur existence à la situation du moment ; le prédicateur en communique au peuple qu'il a eu tout le loisir de classer dans sa tête : les acteurs sont dans un état d'inquiétude extérieure très-réelle, incertains, et irrésolus ; ils sont agités par des idées et par des sentimens variés : la tranquillité extérieure du prédicateur n'est troublée d'aucune manière ; occupé d'un seul objet, il n'a aussi qu'un seul sentiment principal et permanent, qu'il peut développer à loisir. Dans le monologue d'Hamlet sur le suicide, il s'agit d'un objet de la plus grande importance ; l'ame est montée à un ton sérieux ; ce ton, l'attitude, et le geste ont de la dignité : l'orateur sacré ne pourroit-il pas en faire usage ? Non certainement, parceque Hamlet, enseveli dans ses réflexions, ne fait que commencer à examiner sérieusement la question ; en passant d'une idée à l'autre, il se perd dans des doutes, qui se multiplient dans son esprit, et cette situation ne peut jamais convenir à un orateur chargé de l'instruction publique. —Mais je reponds aussi affirmativement à la question proposée ; savoir, en tant que dans le drame il peut se trouver des passages dont les sujets medités auparavant par les personnages sont exposés de suite et sans trouble, et qui par conséquent équivalent à des discours suivis ; et en second lieu, en tant que ces passages peuvent être pleins de dignité, que les caracteres des personnages peuvent avoir un caractere sérieux, noble, et élevé. Les conseils paternels que le *Pere de Famille* de Diderot donne au second acte à sa fille et à son fils, sont de ces discours suivis et médités auparavant; il y regne à la verité beaucoup de sensibilité ; mais qui osera bannir le ton du sentiment de la chaire, et transformer l'orateur sacré en un moraliste froid et insensible ? il suffit que le sentiment dominant des discours en question soit du genre le plus noble, et qu'un père prudent et tendre, qui exprime ce sentiment envers ses enfans chéris, soit à mes yeux le caractere le plus venerable qui existe. Qu'est-ce qui empechera l'orateur sacré de faire du théâtre son école, et d'un excellent acteur l'objet de ses études ? Plut au ciel que beaucoup d'entr'eux eussent vu un Aufresne ou un Ekhoff, et qu'ils se fussent trouvés en état de sentir et d'imiter le jeu vrai, naturel, plein de dignité et de grace de pareils acteurs ! Exiger de l'orateur sacré qu'il accompagne ce ton du sentiment d'un simple jeu de mains insignifiant, et employé au hazard, ce seroit vouloir que ses gestes

qualities of perfect gesture are required. But for rhetorical delivery, we have seen that some of those qualities are unnecessary, and some are improper. If the speaker have judgment sufficient to retrench what is superfluous, o.· improper for his use, the action of the theatre may, no doubt, afford him very useful instruction, and become under proper restrictions the best model. He will learn from the theatre energy, variety, and precision of action. The simplicity of action he must derive from his own unaffected sincerity, and grace from habit and taste. And as to the other qualities, he must know how to use them discreetly, or to retrench them altogether. But he must carefully guard against attempting to introduce the full license of theatrical action into rhetorical delivery of any kind. If he be a mere imitator, and cannot discriminate, his gesture will be the subject of just reprehension.

But the gesture of the public speaker must also vary considerably with the different circumstances of his situation, of his sentiments, and of his audience.[13] If the mere information or instruction of his audience be his sole objects, as when the evidences of religion, and the grounds of Christian duties are

---

taxassent ses paroles de mensonge. Il faut certainement que son jeu soit toujours expressif, pourvu qu'il soit en même tems posé, modéré, et convenable à son état, ainsi qu'au sujet qu'il traite ; et tel fut aussi dans la situation citée et dans nombre d'autres de ce genre, le jeu sublime d'Aufresne et d'Ekhoff. *Engel, Idées sur le Geste, Lett.* 38.

[13] Primum, quid, apud quos, quibus præsentibus sit acturus. Nam ut dicere alia aliis, et apud alios magis convenit : sic etiam facere. Neque eadem in voce, gestu, incessu; apud principem, senatum, populum, magistratum, privato, publico judicio, postulatione, actione similiter decent. Quam differentiam subjicere sibi quisque, qui animum intenderit, potest, tum qua de re dicat et efficere quid velit. . . . . In senatu conservanda auctoritas, apud populum dignitas, in privatis modus. *Qint.*

to be explained from the pulpit; or when the details of calculation and finance are to be laid before parliament; or when facts are weighed, and laws are argued in the courts of justice. He will limit himself to a very small degree of gesture, and that of the class which is named discriminating gestures; these he will exercise with simplicity and precision. He will strip them of all the parade of preparation, and of the graces of transition, and give them only that degree of variety which shall guard them against disgusting sameness. This is far removed from theatrical gesture, and seems rather to approach the colloquial style. And it is worthy of observation, that by far the greatest number of public speakers in the different situations mentioned, confine themselves totally to this humble but most useful and most necessary species of oratory; and nothing can be imagined more incongruous than an attempt (were any one to be found capable of such absurdity) to introduce into their discourses the parade and magnificence of theatrical gesture. The charge which is sometimes made against public speakers, of being theatrical in their gesture, probably arises more from some unsuitableness in the matter to their manner, than from any thing of uncommon majesty, boldness, or grace in their action.

If the public speaker aim at persuasion, as in discourses from the pulpit for public charities, on extraordinary occasions in Parliament, or at the bar, when the advocate desires to influence the opinions of a jury; he will naturally use more graceful, more flowing, and more various gesture. But although between such gesture and that of tragedy, the boundaries are not strictly defined, and although the blending shades intermix, he will not run far beyond the limits, nor fall into the action of the theatre. He may be graceful, but he will be simple; he may be energetic, but he will not affect gestures too strongly significant, much less attempt surprise by attitudes. All his gestures will be regulated by manly decorum suitable to his own true situation, which the orator does not change as the actor must; they will be suitable to the just expression of his sentiments, and to the character of his hearers; of all which he is never to lose sight; nor allow himself to be betrayed into any violent extremes, unbecoming his own place and his objects, or failing in proper respect to those, whom he is called upon only to instruct or to persuade.

CHAPTER XXI.

OF THE SIGNIFICANCY OF GESTURE.

Merely articulate language without gesture or modulation of tones would be very imperfect—The universality of the natural signs—Opinion of Lord Kaims as to their necessity—Natural and instituted gestures according to the Abbé Du Bos—Mr. Engel's division of gestures into classes—The significancy of gesture has principally employed the attention of the ancient writers upon gesture—And also of the moderns, as Buffon, Du Bos, Sheridan, Walker—Examples of significant gestures —Division of them into four classes—Examples of complex significant gestures from Engel—Examples from a great actress—Gestures of this kind the proper objects of the painter's imitation, but not of the orator's—The less shewy gestures suit him best—Collections of gestures as proposed by Sulzer would be of little use to the orator—Some advantages of the present system.

CHAPTER XXI.

Of the Significancy of Gesture.

LANGUAGE, which is so much the boast of rational beings, and has been assumed by the father of poetry as the distinguishing characteristic of men,' derives all its significancy from compact only. And if men were limited in the expression of their wants and desires to the power of language alone, their com munication would also be extremely limited; and a man could not, without danger of every inconvenience, venture beyond the confines of his own tribe, or the narrow local prevalence of his own dialect. And whilst the animals of the same species, of the north and south, and of the east and west, if brought together would readily associate; men, under the same circum- stances, if they had no other means of communicating their thoughts except language, would long remain strangers to the sentiments of each other, even in a greater degree, than they are now to what passes in the minds of some brutes. But all bountiful nature is not such a niggard of her gifts to man, nor leaves in her wisdom her principal work subject to such a defect. She has not abandoned man to the mere resources of his own devices on his most important concerns, but has furnished him with such external signs as indicate universally to his own

---

' Τῷ δ' ἠδὲ δύο μέη γεναὶ μεϱόπων ἀνθϱώπων 'Εφθίαθ'. *Ilias. a.* 250.

species his most pressing wants, and his most interesting feelings.[2] And so expressive are these external signs, that all nature may be figuratively said to understand them, and they are actually capable, by a little instruction, to be made the means of communication between him and many of the most valuable animals which he domesticates for his service.[3,4] These external

---

[2] The external expressions of passion form a language understood by all, by the young as well as the old, by the ignorant as well as the learned. *Elements of Criticism.*

[3] Mutorumque silens positura imitabitur actus. *Dufresnoy.*

> Learn action from the dumb, the dumb shall teach
> How happiest to supply the want of speech.   *Mason's Translation.*

In the note on this passage Sir Joshua Reynolds says,

" Gesture is a language we are born with, and is the most natural way of expressing our-
" selves: painting may be said therefore in this respect to have the superiority over
" poetry.

" Fresnoy, however, certainly means here persons either born dumb or who are become
" so from accident or violence, and the translator has therefore rendered his meaning
" justly: but persons who are born dumb are commonly deaf also, and their gestures are
" usually extravagant and forced, &c."

Sir Joshua was too nice an observer to admit that graceful action could be learned from the dumb; but does not seem to have enquired into the precise reason, nor to have stated exactly what kind of gestures are proper for the imitation of the painter. The gestures of the dumb being almost entirely artificial, and used for the purpose of communicating their ideas in the speediest manner possible, can have little grace to serve as a model for the painter.

The natural gestures, which express the feelings or affections of the mind, are on the contrary often highly graceful; particularly when they are too powerful to submit to any restraint. Then the expressions even of the uncultivated are graceful, and worthy to be observed as a model by the painter or the tragedian. The swelling torrent which breaks all bounds, and sweeps every thing before it, is always a grand object.

[4]
> The man to solitude accustom'd long
> Perceives, in ev'ry thing that lives, a tongue;
> Not animals alone, but shrubs and trees,
> Have speech for him, and understood with ease;
> After long drought, when rains abundant fall,
> He hears the herbs and flow'rs rejoicing all;
> Knows what the freshness of their hue implies,
> How glad they catch the largeness of the skies;

signs are tones, looks, and gestures. The tones of the voice are never misunderstood even by those to whom the language is unknown, and the very animals themselves quickly learn to comprehend the soft accents of man's caressing, and the rude sounds of his anger. The countenance also is a sure indication of the various feelings of the mind, so far as its movements are not forcibly suppressed. Smiles and frowns, anxiety and tranquillity, pain and pleasure, are manifest in the expression of the countenance; and some emotions, as shame or fear, are not to be dissembled, but are known by the betraying blush, or by the paleness, which cannot either of them command the action of the blood. Gestures too, as well as some involuntary agitations, discover the thoughts distinctly. Terror and indignation swell the breast, and oblige the lungs to breath short, and the heart to palpitate; gestures express also in universal language, threatening or invitation, pity or contempt, shame and triumph, submission or command, and many other sentiments, passions and desires.

The ingenious author of elements of criticism has treated this subject so ably, that a few extracts from his chapter on the external signs of emotions and passions will not be unaccept-

---

But with precision nicer still, the mind
He scans of ev'ry loco-motive kind;
Birds of all feather, beasts of ev'ry name,
That serve mankind, or shun them, wild or tame,
The looks and gestures of their griefs and fears
Have, all, articulation in his ears;
He spells them true by intuition's light,
And needs no glossary to set him right. *Cowper. The Needless Alarm.*

able, and may perhaps induce the reader to consult the work
at large.

" The external signs of passion are of two kinds, voluntary
" and involuntary. The voluntary signs are also of two kinds;
" some are arbitrary, and some natural. Words are arbitrary
" signs, excepting a few simple sounds expressive of certain
" internal emotions; and these sounds, being the same in all
" languages, must be the work of nature. But though words
" are arbitrary, the manner of employing them is not altogether
" so; for each passion has by nature peculiar expressions and
" tones suited to it. Thus the unpremeditated tones of admira-
" tion are the same in all men; as also of compassion, resent-
" ment, and despair. . . . . , .

" The other kind of voluntary signs, comprehends certain
" attitudes and gestures that naturally accompany certain
" emotions with a surprising uniformity. Thus excessive joy
" is expressed by leaping, dancing, or some elevation of the
" body, and excessive grief by sinking or depressing it. Thus
" prostration and kneeling have been employed by all nations
" and in all ages to signify profound veneration. Another
" circumstance, still more than uniformity, demonstrates these
" gestures to be natural, viz. their remarkable conformity or
" resemblance to the passions that produce them. Joy, which
" produceth a cheerful elevation of mind, is expressed by an
" elevation of body. Pride, magnanimity, courage, and the
" whole tribe of elevating passions, are expressed by external
" gestures that are the same as to the circumstance of elevation,

" however distinguishable in other respects. Hence it comes,
" than an erect posture is a sign or expression of dignity :

> " Two of far nobler shape, erect and tall,
> " Godlike erect, with native honour clad,
> " In naked majesty, seem'd lords of all.   *Paradise Lost, b. 4.*

" Grief, on the other hand, as well as respect which depress the
" mind, cannot for that reason be expressed more significantly
" than by a similar depression of the body. Hence *to be cast*
" *down*, is a common phrase, signifying to be grieved or dis-
" pirited.

" One would not imagine, who has not given peculiar atten-
" tion, that the body is susceptible of such a variety of attitude
" and motion, as readily to accompany every different emotion
" with a correspondent gesture. Humility, for example, is
" expressed naturally by hanging the head ; arrogance by its
" elevation ; and languor or despondence by reclining it to one
" side. The expressions of the hands are manifold. By different
" attitudes and motions, the hands express desire, hope, fear :
" they assist us in promising, in inviting, in keeping one at a
" distance ; they are made instruments of threatening, of sup-
" plication, of praise, and of horror : they are employed in
" approving, in refusing, in questioning ; in shewing our joy,
" our sorrow, our doubts, our regret, our admiration. These
" gestures, so obedient to passion, are extremely difficult to be
" imitated in a calm state. The ancients, sensible of the advan-
" tage as well as the difficulty of having these expressions at
" command, bestowed much time and care, in collecting them
" from observation, and in digesting them into a practical art,

" which was taught in their schools as an important branch of
" education.

. . . .

" The natural signs of emotions, voluntary and involuntary,
" being nearly the same in all men, form an universal language
" which no distance of place, no difference of tribe, no diver-
" sity of tongue, can darken or render doubtful. Education,
" though of mighty influence, hath not power to vary or
" sophisticate, far less to destroy, their signification. This is a
" wise appointment of Providence. For if these signs were, like
" words, arbitrary and variable, it would be an intricate science
" to decipher the actions and motives of our own species, which
" would prove a great or rather invincible obstruction to the
" formation of societies. But as matters are ordered, the exter-
" nal appearances of joy, grief, anger, fear, shame, and of the
" other passions forming an universal language, open a
" direct avenue to the heart. As the arbitrary signs vary in
" every country, there could be no communication of thoughts
" among different nations, were it not for the natural signs in
" which all agree. Words are sufficient for the communication
" of science, and of all mental conceptions : but the discovering
" passions instantly as they arise, being essential to our well
" being, and often necessary for self-preservation, the author of
" our nature, attentive to our wants, hath provided a passage
" to the heart, which never can be obstructed while our
" external senses remain entire."

. . . . . . " An infant is remarkably affected with the pas-
" sions of its nurse expressed on her countenance ; a smile

" cheers it, and a frown makes it afraid. Fear thus generated
" in an infant, must, like every other passion, have an object.
" What is the object of this passion? surely not the frown
" considered abstractedly, for a child never abstracts. The
" nurse who frowns is evidently the object. Fear at the same
" time, cannot arise but from apprehending danger. But what
" danger can a child apprehend, if it be not sensible that the
" person who frowns is angry? we must therefore admit, that
" a child can read anger in its nurse's face; and it must be
" sensible of this intuitively; for it has no other means of
" knowledge."

. . . . . . " Language no doubt is the most comprehensive
" vehicle for communicating emotions; but in expedition, as
" well as in the power of conviction, it falls short of the signs
" under consideration; the involuntary signs especially, which
" are incapable of deceit. Where the countenance, the tones,
" the gestures, the actions, join with the words, in communicat-
" ing emotions, these united have a force irresistible. Thus
" all the agreeable emotions of the human heart, with all the
" social and virtuous affections, are by means of these external
" signs, not only perceived but felt. By this admirable contri-
" vance, social intercourse becomes that lively and animating
" amusement, without which life would be at best insipid.
" One joyful countenance spreads chearfulness instantaneously
" through a multitude of spectators."

It is impossible to forbear annexing to this long extract the
important conclusion of this most instructive writer, and profound investigator of human nature.

3 P

" Loath to quit so interesting a subject, I add a reflexion,
" with which I shall conclude. The external signs of passion
" are a strong indication, that man, by his very constitution,
" is framed to be open and sincere. A child in all things
" obedient to the impulses of nature, hides none of its emotions :
" the savage and clown, who have no guide other than pure
" nature, expose their hearts to view by giving way to all the
" natural signs : and even when men learn to dissemble their
" sentiments, and when behaviour degenerates into art, there
" still remain checks, which keep dissimulation within bounds,
" and prevent a great part of its mischievous effects. The total
" suppression of the voluntary signs during any vivid passion,
" begets the utmost uneasiness, which cannot be endured for
" any considerable time. This operation becomes indeed less
" painful by habit : but luckily the involuntary signs, cannot
" by any effort be suppressed, or even dissembled. An absolute
" hypocrisy, by which the character is concealed and a ficti-
" tious one assumed, is made impracticable ; and nature has
" thereby prevented much harm to society. We may pro-
" nounce therefore, that nature, herself sincere and candid,
" intends that mankind should preserve the same character, by
" cultivating simplicity and truth, and banishing every sort of
" dissimulation that tends to mischief."

Having established on the authority of the acute and learned
author of Elements of Criticism, the existence of natural signs
and their necessity ; I shall proceed to enquire into their
value, and the manner of discriminating and appreciating the
different kinds of external signs on the authority of other authors,
who appear to me to have treated the subject with the greatest

precision. The Abbé du Bos' division of gesture into *natural and instituted*, seems clear and comprehensive, and his observations on certain passages of Quintilian appear so just, that I shall freely transcribe from his work.

" Let us return to Quintilian. This author observes in " another place, that an orator should not deliver himself like " a player; nor use the gestures of a dancer. The following are " probably his reasons.

" The gestures, which the art called *saltatio* taught, were not " always confined to graceful motions; and if it may be allowed " to say so, to gestures which conveyed no particular meaning; " but they often taught gestures which were to represent dis- " tinctly some particular circumstance, gestures which they " designed as it were to speak. These significant gestures were " of two kinds: the one natural, the other artificial.

. . . . . . " Natural gestures have rarely any distinct signi- " fication when used without words. . . . . they may, however, " when they indicate an affection of the body or mind, as head- " ache or impatience. But the natural gesture at that me " cannot sufficiently express the particular circumstances of " such affection,

. . . . . " If a man would express distinctly by his gestures, " and without speaking, any thing more than a mere affection, he " is obliged to have recourse to those signs and artificial gestures " which do not derive their signification from nature, but from " the compacts of society. And a proof, that they are artificial " signs, is, that they are understood only in a particular country.

" The signs and the gestures which a man uses who either
" does not choose or who cannot speak, are not precisely the
" same as those which he uses when he speaks. If a man
" desired to express by signs, without uttering a word this
" sentence, *my father is just now dead*, he would be obliged to
" substitute for the expression of those words studied signs
" different from those, which he would use, were he to speak
" them. These signs may be called artificial gestures, or to adopt
" the language of logic, gestures *of institution.* Logic, it will be
" recollected, divides all signs into two kinds, natural signs, and
" signs of institution. Smoke, for example, it calls the natural
" sign of fire; but a crown is only a sign of institution, an
" emblem of royalty. In the same manner a man who beats
" his breast, uses a natural gesture indicating a strong affection
" of the mind: but he, who by his gestures describes the fore-
" head encircled by a diadem, makes use of a gesture of insti-
" tution, signifying a crowned head.

" An orator in speaking has no occasion to use these artificial
" gestures in order to make himself understood. And besides
" many of these gestures could not fail to be incompatible with
" the decorum which he ought to preserve in his delivery. And
" this, in my opinion is the reason, why Quintilian so often for-
" bids the orator to imitate the gesticulation of the dancers, or
" pantomimes.

" What Quintilian says in another passage seems to establish
" my conjecture as certain. All the gestures which I have
" mentioned, says Quintilian, should finish with the words.
" But there is another kind of gestures which derive their
" signification from their description of the thing which is

" expressed by their means. Such is the gesture which represents
" the action of a physician feeling the pulse, and which is used
" to signify a sick person. Nothing can be more v icious in an
" orator, continues Quintilian, than to employ in his declama-
" tion gestures of such a kind. The action of an orator ought
" to be altogether different from that of a pantomime. An orator
" ought to suit his gesture to the general sentiment which he
" expresses, and not to the particular signification of the word,
" which he pronounces."[5].[6]

---

[5] *Réflexions Critique sur la Poesie et sur la Peinture, Tom. III. p. 217. Quarto.* PARIS 1755.

Revenons à Quintilien. Cet auteur dit encore, dans un autre endroit, qu'il ne faut pas qu'un orateur prononce comme un comédien, ni qu'il fasse ses gestes comme un danseur. *Non comœdum in pronuntiatione, non saltatorem in gestu facio.* Voici, suivant les apparences, une des ses raisons.

Les gestes que l'art, appellé *saltatio*, enseignoit, n'étoient point toujours des gestes servans uniquement à donner bonne grace ; et s'il est permis de s'expliquer ainsi, des gestes, vuides de sens, mais souvent des gestes qui devoient signifier quelque chose intelligiblement, des gestes qui devoient parler. Or les gestes significatifs sont de deux espèces. Les uns sont des gestes naturels, et les autres sont des gestes artificiels.

. . . . . Mais il est rare que le geste naturel signifie quelque chose distinctement, quand on le fait sans parler. . . . . cela arrive lorsque le geste naturel signifie une affection, comme un mal de tête ou de l'impatience. Mais le geste naturel ne suffit pas même alors pour donner à connoitre les circonstances de cette affection. . . . . . *p.* 218.

. . . . L'homme qui veut exprimer distinctement, sans parler, une autre chose qu'une affection, est obligé d'avoir recours à ces démonstrations, et à ces gestes artificiels, qui ne tirent pas leur signification de la nature, mais bien de l'institution des hommes. La preuve qu'ils ne sont que des signes artificiels, c'est que comme les mots, ils ne sont entendues que dans un certain pays. P. 219.

Les démonstrations et les gestes, dont se sert un homme qui ne veut pas, ou qui ne peut point parler, ne sont donc pas les mêmes précisément dont on se sert en parlant. Celui qui veut dire par signes, et sans proférer aucune parole, Mon pere vient de mourir, est obligé de suppléer par des signes étudiés et différens de ceux qu'il employeroit en prononçant, aux paroles qu'il ne dit pas. Ces signes peuvent s'appeller des gestes artificiels, et en suivant l'ésprit de la Logique, *des gestes d'institution.* On sçait que la Logique divise tous les signes en deux genres, qui sont les signes naturels et les signes d'institution. La fumée, dit-elle, est le signe naturel du feu ; mais la couronne n'est qu'un signe d'institution, un embleme de la royauté. Ainsi l'homme, qui se bat la poitrine, fait un geste naturel qui marque un saisissement. Celui qui décrit en gesticulant, un front ceint du diadême, ne fait qu'un geste d'institution qui signifie une tête couronnée. P. 220.

. . . . L'orateur qui parloit, n'avoit pas besoin d'employer ces gestes artificiels pour se

Among the modern writers upon the art of gesture whose works are accessible to me, none have treated the subject more methodically nor so much at large as Mr. I. I. Engel.[7] The work is expressly designed for the theatre, but many of the observations of course apply equally to public speakers in general; several of which will be found interspersed among the notes in this treatise Mr. Engel'sdivision of gesture into the various kinds arising from the causes of their production or the manner of making them, however in names differing from the voluntary and involuntary, or the natural and instituted gestures of the authors above cited, may be easily reduced to the same descriptions.

---

faire entendre. D'ailleurs, il est comme impossible que plusieurs de ces gestes ne fussent incompatibles avec la decence qu'on devoit garder dans sa déclamation. Voilà, suivant mon sentiment, la raison pour la quelle Quintilien defend si souvent a son orateur d'imiter la gesticulation des danseurs ou des *saltatores*.

Ce que dit Quintilien dans un autre endroit, semble rendre ma conjecture une chose certaine. Tous les gestes dont je viens de faire mention, c'est Quintilien même qu'on entend, partent naturellement avec la parole. Mais il y a une autre espèce des gestes qui ne signifient que parce qu'ils décrivent la chose qu'on veut exprimer par leur moyen. Tel est le geste représentant l'action d'un medecien qui tate le pouls, et dont on se sert pour signifier un malade. Rien n'est plus vicieux dans un orateur, ajoute Quintilien, que d'employer dans sa déclamation des gestes de cette espèce. La déclamation de l'orateur doit être entierement différente de celle du *danseur*. L'orateur doit assortir son geste avec le sentiment qu'il exprime, et non pas avec la signification particulière du mot qu'il prononce. P. 222.

6 The following passage is already quoted, speaking of imitation: Et ii quidem de quibus sum locutus cum ipsis vocibus naturaliter exeunt gestus. Alii sunt qui res imitatione significant, ut si ægrum, tentantis venas medici similitudine, aut citharœdum, formatis ad modum percutientis nervos manibus, ostendas : quod est genus quam longissimè in actione fugiendum. Abesse enim plurimum a saltatore debet orator, ut sit gestus ad sensum magis quam ad verba accommodatus, quod etiam histrionibus paulò gravioribus facere moris fuit. *Quint.* 11. 3.

7 This work, translated from the German into French, is entitled Idées sur le Geste, et l'Action théatrale, par M. I. I. Engel de l'Academie Royale des Sciences de Berlin, &c.

It is printed in a publication named, Recueil de Pieces intéressantes concernant les Antiquités, les Beaux Arts, &c. Paris An. 5 (1796.)

The modifications of the body are divided by M. Engel into two classes ; those arising from involuntary action, or the mechanism of the body only, as quick respiration after running, the closing of the eyelids from drowsiness, and sneezing from the irritation of the pituitary membrane. Those of the second kind depend on the will, and answer to the inflections of the voice, their action falling as the stroke of the gesture described in this work, does on the accented syllable of the emphatical word.

The more particular or determinate modifications of the body he divides into *picturesque* and *expressive gestures.* The *picturesque* are descriptive, and answer to the kind of gestures which Cicero calls *demonstratio*, and the *expressive* relate to the feelings of the mind, and answer to those which he calls significatio.[8] Other movements he names *indicative* when an object is merely pointed out but not described.

Action is *complete* when the imitation is perfect ; as may take place, when one man describes the gestures of another.

Action is *incomplete* when a man describes objects incapable of being adequately represented by his powers, as if he should describe the height and circumference of a mountain.

Action is figurative, when some resemblance in the gesture is substituted for the feelings of the mind, as the thinking of elevation of mind, raises up the body and countenance ; and the idea of obstinacy stiffens the whole person.

---

[8] Omnes autem hos motus subsequi debet gestus, non hic verba exprimens, scenicus, sed universam rem et sententiam, non demonstratione, sed significatione declarans. *Cicero.* de Orat. l. 3. c. 59.

Gestures arising from desire or aversion, which seem as it were to be gratified by their means, he names *gestures of motive* (gestes motives).

Analogous gestures, represent the feelings of the mind, in a manner similar to those of the body, as when in refusing assent the hand pushes as it were the ideas aside. But these seem rather to belong properly to his *figurative gestures*. *Physiological gestures* are involuntary indications of the mind, as blushing, paleness, tears, laughing, &c. these appear properly to belong to his first division.[9]

Such are the principal divisions of gesture according to Mr. Engel; from their various combinations, he very ingeniously accounts for the significancy of gesture, under many different modifications, and gives directions for its proper use. He states the object of his work to be principally an enquiry into the truth of theatrical action, by which is to be understood its significancy, which he complains was neglected, and that in its place was substituted a cold affectation of grace without life or

---

9 Je dois commencer par classer les différentes modifications du corps, que le comédien imite d'après nature. Elles se partagent d'abord en deux espèces principales; savoir, en celles qui sont uniquement fondées sur le mécanisme du corps; comme, par exemple, la respiration difficile après une course rapide, l'affaissement des paupieres à l'approche du sommeil, &c.; et en celles qui, dependant davantage de la coopération de l'ame, nous servent à juger de ses affections, de ses mouvemens et de ses desirs, comme causes occasionnelles et ou motrices. Engel, Tome III. p. 359.

.... Elles répondent aux inflections de la voix dans le récit tranquille.... afin que l'attention de l'auditeur s'attache precisément à ce qui occupe celle de la personne qui parle.

expression.[10] Whatever ground of complaint he might have against the practice or traditions of his theatre on this account; the same charge cannot be made against the writers on this subject, at least those in our hands; for their chief attention has been directed to the significancy and truth of gesture. Mr. Engel has no doubt taken a very comprehensive and able view of this kind of gesture, but the old rhetoricians have also laboured in the same way, as Caussinus Cresollius, Henischius and Curius Fortunatianus; from the two former frequent extracts have been made in the notes, and from the two latter, as containing well condensed abridgments of Cicero and Quintilian

---

. . . . en élevant et renforçant la voix par une prononciation plus lente et plus imposante du mot qui indique l'idée particulierement digne d'être remarquée. *Pp.* 365, 366.

La regle . . . . est la même que celle qui doit determiner l'accent. *P.* 367.

Toutes les modifications du corps d'une signification plus determinée se partagent dans les deux espèces que je viens de nommer; savoir, en gestes *pittoresques* et en gestes *expressifs.* Peutêtre ne devrois-je appliquer le mot *geste* qu'à cette derniere espèce; mais notre langue (Allemande) me paroît aussi bien permettre cette extension du sens que la langue latine. Ciceron qui, dans un endroit, n'applique le mot *gestus* qu'aux signes extérieurs de la situation de l'ame, les *affectiones animi;* parle ailleurs du *gestu scenico, verba exprimente.* Ce que j'appelle *peinture* est sa *demonstratio;* et *significatio* est à-peu près chez lui ce que j'entends par *expression.* A la verité, il y a encore d'autres mouvemens, qu'on pourroit appeller *indicatifs,* lorsque la chose ne doit pas être dépeinte, mais seulement indiquée. *P.* 372.

La peinture de l'art du geste est, comme celle de la musique, complette ou incomplette. *P.* 389 *et seq.*

Je me contenterai d'indiquer seulement une remarque très-intéressante qu'on peut encore faire ici : elle concerne le grand nombre des figures et sur-tout de métaphores, qui se trouvent aussi bien dans le langage des gestes, que dans celui de la parole. *P.* 398 *et seq.*

Quelques-uns de ces gestes sont *motives* ou faits à dessein : ce sont des actions extérieurs et volontaires par lesquelles on peut connoitre les mouvemens, les penchans, les tendences, et les passions de l'ame, quelles servent à satisfaire comme moyens. *P.* 404.

D'autres gestes sont *imitatifs* non en peignant l'objet de la pensée, mais la situation, les effets, et les modifications de l'ame, et je les appellerai gestes analogues. *P.* 405.

Il y a encore d'autres gestes, qui sont des phenomenes involontaires . . . Je réunirai tous ces gestes sous la denomination commune de gestes *physiologiques.* *P.* 407.

with perhaps some valuable additions, large extracts are added
in the Appendix. Johannes Lucas, who wrote a Latin poem on
the gesture and voice of a public speaker, has been put under
contribution in the same manner. The excellence of his precepts,
and the beauties of his poetry appear to better advantage
kept thus together, than scattered, as they might have been,
through the notes. For these additions to the work, it is hoped
that their value, and the rarity of their books will be sufficient
apology. The elegant Count de Buffon, in his natural history of
man, has devoted several pages to the expression of his countenance, and his gestures : a passage or two quoted from this will
induce the reader to consult the eloquent author in his own work
at large. Mr. Sheridan has written also at considerable length
on this subject, in his Art of Speaking, as well as in his Lectures.
Mr. Walker in his Elements of Elocution has improved on that part
of Mr. Sheridan's work, which describes the external characters
of the passions, and has subjoined to each, appropriate examples
selected with his usual judgment and taste. As these books are
or ought to be in the hands of every public speaker, there is the
less occasion to make extracts from them.

Without entering very largely into the subject of significant
gestures, which are not the principal object of this treatise, it
may be necessary to enumerate a few of them.

The Head and Face.

The hanging down of the head denotes shame or grief.
The holding it up, pride or courage. (")

---

[10] . . . La plupart des règles conservées par tradition sur la déclamation théâtrale

To nod forwards implies assent. (")
To toss the head back, dissent. ('²)
The inclination of the head implies bashfulness or languor.
The head is averted in dislike or horror. ('³)
It leans forward in attention.

The Eyes.

The eyes are raised in prayer.
They weep in sorrow. ('⁴)
They burn in anger.
They are downcast or averted in anger.'⁵
They are cast on vacancy in thought.
They are thrown in different directions in doubt and anxiety.

The Arms.

The arm is projected forwards in authority.
Both arms are spread extended in admiration.
They are both held forwards in imploring help.
They both fall suddenly in disappointment.

---

n'ont d'autre objet que la dignité, la beauté et la noblesse du jeu. De-là vient que nous remarquons cette froide élégance, sans ame et sans expression dans le jeu de tant d'acteurs. P. 384.

¹¹ Capitis demissio mœstitiam et luctum consequitur.
  Caput attollere superbientium et arrogantium gestus est.
  Capitis nutus apud Homerum ratæ permissionis signum est. *Caussinus.*

¹² Ἀλλ' ἄγε τῇ κεφαλῇ κατανεύσομαι. *Iliad.* 1.

¹³ Lucian humorously compares the alternate assent and dissent of a man distracted by doubt to the nodding backwards and forwards of persons asleep : ἄρτι μὲν ἐπινεύων ἄρτι δὲ ἀνανεύων ἔμπαλιν. *Menip.*

¹⁴ Tristior et lachrymis oculos suffusa nitentes. *Virg.*

¹⁵ Illa solo fixos oculos aversa tenebat. *Ib.*

The Hands.

The hand on the head indicates pain or distress.

On the eyes, shame.

On the lips, injunction of silence.

On the breast, it appeals to conscience, or intimates desire.

The hand waves or flourishes in joy or contempt.

Both hands are held supine, applied or clasped, in prayer.

Both descend prone in blessing.

They are clasped or wrung in affliction.

They are held forward and received in friendship.

The Body.

The body held erect indicates steadiness and courage.

Thrown back, pride.

Stooping forward, condescension or compassion.

Bending reverence or respect.

Prostration, the utmost humility or abasement.

The Lower Limbs.

Their firm position signifies courage or obstinancy.

Bended knees, timidity or weakness.

Frequent change, disturbed thoughts.

They advance in desire or courage.

Retire in aversion or fear.

Start in terror.

Stamp in authority or anger,

Kneel in submission and prayer. [16, 17, 18, 19, 20]

---

[16] Every part of the human frame contributes to express the passions and emotions of the mind, and to shew in general its present state. The head is sometimes erected, sometimes

These are a few of the simple gestures which may be termed significant. The catalogue may be enlarged at pleasure. They seem to be natural and altogether involuntary, but Buffon does not include them in this description, and that evidently with good reason.

" These movements are so prompt (says he), that they ap-

---

hung down, sometimes drawn suddenly back with an air of disdain, sometimes shews by a nod a particular person or object ; gives assent, or denial by different motions ; threatens by one sort of movement, approves by another, and expresses suspicion by a third.

The arms are sometimes both thrown out, sometimes the right alone, sometimes they are lifted up as high as the face to express wonder, sometimes held out before the breast, to shew fear ; spread forth with hands open, to express desire or affection, the hands clasped in surprise, and in sudden joy and grief, the right hand clinched and the arms brandished, to threaten ; the two arms set a kimbo, to look big, and express contempt and courage. . . .

The legs advance or retreat, to express desire or aversion, love or hatred, courage or fear, and produce exultation or leaping in sudden joy ; and the stamping of the foot expresses earnestness, anger, and threatening. *Sheridan's Art of Speaking.*

[17] For significant gestures of the head see a passage of Quintilian already quoted. Chap. 4, p. 350. *Chironomia.*

[18] La tête en entier prend dans les passions, des positions et des mouvemens différens, elle est abaissée en avant dans l'humilité, la honte, la tristesse ; penchée à coté dans la langueur, la pitié ; élevée dans l'arrogance, droite et fixe dans l'opiniâtreté ; la tête fait un mouvement en arrière dans l'étonnement, et plusieurs mouvemens réitérés de côté et d'autre dans le mepris, la moquerie, la colere et l'indignation. *Buffon. Hist. Nat.* quarto. Tome IV. p. 531.

Lorsque l'ame est tranquille, toutes les parties du visage sont dans un état de repos, leur proportion, leur union, leur ensemble marque encore assez la douce harmonie des pensées, et repondent au calme de l'intérieur ; mais lorsque l'ame est agitée, la face humaine devient un tableau vivant, ou les passions sont rendues avec autant de délicatesse que d'énergie, ou chaque mouvement de l'ame est exprimé par un trait, chaque action par un caractère, dont l'impression vive et prompte devance la volonté, nous décèle et rend au dehors par des signes pathétiques les images de nos secrettes agitations. *Ib. p.* 519.

[19] Les bras, les mains, et tout le corps entre aussi dans l'expression des passions : les gestes concourent avec les mouvemens du visage pour exprimer les différens mouvemens de l'ame. Dans la joie par exemple, les yeux, la tête, les bras, et tout le corps sont agités par des mouvemens prompt et variés ; dans la langueur et la tristesse les yeux sont abaissés, la tête est penchée sur le côté, les bras sont pendens, et tout le corps est immobile : dans l'admiration, surprise, l'étonnement, tout mouvement est suspendu, ou reste dans une même attitude. *Ib. p.* 533.

[20] The reader will find pleasure in consulting the work at large, for many profound and interesting observations on this subject. As the expression of the passions in the counte-

" pear to us involuntary, but we are deceived by the effect of
" habit ; for they depend upon reflection, and are rather to be
" considered as proofs of the perfection of the mechanism of the
" human body, from the promptitude with which all the mem-
" bers obey the commands of the will." ([21]) The significant
gestures may then be divided into four different classes. 1st.
Those which are natural or involuntary, as blushing in shame,
paleness, or trembling from fear. 2nd. The simple significant
gestures of the body as those enumerated. 3rd. Complex significant gestures which are combined of the simple variously
according to the mingled passions which they represent. These
take place principally on the stage, the boldest, and most magnificent of which are termed attitudes. Although the first of these
classes alone is purely natural, yet on account of the facility of
understanding their meaning, even by those who are ignorant
of the language of the speaker, the three classes may properly
be comprehended under the description of gesture, which the
Abbé du Bos calls *natural*. The 4th class is that which he
calls *instituted*. These are gestures deriving their significancy
merely from compact, and such as are altogether arbitrary in
their meaning, and local in their use. They are not understood
by all people, and their meaning is to be learned like that of
words in a new language. They are, however, more easily
acquired, because they can often be made out from the context

---

nance, &c. For this he may also consult Le Brun's drawings of the passions with the description, and also *Dubroca Art de lire a haute Voix,* p. 564.

    [21] Ces mouvemens sont si prompts qu'ils paroissent involontaires, mais c'est un effet de
l'habitude, qui nous trompe, car ces mouvemens dependent de la reflexion, et marquent
seulement la perfection des ressorts du corps humain, par la promptitude avec laquelle tous
les membres obeissent aux ordres de la volonté. *Buff.* 534. *ib.*

of the natural signs, with which they are intermixed: and the knowledge of them is facilitated in the same manner, and with the same advantage as the acquisition of a new language, when a person in possession of a number of its words or roots, or when it is very similar to his own. This class of significant gestures is of vulgar, pantomimic, or comic usage alone. and not having any relation to the nobler kinds of public speaking, will be no farther noticed.

It will not be improper to enumerate here a few instances of complex significant gestures.

Terror excites the person who suffers under it, to avoid or to escape from the dreaded object. If it be supposed to be some dangerous reptile on the ground, and very near, the expr sion is represented by the figure starting back, and looking downwards. If the danger threaten from a distance, the terror arising is expressed by the figure looking forwards, and not starting back, but merely in the retired position. But if the dread of impending death from the hand of an enemy awaken this passion, the coward flies. Of this a fine example will be recollected in the battles of Alexander, by Le Brun.

Fig. 100. Aversion, as already observed, Chap. 16, is expressed by two gestures, first the hand held vertical is retracted towards the face, the eyes and head are for a moment directed eagerly towards the object, and the feet advance. Fig. 101. Then suddenly the eyes are withdrawn, the head is averted, the feet retire, and the arms are projected out extended against the object, the hands vertical.[22]

---

[22] Quand il s'agit de refuser ou de rejetter, et que nous marquons avoir quelque chose ou

Fig. 102. Horror, which is aversion or astonishment mingled with terror, is seldom capable of retreating but remains petrified in one attitude, with the eyes rivetted on its object, and the arm held forwards to guard the person, the hands vertical, and the whole frame trembling.

Fig. 103. Listening, in order to obtain the surest and most various information, first presents the quick and comprehensive glance of the eye towards the apparent direction of the sounds, if nothing is seen, the ear presents itself towards the point of expectation, and the eye is bent on vacancy: but all this passes in a moment. The hand and arm are held vertical extended. If the sound proceed from different quarters at the same time, both arms are held up, and the head alternately changes from one side to the other, with a rapidity governed by the nature of the sound; if it be alarming, with trepidation; if pleasing, with gentle motion   The figure is *listening fear*.

Fig. 104. Admiration, if of surrounding natural objects of a pleasing kind, holds both hands vertical and across, and moves them outwards to the position, extended as in the figure. If admiration arise from some extraordinary or unexpected circumstances, the hands are thrown up supine elevated, together with the countenance and the eyes.

Fig. 105. Veneration crosses both hands on the breast, casts down the eyes slowly, and bows the head.

---

quelque personne en horreur et en exécration, alors en même tems que nous repoussons de la main, nous detournons la tête pour marquer d'aversion.   *Rollin Belles Lettres.*

Fig. 106. Deprecation advances in an extended position of the feet, approaching to kneeling, clasps the hands forcibly together, throws back, the head sinking it betweeen the shoulders, and looks earnestly up to the person implored.

Fig. 107. In appealing to heaven the right hand is first laid on the breast, then the left is projected supine upwards, the eyes first directed forwards, and then upwards.

Fig. 83. In the appeal to conscience, the right hand is laid on the breast, the left drops unmoved, the eyes are fixed upon the person addressed; sometimes both hands press the breast.

Fig. 108. Shame in the extreme sinks on the knee and covers the eyes with both hands: this is a feminine expression of it.

Fig. 109. Mild resignation falls on the knee, crosses the arms on the breast, and looks forwards and upwards towards heaven. This is also a feminine expression of this feeling.

Fig. 116. Resignation mixed with desperation stands erect and unmoved, the head thrown back, the eyes turned upward and fixed, the arms crossed. A fine instance is seen in the figure from an attitude of Mrs. Siddons.

Fig. 84. Grief arising from sudden and afflicting intelligence covers the eyes with one hand, advances forwards and throws back the other hand.

Fig. 85. Attention demanding silence holds the finger on

3 R

the lips, and leans forwards, sometimes repressing with the left hand.

Fig. 86. Distress when extreme lays the palm of the hand upon the forehead, throws the head and body back, and retires with a long and sudden step.

Fig. 87. Deliberation on ordinary subjects holds the chin, and sets the arm a kimbo.

Fig. 40. Self-sufficiency folds the arms, and sets himself on his centre.

Fig. 41. Pride throws back the body, holds the head high, and nearly presents foward his elbow a kimbo.

These few complex significant gestures are some of the most obvious, and principally such as occurred in the illustration of other parts of this system; they serve however in some degree to explain the nature of these gestures. But among the writers who have treated particularly on these, none have written with greater ingenuity than Engel: we will borrow therefore an example or two from him. Fig. 110. Surprise causes the body and lower limbs to retire, and affection stimulates the person to advance; the figure represented is the character of Frederick de Reuss in a German play, who unexpectedly sees his dear friend. He withdraws in surprise his body and lower limbs, and in the ardour of friendship at the same time stretches forwards his head and his arms.[21]

---

[21] Je dois encore observer ici que plusieurs expressions mixtes peuvent produire des gestes et des attitudes qui, ayant des sentimens contraires à réunir, paroissent fausses par la con-

When the thoughts flow without difficulty or opposition, the movement of the limbs is free and direct. But when difficulties occur or obstacles are discovered, a man either arrests his action entirely, or changes it to something altogether different. The direction of his eyes, and the action of his head is also under similar circumstances quite altered. The eyes, instead of moving freely from object to object, become fixed, and the head is thrown back, if before hanging down on the breast. As an example of these effects, which are detailed at large in the extract subjoined in his own words, M. Engel refers to a scene in a play of Lessing, in which an old gentleman is very much puzzled how to manage, under a situation of great difficulty and delicacy. In the commencement of his deliberations he is represented as in Fig. 111, and in the next period of them, as in Fig. 112.[24]

---

tradiction qu'on y remarque, sans pourtant l'être réellement. Vous savez que l'étonnement fait jetter le corps en arrière, et que l'amitié le fait porter en avant : ainsi lorsqu'un ami qu'on ne s'attendoit pas à voir se presente subitement à nous (comme par exemple, Otton de Wittelsbach à Frederic de Reuss) ce sera un jeu très vrai ou plutot le seul veritable, que de faire un pas en arrière, ou du moins de pencher le corps en arrière à cause de l'étonnement ; tandis que les bras se porteront en avant pour recevoir cordialement l'hôte chéri. *Recueil des Pieces Intéressantes. Tom. IV. p.* 256.

[24] Lorsque l'homme developpe ses idées avec facilité et sans obstacle, sa marche est plus libre, plus rapide, et continue davantage dans une direction uniforme. Quand la série des idées se présente difficilement, son pas devient plus lent, plus embarassée ; et lorsqu'enfin une doute importante s'éleve soudain dans son esprit, sa marche est alors entièrement interrompue et l'homme s'arrête tout court. . . . . . . Le jeu des mains est modifié de la même manière que la marche : il est libre, sans gêne, aise, et facile, lorsque les idées se developpent sans peine, et que l'une nait sans difficulté de l'autre ; il est inquiet, irrégulier, les mains s'agitent en tout sens, et se meuvent sans dessein, tantôt vers la poitrine, tantôt vers la tête ; les bras s'entrelacent et se déploient, suivant que la pensée est arrêtée dans sa marche ou poussée vers toutes sortes des routes étrangères et incertaines. Du moment qu'une difficulté ou un obstacle se présente, le jeu de mains s'arrête entièrement. L'œil, qui de même que la tête, avoit des mouvemens doux et faciles tandis que la pensée étoit

These examples are introduced by M. Engel to illustrate his analogous gestures, but they may also be very well applied to illustrate the complex significant gestures, which are the present subject of investigation. The description which he gives of melancholy contrasted with anxiety, to which the following figures refer, is throughout correct, and full of nice discrimination.

Fig. 113. Melancholy is a feeble and passive affection; it is attended by a total relaxation of the nerves, with a mute and tranquil resignation, unaccompanied by opposition either to the cause or the sensibility of the evil. The character externally is langour without motion, the head hanging at the " side next the heart," the eyes turned upon its object, or if that is absent fixed on the ground, the hands hanging down by their own weight without effort, and joined loosely together.[25]

régulière et se développoit avec facilité, ou qui erroit d'un angle à l'autre lorsque l'ame s'égaroit d'idée en idée, regarde, dans cette nouvelle situation, fixement devant lui, et la tête se jette en arrière ou tombe sur la poitrine, jusqu'à ce qu'après le premier choc du doute, s'il m'est permis de m'exprimer ainsi, l'activité suspendue reprenne sa première marche.

Afin de sentir l'analogie des gestes avec plus de clarté, représentez vous le vieux Philto ou Staleno plongé dans la réflexion, lorsqu'ils cherchent ensemble un moyen de parvenir à leur but. Ils voudroient payer la dot de Camille, sans que son prodigue frère pût s'appercevoir de la richesse du coffre-fort du père. La chose est difficile à arranger ; ils cherchent pendant quelque tems, croient avoir trouvé un bon expédient, et l'abandonnent sur le champ. Supposons que le vieux Philto, en poursuivant sa première idée, ait laissé tomber la tête sur la poitrine en fixant la terre et reposant le corps sur la jambe gauche, la droit portée en avant ; il y a toute à parier qu'à la seconde pensée il aura changé de position. Fig. 111. Peutêtre mettra-il alors les mains sur les hanches, ou bien il levera la tête en régardant le ciel, comme s'il vouloit chercher là haut, ce qu'il n'a pu trouver ici bas ; ou il prendra enfin une attitude tout-à-fait opposée, en plaçant sur le dos une main dans l'autre, en jettant en arrière la tête penchée d'abord, en retirant le pied gauche, et en s'appuyant sur la jambe droite. Fig. 112.

[25] L'abbatement ou la melancholie est une affection foible et passive : c'est un relâche-

Fig. 114. Anxiety is of a different character ; it is restless and active, and manifest by the extension of the muscles ; the eye is filled with fire, the breathing is quick, the motion is hurried, the head is thrown back, the whole body is extended. The sufferer is like a sick man who tosses incessantly, and finds himself uneasy in every situation.

Fig. 115. One of the causes of Mr. Engel's gestures of analogy is, as he observes, the " disposition of the mind to refer intel-
" lectual ideas to external objects. When King Lear recollects
" the barbarous treatment of his daughters, who in the midst
" of a stormy night had exposed his hoary hairs to the incle-
" mency of the weather, and when he immediately exclaims,

> O, that way madness lies ; let me shun that ;
> No more of that,————

" there is not in reality any external object from which this
" unhappy prince should avert his eyes with horror, and yet
" he turns his head away to the side opposite that to which it
" was directed before ; endeavouring, as it were, with his hand
" reversed, to banish that cruel and afflicting recollection."[26.27]

But if we seek examples of complex significant gestures, or

---

ment total des forces, une résignation muette et tranquille, sans resistance ni contre la cause, ni contre le sentiment même du mal. . . . . la tête foible et lourde tombe du côté du cœur ; . . . . le mouvement de tous les membres est lent, sans force, et sans vie. . . . . les yeux dirigés vers l'objet qui cause la tristesse ; ou s'il est absent, les regards sont fixés vers la terre ; tout le corps même s'y penche : Fig. 113.

Ad humum mœror gravis deducit.   Hor. de Art. poet.

[26] La souffrance est une affection inquiète et active qui se manifeste par la tension des

attitudes the most noble and expressive, we need not look abroad, the most perfect models perhaps existing of such gestures may be found at home; and may frequently be contemplated with delight and wonder. The consummate art, majesty, and grace of Mr. Kemble can furnish variety on every occasion that calls him to perform his high tragic characters.[26] And his admirable sister has obtained merited and universal

---

muscles. C'est une lutte intérieur contre la sensation douloureuse, et un effort de la surmonter et de s'en debarasser, ... l'œil est rempli du feu . . . la poitrine s'élève rapidement et avec violence; la marche est pressée et pesante, tout le corps s'allonge. . . la tête jettée en arrière, se tourne de côté en portant un regard suppliant vers le ciel. Fig. 114. . . . . . . L'individu qui souffre ressemble à un malade qui éprouvant dans tous les situations des inquiétudes et un mal-aise, espere sans cesse d'en trouver enfin une plus commode; mais qui se tournant de côté et de l'autre, la cherche toujours sans jamais la trouver. *Engel, Lettre 23.*

[27] La seconde raison du geste analogue est dans la tendence de l'ame de rapporter ses idées intellectuelles aux matérielles. . . . . Fig. 115. Lorsque le Roi Lear se ressouvient de l'indigne traitement de ses filles, qui pendant une nuit orageuse ont exposés ses cheveux blancs aux injures du tems, et qu'ensuite il s'écrie tout d'un coup. " Ah, c'est là le " chemin qui conduit au délire! evitons le!" Il n existe véritablement aucun objet extérieur dont ce malheureux prince doive detourner les regards avec effroi, et cependant il se tourne du côté opposé à celui vers lequel il étoit d'abord placé, en cherchant pour ainsi dire, a repousser avec sa main renversée ce cruel et douloureux souvenir. *Engel, Lett.* 11.

[28] Some persons of taste, more fastidious than correct, have complained of Mr. Kemble's art. It is no doubt consummate; his various learning with most laudable propriety is made to bear with its full effect on all his theatrical characters. To their illustration does he direct his readings and his profound knowledge of the *costume,* and to adorn and enforce their sentiments and situations, the truth, the precision, the grandeur and significancy of his action. On the subject of art it may not be amiss to give the sentiments of a late celebrated French actress, Mademoiselle Clairon.

En me rappelant mon plan d'étude, j'espère qu'on me pardonnera de me rappeller aussi que j'ai souvent ri des sottises qu'on disait en me reprochant d'avoir de l'art. Eh! que vouloit-on que j'eusse? Etois-je en effet, Roxane, Amenaïde, ou Viriate? Devois-je preter à ces rôles mes propres sentimens, et ma façon d'être habituelle? Non sans doute. Que pouvois-je substituer à mes idées, mes sentimens, mon être enfin? L'art, parcequ'il n'y a que cela; et si jamais il m'est arrivé d'avoir l'air vraiment naturel, c'est que mes recherches jointes à quelque dons heureux que m'avait fait la nature, m'avaient conduite au comble de l'art.

applause in every dramatic excellence, and particularly in this kind, unattempted, and it would almost seem unattainable by the usual power of female efforts. Many illustrations of the significancy, of the truth and dignity of action, may be observed not only in the performance, but may be found recorded in the pictures and engravings after these great tragedians. But more in proportion of the admired gestures of Mrs. Siddons have been thus preserved, perhaps on account of the partial preference due to her sex. By the favour of a young lady,[29] who has taste to be charmed by the truth and dignity of her action, and who possesses talents to record it, I have been enabled to gratify the reader with a few interesting sketches of this great actress. They, with many others of equal merit, have been drawn from recollection by this young lady, immediately after having seen her in her principal characters. The passages, to which the figures refer, are placed below with the proper notation.

---

[29] Miss M. H———, daughter of the Right Honourable S. H———.

Fig. 116. *Sciolto.* See where she stands like Helen. *Fair Penitent, A.* 5. *sc:* 1.
U. B cr br

U   iz sp—xdx
Fig. 117. This arm shall vindicate a father's cause. *Grecian Daughter, Ac.* 1. *sc. last.*
aR2

U   B cl.eb.
Fig. 118. A widow cries, Be husband to me, heav'n. *King John, A.* 3. *sc.* 2.
R.1

Fig. 119. Scorn'd by the women, pity'd by the men
B   c F—cdx
Oh ! insupportable ! *Fair Penitent, A.* 2. *sc.* 1.
L.1.x

S   iZ sp—pdx
Fig. 120. Wert thou the son of Jupiter. *Imogen, A.* 2. *sc.* 3.
a,R.2

scb—shf
Fig. 121. Jehovah's arm snatch'd from the waves and brings to me my son.
L.1

Douglas, A. 3. *sc.* 2.

D   Bcl ef U   heq bn—hdx
Fig. 122. *Pity* and *forgiveness.* *Venice Preserved, A.* 5. *sc.* 1.
aR.1.K.

In the passage from Douglas it is rather difficult to conjecture the moment of the action, because another is required also on the word " son," but the remainder of the line is necessary to complete the sense, and the action seems properly placed on " Jehova's arm." In the short passage from Venice Preserved, " pity and forgiveness," a previous gesture is added from conjecture on the word " pity." The head cast down, and *both hands clasped elevated forwards* significant of the profound humility implied in the word " pity." The transition from this to the gesture represented would be bold and beautiful; the veil is removed with both hands on the word " forgiveness," and the eyes are turned upon Sciolto; and it seems to require some previous expression of greater submission. For the word " forgiveness," considering the situation of Belvidera, and the natural hope to be formed from a parent's affection, justifies the mixture of humility and submission, with the importunity of demand, and the ardour of filial expectation, all of which are so finely represented in this instance of complex and highly significant action.[30]

Significant gestures appear thus to be the great ornaments of dramatic exhibition, and it must be admitted that the performance will be the most brilliant in which they abound most. And hence significant gestures may seem alone worthy of cultivation; and this opinion seems to be supported by the

---

[30] In these gestures of Mrs Siddons, the hand is boldly raised above the head.

Les régles défendent, disoit Baron, de lever les bras au-dessus de la tête; mais si la passion les y portent, ils seront bien: la passion en scait plus, que les régles. *Marmontel, Elémens de Litérature, Tom. III. p.* 329.

Tolli autem manum artifices supra oculos, demitti infra pectus vetant. **Quint.**

Quintilian is speaking of the gesture proper for an orator; the theatre is allowed greater freedom and boldness.

observation, that painters and writers have confined their attention almost solely to them. It occurs therefore as an obvious question, to ask of what use the investigation can be of the other gestures, concerning which so much has been said in this work. An enquiry instituted on this ground would make it evident that a considerable chasm has hitherto been left neglected in this division of public speaking, which is here attempted to be supplied.

The significant gestures however numerous and correct which a great actor makes in the representation of an entire dramatic character, bear no proportion to the greater number of his gestures which are not significant, and which are no less necessary, though not so splendid nor imposing. The painter is struck by the boldest and finest of the significant gestures which are called attitudes, and he records them; they are the proper objects of his art; they are striking and less evanescent than the other gestures, which pass unnoticed by him, although they make up by far the greater and more important part of the gestures requisite for illustrating the sentiments. These less prominent gestures give to the declamation its precision and force. A slight movement of the head, a look of the eye, a turn of hand, a judicious pause or interruption of gesture, or a change of position in the feet often illuminates the meaning of a passage, and sends it full of light and warmth into the understanding. And the perfection of gesture in a tragedian will be found to consist more in the skilful management of the less shewy action, than in the exhibition of the finest attitudes. Attitudes are dangerous to hazard; the whole powers of the man must be wrought up to their highest energy,

3 S

or they become forced and frigid. Every one will recollect that excellent players have been seen, who have never ventured an attitude, but none deserving the name of excellence have ever appeared whose declamation has been deficient in precision or propriety. Where all the solid foundation of just and appropriate action has been laid, attitude, when regulated with taste and discretion, may be added to ornament the superstructure; but introduced unseasonably or overcharged, it is an evidence of deficiency of understanding as well as of depravity of taste.

An indifferent actor often uses full as much gesture, or perhaps even more, than those who are deservedly esteemed. His fault will be found in the improper use of action: as when there is no precision in the stroke of his gesture supporting the emphasis of the voice, and neither discrimination, nor variety; but a monotony alike, perhaps, of voice and of action. By such actors also significant gestures of the tamer kind are repeated without meaning where they are not required. Thus it is well known that the hand is laid on the breast to signify some relation to the inward sentiments, or when a person speaks of himself. This action often occurs properly. But some actors, singers particularly, grow fond of it, and during the whole course of their song alternately press one hand on the breast, and extend the other arm. The clasping of the hands together indicates distress: but it cannot be proper to clasp and unclasp them incessantly; and even though there may be woe enough to justify the gesture once or twice repeated, it would be better to vary it by introducing something different.

If the significant gestures of the actor are less numerous than those which are less brilliant; the gestures of this kind allowed to the orator are still more rare and more reserved. And this circumstance forms one material point of difference between rhetorical and dramatic action. But if the orator is precluded from the general use of significant gestures, it is evident also that gesture of some other kind is required to illustrate and enforce his sentiments. The gestures more particularly suited to him are enumerated in the 15th Chapter; and they will be found to constitute the great mass of those which must also be introduced on the theatre.[31]

In the very ingenious work of M. Engel, it appears that Sulzer, a German author whom he quotes, proposed as a measure likely to open a just theory of gesture, that certain scenes should be analysed with respect of the pantomime or action suitable to them.[32] And in another place he quotes him as suggesting a plan of making a collection of gestures (evidently those of the significant class,) which should be classed in order,

---

[31] Alii sunt, qui res imitatione significant : ut si ægrum, tentantis venas medici similitudine, aut citharœdum, formatis ad modum percutientis nervos manibus ostendas, quod est genus quam longissime in actione fugiendum. Abesse enim plurimum a saltatore debet orator, ut sit gestus ad sensus magis, quam ad verba, accommodatus : quod etiam histrionibus paullo gravioribus facere moris fuit. Ergo ut ad se manum referre, cum de seipso loquatur, et in eum, quem demonstret intendere, et aliqua his similia permiserim : ita non, effingere status quosdam, et, quicquid dicet, ostendere. Neque id in manibus solum, sed in omni gestu ac voce servandum est. Non enim aut in illa periodo, *stetit soleatus populi Romani*, inclinatio incumbentis in mulierculam Verris effingenda est : aut in illa, *Cædebatur in medio foro Messanæ*, motus laterum, qualis esse ad verba, solet, torquendus : aut vox, qualis dolore exprimitur, eruenda. *Quint. B. p.* 1018.

See also *Quint. B. p.* 1036, already quoted, ch. xv. p. 20.

[32] Le vœu de Sulzer que beaucoup des scenes isolées soient developpées par une sage critique relativement à la pantomime, n'a pas été rempli jusque à ce jour si l'on en excepte quelques légers essais. *Recueil de Pieces intéressantes. Tom. III. p.* 358.

and arranged in the manner of natural history."[33] He does not decide upon the advantages of such a collection: But the probability is, from what may be observed with relation to the favour with which such publications are received as contain portraits of celebrated actors in their most remarkable attitudes, that such a work would prove highly entertaining and very acceptable to the public in general, and might also be of some advantage to theatrical students; if it should not contribute to carry them away by the ambition of attitude, before they studied precision, and all the more laborious but more necessary arts of their difficult profession.

To the orator such collections would be of little service, and to the mere reader of the drama they would convey little more information relative to the entire action of celebrated performers, than portraits and sketches of great actions in history convey concerning the chain of the facts. The portrait, and the attitude, and the historical picture, are pleasing and valuable so far as they delineate the simple action of the individual, or the complex actions of many at some particular and interesting moment of the drama or the history. They support and refresh the imagination through the aid of the " faithful eye" as far as the momentary comprehension of the painting extends: but unless they were carried through a whole drama, or a whole history, in the manner of those little figures which illustrate the connexion and transition of gesture in the portion of the fable of the Miser and Plutus, they must leave many unavoidable chasms. Now to execute a whole play according

---

[33] Pourquoi une collection de gestes expressifs ne seroit-elle aussi possible et aussi utile qu'une collection des desseins de coquilles, de plantes, et des insectes ? *Ib. p.* 381.

to that plan would be a work of enormous expense and difficulty; this system of notation precludes in a great measure the
necessity for such labour and expense: for if it were desired, a
great orator or actor by its means could with little trouble
record every action as faithfully as if each was correctly
depicted. This system has also the advantage over all possible
collections of particular gestures, however extensive, in much
the same manner, and nearly in the same degree, as the communication of ideas by words formed of elementary or alpha-
betic characters has over hieroglyphic or picture writing. And
it will not be considered unimportant that it possesses this
further advantage, that it is not to be considered as assuming
any exclusive power of illustration. On the contrary, it is
offered only as an additional and intermediate bond of connection, and as an auxiliary both to the literary and to the representative art, with each of which it coalesces perfectly, uniting
the facility of execution and of reproduction of the one, with
something of the vivacity and precision of the other; and it is
at the same time free from some unavoidable imperfections of
both. The description of gesture, but especially of many gestures in words at large, however possible, we have already seen
would be attended with such a diffuseness of writing, as would
rather disgust than inform. And painting, whatever may be
its powers, is subject to interruption and chasms, and is besides
operose, expensive, confined to the powers of the artist alone, and
limited to the single attitude or moment of the action. Whereas
this art of notation is much more brief than the written expressions
which it is calculated to illustrate; and may be used, according
to the pleasure of the annotator, either for marking precisely
with their proper gestures and tones, every passage throughout

a whole drama or oration, from the beginning to the conclusion; or, which is perhaps the better method for annexing them, according to the most deliberate judgment, to such passages only, as require in the delivery more particular energy or expression.

CHAPTER XXII.

OF GRACE.

Grace depends partly on the person and partly on the mind—Must be acquired by imitation of the best models—Natural grace may appear when the mind is agitated beyond the power of all restraint—The influence of graceful delivery—Wherein the grace of oratorical action consists—Of timidity—its effects injurious to grace—Conditions necessary to graceful delivery—Of affectation and vanity—Why the action of children is never deficient in grace—Hogarth's opinions concerning grace—Grace of decorum or suitableness—Quintilian's directions relative to grace—The speaker should study his own powers.

CHAPTER XXII.

Of Grace.

THE gracefulness of rhetorical action depends partly on the person and partly on the mind.[1] Some are so happily formed in person, that all their motions are graceful;[2,3,4,5] and some minds are so noble, that they impart genuine grace to the most uncouth forms: but both these cases are comparatively rare: the person in general requires to be practised into grace, and the mind to be instructed and encouraged. Grace, like the ideal beauty of the painter and of the sculptor, is not commonly to be found in the individual living model, but to be collected from the various excellencies of many. Most forms of the human figure are capable, in a considerable degree, of graceful motions, but if not trained and educated in the most perfect, are

---

If hearers are amaz'd from whence
Proceeds that fund of wit and sense,
Which, though her modesty would shroud,
Breaks like the sun behind a cloud;
While gracefulness its art conceals,
And yet through ev'ry motion steals.   *Swift.*

[2] Short and ungraceful gestures, not to give them any harsher character, are now affected by young men of fashion. When to these are added the further affectation of apathy of countenance, the hope of seeing the graces and persuasive ornaments of eloquence revived is distant.

[3] Decor quoque a gestu atque a motu venit. *Quint. B.* 1013.

[4]   Illam, quicquid agit, quoquo vestigia flectit
          Componit furtim subsequiturque decor.   *Capperonius in Quintil.*

3 T

more apt to imitate the awkward and the vulgar; because their manners abound among the majority or the less cultivated, and because they are the short, the inattentive, and the most direct expressions of the feelings. If the vulgar at any time attempt circuitous or ceremonious motions, they discover the habits of obsolete, and of bad taste.

The mind also may be capable of every dignified sentiment, but when untaught, not being acquainted with the manner of suitable expression, and either dubious, or conscious of its own deficiency, it betrays in every motion of the person constraint and apprehension, with consequent awkwardness and want of grace. This happens principally to the young and timid.[5] Men, who are seriously affected, and express their feelings in public according to their natural impression, if previously uninstructed, may in some measure be ungraceful; but, when so much in earnest, as to cease to think of appearances, or of any thing but the accomplishment of their particular object, they never fail to be energetic and impressive in proportion to their

---

[5]   Grace was in all her steps, heav'n in her eye,
        In ev'ry gesture dignity and love.   *Milton.*

[6] A late noble lord, in his observations on parliamentary speaking, seems to coincide in opinion with Demosthenes, that action is the great requisite. Action is to be understood, in order to perceive this coincidence, in its utmost extent as comprehending all the externals of oratory.

When you come into the house of commons, if you imagine that speaking plain and unadorned sense and reason will do your business, you will find yourself grossly mistaken. As a speaker you will be ranked only according to your eloquence, and by no means according to your matter; every body knows the matter almost alike, but few can adorn it. I was early convinced of the importance and powers of eloquence, and from that moment I applied myself to it. . . . . . . Ornaments are at present your only objects. Your sole business now is to shine, not to weigh. Weight without lustre is lead. *Chesterfield's Letters by Gregory, p.* 309.

sincerity, their good sense, and the extent of their information. It will be here observed, that no comparison is made between sincerity, good sense, and information on the one hand, as opposed to grace on the other; the influence of the truth, however presented, it is hoped will always be victorious in every wise assembly. But it may not be amiss above all other orna · ments to recommend it by the simple grace and dignity which so much become it, and so admirably suit its character. And the observation goes only so far as to shew that nothing less than the irresistible force of sincerity, and fact can bear out a public speaker when divested of grace, the proper garb and ornament of truth. A silly fellow, however capable of imitating a graceful manner, can never be an impressive speaker; his attempts degenerate into vapid affectation, and impose only on the weak and ignorant; yet, as such descriptions of people make no inconsiderable portion of a popular audience, the affected graces of a fluent coxcomb will not be altogether disregarded. Such is the influence of the exterior in oratory.[7]

But genuine oratorical grace can only be the result of refined cultivation adorning a superior understanding, or the

---

[7] In some passages the noble Lord has delivered his opinions with perhaps an unjustifiable boldness. "If you would either please in a private company or persuade in a public assembly, air, looks, gestures, graces, enunciation, proper accents, just emphasis, and tuneful cadences, are full as necessary as the matter itself. Let awkward, ungraceful, inelegant, and dull fellows say what they will in behalf of their solid matter, and strong reasonings; and let them despise all those graces and ornaments which engage the senses, and captivate the heart; they will find (though they will possibly wonder why) that their rough unpolished matter, and their unadorned, coarse, but strong arguments, will neither please nor persuade; but on the contrary will tire out attention and excite disgust. We are so made that we love to be pleased, better than to be informed; information is, in a certain degree, mortifying, as it implies our previous ignorance; it must be sweetened to be palatable.

To bring this directly to you; know that no man can make a figure in this country, but

rare gift of nature to a pure and exalted mind, expressed by the actions of a distinguished person.

But though true external grace can hardly be either assumed by, or imparted, except to a mind of a generous and noble nature, yet cultivation will do as much towards the improvement of the person, in this respect, as education can effect towards the improvement of the mind, and the bringing into action the internal powers of oratory.[s] Not every public speaker

by parliament. Your fate depends on your success as a speaker: and take my word for it, that success turns much more upon manner than matter. Mr. Pitt, and Mr. Murray, the solicitor general, uncle to Lord Stormont, are beyond comparison the best speakers. Why? only because they are the best orators. They alone can inflame or quiet the house; they alone are attended to, in that numerous and noisy assembly, that you might hear a pin fall while either of them is speaking. Is it that their matter is better, or their arguments are stronger than other people's? Does the house expect extraordinary information from them? Not in the least; but the house expects pleasure from them, and therefore attends; finds it, and therefore approves. Mr. Pitt, particularly, has very little parliamentary knowledge; his matter is generally flimsy, and his arguments are often weak; but his eloquence is superior, his action graceful, his enunciation just and harmonious, his periods are well turned, and every word he makes use of is the very best, and the most expressive, that can be used in that place. This, and not his matter, made him paymaster in spite of both king and ministers. *Chesterfield's Letters by Gregory,* p. 294.

[s] The historian may not be satisfied with some observations here, and the student may not agree in the full extent of all; but the whole letter deserves his perusal, and is important to him who intends to speak in public. The following passage is singular.

To govern mankind, one must not over-rate them; and to please an audience as a speaker, one must not over value it. When I first came into the house of commons, I respected that assembly as a venerable one; and felt a certain awe upon me: but upon better acquaintance, that awe soon vanished; and I discovered that of the five hundred and sixty, not above thirty could understand reason, and that all the rest were *people:* that those thirty only required plain common sense, dressed up in good language; and that all the others only required flowing and harmonious periods, whether they conveyed any meaning or not; having ears to hear but not sense enough to judge. These considerations made me speak with little concern the first time, with less the second, and with none at all the third. I gave myself no farther trouble about any thing, except my elocution and my style; presuming without much vanity that I had common sense sufficient not to talk nonsense. *Ib.* p. 435.

will become a Demosthenes, nor every actor a Roscius; yet will it be admitted to be of no small advantage to have duly studied the institutes of eloquence, and to hold up to view for imitation the great models of perfection.[9] And although neither true grace nor consummate eloquence can be acquired by those who are totally deficient in natural qualifications, yet they to whom nature has not denied some portion of talents and dispositions may improve in both, precisely according to the degree of their application: and these last constitute a considerable proportion of the well educated amongst men. Supposing then that there are no impediments of unconquerable obstinacy to be encountered, it may be of use to the public speaker to consider the principal constituents, in which grace consists, that he may labour for their acquisition; and also to mention the principal points in which it is violated, in order that he may guard against faults.

The grace of oratorical action consists chiefly in the facility, the freedom, the variety, and the simplicity of those gestures which illustrate the discourse. Graceful position precedes

---

[9] Whatever may be said at Paris of my speech upon the bill for the reformation of the present calendar, or whatever applause it may have met with here, the whole, I can assure you, is owing to the words, and to the delivery, but by no means to the matter; which, as I told you in a former letter, I was not master of. I mention this again to shew you the importance of well chosen words, harmonious periods, and good delivery; for, between you and me, Lord Macclesfield's speech was, in truth, worth a thousand of mine. It will soon be printed, and I will send it you. It is very instructive. *Chesterfield's Letters, p.* 315.

Nothing can be more candid!

graceful action; of this something has been already said in the chapter on the positions of the feet.

Graceful action must be performed with facility, because the appearance of great efforts is incompatible with ease, which is one constituent part of grace. A man of great corpulency cannot bend downwards without extreme difficulty, nor run without labouring; whilst the bow of a light figure may be both profound and graceful, and in running, the facility of his motion may almost compare with the gracefulness of the flight of some birds. Since much of the facility of action consists in the due proportions of length, in the different parts of the form, those whose arms and necks are short and thick, must be void of grace; whilst the motions of those, whose limbs are long, and whose neck is well proportioned, and well set on, are generally graceful, as well from the apparent ease, with which they are performed, as from the ample space through which they pass. The motions of the former are short, unmarked, and round; of the latter the motions are flowing, decided, and distinct.

Freedom is also necessary to gracefulness of action. No gestures can be graceful, which, are either confined by external circumstances, or restrained by the mind. If a man were obliged to address an assembly from a narrow window, through which he could not extend his arms and his head, it would be in vain for him to attempt graceful gesture. Confinement in every lesser degree must be proportionably injurious to grace; thus the crowded bar is injurious to the action of the advocate, and the enclosed and bolstered pulpit, which often cuts off more than

half of his figure, is equally injurious to the graceful action of
the preacher. The gracefulness of action will also be prevented,
if the speaker actually suffer from the pain of a wound, or from
chronic pains, which disable him from raising his arms or
moving his legs, or bending his body. The sentiments which
he delivers may derive considerable interest from their solidity
and soundness, and from other circumstances, but cannot
borrow any recommendation from the manner, since grace, the
most powerful of all external additions to oratory, must be
wanting, where every motion must indicate restraint and pain.
But not only they, who labour under present indisposition or
injury, are disqualified from graceful rhetorical action; they
are also to be included in this disqualification who have been
in the smallest degree injured or mutilated; whose muscles
have been deranged by any permanent contraction, or who
have suffered even the loss of a finger; and so on in proportion
to the greatness of the injury. And it may be said almost
without a figure, that the sacrifices to the Graces must consist of offerings, perfect and free from b lemish. The reason is
evident. The action of the limbs can seldom be considered
to originate from, and be referred solely to, their own immediate muscles. The most energetic actions of the arm arise
from the muscles of the body, and the connection of the lower
limbs with the trunk, is equally strict and important."[10] In the
soundness and vigour of health the muscles which are brought

---

[10] Latera cum gestu consentiant. Facit enim aliquid, et totius corporis motus : adeo
ut Cicero plus illo agi, quam manibus ipsis putet. Ita enim dicit in Oratore, Nullæ
argutiæ digitorum, non ad numerum articulus cadens, *trunco magis toto se ipse moderans,
et virili laterum flexione.* Quint B, 1025. et Cic. Orat. Cap. 18.

into action, influence involuntarily all the others connected with their motions. But if any, even the smallest of these, have suffered injury or feel pain, a consciousness seems to be imparted to the muscle originating the motion, so that it sympathetically checks its own action, lest it should distress the morbid sensibility of its associates. Rigidity or mutilation causes more laborious action of the muscle, which is deprived of its associates. Such labour or even interruption without reference to the matter of the discourse, is incompatible with grace. But if, in public speaking, the gesture should be suddenly arrested from surprise or any similar feeling, the effect may even be graceful, and will be altogether different from that which arises from bodily pain or infirmity.

Art may, however, conceal imperfections for a time, if they are not of considerable magnitude; and it may happen that gesture may be graceful, where the injured part is not called into action. Thus if the injury should be only in the lower limbs, as the arms and hands are the principal instruments of the orator, it may continue in a great measure unperceived, so long as he has not occasion to change the position of the feet; or if he deliver his oration sitting, as a judge does his charge to the jury.

This precept of Quintilian, " that the gesture of the arms shall accord with the motions of the body," is worthy of attention. And Cicero's, " manly inflexion of the sides," which Quintilian says he laid more stress upon, than upon the gestures of the hands themselves, appears to be supported by the observation of the important muscles of the trunk, which govern the motions of the arms. Without due attention to the easy bending of the trunk, the action of an orator would not be different from the rigid absurdity of a puppets motions; and if carried into extreme, it would be unsuitable to the decorum of oratorical action, and degenerate into the gesticulations and the contortions of the common pantomine.

But the restraint arising from timidity of mind, or bashfulness, is equally prejudicial to grace: it has, however, this advantage, that it may be effectually corrected by perseverance;
it is usually the fault of youth and inexperience. The effect
of timidity is to check the action of those muscles, which
should consent and harmonize in the gesture. The arms
cling to the sides, and abridge the gesture, or when the gesture,
by a manifest effort, is sufficiently extended, it is precipitately
retracted, the head sinks between the shoulders and droops
forwards, the knees bend, and there appears in the figure a
mixture at once of rigidity and relaxation; and innumerable
muscles are apparently set at variance, some being relaxed, which
ought to be braced; and others rigid, which ought to be perfectly
at rest. The action of the arm is shortened, the preparations are
retrenched, they become feeble, frigid, and as it were convulsed.
In the dance, plate II. of Hogarth's Analysis of Beauty, the young
lady in the second couple is a good illustration of this restraint
of awkward bashfulness: the little man her partner is ungraceful
from a very different cause. He appears to be ungraceful from
presumption and vulgarity, which are generally hopeless and
incurable. And although timidity may often fall short of grace,
presumption is not the proper corrective for it; but judicious
precepts followed by practice and by a just confidence in its own
powers. Modesty and even timidity in the exordium of an oration
are decorous and prepossessing in the highest degree; but as he
advances, the speaker may with great propriety change them into
a just and manly confidence in the truth and reasonableness of
his own sentiments, which he desires to impress on his hearers.
Such a feeling will divest him of false timidity, and give to his

manner a boldness, an energy and grace, which are at once most becoming to the truth, and the most persuasive characters of eloquence.

For the maintenance of grace in rhetorical action, variety is also indispensable. The iteration of the same gesture or set of gestures, however graceful in themselves, betrays a poverty of resources, which is altogether prejudicial to the speaker. They have an effect even worse than monotony of tones, which may be pardoned as arising from natural deficiency, but a fine gesture or two can be assumed only for ornament, and may be repeated to disgust.

But simplicity and truth of manner, if not constituting grace in themselves, are inseparable from it. The gesture must appear to be used only for the better supporting the sentiments of the mind, and for no other purpose. Gestures which are manifestly contrived for the mere display of the person, or for the exhibition of some foppery, as a fine ring, instantly offend. Fine gestures are to be used only, when the mind is elevated and the sentiments magnificent, and energetic gestures, when it is ardent and earnest. Attitudes are not permitted to the orator, and rarely even to the actor, except in the extremes of passion, as when he is petrified with horror. But as all his subject is known to the orator beforehand, so he cannot be surprised into any thing of this kind.

To simplicity of gesture is opposed affectation, that falsehood of action, which destroys every pretension to genuine grace. The more shewy and fine the gestures are, unless they belong indispensably to the subject, to the affection of the mind, and to the character of the speaker, the more do they offend the judicious by their manifest affectation. When the profligate speaks of piety, the miser of generosity, and the coward of valour, and the corrupt of integrity, they are only the more despised by those who know them. To these faults of character, the faults of manner are analogous and almost equally disgusting. If dignity be assumed where none is found in the sentiment, pathos without any thing interesting, vehemence in trifles, and solemnity upon common place ; such affectation may impose on the ignorant, but makes " the judicious grieve." Simplicity, which constitutes the true grace in manners and in dress, should equally be observed in the action of an orator. Early good instructions with constant practice and imitation of the best models will establish habits of graceful action : in the same manner as the personal accomplishments, however, at first, the cause of constraint, become, after sufficient exercise, easy and agreeable; and distinguish, in all their motions and manners, those who have been cultivated, from the awkward and affected vulgar. It is an observation founded in fact, that the action of young children is never deficient in grace ; for which two reasons may be assigned : first, because they are under no restraint from diffidence or from any other cause, and therefore use their gestures with all sincerity of heart only to aid the expression of their thoughts : and next, because they have as yet few ideas of imitation, and so are not deprived of the graces of nature by affectation, nor perverted by bad models.

The grace of action, according to Hogarth, in his ingenious

Analysis of Beauty, consists in moving the body and limbs in that curve which he names the line of beauty. When action is considered independant of language and sentiment, his observation will perhaps be found generally correct. But rhetorical action, which is intimately concerned in these circumstances, derives its grace not only from the actual motions of the speaker, but also very much from the congruity of his motions with the sentiments which he delivers. They must accord with them in every character, and vary according to all the different situations as well as sentiments, not only of the same person, but of different persons. The dignity and sobriety of deportment, which is becoming grace in a judge, would be quaint affectation in a young barrister. And the graceful, but colloquial familiarity of action, even of the court, would be highly indecorous in the pulpit. So that it will be allowed, according to the very just maxim of Cicero and Quintilian, that decorum constitutes true oratorical grace. And accordingly this decorum admits great variety, and allows great scope for the action of the orator under different circumstances. Vehement action is sometimes both decorous and graceful, but outrageous extravagance can never be allowable. Abrupt and short and dry action, if it bear the impression of truth, will so far be decorous, and have a grace of suitableness. Such are the gestures of an old man when he is irritated. But the most flowing and beautiful motions, the grandest preparations, and the finest transitions of gesture ill applied and out of time, lose their natural character of grace, and become indecorous, ridiculous, or offensive. The observations of Quintilian, conceived in such good taste, and delivered with such correct judgment at the conclusion of his discourse on gesture, will properly close this subject.

" One observation more is to be added; that as decorum is
" principally to be attended to in gesture, so a different style will
" often become different speakers. There is some latent and
" inexplicable reason for this : and as it has been truly observed
" that the summit of art consists in this, that your action should
" become your character; so neither can that decorum be
" acquired without the assistance of art, nor yet be altogether
" delivered by the rules of art. In some persons, absolute
" perfections are void of grace, whilst in others their very
" faults afford delight . . . . . . Let every one therefore make
" himself acquainted with his own talents, and adopt the plan
" of forming his action, rather according to the nature of his
" own peculiar powers, than merely according to the usual
" precepts. It is not indeed impossible that every kind of
" action, or at least a great variety may be gracefully performed
" by some persons : but let the conclusion on this subject be
" the same as it should be on others, that above all the most
" necessary rule is moderation. For it is not an actor whom
" I wish to form, but an orator. Therefore in gesture, let us
" not pursue every affectation; nor in speaking use too many
" discriminations, pauses, or emphasis, as if we were acting a
" part in a play like this : What then shall I do ? shall I go ? or
" shall I even refuse her, now when she invites me herself? or
" shall I not rather so govern my passion, that I may no longer
" suffer the insolence of a wanton ?—For here the actor will
" express the delays of doubt, the inflexions of the voice,
" and variety of gestures, and different motions of the head.
" An oration has another character, it must not be too highly
" seasoned. For this reason the delivery is justly condemned as

" vicious, which is deformed by grimace, which offends by
" gesticulations, and breaks unequally by affected changes
" of the voice . . . . . . We must regulate our gesture, in
" this manner ; lest, whilst we aim at the graces of the player,
" we should lose the dignity of the grave and respectable
" man."[1]

---

[1] Unum jam his adjiciendum est, cum præcipue in actione spectetur decorum, spe aliud alios decere. Est enim latens quædam in hoc ratio et inenarrabilis : et ut vere hoc dictum est, caput esse artis, decere quod facias : ita id neque sine arte esse, neque totum arte tradi potest. In quibusdam virtutes non habent gratiam, in quibusdam vitia ipsa delectant. . . . . *Quare norit se quisque, nec tantum ex communibus præceptis, sed etiam ex natura sua capiat consilium formandæ actionis.* Neque illud tamen est nefas, ut aliquem vel omnia vel plura deceant. Hujus quoque loci clausula sit eadem, necesse est, quæ cæterorum est, regnare maxime modum. Non enim comœdum esse, sed oratorem volo. Quare neque in gestu persequemur omnes argutias, nec in loquendo distinctionibus, temporibus, affectionibus moleste utemur : ut si sit in scena dicendum,

> Quid igitur faciam ? non eam, ne nunc quidem
> Cum accersor ultro ? an potius ita me comparem,
> Non perpeti meretricium contumelias ?

Hic enim dubitationis moras, vocis flexus, varias manus, diversos nutus actor adhibebit. Aliud oratio sapit, nec vult nimium esse condita. Quare non immerito reprehenditur pronunciatio vultuosa et gesticulationibus molesta et vocis mutationibus resultans. . . . . . . ita tamen temperanda (est actio) ne, dum actoris captamus elegantiam, perdamus viri boni et gravis auctoritatem. *Quint. l. xi. ad finem.*

CHAPTER XXIII.

ILLUSTRATIONS.

Observations on the gesture suited to the recitation of descriptive poetry —Part of Gray's Elegy in a country churchyard with the notation. Observations on it—The speech of Brutus on the death of Cæsar with the notation—Observations—Passage from Young's Night Thoughts with the notation—Observations—Additions to the synoptical table.

CHAPTER XXIII.

Illustrations.

However fully the method of notation of gesture has been already explained in detail, as it may possibly be rendered still more intelligible by additional illustrations, I here present the reader with three pieces of different characters noted in *one* manner in which they may be recited or delivered: and have annexed observations at large upon every passage which appears to require explanation.

In order to render every circumstance the more clearly intelligible, I have marked the notation more minutely, than necessary for general use. For general use it is sufficient to note the most prominent and important circumstances, leaving the filling up to the judgment of the speaker, and even to accident; which method, whilst it furnishes, as it were, certain landmarks, and supplies confidence, gives also the character of greater freedom to the speaker. The teachers of music proceed somewhat in the same manner. At the beginning of their lessons they write down every most minute particular, and mark the fingering of every note; but as the scholar advances, they pass over what is obvious, and mark the difficult passages only, and when he is far advanced, they supply only the more brilliant ornaments and cadenzas. In the use of our species of notation, we may proceed through similar gradations; and I hope on this account my diligence in the explanation of the first rudiments of a new art will not be thought too minute and tedious.

I have chosen to illustrate this art, first by a simple fable, aided both by engraved figures and notation. A descriptive poem, such as that which here follows, appears to be the next exercise in progressive facility: because the delineations of natural description suggest a variety of gestures, the propriety of which is easily conceived. And I have chosen a serious poem of this kind, because the changes of gesture are made slowly, and are therefore more suitable for practice and experiment.

In the recitation of descriptions of any kind, the speaker must, in imagination, have the picture placed before his eyes, and each object must be disposed in the same order, as if actually painted. If this imaginary picture in the speaker's mind be faulty in the composition, confused, or ill grouped, his gesture will confound rather than illustrate; but if it be well conceived, and well disposed in all its parts, the speaker will seem to give it the interests of life by his skilful gesture and recitation; and the imagination of the hearer will be charmed and enlightened, so that he will seem almost actually to contemplate all that the speaker describes.

Impassioned compositions delivered with proper feeling and expression open in like manner to the view of the hearer the internal operations of the speaker's mind, a contemplation still more interesting than any scenes of external nature which can be presented in description.

If upon trial and consideration, the gestures marked on any of the following pieces should appear too numerous, they may be omitted; or if they appear in any instances incorrect, they may be altered at pleasure.

As in writing, even an appropriate term must not be used too frequently, so in this art, the same gesture, however expressive, must not be too often repeated. Variety is graceful, and requires that both similar words and similar gestures should be separated by those which are diverse.

In action it is a general rule that each new idea requires a new gesture. But important ideas only require distinguished gesture. For these last, therefore, should be reserved the species of gestures named *emphatical;* for the former, which are the most numerous, the *discriminating* will be sufficient. As to frequency, the propriety of gesture will be found to depend on the deliberation and expression of the feelings of the speaker. If the feelings are not alive, and if the lines are not delivered with due deliberation, the gestures will appear too numerous and overcharged in all cases. In the following illustrations they may seem also to have this fault from this circumstance, that it is the object here to exhibit at large the greater part of their minute connections and transitions. A little attention however will shew that much has been still left to be supplied by the judgment of the reader.

An Elegy written in a Country Church Yard.

GRAY.

I.

Ls   veq—vhx   a————B pef——,——d

The curfew tolls the knell of parting day,
    aR2

F   phf— . . . . . q x

The lowing herd winds slowly o'er the lea,
    rR1

. . . . . —phf————————q   B veq

The ploughman homeward plods his weary way,
    V   B nef————————d————B.R

And leaves the world to darkness and to me.

II.

R   B phc————————————q———————————x

Now fades the glimmering landscape on the sight,
      Bvef——————————q

And all the air a solemn stillness holds,
      iec———————————q

Save where the beetle wheels his drony flight,
        phf p—   R

And drowsy tinklings lull the distant folds;
       aR2

III.

     —ieq n

Save that from yonder ivy mantl'd tow'r,
    R 1

     —veq   U   —seb

The moping owl does to the moon complain
        rL1

       —shq

Of such, as wand'ring near her secret bow'r,

     —veq————p

Molest her ancient solitary reign.

IV.

shf n . . . . . .—shf n
Beneath those rugged elms, that yew-tree's shade,

Bbdf a————— —————vhf
Where heaves the turf in many a mould'ring heap,

D   a ———B nef sp————
Each in his narrow cell for ever laid,

F   B phf————— ——d ——B.R
The rude fore-fathers of the hamlet sleep.

V.

shf—   veq w
The breezy call of incense breathing morn,

rR1
ieq————a—————————n
The swallow twitt'ring from the straw-built shed,

idq——   veq w——
The cocks shrill clarion, or the echoing horn,

a—————B nef sp   B sdf d
Nor more shall rouze them from their lowly bed.

       aR2

VI.

shf n——
For them no more the blazing hearth shall burn,

rR1
      vhf——
Or busy housewife ply her ev'ning care;

B shf p
No children run to lisp their sire's return

aR2
B nef a   D   F   B shf n
Or climb his knees, the envied kiss to share.

      rR1

VII.

phc—————————q
Oft did the harvest to their sickle yield,

sdf st
Their furrow oft the stubborn glebe has broke;

sec sw——————————————phq sp
How jocund did they drive their team a field!

ceb bn—————————chf st
How bow'd the woods beneath their sturdy stroke!

VIII.

ief———————ihf n—
Let not ambition mock their useful toil,
rL1

pef————pdf d—
Their homely joys, and destiny obscure;

oec——————————q rj
Nor grandeur hear with a disdainful smile,
rR1

a———— vef————d —— R
The short and simple annals of the poor.

IX.

vef sp—   ief fl—
The boast of heraldry, the pomp of pow'r,
aR2

B shf p———————q
And all that beauty, all that wealth e'er gave,

B vhq sh
Await, alike, th' inevitable hour;
rR1

a———vef——a————d   sdq n R‖
The paths of glory lead but to the grave.‖
aR2

X.

B phc————q   a————shf n—
Nor you, ye proud, impute to these the fault,
rL1

veq w
If mem'ry o'er their tomb no trophies raise
L2

vhf p—   sec————q
Where thro' the long-drawn aisle and fretted vault,

a———B nef—— a————d————B.R
The pealing anthem swells the note of praise.

XI.

ihf— . . ; . . . . . . —vhq n
Can storied urn, or animated bust,
rR1

i————BL tc——————oq
Back to its mansion call the fleeting breath?

a———————veq————d   sdf—R
Can honour's voice provoke the silent dust,
aR2

B shf sh   a——vef————vdf p
Or flatt'ry sooth the dull cold ear of death?

XII.

idf———n
Perhaps in this neglected spot is laid
rR1
          br—R   veq w—
Some heart once pregnant with celestial fire:
B nef———————————————B shf st
Hands, that the rod of empire might have sway'd,
              pec sw———————————veq sw
Or wak'd to ecstasy the living lyre

XIII.

            shf d————q
But knowledge to their eyes her ample page,
          phc——————————   x
Rich with the spoils of time, did n'er unroll;
      B vhf rt ———· rp   ——————q
Chill penury repress'd their noble rage,
      B vhq c   B nhf p   B.br.
And froze the genial current of the soul.

XIV.

          ihf—
Full many a gem, of purest ray, serene,
      a·———B pdf d   ——————q
The dark unfathom'd caves of ocean bear;
          aR2
                shq—p
Full many a flow'r is born to blush unseen,
      phc——————q——————x
And waste its sweetness on the desart air.

XV.

          vef—   br—R
Some village Hampden, that with dauntless breast
          rL1
      ihf—   veq w
The little tyrant of his fields withstood,
          a———B nef———d————B sdf
Some mute inglorious Milton here may rest;
              aR2
      B vhf rt———p   A   B vhc———x
Some Cromwell guiltless of his country's blood.
      rR1

XVI.

B shf p————————q————————x
Th' applause of list'ning senates to command,

phf p————a   a————vef—rj
The threats of pain and ruin to despise,

Bphc——q   ————————Bvhx sp
To scatter plenty o'er a smiling land,

B shc————————q————————x
And read their history in a nation's eyes;

XVII.

phf st— R | phc————————q—
Their lot forbad : | nor circumscrib'd alone

————————————— x   Bvhf rt
Their growing virtues, but their crimes confined;

B bdf ad————————— vhf————————eb
Forbad to wade through slaughter to a throne,

B vhf p ————————a————d—BR.
And shut the gates of mercy on mankind.

* *

ANALYTICAL OBSERVATIONS ON THE NOTATION OF PART OF GRAY'S ELEGY.

STANZA I.

The unavoidable repetitions in these explanations will be excused.

L. 1. Ls. listening. See complex significant gestures. In this action the eyes are turned first towards the direction from whence the sound proceeds, and the hand is presented vertical in the same direction; but the eye quickly discovers its own insufficiency, and then the ear, the proper organ, is turned towards the sound, whilst the eyes are bent on vacancy, the hand remaining as before. The body leans forwards more or less according to the earnestness of the attention. The attitude is expressed by the notation *veq—vhx*, which shews the position of both hands. a.R2 shews the action of the feet.

" Knell," the small *a* over this word is connected with the set of letters *B pef* over " parting," and the small *d* is also connected with the same set. Each is considered a 4th small letter separated from its set, the first *a* is the preparation, and the last *d* the termination of the motion of the gesture.

In the second line, the set of letters relates to the right hand, which finishes its action at *x* and falls slowly to rest. In the third line, the left hand takes up the principal gesture for a short space. This is called *alternate* gesture, and is distinguished by forming the connecting line of dots. Both hands unite their action on " weary."

Line 4. V. The eyes bent on vacancy.

STANZA II.

" Now fades," l. 1. The several gestures which are connected together by long dashes are to be considered as the flowing variation of continued motion, till either one or both hands fall to rest. Gestures connected thus, may be named *continuous;* they are generally of that kind which are called *discriminating.* See Chapter XVII. p. 390.

The position on " fades," *B phc* is the preparation for sweeping round the horizon. The head and eyes are to begin (as marked by R at the beginning of the line) to turn towards either extreme; (towards the right or left,) whilst the hands proceed to the position noted *B phc*. Whilst the arms move from this to the different positions *q* and *x*, the head and eyes rather precede their action. If the right hand perform the principal action, the head follows its motion and turns from left to right; if the left, the contrary. The long dashes, as usual, connect the positions with the preceding set of letters: and the words, on which *q* and *x* are respectively noted, shew where those positions are to take place. That is the gestures are not to take place considerably before, or considerably after those words are pronounced. A trial will prove, that such ill-timed gesture would be attended with a very bad effect.

Line **3**. The left hand drops here, and the index of the right is prepared to point across. The eye is to follow the object, at which the finger seems to point, a little above the finger and at a small distance; as at a beetle which may be supposed to be seen to fly.

Line 4. The preparation for the *manner of motion* marked *p, pushing*, is always *retracting*, and that with energy in propor-tion to the sentiment. The notation of this word *retracting, rt,* ought to have been marked in the synoptical table among the expressions named manner of motion. The reader can insert it with a pen. He will find this and a few other omissions mentioned at the end of this chapter. This preparation would be *vef rt*, and would fall on the word " lull." The hand is gradually with-drawn from the position in the third line, and then pushed for-wards on the word " distant," as noted. But all this is omitted, as it is easily understood that in order to make the motion marked on " distant," it is necessary to withdraw the hand a convenient space. See the chapter on the preparation of gesture.

STANZA III.

Line 1. In order to vary the gestures, and the better to distribute the objects in the picture, the " tower" is here supposed to be placed on the left side, and the left hand assumes the principal gesture: this is indicated in the notation by the short dash which precedes the set of letters.

Line 2. " moon." The eyes look upwards at the moon, as if high in the heavens, the hand which was *vertical* in the former gesture, by throwing back the arm becomes *supine.*

Line 4. " Ancient, solitary." Substantives may be considered as the outlines or images of things, adjectives as the colouring or circumstances added to those images, or limitations deducting something from them. In poetical language they are called epithets. Gray has indulged in the use of them perhaps to a fault. But however that may be, whenever they occur they almost constantly rob the principal image or substantive of its emphatical distinction, and claim it to themselves; perhaps because the circumstances alone give individuality to the image which in itself is a general term. For these reasons the action or gesture also falls rather on the epithet, and if two epithets or more are added to the same image, each must be distinctly marked both by emphasis and by action: if so pronounced, they serve to illustrate the idea; but if they are hurried over, they cause only confusion. Therefore the words " ancient solitary reign" require two gestures, one on each epithet; but in order to avoid affectation, the transition should be the easiest possible; and this will be, when, as in this case, the gesture on the preceding word is made the preparation for that on the subsequent. When two epithets are applied to a name, the latter should be the stronger, and in this view also it is proper to reserve the emphatical gesture for it, as the principal.

Stanza iv.

Line 1. " Elms." The right hand again resumes the principal gesture. It is here alternate or auxiliary, as appears from the dotted line of connection.

Line 2. " Heaves," the backs of the hands are presented forwards, the hands hanging down, and in the action they ascend gradually towards *vertical elevated* on the word " mouldring."

Line 3. " Each in his narrow cell for ever laid," the arms gradually ascend to the highest point on the word " ever," and then in the same manner descend to rest on the word " sleep," making in their progress a momentary arrestation on " forefathers." It seems to be an incongruity to raise the arms in speaking of the grave, which is below ; but this is removed by the downward inclination of the head, and look of the eyes, as noted; and is not an uncommon action in looking into any thing dreadful below. This is also the preparation for the following gesture, which requires the arms to fall to rest. From the 3d line to the end of the stanza the gestures are continuous.

Stanza v.

Line 1. " Breathing," the *graceful wave* is here marked.

The *wave* may be considered of three kinds; the *graceful,* as here; the wave of triumph, and in a lesser degree, of joy ; and the wave of scorn or contempt. The subject will always sufficiently determine the character to be adopted, though the notation is the same for all.

Line 2. " Swallow," the index is raised to point at the object; at *a* over " twittering" it ascends to the highest, or is retracted so as almost to touch the head, and then on the word " straw-built" it makes the action of *noting*.

Line 3. " Echoing," the joyful *wave* approaching to triumph; the voice should here mark the *crescendo*, which will be contrasted with the gravity of the following line.

Line 4. " Rouse," *sp* the 4th and 5th small letters in this notation mean *springing*. In order to execute this action, the arms begin to ascend from " more," and having arrived near the word " rouse" the wrists make on it the *stroke* of the gesture by springing backwards and upwards. See this action described in its place.

STANZA VI.

Line 4. " Climb," a suspended gesture preparatory to that on " kiss." The eyes look downwards on " climb," and forwards on the next gesture. The points of the fingers approach the mouth a little on " kiss," and then the hands are advanced *supine noting*.

Line 2. " Stubborn," the preparation for this gesture is *neq rt* which would fall on " oft," but is here omitted as taking place of course when the gesture marked on " stubborn" is executed. It will be observed that several emphatical gestures imply a proper suspended or preparatory gesture, and reciprocally the latter the former. Thus when a *stroke* is required to be made, the arm must of course be raised, therefore *shf st*— must necessarily imply *nef bn—inwards, elevated, forwards, bended* as nearly expressed Fig. 95,—*veq w*—implies *bhf a— backwards, horizontal, forwards, ascending*, as may be seen in the dotted lines of Fig. 91. And *vhx rj*—implies *vhx rt*— as expressed the first, in Fig. 101, and the second Fig. 100. In the notation the preparatory gestures are often omitted when they are not required to mark a preceding less emphatical word : in which case they are prepared with less decision, and their *stroke* is softened. If the suspended or preparatory gesture be used as the principal, which it sometimes is, as in terror, where the arms are retracted violently, and in surprise, where they are elevated forcibly, the subsequent gesture is also softened, and the emphasis of its stroke is remitted.

Line 3. " Jocund," this *sweep* is nearly the same as that described by Quintilian, and represented Fig. 55.

Line 4. " Woods," this preparation might possibly have been omitted, if the word " woods" should not be pronounced with strong emphasis.

STANZA VIII.

Line 1. " Ambition," the first gestures in the three first lines of this stanza are the *preparatory* of the decided kind, and the last in each *emphatical*. As all the words, which are noted, are important, they all require the enforcement of gesture ; and the connection of suspended or preparatory and emphatical gestures renders the transitions easy and unaffected.

Line 2. " Destiny;" this substantive here placed before its adjective or epithet may obtain both the emphasis and action. They might also be reserved for the epithet " obscure."

Line 4. " Short and simple;" the first epithet is distinguished by a slight *discriminating* gesture produced by a small change in the elevation of the arm and hand as marked *a*. This is made the commencement of the gesture *vef*—which is completed by a suspended gesture on " simple," the second epithet, and which descends to *rest* on the word " poor," with an emphatical and terminating gesture.

Stanza IX.

Line 1. " Power;" the *flourish* is here marked. The flourish as expressed Fig. 92. is performed principally by the wrist. In order to execute this action, the hand with the index is dropped down, a little above the head, nearly at right angles to the fore arm, and is then flung forcibly upwards and sweeps round as marked by the dotted line in the figure. To advance boldly indicates confidence, pride, &c. to advance slowly, on the contrary, implies solemnity, grief, resignation. The notation is the same in either case, as the sentiments sufficiently shew in what manner the speaker should advance. Of the former, bold advance, an instance is observed on the word " power" in this line. Of the latter, slow advance, an instance is seen on the word " grave," in the last line.

Line 3. " Inevitable," *sh* shaking. The shake is not to be made by frequent tremulous motions, lest it appears ridiculous:

it is sufficient that the hand should move twice suddenly backwards and forwards.

Line 4. " Glory;" the gestures in this line are continuous. The first *a* is a discriminating gesture leading to the suspended gesture on " glory." The second *a* is the preparation for that which descends *d* to " grave," on which falls the emphatical and terminating gesture. The advance, noted in this line *aR2*, for the step, combines with the descending arms, and aids in look-ing resignedly down. But it might be also *rR*1 or *rL*1 which would express terror or alarm. I prefer the former as marked. The double perpendicular stroke is a long pause, or the end of a paragraph.

Sanza x.

The observations made on the former part of the last line of the foregoing stanza will apply to the last line of this.

Stanza xi.

To the *fourth* and *fifth* small letters in the synoptical table, at *manner of motion* should be added *i.* inwards, and *o.* out-wards.

Line 2. " Back," *i.* inwards. Both hands the palms inwards, and moving inwards, so that at " mansion" both nearly touch the lips, as noted; they then move outwards to the position *oblique* on the word " fleeting."

Stanza xii.

Line 3. " Hands," a suspended gesture, and the preparation

for the subsequent. It might have been omitted as necessarily implied; were it not thought proper to mark hands with some force; which word obtains thus, the distinction of gesture, without extravagance or unnecessary waste of gesture. If this preparatory gesture was not marked, the hands would gradually and imperceptibly ascend to " rod," and then make the stroke on " empire," which would be feeble, and if noted at large, would be thus. See observations on Stanza VII.

B shf sh
Hands that the rod of empire might have sway'd

L. 4. " ecstasy ;" the double *sweep* first inwards and then outwards.

STANZA XIII.

L. 3. " penury," the gesture here marked is *suspended*, its 4th and 5th letters, *rp*, which express the manner of motion, being separated in order to place them over their proper syllable. The notation at large would be thus,

B vhf rt   B vhf rp
Chill penury repress'd

the first *retracting* the last *repressing;* but this is understood, L. 4. " froze," the *fourth* small letter *c* contracted. The notation on " current" serves as a preparation for placing the hands on the breast. This notation *B nhf p* begins to advance on " genial," and stretches out both arms with some force *p projecting* on " current."

STANZA XIV.

L. 3. " flow'r," on this word might be marked *shf rt* as the preparation for the gesture on " blush," but the word not requiring a strong emphasis it is omitted in the notation ; however, it is implied. See obs. on Stanza VII.

3 Z

STANZA XV.

Line *3*. " Milton," continuous gestures.

L. *4* " country's," when, from the transverse position *c*, the arms move directly to *x*, without noting the immediate position *q*, as here, on "country's blood," the motion is understood to be rapid and decided, expressing vehemence or horror.

STANZA XVI.

L. *2*. " threats" *phf p* projecting. The gestures necessary to be marked on this line are four : of which the second on " pain" and the third on " ruin," are made by the momentary arrestation of the hand at the different points of its ascent, to *vef* on the first syllable of " despise," *rj, rejecting*, on the last syllable finishes the whole with the emphatical stroke. Thus sufficient discrimination is made simply without falling into quaintness of gesture, or affectation. These small *discriminating* gestures produced, by slight arrestations of motion, and often by merely turning the position of the hand, are more frequent, and more important to the orator, than the more shewy gestures, and should be particularly attended to.

STANZA XVII.

The two last lines have each a series of continuous gestures. From this analysis and notation it will be observed that the *discriminating* gestures are principally requisite for the reciting of this poem. The *suspended* are frequent, and the *emphatical* also occur often; but these last seldom require to be strongly marked, as the general character of the sentiments is calm and tender. Of *significant* gestures there are very few. The first marked *Ls, listening,* over " curfew" is of this class, and perhaps a few others may also be reckoned to belong to it, as when the hand is laid on the breast ; but there are not many more.

As these gestures may be varied, it may be said, infinitely, so there can be no fixed standard, as to the manner of delivering this or any other poem or oration, which should be considered exclusively appropriate. The sentiments require indeed to be delivered with suitable tones of voice, and expression of coun-tenance ; but great variety of gesture may consist with propriety, provided general rules are not violated : as, that decorum and simplicity be observed, that the transitions, connections, the time of, and precision in the stroke of the gesture be attended to, and other obvious precautions of general import already sufficiently detailed. The notation will accommodate itself to every variety in the speaker's manner, and this must prove a recommendation to its use.

THE SPEECH OF BRUTUS ON THE DEATH OF CÆSAR.

Julius Cæsar, Act 3. S. 2.

p. 392 393.

B shf p ———— q ———— vex sp   B nef ———— B shf st
Romans, countrymen, and lovers ! hear me for my cause;
a R 2   r R 1

pef—phx   phf st—R   B shf p—   br—R
and be silent that you may hear: believe me for mine honour ;
a R 2

br. pr.—veq sp   B shf n
and have respect unto mine honour, that you may believe :

D Bpef   B nhx   B vef sp
censure me in your wisdom; and awake your senses, that you
r R 1

B shf n   B she ————x ————
may the better judge. ‖ If there be any in this assembly, any
a R 2

sdf d   vef sp—   br—R

dear friend of Cæsar's, to him I say, that Brutus' love to Cæsar

r R 1

shf st   ief —— n—   veq—

was no less than his. If then that friend demand, why Brutus

B shf p ———————q

rose against Cæsar, this is my answer,—Not that I loved

nef— shf st—   B veq w.   shf p—

Cæsar less, but that I loved Rome more. Had you rather

peq sp—   phf st—

Cæsar were living, and die all slaves; than that Cæsar were

B shf st   B nhx   r L 1   sef—   E—R

dead, and live all freemen. ‖ As Cæsar loved me, I weep for

a R 2   r L 1

veq w—   br—   veq—vhq

him; as he was fortunate, I rejoice at it: as he was valiant, I

B sdf d   cef—   chf st—   D

honour him: but as he was ambitious, I slew him: There are

L 2   a R 2

B nef   shf d U br—R   veq w—   D B pef   B veq sp—

tears for his love; joy for his fortune; honour for his valour;

r R i

ceb—   chf sh—— B R ‖ shf ———————p   ohc —

and death for his ambition. ‖ Who's here so base, that would

r L 1   a R 2

—— x   rj   pef— pdf st—   ihf rc   R—

be a bond-man? If any, speak; for him have I offended.

phc ——————————————x   shf

Who's here so rude, that would not be a Roman? If any,

r R 1

——n   vef sp—   B vhf p

speak; for him have I offended. Who's here so vile, that will

r L 1

B veq w   B shf n   A Bvhf sh

not love his country? If any, speak; for him have I offended.

B. R.   veq w—   shc sw ———

I pause for a reply. ‖ None! Then none have I offended.

a R 2

shf n—   nef   br—R

I have done no more to Cæsar, than you shall do to Brutus.

r L 1

a ——————— ihf n   a ——————— ieb n

The question of his death is enrolled in the Capitol: his glory

phf d ——————————————— q   ihf—

not extenuated, wherein he was worthy; nor his offences

vef sp—   a ——————— phf st

enforced, for which he suffered death.

B   —ihb . . . . . . shc—   F shc—shb n
Here comes his body, mourned by Mark Antony : who,
r R 1

shf—R   nef—
though he had no hand in his death, shall receive the benefit of

shf n—   B shc ——— q ———— x
his dying, a place in the commonwealth, as which of you shall
a R 2

Bnef ————B R   cef—
not? With this I depart; that, as I slew my best lover for the
r R 1   r L 1

B shf n   chf sh —   br. st — R
good of Rome, I have the same dagger for myself, when it

a ——— B pef   d ————— B. R. st
shall please my country to need my death.
r R 1

OBSERVATIONS.

Both Warburton and Steevens in their observations on this
speech condemn it as artificial, and abounding in forced antitheses. I cannot subscribe to the united opinion of these learned
commentators, but look upon it as characteristic, and manly;
and distinguished by touching boldly and briefly on the circumstances, which must be conceived to have agitated the mind of
Brutus on the occasion. It appears to me not less worthy of
its great author, than the inimitable and subtile eloquence of
Antony, with which it is evidently contrasted. At all events,
it suits my present purpose better than any other passage,
which I can recollect. I have introduced this speech, and
noted it for the purpose of supporting what I have advanced,
page 393, which is, that the gestures necessary for delivering it
in the true spirit, are those principally, which I have named
suspended and *emphatical :* an inspection of the notation will
make this evident; for even although the reader may wish to
alter many particular gestures, which are here noted, he must

change them for others of the same nature, if he would preserve
the character of the speech.   The *suspended* and *emphatical*
gestures must still abound, and he will find little opportunity
for introducing the other descriptions, which are in general too
tame for the abrupt and vehement style of this speech. Near
the close indeed he becomes submissive, but the last sentence
ends with the same vehemence as the beginning.

" Be silent that you may hear ;" on these words I have
marked the gesture for both left and right hand, as also on the
words " have respect unto mine honour ;" this last is an auxiliary
gesture, but of the vehement kind.   The exordium of this
singular oration ends at " better judge." After which the arms
should fall to rest, and there should be a considerable pause, as
marked by the double perpendicular lines. Another division,
which may be called the proposition, takes place at " live all
freemen ;" another, the narration, at " death for his ambition."
And that which may be called the pathetic, or appeal to the
passions, finishes at, " I pause for a reply." The argument or reasoning ends at " suffered death."   And the peroration follows.

" I weep for him ;" this is noted **E—R.** the right hand on the
eyes, the left at rest.

" Him have I offended," noted on " him" *ihf rc, recoiling :*
in this action the finger is pointed suddenly and scornfully,
and is then immediately withdrawn.   See p. 344.

Frequent changes in the positions of the feet indicate anxiety,
as observed, p. 303, and are therefore noted in this speech.

" His body mourned," *auxiliary* gesture : when the right
hand is brought up on " mourned," both hands become supine ;
and on the next words, " Mark Antony, " they make the
action of *noting*. At the beginning at B, the speaker looks back ;
at F, " before Mark Antony," he looks forwards to those whom
he addresses. It would be tedious to point out all the *suspended*
gestures, succeeded immediately by the *emphatical*, for they
abound. In all the antheses, which are numerous, the *suspended*
will be found over the first member, and the *emphatical* over
the last.

The method of notation, as may be clearly seen, requires for
each gesture not more than five symbolic letters, sometimes
fewer ; and the use of these letters has a farther advantage,
which is, that each suggests an appropriate term, of which it is
either the commencing or a distinguished letter : so that the
most complicated gestures, represented by five symbolic letters,
can also be enounced in four words, or even fewer. A teacher
may therefore equally use his pen or words for conveying his
instructions : and whatsoever he delivers in this way will be
both short and precise.

Mere symbols not capable of being enounced in words, however they might suffice to convey information to the eye,
would not be attended with equal advantage, as the symbolic letters, and the language belonging to them. It is
admitted that every gesture is capable of being accurately
described in common language, but the description of any
single gesture requires a multitude of ordinary words ; so, that
such language is not convenient, and therefore seldom used,
must be allowed on the evidence of fact. Language, as is well
observed by the ingenious author of the *Epea Pteroenta*, requires

abridgment as well as expression. The language here explained is a methodical abridgment, by which those ideas, which would overflow numerous pages, are compressed within the bounds of the ordinary writing, which records the thoughts themselves.

PASSAGE FROM YOUNG'S NIGHT THOUGHTS.

U　　　　vef n　　F　　　　　　B nef
The bell s trikes one. We take no note of time
　　　　　　a R 2　　　　　　　　　　　　r R 1
———— -　　B shf st　　　　.　　U　　ief—
But from its loss. To give it then a tongue

　　shf n —　　　　　V　B phq
Is wise in man. As if an angel spoke

U　br—R　　　　　　　　　　ihf—
I feel the solemn sound. If heard aright,

———————— ief ———————— idq ——— R st
It is the knell of my departed hours.　　　　　　　　　5

R　B vhc ————q　　　　　rt ——— - B vhf p
Where are they? with the years beyond the flood.

V　　　ieq—　　　　　　phf st—
It is the signal that demands dispatch:

　　B phf x　　　　　　　　B vhq ——— a—
How much is to be done? My hopes and fears

—sp ——— ——— ——— a ——— ——— Z
Start up alarm'd, and o'er life's narrow verge
　　　　　　a R 2
D　　　　B phf st　　　B nef sp ———— ——
Look down.—On what? A fathomless abyss;　　　10
　　　　　　　　　　　r R 1
———————— B vef p———— a ———— B R st
A dread eternity! how surely mine!

　　　vef—　　　　　　br...
And can eternity belong to me,

...... — vef　　　　B nef ———— B R
Poor pensioner on the bounties of an hour?

U　　nef c — F　shf st — A　ohc — vhfc　F　B veq w
How poor, how rich; how abject, how august;

　　B vhc ———— ——— x
How complicate, how wonderful is man?　　　　15

U   a ———— B vef sp ———— d   B R
How passing wonder he who made him such?

      B tc. br. ———————— B nhx sp
Who center'd in our make such strange extremes

    B vhc ———————— q
From differing natures marvellously mix'd,

   B nef rt———————pef p ———— q
Connexion exquisite of distant worlds!

shf p ———————————— a ——— nef sp —
Distinguish'd link in being's endless chain   20

    idf n ———————— i Z —
Midway from nothing to the Deity!

   U   shf —   vhf ———— vef
A beam ethereal sully'd and absorpt:

   d ———— phf st ———— a —— vef sp — vhx
Though sully'd and dishonour'd, still divine!

  vhf c —   U   veq w —
Dim miniature of greatness absolute!

   B nef ———— d ————   B sdf n
An heir of Glory! a frail child of dust!   25

F B phf U B veq sp D idf— U veq w —
Helpless immortal! insect infinite!

idf n — U vef sp   B shf sh ————
A worm, a God! I tremble at myself,

V   B br   vef — br
And in myself am lost. At home a stranger,

U F st—R ———————— V   vef sp —......— vhx sp
Thought wanders up and down surpriz'd, aghast;

V   B vhf sh   B vec ———— x
And wondring at her own. How reason reels!   30

   vef c —   phf n —   br — R
O what a miracle to man is man!

B veq w ———— B R   vef sp —   vhf sh —
Triumphantly distress'd; what joy, what dread!

  B shf p ———— B vhf rt
Alternately transported and alarm'd.

             r R 1
  B br   B vhc ————   x
What can preserve my life, or what destroy?

4 A

<pre>
a ——— ———— nef sp —   d ——— pdf n
</pre>
An angel's arm can't snatch me from the grave   35
<pre>
B veq w ————   B nef————   B sdf st
</pre>
Legions of angels can't confine me there.

The peculiarities of Young's style, especially in his Night Thoughts, render his poetry particularly difficult for recitation. His use of epithets is faulty to excess. He heaps them profusely, and in every manner, on the principal idea. Man is here his subject, which he colours with every variety of tint, exhibits in every light, and touches and retouches almost to disgust. And yet he has produced here many sublime images; and his very faults, his labour, his antitheses, and his catachreses are the source of his beauties. This passage is particularly celebrated as an exercise in recitation, and it is particularly difficult. The difficulty arises chiefly from the multiplicity of the images, and the brevity of the expression; consequently, if the speaker is not careful to pronounce every passage with due deliberation, his gesture makes only confusion, and gives an air of mummery to his recitation. This condensation of images occurs in almost every line; but the 26th line, which consists of only four words, is remarkable. Each word contains an image contrasted with that which follows, and each consequently requires distinct and contrasted gesture:

Helpless immortal! insect infinite!

To give force and variety, and at the same time simplicity and gracefulness to gestures so heaped on each other, is attended with no inconsiderable difficulty. But even should the speaker's manner in the recitation of these lines prove unexceptionable in this respect, the difficulty is but half conquered. They do not indeed require any considerable variety of voice, but the eye and the countenance of the speaker must be full of expression and intelligence : he must appear to be rapt in meditation, which rises into sublimity as it proceeds, and inflames as it catches the rapid succession of thought. On these accounts this passage is seldom recited successfully.

After what has been already said in the analysis of the other pieces, a very few observations will suffice for this.

L. 4, " aright," continuous gesture to the end of the 5th line, where the hand falls to rest with some degree of force, marked **R. *st. Rest, striking.*** The hand generally in falling to rest drops quietly and imperceptibly by its own gravity, and it is then noted with a simple R; but sometimes the hand is struck down forcibly, and then it is noted as above, R. *st.* Homer's heroes and even his Gods, used this smiting of the thigh, when sudden and great calamity befel them. Thus when Mars hears from Juno that his favourite Ascalaphus was slain,

'Ως έφατ'. αυτάρ Άρης θαλερώ πεπλήγετο μηρώ
Χερσὶ καταπρηνέσσ', ὀλοφυρόμενος δὲ προσηύδα. *Il.* O. 113.

She spake ; and with expanded palms his thighs
Smiting, thus, sorrowful, the God exclaim'd. *Cowper.*

See notes 7 and 8 from Quintilian and Cresollius, Chap. 18.

L. 8. " How much," the x in the fourth place means that the arms are to be extended forwards eagerly,

L. 14, 15, 16, six epithets, antithesis, and climax : the voice and gesture must encrease in energy, and on " he" in the 16th line complete the climax. The first in each pair of gestures is preparatory to the subsequent in the antithesis. L. 25 to 33, Antithesis and catachreses heaped on each other, each requiring a separate gesture strongly contrasted with that to which it is opposed.

L 29. F. *st.* the hand striking the forehead.

From what has been said, the rest of the notation will be easily understood.

The notation and the analytical observations on the three foregoing pieces, together with the fable of the Miser and Plutus in the former part of the work, will, it is conceived, afford sufficient information to such as may desire to assist their rhetorical studies by this invention. The method of using the notation to the best advantage, is not, that the young speaker should note every possible passage in his discourse, in the manner of those illustrations, for such minuteness would lead to embarrassment, unless preceded by immense labour. If the discourse is to be delivered from a writing, as our sermons generally are, the utmost adviseable notation should not be more than a few marks on particular passages, and those separated considerably from each other, the filling up of which should be trusted to the feelings of the moment. But the best method in all respects for acquiring a finished rhetorical delivery is the private practice of declamation, which is supported on the authority of the great masters and models of oratory, Demosthenes and Cicero. For this purpose the system of notation here delivered, it is conceived, will prove of singular advantage. The aspiring rhetorical student will select one or more celebrated orations in the style, which he wishes to adopt; these he will carefully subject to all the rules of notation; he will study and commit them to memory; he will exercise on them the whole powers of his voice, his countenance, and gesture; and like Demosthenes, consult his glass, and take the opinion of a judicious friend on his performances. The knowledge and facility, which, by repeated exercises of this kind he will acquire in rhetorical delivery, may be transferred with advantage to his own compositions, which are to be delivered in public; and without hazarding the inconveniences of particular notation, he will find himself possessed of such a rich store of various, forcible, and expressive action, that whatever his feelings shall suggest on the moment, he will be able to execute in perfection.

ADDITIONS.

It has been said at the end of Chap. XIII. p. 345, that many other gestures may be named and marked, besides those there described. The following having been found necessary in the illustrations, it will be convenient to suppose them to be added.

Add page 345 after *pressing.*

Retracting (*rt*) is when the arm is withdrawn preparatory to projecting or pushing: as may be imagined in fig. 39, if supposed to prepare to push towards the star, and as in the dotted hand and arm of fig. 90, or in the right arm of fig. 100,—or in order to avoid an object either hateful or horrible, as in fig. 99 and 102.

Rejecting (*rj*) is the action of pushing the hand vertically towards the object, and at the same time averting the head, as in fig. 101, for which the former fig. 100 is preparatory.

Bending (*bn*) is the gesture preparatory to *striking.* It is represented by the uppermost dotted hand and arm of fig. 94, and by the strongly marked and elevated right arm of fig. 95.

Additions to the Synoptical Table, p. 364.

Add to the symbolic letters for the 4 and 5 small letters,

Direction of Motion.

i. inwards.   *o.* outwards.

Manner of Motion.

rt. retracting.   *rj.* rejecting.   *bn.* bending.

APPENDIX.

No. I.

The Qualities of the Voice are thus enumerated by Julius Pollux, *Onomasticum*, L. ii. c. 4. *Amstel*, 1706. Ἔιποις δ᾽ ἄν φωνὴν. You may call the voice,

As to the good Qualities,

1.	ὑψηλην, — —	altam, — — — —	high.
2.	ὑπέρογκον, — —	excelsam, — — —	powerful.
3.	λαμπρὰν, — —	claram, — — — —	clear.
4.	πλατεῖαν, — —	latam, — — — —	extensive.
5.	βαρεῖαν, — —	gravem, — — — —	deep.
6.	λεύκην, — — —	splendidam, — —	brilliant.
7.	ἐκκεκαθαρμένην,	mundatam, — — —	pure.
8.	ἡδεῖαν, — —	suavem, — — — —	sweet.
9.	ἐπαγωγὸν — —	illecebrosam, — —	attractive.
10.	ἐυμελῆ — —	exquisitam, — — —	{ melodious. cultivated. }
11.	ἐυπειθῆ, — —	persuasibilem, — —	persuasive.
12.	ἐυάγωγον, — —	{ pellacem, tractabilem, }	{ engaging. tractable. }
13.	ἐυκαμπῆ, — —	flexilem, — — —	flexible.
14.	ἐυέλικτον, — —	volubilem, — — —	executive.
15.	γλυκεῖαν, — —	dulcem, — — — —	sweet.
16.	λιγυρὰν, — —	stridulam, — — —	{ sonorous. harmonious. }
17.	σαφῆ, — — —	manifestam, — —	distinct.
18.	διαφανη, — —	perspicuam, — — —	{ perspicuous. articulate. }

4 B

As to the bad Qualities.

19.	μέλαιναν, - -	nigram, - - - -	obscure.
20.	φαιάν, - - -	fuscam, - - - -	dull.
21.	ἀηδῆ, - - -	injucundam, - -	unpleasing.
22.	σμικράν, -	{ exilem, } - - { small.
		{ pusillam, } { feeble.
23.	στενήν, -	angustam, - - -	thin.
24.	δυσήκοον, -	{ difficilem auditu, }	faint.
		{ molestam, }	
25.	ἀσαφῆ, -	{ subsurdam, } - { hollow.
		{ obscuram, } { indistinct.
26.	συγκεχυμένην, -	confusam, - - -	confused.
27.	ἐκμελῆ, - -	absonam, - - -	discordant.
28.	ἀμελῆ, - -	{ inconcinnam, } { unharmonious,
		{ neglectam, } - { uncultivated.
29.	ἀνάγωγον, - -	intractabilem, - { unattractive.
		{ unmanageable.
30.	ἀπειθῆ, - -	impersuasibilem, -	uninteresting.
31.	δυσκαμπῆ, - -	rigidam, - - -	rigid.
32.	τραχεῖαν, - -	asperam, - - -	harsh.
33.	διασπαρμένην, -	distractam, - -	cracked.
34.	λυπηράν, - -	tristem, - - -	doleful.
35.	βραγχώδη, -	{ infirmam, } - { unsound.
		{ raucam, } { hoarse.
36.	χαλκίζουσαν, -	æneam, - - - -	brassy.
37.	ὀξεῖαν, - - -	acutam, - - - { shrill.
		{ sharp.

In the same chapter the curious may find many other appellations for the exercise of the voice, and what relates to articulation and delivery.

The qualities of the voice here enumerated chiefly relate to its exercise in speaking. The singing voice resembles it in many respects, but is not here the object of research. The three principal descriptions, however, of the singing voice, as nearly related to the speaking voice, may be mentioned. The *voce di petto*, which proceeds from the breast, is the voice of the finest quality. The *voce di testa*, proceeding chiefly from the head, of an inferior character; and the *falsetto*, or feigned voice; this last, if it enter at all into public speaking, is very disagreeable. The reader is referred for the qualities and management of the singing voice, to the very ingenious work—" An Introduction to the Art of Sol-fa-ing and Singing,"—by J. Jousse, London, Goulding and Co.

No. II.

THE account of the Phonasci, by Cresollius, which is very curious, being too long to insert in a note, I have reserved it for this place: and also some precepts of Curius Fortunatianus relative to the voice. As the books of these authors are rare, the following extracts will not be unacceptable to the reader.

Ludovici Cresollii Vacationes Autumales, *Chapter* xi. p. 516.

De Voce tuenda.

Speaking of things injurious to the voice, he mentions figs, apples, pears, and nuts; Suetonius says of Nero,—abstinere pomis cibisque (voci) officientibus solebat. (Suet. in Neron. c. 20.) Athenæus says, Hegesianax retained a fine voice by abstaining from figs. Thrasybulus, when corrupted by a bribe, said he had got a hoarseness (ravim) by eating wild pears, and did not speak in public. The Phonasci abstained from cold drinks (mulsum frigidum). Addo libidinem omnem voluptatis, non minus voci quam animæ labem et damnum inferre. Itaque scribit Aristoteles, lib. 7. de animal. Cantores abstinere solitos a veneris obscenitate, ut diutius, sine ulla mutatione vocem retinere possent suavem et canoram, quæ flagitio corrumperetur. (Revera compertum habemus vocem maxime rebus venereis affici. Pubescente enim ætate quando primum aptus est adolescens ad has voluptates aggrediendas vox frangitur. Eunuchi vero vocis puerilis suavitatem et exilitatem usque ad vitæ finem retinent.) Et Calvus Orator plumbeas laminas de nocte adhibebat corpori, ad cohibendos libidinum sensus, et ludificationes, quæ in somno contingerent, quo vegetior deinde laborem studiorum et dicendi contentionem sustineret.——Vinolentia—drinking to excess is injurious, the voice being more easily broken by the repletion of the vessels. Speakers should guard against cold; and not devote themselves to severe study. Portius Latro is spoken of by Seneca, (pref. l. 1. cont.) as careless of his health and voice in this respect. Sæpe cum per totam lucubraverat noctem, ab ipso cibo, statim ad declamandum perveniebat. It is bad for the voice to speak immediately after a full meal.

P. 519. Medici rerum aiunt esse duo genera quæ vocis claritatem augere possint, suavitatemque efficere. Quædam enim arterias et pulmonis asperitatem leniunt, ut pruna dulcia, cremor hordei, succus amygdalarum dulcium, semen malvæ, viola, glycerhiza, mel coctum, saccharum. Quædam vero non leniendo, sed detergendo et extenuando vitia pectoris et pulmonis tollunt, uva passa, ficus, hyssopus, satureia, thymus, cepa, porrum, allium. De porro quidem et allio, magnus naturæ mystes consentit, ea enim quod extergendi vim habeant, ait, πρὸς ἐυφωνίαν συμφέρειν, canoram vocem efficere. (Arist. sect. xi. prob.) Adeoque nobilitavit Nero princeps stulta et ignobili sua diligentia, de qua Plinius (l. xix. c. 6.) in hunc modum: Porro sectivo nuper auctoritatem dedit princeps Nero, vocis gratia ex oleo, statis omnium mensium diebus, nihilque aliud, ac ne pane quidem vescendo. Et alio loco Plinius (l. xx. c. 6.) porrum voci splendorem afferre dicit. Eandem etiam vim portulacæ tribuit. De leguminibus idem putat Sanctus Isodorus (2 de divin. Offic.) Psallentes, inquit, legumine in causa vocis assidue utebantur : unde et cantores apud Gentiles *fabarii* dicti sunt. (Rabau. de instit. cler. l. ii. c. 48.) Ovorum quoque lutea prosunt faucium scabritiæ, ait Beroaldus ad Suetonium (in Nerone.) Clearchus item poeta candidum congrum et viscidos omnes pisces alere spiritus aiebat et efficere τὸ φονάριον περὶσαργον, celeriorem et expeditam magis vocem. Itaque Fortunatiani Rhetoris considerata illa est et audienda monitio, firmam efficit vocem et suavem, observantia cibi potus et veneris continentia. E baccis commendatur maxime in eam rem, carpesium (cubebs), de quo Hermolaus Barbarus ita memorat, Carpesium, si ore contineatur, claram vocem facit pronunciantibus : ob id Bernardus Justinianus homo imprimis doctus et eloquens nunquam sine hoc semine concionabatur. (Hermol. Bar. c. 4. Coroll. in Dioscorid.)

The ancients had some kind of drink which they called plasma (gargle) for assisting the voice.

> —————————— liquido cum plasmate guttur
> Mobile prolueris.　　　　　　　　　　*Pers. Sat.* I.

Cresollius cannot conjecture what this drink was composed of. Martial seems to speak of it as merely warm water.

> At tu multa diu dicis, vitreisque tepentem
> Ampullis potas semisupinus aquam.

Cresollius supposes that it was wine, not plain, but mixed with water and medicated (mulled wine), which St. Jerome and Pope Gregory complained that the singers used too freely, before they went in to perform the service of the church.

> Deo non voce, sed corde cantandum.——*Hieron.*
> Dum blanda vox quæritur, quæri congrua vita negligitur.——*Greg.*

The drink was however supposed to have a good effect on the voice : hence these monkish lines,

> Non vox, sed votum ; non chorda musica, sed cor,
> Non clamans, sed amans, cantat in aure Dei.

Two complaints of the throat affecting the voice are mentioned by Galen : the one κόπον τονώδη, rendered lassitudinem intensivam, fatigue from over exertion or overstraining : the other κόπον φλεγμονώδη, lassitudinem inflammatam (inflammation), cum eæ partes plurimum ignis calorisque sentiunt ob recrementa circumfusa. Cum igitur hoc congerit, ait Galenus uti Phonascos solere cibis, qui ex lacte, amylo, alica ovis et τοῖς ἰκρίοις componuntur. Τὰ ἴκρια exponunt quidam πρεμμάτια καὶ τραγήματα, hoc est placentulas et bellaria : addunt alii διὰ σεσάμυ καὶ μέλιτος γενόμενα quæ ex sesamo et melle parantur. Others understand sweetmeats called marzepanes, (quasi massa panis). Galen advises, dulce vinum theræum aut sybelites bibere, light wines, a drink consisting of, lacte et melle diutius coctis, amylo injecto. Quintilian recommends, ambulatio, unctio, veneris abstinentia, facilis ciborum digestio, id est frugalitas. Beroaldus in Suet. alitur autem vox, si a lectulo statim corpus deambulando moveamus. He desires also, if the voice be fatigued (vexata) dormituris laser instillare. Exercise of walking is beneficial. But exercise of the voice itself most of all. Bona vocis augentur cura, negligentia minuuntur. *Quint.* Reading aloud is a good exercise of the voice. Omnes qui vocis curam olim habuerunt ἔοθεν τὲ καὶ νήςεις ὄντες mane et jejuni consuetam exercitationem capiebant. (Arist. xi. prob. 22 and 36.)

The *mute exercise* of the voice, he reckons another useful practice. This he explains by relating the story of the Roman magpie from Plutarch, already mentioned (note 15, chap. ii.). Marcus the Byzantine orator is said to have much practised this silent exercise of the voice. He told his friends that he practised energetic silence : σιωπῇ ἐνεργῳ χρᾶσθαι,

A celebrated actress in the preparation of her characters is said only to use this silent meditation, and not to declaim aloud.

This practice may be used to great advantage for determining where the voice is to be raised or lowered, what inflections are to be used, and where the voice should be encreased or diminished in volume or body : so that a speaker, though he may not have time or opportunity to declaim aloud, may not be altogether unprepared for the proper management of his voice. But evidently improvement of the voice cannot be expected hence.

Φονασκοὶ, Φονασκηταὶ, Phonasci, Vociferarii et Vocales, were the common appellations of those who taught the exercise and management of the voice. Tertullian calls them Edomatores vocis. Galen says they recommended to their disciples the frequent use of the warm bath. Cresollius mentions other practices of the Phonasci, some of which are curious, and some he considers useful. P. 557. Quanquam non omnia ut paulo ante aiebam, quæ ab illis exercitoribus fiebant, jam in usum revocanda esse putaverim. Adhibebant ἐωθινὰς μιλέτας et quotidianas, ut auctor est Aristoteles, quæ forte delicatæ nostræ adolescentiæ molestiores videantur : (very probably indeed !) laminam ad pectus admovebant, quam per me, licet orator abjiciat ; stata tempora spatiandi habuerunt quæ religiose observarent, quæ omittere jam mihi nulla sit religio, abstinebant a certis cibis et dilectum genus potionis habuerunt, ea de re quid ego sentiam superiori jam capite exposui.

Quid igitur est quod sumendum ab illis mutuandumque existimem ? Illas profecto ut Galeni verbis utar, καλουμένας ἀναφονήσεις, haud dubitem ad tempora hæc nostra et consuetudinem accommodare. Solebant enim sensim vocem et veluti per gradus attollere, mox deponere, tum molliendæ arteriæ causa et firmandæ, tum conciliandæ varietatis, ut nulla esset flexio, quam non commode, prout causa ratioque postulavisset, adhiberent. Id non modo usurpatum a Græcis, verum etiam et Latinis oratoribus, e Seneca patre, homine eruditissimo cognoscimus : qui de Porcio Latrone memorans, qui inusitatum eloquentiæ cursum et vitæ modum sequebatur, ait ipsum nil vocis causa facere solitum, *Non illum* per gradus paulatim ab imo usque ad summum perducere, non rursus à summa contentione paribus intervallis descendere, (Senec. Proem. Cont.) quod fuisse aliorum dicentium commune videtur. Id proprie doctoribus Græcis est παιωνίζειν, de quo sic Alexander Aphrodisieus Οἱ Φονασκοὶ δὲ παιονίζοντες προμαλακύνεσι τα ἀναπνευςικά, Phonasci pæanam citantes arterias præmolliunt. Ex eorum mente autor ad Herennium, arterias, ait, lædi, si antequam vox præmulsa est, acri clamore compleantur.

No. III.

Antiqui Rhetores Latini.   Paris, 1599.

Curii Fortunatiani Consulti Artis Rhetor Scholicæ.   Lib. iii.

De Pronuntiatione.

PRONUNTIATIONEM quid Tullius vocat? Actionem.—Ea quid præstat? Ut conciliemus, persuadeamus, moveamus.—His generaliter et naturaliter quid accidit? Delectatio.—Pronuntiatio quibus modis constat? Voce, vultu, gestu.—His quid accidit? Cultus sive habitus.—Vox quibus constat? Natura et scientia.—In natura vocis quid observabo? Qualem vocem habeas.—Ea quibus constat? Quantitate et qualitate.—In vocis scientia quid observabo? Quomodo ea utaris.—Bonitas vocis quibus constat? Claritate, firmitate, suavitate.—Claram qua res efficit? Anaphonesis.—Quid firmam, quid suavem? Observatio cibi et potus, et veneris continentia.—Hæc omnia quæ res præstat? Natura quæ augetur diligentia.—Quæ est diligentia et cura vocis? Triplex, alendi eam, custodiendi, restituendi.— Vox quomodo alitur? Si a lectulo statim corpus deambulando moveamus intra mille passus: quia si quid adhuc insidet indigestum, parva exercitatio per corpus deducit: nam nimia extenuat et fatigat.—Post ambulationem quid faciendum est? Statim ad studia nos conferamus: et priusquam scribere incipiamus, ut animus legendo calescat, legemus aliquid tacite, vel cum tenui murmure, tunc deinde scribemus, sed non clara voce ut quidam.—Post illud quid faciendum est? Ad curam vocis nos transferemus.--Quæ est hæc? Ut sedentes versus paucos pronuntiemus.—Quæ ratio est elocutionis, ea est et pronunciationis? Cur ita? Quoniam ut elocutio emendata esse debet, dilucida, ornata apta, ita et pronunciatio.—Quomodo erit emendata? Si vitio careat.—Quid dilucida? Ut sonus vocis medius sit, nec gravissimus, nec acutissimus.--Quid ornata? Ut virilis.--Quid apta? Ut monotoniam vites, id est ut varia utaris pronunciatione.—Id quemadmodum faciam? Pro qualitate rerum, id est negotiorum.—Rei observatio qualis est? Quadruplex, una in tota causa, ubi sunt et genera dicendi: altera in partibus orationis: tertia in sensibus: quarta in verbis: nam pro qualitate horum omnium pronunciatio esse debet.—Huic distributioni quid accidit? Ut personarum etiam et locorum et temporum servemus qualitatem.—Apte principia quemadmodum pronuntiabo? Si qualitatem figurarum, id est schematum diligenter inspexeris: aliter enim in causa eudoxo et amphidoxo et adoxo et disparacolutho pronuntiandum est.—Quid narrationem? Si omnes ejus partes consideravimus.—Quid partitionem? Expedite ac simpliciter.—Quid argumentationem? Varie, agiliter, acriter, pugnanter et instanter. —Quid sensus? Si locos quoque communes lenta et gravi voce, deinde per gradus paulatim. extollamus, ut quantum potest surgunt: tunc rursus per eosdem gradus eam paulatim revolverimus, donec sine damno ad murmur usque perveniat.— In exercitatione ista qui modus erit? Non amplius quingentorum versuum, quia plus vox laborat in lectione, quam in actione, si tamen angustia temporum toleret res pronunciantis.—Vox quomodo custo-

dienda est? Quoties declamandum fuerit, si occupationes permiserint, aliquid ante pronun-
tiabis ut vocis itinera mollias.—Quid si fuerit repente dicendum? hoc idem consequi poteris
in ipsa moderatione actionis: ut in principiis vox tua submissa sit, deinde paulatim se
intendat.—Quid in desinendo observandum est? Sicut vitandum est, ne vox in clamorem
subitum prorumpat: ita etiam ne a clamore subito considas.—In cibo capiendo sunt
aliqua observanda? Sunt, ut stomacho inservias; nam si melius prandio valet, prandendum
est sæpius, non tamen semper, sed cibo tenero et exiguo, qui in cœnæ tempus dissipetur:
in cœnando autem nec multis nec gravibus utendum est.—Quid in potu? frigidis potionibus
abstinebis, quia his *inuruntur* arteriæ, calidis autem aperiuntur: nam per illas vox fluit.—
Si leviter vexata fuerit vox, quid faciam? Utere acrioribus cibis; quibus si quid obstat
voci et obstrepit, perrumpatur: nam medici dormituris lasar instillant et experrectos
jubent sorbere aliquid aceti acris.—Quid si vehementer fracta vox fuerit, quemadmodum
eam restituam? Siti, ut ejus itinera siccentur. Item ambulatione multâ, ut humor in
inferiora loca ex superioribus evocetur; et vini abstinentia, quod est voci læsæ infestissi-
mum; quod si non possumus, utemur dulci ac diluto potius: cibus quoque lenissimus
arteriæ prodest.—Quid si simplex? Nec multis medicamentis impedito, maxime glycerhiza utendum est, vel (si possis) succi ejus modice sub lingua habeto, ad imaginem len-
ticulæ vel pisi.—In summa quid observabo? Ne operosam vocis tutelam habeas, ne ei
nimium indulgeas, et tamen parcas, ut et arteriæ ne desit humor, nec supersit, oportet enim
illas non humidas esse, sed lubricas. Intuearis inventivi sint an defensionales, descriptivi,
an nativi, an minus, item, si figuras schematum spectes.—Verba quoque quam in se vim
habeant considerabo? Utique: nam ut res ex sensibus constat; ita et sensus verbis explicantur.—Omnibus verbis pronunciationem accommodabo? Non omnibus, sed necessariis.—
Personarum qualitatem quemadmodum spectabo? Ut scias quid agas, pro quo, adversus
quem, quibus presentibus, quibus oppugnantibus, quibus faventibus.—In locis quid observabo? Ut scias ubi agas.—Quid in tempore? Ut videas quando tibi sit promenda oratio,
ne temporis competat qualitas.

No. IV.

Chapter XIII. p. 327 and 331.

In order to afford assistance in correcting my own translation of the passage of Quintilian
in which he describes the different positions of the hands, I subjoin the French translation
by Gedoyn, from the edition in 12mo. Paris 1752. The English translation by Guthrie
omits the greater part of this difficult passage. I know of no other translations of
Quintilian.

Est autem gestus ille maxime communis, &c.

Pour entrer dans le détail, un geste fort commun est celui, où le doit du milieu plié
contre le pouce, on alonge les trois autres. Ce geste est assez d'usage, quand on entre en

matiere, et alors il est plus mesuré, se portant modestement à droite et à gauche, la tête et les épaules ne faisant de leur côté autre chose, que se laisser aller insensiblement au mouvement de la main. Si l'on donne à ce même geste un peu plus d'étendue, il a je ne sçais quoi de positif et d'assuré. Enfin dans les reproches et les invectives il est vif et pressant, se déployant alors avec une liberté entiere. Mais plusieurs le corrompent, en l'avançant jusques vers l'épaule gauche. Quelques-uns font encore pis, ils mettent le bras en travers et prononcent du coude.

Non seulement le doit du milieu, mais aussi celui qui le précéde, se plie fort bien contre le pouce conjointement avec lui. Cela fait un geste qui est encore plus pressant que le dernier, et qui par cette raison est moins propre pour l'exorde et pour la narration.

Quelquefois on tient les trois derniers doits fermez sous le pouce et alors le premier, celui dont Cicéron dit que Crassus se servoit avec tant de graces, demeurant alongé, a plus d'un usage. Car panché de côté il reproche, il indique, d'où même il a pris son nom. Si l'on tient la main haute, et que ce doit soit un peu baissé en dedans vers l'épaule, il affirme. Tourné contre terre et presque renversé, il presse. En quelques rencontres il signifie un certain nombre; et si vous le prenez par l'extrémité d'en haut, en courbant un peu les derniers, mais le petit moins que les autres, vous trouverez qu'il est fort propre pour la dispute. Cependant il me semble que quand on dispute vivement, il est encore plus naturel de tenir ce doit par le milieu, en fermant les derniers d'autant plus fort, que les premiers descendent plus bas.

Un autre geste qui convient particuliérement à un discours modeste, est celui où les doits se joignant foiblement par en haut, l'orateur porte la main vers lui pas loin de la bouche ou de l'estomac, puis l'éloignant un peu, la laisse aller doucement en bas. Telle fut, je m'imagine, la maniere dont Demosthéne prononça cet exorde si timide et si soumis de son oraison pour Ctesiphon. Et Ciceron, je crois ne tenoit pas la main autrement quand il disoit, *Si j'ai, Messieurs, quelque sorte d'esprit et de talent, et je sens mieux que personne combien peu j'en ai,* &c.

Il y a un autre geste, où il semble que la main profere elle-même les paroles. C'est lors qu'après avoir été pendente un moment, elle se ramasse en quelque façon pour se porter vers la bouche, et qu'ensuite elle s'ouvre et se deploie librement en dehors.

A l'égard des doits, tantôt on les partage, mais sans y joindre le pouce; ensorte que les deux derniers panchent en dedans, et que les premiers ne soient pas même aussi droits, aussi alongez qu'ils pourroient l'être. Tantôt on couche les deux derniers contre l'extrémité du pouce, et le pouce se joint lui-même aux premiers vers le milieu. Tantôt le quatriéme demeure plus courbé que les autres. Tantôt enfin nous tenons tous les quatres médiocrement alongez, et le pouce incliné; ce qui nous donne deux facilitez, l'un pour distinguer les choses que nous disons, en les computant par nos doits, s'il est besoin; l'autre pour indiquer à droite et à gauche, la main n'ayant qu'à se porter d'un et d'autre côté. Quelquefois aussi la main peu avancée, et à demi tournée imite l'attitude, où l'on peint ces personnes qui font quelque vœu. La main dans cette assiette se meut par intervalles, et comme à la dérobée en trainant avec soi un leger mouvement des épaules. Cela fait un petit geste qui est fort propre dans les occasions, où il faut parler avec crainte et retenue.

L'admiration a son geste particulier. La main élevée à une certaine hauteur forme avec ses cinq doits une manière de cercle ; puis elle s'ouvre, et se retourne tout d'un tems en dehors, pendant que le bras, de plié qu'il étoit s'alonge et se déploie. L'interrogation s'exprime diversement. Cependant c'est d'ordinaire par un tour de main, de quelque maniere qu'il se fasse.

Le premier doit apuyé contre le pouce, et les trois autres médiocrement alongez avec un leger mouvement de la main, font un geste qui a de la grace, et dont on se sert fort bien, soit pour distinguer, soit pour aprouver, soit pour narer. Les Grecs en ont qui n'est pas fort différent, et dont l'usage leur est aujourd'hui très-familier, lorsque dans une dispute vive et serrée ils poussent leurs enthymèmes. Car ils allongent le pouce et le doit qui suit, fermant les trois autres. Ils font même ce geste des deux mains tout à la fois ; ce qui forme deux cornes, dont vous diriez qu'ils menacent leur adversaire.

Un mouvement de la main doux et modéré, est bon quand on promet, ou quand on flatte ; comme un mouvement plus fort, est d'usage quand on exhorte, quelquefois aussi quand on loue. C'est encore un geste des plus communs, mais néanmoins fort pressant, que celui où la main s'ouvre et se ferme alternativement avec vitesse. Enfin il y a un geste pour encourager ; c'est une main creuse que l'on éleve plus haut que l'épaule, en écartant les doits, et que l'on accompagne d'un certain mouvement. Ce geste nous est venu des écoles étrangères, et je vois qu'il s'introduit. Je ne parle point d'une main tremblante, parce qu'elle sied mieux à un bouffon qu'à un orateur.

Quelques-uns n'aprouvent pas qu'on porte à sa bouche une main, dont les doits soient joints par le bout. Je ne vois pas pourquoi. Car il me semble que nous faisons naturellement ce geste pour marquer de l'admiration, ou lors qu'une juste indignation nous jette tout-à-coup dans une sorte d'effroi, ou que nous demandons grace. On peut même apuyer fort bien contre son estomac une main fermée, soit dans un mouvement de colère, et alors quelque mots prononcez d'une voix sourde, et comme entre les dents, ne deplaisent pas, *que ferai-je maintenant ? Quel parti prenderai-je ?* Pour ce qui est de montrer quelque chose avec le pouce tourné en dehors, c'est un geste qui est plus usité que bienséant.

No. V.

Chapter XIII. pp. 330, 331, 332. Fig. 56, 62, 63.

Pollici proximus digitus, &c. both Burmannus and Capperonier have adopted on this passage the following note :

Arbitror ab hoc gestu inolevisse proverbium antiquum ; *premere pollicem* pro *approbare*, atque *favere* : contrarium autem est, *pollicem invertere*, id est, *improbare.* BURMAN.

4 G

A note of Baxter upon the following line,

" Fautor utroque tuum laudabit pollice ludum"

is attributed by mistake to Juvencus, p. 333. *Hor.* Epist. l. 1. 18. 65 ; it is this :

Utroque pollice, compresso significare volebant deosculandum esse eum qui bene luserat ; contra conversis pollicibus ignave devictum necari jubebant : *Eo autem modo necantur pulices.* Et verso pollice vulgi quemlibet occidunt populariter. *Juvenalis.* Frustra se hactenus torserunt eruditissimi. Quid apertius ?

The note of Juvencus on the same passage is more intelligible and more explicit, notwithstanding this self-complacency of Baxter. P. 426. Edit. Rotamagi, 1706. *Pollice.* Cum Romani favebant alicui gladiatori generoso in arenâ certanti, si accideret ut ab adversario superatus veniret in vitæ discrimen, jubebant eum vivere ; et eum favorem significabant ambos pollices premendo, ut diserte docet Plin. l. 28. cap. 2. Contra vero, si cui essent infensi, si quem occidi juberent, alterum pollicem vertebant. Porro pollicem premere nihil aliud erat quam utrâque manu sublata pugnoque facto pollices ipsos intra pugnum arcte vehementerque comprimere. Pollicem vertere : erat, altera manu sublatâ inque pugnum pariter contractâ, pollicem à pugno reductum attollere, eumque vel in gyrum vertere, vel ad eum qui manum attollebat retrò flectere ac detorquere. Ita explicat Bernardinus Ferrarius in erudito opusculo de favendi ac plaudendi formulis.

The expression *premere pollicem*, by which the Gladiator was delivered from the sword of his adversary, according to Juvencus, does not suit with my idea of the passage in Quintilian, which I have illustrated by fig. 56. It must in this view be the fist, clenched and enclosing the thumbs pressed closely by the fingers of both hands. And this explanation seems to agree well with the words *utroque laudabit pollice.* Figures 62 and 63 very well represent the disposition of the thumb for condemnation, particularly 63, as may be collected from the explanation (not very delicate) given by Baxter of this passage as above.

Pliny's observation merely relates to the custom, and not to the manner of using the thumb or fingers, he speaks of a practice in his time well known. Pollices, cum faveamus, premere etiam proverbio jubemur. But along with the cessation of the practice, the manner seems to have been lost, as we may judge by the different interpretations of different commentators.

Le Pere Sanadon explains this passage thus :

Quand les Gladiateurs combattoient, si les spectateurs pressoient les pouces ensemble en joignant les deux mains, et entrelaçant les doigts c'étoit encore une marque de faveur, le vainqueur donnoit la vie au vaincu. Mais s'il tournoit les pouces en dejoignant les mains c'étoit un signe de haine, et il n'y avoit plus de quartier. , ...

. . . . On a donc eu tort de croire que *premere pollicem* étoit ce que nous faisons en mettant le pouce sur le troisième doigt, et en le faisant tomber avec quelque bruit sur le second.

This last observation is aimed against Cruquius, who considered *premere pollicem* to signify the snapping of the fingers. See below ; as to the former part of the Pere Sanadon's explanation, it seems as if he understood that the hands were to be clasped as in fig. 76, and the thumbs pressed together, but not crossed as in the figure. Others, as Watson, represent the act of condemnation as in fig. 62, and the mark of favour as fig. 63.

Pollice ad medium digitum presso, inque indicem relapso, signum clarum sonitumque damus, favoremque significamus : quod si fiat utroque pollice ; maximi id favoris est : et hoc est premere pollicem. *Cruquius, ad locum Horat. a Bond.*

Erasmus in his Proverbs, p. 315, Ludg, 1703, says that Porphyrion and Acron seem to consider the passage of Horace abovementioned to mean, that he will applaud in the modern manner by clapping hands, or perhaps by flourishing the hands, for by these means the thumbs are brought into contact.

Porphyrion enarrat hunc ad modum : *utroque pollice,* i. e. utraque manu, συνεκδοχικῶς. Synecdoche a parte totum. An qui vehementius laudat, manus jungens, jungit pollicem eum proximo. Acron hoc pacto : utroque pollice συνεκδεχικῶς, manu utraque, sublataque pariter ac sæpius mota. Hic enim gestus valde laudantium est. But Erasmus does not agree with them, although he has not accurately expressed his own sense of the manner of the action ; he concludes thus : sane utrumque, sicut ex iis conjici licet, proverbii origo fugit.

No. VI.

Actio Oratoris, seu de Gestu et Voce Libri duo, Auctore Joan. Lucas, S. J. Paris, 1749.
Liber 1.

Qui nondum justo moderari corpora motu,
Et regere artifici didicit modulamine vocem,
Actorem aggredior, facilis si Musa laborem
Adjuvat, ignotas cantu deducere ad artes.

Address to Advocates and Preachers, and Importance of Action.

Vos mihi, sive forum, seu pulpita sacra vocabunt,   5
Ferte pedem properi, et pronas his vocibus aures
Adjicite, ô pueri. Nec vos didicisse pigebit,
Spero equidem, quâ se tollit facundia voce,
Quis capitis situs orantem, quæ gratia vultus,
Quis flexus laterum, reliqui quis corporis usus,   10
Quis status incessusque decet. Namque actio primas
Divitis eloquii partes, eademque secundas,
Et quantum est primis quod partibus atque secundis
Additur, una potest in se complexa videri :
Ni Graiæ ac Latiæ fallunt oracula linguæ.   15

The lines are numbered without interruption, for the convenience of reference ; much of the original poem is omitted.

Rules follow for the carriage of the head ; and faults are enumerated.—Such as staring at the cieling, keeping the eyes fixed upon the ground, stiffness of the neck, and tossing of the head. The fable of Proteus explained by reference to Oratory and its various changes.

The Eyes.

Erudienda tibi sic sunt tua lumina ad omnes
Quos intus pateris, quos vis effingere, motus.
Namque alios dabit ira, alios clementia visus.
Hos stupor affixosque solo immotosque tenebit :
Dejiciet dolor : at rebus recreata secundis   20
Lætitia attollet cœlo, et quocumque movebit
Exultans animis : gravis indignatio torvos ;
Et conniventes faciet miseratio : siccos
Risus et humentes gemitus sibi tristis habebit.

The Hands.

Nunc mihi fas docilesque manus et cerea flecti,   25
Quo lex cumque vocat nunquam violanda decori,
Brachia circumagere, et justo disponere flexu.
Tu ne fingentis ductum accepisse recusa,
Neve resiste operi : sic te exoptata manebunt
Appensæ ante fores, actorum præmia,* palmæ.   30
Actio multa quidem diversaque munia fungi
Dicitur, in manibus tamen omnis, et omnis in uno
Pæne sita est gestu.   Linguam manus adjuvat, infans
Illa licet, licet ista parens sit vocis, et omnes
Docta soni modulos objectu frangere dentis.   35
Verum hoc principium tibi ponitur et caput artis,
Nosse istos variare situs.   Nam lingua loquendo
Non plura expediat diversis nomina rebus ;
Congrua nominibus variis quam signa reponat
Æmula, nec vinci patiens manus.   Ilicet omnia   40
Circuitu verborum et longa ambage laborans
Quæ segni lingua eloquio demittit in aures,
Dextra cito vigiles oculos docet indice gestu :
Dextra, potens celeris motum prævertere linguæ ;
Atque eadem, dum pulmo animæ vitalis egenus   45
Plura locuturi non sustinet oris hiatum,
Semper inexhausta et nunquam defessa moveri.
Ergo tibi labor is primum impendendus, ut omnis
Quid facunda velit manuum sibi motio, noris.
Nec tenuis labor iste : tibi nam mille figuræ,   50
Signorum innumeræ species et nomina mille
Ediscenda prius, quæ paucis deinde docebo.

---

* Palmas dari solitas ædilium judicio histrionibus, qui bene personam sustinuissent, patet
ex prologo Amphitryonis et Pænuli.   Vide etiam. Juv Sat. 7.

Significant Gestures.—Both Hands.

Ambæ dum passis nituntur ad æthera palmis,
Consistuntque manus; præsentia rebus egenis
Adfore declarant non cassis numina votis.   55
Deciduâ dum mole premunt latus : irrita monstrant
Vota nec auritos potuisse advertere Divos.
Pectinis in morem digitis coeuntibus, antè
Dum pendent; tristem : dum convertuntur, anhelum :
Dum lumbos super et turgenti tergore tortæ   60
Pone sedent ; tumidum : dum ansas hinc inde figurant
Præfidentem animi : dum pandunt longius alas ;
Audentem ; lætum, dum crebris motibus errant ;
Attonitumque decussatæ : in spiramque volutæ,
Plurima volventem secum : abjectumque remissæ,   65
Sive vaccillantes dubio libramine dicunt.
Atque hæc signorum manibus quæ forma duabus.

Use of the Right Hand.

Jam quibus indiciis se dextera ventilet, audi.
Usus erit dextræ primum cognoscere motus :
Quæ sæpe, ut lævâ potior, solet una moveri.   70
Illa quidem explicitæ dum porrigit intima palmæ,
A labiisque ad humum lente dimittit ; honorat
Et salvere jubet.   Retro conversa repellit :
Et vos este, inquit, procul hinc ; procul este profani.
Miratur resupina : levi circumacta rotatu,   75
Si paullum assurgit, dicta elevat ; et tua teque
Spernit : adulatur, si tantum circinat auras,
Et tenui in sese gyro sinuata recurrit.
Imperium exercet, si cessat tensa moveri ;
Sin agitat sese alternis sursumque deorsumque ;   80
Indicit calidæ tranquilla silentia turbæ
Majestate suâ : quæ mitius imperat, ora
Dum media occludit, transversoque indice signat,
Ut qui Sigalion* servat tua sacra, Serapi !
Verum hæc ante alias vox est blandissima voces   85
Sensa animi dextræ vulgantis, sæpe supremam
Hinc atque inde cutem frictu quæ mulcet amico
Palpatrix, vel dum candentia colla, humerosque,
Atque repercussum tremulo latus impete plaudit,

---

* Simulacrum apud Ægyptios, in sacra Isidis et Serapidis, digito labris adpresso, silentium imperans.

Dulce cavo tenui resonans. Sic nempe jocosque,   90
Deliciasque, et amicitias, atque omnia suevit
Blandimenta loqui. Sed non ita : dum redit in se
Applicitisque volæ pugnum facit unguibus. Audin'
Compressi in palmam digiti quas protinus iras,
Et quæ flammati jam proxima prælia Martis   95
Intentu graviore canant ? Non ludimur, ecce
Prædicta exarsit subito discordia motu.
Et jam cum rubra dentes spuit ille saliva :
Iste cruentatas deformi vulnere nares
Ardet inexpletum vulsis pensare capillis.   100
Nigrescunt oculi, frons livida turget : et auris
Pulsa calet, crebroque rubens male tinnit ab ictu :
Et velut hyberna crepitat sub grandine dorsum.
Has nimirum inimicitias et prælia pugnus
Dixerat. Usque adeo, quamvis sit muta, fideli   105
Dextra oculo narrat non mutis omnia signis.

The Fingers.

Nec tantum manibus concessa locutio totis :
Sunt quoque vocales digiti, articulique loquaces.
Quorum ne fugiat tacitus tua lumina sermo,
Quid positus monstrent varii præscire labora.   110
Te docet, interior dextro si pollici adhæsit,
Tresque alios à se digitos procul expulit index.
Te vocat admotus labris, vola pressa coërcet
Tres superimposito digitos cum pollice. Sed cum
Obliquus se crebra movet, fuge : namque minatur   115
Intentatque malum. Si recta porgitur, ito :
Quid cessas ? tibi monstrat iter : de millibus unum
Ni te fortè notat. Frustra sonat auribus, hic est,
Hic vir, hic est, clamas iterumque, iterumque tot inter
Quem loqueris tamen ignoro : si dixerit index   120
Eloquio meliore, hic est ; sint millia centum,
Ille patet quemcumque notat, mihi cognitus hic vir.
Tanta vel in digito facundia cernitur uno.

Time of Gesture.

Quod superest, manibus tu caute utare disertis,
Ut quæ lingua sonat gestu propiore sequaris,   125
Non præeas. Nescit menti vox sana præire,
Nec voci novit sapiens præcurrere gestus.
Ponè sequi dominam gaudet vox sobria mentem :

Ire comes voci motu famulante laborat,
Et paribus spatiis menti succedere gestus,
Tu ne communis famulatûs jura resolve,
Sed magis officiique vices et tempora serva.
Nam quandoque amens turbat discordia foedus :   130
Dum gestum opponit voci, vocemque vicissim
Cum gestu bellare facit : deformia bella
Scilicet, et menti nunquam placitura magistræ.
Quæ sint bella rogas ? dum vox petit ardua cœlum,
Juppiter ! ingeminans : gestu petit ima rebelli,   135
Indictumque notat malè concors dextera Ditem.

   The Direction of the Eyes and Gesture to correspond.

At ne lucis egens nullo ductore feratur
Gestus in incertum, nec te convertere visus
Huc pigeat, quo mens vocem gestumque vocabit.
Nam, nisi quem reicis tactu procul accessuque,   140
Est licitum commotæ occulos non jungere dextræ.

   The left Hand. The limits of Gesture, and various faults.

Læva sibi rarò tantum me judice sumat,
Ut si sola potest, tamen ausit sola moveri.
Conjunctis aptè digitis se dextera solvat
In gestum : nec supra oculos amet ire, nec infra   145
Se cinctum valde abjiciat : nec longius, aut se
Latius effundat : ne remiget ; aut natet, orbes
Orbibus impediens varios : ne pulpita tundat,
Aut strepera alterius percellat concava palmæ.
Qui sibi sic plaudit, mihi jam ludibria debet,   150
Et referet stolidus meruit quæ sibila plausor.
   Nec latum digitos discriminet intervallum ;
Nec coëant in se glomeratis unguibus : intus
Nec palmâ lateant, dum pugnus cogitur, imâ :
Neve micent celeres, veluti si spretus Alexim   155
Vocales doceat Coridon resonare cicutas ;
Dum premit alterno ventosa foramina tactu,
Queis iter est animæ.   Vitia in contraria proni
Offendunt pariter, pressas muliebriter ulnas
Et qui continuat lateri ; et qui subrigit altè   160
Axillæ gibbos ; et dimidiata refringit
Brachia qui cubiti nodo ; et qui brachia laxis
Distendit nervis : cui gestu languida nullo
Diriguit manus ; aut nimium manus emicat ardens,
Otia nec docilis nullo unquam ducere motu.   165

Frequency of Gesture.

Garrulus ut nescit, teneras ne subruat aures
Flumine verborum, torrentem sistere linguam :
Sic, ne multiplicis confundat imagine gestus
Intentas spectantûm acies, nec parcere dextræ,
Nec certo dare compositos in tempore gestus   170
Gesticulator amet. Rabidæ sed Phœbados instar
Quam Deus intus agens majori numine rumpit,
Incertus qua parte ferat, fert brachia, dextramque
Et lævam quocumque rapit malesana libido.
Hoc felix uno, sic omni ex parte beatus,   175
Præ manibus torpere celer si lingua videtur.

The Inflections of the Trunk.

Forsitan et flexus truncum qui corporis ornet,
Dedecoretque canam :* laterum inclinatio qualis
Dedeceat, deceatve : aut qualis denique forma,
Quique modus summos nutu coxendicis artus   180
Leniter, ut prudens statuit natura, movendi.
    Namque ego florentes ætatibus et genus alto
Sanguine ducentes procerum vidisse recordor,
In tantum qui se declivi corpore deorsum
Projicerent medios ; ut centum ferre putares   185
Annorum incumbens humeris, quod spissius Ætna est,
Si qua fides senibus, minus et tolerabile pondus.
    Nec minus à summis thoraca revellere coxis,
Alter in oppositum resupino corpore visus ;
Nec secus ac crescentum uterum quæ foemina gestat,   190
Abdomen longè reliquis præponere membris.
    Quin etiam deprensi, habitu qui cætera recto
Se tamen agresti nimium molimine torquent ;
Intersistentes offensantesque subinde.
Duriter, et vasto projectu immania terga   195
Discordesque humeros, nec non incongrua foedo
Succussu latera, et compagem dentique totam
Librantes incompositis incessibus : ut qui
Verna boves inter, turpesque adoleverit hoedos,
Collibus in patriis et solo in gramine villæ,   200
Nulla incedendi nisi prava exempla secutus.
    Nec rari sunt adeo qui summo vertice ad imos
Usque pedes, verubus transfixi hærere colurnis,

---

* The Author in this part of his subject seems to have had Cresollius in view ; see introduction, notes 15 and 16.

Et stare induti thorace putantur aheno.
Sic commissuræ, sic nervi, et musculus omnis   205
Sic tori, et in collo lumbisque ac poplite nodi,
Et medium postica secat quæ vertebra dorsum,
Machina sic omnis curvari ignara rigescit.

The Feet.

Postquam autem parte ex omni concinna nitebit
Actio, tum pedibus certas conscribere leges
Profuerit. Pedibus debetur cura regendis   210
Non postrema : illos nam cætera membra sequuntur ;
Nec recto corpus positu constare videbis,
Ni bene firma situ constent vestigia recto.
Ergo dum scenæ prætenta aulæa relinques,
Teque in conspectum caveæ dabis : incipe primum   215
Orchestra in media firmo consistere gressu,
Nec pede tange pedem, nec calcem calce fatiga,
Nec tortos in se digitos committe, nec ungues
Applicitos plantæ talo postpone prioris,
Nec plantam ferre alterius sola præcipe plantæ.   220
Hæc turpis ratio est : et non magis apta moveri,
Quam quæ diversas in partes dissita longè
Crura nimis magno divaricat intervallo,
Et Græcum positu deformi lamda* figurat.
Sic bene constiteris : si paulum aversus uterque,   225
Sed tamen haud longè pes respicit ; atque sinistro
Posterior retro didicit succedere dexter.
E regione nefas sibi respondere sinistrumque
Et dextrum : simul hos vetuit natura moveri ;
Ars vetat hos pariter versu consistere eodem.   230

Precepts for Steps, and the Time of making them.

Hæc ubi rite memor dudum provisa tenebis :
Perge age, et ingenti nunc ora resolve theatro,
Principio immotus : nisi forte exæstuat intus
Mens furiis incensa. Aliquot sententia verbis
Verum ubi prodierit rectè conclusa, juvabit   235
Inde referre pedem. Rari, dum lingua movetur,
Sint pedibus motus ; motus, dum lingua quiescit,
Esto pedum. Tacito dum ducitur halitus ore

---

* Ab eo vitio Cypseli Corynthii mater et Eteonis conjux, dicebatur ΛΛΜΔΑ   Cœl. l.
13. c. 2.

Tum, vacuas aures quoniam vox languida fugit,
Tempus erit turpi succumbere nescia somno   240
Lumina progressu, atque habili recreare palæstra.
   Verum ista imprimis memori sub pectore conde,
Non simili libranda modo vestigia, quicquid
Dixeris. Incedunt alio luctusque, pavorque;
Atque alio risus, præcepsque audacia ritu.   245
Genua labant tristi, protensa volumina crurum
Audax figit humo, lætus vix libat arenam.
Spes volat, ira ruit, ceu nubem ruperit ignis
Quem gremio algenti dudum complexa tenebat.
Nec pater Anchises Æneam passibus æquet   250
Nec, non antevolet Thersitem pulcher Achilles :
Aut incessum habeat grandævi Nestoris Ajax,
Dum nota insanis concîdit terga flagellis.

Several faults are enumerated ; he compares to a tree those who stand unmoved in the same position.   Then proceeds.

   Nec vero pauci, queis plumbea crura pedesque
Marmoreos, stupidoque artus torpore rigentes
Non natura dedit ; nimium sed cultus agrestis,
Et coram populo dicendi rarior usus,
Infestusve pudor. . . . .
. . . . Quid mole tua stas,
Increpitans inquam ? quid tantum immobilis hæres ?   260
Eia age, quid cessas ? Clavo vel adacta trabali
Membra leva, pigrumque pedem procul inde reporta.
Non pudet hic horam consistere ?

Other faults of the positions and motions of the Feet enumerated. As frequent changes, and at regular Intervals.

   . . . . . . dein simul ambas
Fullonis saltu paulum erigit ; et modo talis,   265
Et digitis modo se, dubius qua parte quiescat,
Qua moveatur, agit : demum argutatur inepte,
Atque eodem titubata solo vestigia mutans,
Multum, immutatâ quamvis statione, mutatur.

Other faults, tripping over the Stage ; stumping heavily ; bended and stiff Knees.

   Prætereo molli duplicant qui poplite crura.   270
Hoc ollis solitum, quos et status extulit ingens
Corporis, et nimium dispersæ in corpore longo
Destituunt vires.   Nam quos compegit in arctum,
Et strictis nodosa toris natura ligavit,

Scilicet his amor est breviora extendere membra ;   275
Et cum damna aliter nequeant sarcire figuræ,
Quicquid habent ex articulis ostendere summis.

Above all, the poet condemns the affectation of the dancing-master. He recommends to public speakers to make observations with their own eyes, and to form themselves accordingly. He thus speaks of himself :

Ipse ego, nam sponte hæc non inficianda fatebor,
Sic didici quæ jam doceo, dum nota frequento
Orantum suggesta. Fuit mihi prima voluptas   280
Scilicet, et primæ studium nec inutile vitæ
Conferta in turba pendere loquentis ab ore ;
Dumque animus speciosa haurit consultaque dicta,
Et numeris aures et lumina pascere gestu.

He took for his models La Moine and his son, whom he thus celebrates :

Jamque opus ordibar, summus cum rite sacerdos   285
Liligeræ Themidis medio, de more, Novembri
Sacra recludebat dicundo limina juri
Lamonius.*   Quanta in roseis tum gratia labris
Quo se tum gestu, quo se tunc ore ferebat ?
Nec minus et patrii Natus non degener oris   290
Lamonides, regni eloquio qui jura tuetur,
Auditus ; magna ingentem dum personat aulam
Voce : stupent omnes, arrectisque auribus astant.
Hoc specimen dicendi, hæc exemplaria primum
Ut vidi, ut nostro dixi pars magna laboris   295
Demitur ? Ecce mihi toties quæsita, neque antè
Visa, oratoris species et forma loquendi
Ante oculos.

Liber II.

De Voce.

Actio si niteat gestu spectanda decoro,
Non tamen exhaustus labor omnis. In ardua scenæ   300
Orandi quemcunque trahit laudata cupido,
Huic quoque vox fingenda : penes vocem omnia sunto.
Gallicus Alcides populos vinxisse catenis
Dicitur (actor erat, tantum cui Gallia nomen
Addidit) ast uno pendebant ore catenæ :
Et qua vocis iter patula dabat auris hiatus,
Annulus huc sese mollito ductilis auro
Insinuans, mentes implexaque corda trahebat.
Vox igitur gestu utilior. Nec pulpita quisquam

---

* Premier President du Parlement, in 1674.

Sacra, profana, actor scandat, me judice, quamvis   310
Concinnoque placens gestu, gressumque decorus,
Ni didicit voci quæ sint præcepta regendæ.

A sound voice is indispensable to a public speaker.

. . . . Quod si vox absona surdas
Destituit fauces : heu, contra absiste moveri.

A person not possessed of a good voice should not devote himself to public speaking,
but rather to private instruction. The poet speaks of his talents slightingly.

Nil vires ultra : dum res est integra, curent   315
Quid valeant, quid non, certis prædiscere signis,
Quorum laus agitur. Porro hæc longe optima signa
Spiritus, et laterum compages, et sonus oris.
Tu cave contemnas . . . . . .
. . . . Artis sunt hac primordia nostræ.   320
Si cui molle latus, gracilis si vocula tantum :
Non illum suggesta petunt. . . . . .
t . . . .
  Verum Pancraticæ studia irrequieta palæstræ
Occupet elumbis nemo : nemo oris honore
Magna sonaturi quem non natura beavit,   325
Occupet ingentis vocalia munera suadæ.
Hæc iterum iterumque tibi prædicta momento.
Non alia se dote magis facundia jactat
Quam vocis.

Having enumerated the imperfections of the voice he says,

. . . . istis quicumque laborat   330
Edico propere mutas descendere ad artes.

Upon *mutas artes* he quotes Virgil, where Iapis comes to heal the wound of Æneas :

Ille, ut depositi proferret fata parentis
Scire potestates herbarum usumque medendi   335
Maluit, et mutas agitare inglorius artes.   Æn. 12. 395.

But the voice may in some cases be improved.

Quanquam naturam meliore refingere cultu
Artis opus, nec successu memorabile nullo.
Annon flexanimæ quondam stupuistis Athenæ
Facundi linguam Demosthenis ? . . . , .   340

The labour of Demosthenes stated, and his example recommended.

Qua cum sic fuerint usu præscita magistro,

Macte animis : vel si moles ignava saginæ
Oppressam retinet sub iniquo pondere linguam :
Seu nimium celeres quatit inconstantia malas :
Ferrea seu nimium riget et nimis ampla dehiscit,   545
Et tinnit nimiùm exilis, nec libera vox est.
    Nonne vides sulco ut tritus splendescere vomer
Incipit : ut gladius scabie et ferrugine salsa
Exuitur pingui tinctu purgantis olivi :
Cotis ut affrictu teli gracilescit acumen.   350
Sic rigidam flecti, fuscamque nitescere, puram
Sic labis tandem ingenitæ mirabere vocem.

Management of the Voice.

    Non satis est vitioque carens et libera fandi
Copia, ni voci mens ingeniosa regendæ   355
Præfuerit.   Nam grandiloquum post terga relinquit
Sæpe alius, qui scit concessis cautius uti.
Quæ porro cautum reddant nunc ordine dicam.
    Imprimis facito te turba exaudiat omnis,
Quam magna est. Decet huc primam convertere curam. 360
Quare oculis metire locum, dum pulpita primum
Summa tenes : et vox quâ parte offensa resultat
Undique, in alterutram quâ parte reflectitur alam,
Contemplator : et huc, melius pulsa unde reclamant
Septa loci, dispone animam. Fuge marmora surda,   365
Et quæcunque silent mutis ingrata columnis.

Vociferation to be guarded against, and the Quantity of Voice to be issued in proportion to the Place.

    Voce igitur si fortè minor tibi panditur unquam
Dicturo locus, ah ! si qua est prudentia, parce
Parietibus nimium angustis, circloque minori
Insultare. Capax non totius area vocis,   370
Da quantum satis est. Positas attingere metas
Cursor amat : quantum campi jacet, aspice nitens
Ut pede decurrit propero : sed linea cursum
Extremo reprimit stadio, nec tenditur ultrà.

Moderation in the Rate of Utterance.

    Sufficit attentas si vox allabitur aures.   375
At bene præscriptam solet hæc contingere metam,
Quæ neque pigrescit, nec præceps fertur eundo.
    Est cui tarda riget duro gingiva metallo.
Pondus inest mento. Labor huc convertere et illuc,

Quas solido credas adamante rigescere malas.   380
Unde intersistens numeratis syllaba prodit
Articulis : mediam dum clepsydra depluit horam,
Ad summum bis dena vides procedere verba.
Verba tamen pennata* vigil cantavit Homerus,
Ocyius ut cupidas possint se sistere ad aures.   385
Quis ferat auditor vulsis sic repere pennis
Aeris et linguæ segni sub Rhetore prolem ?
  Nil tamen hic quidquam nimium. Quippe omnia iniquo
Sunt extrema loco. Cui lingua volubilis, ille
Non erroris egens culpaque remotus ab omni   390
Sentiet, undantes linguæ si immittat habenas.
Sæpe orator enim rapido torrentior ore
Gyrum extra et rectæ fines rationis aberrat,
Ut celer Hatterius : cujus sufflamine currum
Augustus medio sisti sermone jubebat   395
Nequicquam. Pulmonem haurit properatio, vocem
Dein intercidit, crebro tum plausa tremore
Ilia conquassat ; quodque his affine putabis,
Plenis ire jubet turmatim verba labellis :
Sed sibi turba obstat, nec iter dat copia. Qualis   400
Sistit ad os versæ circumflua lympha lagenæ.

The poet observes that the length of the sentences should be adjusted to the power of
the lungs, and gives directions for marking a speech as it ought to be pronounced by the
voice. Variety of voice follows.

. . . . . . Sed enim juvat hoc ante omnia : crebro
Si flexu interdum vox sit diversa ; neque una,
Uniusve modi. Tu commutare labora
Qua potis arte sonos : varium et mutabile novi   405
Ingenium auditûs : teretem vel dulcia sensum
Invariata gravent : nec si vel Thracius Orpheus,
Vel mihi si chorda Dircæus oberret eadem
Amphion, placeant. . . . . .

If the cuckoo could vary her voice like the nightingale, she would please.

Si tantum posses variare, cucule, placeres.   410

Cadence.

. . . . . . Extrema vocabula presso
Inferius demitte sono. Magis omnibus una

---

* ἔπεα πτερόεντα.

Auribus incumbit, quæ claudit syllaba versum :
Hanc neque tu sublime sinas evadere cantor,
Vel nimium gelidos inter torpescere dentes.   415
Omnis in hoc cardo prope vertitur, ut cadat apte
Litera, quæ vocem claudit, quæ syllaba versum.

Simplicity of Tones without Affectation or Cant.

Actor ades, Loquere. Hoc vitium commune, loquatur
Ut nemo : at tensâ declamitet omnia voce,
Declamatoris vano qui nomine gaudet.   420
Tu loquere, ut mos est hominum. Boat et latrat ille,
Ille ululat, rudit hic (fari si talia dignum est)
Omnia cum volucrum sonet, omnia quadrupedantum,
Non hominem vox ulla sonat ratione loquentem.
Sibilat, exclamat, ridet, gemit, ejulat, actor   425
Humano nil more loqui juratus : at esto
Cautior his monitis. Nubes et inania captat
Alter magniloquus. Vulgi capita infima supra
Sermo elatus abit, tanquam si numina et astra
Dignetur tantum alloquio. Prompta ultio. Non me   433
Alloqueris ? Nec te auditor sequar usque loquentem.

Marks of Disgust from the Audience.

Quod faciam his signis ne non cognoscere possis.
Aspice, diducit vegrandem ut nausea rictum ;
Cerne, invitatus nictantes somnus ocellos
Ut premit ; ut scalptum caput impatientia torquet.
Quod si me excutio, stricto si mordeor ungui
Ad vivum, pando invitam si pervigil aurem :
Rideo dum ploras ; dum rides, torqueor intus ;
Et ventis permitto ferant tua dicta per auras ;
Quo libitum. Levis est veniæque simillima pæna,   440
Quam subterfugiat sub amico judice nemo,
Omnia cum dicas alienâ voce, alienâ
Ut mente auscultans, fida nec prosequar aure.

The tones of the voice are to vary according to the occasion, as in giving counsel, in congratulation, in reprehension, and in the different circumstances of pleading a cause. This last merits attention.

At si ponè cliens tremit, et sub judice lis est :
Suggeret ipsa tibi quem vult oranda sonorem   445
Pro se causa. Decent actorem fervida bilis,
Os tumidum, streperæ fauces, et pectus anhelum ;
Defensorem æqui placidæ modulamina vocis,

Sincerusque tenor, quem nec tremor arguat ulli
Affinem noxæ, nimium nec sedula cura   450
Suspectum fraudis.   Si sunt contraria jura :
Vox blanda excusat, veniam inclinata precatur,
Implorat lacrymosa fidem superumque hominumque.

The manner of suiting the Voice to the different parts of an Oration—first the Exordium.

.... Gaudent affatu exordia molli
Nam licet abruptum excusent furor iraque sensum,   455
Plus moderata juvant.

Narration, Confirmation, Peroration.

Post exorsa venit narratio simplice cultu :
Quæ satis officium potuit perfuncta videri,
Si satis audiri potuit. Pugnam pede presso   460
Occupat inde, solet quæ confirmatio dici,
Bellatrix semper, nec non in utrumque parata,
Inque alios torquere, et missa repellere tela.

Orandi tum finis, at hic calefacta madebunt
Ora perorantum lacrymis : nec jam sonus unus,   465
Ast adhibenda tibi quot sunt exempla sonorum;
Si qua homines, si qua Deos, quod denique restat,
Ipsum si qua etiam possunt Acheronta movere.

Three principal keys of the Voice, and the proper time for the commencement of Learning.

Tres statuit natura sonos, imumque, supremumque,
Et medium : sed de medio descensus ad imum,
Ad summum ascensus quot habet, nunc quærere noli.
Hactenus hæc : melior dein cætera suggeret usus :
Sint modo, qui teneris vocem formare sub annis
Tractando studeant.   Hominis sunt omnia primum
Cerea ; vox, digiti, cervix, plantæque, lacertique.
Omnia durescunt, cum prima ebulliit ætas :
Ut cera admotos quæ jam non ebibit ignes,
Indocilis fit deinde novæ succedere formæ.

Teachers of Declamation.

*Declamare doces, ó ferrea pectora Vecti ?** 　　　　　　　475
Triste ministerium miseri deflere magistri
Suetus ait grandis Satyræ pater.   Attamen ingens
Hoc pretium est operæ, tenerum si Nestora fingas,

---

* Juv. 7, 150,

Nestora præsidiumque suis, certamque futurum
Hosti perniciem. Quicumque es Vectius, ergo   480
Tironem quoties peccat revocabis, idemque
Bissenis verbum vicibus resonare jubebis
Quo præeas modulo. Neque enim quærenda voluptas
Hoc studio tantum. Vires tractatio vocis
Dicendis etiam superadjicit. Omnia mentis
Frivola sunt sine voce. Tenor dat pondera rebus.

The exercise of the Voice important, and practised by Augustus in the height of his power.—
Boys were exercised weekly in Declamation.

Tu vero istius quicumque novitius artis
Exercende venis, curis puerilibus istam
Ne, moneo, curam adnumera. Rerum ipse potitus
Tum bello Parthos exercet et imperat orbi   490
Augustus, vocemque exercet et imperat ori.
*Sexta quâque die teneri dixere Quirites
Sub Fabio, pater adductis quæ audiret† amicis :
Sic visus labor iste viros puerosque decere.

The passage from Persius to which Lucas alludes is the following : he speaks of his dislike of this practice of recitation, and his pretence of sore eyes in order to excuse himself.

Sæpe oculos memini tangebam parvus olivo,
Grandia si nollem morituri verba Catonis
Discere, ab insano multum laudanda magistro,
Quæ pater adductis sudans audiret amicis.†

The Voice must be kept in constant exercise.

. . . . . . Nec, publica tantum
Concio cum condicta premit, voce utere ; nam vox
Si fuerit multos ignava et inutilis annos,
Comperies sensim vanescere : sive meatum
Præpedit aggestus desuetis faucibus humor,
Seu vox ipsa fugit. Vocem experiere colendo
Durare, et longo se conservare labori.   505
Ne tamen assiduo stomachum clamore fatiga,
Neu jubeo, æternum recitando guttura frangas.

The poet concludes his instructions by enumerating the remedies for the voice, the same nearly as those mentioned by Curius Fortunatianus, and also cautions the speaker against the use of certain things, as nuts, figs, cheese, and olives.

---

* Juv. 7, 160.   † Persius, 3, 44.

No. VII.

The following extract, containing a convenient abridgment of the precepts of Cicero, Quintilian, and others upon delivery, will prove, it is hoped, not unacceptable to the reader. The work is scarce.

Præceptionum Rhetoricarum Libri v.
Autore Georgio Henischio.
Augustæ, 1593.

Henischius divides *pronuntiation* into grammatical and rhetorical.
Rhetorical into the voice and gesture.
Gesture into what relates to the countenancé and to the body.
His rules are either general (in genere), or particular (adjacentia).

Lib. v. p. 318.   *De rhetorica pronuntiatione.*

Quid ?
Rhetorica pronunciatio est vocis, vultusque et gestus moderatio cum venustate.

. . . .

Quæ adjacentia ? (vocis scil.)

Vocem commendari magnam, non parvam : virilem et a pectore resonantem, non effeminatam ; claram et secantem aera, non obscuram ; sufficientem auditori, et exauditu facilem ; et loci qualitati, et auditorum multitudini et distantiæ eorundem accommodatam ; firmam et durabilem ; non decrescentem, sed firmiter manentem, et sæpe augescentem ; æquabilem, non subsultantem imparibus spatiis ac sonis ; sicut misceat longa brevibus, graviora acutis, elata submissis ; mediocrem, non acutissimam, nec gravissimam, nec unius soni ac spiritus ; sed mollem et mutabilem ; non præcipitatam, sed tardam et distinctam. p. 319.

Rules for Gesture.

Quæ adjacentia ? (gestus scil.) p. 321.

In genere requiri non scenicum et immoderatum, sed oratorium et moderatum, qui motu corporis totius vel partium modestiam atque verecundiam cum gravitate conjunctam præ se ferant.

In specie gestum totius corporis commendari secundum naturam excelsum et erectum, non incurvatum, aut immodice erectum, aut nutantem aut vaccillantem : in dextram tamen ac sinistram partem dicentem se vertere, non indecens videri, ut et commodius ab omnibus audiatur, et universos ad attentionem provocet.

Gestum totius capitis laudari, si sit illud cum statu corporis consentaneum : si sit rectum, si non concutiatur crebris motibus, si non illo solo fiat gestus, aut frequenter non fiat ; si quoties exclamandum sit, conatus ille sit lateris, non capitis.

Faciei dicentis convenire, ut sit recta : ut eo vertatur quo gestus corporis.

Oris non esse nimium mutandam speciem, ne aut ad ineptias, aut ad pravitatem aliquam deferamur.

Labra et porrigi male, et scindi, et astringi, et diduci, et dentes nudari, et in latus ac pene ad aures trahi, et velut quodam fastidio replicari, et pendere, et vocem tantum altera parte dimitti, lambere quoque ea et mordere esse indecorum.

Oculos opertos compressosque in dicendo neminem nisi plane rudem et stultum habere : inæqualem illorum motum, qualem in Pisone fuisse ait Cicero, item rigidos et extentos, aut languidos et torpentes, aut lascivos aut mobiles, aut limos reprehendi.

In superciliis vitium esse, si aut immota sint omnino, aut nimium mobila, aut inequælitate dissident.

Naribus ut et labris non fere quicquam decenter ostendi : indecorum esse, et corrugare nares, et inflare, et movere, et digito inquietare, et impulsu subito spiritum excutere, et diducere sæpius, et plana manu resupinare et emungere frequentius.

Cavendum esse ne mentum pectori sit affixum.

Cervicem commendari rectam, non rigidam aut supinam : sicut et caput et collum diversa quidem, sed pari deformitate et contrahi et tendi.

Pectus et ventrem nequaquam projiciendum, latera tantum cum gestu consentire oportere : pectus cædere, scenicum esse.

Humeros raro elevandos atque contrahendos. Exemplo esse Demosthenem, qui cum humeros jactare soleret, hoc vitium tandem metu hastæ humero imminentis emendavit.

Brachia moderate projicienda esse remissis humeris, atque explicantibus se in proferenda manu digitis. Vitiose transversum brachium proferri et cubito pronuntiari.

Manus nec non movendas, nec more levium histrionum indecore movendas : ad sensum magis quam ad verba accommodandas esse, hoc est, *non proferendas ante sensum, neque sensum sequi oportere.* Non quicquid dicitur manibus ostendendum esse. Nunquam ultra oculos, neque infra pectus seu suggestum movendas esse. Sinistram manum per se nunquam facere gestum. Neque ultra humerum moveri debere, neque etiam ultra latus. Neutram manum in posteriora agendam esse. Complodere manus scenicum esse.

Digitorum argutias vitandas esse, ne ad numerum cadat articulus.

Pedum complosionem nimis frequentem ut ridiculam rejici. Vitanda illorum varicationem, in statione turpem, in motu obscenam. Rarum incessum, neque ita longum probari.

P. 324. In genere vultum motumque pronunciantis et ipsi voci et animo consentaneum esse oportere. In specie pronunciationem propriam prudenti consilio pro loco et tempore, causæque et auditorum respectu moderandam esse. Sic in brachiorum jactu plus apud Italos quam Germanos dicturis permittitur.

Pronunciatio fidei est, qua cum docemus aut fidem facimus utimur. Huic convenit ea pronunciatio, quam contentionem autor ad Herennium appellat.

Partes hujus duæ : continuatio et distributio.

The voice in this action should encrease in force. The action should be rapid, and the aspect ardent and fixed (aspectu acri et defixo.)

Delivery for the purpose of pleasing or delighting follows. This is divided into dignity, demonstration, narration, and jesting.

Sermonis cum dignitate, quod ad figuram vocis hæc sunt adjacentia : gravitas, tarditas, humilitas, modus. Gravitatem fauces efficiunt plenæ. Vox tarda est, quæ non habet anfractus et accelerationem. Vox humilis est, quæ non est alta. Modus est ut servetur mediocritas ; ne ab oratoria consuetudine ad tragicam transeamus.

Quod ad motum corporis attinet, status oratoris erectus erit, ut non modo vultus, sed corpus etiam totum conspiciatur. Deinde non sinistræ quod est malæ educationis indicium sed dextræ motu loqui oportebit : sed ut absit gesticulatio. Tertio, vultus ad sermonis sententias accommodatus erit, quæ vel sunt tristes, vel hilares, vel mediæ.

Sermonis cum est in demonstratione quod ad figuram vocis, hæc sunt adjacentia. Primum vox debet esse attenuata, quæ fit faucium contractione.

Deinde utendum est intervallis et divisionibus crebris, membrorum scilicet et incisorum, ut ipsa pronunciatione eas res quas demonstrabimus, inserere atque intersecare, id est, sigillatim inferre videamur in animos auditorum.

Quod ad motum corporis hæc sunt adjacentia. Paululum corpus a cervicibus demittemus, vultumque quam proxime admovebimus ad auditores, quos docere et vehementer instigare velimus.

Sermo cum est in narratione, quod ad figuram vocis, varietatem vocum postulat, ut quo quidque pacto gestum sit vel strenue, vel ociose, vel acriter, vel clementer, vel mœste, vel hilariter ita narrari videatur. Quod si occurrant vel rogata vel responsa vel admirationes, hæc quoque alia atque alia pronunciatione sunt mutanda. Quod ad motum corporis attinet, is motus poterit idoneus esse, qui demonstratus est in dignitate, ut scilicet stantes in vestigio, leni motu dextræ loquamur, hilaritate vultus, tristitia, mediocritate ad sermonis sententiam accommodata.

P. 328.

. . . . Sermo cum jocatione. . . . vitetur scurrilitas.

Pronunciatio motus est, qua in movendis et sedandis affectibus utimur. Hæc pronunciatio ab autore ad Hercenium amplificatio appellatur. . . . Partes quatuor, una, qua voluptas, secunda qua molestia exprimitur ; tertia cohortatio, quarta conquestio. . . . . .

Pronunciationis, qua voluptas exprimetur, vox debet esse effusa, lenis, tenera, jucunda. Quod ad motum attinet, requiritur frons exporrecta, vultus hilaris, gestus exultans, supercilia et oculi diducti et placidi, dextra sublata ac vibrata. Eadem est pronunciatio cupiditatis.

Pronunciationis, qua molestia exprimitur, vox debet esse fusca, id est obscura intra fauces ; et tarda, quæ res mirifice animos hominum frangit et ad luctum impellit. Quod ad motum attinet, requiritur vultus tristis, oculi contracti, manus inter se complicatæ. Huic cognata est metus pronunciatio, quæ deprimit vocem, et sæpe intersistit et interspirat, et relaxat, ita ut illam abjicere videatur.

Cohortationis, quod ad vocem hæc sunt adjacentia. Primum ut sit vox attenuatissima, quæ fit faucibus contractis : deinde clamor lenis, non obstreperus : tertio sonus æquabilis, id est, sui similis, non subsultans : quarto commutationes crebræ, quæ fiunt sermone graviore in remissionem et contra. Postremo celeritas. Neque enim est apta ad iracundiam tarditas.

Quod ad motum corporis, primum gestus debet esse tardior, ut appareat aliqua prudentiæ gravitas: cui celeritas est contraria: Deinde etiam consideratior, ut nullum videare membrum movere sine causa. Tertio utemur brachio celeri, mobili vultu, aspectu acri, non secus ac in continuatione.

Conquestionis, quod ad vocem attinet totidem adjacentia quot cohortationis. Utendum est enim voce depressa, inclinato sono, crebris intervallis, longis spatiis, magnis commutationibus. Quod ad motum corporis attinet, primum fæmineo plangore, mœsto et conturbato vultu: uti oportebit, quoniam conquestio finem habet misericordiam. Sed quia in conquestione etiam incommodorum est commemoratio, ideo nonnunquam sedato et stanti gestu, nonnunquam capitis ictu uti conveniet, qua indignationem significamus. Fit autem illa capitis concussio, vel inclinatione vel declinatione..

. . . .

Pronunciatio generum causarum, quæ in specie generibus causarum accommodatur, quadruplex est. Alia generis didascali, alia demonstrativi, alia deliberativi, alia judicialis.

In genere vehementia convenit fere in judiciali: lenitas et mediocritas in cæteris generibus. In specie, in laudationibus (nisi si funebres erunt) gratiarum actione, exhortatione, similibusque, læta et magnifica, et sublimis est actio. Funebres conciones, consolationes, plerumque causæ rerum, tristes ac submissæ. In senatu conservanda autoritas, apud populum dignitas, in privatis modus.

. . . .

Pronunciatio partium orationis, quæ in specie partibus orationis accommodatur, quintuplex est. Alia Exordii, alia Narrationis, alia Propositionis, alia Confirmationis et Confutationis, alia Perorationis.

Exordii in genere ea est pronunciatio, quæ delectationis. In specie primum observandum, ut ante exordium demisso capite mora aliqua adhibeatur, quo et dicturus se colligat, et auditor attentior reddatur.

Deinde vox sit parva, nec tantum infima et inaudita, sed quæ possit pedetentim augeri.

Tertio, manus sit explicata, digitis tamen non tensis et pollex incumbat extremo articulo indicis.

Quarto, motus sint breves ad commata et cola: vel ut aliis placet, in latentibus sermonis percussionibus: ut in Ligariana Ciceronis, *Novem crimen,* est una percussio: altera est, C. *Cæsar*: tertia, *et hactenus inauditum,* et ubicunque subaudiendum videtur comma, tametsi non exprimatur: At in progressu et ubi oratio jam incaluerit: et cum affectus incremento increscat etiam motus.

Narrationis in genere ea est pronuntiatio, quæ sermonis in narratione positi, de qua supra dictum est. In specie vox narrationis debet imo gradu ferri, et familiari colloquio similis esse: sic tamen ut rerum et personarum proprietates in ipsa repræsententur. Aliter enim in læta narratione, aliter in tristi vox attémperanda est.

Propositionis, ut et partitionis pronuntiatio est sermoni proxima, simplex et expedita.

Eadem est ratio contradictionis. Nam ea quoque diversa propositio est. Sed hæc tamen aliquando irridentes, aliquando imitantes pronuntiamus.

Confirmationis et confutationis in genere eadem est pronuntiatio, quæ contentionis supra exposita. In specie argumentatio plerumque agilior et acrior et instantior consentientem orationi postulat etiam gestum, id est, fortem celeritatem. Instandum quibusdam in partibus et densanda oratio. *Egressiones* fere lenes et dulces et remissæ, ut raptus Proserpinæ, Siciliæ descriptio, Cn. Pompeii laudes. Medii digiti unguis sub pollice demittendus, indice laxato, et reliquis duobus digitis tensis quidem sed tamen leviter incurvatis. Indicamus et demonstramus dupliciter, semel odiose, tribus posterioribus digitis, minimo, annulari et infami coeuntibus sub pollicem. Cum veneratione demonstramus sublatis manibus in latus tensis et dispositis ut in exordio. Distinguimus vero tripliciter, vel cava manu delata supina in sinistrum latus, et relata prona in dextrum latus : vel quando in utroque latere pollice comprehendimus indicem, et in suum latus quamque manum distendimus : vel manum dextram quomodocumque dispositam in sinistrum prius, deinde in dextrum latus reducimus. Pedis supplosio ut loco est opportunus, ut ait Cicero, in contentionibus aut incipiendis aut finiendis, ita crebra et inepti est hominis et desinit judicem in se convertere.

Perorationis in genere eadem est pronunciatio quæ amplificationis supra expositæ. In specie vero vox perorationis requiritur mediocris cum claritate pronuntiandi : sed sine anhelitu ne spiritus defatigetur : item tardior, ut intelligatur quid concluditur. Illa quoque mire facit in peroratione velut deficientis dolore et fatigatione confessio, ut Cic. pro Milone. *Sed finis sit : neque enim præ lachrymis jam loqui possum.* Quæ similem verbis habere debent etiam pronuntiationem. P. 333.

P. 334. In genere non omnibus verbis accommodanda pronunciatio, sed necessariis solum. In specie tot sunt adjacentia, quot rerum discrimina.

Here follows a description of various different affections and circumstances requiring difference in voice and gesture.

Denique qui res supremas nominabit, indicem et oculos attollet : qui res infimas, ad inferiora motum potest inclinare, idque non semper, sed interdum, si quando affectuum magnitudo postulabit. Sic qui dextra dicit, ad dextram, qui quippiam intimum significare cupit, pectori manus admovebit.

. . . .

P. 336, 337.

Rapidity of Utterance.

Ad numeros quod attinet sunt illi triplices : vel magni et graves, qui graviter pronuntiandi ; vel communes qui proferendi celeriter : vel medii, qui pronunciationem quoque intermedium desiderant.

Pronunciationis schematum dianæas varia est ratio. Interrogantes non uno modo gestum componimus, plerumque tamen vertentes manum utcunque composita sit; Humerorum allevatio admirationis est indicium, contractio adulationis : Aversamur et detestamur objectis ante nos manibus et facie nonnihil aversa. Idem est gestus verecundiæ, dubitationis, admirationis, et indignationis.

P. 341. Precepts for forming, preserving, and restoring the voice are here given very much at large, similar to those extracted from Fortunatianus et Cresollius.

. . . .

P. 350. The faults of delivery enumerated in general. Ἰσχνότης vocis gracilitas. μογιλαλία linguæ hæsitantia. Κοιλοσομία vox in specu. Τραυλότης blæsitas. Ψελλότης balbuties, cum syllaba vel litera supprimatur.

ERRATA.

Page	line	for	read
22	7, from bott.	learner	hearer
29	last	emittens	remitttens
155	8,	is	of
261	9,	were	where
ib.	3 from bott.	μγάλη	μεγάλη
333	12 from bott.	Juvencus's	Baxter's
351	last	sapenitia	sapientia.

INDEX.

4 F

E

G

H

INDEX.

INDEX.

T

W

Walking and running, their difference, n. 18, 303.

Warm bath recommended by the Phonasci for the voice, **App.** II.

Way, the particular manner of a speaker so called, 5.

West, his picture of Oliver Cromwell, 416.

Weight without lustre, lead, n. 6. p. 506.

Whisper, its nature, 78—theatrical, what, n. 19, *ib.*

Words should rather follow than precede gesture, why, 377—important, should each be marked with gesture, 435.

Y

Young's Night Thoughts, a passage with the notation, and observations upon it, Chap. XXIII.

TABLE OF REFERENCES TO THE FIGURES.

---

* Hodie eadem de causa (jurandi scil.) duos attollunt digitos, indicem et medium. Voss. Inst. Orat.
p. 520, chap. IV. lib. vi. See also Flaxman's Æschylus. The seven Chiefs against Thebes, Plate I.

TABLE OF REFERENCES TO THE FIGURES.

Places on which the Hands are laid.